Philo's Portrayal

of

Moses

in the

Context

of

Ancient Judaism

Christianity and Judaism in Antiquity Series

Gergory E. Sterling, Series Editor

VOLUME 15

The University of Notre Dame Press gratefully acknowledges the generous support of Jack and Joan Conroy of Naples, Florida, in the publication of titles in this series.

LOUIS H. FELDMAN

Philo's Portrayal *of* Moses *in the* Context *of* Ancient Judaism

University of Notre Dame Press

Notre Dame, Indiana

Notre Dame, Indiana 46556
www.undpress.nd.edu

Manufactured in the United States of America

Designed by Wendy McMillen, type set in 10.6/13.5 Garamond MT
Printed on 55# Nature's Natural recycled paper in the U.S.A. by Sheridan Books, Inc.

Library of Congress Cataloging-in-Publication Data

Feldman, Louis H.
Philo's portrayal of Moses in the context of ancient Judaism / Louis H. Feldman.
p. cm. — (Christianity and Judaism in antiquity series ; v. 15)
Includes bibliographical references and index.
ISBN-13: 978-0-268-15951-1

1. Moses (Biblical leader) 2. Philo, of Alexandria. 3. Pseudo-Philo. 4. Josephus, Flavius. 5. Rabbinical literature—History and criticism. 6. Greek literature, Hellenistic—Jewish authors—History and criticism. 7. Dead Sea scrolls. 8. Christian literature, Early—History and criticism. I. Title.
BS580.M6F43 2007
222'.1092—dc22

2007017368

Christianity and Judaism in Antiquity Series (CJAS)

The Christianity and Judaism in Antiquity Program at the University of Notre Dame came into existence during the afterglow of the Second Vatican Council. The doctoral program combines the distinct academic disciplines of the Hebrew Bible, Judaism, the New Testament, and the Early Church in an effort to explore the religion of the ancient Hebrews, the diverse forms of Second Temple Judaism, and its offspring into religions of Rabbinic Judaism and the multiple incarnations of early Christianity. While the scope of the program thus extends from the late Bronze and Early Iron Ages to the late antique world, the fulcrum lies in the Second Temple and Early Christian periods. Each religion is explored in its own right, although the program cultivates a History-of-Religions approach that examines their reciprocally illuminating interrelationships and their place in the larger context of the ancient world.

During the 1970s a monograph series was launched to reflect and promote the orientation of the program. Initially known as Studies in Judaism and Christianity in Antiquity, the series was published under the auspices of the Center of the Study of Judaism and Christianity in Antiquity. Six volumes appeared from 1975 to 1986. In 1988 the series name became Christianity and Judaism in Antiquity as the editorship passed to Charles Kannengiesser, who oversaw the release of nine volumes. Professor Kannengiesser's departure from Notre Dame necessitated the appointment of a new editor. At the same time, the historic connection between the series and the CJA doctoral program was strengthened by the appointment of all CJA faculty to the editorial board. Throughout these institutional permutations, the purpose of the series has continued to be the promotion of research into the origins of Judaism and Christianity with the hope that a better grasp of the common ancestry and relationship of the two world's religions will illuminate not only the ancient world but the modern world as well.

Gregory Sterling, *Series Editor*

To our grandchildren: Yossie, Yair, Shalom, Yehuda, Shmulie, Ari, Shoshanah, Elana, Eliana, Zevi, and Abby, in the fervent hope that they will continue to learn and to love and to transmit our Torah tradition.

אל תקרא בניך אלא בוניך

"Do not read 'your children' but 'your builders.'"

—*Berakot* 64a

Contents

Preface

There is no figure in the Bible who is both greater and more enigmatic than Moses. How do we square his greatness as a Jewish political and religious leader with the fact that he was brought up in the palace of the Egyptian pharaoh, that we hear nothing of his Israelite education, that he was guilty of the murder of an Egyptian, even if that Egyptian was cruel, that he married a non-Israelite woman, Zipporah, whose father, Jethro, was a pagan priest, that he failed to circumcise his son so that G-d was on the verge of killing him, that we hear almost nothing about his children, that he apparently divorced his wife and married an Ethiopian woman, that he was chosen by G-d to be the chief negotiator with the Pharaoh and to lead and inspire the Israelite people even though he was eighty years old and suffered from a speech impediment, that he lost his temper and smashed the G-d-given tablets of the Law when he found the Israelites worshipping a golden calf, that he who spent forty days in communion with G-d and who conveyed the entire Torah to the Israelites did not know how to rule in the cases of the blasphemer or of those who had been unable to make the paschal offering at the appointed time because of ritual defilement and who sought a second opportunity to do so or of the complaint of the daughters of Zelophehad with regard to their inheritance, and that he disobeyed G-d and consequently was forbidden to enter the Promised Land? Indeed, we may well ask why G-d chose as the vehicle of His revelation a shepherd rather than a trained philosopher or theologian. We may also ask how to explain that Moses was in charge of the priestly establishment and yet was not high priest.

The only attempt at a comprehensive account of Moses in the context of ancient Judaism is the dissertation by Lierman (2002), which focuses on the New Testament. The only comprehensive account of what pagan writers say about Moses is that by Gager (1972). The only systematic, though relatively brief, study of the depiction of Moses in Philo's *Mos.* with brief reference to pagan and other Jewish accounts is the dissertation by Robbins (1947); but this is largely a summary, with minimal analysis, of what Philo has to say about Moses. A briefer study, concerned primarily with tracing Philo's sources for his depiction of Moses as a philosopher-king, is Cukrowski (1994, 149–66). We may also call attention to brief introductory surveys by Goodenough (1933, 109–25); and Botte (1954, 173–80). No study of Moses as found in Pseudo-Philo's *LAB* has yet been attempted. I have written a study of Moses as interpreted by Josephus in my *Josephus's Interpretation of the Bible* (1998, 374–442).

This volume's chief concern is Philo's biography of Moses in *De Vita Mosis*. Just as that biography is in two books, the first, in the style of Plutarch proceeding chronologically, the second, in the style of Suetonius proceeding topically, so this volume, after a first chapter containing a series of introductory sections, proceeds in the second chapter to discuss the life of Moses chronologically, and in the third chapter to discuss it topically. To discuss the particular features of Philo's portrait of Moses this volume attempts to compare them with the way in which Moses is viewed by others in antiquity both by Jews—notably Pseudo-Philo, Josephus, alleged Graeco-Jewish historians, poets, and philosophers, Apocrypha, Pseudepigrapha, Samaritan tradition, Dead Sea Scrolls, and rabbinic tradition—and non-Jews—notably Greek and Roman writers who mention him.

I am particularly grateful to Professors Naomi Cohen, Alan Mendelson, Maren Niehoff, Gregory Sterling, and David Winston for reading through an earlier version of portions of the manuscript of this book and for very many comments and suggestions. I am especially grateful for technical support, far beyond the call of duty, to Steve Siebert of Nota Bene. Portions of this work have appeared in a preliminary form as "Philo's View of Moses' Birth and Upbringing," *Catholic Biblical Quarterly* 64 (2002) 258–81; "The Plague of the First-born Egyptians in Rabbinic Tradition, Philo, Pseudo-Philo, and Josephus," *Revue Biblique* 109 (2002) 403–21; "Philo's Interpretation of Korah," *Revue des Études juives* 162 (2003) 1–15; "The Portrait of Sihon and Og in Philo, Pseudo-Philo and Josephus," *Journal of Jewish Studies* 53 (2002) 264–72; "The Portrayal of Phinehas by Philo, Pseudo-Philo, and Josephus," *Jewish Quarterly Review* 92 (2001–2) 315–45; "Moses in Midian, according to Philo," *Shofar* 21.2 (2003) 1–20; "The Death of Moses, according to Philo," *Estudios Biblicos* 60 (2002) 225–54.

Abbreviations

AAASH	*Acta Antiqua Academiae Scientiarum Hungaricae*
ABD	*The Anchor Bible Dictionary*, ed. D. N. Freedman (New York: Doubleday, 1992), 6 vols.
'Abod. Zar.	*'Abodah Zarah*
'Abot R. Nat.	*'Abot de-Rabbi Nathan*
Abr.	Philo, *De Abrahamo*
Aen.	Virgil, *Aeneid*
Agr.	Philo, *De Agricultura*
AIPhHOS	*Annuaire de l'Institut de Philologie et d'Histoire Orientales et Slaves*
A.J.	Josephus, *Antiquitates Judaicae*
AJP	*American Journal of Philology*
Anim.	Philo, *De Animalibus*
ANRW	*Aufstieg und Niedergang der römischen Welt*
Ant. Rom.	Dionysius of Halicarnassus, *Antiquitates Romanae*
Ap.	Josephus, *Contra Apionem*
Apol.	Tertullian, *Apologeticus*
'Arak.	*'Arakin*
Arist.	Letter of Aristeas
Art.	Artapanus
Ass. Mos.	Assumption of Moses
AUSS	*Andrews University Seminary Studies*
b.	*Babylonian Talmud*
Bar.	Baruch
B. Bat.	*Baba Batra*
B. Qam.	*Baba Qamma*
Bek.	*Bekhorot*
Ber.	*Berakhot*
B.H.	Diodorus, *Bibliotheca Historica*
B.J.	Josephus, *Bellum Judaicum*
BJRL	*Bulletin of the John Rylands Library*
B. Mez.	*Baba Mezia*

Cant.	Canticles (Song of Songs)
CD	*Cairo Damascus Document*
Chaer.	Chaeremon
Cher.	Philo, *De Cherubim*
Chr.	Chronicles
Cohort.	Pseudo-Justin, *Cohortatio ad Gentiles*
Conf.	Philo, *De Confusione Linguarum*
Congr.	Philo, *De Congressu Eruditionis Gratia*
Contempl.	Philo, *De Vita Contemplativa*
Cor.	Corinthians
CPJ	*Corpus Papyrorum Judaicarum*
CS	*Cahiers Sioniens*
Dan.	Daniel
Decal.	Philo, *De Decalogo*
Dem.	Demetrius
Det.	Philo, *Quod Deterius Potiori Insidiari Soleat*
Deus	Philo, *Quod Deus Immutabilis Sit*
Deut.	Deuteronomy
Diod.	Diodorus Siculus
DJD	*Discoveries in the Judaean Desert*
DSD	*Dead Sea Discoveries*
Ebr.	Philo, *De Ebrietate*
Eccl.	Ecclesiastes
EJ	*Encyclopaedia Judaica* (Jerusalem: Macmillan, 1971), 16 vols.
EN	Aristotle, *Ethica Nicomachea*
EQ	*Evangelical Quarterly*
Esdr.	Esdras
ET	*Expository Times*
ETL	*Ephemerides Theologicae Lovanienses*
Eus.	Eusebius
Exod.	Exodus
FJB	*Frankfurter Judaistische Beiträge*
Flacc.	Philo, *In Flaccum*
frag.	fragment
Frg. Tg.	*Fragmentary Targum*
Fug.	Philo, *De Fuga et Inventione*
Gal.	Galatians

Gen.	Genesis
Gig.	Philo, *De Gigantibus*
Giṭṭ.	*Giṭṭin*
GRBS	*Greek, Roman and Byzantine Studies*
Hdt.	Herodotus
Heb.	Hebrews
Hec.	Hecataeus of Abdera
Her.	Philo, *Quis Rerum Divinarum Heres Sit*
Hist.	Herodotus, *Historiae*
Hist. Phil.	Justin, *Historiae Philippicae*
HTR	*Harvard Theological Review*
HUCA	*Hebrew Union College Annual*
Ḥul.	*Ḥullin*
Hypoth.	Philo, *Hypothetica*
ICS	*Illinois Classical Studies*
IJCT	*Internation Journal of the Classical Tradition*
Il.	Homer, *Iliad*
Ios.	Philo, *De Iosepho*
Is.	Plutarch, *Isis and Osiris*
Isa.	Isaiah
JBL	*Journal of Biblical Literature*
Jer.	Jeremiah
JHI	*Journal of the History of Ideas*
JJS	*Journal of Jewish Studies*
JNES	*Journal of Near Eastern Studies*
Jos.	Josephus
Josh.	Joshua
JQR	*Jewish Quarterly Review*
JSJ	*Journal for the Study of Judaism*
JSNT	*Journal for the Study of the New Testament*
JSOT	*Journal for the Study of the Old Testament*
JSP	*Journal for the Study of the Pseudepigrapha*
JTS	*Journal of Theological Studies*
Jub.	Jubilees
Judg.	Judges
Just.	Justin, *Historiae Philippicae*
Juv.	Juvenal

Ket.	*Ketubbot*
LAB	Pseudo-Philo, *Liber Antiquitatum Biblicarum*
Leg.	Philo, *Legum Allegoriae*
Legat.	Philo, *Legatio ad Gaium*
Lev.	Leviticus
LS	*Louvain Studies*
LTP	*Laval Théologique et Philosophique*
LXX	Septuagint
Lys.	Lysimachus
m.	Mishnah
Macc.	Maccabees
Man.	Manetho
Matt.	Matthew
Meg.	*Megillah*
Mek.	*Mekhilta*
Mek. R. Ish.	*Mekhilta de-Rabbi Ishmael*
Mek. R. Shim.	*Mekhilta de-Rabbi Shimon b. Yoḥai*
Memar	Samaritan, *Memar Marqah*
Men.	*Menaḥot*
MGWJ	*Monatsschrift für Geschichte und Wissenschaft des Judentums*
Midr.	*Midrash*
Midr. Deut. Rab.	*Midrash Deuteronomy Rabbah*
Midr. Exod. Rab.	*Midrash Exodus Rabbah*
Midr. Tann.	*Midrash Tannaim*
Migr.	Philo, *De Migratione Abrahami*
MJS	*Münsteraner Judaistische Studien*
Mo'ed Q.	*Mo'ed Qatan*
Molad	Samaritan, *Molad Mosheh*
Molon	Apollonius Molon
Mos.	Philo, *De Vita Mosis*
Mut.	Philo, *De Mutatione Nominum*
Ned.	*Nedarim*
Neh.	Nehemiah
Nid.	*Niddah*
NT	*Novum Testamentum*
NTS	*New Testament Studies*
Num.	Numbers

Od.	Homer, *Odyssey*
OLZ	*Orientalistische Literatur-Zeitung*
Opif.	Philo, *De Opificio Mundi*
OTE	*Old Testament Essays*
P.	Papyri
PAAJR	*Proceedings of the American Academy for Jewish Research*
PE	Eusebius, *Praeparatio Evangelica*
Pes.	*Pesaḥim*
Pesiq. Rabbati	*Pesiqta Rabbati*
Pesiq. Rb. Kah.	*Pesiqta de-Rab Kahana*
Pet.	Peter
PG	*Patrologia Graeca,* ed. Jacques-P. Migne (Paris, 1857–86)
Pirqe R. El.	*Pirqe de-Rabbi Eliezer*
Plant.	Philo, *De Plantatione*
Plut.	Plutarch
PMG	*Papyri Magicae Graecae*
Pomp.	Pompeius Trogus
Post.	Philo, *De Posteritate Caini*
Praem.	Philo, *De Praemiis et Poenis*
Prob.	Philo, *Quod Omnis Probus Liber Sit*
Prov.	Philo, *De Providentia*
Ps.-J.	*Pseudo-Jonathan*
QE	Philo, *Quaestiones et Solutiones in Exodum*
QG	Philo, *Quaestiones et Solutiones in Genesin*
Qid.	*Qiddushin*
R.	Plato, *Republica*
Rab.	*Rabbah*
RE	*Realencyclopädie der klassischen Altertumswissenschaft*, ed. A. Pauly, G. Wissowa, W. Kroll, and K. Mittelhaus (Stuttgart: Metzler, Druckenmüller, 1893–1978), 1st ser., 47 vols.; 2d ser., 18 vols.; 15 suppl. vols.
RecSR	*Recherches de science religieuse*
REx	*Review and Expositor*
Rev.	Revelation
Rhet.	Aristotle, *Rhetorica*
RHPR	*Revue d'Histoire et de Philosophie Religieuses*
Rom.	Romans

Rosh Ha-Sh.	*Rosh Ha-Shanah*
RR	*Review of Religion*
RSC	*Rivista di Studi Classici*
RSR	*Revue des Sciences Religieuses*
Sacr.	Philo, *De Sacrificiis Abelis et Caini*
Sam.	Samaritan
Sat.	*Satires*
Sanh.	*Sanhedrin*
SBLSP	*Society of Biblical Literature Seminar Papers*
SC	*Syllecta Classica*
SH	*Scripta Hierosolymitana*
Shab.	*Shabbat*
Sib. Or.	Sibylline Oracles
Sir.	Ben Sira (Ecclesiasticus)
SJT	*Scottish Journal of Theology*
Sobr.	Philo, *De Sobrietate*
Somn.	Philo, *De Somniis*
Soṭ.	*Soṭah*
SP	*Studia Patristica*
SPA	*Studia Philonica Annual*
Spec.	Philo, *De Specialibus Legibus*
ST	*Studia Theologica*
Stob.	Stobaeus
Strom.	Clement of Alexandria, *Stromata*
Suet.	Suetonius
SVF	*Stoicorum Veterum Fragmenta*
Suk.	*Sukkah*
Sym.	Plato, *Symposium*
t.	*Tosefta*
Tac.	Tacitus
Ta'an.	*Ta'anit*
Tan.	*Tanḥuma*
Tan. Sh.	*Tanḥuma Shemot*
TAPA	*Transactions of the American Philological Association*
TDNT	*Theological Dictionary of the New Testament*, ed. G. Kittel and G. Friedrich, trans. G. W. Bromiley (Grand Rapids: Eerdmans, 1964–76), 10 vols.

Tg.	*Targum*
Tg. Neof.	*Targum Neofiti*
Tg. Onq.	*Targum Onqelos*
Tg. Ps.-J.	*Targum Pseudo-Jonathan*
Tg. Yer.	*Targum Yerushalmi*
Thucy.	Thucydides
Ti.	Plato, *Timaeus*
Tim.	Timothy
TU	*Texte und Untersuchungen zur Geschichte der altchristlichen Literatur*
Virt.	Philo, *De Virtutibus*
VT	*Vetus Testamentum*
Wis.	Book of Wisdom of Solomon
y.	Jerusalem Talmud
Yad.	*Yadayim*
Yal.	*Yalqut*
YCS	*Yale Classical Studies*
Yeb.	*Yebamot*
Zeb.	*Zebaḥim*
Zec.	Zechariah
ZNW	*Zeitschrift für die neutestamentliche Wissenschaft*

I. General Considerations

1. The Importance of Moses in Classical Antiquity

The one figure in Jewish tradition who was well known to the pagan world was Moses (see Gager 1972). When Quintilian (3.7.21), at the end of the first century, refers to "the founder of the Jewish superstition," he, like Pseudo-Longinus, does not deem it necessary to name him, because Moses was apparently well known.[1] When Juvenal (14.101–2) wishes to satirize converts to Judaism he speaks of what they learn as "Moses' arcane book." Moses' connection with Egypt, known for its antiquity, its learning, and its wealth, undoubtedly gave him a certain prominence, especially during the Hellenistic period, when Alexandria was the chief center of scholarship. Philo asserts that while the fame of Moses' laws had spread throughout the world, not many knew him as he really was, since Greek authors had not wanted to accord him honor, in part out of envy[2] and in part because the ordinances of local lawgivers were often opposed to his (*Mos.* 1.1–2).

In an age and place where grammarians and Homeric scholars were leaders of the intellectual community, one of the important figures of the intellectual scene in Alexandria in the first half of the first century C.E., Apion, known for his glosses on Homer[3] and as Philo's counterpart as a leader of the Alexandrian anti-Jewish delegation to the Emperor Gaius Caligula, was a major advocate of such revisionist views of Moses, as we see in Josephus' reply (*Ap.* 2.10–27) to these charges. In view of Apion's intellectual prominence, it was, therefore, all the more important for Philo to refute his charges.

Galen (*De Usu Partium* 11.14), who wrote a century after Philo, adds a further reason why Moses was not accorded honor, namely because he failed to recognize that G-d does not do what is physically impossible but merely chooses the best out of available possibilities. His criticism of Moses as a scientist and philosopher may well go back to an earlier period, and Philo may well have been motivated to challenge such views. Moreover, inasmuch as mystery religions turned out to be particularly attractive during the Hellenistic period, Philo feels that it is his duty to explain that Jews did not have to go outside of Judaism to find a mystery cult and did not have to seek mystagogues, since they had the greatest of all, Moses, the most ancient of great religious leaders and the founder of the Jewish mystery cult. According to Goodenough (1935, 197) Moses thus bridged the gulf between mortal and immortal.

According to Josephus (*Ap.* 2.145), the first-century Apollonius Molon and Lysimachus maligned Moses as a charlatan and impostor, partly from ignorance, though mainly from ill will. Rather, says Josephus (*Ap.* 2.161), Moses is comparable to the Cretan lawgiver, Minos, and to later legislators, who attributed their laws to a god, whether Zeus or Apollo, either being convinced themselves of this as a fact or hoping thus to facilitate the acceptance of the laws. But as to who was the most successful legislator, this can be answered by comparing the laws themselves with those of others.

The repetition of the charge of superstition[4] against Moses in Quintilian's younger contemporaries, Tacitus and Juvenal, is evidence that a new image of Moses, prompted by the conflicts between the Jews and the Roman emperors, starting with Tiberius, had established itself in this period. We must, however, reserve judgment, inasmuch as all three of these critics are rhetoricians or satirists and hence tend to exaggerate. That Philo was aware of such charges is evident in the introduction to his *Mos.* (1.2), where he states that he is writing his biography of Moses to refute those men of letters who have refused to treat him as worthy of memory.

In his attempt to raise the stature of Moses in the eyes of his audience Philo was confronted with a dual problem. On the one hand, the Bible seems to offer detractors considerable indications that Moses was really not so great a figure. As Silver 1982, 3–43, summarizes them: "Moses never devised a war plan or sat on a throne, or promulgated laws (he only reported what G-d told him); he had no mausoleum, founded no dynasty, left no important offspring; the Torah does not say Moses freed Israel, that he did miracles, or that he led the people in the desert (G-d is always the subject of those activities); Moses is not depicted as a self-reliant leader but as a man without freedom of judgment and action, a faithful courier who did only what he was told; he was only an agent, not a leader, ambassador, or principal; in Exod. 2:14–15 we read that Moses struck down an unsuspecting victim, hid his act, and fled in fright into the night; and Exodus reports no plan of Moses to return and help his people until G-d appeared to him in the bush."

To these observations, which seem to diminish his stature, we may add that the one virtue of Moses that is singled out by the Bible (Num. 12:3), where he excelled all other people, namely humility, is not one that many or most in his non-Jewish audience would have viewed as a virtue. We need but recall what Aristotle (*EN* 4.3.1125a19–23) says: "The unduly humble man, being worthy of good things, robs himself of what he deserves, and seems to have something bad about him from the fact that he does not think himself worthy of good things, and seems also not to know himself; else he would have desired the things he was worthy of, since these are good."

To answer the charges of those who had sought to disparage Moses, Philo, at the very beginning of his biography of Moses (*Mos.* 1.1–2), boldly asserts that he is seeking in his essay to bring the story of this man, greatest in all respects (τὰ πάντα μεγίστος) and most perfect (τελειότατος)[5] of men, to the attention of learned (λόγιοι) Greeks.[6] These superlatives—"greatest in all respects" and "most perfect"—definitely go beyond what we find in the Bible, which limits his superlative qualities to his being the humblest of men (Num. 12:3) and the greatest prophet that has arisen among the Israelites (Deut. 34:10). Philo even goes beyond the encomium that we find in Josephus (*A.J.* 4.328), who limits Moses' greatness to his having surpassed in understanding (σύνεσις) all men who had ever lived and his having utilized his thoughts (νοηθεῖσιν) in the best (ἄριστα) possible way. Since, as Philo (*Mos.* 2.2) says, following Plato (*R.* 5.473D), the ideal state comes into being only where a king is a philosopher or a philosopher is king, Moses is the ideal ruler, inasmuch as he combines both the kingly and the philosophical in his single person. As the ideal philosopher-king (*Opif.* 2) he is the supreme philosopher in exploring his subject thoroughly, in refraining from stating abruptly what should be practiced or avoided, in preparing his subjects, who are to live under the laws of which he is the agent, and in refraining from devising myths invented by himself or in acquiescing in those composed by others.

Philo (*Mos.* 1.3), as we have noted, felt that he had to refute those Greek writers who had actually shown malice (βασκανία, "slander") toward him. The fact that immediately after this statement Philo asserts that most of these authors have composed, whether in verse or prose, comedies and pieces of voluptuous license implies, though he does not say so directly or give specific examples, that they have attempted to ridicule Moses through these writings. We may see evidence of this malice in such remarks as that of Diodorus in the first century B.C.E. (*Bibliotheca Historica* 34–35.1.4), who sneers that Moses had ordained for the Jews their misanthropic and lawless customs. Josephus (*Ap.*

2.145) declares that Lysimachus and others, partly from ignorance and partly from ill will, had cast aspersions upon Moses and his code, maligning him as a charlatan (γόης, "juggler," "cheat," "sorcerer") and an impostor (ἀπατεών, "cheat," "rogue"). In particular, Apollonius Molon, the renowned and extremely influential rhetorician, who included Cicero and Caesar among his pupils,[7] is reported by Josephus (*Ap.* 2.145) to have maligned Moses as a charlatan. Philo (*Hypoth.* 6.2) similarly refers to some people, though without naming them, who abused Moses as a charlatan (γόης) and a man-monkey (κέρκωψ). Philo sarcastically reduces these charges to absurdity: "Well, that was a fine kind of imposture and knavery which enabled him to bring the whole people in complete safety amid drought and hunger and ignorance of the way and lack of everything as well, as if they had abundance of everything and supplies obtainable from the neighboring nations, and further to keep them free from internal factions and above all obedient to himself." Such Alexandrian non-Jewish writers as Manetho, Chaeremon, and Lysimachus, in their attack upon the Jews had focused, in particular, on denigrating the greatest Jewish leader, Moses, as a leader of polluted cripples and lepers (*Ap.* 1.260–66, 289–90, 305–11) and as one who had been expelled from Egypt because of his leprosy (*Ap.* 1.279). Even the first-century Pompeius Trogus (*ap.* Justin, *Hist. Phil.* 36, *Epitoma* 2:11–13), who praises Moses for his knowledge and handsomeness of person, declares that he was expelled, together with those Israelites who were diseased with scabies and leprosy, by the Egyptians, and that it was by stealth that he carried off the sacred vessels of the Egyptians.

As to Alexander Polyhistor's extraordinary statement (*ap.* Suda, *s.v.* Ἀλέξανδρος ὁ Μιλήσιος) that the laws of the Hebrews had been composed by a Hebrew woman named Moso, on the surface this would seem to be an attempt to ridicule the lawgiver of the Jews.[8] We may here suggest that perhaps Polyhistor or his source saw a similarity of sound between Moses and Musaeus, the teacher or pupil of the revered Orpheus,[9] and Μῶσα (Doric for Μοῦσα, "muse," a feminine noun) and hence drew the conclusion that Moses was feminine. Or he may have known the tradition that the great Roman king and lawgiver, Numa Pompilius, had received inspiration from the nymph Egeria. Or he may have been influenced by the tradition of the prophetic Sibyls. Or Polyhistor may have believed that divinely inspired men, like divinities, were bisexual, as we find in the case of such deities as Hermaphroditus and Dionysus.

The opponents of the Jews, according to Josephus, had apparently also reviled Moses as utterly unimportant (φαυλότατος) (*Ap.* 2.290). Braun (1938, 68) has pointed out the significance of the omission of Moses' name from the list of Oriental national heroes cited by Plutarch (*Is.* 24.360P), otherwise a relatively impartial authority (see Feldman 1996a, 529–52). In response to this attempt to belittle Moses, Josephus (*A.J.* 2.216) introduces a scene in which G-d Himself appears to Moses' father, Amram, predicting that a son will be born to him who will be remembered as long as the universe shall endure and not only among Hebrew men but also among foreigners.

And yet, despite attempts to denigrate Moses, we may see the importance of Moses in the writing of the third-century B.C.E. Egyptian priest Manetho. The fact that Manetho (*ap. Ap.* 1.250), himself an Egyptian priest, identifies Osarsiph, whom he refers to as the lawgiver of the Israelites, with Moses as a priest, even though the name seems more reminiscent of Joseph, shows how central Moses was to Manetho.[10] The fact that he identifies Moses as a priest is a great compliment, since the priests in Egypt were said to possess esoteric knowledge; and Herodotus, for example, as he shows throughout the second book of his *Histories,* was very much impressed with this wisdom. We may conjecture that the basis of this tradition is the upbringing of Moses, according to the Bible, at the court of the Pharaoh, who was regarded as a god. Hence, it was readily assumed that Moses must have learned the esoteric lore of the Egyptians. In addition, he had sojourned with Jethro, the priest of Midian, whose daughter Zipporah he had married; and, furthermore, he himself was the brother of Aaron, the progenitor of the high priests among the Israelites. According to Manetho (*ap. Ap.* 1.238) it was the rebellious Israelites (rather than G-d) who appointed Osarsiph (Moses) as their leader.

It was Freudenthal (1874, 1.143–74) who contended that Artapanus, with his emphasis on the importance of Moses, influenced Second Temple Judaism greatly. He was convinced that legendary elements in the amplification of the personality of Moses became the basis for most, perhaps even all, later accounts of Moses both in the Diaspora and even in midrashic accounts in Palestine. Nevertheless, it would seem surprising, if this were the case, that Artapanus is mentioned nowhere by name, let alone quoted or paraphrased by Philo[11] or Josephus[12] or for that matter in any other source, whether pagan[13] or Jewish, until he is quoted by the third-century Clement of Alexandria and the fourth-century Eusebius. Indeed, it is hard to imagine that Philo or Josephus would have used as a model for rewriting the Bible a writer who identifies Moses with the mythical Musaeus and who declared that Moses became the teacher of Orpheus (*ap.* Eus. *PE* 9.27.3–4), that he assigned cats, dogs, and ibises as gods (*ap.* Eus. *PE* 9.27.4), and that he was actually deemed worthy of divine honors by the priests and was called Hermes (*ap.* Eus. *PE* 9.27.6). Hence, it is difficult to adopt the view of Freudenthal and his followers, including, most recently, Lierman (2002, 12–13), that Artapanus enjoyed a wide readership and that it was his view of the centrality and exaltation of Moses in Judaism (and in the Jewish history of the world) that was widely endorsed.

Most scholars have concluded that Artapanus was a Jew,[14] inasmuch as his portraits of Abraham, Joseph, and Moses are embellished, and inasmuch as Moses is exonerated in the slaying of the Egyptian, since it is presented as an act of self-defense; but it is hard to believe that a Jew, however liberal, could have said that Moses consecrated Egyptian deities, especially the worship of animals. It is also hard to believe that Artapanus, if he had been a Jew, would have modeled his Moses, as Tiede 1972, 153–67 (see Niehoff 2001, 72–73) postulates, in conspicuous details, on the most popular Egyptian hero, Sesotris. Holladay 1983, 193, and Barclay 1996, 132, suggest that perhaps his liberal attitude toward the Egyptian religion was more common than we realize and that he represented a popular Egyptianized Judaism; but we have no evidence that such an attitude was popular. Niehoff 2001, 73, contends that only a Jew would have claimed Graeco-Egyptian culture for the Jews; but Artapanus (*ap.* Eus. *PE* 9.27.3) portrays Moses not so much as a Jew as, in reality, an Egyptian by adoption. Moreover, there is no indication of Moses' Jewish education; and the emphasis is on his popularity among the Egyptians and on the Pharaoh's jealousy toward him. Indeed, we may suggest that the very fact that Artapanus entitled his book Περὶ Ἰουδαίων ("Concerning Jews") would seem to indicate that the author was not a Jew but an outsider.

We may see this elevation of the stature of Moses in his representation in the third-century murals of the synagogue at Dura-Europos (see Goodenough 1964, 10:119), where his figure is much larger than those that surround him. Indeed, as Goodenough (121) has suggested, his rod resembles that of a club and indicates that Moses is comparable to Heracles, who was known for his club; and scenes from Moses' life dominate the paintings in the synagogue (see Lierman 2002, 146–47), as they do in Philo's representation.

During the period that Philo lived there is every reason to believe that Jews welcomed converts to Judaism (Feldman 1993a, 288–341), as we see in

Philo's account (*Mos.* 2.25–27) of the origin of the LXX. To attract such converts the Jews needed a charismatic national hero, and that hero was Moses.

In sum, Moses is the one biblical figure who does seem to be well known to Greek and Roman intellectuals. His antiquity and his connection with Egypt gave him a definite prominence, though opinions about him differed. In Philo's effort to point out the virtues of Judaism, the personality of Moses was an important means to attract attention, to correct misapprehensions, and to impress potential proselytes.

2. The Antiquity of Moses

To establish the stature of a people, it was first of all necessary to establish its antiquity (Feldman 1993a, 177–200). As Josephus states, every nation attempts to trace its origin back to the remotest antiquity in order not to appear to be mere imitators of other peoples (*Ap.* 2.152). In his apologetic essay *Ap.* (1.7–8), Josephus stresses that the Greeks are relative newcomers to civilization, "dating, so to speak, from yesterday or the day before," whereas in the foundation of cities, the invention of the arts, and the compilation of a code of laws they were anticipated by the Egyptians, the Chaldeans, the Phoenicians, and, above all, the Jews. One remembers how impressed Herodotus (2.142) was when the Egyptian priests showed him records covering 341 generations. One recalls the remark of the aged Egyptian priest to Solon, "You Greeks are always children; in Greece there is no such thing as an old man" (Plato, *Ti.* 22B). The Egyptian sneers at the genealogies of the Greeks, which, he says, are little better than nursery tales (Plato, *Ti.* 23B).

Greek philosophers such as Pythagoras (*Ap.* 1.162–65), Theophrastus (*Ap.* 1.166–67), and Aristotle (*Ap.* 1.176–82), historians such as Herodotus (*Ap.* 1.168–71), Hecataeus (*Ap.* 1.183–204), and Agatharchides (*Ap.* 1.205–12), poets such as Choerilus (*Ap.* 1.172–74), and many others cited only by name by Josephus (*Ap.* 1.216) establish the antiquity of the Jews and often express admiration for their wisdom and piety. Indeed, in the very first statement in the treatise *Ap.*, Josephus emphasizes that he had, in the *A.J.*, made clear the extreme antiquity of the Jewish people. The very title of the *A.J.*, Ἰουδαικὴ ἀρχαιολογία, literally "ancient lore," underlines this. Furthermore, the title *Ap.* is not Josephus' own; and one of the titles in the manuscript, Περὶ ἀρχαιότητος Ἰουδαίων, *De Iudaeorum Vetustate*, emphasizes this theme.

Josephus himself says (*Ap.* 1.2–3) that his purpose in writing the treatise is to disprove those who discredit the statements in his previous historical work concerning the antiquity of the Jews and who claim that the Jews are relatively modern. It is significant that in the first four sections of the treatise Josephus uses the word ἀρχαιολογία three times (1.1, 2, 4) and the word ἀρχαιότης, likewise meaning "antiquity," once (1.3).[15]

The earliest Greek philosophers to deal with celestial and divine phenomena, such as Pherecydes of Syros, Pythagoras, and Thales, are presented by Josephus as being, by universal agreement, disciples of the Egyptians and Chaldeans (*Ap.* 1.14). In Josephus' version, the Egyptians turn out to be students of Abraham in mathematics and astronomy (*A.J.* 1.166–68), generally regarded as the most important of the sciences in ancient times (see Marrou 1956, 176–85). When Josephus wishes to emphasize the great wisdom of Solomon, he compares him with the Egyptians and says that even they, "who are said to excel all men in understanding, were not only, when compared with him, a little inferior but proved to fall far short of the king in sagacity" (*A.J.* 8.42). Josephus takes pains to stress that even such critics of the Jews as the Egyptian Manetho, as well as the Tyrian archives, Dius, Menander of Ephesus, and the Chaldean Berosus, bear witness to the antiquity of the Jews (*Ap.* 1.69–160).

The importance that the Romans attached to establishing their antiquity may be seen from the determined attempt of Virgil in his *Aen.* to trace the ancestry of the Romans back to the famed Trojans and specifically to Aeneas, who was said to be the son of Venus, the daughter of Jupiter. We may recall Livy's famous comment in his preface (7) that if any nation deserves the privilege of claiming a divine ancestry, that nation is Rome.

When Hecataeus (*ap.* Diodorus 40.3.2) cites the leaders of those who were expelled from Egypt he refers to them as notable (ἀξιόλογοι, "worthy of mention," "remarkable") men, whereupon he names Moses, together with such famous Greek leaders as Danaus, the mythical king of Argos, after whom the inhabitants were called Danaoi, and Cadmus, the founder of Thebes and the person responsible for the introduction of the alphabet to Greece. To make Moses a contemporary of Danaus and Cadmus gives tremendous antiquity to Moses.

Consequently, we can understand why Josephus placed such stress, in his apologetics, on his claim that Moses was the most ancient legislator who ever lived (*Ap.* 2.154),[16] next to whom such famous lawgivers as Lycurgus of

Sparta, Solon of Athens, and Zaleucus of Locris "appear to have been born yesterday," whereas an infinity of time has passed since Moses (*Ap.* 2.279). It is significant that in a fiercely apologetic treatise, *Ap.*, Josephus sees no need to reply to a charge that Moses never lived. Indeed, his existence is never questioned by any ancient writer, Jewish or non-Jewish.

Moses' reputation was further enhanced by Manetho's dating of the Exodus (*ap. Ap.* 2.16) as occurring in the reign of Tethmosis, 393 years before the flight of Danaus to Argos. Inasmuch as Danaus was the son of Belus, who was said to be the son of Poseidon, this lent the great prestige of antiquity to him.

In view of the fact that the ancients placed such a premium upon antiquity, the statement of the first-century Ptolemy of Mendes (*ap.* Tatian, *Oratio ad Graecos* 38, and Clement of Alexandria, *Strom.* 1.21.101.5), an Egyptian priest who was the author of a chronicle of the Egyptian kings, is of importance. He states that the Exodus of the Israelites occurred under the leadership of Moses in the time of King Amosis, who lived in the time of King Inachus, the first king of Argos, who was said to have been the son of Oceanus (the son of Ge and Ouranos, the very first divinities) and Tethys (likewise the daughter of Ge and Ouranos). Thus Moses' ancestry is traced back to the very beginning of creation. The statement that Moses lived at the time of Inachus is also found in Apion (*ap.* Africanus, *ap.* Eus. *PE* 10.10.16) and Tertullian, *Apol.* 19.3. According to Polemo of Ilium, who lived in the second century B.C.E., the Exodus occurred during the reign of Apis, the king of Argos, who was the son of Phoroneus, who was the son of Inachus. The fourth-century Porphyry (*Adversus Christianos*, *ap.* Eus., *Chronica*, *ap.* Jerome, *Chronica*, 7–8) assigns an even greater antiquity to Moses, since he says that Semiramis, who reigned 150 years before Inachus, lived after Moses; and it thus follows that Moses preceded the Trojan War by almost 850 years.

Lysimachus, who lived apparently in the second or first century B.C.E. (see Stern 1974, 1:382), has an account of the rise of the Israelites that seems to be independent of Manetho or Chaeremon or their sources.[17] It is more anti-Jewish than any account that has come down to us, with the exception of that of Apion. Indeed, Josephus (*Ap.* 1.304) says that he surpasses Manetho and Chaeremon in the "incredibility of his fictions." By placing the Exodus in the reign of the Pharaoh Bocchoris (*ap. Ap.* 1.305), a king of the twenty-fourth dynasty, that is, in the eighth century B.C.E.,[18] Lysimachus no longer accords Moses the compliment of antiquity;[19] but his is clearly a minority opinion.

Unlike Manetho, Apion (*ap.* Josephus, *Ap.* 2.17) dates the Exodus in the year 752 B.C.E., the first year of the seventh Olympiad and the year in which the Phoenicians founded Carthage, a much later date than that assigned by Manetho. Apion's date for the Exodus is thus in approximate accord with that assigned by Lysimachus.[20] This clearly contradicts the statement of Apion (*ap.* Africanus, *ap.* Eus. *PE* 10.10.16) that Moses lived at the time of Inachus. Apion is apparently getting his information here from different sources.

Like Eupolemus and Artapanus, the identity of Thallus, whether pagan, Hellenistic Jewish, or Samaritan, has been much debated (see Holladay 1983, 1:343–44). His date is probably somewhere between the first century B.C.E. and the first century C.E. In view of the great regard that the ancients had for antiquity, the fact that Thallus (*ap.* Theophilus, *Ad Autolycum* 3.29) states that Moses is the most ancient of all writers, since he says that Moses antedates the capture of Troy (the traditional date for which is 1193 B.C.E.) by 900 to 1000 years, is a tremendous compliment, inasmuch as a much later date of approximately 1270 B.C.E. for the Exodus seems more likely (see Oded 1971, 6:1042–48). Elsewhere Thallus (*ap.* Pseudo-Justin, *Cohortatio ad Gentiles* 9) asserts that of all the Greek teachers, "whether sages, poets, historians, philosophers, or lawgivers, by far the oldest, as the Greek histories show us, was Moses."

Thallus cites the evidence of Polemon, who lived in the second century B.C.E., in the first book of his *Hellenica*, and of Apion in his book against the Jews and in the fourth book of his history, where he says that during the reign of Inachus in Argos the Jews revolted from Amosis, the king of Egypt, and that Moses led them. Ptolemy of Mendes (*ap.* Tatian, *Oratio ad Graecos* 38 and *ap.* Clement of Alexandria, *Strom.* 1.21.101.5), who lived before Apion, who cites him, likewise asserts that the Exodus occurred, under the leadership of Moses, in the time of King Amosis, who in turn lived in the time of King Inachus. Pseudo-Justin, *Cohortatio ad Gentiles* 9, whose date is thought to be the third century C.E., likewise attests to the antiquity of Moses in his statement that the historians Hellanicus, who lived in the fifth century B.C.E., Philochorus, who dates from the fourth to the third centuries B.C.E., Castor of Rhodes and Alexander Polyhistor, who lived in the first century B.C.E., "and, moreover, the very wise (σοφώτατοι) Philo and Josephus, the historians of the Jews, have mentioned Moses as a very ancient (σφόδρα ἀρχαῖος) and old (παλαιός) leader of the Jews."[21]

Thus, the fact that Philo (*Mos.* 1.5) begins his biography of Moses with the statement that he was a Chaldean and that he was born and raised in

Egypt is his way of calling attention to the fact that Moses was thus associated with the two most ancient and most respected civilizations, those of Mesopotamia and Egypt.

In sum, Josephus establishes that many Greek philosophers and historians attest to the antiquity of the Jews. In particular, a number of writers attribute tremendous antiquity to Moses, some dating the Exodus back to long before the Trojan War. Consequently, Philo and Josephus can claim that Moses was the most ancient legislator who ever lived.

3. Philo's Audience in *De Vita Mosis*

In order to determine Philo's attitude toward Moses we must first address the important question as to whom he is addressing his comments in the most important essay dealing with Moses, *Mos.* Furthermore, if we could, we would want to distinguish between his intended audience and his actual audience. Quite clearly, as we can see from the contradictory views that he expresses in other essays about such figures as Joseph and Jethro, not all the treatises were addressed to the same audience. Some of Philo's works, however, are more intelligible when it is recognized that they were directed also or even primarily toward Gentiles, though admittedly it is usually impossible to determine whether Philo is interested in converting Gentiles or in merely explaining the Bible.[22] Such treatises as *Contempl.* and *Prob.* are definitely addressed to Gentiles, as Nock 1933, 79, admits (the latter essay being, in substance, a popular Hellenistic diatribe), and as we can see from the approving reference in the latter treatise both to companions of "the Olympian gods" (42) and to "the legislator of the Jews" (43)—phrases one would hardly use in addressing Jews. We may add that the *Hypoth.* is apparently addressed to Gentiles, as it is probably meant to meet the hostile criticism of the Gentiles by giving a rationalistic version of Jewish history. Indeed, the opening sentence (6.1) in the first fragment that has come down to us states that "*Their* original ancestor belonged to the Chaldeans," where *their* must have been written by a Jew addressing a non-Jewish audience, since a Jew would have written *our.* The apologetic works *Flacc.* and *Legat.* likewise seem to have been addressed to Gentiles.

Probably intended for a non-Jewish audience are Philo's statements that Moses attained the summit of philosophy (*Opif.* 8), that the pre-Socratic philosopher Heraclitus stole his theory of opposites from Moses (*QG* 4.152), that Moses excelled the Greek philosophers in assigning the task of giving names not to some of the men of old but to the first man created (*Leg.* 2.15), and that Moses (like Socrates) was opposed to sophistry (*Det.* 38–39), though admittedly such statements would also have delighted Hellenized Jews.

Still, the theory that such treatises and statements were intended primarily for Jews who were on the threshold of apostasy seems less likely in view of the infrequency with which the issue of apostasy is mentioned explicitly by Philo (see Feldman 1993a, 79–83; Barclay 1996, 104–6). Indeed, Philo (*Virt.* 217) praises the example par excellence of the missionary, Abraham, as one whose voice was invested with persuasiveness and whose hearers were endowed with understanding by the Divine spirit. Sandmel 1979, 47, moreover, has suggested that if we conceive of the presence in Alexandria of Jews nearly on the verge of leaving the Jewish community, as did Philo's nephew, Tiberius Julius Alexander, with whom he has a dialogue in his *Prov.*, he may have had an obliquely related purpose to counter this threat.

There are some scholars, such as Tiede 1972, 107, who contend that Moses may be praised by Philo as much to encourage the cultured Jew who tends to be embarrassed by his tradition as to win respect from the non-Jew who has preconceived notions about Judaism. However, it would seem that *Mos.* is an apologetic treatise addressed primarily to non-Jews (Goodenough 1933, 109–25; 1940, 37–38),[23] or that it was addressed to wayward Jews who had imbibed Greek culture and who had raised questions about the Bible. If, indeed, it is addressed to non-Jews it seems to differ from Philo's other apologetic works—*Hypoth.*, *Flacc.*, and *Legat.*—in that, unlike them, *Mos.*, though it begins with a refutation of the misrepresentation of the Jews by non-Jewish writers, is not primarily concerned with refuting the charges of these writers. Rather, it appears to be an introduction to the ideals of Judaism as exemplified by Moses (Goodenough 1933, 109).

Nevertheless, Tcherikover 1956, 169–93, questions whether widespread Jewish literary propaganda among the pagans was technically possible, and he challenges the widespread views that the distribution of books in the ancient world was similar to that in modern times, that books were produced in large numbers of copies and were sold in thousands of shops and sent to distant countries, and that famous authors had their own "publishers" who profited from these sales. I have challenged Tcherikover on almost every basic point (Feldman 1987–88, 187–251). The fact is that by the middle of the first century not only public but also private libraries had become numerous (Kenyon

1951, 80–81). The fact that Pseudo-Longinus (*On the Sublime* 9.9) not only paraphrases Gen. 1:3 and 1:9–10 but cites it as an example of the most sublime style makes it unlikely, as we have noted, that the quotation would be utterly unknown to his readers. In addition, from the way that he refers to Moses without bothering to identify him by name, presumably because his readers knew who the "lawgiver of the Jews" was, we may gather that he was acquainted with much more from the Bible than this passage alone.

That *Mos.* was apparently directed primarily to non-Jews seems likely from the fact that at the very beginning of the treatise (1.1) Philo declares, as we have noted, that he hopes to bring the story of Moses to the attention of such as deserve not to remain in ignorance of it. Again, at the very beginning of the treatise (1.2) he complains that Greek authors have refused to treat Moses as worthy of memory, the implication being that Philo in this treatise is seeking to correct this; and he can do this only by directing his comments to the non-Jewish readers who have a distorted picture of Moses. In the second book of this treatise Philo (2.25–44) tells the story of the translation of the Pentateuch into Greek even though this is, strictly speaking, not directly relevant to the account of the life of Moses. He does this in order to show that King Ptolemy Philadelphus of Egypt conceived an affection for the Jewish laws to the point that he sought to have a copy in the library that he was building. The implication is that other non-Jews would likewise find it of interest. Just as, according to Philo, the Arist. (9–11), and Josephus (*A.J.* 12.12–16), the Pentateuch was translated into Greek upon the order of a non-Jew, Ptolemy Philadelphus, so the *Mos.*, which tells the story of the translation, may have been intended for a non-Jewish audience; and just as the translation of the Pentateuch received recognition throughout the civilized world (*Mos.* 1.2), so Philo writes his essay in order that the hero of that work, Moses, who had hitherto been neglected, might receive due recognition (ibid.). The fact that this treatise presents a rewritten version of the Pentateuch, in this respect similar to Josephus' *A.J.*, will explain the relatively straightforward narrative style, with few philosophical and allegorical interpretations, such as we find in most of Philo's other works. It would seem, therefore, that *Mos.* is presented as a kind of official biography of by far the most important figure in Judaism, Moses, intended for the non-Jewish world in the hope, if not of actually winning it to convert to Judaism, at least of explaining to an intelligent and scientifically sophisticated audience, in a rational and credible fashion, the key events reported in the central book in Judaism, namely the Pentateuch.

Goodenough 1933, 109–25, has contended that *Mos.* served as the first presentation of the Jewish point of view to be given to Gentiles who showed genuine interest in the Jews but as yet knew little about them. This would seem to be borne out, as we have noted, by the extraordinary digression in *Mos.* 2.25–44 concerning the translation of the Pentateuch into Greek, which, significantly enough, starts with the statement "That the sanctity of our legislation has been a source of wonder not only to the Jews but also to *all other nations* [my emphasis], is clear both from the facts already mentioned and those which I proceed to state." The key point of this passage is the statement (*Mos.* 2.41) that every year a feast and general assembly are held on the island of Pharos, "whither not only Jews but *multitudes of others* [my emphasis] cross the water, both to do honor to the place in which the light of that version first shone out, and also to thank G-d for the good gift so old, yet ever young." The pericope ends with a call to the Gentiles for conversion to Judaism (*Mos.* 2.44): "But if a fresh start should be made to brighter prospects, how great a change for the better might we expect to see! I believe that each nation would abandon its peculiar ways, and bidding farewell to their ancestral customs, turn to honoring our laws alone. For when the brightness of their shining is accompanied by national prosperity, *it will darken the light of the others* [my emphasis] as the risen sun darkens the stars." This can refer only to the hope of mass conversion to Judaism, even if there is no indication of actual missionary activities. Fischer 1978, 186, says that Philo is here speaking of a spiritual and universal eschatology rather than a national Jewish eschatology, but, as Borgen 1992, 346, n. 7, concludes, the passage indicates that all nations will become proselytes. We would call attention to Philo's language, namely, that all nations will bid farewell to their ancestral customs and adopt Jewish laws alone. This indicates a metamorphosis, a mass conversion to Judaism.

It is significant that in an essay on the life of Moses, Philo (*Mos.* 2.12–14) digresses to compare the laws promulgated by Moses with *all* the other laws that have ever arisen among the Greeks and barbarians in *all* other countries. He makes a special point of noting that the laws of the Jews alone are "firm, unshaken, immovable, stamped, as it were, with the seals of nature itself." This is an indication that he is addressing a non-Jewish audience, who are, in effect, invited to compare their laws with those of the Jews. As if to answer those who would disparage the Pentateuch, he admits (*Mos.* 2.15) that the Jewish people have undergone many changes, both increased prosperity and the reverse, yet "nothing—not even the smallest part of the ordinances—has been disturbed, because *all* have clearly paid high honor to their venerable and godlike character."

That Philo is directing his remarks to non-Jews seems evident from his statement (*Mos.* 2.43) that "the laws of the Jews are shown to be desirable and precious in the eyes of *all*, ordinary citizens and rulers alike, and this despite the fact that our nation has not prospered for many years." The fact that he says that rulers praise the laws must refer to non-Jewish rulers, and consequently the reference to ordinary citizens must be to non-Jews as well.

It is striking that in a biography of Moses Philo sees fit to include at some length an account of the translation of the Pentateuch into Greek, which, strictly speaking, as we have noted, is really only tangential. This is still another indication that he is directing his essay to non-Jews, since it includes his statement (*Mos.* 2.27) that some people—a clear reference to Ptolemy Philadelphus—thought that it was a shame that the laws should be found in only one-half of the human race, the barbarians—that is, the Jews—and denied to the other half, that is, the Greeks, and consequently arranged to have it translated into Greek. Although Philo's account of the translation is clearly dependent upon that in the Arist., his addition about the annual celebration of the translation on the island of Pharos surely underlines the fact that non-Jews regularly participate in this celebration. Indeed, in his account of the translation, Philo (*Mos.* 2.36) makes a point of adding that the translators prayed that G-d assist their aim, namely that the greater part, or even the whole, of the human race—another indication that Philo has non-Jews in mind—might be led to a better life through adopting the laws in the Pentateuch. It is significant that *to Philo* the reason for the translation was not, as many modern scholars postulate, that the Jews of Alexandria lacked the knowledge to understand the Pentateuch in the original Hebrew, but rather that it should be made known to all nations so that they might be converted to Judaism, although, in point of fact it might have served both purposes (see Borgen 1997, 140–44).

Furthermore, though this is an *argumentum ex silentio*, we may suggest that if the *Mos.* had been written for wayward Jews, Philo would have inserted a comment, such as his unusual interpretation (*Spec.* 4.149) of the biblical prohibition (Deut. 19:14) against removing one's neighbor's landmark that one's forefathers have erected, namely that this applies not only to boundaries of land but also to the safeguarding of ancient customs. Or we would have expected him to criticize such wayward Jews as he does extreme literalists

(*Somn.* 2.301, *Cher.* 42, *Conf.* 2, 9–10, *Deus* 21, 52, *Virt.* 10, *Mut.* 61) and extreme allegorists (*Migr.* 89, 91; *Post.* 42, *Migr.* 90, 93). Or we should have expected him to criticize such wayward Jews as he does those who rebel from the holy laws (*Virt.* 182, *Praem.* 152) or who intermarry (*Spec.* 3.29). Moreover, if *Mos.* were directed toward Jews we would expect it to comment on contemporary issues and events, particularly anti-Semitism and the relationship with the non-Jewish community.

In sum, *Mos.* is best seen as an official biography of Moses, primarily addressed to non-Jews, as we see from the very beginning of the treatise, where Philo says that he hopes to bring the story of Moses to the attention of those who deserve not to remain in ignorance of it. The fact that it includes an extraordinary digression concerning the translation of the Pentateuch into Greek, with the striking call to Gentiles to give up their ancestral customs and to turn to the laws of the Jews, is an important clue to one of the purposes of the treatise.

4. Philo's Life of Moses as an Aretalogy and as an Encomium

Moses Hadas and Morton Smith (1965) have discussed the genre of ancient biographical writing called aretalogy,[24] which praises a hero's virtues and excellence. Hadas 1965, 3, who is the author of the first part of this volume, defines "aretalogy" as "a formal account of the remarkable career of an impressive teacher that was used as a basis for moral instruction." Examples may be found in Diogenes Laertius' *Lives of Eminent Philosophers* and Philostratus' *Life of Apollonius of Tyana.* Najman 2003, 90–91, calls attention to three notable characteristics of aretalogies: the hero's education is depicted as including travel and initiation into mysteries, notably those of Egypt; he is outstanding for his treatment of others and his formulation of a code of behavior; and he is portrayed as so superior to ordinary humans that he is practically divine. All of these are found in the case of Philo's *Mos.* To be sure, Moses does not actually travel abroad, but he has teachers who come from other lands to instruct him. We would add a fourth characteristic, namely, that the sole focus of the biography is on the hero; and a fifth characteristic, namely, that the perfect copy of the Law of Nature is to be found in the life of the sage. Indeed, the focus in Philo's *Mos.* is solely on Moses; his father and mother are referred to merely as "father" and "mother" and never identified in this essay by their names, Amram and Jochebed (*Mos.* 1.7). His sister is identified merely as his "sister" and never identifed by her name, Miriam. His brother is identified merely as his "brother" and never by his name, Aaron (*Mos.* 1.84–85). His wife is never identified by her name, Zipporah, nor is her father, Jethro (*Mos.* 1.59). His sons are identified merely as "sons" and never identified by their names, Gershom and Eliezer (*Mos.* 1.150). The great conspirator against Moses is never identified by his name, Korah (*Mos.* 2.275–87). The soothsayer who was sent to curse the Israelites is never identified by his name, Balaam (*Mos.* 1.264–300). Thus Moses is the complete center of attention. Whereas Plato speaks of the philosopher-king (*R.* 5.473D) of the ideal state, Philo says that the Jews have already had him in the person of Moses, just as Cicero in his *De Republica*, Book 2, says that the ideal state has already come into existence, namely the Roman Republic.

In ancient aretalogies the person often has a miraculous birth, works wonders, and encounters the hostility of a tyrant, whom he confronts with courage and at whose hands he sometimes suffers martyrdom. The original prototypes for such aretalogies are divine and heroic figures such as Dionysus, Heracles, and Theseus (see Hadas 1965, 17–26). Others who contributed to what may be called the institution of heroization are Orpheus, Pythagoras, and Empedocles. As examples of such aretalogies Hadas and Smith have selected, in addition to Philo's biography of Moses, Porphyry's *Life of Pythagoras*, the life of Jesus in Luke's Gospel, and Philostratus' *Life of Apollonius of Tyana.*

Inasmuch as Philo again and again uses the term Tὸ ὄν, "Existence," with reference to G-d, in such an intellectual world G-d is pure being, an unmoved mover, and pure existence. It is thus really impossible to conceive of such a G-d by reciting His attributes. Such a G-d cannot realistically be a model for human beings. Philo (*Virt.* 168; cf. *Spec.* 4.188 and *Fug.* 63), to be sure, does say that one should imitate G-d as much as one can, and "leave nothing undone that may promote such assimilation as is possible." But since this is really very difficult, Philo, from a purely practical point of view, set up human models, namely the patriarchs and especially Moses as examples of virtuous behavior, just as the Greeks set up the seven wise men. In effect, such men become divine.

But the full-fledged paradigm for aretalogy is Socrates (Hadas 1965, 49–56), as idealized in the writings of Plato, especially the *Symposium* and the *Phaedo.* Sigal 1984, 171, objects that Philo's biography of Moses cannot be considered an example of an aretalogy because the paradigm for aretalogy was the life of Socrates, the culmination of which was his martyrdom for truth, whereas martyrdom is in no way associated with the life of Moses.[25] But Philo's biography does, on the whole, fit the definition of aretalogy as formulated by Hadas, namely the remarkable career of a teacher that serves as the basis for moral instruction. Martyrdom is not necessarily part of such a career, and, as we see in Philostratus' *Life of Apollonius of Tyana* (8.29–30), neither did Apollonius die a martyr's death. Philo's life of Moses does fit the common denominator of an aretalogy, namely that he is precocious as a child, is taught the ancient wisdom of the Egyptians and Greek philosophy and Chaldean astrology, lives a life of asceticism, despises sexual relations, is constantly involved with the study of philosophy, is suspected, as philosophers often were, of plotting a revolution, and consequently had to flee Egypt, all of which details are, significantly, additions to the biblical narrative. Philo's Moses may not have been martyred, but Philo certainly emphasizes, even beyond the biblical text, the pain and suffering Moses experienced at the hands of the masses of the Israelites, forever grumbling and rebelling.

If we are looking for a single term to classify *De Vita Mosis*, that term would be "encomium." As Shuler 1990, 88, notes, the role of the encomium in the development of biography in the ancient world has been well documented.[26] The rules for writing encomia were set forth by Aristotle, *Rhet.*, Book 1; Aristotle, *Rhetorica ad Alexandrum*, 3–4; Cicero, *Rhetorica ad Herennium*; Cicero, *De Partitione Oratoria* 21; Quintilian, *Institutio oratoria* 3.7.3; Theon (in Spengel 1854, 2:60ff.); and Hermogenes, *Progymnasmata* (in Rabe 1913). In particular, we may call attention to Cicero, *Epistulae Ad Familiares* 5.12, in which he sets forth the thesis—and, indeed, cites the great Polybius in support—that in a general history one must adhere strictly to the truth but that in a monograph dealing with a period or event or biography of an individual one is permitted to take liberties with the facts.

According to these rhetorical handbooks, an encomium would include many or most but not necessarily all of the following: genealogy, place of birth, omens before birth, events on the occasion of birth, nurture, childhood excellence, education, physical attributes, adult career, virtues, events surrounding death, and occurrences after death (cited by Shuler 1990, 88–89). Two techniques employed by the author of the encomium are comparison with another person whom the subject excels and amplification of the qualities of the subject. That *Mos.* comes under the category of encomium and epideictic literature was already noted by Priessnig 1929, 143–55. Philo uses the word encomium in praising the virtues of Abraham (*Abr.* 217 and 255) and of Joseph (*Ios.* 205); but, to be sure, he does not actually use this word with regard to the merits of Moses. However, we may note that Josephus (*Ap.* 2.147) specifically states that his object is not to write an encomium for the Jews, whereupon he proceeds to do just that, as Balch 1982, 102–22, has convincingly shown. That *Mos.* fulfills the definition of encomium is clear from the facts that he includes most of the topics listed above as appropriate to an encomium and that he enhances Moses' qualities, especially when we compare his depiction with the bare data cited in the Bible.

In sum, by omitting in his *Mos.* the names of Moses' parents, siblings, wife, and sons, Philo focuses solely on Moses. The *Mos.* is best classified as an encomium and includes most of the topics customarily found in this genre.

5. Philo's Method as a Biographer of Moses

If we define a biography as a work devoted exclusively to delineating the life of a person from birth to death (Momigliano 1971a, 11), the essay *Mos.* is the first known biography of Moses, but it is not the first biography, which goes back to Isocrates' *Evagoras* and Xenophon's *Agesilaus* and *Cyropaedia* in the fourth century B.C.E.[27] The fact, noted by Momigliano 1971a, 54–57, that true biography, such as we find in Xenophon's *Cyropaedia*, was preceded or at least accompanied by fiction, such as we find in Herodotus and Ctesias, will help us to understand Philo's aim in writing his biography of Moses, namely to present the man as he really was (*Mos.* 1.2).

The first collection of biographies that we possess is by Cornelius Nepos, who lived half a century before Philo; and the next biography is that of Augustus (based on Augustus' autobiography) by Nicolaus of Damascus, an older contemporary of Philo. Yet, even in the fifth century B.C.E., as Westlake 1968 (cf. Wardman 1974, 5–6) has argued, Thucydides had become more interested in the character of his personalities as his work progressed. Indeed, as Momigliano 1971a, 1–7, has stressed, the distinction during the Hellenistic period between history and biography was less than generally accepted; instead biography came to be recognized as a type of history.

Isocrates had pioneered in the writing of eulogistic biography in his *Evagoras*, the purpose of which was to show that Evagoras, king of Salamis in Cyprus, surpassed even the legendary princes of ancient times in valor, piety, and justice, three key qualities that Josephus singles out for praise in his biblical heroes (see Feldman 1998a, 96–129). That Plutarch knew the works of Isocrates and was influenced by them, particularly his views on education and political philosophy, seems most likely in view of the fact that he cites him thirty-five times (see Helmbold and O'Neil 1959, 49).[28] But the dividing line between the Isocrateans and the Peripatetics was not so clear-cut; and we hear that one of Isocrates' successors, Theodectes, followed his father in going from the Isocratean to the Aristotelian school. Another of the pupils of Isocrates, Ephorus, was noted for the incorporation of sweeping panegyrics, precisely what we find at times in Philo's and Josephus' portraits of their major biblical figures. It is precisely the tendency to abandon the time-honored distinction between history and biography and to convert history into biography—one is almost tempted to say psycho-history—that we see in the very title, *Philippica*, of the work of another of Isocrates' disciples, Theopompus, which indicates that he had departed from the interest in traditional history and had turned to biography and psychology. Theopompus is actually criticized by Polybius (2.8.10) for building his history around a man, Philip II, rather than around Greece. In fact, with Theopompus the goal of history was no longer restricted to the narration and explanation of great events but also included and even emphasized the evaluation of the feelings and motives of major characters in history (see Connor 1967, 133–54). Indeed, this school frequently sought to reveal the conscious, rational motives behind men's actions. In particular, Theopompus is fond of comparing the reaction of two historical figures to similar circumstances. It was this comparative approach that Plutarch made famous and that we also see, for example, in Josephus' comparison of Agrippa I and Herod (*A.J.* 19.328–31). In fact, Theopompus is important for introducing a personal, almost a biographical, history; and this approach had a profound, though perhaps indirect, influence upon historians such as Josephus, as well as upon later biographers such as Plutarch.

Aristotle's followers, the Peripatetics, starting with his successor Theophrastus, tried to classify types of lives, just as they did types of animals and plants; and they thus proceeded to write biographies illustrating these various types of life. To this end, as we see in Plutarch, Philo, and Josephus, they used anecdotes and historical incidents. In fact, in research into the history of philosophy, the Peripatetics used biographical details as offensive and defensive weapons (Momigliano 1971b, 14). Indeed, Dihle (1956) has suggested that Aristotle's *EN* was the main influence on later biography. There is surely significance in the fact that Nicolaus of Damascus, who was Josephus' main source not only for the large part of the *A.J.* pertaining to Herod but also for much else, was a Peripatetic philosopher who wrote, as we have noted, a biography, now lost, of the Emperor Augustus, though Momigliano (1971a, 120) concludes that Aristotelianism alone was neither a necessary nor a sufficient presupposition of Hellenistic biography.[29]

During the Hellenistic period the gap between historical encomium, biography, and history had narrowed, so that, in effect, it became impossible to separate them (Momigliano 1971a, 83). Hence, despite Cicero's attempt to justify stretching the truth in a proposed monograph about his consulship (*Ad Familiares* 5.12), for practical purposes the difference had diminished. Even Polybius himself, who is so critical of the Isocratean school, wrote an encomium of Philopoemen, which has an emotional and tragic component. Presumably, he felt that his encomium was justified so long as the panegyric was not included in his history. Philo and Josephus, like Dionysius of Halicarnassus, seem to have fused panegyric and history.

To be sure, Plutarch himself (*Alexander* 1.2) seems to make a sharp distinction between history, with its emphasis on events, and biography, with its emphasis on character, as revealed even by minor events. As Momigliano (1971a, 110) remarks, the principal form of biography was the encomium,[30] not a form of which Thucydides would, in general, have approved; and yet it is precisely this form that we find in Philo and in Josephus' *A.J.* (see Feldman 1998a, 80, 82), as we do, of course, find in Plutarch's lives. Indeed, Josephus himself, in his account of the war of the Jews against the Romans (*B.J.* 1.1–2), follows the model of Thucydides in its interest in contemporary events and in its critical, scientific approach to the writing of history, and sharply criticizes the inclusion in history of invectives or encomia. Similarly, Lucian (*Quomodo Historia Conscribenda Sit* 7) emphatically asserts that history and encomium are separated by a high wall. But his very emphasis would seem to indicate that the distinction had broken down.

As to the difference between history, as seen in Josephus, and biography, as seen in Plutarch, that difference is sometimes blurred. Josephus (*A.J.* 1.15–16), in his proem to the *A.J.*, insists that Moses kept his words concerning G-d pure of the unseemly mythology current among others, although in dealing with ages so remote he would have had ample license to invent fictions. Philo similarly and vehemently objects to those who view the biblical stories, such as the account of the building of the Tower of Babel, as similar to Greek myths, such as the piling of Pelion on Ossa on Olympus by the Aloeidae (Aloadae) (*Conf.* 4–5). In the introduction to his life of Theseus (1.5), Plutarch admits that in biography, where the emphasis is on the virtues of his characters and where he enjoys citing insignificant acts and casual remarks or jests (*Alexander* 1.2), one has the latitude with the facts that one does not have with history, where the emphasis is on events and on factual accuracy. Plutarch is well aware of this contrast. "May I therefore succeed," he says, "in purifying fable, making her submit to reason and take on the semblance of history. But where she obstinately disdains to make herself credible and refuses to admit any element of probability, I shall pray for kindly readers, and such as receive with indulgence the tales of antiquity." Josephus, in the introduction to his *B.J.* (1.2), like Philo in the proem to *Mos.*, criticizes predecessors who were guilty of misrepresenting the facts, "their writings exhibiting alternatively invective and encomium, but nowhere historical accuracy." But *Lycurgus* is not *Theseus*, which clearly is dealing with myth. Indeed, in *Lycurgus* Plutarch is well aware of the difference, since he asserts at the very beginning (1.1) that there is least agreement among historians as to the times in which Lycurgus lived; and he certainly talks like a critical historian when he says (1.3) that although the history of those times is such a maze, he will try to follow those authors who are least contradicted or who have the most notable witnesses for what they have written about him. One guesses that the Plutarch who writes thus should have felt a certain kinship with the Philo of *Mos.*, who claims to be true to the facts of history.

In the case of Philo's *Mos.*, we may suggest that it is actually a compromise: Book 1 is a factual history, "Plutarchian" in style, that deals with political and military events and is chronologically ordered, whereas Book 2 is a biography, "Suetonian" in style, that is, systematically ordered and concentrating on the virtues of Moses. We may note that in the second book of his biography of Moses Philo does not proceed chronologically but rather topically, so that he actually (*Mos.* 2.253) repeats the account of the crossing of the Sea of Reeds, since he is here dealing with the aspect of Moses as a prophet. Momigliano 1971a, 77–89, has demonstrated that both types of biography existed in the Hellenistic period in the third and second century B.C.E., certainly prior to Philo.[31] The Pythagorean and later Aristotelian Aristoxenus of Tarentum, who lived in the fourth century B.C.E. and who wrote biographies of Pythagoras, Archytas, Socrates, and Plato, is basically a "Plutarchian" (see Momigliano 1971a, 74–76); among "Suetonian" biographies, as Momigliano

(1971a, 86) has indicated, the abridged *Vita* of Sophocles must have been written in the Hellenistic period, as we can see from the fact that it never quotes any authority later than the second century B.C.E. Moreover, two of the biographies by the first-century B.C.E. Cornelius Nepos, namely those of Epaminondas and Iphicrates, are closer to the Suetonian than to the Plutarchian type (Momigliano, 1971a, 87).

In fact, though the Bible contains histories in which individuals, such as Moses, figure prominently, it does not contain any biography as such. Indeed, the species of biography is foreign to the rabbis as well (see Silver 1982, 92). Where we have biographical details they are brief incidental digressions, since the chief goal of the rabbis is to present commentaries on biblical passages and discussions of the various commandments. It is not until the Christian tradition that we find biographies of Jesus and of the saints, where biography becomes hagiography and is used as a tool of evangelism. Philo's biography of Moses, together with his lives of Abraham and of Joseph, constitute the first Jewish biographies. Josephus, two generations later, wrote an autobiography, but he apparently never attempted a biography, as such, of a biblical figure, though the first half of the *A.J.* contains many quasi-biographies of biblical personalities within a historical framework. Philo thus merits comparison with Plutarch, who lived later in the first century and who likewise used biography as a means of supplying role models of virtue for his readers rather than as a source of mere fact. But after Josephus' autobiography we do not find biographies written by Jews until modern times. However, if Plutarch had written a biography of Moses he would have been interested in the man, and especially his character.

One would expect that Philo's life of Moses would be similar in method and style to his biographies of Abraham and Joseph, but such is not the case. Botte 1954, 173–80, calls attention to the fact that whereas in his biography of Abraham, Philo also describes the lives of Enosh, Enoch, and Noah, in his biography of Moses Philo concentrates on the life of Moses. What distinguishes the biography of Moses from the other essays of Philo, including the biographies of Abraham and Joseph, is that he is here presenting a direct interpretation of the biblical text and avoids allegory. In fact, the words ἀλληγορία ("allegory"), ἀλληγορικός ("allegorical"), and ἀλληγορέω ("to allegorize") do not occur even once in either of the two parts of the biography of Moses. Nikiprowetzky 1977, 196, objects that *Mos.* is not primarily a biography, inasmuch as the exposition of the law plays a prominent role. However, we must note that it is only in the second book of the *Mos.* that we have the digression (*Mos.* 2.25–44) about how the LXX came into being, the description of the Tabernacle and the high priest's vestments and the sacrifices (*Mos.* 2.76–158), and the exposition of the laws of the punishment of the blasphemer (*Mos.* 2.192–208), the Sabbath-breaker (*Mos.* 2.209–20), the regulations concerning Passover (*Mos.* 2.221–32), and the laws of inheritance (*Mos.* 2.233–45). The very fact that Philo repeats in Book 2 some of the same stories, such as the crossing of the Sea of Reeds (1.163–80, 2.247–57) and the manna (*Mos.* 1.191–208, 2.258–69), that he has recounted in Book 1 would indicate that the purposes of the two books are different. Geljon 2002, 31, has characterized *Mos.* as a philosophical biography and asserts that just as in the philosophical schools the life of the philosopher was read before studying his writings with the help of a commentary, so in Philo's school *Mos.* was intended to be read before studying his commentaries on the Pentateuch. We would add, however, that this is true particularly for Book 1 of the treatise. Geljon 2002, 27, concludes that the structure of *Mos.*, determined by the four offices of Moses as philosopher-king, legislator, high priest, and prophet, shows that it is a philosophical treatise rather than a biography, but, we may respond, this is really true only for Book 2. Only once (*Mos.* 2.99), when he refers to the symbolism represented by the cherubim in the Tabernacle, does Philo say that they are allegorical representations (ὑπόνοιαι) of the two most august and highest potencies of G-d, the creative and the kingly.[32]

To be sure, in the biography of Abraham (*Abr.* 88) Philo mentions and differentiates between two expositions, the literal and the allegorical, of Abram's migration from Chaldea. Again (68), after describing Abram's migration from Chaldea according to the literal interpretation, he does mention, though he does not elaborate, how this migration is to be interpreted according to the laws of allegory (κατὰ . . . τοὺς ἐν ἀλληγορίᾳ νόμους), namely, as he says, as a virtue-loving soul in search for the true G-d.

Philo is clearly aware that the allegorical method is separate and distinct from the literal interpretation, as we see in his remark (*Abr.* 99) that he has heard (ἤκουσα) that some natural philosophers interpret the episode of Abraham and Sarah in Egypt allegorically (ἀλληγορούντων), not without good reason (ἀπὸ σκοποῦ, "away from the mark"); and he then proceeds, indeed, to present this allegorical interpretation. Occasionally, as, for example, in his account of the visit of the angels to Abraham (*Abr.* 119, 131), he tells or warns the reader that he is about to leave the literal exposition and is about to begin the allegorical. He asserts (*Abr.* 147), after his discussion of the destruction of Sodom, that what he has presented is the obvious (φανερός) rendering of the narrative as suited for the multitude (πρὸς τοὺς πολλούς). After this he presents at length (*Abr.* 147–66) the hidden, symbolic meaning which appeals to the few (πρὸς ὀλίγους). Likewise, after presenting the literal interpretation of the account of Abraham's readiness to sacrifice his son Isaac, Philo (*Abr.* 200) remarks that there is also a further explanation, obscure to the many but recognized by those who prefer the mental to the sensible and which he then proceeds to set forth. Again, after narrating the separation of Abraham from Lot, he proceeds to the allegorical exposition (*Abr.* 217–24). Likewise, after narrating the story of the war of the five versus the four kings according to the literal sense, Philo expounds the allegorical interpretation (*Abr.* 236–44).

In *Ios.* (28–36), after presenting the narrative of the sale of Joseph by his brothers according to the literal interpretation, Philo, as in *Abr.*, turns to explain the underlying meaning (ἐν ὑπονοίαις, *Ios.* 28), since, as he says, all or most of the Pentateuch is an allegory. Then, after resuming the literal interpretation of the narrative of Joseph's service under Potiphar (*Ios.* 37–57), he interrupts himself (*Ios.* 58–79) with the comment that he should now, in due course, show the lessons revealed by the story. He thereupon (*Ios.* 80–124) resumes the narrative of Joseph's incarceration and liberation, after which he examines the allegorical import of this pericope (*Ios.* 125–50). He then, in a most unusual turn, gives an alternate allegorical explanation (*Ios.* 151–56). Philo now resumes his literal interpretation (*Ios.* 157–270) until the end of the story. We may wonder why Philo does not present an allegorical interpretation of this, the largest segment of the Joseph narrative.

But even more remarkably, we may wonder why Philo generally avoids presenting an allegorical interpretation of the Moses narrative, at least in *Mos.* Perhaps the answer may be found in Philo's statement (*Mos.* 1.1) that his aim, as we have noted, is to bring the story of Moses to the attention of those who deserve not to remain in ignorance of it. It seems clear from the remark that follows, namely that Greek writers have refused to treat him as worthy of memory, that Philo seeks to correct this by informing these Greek writers, clearly non-Jews, of the truth about Moses' greatness. Apparently, since, as we have seen, the *Mos.* is intended for a wider, non-Jewish audience, Philo avoids the esoteric, allegorical approach, which would be understood only by a much smaller circle of Jews. It is only when he comes to the description of the high priest's vestments and the apparatus of the Tabernacle that he feels the need to present an allegorical interpretation, since a literal interpretation would most likely leave the non-Jewish reader wondering why these vestments and apparatus must be as they are in their intricate details.

On the other hand, there is no statement at the beginning of the biographies of Abraham and of Joseph that Philo is seeking to correct misrepresentations of these biblical figures; and if he presents allegorical in addition to literal interpretations, he intends the allegorical reading for the few (*Abr.* 147, 200) who seek the hidden meaning. These would most likely be Jews.

If, exceptionally, we find that Philo (*Mos.* 1.67) does offer an explanation of the symbolism of the burning bush (Exod. 3:1–6), it is because the Bible does not explain the connection between the fact that the bush was burning but was not consumed and G-d's statement to Moses (Exod. 3:7–9) that He has seen the affliction of the Israelites being oppressed in Egypt and that He was sending Moses to Pharaoh to take the Israelites out of slavery. Philo (*Mos.* 1.2), at the very beginning of his treatise, asserts that Greek writers have hitherto refused to treat the story of Moses as worthy of memory; and we may gather that one of the reasons for this neglect and misrepresentation is that Greek writers found the biblical narrative to be difficult to understand or even irrational. Hence, Philo here corrects this by explaining the connection between the burning bush and G-d's assurance to Moses, namely that the bush symbolizes the suffering Israelites and that the fact that the bush was not consumed symbolizes that the sufferers would not be destroyed by their aggressors. Significantly, at the beginning of his essay (*Mos.* 1.4), Philo asserts that he will tell the story of Moses on the basis of what is written in the Bible, as complemented by what he has heard from the elders of the nation. In this case, the explanation of the symbolism, significantly enough, is paralleled in the midrashic tradition.[33]

Arnaldez and his co-editors (1967, 11) have noted the unique position of *Mos.* among Philo's works in its almost total avoidance of allegory, so that sometimes it has even been doubted that it was written by Philo. However, as they point out, the fact that Philo elsewhere (*Virt.* 52) says specifically that he has already set forth the actions of Moses from his earliest years to old age in two treatises (συντάξεσιν) which he has written about the life of Moses clearly indicates that the biography of Moses, which indeed consists of two books, was authored by Philo.

In general, especially as compared with Josephus' interpretation of the Bible, Philo in his biography of Moses is more faithful to the biblical narrative, though he does indicate, as we have noted, that he has drawn upon the tradition of the elders (*Mos.* 1.4), presumably the oral tradition parallel to that of the rabbis. Since, indeed, his primary aim in the essay on Moses is to reach non-Jewish readers, he may have felt that he would lose credibility with those of his readers such as the anonymous author of *On the Sublime* (see Feldman 1993a, 533–34, n. 21) who were familiar with the LXX, if he radically changed the interpretation of the text of the Pentateuch. If we ask why Josephus, who is similarly addressing his *A.J.* primarily to a non-Jewish audience, is not afraid that he will lose his credibility by virtue of the fact that he takes such liberties with the biblical narrative (see Feldman 1998a and 1998b), we may reply that Josephus is, indeed, in the prooemium of his *A.J.* extremely conscious of this charge, since he insists (*A.J.* 1.17) that, in point of fact, he is not adding to or subtracting from the biblical text. Moreover, he is even more concerned with apologetics than Philo (so also Heinemann 1935, 374), who is particularly eager to reach his philosophical audience.

In sum, during the Hellenistic period the gap between encomium, history, and biography had narrowed. Unlike his biographies of Abraham and Joseph, Philo's biography of Moses presents a direct interpretation of the biblical text and avoids allegory.

6. Philo's Knowledge of Oral Tradition

Heinemann 1927, 152–59, disputes the thesis of Hirzel (1900) that Philo's reference to the "unwritten law" (ἄγραφος νόμος) (*Abr.* 5, 16, etc.), as embodied by the patriarchs, is a Jewish concept and is equivalent to the rabbinic oral law. He points out that the important difference is that the latter is not antecedent to the written law but parallel to it. But, as Marcus (1935, 467) points out, at the very least there is a similarity between Philo's "unwritten law" and the Noachian commandments mentioned in rabbinic tradition (*b. Sanh.* 56–60).

In a very important and little noticed remark, Philo (*Mos.* 1.4) states that his account of Moses will be drawn from two sources—from the sacred books, that is, the Pentateuch, that he has left behind him, and from some of the elders of the nation (παρά τινων ἀπὸ τοῦ ἔθνους πρεσβυτέρων). He then adds that he always interweaves what he has been told (τὰ λεγόμενα), presumably oral tradition, with what he has read, and that he consequently believes that he has a more accurate knowledge of Moses' life's history than others.

The fact that he uses the word "always" (ἀεί) indicates that this combination of written and oral sources is to be found throughout his writings.

In thus seeking to compare his account with that of others who have preceded him, he specifically says here that he has drawn upon oral sources, namely "the elders of the nation." Who are these "elders of the nation"? Borgen 1997, 21, says that since Philo did not seek to assert the independence and greatness of Alexandrian Judaism over Palestinian Judaism, the elders whom he here mentions were probably in fact primarily Alexandrian teachers. The term "elders" also, however, is used as a technical term to designate the exponents of the oral law in Palestine (see Wolfson 1947, 1:189–90). That the rabbis did issue rulings that were applicable in Egypt in particular may be seen from the statement in the Mishnah (*Yad.* 4:3) ascribed to the second-century Rabbi Tarfon, that they, that is the rabbis, have made Egypt liable for the poor man's tithe, so that the poor of Israel may depend on it in the Sabbatical year. Of course, to what extent such Palestinian teachers succeeded in their efforts and to what extent they were preceded by similar claimants remains uncertain.

Elsewhere, at the very beginning of his essay *Decal.* (1), Philo mentions the distinction between the written and the unwritten laws, noting that in preceding treatises, presumably such as *Abr.*, *Ios.*, and *Mos.*, he had related the lives of those who are presented in the sacred books (αἱ ἱεραὶ βίβλοι) as founders of the Jewish people, and who are themselves unwritten laws (νόμοι ἄγραφοι), a reference to his thesis that even before the revelation of the written law at Sinai the patriarchs followed the laws laid down by nature (*Abr.* 16).

Philo (*Mos.* 1.162) says that since Moses was destined to be a legislator, G-d caused him, long before he was actually appointed to that position, to be the reasonable and living impersonation of law, just as Abraham was himself a law and an unwritten statute (*Abr.* 276). Indeed, says Philo (*Mos.* 2.4), since to command what should be done and to forbid what should not be done is the peculiar function of law, the king, whose duty it is to issue such commands, is a living law, and the law is a just king. This is the view of such Hellenistic non-Jewish philosophers as Archytas (*ap.* Stob., 43.132), Musonius (*ap.* Stob., 47.67), and Diotogenes (*ap.* Stob., 4.7.61) (see Goodenough 1928, 55–104).

But in addition to these unwritten laws, which are identified with the patriarchs themselves, Philo (*Spec.* 4.149–50) mentions decisions (δόγματα) of men of old (παλαιοὶ ἄνδρες) which he speaks of here as customs (ἔθη) that are unwritten laws (ἄγραφοι νόμοι) which children inherit from their parents and by which they should still abide.[34] The divinely gifted (θεσπέσιοι) men who ordained these customs and who, he says, are greater than those of his own time (*Migr.* 90) would appear to refer to elders such as the rabbis. Philo (*Spec.* 4.150), moreover, like the rabbis (*y. Sanh.* 11.6.30a), goes so far as to say that one who obeys the unwritten laws deserves even more praise than one who obeys the written laws.

Philo proceeds to admit that countless multitudes of Jews from the Diaspora made pilgrimages to Jerusalem (*Spec.* 1.69) and that friendships were formed there with those who had not previously known one another. On at least one occasion Philo himself (*Prov.* 2.64) visited the Temple in Jerusalem and offered up prayers and sacrifices there. It would seem likely that while there he heard oral interpretations of the Pentateuch; but whether these sources were Palestinian or Alexandrian, they represented an oral tradition, which ultimately may have gone back to Palestinian sources. Indeed, as Belkin (1940) and Cohen (1995) have noted, Philo's intepretations of Jewish law are often parallel to Palestinian Oral Law.

In sum, when Philo says in *Mos.* that he has drawn from some of the elders of the nation, he is referring to the exponents of the oral law in the Land of Israel. Elsewhere, he refers to customs that are unwritten laws that were ordained by divinely gifted men who are greater than those of his own time. This would appear to be a reference to the rabbis who expounded the oral law.

7. Philo as Midrashist

One of the fiercest debates in modern Philonic scholarship is on the question of Philo's relationship in his biblical essays with the midrashim that have come down to us.[35] As Cohen (1995, 14) has pointed out, midrash is the literary form that Jewish thought and theology have most often adopted as the best vehicle for the exposition of ideas. What inspires its use is the positive emotional link to the sacred text felt by the speaker, the writer, and the audience. Since Scripture was regularly expounded in the synagogues and schools, it was the natural means to transmit contemporary moral messages. If, indeed, Philo's essays on biblical episodes are, in effect, like sermons, we should not be surprised if they sometimes incorporate midrashic-like expositions.

To a considerable degree, Philo's biblical expositions and Josephus' *A.J.* seem to belong to the genre of midrash, in the style of the "rewritten Bible," in that they retell the biblical narrative by arranging and supplementing it, by explaining difficult passages, and by defending the Jews against charges that had been made against them on the basis of the biblical text (Feldman 1998a, 16–17).

One common feature of both Philo and rabbinic exegesis is that they are often in the form of question and answer. Thus, in an example that Borgen 1997, 86–88, cites, Philo (*Opif.* 77) asks why man was the last in the world's creation. The same question is asked in *t. Sanh.* 8.7. Philo's answer (*Opif.* 78) is in the form of an analogy: just as in the case of a banquet, one does not send out invitations until everything has been prepared, so also in the case of G-d's creation. Precisely the same analogy is found in rabbinic exegesis (*t. Sanh.* 8.9), and even the wording is similar. Furthermore, Philo (*Opif.* 77) implies that his answer is based on tradition, quite conceivably the same tradition that is represented in the *Tosefta*: "Those, then, who have studied more deeply than others the laws of Moses and who examine their contents with all possible minuteness, maintain" the answer that he gives.[36]

If we accept the definition of Porton 1979, 112, in midrash the original verse is explicitly cited or clearly alluded to. This, indeed, is generally the way of Philo. Josephus, though he may be explaining the verses as does the midrash, does not cite the original verse as such. Moreover, midrashim are not, or at least originally were not created to be, a running commentary but, like modern sermons, digress, frequently at length. Though they omit relatively little, they are not intended to be systematic and comprehensive. Furthermore, it is the way of the rabbinic midrashim to present more than one comment or interpretation of a given incident. However, one remarkable respect in which Philo's midrashic-like interpretation differs from that of Josephus is that Philo actually presents contradictory interpretations of the same biblical passages, such as those with regard to Joseph.[37] Moreover, Philo does present muliple views in *QG* and *QE*, whereas Josephus does not do so. Furthermore, in rabbinic literature the comments are generally assigned to specific rabbis, whereas Philo and Josephus never cite any rabbis as sources for their explanations. While it is true that the earliest extant rabbinic midrashim date from the fourth century, there is reason to think, especially if we note the midrashic-like additions in Philo and Josephus, that they go back to an earlier period.

Perhaps the closest analogue to Philo's biblical essays and Josephus' *A.J.* is to be found in the Targumim, written in Aramaic, the earliest datable of which are a Targum of Job (covering Job 37:10–42:11) and some fragments of

Lev. 16:12–15, 18–21, found among the Dead Sea Scrolls and apparently written in the first century C.E. In Targumim, as in Philo's and Josephus' paraphrases, it is impossible, without looking at the original biblical text, to discern what is the base text and what has been amplified or omitted, so seamlessly have the additions, for example, been made to the biblical text.

It has often been suggested that a considerable knowledge of Hebrew or of Aramaic was necessary for contact with midrashim. But, as Cohen 1995, 16–17, has noted, a broad spectrum of literature had been translated into Greek from Hebrew or Aramaic by Philo's time, and, indeed, much of the Pseudepigraphic literature that has survived has come down to us only because it was translated into Greek. When a papyrus was found that listed etymologies of names parallel to those of Philo, to be sure, Rokeah 1968, 70–82, suggested that rather than regard this as evidence of a common Palestinian-Alexandrian tradition, rabbinic exegesis and etymological interpretation might have independently produced similar results; and if we find similar interpretations of names, such as Abel (Philo, *Migr.* 102; Josephus, *A.J.* 1.52) and Ishmael (Philo, *Mut.* 202; Jos., *A.J.* 1.190), this may well be due to mutual dependence upon onomastica such as have been found in papyri in Egypt (Rokeah 1968, 70–82). The fact that several of Philo's etymologies agree with such a list even in their linguistic peculiarities is a strong argument for the view that Philo was dependent upon it.[38]

Borgen 1965, 7–20, has demonstrated how a tradition about manna was common to Palestinian midrash and Philo. He examines six texts for the tradition about bread from heaven—*Midr. Exod. Rab.* 25.2, *Midr. Exod. Rab.* 25.6, *Mek. Exod.* 16.4, *Petirat Mosheh* (in Adolf Jellinek, ed., *Bet ha-Midrasch*, 1.119), and Philo, *Mos.* 1.201–2 and 2.267. All six versions speak of bread coming from heaven and from earth; all mention water from heaven and from earth; and all agree in making heaven and earth interchange their normal function when the manna came down. In addition, *Mid. Exod. Rab.* 25.6 and *Mos.* 1.201–2 employ the term "from below" (מלמטן, κάτωθεν), meaning "from the earth." That the tradition originated from Palestine rather than from Egypt can be deduced from the fact that it is unlikely that Philo, living in Egypt, where there is so little rain, would think of rain coming from heaven as the common order of nature. Since, however, the tradition from Palestine gave this usual picture, he had to either omit the part about rain, as he did in *Mos.* 2.267, or reinterpret it rather awkwardly by referring to the Nile River as rain from below, as he did in *Mos.* 1.201–2. Hence, Philo adjusted the haggadic tradition to his own outlook. Since the versions in *Midr. Exod. Rab.*, *Mek. Exod.*, and *Petirat Mosheh* represent the same tradition that we find in Philo, they must go back to at least the time of Philo.

In addition, Borgen 1965, 51–58, has noted that the same five-fold pattern is to be found in Philo's homilies and in those of Palestinian midrash: the text, with the first verse of a pericope from the Pentateuch; the connecting formula between the text and a second text cited in the proem; the second text, the prooemial text, followed by an exposition; the connecting formula between the exposition and the close; and the text from the pericope repeated.[39]

Muffs 1975, 30–32, has cited another example where Philo seems to reflect the rabbinic midrashic tradition. In Exod. 4:14 we read that when Moses tells G-d that he has a speech defect and asks that He send another person to go to the Pharaoh, G-d is angry and exclaims: "Is there not Aaron, your brother, the Levite? I know that he can speak well; and behold, he is coming out to meet you, and when he sees you he will be glad in his heart." Then we read (Exod. 4:27) that G-d said to Aaron: "Go into the wilderness to meet Moses." The text continues: "So he went and met him at the mountain of G-d and kissed him." Philo (*Mos.* 1.85), in his paraphrase of these passages, adds an extra-biblical statement, namely, that when Moses and Aaron met, Aaron's soul had, in fact, been prepared beforehand (προυπεἰργαστο) through the watchful working (ἐπιφροσύνη, "thoughtfulness," "wisdom") of G-d to obedience (πειθαρχία, "obedience to the command of someone in authority"), so that without hesitation (ἀνενδοιάστως, "unequivocally," "without doubt") he assented and readily followed. It is clear from Philo's language that Aaron's agreement could not be taken for granted, perhaps because, as Moses' older brother, he felt that he should have been chosen by G-d. In any case, Philo has added that G-d had to use His power of persuasion to overcome his hesitation so that he might assent to his role unequivocally. This Philonic addition is paralleled in the midrashic tradition (*Tan. Yashan* on Exod. 4:27), to be sure not recorded until much later but, we may conjecture, reflecting an early tradition. There we read that G-d revealed Himself to Aaron and told him: "Go out to meet Moses, your brother, in order to let him know that you are happy concerning this matter." This is parallel to Philo's addition that G-d predisposed Aaron so that he would agree. Whereas the biblical phrase (Exod. 4:14) declares that Aaron would be glad in his heart, in both Philo and the midrashic tradition G-d played a key role in predisposing Aaron to assenting unequivocally to his role. Muffs 1975, 32, closes his discussion of the parallel with the following statement: "The light that they [the Philonic and midrashic passages] shed on each other is not an isolated phenomenon. It is obvious that the last word on the subject is yet to be said."[40]

In sum, to a considerable degree Philo's biblical expositions seem to belong to the genre of midrash in that they arrange and supplement the biblical narrative. Borgen and Muffs have demonstrated how a tradition was common to rabbinic midrash and Philo. The fact that Philo says that he has drawn upon the elders of the nation would appear to be a reference to exponents of the oral tradition such as we find in midrashim.

II. The Life of Moses

1. Moses' Genealogy

In the first book of his essay *Mos.*, Philo's goal is to present Moses as the perfect representation of the ideal of the kingly character (Goodenough 1935, 181). Ancient biographies, as Momigliano 1971a, 82–83, notes, regularly include discussion of the person's ancestry, childhood, and education.[1]

Accordingly, we must start with the genealogy of the kings and heroes. With regard to genealogy, the first-century Greek rhetorician Aelius Theon of Alexandria declares that the first of the thirty-six stages of praising a person is to laud his ancestry (Spengel 1854, 2:60–130; Talbert 1980, 135).[2] Indeed, the Greeks made a virtue of good birth in and of itself. When Plato (*Hippias* 285D) defines the term ἀρχαιολογία ("ancient history," "antiquarian lore"), the first subject which he says it includes is genealogies of heroes and of ordinary men. The importance of genealogy is seen in the *Menexenus* (237A) ascribed to Plato, where he says: "They were good because they sprang from good fathers." We see the same emphasis in Aristotle's description of the great-souled man (μεγαλόψυχος) as well-born (εὐγενής) (*EN* 4.3.1124A21–22). When Aristotle considers the gifts of fortune by which human character is affected, his first topic of discussion is good birth (*Rhetorica* 2.15.1390B11–30). The well-born will look down, he says, even on those who are as good as their own ancestors. So much stress was placed on genealogy that the matter became a fit subject for satire, as we see in the fifth century B.C.E. parody of Homer known as *Batrachomyomachia* ("The Battle of the Frogs and Mice"), attributed to Pigres of Halicarnassus, where (line 13) a frog asks a mouse: "Who are you, stranger? Whence do you come to this shore? And who is the one who begot you?"

Philo, after his general introduction to the essay *Mos.*, begins his account of Moses (1.5) with the statement that Moses was by race (γένος) a Chaldean (Χαλδαῖος). Philo seems to use the terms "Chaldean" and "Hebrew" interchangeably,[3] as we see in the account of the discovery of the infant Moses by the Pharaoh's daughter (*Mos.* 1.15), where we are told that she recognized that he belonged to the Hebrews (Ἑβραῖοι). Wong 1992, 13, suggests that as time went on, Philo felt compelled to be more precise in his use of the word "Chaldean," seeking to dissociate himself from the identification of the Jews with the Chaldeans, notably after leading an embassy to Rome in 39/40, because of the association of Chaldeans with astrology, inasmuch as the Chaldeans were often the source of riots and troubles in Rome. But we may note that the expulsion of the Jews and astrologers from Rome is said to have occurred in the year 139 B.C.E. (Valerius Maximus, *Facta et Dicta Memorabilia* 1.3.3, according to the epitomes of Januarius Nepotianus and Julius Paris), long before the birth of Philo; and Jews and astrologers are not coupled in any of the accounts of the expulsion of the Jews from Rome in 19 C.E. (Josephus, *A.J.* 18.81–84; Tac., *Annals* 2.85.4; Suet., *Tiberius* 36.1; and Dio Cassius 57.18.5 a). On the contrary, we may suggest that by denominating Moses a Chaldean, Philo is accomplishing two purposes: in the first place, he is ascribing further antiquity to Moses, since the Chaldeans were more ancient than the Hebrews; and, in the second place, he is associating Moses with Chaldean astronomy, the greatest achievement of the Chaldeans (*Migr.* 178; *Somn.* 1.53; *Abr.* 69),[4] in which the youthful Moses is said by Philo to have been instructed (*Mos.* 1.23). That the Greeks prized astronomy so highly we may see from its position in the curriculum of the higher education of the philosopher-kings in Plato (*R.* 7.528E–530C). Significantly, moreover, when Philo discusses the translation of the Pentateuch into Greek, again he appears to want to indicate its antiquity, since he refers to the language of the Pentateuch as Chaldean (*Mos.* 2.26, 31, 38, 40 [*ter*]).

Whereas the Bible (Exod. 2:1) introduces the parents of Moses with the bland statement that "a man from the house of Levi went and took to wife a daughter of Levi," Philo (*Mos.* 1.5), realizing how much attention was given in antiquity to genealogy, says that he will start with what is necessarily the right place to begin. He then proceeds to note (*Mos.* 1.7) that Moses had for his father and mother the best of their contemporaries, members of the same tribe, whereas when Josephus first mentions Amram, the father of Moses, he is content merely to state that he was one of those well-born among the Hebrews (*A.J.* 2.210).[5] However, whereas Josephus greatly elevates the status of Amram by having G-d Himself appear to him and prophesy the future greatness of the son to be born, Philo has no such scenario and, in fact, does not even mention the name of Amram, so concerned is he to focus completely on

Moses alone. The rabbis, like Josephus, greatly exalt the position of Moses' father, Amram; indeed, they state (*b. Soṭ.* 12a, *Midr. Exod. Rab.* 1.19) that Amram was the greatest man of his generation. According to one view (*Midr. Exod. Rab.* 1.13), he was even the head of the Sanhedrin, the supreme judicial authority of the Jews.

Furthermore, when the Bible finally does give the genealogy of Moses (Exod. 6:16–20), it lists Moses as the fifth generation from Jacob. Philo, like Demetrius (*ap.* Eus. *PE* 9.29.2), Josephus (*A.J.* 2.229),[6] the rabbis (*Midr. Gen. Rab.* 19.7, *Midr. Cant. Rab.* 5.1, *Pesiq. Rb. Kah.* 23.10 [Mandelbaum ed., 2.343–44]), and the Samaritan tradition, lists Moses as the seventh generation from Abraham, the founder of the whole Jewish nation.[7] Indeed, Josephus is critical of Lysimachus for not establishing Moses' descent and parentage (*Ap.* 1.316). He is particularly upset because the eminent genealogy of a hero was crucial to establishing his greatness.

Taking note of the report in Exod. 2:19 that Jethro's daughters tell their father that an Egyptian man had saved them from the shepherds, Philo (*Mut.* 117) emphasizes that Jethro's daughters called Moses an Egyptian. On the contrary, he says, Moses was not only a Hebrew, but he was of the purest race of the Hebrews (that is, the Levites), which alone is consecrated. Elsewhere Philo (*Congr.* 131–32, *Leg.* 2.51–52), commenting on the statement (Exod. 2:1) that a man from the tribe of Levi married a daughter of Levi, says that the child of this marriage, Moses, being from the tribe of Levi on both his father's and mother's side, has a double link with truth. As evidence he cites the fact that the Levites, in their loyalty to G-d alone, did not show favoritism toward their own kin but slew all those who had worshipped the Golden Calf.

In sum, the ancients placed a great premium on genealogy. By denominating Moses a Chaldean, Philo ascribed further antiquity to him, since the Chaldeans were even more ancient than the Hebrews and were particularly distinguished in astronomy, so prized by the Greeks. Philo stresses that Moses had for parents the best of their contemporaries, who were of the purest race of the Hebrews.

2. Moses' Birth

Both the biblical text (Exod. 2:7) and Philo (*Mos.* 1.8) indicate that the Pharaoh was afraid that the Israelites, who kept on increasing, might revolt against him.[8] Consequently, he gave orders to put the male infants to death but to rear the females.[9] Philo, however, has rearranged the order of events: he places the enslavement of the Israelites, which in the Bible appears before the issuance of the murder decree by the Pharaoh, at the end of the narrative of Moses' birth.[10] As Cohen 1993, 10–11, remarks, the biblical account raises the question as to why the Egyptians, after enslaving the Israelites, would seek to decrease their population, inasmuch as a slave owner's supreme interest normally is in increasing the number of his slaves. Moreover, if the Pharaoh was interested in decreasing the number of the Israelites, it would have been more effective if he had done away with the females. Furthermore, if the Pharaoh's concern was with decreasing the birthrate of the Israelites, it seems strange that after the account of the birth of one child we hear nothing more about the Pharaoh's decree. On the contrary, the center of attention is the Pharaoh's desire that the Israelites remain in Egypt. Hence, Philo detaches the enslavement from the biblical explanation, which accounts it to the tremendous increase in population of the Israelites. In Philo's version, the Israelites are enslaved due to the Pharaoh's cruelty, which is thus emphasized; and this cruelty is highlighted by the contrast with the hospitality that the king should have granted to the Israelites as strangers and suppliants (*Mos.* 1.35–36).

Indeed, in treatise after treatise Philo presents a uniformly derogatory picture of the Egyptian pharaohs.[11] The Pharoah is the mind that is the king of the body, namely Egypt.[12] He is steeped in greed, is licentious and unjust (see Feldman 1998b, 44–45), and is the very antithesis of G-d (*Somn.* 2.183) (see Feldman 1998b, 75–78). Josephus (*A.J.* 2.201) goes so far as to place the blame not on the Pharaoh but on the Egyptians, who are described as a voluptuous and lazy people, and on the Pharaoh's scribes (*A.J.* 2.205) (Feldman 1998b, 82–88). On the other hand, the rabbis, while magnifying the Pharaoh's brutality, depict G-d as telling Moses to treat the Pharaoh with the deference and respect due to a sovereign (Feldman 1998b, 78–82).

In both the Bible and Philo, the Pharaoh is fearful of the growing numbers of the Israelites. There is a difference, however, in that in the former we read (Exod. 1:10) that it is the Pharaoh's fear that the Israelites become more numerous and that if a war should occur, they would join the enemies of the Egyptians and leave the land. In Philo's version (*Mos.* 1.8), the Pharaoh's fear is that, far from leaving the country, the Israelites would try to take over the country. This would fit in with the view of such anti-Jewish writers as Manetho, Chaeremon, Lysimachus, and Apion, as we see in Josephus' *Ap.* (1.228, 1.290, 1.306, 2.20), that the Israelites were actually expelled from Egypt. This would also fit in with Philo's apologetic goal of defending his Egyptian Jewish constituency against such charges in his own day. A major aim of Philo in his *Mos.* is to answer the charge that the Jews are aggressive and expansionistic.

In Pseudo-Philo's version (9.1), the Pharaoh is concerned because of the increase in the number of the Israelites, but no reason is given as to why he is concerned. Josephus, however, strikingly omits all mention of the increase in numbers of the Israelites, presumably because he is sensitive to the tremendous increase in the number of Jews during the first century B.C.E. and the first century C.E. and to the implications of this (see Feldman 1993a, 288–341). Instead, he contends that the Egyptians became bitterly disposed toward the Israelites through envy of their prosperity (*A.J.* 2.202). Moreover, whereas, according to the Bible and Philo (*Mos.* 1.8), the Pharaoh's aim in giving the command to kill all Israelite males is to prevent the Israelites from becoming so numerous, the Pharaoh's motive in Josephus (*A.J.* 2.215) is to prevent the birth of the great Moses.

Moreover, whereas the Hebrew text and the LXX version of Exod. 1:15 specifically state that the midwives whom the Pharaoh appointed to enforce his edict of the male children's slaughter were two Hebrews and give their names as Shifrah and Puah, Josephus (*A.J.* 2.206), without giving the women's number or their names, identifies them as Egyptians. He was apparently troubled by the question as to how two midwives could supervise so huge a population of Israelites, since according to Exod. 12:37 the number of adult men alone who left Egypt was 600,000. Moreover, it would seem unlikely that an Egyptian king would entrust Hebrew women with carrying out such a cruel decree against their own people. Philo (*Her.* 128) is apparently untroubled by such considerations and, on the contrary, is aware that non-Jewish readers might well be aware of the LXX version of the Pentateuch and might well be present at the annual celebrations of its completion on the island of Pharos, which they attended in large numbers (*Mos.* 2.41). Consequently, he omits mention of the midwives altogether in his biography of Moses (*Mos.* 1.8) but remains true to the biblical text and gives the names of the two midwives (*Her.* 128), though not in *Mos.*, and identifies them as Hebrews. Jub. (47:2) and Pseudo-Philo (9.1) do not mention the midwives at all, let alone give their names and identities.

Philo (*Mos.* 1.8) says nothing about a debate among the Israelites as to whether they should continue to have children in view of this terrible decree. According to Josephus (*A.J.* 2.210), Amram, Moses' father, was in a quandary since he feared that the Israelites would become extinct through lack of a young generation, but he does not indicate what measures he proposed to take to counter the Pharaoh's decree. Instead, Josephus notes that Amram was troubled because his wife was pregnant.[13]

Presumably basing himself on the midwives' statement to the Pharaoh (Exod. 1:19) that the Hebrew women, unlike the Egyptian women, give birth before the midwife comes to them, Philo (*Migr.* 142) furnishes the extra-biblical detail that Jochebed, Moses' mother, gave birth to Moses without requiring a midwife's skill.[14]

The Samaritan *Molad* (p. 19, ll. 2–3) records that there had been a buoyant expectancy that Egypt would be destroyed through the hand of an Israelite prophet, to whom there would be none his equal and who would live to the age of 120. The *Molad* reports that the Israelites had two or three or even four children at one time. The rabbinic tradition[15] goes even further and asserts that Israelite women bore as many as six or twelve or even sixty or seventy children at one time. Philo focuses on the one child, Moses.

The Apocryphal Book of Wis. (18:5) refers to the fact that since the Egyptians had sought to kill the infants of the Israelites by drowning them in the Nile, the exposure and rescue of a single child, Moses, was enough to convict them and to result in the destruction of his would-be murderers through their being drowned in the Sea of Reeds. Indeed, Josephus (*A.J.* 2.205–6, 234) reports that one of the Egyptian sacred scribes had prophesied that someone would be born to the Israelites who would humble the Egyptians—a prophecy that resulted in the slaughter of innocent babes. However, unlike Josephus, who adds Moses' father's dream confirming Moses' future greatness (*A.J.* 2.212–16), Philo, in his account of Moses, in accordance with his tendency to remain true to the biblical narrative and, in general, to reduce or rationalize such miraculous elements, does not have such a prophecy. Moreover, he specifically says that Moses' parents were ignorant of the future (*Mos.* 1.12).

The Samaritan *Molad* (p. 20, ll. 15–17) states that the Israelite wives wept, asking G-d to give them fast delivery of their babies. Indeed, when their labor pains began, the Israelite women went out to the desert, and G-d gave them health and recuperative powers. If the child turned out to be a male, the mother would leave it in the desert under the care of angels, who would feed the baby with honey and oil; and she herself would return to her home. In time the angel would lead the baby to his father's house. We find a similar tradition in rabbinic literature (*b. Soṭ.* 11b), namely, that when it came time for the Israelite women to give birth, they went into the field beneath the apple trees; and G-d sent down someone from the high heavens who washed and straightened the limbs of the child and who fed the baby with honey and oil.[16]

The New Testament account (Matt. 1:8–2:23, Luke 1:5–35) of the birth of Jesus bears an obvious resemblance to the biblical and later accounts of the birth of Moses. In both the New Testament account and in the biblical account there is an edict against male babies, preceded by an attempt to achieve the same objective secretly by a devious design (in the Moses story by means of midwives, in the New Testament by means of wise men), divine intervention, and the rescue of a single son. In particular, we find the statement (Matt. 1:20–23) that an angel appeared in a dream to Joseph, to whom Mary had been betrothed, and assured him that Mary would bear a son who would save his people from their sins. This is similar to the tradition recorded by Josephus (*A.J.* 2.210–16) that after Amram's wife, Jochebed, had become pregnant, G-d appeared to him in a dream and assured him that she would bear a son who would deliver the Hebrews from their distress among the Egyptians. The wise men (Matt. 2:7) who are summoned by King Herod and who are told to examine the stars are paralleled by the sacred scribes who are skilled in their ability to predict the future; according to Josephus (*A.J.* 2.205), by the astrologers, according to the midrashic tradition (*Midr. Exod. Rab.* 1.22), by the magicians, according to *Pirqe R. El.* (48), and by the chief magicians Jannes and Jambres, according to the *Tg. Ps.-J.* (on Exod. 1:15). Herod's decision, to kill all male children who were two years old and under, parallels the Pharaoh's edict to kill all Israelite baby boys.[17]

Josephus (*A.J.* 2.218) and the rabbis (*Soṭ.* 12a, *Midr. Exod. Rab.* 1.20) say that Moses' mother, Jochebed, miraculously gave birth to him without pain; but Philo, whether or not he knew it, does not report such a tradition, nor does Pseudo-Philo. The rabbis give further miraculous details in connection with Moses' birth—that Jochebed was 130 years old[18] at that time (*Midr. Exod. Rab.* 19, *b. B. Bat.* 120a, *b. Soṭ.* 12a),[19] that when he came out of his mother's womb he was already circumcised (so also Pseudo-Philo 9.13), that when he was only three days old he not only walked but that he even talked with his parents, and that he actually refused to drink milk from his mother's breasts until she had received her payment from the Pharaoh's daughter (*Midr. Exod. Rab.* 11.20, *Midr. Deut. Rab.* 11.10); but neither Philo nor Josephus gives such miraculous details. The Samaritan *Molad* (p. 25, ll. 8–10) says that during the three months after Moses' birth, his light grew larger and larger, and all the other lights dimmed before his appearance, so that even the sun itself was eclipsed by his light.

Pseudo-Philo (9.14) adds that when the baby was born, the Israelite elders assembled and complained to Amram saying that it was preferable to die without having children than for the baby to be killed. Whereas the Bible (Exod. 2:2) says that Moses' mother hid him for three months, Philo (*Mos.* 1.9), without indicating that it was his mother who hid him, says that he was kept at home; and Josephus (*A.J.* 2.218), concerned that the father's role not be diminished, follows the LXX in saying that they, Moses' father and mother, hid him for three months.[20] Josephus, indeed, places the spotlight to a much greater degree on Moses' father, Amram, reporting at great length, in an extrabiblical addition, G-d's words of assurance and prediction of Moses' greatness (*A.J.* 2.212–17), as well as the additional detail that Amram had fallen under the wrath of the Pharaoh (*A.J.* 2.219).

A portion of a drama, *The Exodus*, by Ezekiel the Tragic Poet, has been preserved by Eus. (*PE* 9.28–29), who quotes it from the first-century-B.C.E. pagan Alexander Polyhistor. Part of this is also preserved by the third-century Christian Clement of Alexandria (*Strom.* 1.23.155.1–7, 156.1–2).[21] The central figure of the play is clearly Moses, and the major event is the Exodus (Exod. 1–15). Ezekiel has almost completely omitted miraculous and supernatural elements in his account of Moses' birth (see Jacobson 1983, 81). Thus, whereas the Bible (Exod. 2:2) states that his mother hid him for three months, Ezekiel adds (*ap.* Eus. *PE* 9.28.2) "as she told him." Moreover, whereas the Bible (Exod. 2:3) says that his mother took a wicker basket and smeared it with clay and pitch and placed the child in it, Ezekiel, as did Philo (*Mos.* 1.10) later, omits the wicker basket, clay, and pitch, presumably as unbecoming one who was to become heir apparent to the Egyptian throne. Instead we read that she wrapped him in an ornamental covering (κόσμος). Furthermore, whereas the Bible (Exod. 2:3) states that his mother placed the baby among the reeds at the bank of the river, Ezekiel, concerned that parents would thus expose an infant, adds that she placed him at the edge of the river in a thickly grown marsh (εἰς ἕλος δασύ), as we see also in Philo (*Mos.* 1.14: ἐν τῷ δασυτάτῳ τῶν ἑλῶν, "in the thickest part of the marshes").

The biblical account, in its brevity, does not explain why Moses' parents ceased to conceal him and exposed him on the river. Josephus' explanation (*A.J.* 2.219) is that Amram began to fear lest he be detected and perish with the child, having himself fallen under the wrath of the king. Philo's explanation (*Mos.* 1.10) is that, as is often the case under a monarch, there were persons prying into holes and corners, eager to report news to the king. Consequently, Moses' parents realized that their continuing to save the child would cause even greater sorrow, inasmuch as they themselves would forfeit their lives.[22] In the Bible (Exod. 2:3) it is Moses' mother who takes a wicker basket, smears it with clay and pitch, places the child in it, and puts it at the bank of the Nile River. In Philo (*Mos.* 1.10), on the other hand, as in Josephus (*A.J.* 2.221), both parents place the child on the bank of the river, perhaps because neither author wanted to ascribe to a woman alone the daring and heroic action of exposing the child on the river. Thus Philo and Josephus apologetically are calling attention to the difference between Jews, who raise all their children, and pagans, who do not (see Tacitus, *Histories* 5.3).

In addition, Philo paints psychological portraits of Moses' parents at this time of crisis, perhaps under the influence of the tragedians, notably Euripides, with whose works he was so well acquainted and who were so popular in the Alexandria of his day (see Feldman 1998a, 175). Indeed, we read in the Arist. (284) that when King Ptolemy Philadelphus asked one of the seventy-two translators of the Pentateuch what he should make his pastime in his hours of relaxation, the translator replied, "To watch plays performed with propriety and to set before one's eyes scenes from life presented with decency and restraint is profitable to one's life and appropriate." Philo (*Ebr.* 177) himself remarks that he has often been to the theater, where he has noticed the diverse effects of the same music on various people. He also notes (*Prob.* 141) how enthusiastically the audience in a theater, some of whom were presumably Jewish like himself, received a play of Euripides. Hence, Philo delves into the human feelings of Moses' parents and presents a much more poignant scene, adding that when they exposed the baby they did so with tears and that they departed groaning. They pitied themselves on being forced, as they said in self-reproach, to be the murderers of their own child, and pitied the child also on being left to perish in this unnatural way. He thus, apologetically, stresses that Moses' parents really had no other choice. He further adds an extra-biblical scene (*Mos.* 1.11) in which the parents accuse themselves, asking why they had not cast him away as soon as he was born. A child, they note, who has not survived to enjoy a normal nurture is not usually reckoned a human being. By nurturing him for three months they had procured more abundant affliction for themselves and torture for him, inasmuch as he would die when he was fully capable of feeling pleasure and pain. In this Philo may be reflecting the tradition later mentioned by Maimonides (*Mishneh Torah, Avel* 1:6), which, we may suppose, goes back to an earlier time, that a child who died before living for thirty days is regarded as not viable and that the laws of mourning do not apply in such a case.[23]

Philo (*Mos.* 1.12), realizing that the reader might well ask about the coincidence that the Egyptian princess just happened to be at the river when Moses was floating in a basket, adds to the Bible and remarks that all that now happened was brought about by G-d's providential concern (προμηθούμενος), though he is careful to qualify this with the phrase ἅ μοι δοκεῖ ("as it seems to me"). It is significant, as Cohen 1993, 41, has remarked, that while Philo does not refrain from ascribing the wonderful confluence of events to G-d, nevertheless he makes few references to G-d. When he does do so, as here, he is careful to defer to his sophisticated non-Jewish audience and to present the explanation of events as his own opinion or as a suggestion of others (*Mos.* 1.17, 1.19). The implication is that readers are entitled to draw their own conclusions, an attitude that we also find frequently in Josephus.[24]

The princess' name is not given in the Bible. In the Book of Jub. (47:5) her name is Tharmouth. Josephus (*A.J.* 2.224) gives her a name, Thermouthis, that is very similar. Philo, who, as always, is concerned to keep the focus on Moses, does not mention her name.[25]

Philo follows the biblical text (Exod. 2:5) in stating that the Pharaoh's daughter went down to the river to bathe. Pseudo-Philo remarks that she did so in accordance with what she had seen in a dream. Josephus (*A.J.* 2.224), drawing the Pharaoh's daughter according to what is a typical female image in his view, is more romantic in asserting that she played by the river. Philo (*Mos.* 1.13), however, adds several details concerning the Pharaoh's daughter, which serve to add drama to her rescue of Moses. Thus he adds that she was an only child of the Pharaoh, that she had been married for a considerable time but had never conceived a child,[26] that she naturally desired a child, particularly of the male sex, to obtain the magnificent inheritance of her father's kingdom, which threatened to go to strangers if she did not give him a grandson. He supplies the romantic touch that she was always depressed and loud in lamentation, but that on this particular day, though she customarily remained at home, she had set off with her maids to the river, presumably to seek solace for her aching heart. A similar portrait of the Pharaoh's daughter is found in Artapanus (*ap.* Eus. *PE* 9.27.3) and Josephus (*A.J.* 2.232), both of whom report that she was barren. This will explain why Pharaoh's daughter so quickly decided to adopt the Hebrew baby.

According to the Bible (Exod. 2:5), Philo (*Mos.* 1.14), and Josephus (*A.J.* 2.224), Pharaoh's daughter sent her maidservant to fetch the basket, whereas, according to Ezekiel (Eus. *PE* 9.28.2), as soon as Pharaoh's daughter saw Moses she herself lifted him from the water. Whereas the Bible (Exod. 2.6), Ezekiel (*Eus. PE* 9.28.2), and Philo (*Mos.* 1.15)[27] say that she recognized him as a Hebrew child, Josephus (*A.J.* 2.224), like Philo, states that she was impressed with his beauty, but apparently wonders how she could have known that he was a Hebrew child. Consequently, he postpones her recognition of that fact until Miriam (*A.J.* 2.226) explains to her that, whereas Moses did not accept the breast of the Egyptian women who were brought to feed him, he would perhaps accept the breast of someone of his own nation.

Philo (*Mos.* 1.15) adds that when the sorrowing princess saw the baby weeping, her heart was moved to feel for him as a mother for her own child. The Bible (Exod. 2:6–7), Philo, and Pseudo-Philo (9.15) report that she recognized that he was a Hebrew. The Bible (Exod. 2:7) immediately follows this with Miriam's question to the Pharaoh's daughter whether to summon one of the Hebrew women to nurse the baby. Philo (*Mos.* 1.16) again adds to the drama of the situation by stating that the Pharaoh's daughter was debating with herself as to what to do, since she realized that it would not be safe to take him to the palace, whereupon Miriam, who guessed her difficulty, ran up to her and asked whether she would take as a foster-mother a Hebrew woman who had recently given birth to a child.

Josephus (*A.J.* 2.224) apparently asked the question as to how the princess could have recognized that the baby was a Hebrew; and he is aware of the fact that even if he was circumcised this would not prove that he was a Hebrew, inasmuch as he knows the passage in Herodotus (2.104), that the Egyptians had practiced circumcision from the beginning (ἀρχῆς) and that it was from them that the "Syrians of Palestine" learned the practice (cf. Josephus, *A.J.* 8.262 and *Ap.* 1.168–70). Consequently, whereas Philo follows the biblical text in having the princess assert that the baby was a Hebrew but does not explain how she knew it, Josephus simply omits this detail. Pseudo-Philo (9.15) explains how she knew that he was a Hebrew, namely that she saw that he was circumcised. The rabbinic tradition (*b. Soṭ.* 12b) likewise apparently posed the question; and it asserts, in explanation, that Moses was born circumcised.

Josephus (*A.J.* 2.225–26), apparently wondering how Pharaoh's daughter could have accepted Miriam's bold and dangerous suggestion, adds that the princess first called many, presumably Egyptian, women,[28] but that the baby refused to be nursed by them, whereupon Miriam approached the princess. Both Philo and Josephus were apparently troubled by the question as to how the princess would not have known that the woman brought by Miriam was Moses' mother, Jochebed. Philo adds that Miriam brought the baby's mother in the guise of a stranger, who readily and gladly promised to nurse him (*Mos.* 1.17). Josephus (*A.J.* 2.227) is careful to add that Jochebed was known to no one. Philo, realizing that the reader might well wonder at the amazing coincidence that the nurse happened to be Moses' own mother, further explains (*Mos.* 1.17) that it was by G-d's design (ἐπίνοια) that it turned out that the child's first nursing came from the natural source.

In the Bible Pharaoh's daughter does not bestow the name of Moses upon the child until after we are told that the boy grew up and Moses' mother brought him to her and he was a son to her; in Ezekiel (*ap.* Eus. *PE* 9.28.2), Philo (*Mos.* 1.17), and Josephus (*A.J.* 2.228) she bestows the name upon him immediately after entrusting him to his mother for nursing. In explaining the etymology of the name, Ezekiel adheres to the Bible (Exod. 2.10) in deriving it from the Hebrew word משה ("drew," i.e., from the water). Philo (*Mos.* 1.17) apparently realized the unlikelihood that an Egyptian princess would give a child a name derived from Hebrew, as we find in the Bible (Exod. 2:10): "She called him Moses (משה), for she said, "Because I drew him out (משיתהו) of the water." Hence, Philo has an Egyptian etymology, remarking that she called him Moses, "for *Mōu* is the Egyptian word for water."[29] Similarly, Josephus (*Ap.* 1.286), in refuting Manetho's assertion that Moses' name was Osarsiph, insists that his name signifies "one saved out of the water" and repeats that "water is called by the Egyptians μῶυ." Philo (*Mut.* 126) gives another etymology, namely, from μεταληφθείς ("receiving") or ψηλάφημα ("handling"), presumably from the Hebrew משא ("burden").[30] Pseudo-Philo (9.16) likewise reports that he was given the name Moses by Pharaoh's daughter; but, concerned that the greatest leader of the Israelites should have an Egyptian name, he declares that Moses' mother gave him the name Melchiel.

The Bible, in telling the story of the birth and the exposure of the infant Moses (Exod. 2:1–10), does not at this point mention by name Moses' father, mother, and sister, or the Pharaoh's daughter, all of whom play crucial parts in the story. Josephus (*A.J.* 2.210–28), in elaborating the story, supplies the names of all of them (Amarames [*A.J.* 2.210], Iocabele [*A.J.* 2.217], Mariame [*A.J.* 2.221], and Thermouthis [*A.J.* 2.224]); and Pseudo-Philo (9.3, 9.12, 9.9) gives the name of the first three. What is significant in all of this is the fact that Philo never, in this whole pericope (*Mos.* 1.5–17), mentions the names of Moses' father, Amram, his mother, Jochebed, his sister, Miriam, or the Pharaoh's daughter. The fact that three of these are women may reflect Philo's prejudice against women.[31] One can hardly explain that their names are omitted because they play an insignificant role in the story, since they all, and especially the Pharaoh's daughter, play a crucial role. Apparently, Philo wishes to keep the spotlight focused upon Moses alone. Moreover, as Cohen 1993, 44–45, has noted, "Moses' deliverance is not an end in itself, as in the biblical narrative, but is directed at the savior being raised and educated in the style of Hellenistic royalty."

In sum, whereas in the Bible the Pharaoh's motive in seeking to kill all Israelite male babies is to prevent the Israelites from becoming so numerous, in Philo it is to prevent the birth of the great Moses. Unlike the rabbinic and Samaritan traditions, Philo, like the tragedian Ezekiel, minimizes or rationalizes the miraculous elements in connection with Moses' birth and minimizes G-d's intervention. He avoids mention of the names of Moses' father, mother, and sister, and of the Pharaoh's daughter, thus keeping the focus solely on Moses.

3. Moses' Upbringing

One of the subjects with which an encomium was to deal was the celebrated person's nurture and training (Neyrey 1994, 182–83). Menander of Laodicea (Περὶ ἐπιδεικτικῶν 2.371.17–372.2) cites, as a topic to be covered, whether the person was reared in a palace and was brought up from the very beginning in a royal setting. The encomium should speak of his "love of learning, his quickness, his enthusiasm for study, his easy grasp of what was taught him." It is precisely these qualities, as we shall see, that Philo emphasizes in his biography of Moses (*Mos.* 1.21–22).

One of the typical motifs of the biography of a hero, whether that biography was Hellenistic, Roman, Christian, or rabbinic,[32] was the hero's exceptional physical development, beauty, self-control, and precocious intellectual development as a child.[33] Thus, it is while still a boy that Alexander shows such remarkable self-restraint when it comes to pleasures of the body and keeps his spirit serious and lofty in advance of his years, despite his tendency to impetuosity and violence in other matters (Plutarch, *Alexander* 4.8). Likewise, in the case of a hero such as Romulus, it is his superiority of stature and strength of body that impress his grandfather Numitor when his identity is not yet known (Plutarch, *Romulus* 7.3–4).

In the Bible (Exod. 2:10) we are told merely that when Moses grew up his mother brought him to the Pharaoh's daughter, and he was a son to her. The accounts of both Philo and Josephus leave us wondering how Moses came to be aware of his Hebrew origin. Ezekiel (*ap.* Eus. *PE* 9.28.3) fills in this lacuna by mentioning that when, after his infancy had passed, his mother brought Moses to the princess she recounted everything and told him about his ancestral origin (γένος πατρῷον) and the gifts of G-d. What role did his father play in his education? The Bible tells us nothing. The only source that tells us anything about this is Jub. (47:9), which reports that his father taught him writing. The Bible (Exod. 2:10) tells us only that Moses was a son to the princess, but we hear nothing about his upbringing and education.

Moses' precocity is recognized by Philo, who notes that the young Moses did not engage in fun, frolic, and sport like an infant, even though his guardians were utterly lenient, but "applied himself to learning and seeing what was sure to perfect the soul" (*Mos.* 1.20). One is tempted to think that Philo may also have molded his biblical heroes in his own image, but he says so little about himself that one must reserve judgment. Josephus also remarks that Moses' growth in understanding (σύνεσις) far outstripped his physical growth, and that even in his games he displayed his superiority (περιουσία), so that his achievements even at that tender age gave promise of greater deeds yet to come (*A.J.* 2.230). The detail that as a child Moses showed his excellence even in his games is paralleled by the anecdote of Cyrus, the king of Persia, who as a mere child played at being king and who ordered one of the village boys to be beaten because he had disobeyed his command (Herodotus 1.114). Similarly, the *m. Ned.* 2:1 and *b. Ket.* 60a remark that G-d gave wondrous increase of Moses' stature. His precocity is also recognized in rabbinic literature (*Midr. Cant. Rab.* 1.26).

We are told by Philo (*Mos.* 1.18) that Moses was weaned at an earlier date than his mother had reckoned.[34] Josephus (*A.J.* 2.230) goes even further and states that when he had attained the age of three, God gave him wondrous increase of his stature.[35] Ezekiel (*ap.* Eus. *PE* 9.28.3) fills in the gap of Moses' early years by remarking that during his childhood the princess undertook to provide Moses with a royal upbringing (τροφαὶ βασιλικαί) and education in every respect. At the very beginning of Philo's account of the upbringing of Moses (*Mos.* 1.8) we are told that Moses was deemed worthy (ἠξιώθη) of a royal nurture (τροφὴ . . . βασιλική), the very words that Ezekiel uses, and that he was given this nurture by G-d's providence (*Mos.* 1.20). Since it was generally expected that he would succeed his grandfather as king, he was regularly called the young king (ὁ νέος βασιλεύς, *Mos.* 1.32). Ezekiel says that the princess raised him as if he were her own child, whereas Philo (*Mos.* 1.19) and Josephus (*A.J.* 2.232) state that the princess actually adopted him as her own son.[36]

As for the period between the birth of Moses and the time when he took up the leadership of the Israelites to get them out of Egypt, the Bible tells us only of Moses' slaying of the Egyptian overseer and his escape to Midian (Exod. 2:11–22). Josephus (*A.J.* 2.232–36) adds a fascinating incident, presaging the leadership of Moses in defying Pharaoh, in which the princess placed the newborn child in the hands of her father. The Pharaoh, in a manifestation of affection, placed his crown upon him, but Moses threw it down and stepped upon it.[37] Thereupon the sacred scribe who had predicted that his birth would lead to the humiliation of the Egyptians rushed to kill him, but the princess snatched him away, and the king was hesitant to slay him. If Philo was acquainted with such a tradition, he does not include it, perhaps because it would support the view of anti-Jewish writers, such as the Egyptian Apion, that the Jews were aggressive in seeking power, a point on which Philo, who was a leader of the Jewish community in Egypt, was very sensitive. If we ask whether Josephus may not have had less reason than Philo to fear pagan suspicions about Jewish claims to power, especially after the great Jewish revolt of 66–70, we would reply that Josephus himself, at any rate, had less to fear since he had done his best to persuade the revolutionaries to give up their revolt. Moreover, Philo had a greater sense of responsibility and was more concerned because he was a leader of the Jewish community, whereas Josephus in Rome had apparently sundered himself from the Jewish community, or the Jewish community had sundered itself from him.

Nevertheless, Moses did not behave like the infant that he was and did not take pleasure in scoffing and laughter and games.[38] Teachers allowed him relaxation and were not strict with him. Modestly and seriously, he gave himself to hearing and seeing what was likely to help his soul (*Mos.* 1.20).

A reader would almost certainly ask how so great a leader was educated and trained, but the Bible tells us nothing about this; and Exod. 2:11 is content to say merely that "one day, when Moses had grown up, he went out to his people." Philo, like Josephus (*A.J.* 2.230–53), adds many extra-biblical details to fill in this period of Moses' life, but Josephus' additions, as one might expect from one who himself had served as a general, are concerned with presenting a background for Moses' political and military career and with explaining the Egyptian jealousy that motivated his departure from Egypt. Philo, on the other hand, emphasizes Moses' training in the liberal arts, as one would expect from one who developed a deep interest in philosophy. Teachers, we are told, in an extra-biblical addition (*Mos.* 1.21), arrived at once, of their own accord, from neighboring countries and from the provinces of Egypt. In addition, Philo apparently assumed that as a future philosopher-king Moses must have been educated by Greek philosophers, inasmuch as he believed that the Greeks excelled in philosophy. Hence, he adds that some teachers were sent for from Greece with the promise of great rewards. In contrast, the Book of Jub. (47:9) states that Moses' father taught him writing and makes no mention of the education that he received at the royal court of the Pharaoh.

It did not take long, according to Philo, before the princely Moses surpassed the capacities of his teachers due to his native gifts, so that he actually anticipated their instruction (*Mos.* 1.21).[39] He seemed to recall, in a manner reminiscent of Plato's theory of ἀνάμνησις, what he had previously known,[40] rather than learning things afresh, the implication being that he was really self-taught, being in this respect like Isaac, whose usual epithet in Philo is αὐτομαθής.[41] Such people, as Philo remarks (*Sacr.* 64) in connection with Jacob's reply to Isaac as to how he was able to find venison so quickly (Gen. 27:20), acquire their knowledge rapidly, because their source of wisdom is G-d Himself, who does not need time for His work. Moreover, they acquire their knowledge without effort (Philo, *Sacr.* 7) (see Völker 1938, 281). In fact, Moses even appeared, in addition, to devise problems that were difficult to understand. Indeed, Philo (*Mos.* 1.22) says that as soon as he grasped the first principles of knowledge he pressed forward like the proverbial horse to the meadow.

As Mansfeld 1988, 95, has pointed out, Philo seems to contradict himself, since he could not really have said that the Greeks had taught Moses philosophy, inasmuch as all such philosophy, according to Philo, is later and, in fact, is derived from Moses (*QG* 4.152). Nor could he have said that Moses derived his knowledge from the study of the Torah, since the Torah had not yet been revealed. Nor could he have said that Moses had derived such knowledge from Jewish teachers, inasmuch as that was not possible in the context of the education of an Egyptian prince. He could have said that Moses had derived such knowledge through the study of nature, as in the case of the forefathers, Abraham, Isaac, and Jacob (*Abr.* 16); but he prefers to present Moses as, in effect, a Platonic-like, essentially self-taught philosopher-king, since this would give him a still higher stature in the eyes of the non-Jewish audience to whom, as we have suggested, the *Mos.* was addressed.

According to Philo (*Mos.* 1.23), who does not state the source of his information, learned (λόγιοι) Egyptians instructed Moses in arithmetic, geometry, rhythms, harmony, metrical theory, and the whole subject of music,[42] as these disciplines are described in textbooks and in treatises of a more special character. Despite the fact that Philo here ascribes the education of Moses in these subjects to the Egyptians,[43] it is surely striking that these are the very subjects, indeed in the very order, that Plato (*R.* 7.521C–531C)[44] prescribes for the higher education of his philosopher-king.

Philo is very likely reflecting his own education, as we see from his statement, spoken in the first person, that in his youth he studied grammar, geometry, and music in that order (*Congr.* 74–76) (Colson 1935, 6:286–87, n. c).[45] He may have derived this information as to the scope of Moses' education in Egypt from his own experience or perhaps also from Plato.

As to the Greeks, according to Philo, they taught Moses the rest of the regular school course (ἐγκύκλιος παιδεία).[46] Philo indicates in another place (*Congr.* 11) that the regular school course included grammar, geometry, astronomy, rhetoric, music, and all the other branches of intellectual study (Mendelson 1982, 1–24). Grammar, as he asserts (*Somn.* 1.205), embraced reading, writing, poetic literature, and ancient history. Arithmetic and geometry inculcated absolute accuracy in making calculations and noting proportions. Music embraced rhythms, meters, and melodies. Rhetoric included conception, expression, arrangement, treatment, memory, and delivery. The other branches of intellectual study are subsumed under philosophy (ibid.).

According to Philo (*Mos.* 1.23), Moses was instructed by learned Egyptians in the philosophy conveyed in symbols[47] as displayed in the hieroglyphics[48] and in the regard to be paid to animals, to which they even paid divine honors. One wonders how Philo, who elsewhere so vehemently ridicules the Egyptian worship of animals (*Decal.* 76–80),[49] could have included this in his account of Moses' education without offering some specific objection or explanation. But as Braun (1938, 30) has noted, Philo seems to be reacting to the view of Artapanus (*ap.* Eus. *PE* 9.27.4) that Moses taught the Egyptians to worship cats, dogs, and ibises. Philo, on the other hand, after mentioning (*Mos.* 1.24) the Greek and Chaldean intructors whom Moses had, stresses that he absorbed this instruction in a critical fashion, both where the Egyptians and Greeks agreed and where they disagreed, seeking only the truth. His mind, Philo remarks, was incapable of accepting any falsehood, such as we find among sectarians, who, he says, defend the doctrines that they have presented, without considering whether they can pass critical examination. In stating that Moses accepted instruction from various sources, Philo, perhaps viewing himself as an eclectic, may be speaking autobiographically. Moses, according to Philo (*Mos.* 1.29), exemplified sincerity: his words expressed his feelings honestly, and his actions were in accord with his words, so that, in Philo's musical terminology, his speech and his life were in harmony and made, as it were, a joint sound (συνηχοῦντες) as on a musical instrument.

In this connection, we may note that, according to Artapanus (*ap.* Eus. *PE* 9.27.4), whether or not he was of Jewish origin (see Holladay 1983, 1:189, 194–95, nn. 6–9), Moses bestowed on humanity many useful contributions, including the invention of philosophy. In addition, according to Philo (*Mos.* 1.24), Moses acquired from the inhabitants of the neighboring countries a knowledge of Assyrian letters (presumably Aramaic), as well as the Chaldean science of the heavenly bodies. The latter he also acquired from the Egyptians, who were especially skilled in astrology.[50] Significantly, Pseudo-Philo, for whom, as for Philo, Moses is the central figure in his whole work, has nothing at all to say about Moses' upbringing and education beyond that Moses grew up and became glorious above all other men (9.16). He apparently regarded such secular studies as inimical to the life of piety.

Both Philo (*Mos.* 1.32) and Josephus (*A.J.* 2.232) assert that Moses was expected to succeed his grandfather as king, Philo adding that he was regularly called the young king. Moreover, in an extra-biblical addition, Philo (*Mos.* 1.20) asserts that Moses, already as a child, and with a modest bearing, applied himself to hearing and seeing what was likely to profit his soul.

Artapanus (*ap.* Eus. *PE* 9.27.7–19) and Josephus (*A.J.* 2.238–57) fill in the gap of these years with an account of the campaign of Moses on behalf of the Egyptians against the Ethiopians and of the jealousy that he encountered from the Egyptians. Philo (*Mos.* 1.45–47) has no mention of a campaign against the Ethiopians, if indeed he was aware of this tradition, since his emphasis is not, as is Josephus', on Moses the general but on Moses the lawgiver. He does, however, note that after Moses had killed the Egyptian overseer, those in authority in Egypt poured malicious suggestions into the ears of the Pharaoh that Moses was highly ambitious, that he flattered some, that he threatened others, that he killed some without a trial (δίκη), that he accused those who were especially well disposed to the Pharaoh, and that he was eager to seize the kingship. As a result, Moses escaped to Arabia.

We would like to know how Moses related to his biological parents and to his adoptive family. One would expect that he would feel considerable conflict. The Bible is silent about this possible conflict, and Josephus is likewise. It is Philo, sensitive to human issues, who states (*Mos.* 1.32–33) that Moses carefully balanced the claims of his real and his adopted parents, that he requited the former with good feeling (εὔνοια) and profound affection, and that he showed gratitude (εὐχαριστίαι) toward the latter.

On the other hand, Philo (*Mos.* 1.39) elaborates on the inhuman treatment meted out to the Israelites by the Egyptians: "They died one after the other, as though they were the victims of a pestilence, to be flung unburied outside the borders by their masters, who did not allow the survivors even to collect dust to throw upon the corpses or even to shed tears for their kinsfolk or friends thus pitifully done to death." One would wonder how Moses could have continued to show such respect and warm feeling for a king who treated his fellow Israelites so harshly; and so Philo is quick to add that he would, indeed, have continued to show such deference had he not beheld in the Pharaoh the greatly impious behavior (ἀσέβημα) that the latter had newly adopted (καινουργηθέν)—perhaps an allusion to the statement of Exod. 1:8, "Now there arose a new king over Egypt."

The Bible (Exod. 2:11–15) has no discussion of Moses' adulthood before his escape to Midian beyond the incident in which he killed the Egyptian overseer. Josephus omits this incident, presumably for apologetic reasons, since he did not want to portray the greatest leader of the Israelites, the future lawgiver, as taking the law into his own hands, even if the slaying may have been justified. He mentions only (*A.J.* 2.237) that the Egyptians regarded Moses with suspicion, presumably because they thought that he had ambitions to overthrow the Pharaoh and to establish himself as king. Pseudo-Philo omits the incident, but Philo (*Leg.* 3.37–39, *Fug.* 148) does include it, justifying Moses' action by the extra-biblical addition that the Egyptian had persecuted

Hebrews to the point of death (*Mos.* 1.44). Philo also elsewhere (*Leg.* 3.38) mentions the incident in order to allegorize the Egyptian as the equivalent of passion. Indeed, there is a rabbinic tradition (*Midr. Exod. Rab.* 1.28 and parallels)[51] that the Egyptian seduced the wife of the Israelite whose name was Dathan. Whereas the Bible states that after killing the Egyptian Moses hid his body in the sand, Philo again allegorizes and says that he hid the lover of pleasure in the Egyptian's mind.

After the account of Moses' slaying of the Egyptian overseer, the Bible (Exod. 2:13–15) relates that during a quarrel between two Israelites in the presence of Moses, the wicked one said to Moses, "Do you propose to murder me, as you did the Egyptian?" Philo, however, like Josephus, omits the account of the two Israelites fighting, presumably since such an account would not redound to the credit of the Israelites. Artapanus (*ap.* Eus. *PE* 9.27.18) seeks to defend Moses by presenting a scenario in which Moses, in self-defense, slays a certain Chanethothes, who had been designated by the jealous Pharaoh to kill him. According to Josephus (*A.J.* 2.237), the Egyptians refrained from slaying him, since there was no other possible successor in whom they could put more confidence to act in the interest of the Egyptians.

Philo offers, moreover, a lengthy extra-biblical discussion of the temperance and self-control (σωφροσύνη καὶ καρτερία) that Moses exercised during this period and the good sense (φρόνησις) that he cultivated, taming and soothing his passions (*Mos.* 1.25–31). Philo notes especially that whereas palaces, such as the one where he was brought up, gave numerous opportunities for fostering the flame of adolescent lust, Moses kept a tight rein on this. He likewise tamed (τιθασεύων) and calmed (ἐπράυνεν, "soothed") the other passions, reducing them utterly to mildness (κἀξημερῶν, "taming entirely"), chastising them, if they so much as stirred, more sternly than any rebuke of words, and watching for their first appearance as one would a restive horse, always making sure that his impulses obeyed the guidance of reason (λογισμός) (*Mos.* 1.26).

During this period of his youth, Moses, whose ideal was apparently asceticism, gave only as much attention to the pleasures of food as nature required. Because this self-control was so novel, he amazed everyone to the point that they wondered whether his mind was human or divine or a mixture of both (*Mos.* 1.27).[52] Philo (*Mos.* 1.29) says that Moses made a special practice of being content with little (ὀλιγόδεια), scorning, as no one else, the life of luxury, and longing to live with his soul alone and not with his body. Moses said what he thought and acted in harmony with his words. Unlike most people he realized that nothing is more unstable than fortune, and so he did not boast himself as bigger than those more obscure than he (*Mos.* 1.30–31). Unlike others, says Philo, in an editorial-like comment, including, presumably, some Jews of his own day, who look down on their relations and friends, forget the past, think only of the present, disregard their ancestral customs[53] and scoff at the law under which they were born and bred, Moses, even though he was the exceedingly prosperous heir apparent to the throne, showed zeal (ἐζή-λωσε, "desired emulously," "strove after," "admired") for the culture (παιδεία) of his kinsmen and ancestors. In stating such a contrast Philo might have had in mind his own nephew, Tiberius Julius Alexander, who, as Josephus puts it (*A.J.* 20.100), did not stand by the practices of his people.[54] On the one hand, Moses regarded the good fortune of his adopters as spurious;[55] and, on the other hand, though his natural parents were less distinguished, he looked upon them as his own and genuine.

In sum, like any Hellenistic or Roman hero, Moses is depicted by Philo as having exceptional physical and intellectual development as a child. Philo even adds that the Egyptian princess adopted him as her own son. He apparently assumed that as a future philosopher-king Moses must have been educated by Greek philosophers. In accordance with the Platonic theory of learning as recollection, Moses seemed to recall what he had known before he was taught. According to Philo, very likely reflecting his own education, Moses was taught the very subjects prescribed for the higher education of Plato's philosopher-king. In his youth Moses, attracted to asceticism, showed extraordinary self-control. He carefully balanced the claims of his real and adoptive parents.

4. Moses' Handsomeness

While it is true, as we shall see, that the importance of the quality of beauty is noted by pagan and Jewish sources alike, it is probably the view of Plato, whom Philo admired so much and whom he described as "most sacred" (ἱερ-ώτατος) (*Prob.* 13), that had the deepest influence upon him. Plato asserts (*R.* 7.535A) that the ideal ruler should be, as far as possible, very good-looking (εὐειδέστατος, "well-shaped," "comely," "beautiful"), since the Greeks apparently assumed that good looks were a reflection of inner worth,[56] this despite the fact that Alcibiades compared his teacher Socrates to the busts of

Silenus, which were not at all good-looking (Plato, *Sym.* 215A) and despite the fact that Socrates himself (216D-E) utterly despised physical beauty.

Artapanus (*ap.* Eus. *PE* 9.27.37) closes his account of Moses with a description of him as being tall, with a ruddy complexion and long, flowing gray hair, and being dignified (ἀξιωμάτικος) in appearance. This clearly supplements the Bible (Deut. 34:7), which says merely that Moses' eyesight, just before his death at the age of 120, was not dimmed and that his vigor was undiminished.

Even before Moses was born, his mother, Jochebed, while she was pregnant, grew each day, according to the Samaritan *Molad* (p. 24, ll. 18–19), in beauty, charm, stature, and symmetry, so that she amazed those who saw her because of the shining of the lights, inward and outward, of her embryo. Similarly, the Midrash states that because Moses was so beautiful, everyone wished to look upon him; and whoever saw him could not turn from him (*Midr. Exod. Rab.* 1.26 on Exod. 2.10, *Tan. Exod.* 8 [p. 213]; cf. Sir. 44:22–45:1). According to the midrashic tradition (*Tan. Exod.* 8 [p. 213]), such was Moses' beauty that the Pharaoh's daughter did not allow him to leave the palace, since whoever saw him could not detach himself from the sight. Stephen (Acts 7:20) likewise refers to Moses' charming (ἀστεῖος) appearance.

Apparently, this tradition of Moses' beauty had even reached the non-Jewish world, inasmuch as we find Pompeius Trogus (*ap.* Just. 36, *Epitoma* 2:11), who lived at the end of the first century B.C.E. and at the beginning of the first century C.E.,[57] commending Moses not only for the knowledge that he had inherited from his father, whom he identifies as Joseph,[58] but also for the beauty of his person.[59]

At Moses' birth, according to Exod. 2:2, Moses' mother saw that he was good (טוב). That Philo placed a premium upon beauty may be seen in his remark (*Abr.* 168) that Isaac, even as a child, was of very great bodily beauty (τό . . . σῶμα κάλλιστος). Since Plato (*R.* 7.535A) prescribed that the philosopher-king, if at all possible, should be handsome, Philo stresses Moses' beauty. At his birth, according to Philo (*Conf.* 106, *Mos.* 1.9), Moses was more than ordinarily ἀστεῖος,[60] that is, "pretty," "charming," "handsome," "graceful," so that his parents, as long as they could, disregarded the edict of the Pharaoh, which required that male babies be put to death.[61]

Furthermore, we learn, from an extra-biblical addition (*Mos.* 1.15), that when the baby Moses was brought to the Pharaoh's daughter, she surveyed him from head to foot and approved of his beauty of form (εὐμορφία) and his good state of health (εὐεξία). This observation is all the more effective, since it comes from a non-Jew. Indeed, according to the Samaritan *Molad* (p. 26, l. 19), when the princess took Moses from the ark she was cured of her sickness. Similarly, Josephus (*A.J.* 2.224) notes that when Pharaoh's daughter first beheld the baby Moses, she loved him very much because of his size and beauty (κάλλος).[62]

In connection with Jethro's first meeting with Moses after the latter had watered the sheep for his daughters, Philo (*Mos.* 1.59), in an extra-biblical addition, states that Jethro was immediately struck, on the one hand, by his appearance (ὄψις) and a little later by his intent (βούλημα), since, as he remarks, great natures are manifest and do not need much time to be recognized. Here the reference is not so much to Moses' physical beauty as to the facial expression of his character and especially qualities of leadership.

Moreover, on Moses' descent from Mount Sinai after spending forty days communing with G-d, Philo (*Mos.* 2.70) describes his countenance (ὄψις) as far more beautiful (καλλίων) than when he had ascended, so that those who saw him were astounded (τεθηπέναι) and amazed (καταπεπλῆχθαι) and could no longer with their eyes endure the impact of the luster flashing forth like the sun. Here again the reference is not so much to Moses' physical beauty as to his spiritual illumination.

In sum, Philo, aware that a philosopher-king, as Plato says, should, if at all possible, be handsome, depicts Moses as unusually beautiful at birth and as an adult. He does not, however, go to the lengths that the rabbis and the Samaritan tradition go in describing his beauty.

5. Moses' Attitude toward Wealth

In antiquity, certainly in the case, for example, of King Croesus of Lydia (Herodotus 1.30) and the Emperor Augustus (Suet., *Augustus* 101) and his successors, wealth was often one of the characteristics of a great leader; and Josephus, in particular, emphasizes this in his portraits of biblical heroes. Thus, Josephus calls attention to the wealth of Abraham in his mention of the rare gifts that he sent to Rebekah's family (*A.J.* 1.243). Jacob, we are told, attained an unparalleled degree of prosperity (*A.J.* 2.7). When G-d appears in a dream to Moses' father, Amram, He reminds him of Jacob's fame even among alien nations for his prosperity and notes that he bequeathed this wealth to his descendants (*A.J.* 2.214). Josephus highlights Korah's grief at his frustration at not being designated to be high priest, despite his greater right to enjoy the highest honors because he was richer than Moses without being his inferior in birth (*A.J.* 4.14). David, according to Josephus, left behind greater wealth than any other king, whether of the Hebrews or of other nations (*A.J.* 7.391). The impression of Solomon's great wealth is magnified with Josephus' striking portrayal of Solomon's horsemen with their extraordinary height, extremely long hair, tunics of Tyrian purple, and gold dust sprinkled in their hair (*A.J.* 8.185). The formula for royal happiness, as illustrated in Josephus' summary of King Josiah's career (*A.J.* 10.73), is to possess wealth and to be held in good opinion by all men.

Philo was a member of an extremely wealthy family (his brother Alexander Lysimachus was able to lend 200,000 drachmas to Agrippa I [Josephus, *A.J.* 18.159] and to decorate the gates of the Temple in Jerusalem with gold and silver [*B.J.* 5.205]). Moreover, Philo's great personal wealth must have allowed him much time for study and writing and undoubtedly played a role in his becoming a leader of the Jewish community. Hence, we would expect him to have defended the possession of wealth. Indeed, there is a tradition (*b. Ned.* 38a) that all the prophets, including Moses, were wealthy. In fact, according to rabbinic tradition, Moses became extraordinarily wealthy, since G-d pointed out to him a diamond quarry from which he obtained the second tablets of the Law and from which he was permitted to keep for himself the chips that fell (*Midr. Num. Rab.* 9.48 and parallels cited by Ginzberg 6:59, n. 306).

Nevertheless, Philo strongly disparages wealth in no fewer than 38 passages in his works (Schmidt 1983, 85). Thus, he belittles in the strongest terms "gold, silver, glory, honors, offices, the materials of objects of sense, the mechanical arts, and all other arts in great variety that minister to pleasure" (*Leg.* 2.107). Indeed, Philo (*Mos.* 1.151) emphasizes that Moses, as leader of the Israelites during the forty years in the wilderness, had as his sole aim to benefit his subjects. In contrast to others who had similar authority, we are told in additions to the biblical account, that he did not treasure up gold and silver, did not levy tributes, did not possess houses or chattels or livestock or a staff or slaves or any other accoutrements of luxurious living, though he might have had them all in abundance. He believed that wealth was blind and that to prize wealth betrayed poverty of soul, whereas he highly honored and zealously pursued the wealth of nature perhaps more than any other man. He was not extravagant in dress or in food and did not display his grandeur. As a private citizen he practiced economy, but, in contrast, he was liberal in his expenditures on behalf of his people (*Mos.* 1.153). Consequently, since he refused to accumulate wealth, which gives people mighty influence, G-d rewarded him by giving him the greatest wealth, namely the wealth of the whole earth and sea and all the elements. Thus G-d made him, as a world citizen (κοσμοπολίτης,[63] *Mos.* 1.157), a worthy partner of all His possessions, so that each element obeyed him as its master.

Elsewhere (*Spec.* 2.23) Philo speaks of a blind wealth against which people have stumbled, "and taking it for their support, they fail of necessity to see the road before them and wander away into pathless wilds, admiring what deserves no serious respect and mocking at what nature would bid them honor." As Cukrowski (1994, 163–64) remarks, in his disdain for wealth and luxury, Moses parallels Socrates (*Apology* 23C, 30A-B, 31C, 36D) and Demonax, as later described by Lucian (*Demonax* 4, 5, 8, 63). It is not, however, that Philo, in disparaging wealth, does so because he is influenced by the Stoics and Cynics, as Mealand 1978, 258–64, would have it. Rather, he looks down upon acquisitiveness as such and regards proper wealth as a divine gift (so Schmidt 1983, 87).

In sum, in contrast to the prevalent view of antiquity and of Josephus that wealth was a prerequisite of a great leader, Philo says that Moses did not treasure wealth as such, since his sole aim was to benefit his subjects. In this attitude Philo's Moses parallels Socrates. As a reward, G-d gave him the greatest wealth possible, namely, the entire wealth of the world. By following a more severe mode of life, Moses was the role model for his people.

6. Moses' Career as Leader of the Israelites

a. Moses before His Departure for Midian

The Bible (Exod. 1:7), at the very beginning of the Book of Exodus, asserts that the Children of Israel in Egypt were fruitful, teemed, increased, and became strong, so very much so that the land became filled with them. It notes the statement by the new king of Egypt advising his people to outsmart the Israelites lest they become even more numerous and may even in a war join the enemies of the Egyptians and then leave. Whereas the Bible (Exod. 1:11) speaks of the enslavement of the Israelites by the Pharaoh before it mentions the birth and upbringing of Moses, Philo (*Mos.* 1.5–33), as we have noted, first mentions the birth and upbringing of Moses and only later refers to their enslavement (1.36). He thus puts greater focus upon Moses and emphasizes the cruelty of the Pharaoh. He stresses the fact that instead of treating the Israelites as suppliants and friends who were eager to obtain equal rights with the other Egyptians and who were near to being citizens because they differed so little from the original inhabitants of Egypt, the Pharaoh showed no shame before or fear of the G-d of liberty, hospitality, and justice to guests and suppliants and enslaved them in the most unspeakable fashion (*Mos.* 1.35–36). This had obvious contemporary implications for the Jews living in Egypt in Philo's time, who were seeking equal rights with the other inhabitants of Egypt.[64] Surprisingly enough, Philo, perhaps because he sought to keep the focus solely upon Moses, does not mention here the tremendous services noted by the Bible that Joseph had done for the Pharaoh and for which the Pharaoh should have been grateful, possibly because the historicity of these services had been questioned by detractors of the Jews or, in any case, are mentioned only by Philo's contemporary Pompeius Trogus (*ap.* Justin, *Historiae Philippicae*, Prologue, 36.2.6–10) among non-biblical authors.

Philo (*Mos.* 1.32) says that Moses was zealous for the discipline and culture of his kinsmen and ancestors without explaining how and why he apparently suddenly came to this realization, except that he saw the king adopting a new and highly impious course of action (*Mos.* 1.33). There is a similar lacuna in Josephus (*A.J.* 2.238). The tragedian Ezekiel (*ap.* Eus. *PE* 9.28.3) explains that Moses left the royal palace because his spirit (θυμός) alerted him to the works and wiles of the Pharaoh. The New Testament (Heb. 11:24), apparently aware of the charge as to why Moses did not act sooner to help his oppressed brethren, states very emphatically that when he grew up Moses refused to be called the son of the Pharaoh's daughter and preferred to suffer hardship with his people rather than to enjoy the transient pleasures of sin.

On the other hand, in the first place, Philo (*Mos.* 1.34–39) describes at much greater length the suffering to which the Israelites were subjected. He mentions the terrible oppression of the Jews, adding (*Mos.* 1.37–38) that the Pharaoh chose as superintendents of their labors men of the most cruel and savage temper who showed no mercy to anyone, that the Israelites built houses, walls, cities, and canals, and carried the materials themselves without respite day and night without being allowed even to sleep, so that they died one after the other, as though in a pestilence, and that they were not even given the minimal rights of burial. The phrase "as though in a pestilence" would appear to be Philo's implied answer to the false anti-Israelite versions of Manetho (*ap.* Josephus, *Ap.* 1.233–35), Apion (*ap.* Josephus, *Ap.* 2.15), Chaeremon (*ap.* Josephus, *Ap.* 1.289), and Lysimachus (*ap.* Josephus, *Ap.* 1.304–5) that the Pharaoh had actually expelled the Israelites as polluted people and lepers. The Jewish community in Egypt, in Philo's day, sizable though it was, was a minority of the population. Philo, undoubtedly influenced by his position as a leader in that community, in language that would remind the reader of the epithet ξένιος, the protector of strangers, as applied to Zeus, is deeply critical of the Egyptians for disregarding the rights of Jews as strangers. We may here suggest, though there is no indication as to when Philo composed his *Mos.*, that if Philo is, indeed, here answering the charges of the anti-Semites noted above, he may have composed this work during the buildup of tensions between the Jews and the Egyptians (see *Legat.* 120) or even possibly after the pogrom of 38.

Philo (*Mos.* 1.40), however, is clearly aware of the objection as to why Moses did not do something to help his brethren; and he explains that Moses continued (διετέλει) to be depressed (ἀθυμῶν, "to be disheartened," "despond") and to be angered (δυσχεραίνων, "be disgusted") at these sufferings, but that he had no power to punish the wrongdoers or to help those who were wronged. What he was able to do, says Philo, he did with words,[65] exhorting the overseers to show moderation (μετριάζειν) and to relax a little (ὑπανιέναι) and to slacken (χαλᾶν) the excessive violence (σφοδρόν) of their orders. Moreover, he urged the workers to endure their present condition nobly (γενναίως, "bravely") and to be manly in their thoughts (φρονήματα) and not to let their souls suffer with their bodies but to await good things after their evils. "All things in the world," he told them (*Mos.* 1.41) encouragingly, "change to their opposites: clouds to open sky, violent winds to tranquil weather, stormy seas to calm and peaceful, and human affairs still more so, even as they are more unstable."[66] In so encouraging his people he reminds us of Aeneas' consoling words to his men when, after they land on the coast of Africa, he recalls to them that they have endured more grievous obstacles and bids them to persevere (Virgil, *Aen.* 1.198–207). With his soothing words Moses is compared to a good physician who seeks to relieve the sickness of his patient (*Mos.* 1.42).[67]

The Bible (Exod. 2:11–15) states merely that Moses went out to his brethren and observed their burdens and killed an Egyptian whom he saw striking a Hebrew. The question, as we have noted, might well arise as to why Moses did not do more to help his fellow Jews when they were so terribly oppressed and why the biblical text mentions only a single incident (Exod. 2:11–15) where he did intervene. The biblical text (Exod. 2:11) says merely that Moses saw an Egyptian man striking a Hebrew, without indicating precisely what the Hebrew was doing and what the Egyptian was doing, why he was striking him and whether there was a pattern of oppression by this Egyptian. Thereupon, when he saw that no one was looking, Moses struck down the Egyptian and hid him in the sand.

Demetrius, who lived in the third century B.C.E. and who is the first Hellenistic Jewish historian of whom we have record, remains close to the LXX, as we see, for example, in his handling (*ap.* Eus. *PE* 9.29.1) of the episode concerning Moses' slaying of the Egyptian (Exod. 2:11–15). On the other hand, Josephus and Pseudo-Philo omit the episode (*A.J.* 2.237), presumably because they were embarrassed by the fact that Moses, the great leader of the Israelites, who was destined to become a great lawgiver, was actually, ironically, a murderer, who showed such a lack of respect for judicial procedure that he took the law into his own hands in his impulsive slaying of the Egyptian overseer. All other accounts of this incident, such as Jub. 47:10–12, Acts 7:24, and midrashic accounts,[68] either confirm or expand the biblical account, which places the blame solely on the Egyptian. Artapanus (*ap.* Eus. *PE* 9.27.18) seeks to defend Moses by presenting a scenario in which Moses, in self-defense, slays a certain Chanethothes, who had been designated by the jealous Pharaoh to kill him.

Philo, however, though adhering more closely, as usual, to the facts of the biblical text, is aware that even under those circumstances there is a real question as to whether Moses was justified in taking the law into his own hands. Hence, he paints a picture of the Egyptian overseers as "exceedingly harsh and ferocious, in savageness differing nothing from venomous and carnivorous animals, wild beasts in human shape who assumed in outward form the semblance of civilized beings only to beguile and catch their prey, in reality more unyielding than iron or adamant." The one whom Moses killed (Exod. 2:12) was, he says, the cruelest (βιαιότατος, "most violent") of all, who was rendered harsher than ever by Moses' exhortations, beating those who did not execute his orders with breathless (ἀπνευστί) promptness (ὀξυχειρία, "quickness of hand"), persecuting them (προπηλακίζων, "bespattering with mud," "treating with insolence") to the point of death and torturing (αἰκιζόμενος) them with every outrage (αἰκία) (*Mos.* 1.44). Moses, he says (ibid.) justified his killing as guiltless (εὐαγές, "pure," "holy," "lawful"); and guiltless it was, as he remarks, in an editorial-like comment, to destroy a man who lived only to destroy men. In other words, Moses was not really guilty of murder, since he had killed one who was more like a wild animal rather than like a human being.[69] The Pharaoh, he continues, was particularly angry (ἠγανάκτει) not because someone had killed another, whether justly or unjustly, but because his own daughter's son was not of one mind (συμφρονεῖ) with him and did not have the same enemies and friends that he had, but hated those for whom the Pharaoh had affection and loved those whom he censured and pitied those toward whom he was inflexible (ἀτρέπτως) and unmerciful (ἀπαραιτήτως) (*Mos.* 1.45). Philo's Moses can hardly be criticized as unfeeling.

Acts 7:23–24 follows the biblical text (Exod. 2:11) in making it clear that the Israelite was being oppressed by the Egyptian. Ezekiel's version (*ap.* Eus. *PE* 9.28.3), uniquely, as Jacobson 1983, 79, observes, neutralizes the blame, since he speaks of two men fighting, one a Hebrew and the other an Egyptian; but there is no indication that the Egyptian was oppressing the Hebrew. Rather, Ezekiel wishes to emphasize that, even though Moses had been brought up in the Pharaoh's palace, he was far from unmindful of the fact that he was an Israelite and hence, as Ezekiel puts it, he rescued his brother (ἀδελφός) simply because he was a fellow Israelite. The fact that Ezekiel says merely that Moses killed the Egyptian without indicating the provocation is a harsh judgment against Moses and raises the question why in a play that is intended to glorify Moses Ezekiel should apparently denigrate his hero. Indeed, to Jacobson 1983, 79, the editor of an extremely erudite and careful edition of Ezekiel, this remains a puzzle. We may suggest that the problem is really closely connected with the question as to what was Ezekiel's projected audience, whether it was Jewish, non-Jewish, or both (see Jacobson, 1983, 17 and 181–82, nn. 1–3). To the extent that he intended it for Jews he may well have been bothered, as Philo (*Mos.* 1.40) was, by Moses' apparent failure to act previously to assist his brethren during the time that they were so cruelly oppressed. Philo's defense there is that Moses did assist them with words through exhorting the Egyptian overseers to show more clemency. Ezekiel apparently found such a defense inadequate. By presenting Moses as one who did care for his brethren to the extent that he murdered the Egyptian without seeking to determine whether that particular Egyptian was oppressing the Israelites, Ezekiel is apologetically telling the Jews, who were at least part of his audience, that Moses was far from indifferent to their plight. Philo, on the other hand, writing for a non-Jewish audience, had to justify Moses' killing of the Egyptian.

The incident that follows (Exod. 2:13–14), in which Moses saw two Hebrews fighting each other and berated the wicked one, clearly does not speak well of the Hebrews. Likewise, it does not redound to the credit of the Hebrews that one of them informed against Moses to the Pharaoh. Moses concluded that one of them was the wicked one and asked him why he was striking his fellow, whereupon the wicked one retorted, "Who made you a prince and a judge over us?"[70] In Ezekiel's version (*ap.* Eus. *PE* 9.28.3), in contrast to the plain biblical statement and to the version in Acts 7:25–28, there is no indication that the two men are Hebrews, since we are told only that they are kinsmen, so that a Jewish audience, being aware of the biblical version, would see them as Jews, whereas an Egyptian audience could easily regard them as Egyptians (Jacobson 1983, 79–80). This apparently resolves the difficulty as to why a Jew would inform on a fellow Jew. Moreover, whereas the Bible speaks of one of the men as wicked, Ezekiel uniquely says that one was weaker than the other. Whereas the Bible (Exod. 2:15) states that the Pharaoh heard about this matter, with no indication as to who told him, Ezekiel indicates that it was the one who had replied thus to Moses.

Philo, like Josephus after him,[71] but in an unusual departure from his own general tendency to follow the biblical text, omits the incident in which Moses saw two Hebrews fighting each other.[72] The bibical text then asserts that the Pharaoh heard about Moses' murder of the Egyptian and sought to kill Moses, whereupon Moses fled to Midian. Philo, however, as a leader of the Alexandrian Jewish community, always the conservative upholder of the importance of obeying the ruler of the nation, while recording the Pharaoh's indignation, puts the emphasis on the Pharaoh's advisers (*Mos.* 1.46), who, we are told, poured (ἐπήντλουν) myriads of slanders into the open ears of Moses' adoptive grandfather, the Pharaoh, so as to make him fear that Moses would seek to usurp the rule. They claimed that he thought nothing small and that, in his eagerness to rule before his time arrived, he was always busy with something more. "He flatters some," they asserted, "threatens others, kills without a trial [clearly an allusion to his slaying of the Egyptian], and accuses those who are especially well-disposed to you. Why do you linger rather than cut short what he intends to do? The delays on the part of those who are plotted against are a great service to those who are attacking."

Artapanus (*ap.* Eus. *PE* 9.27.7–11) adds a new element in his account of the jealousy harbored by the Pharaoh, Chenephres, against Moses. He says that Chenephres appointed Moses as general against the Ethiopians in the hope that Moses would thus be killed. Moses, we are told, in a war that lasted ten years, won every battle with distinction. Moses and his followers, he says, founded a city in Heliopolis which they named "The City of Hermes," perhaps, we may suggest, in allusion to the fact that this was the name by which Moses was called (*ap.* Eus. *PE* 9.27.6). There they consecrated the ibis because the ibis is reputed to kill those animals that are harmful to humans, presumably in allusion to the role by the ibis in the campaign against the Ethiopians. Though the war had been fought against the Ethiopians, the latter now came to love Moses and they, together with the Egyptian priests, adopted from him the practice of circumcision.

Chenephres now welcomed back Moses, though he continued to plot against him. When Chenephres asked Moses whether he knew of anything else that might be useful to mankind, Moses suggested a breed of oxen that would be useful in tilling the land. In his jealousy and in his eagerness to conceal Moses' achievements, Chenephres ordered that the animals that had been consecrated by Moses should be buried; and he plotted to kill Moses. Upon the advice of his brother, Aaron, who had learned of the plot, Moses decided to flee to Arabia. In an episode that corresponds to the biblical account of Moses' slaying of the Egyptian taskmaster (Exod. 2:11–12), a certain Chanethothes, whom Chenephres had designated to kill Moses, drew his dagger on him, but Moses, in self-defense, as we have noted above, drew his own sword and killed him.

But while Artapanus (*ap.* Eus. *PE* 9.27.7–10) and Josephus (*A.J.* 2.239–53) depict Moses as a great general who succeeds against great odds in defeating the Ethiopians, Philo has no reference to any such campaign, although it would seemingly have enhanced the status of Moses. Instead, he downplays his military achievements. Moreover, as Niehoff 2001, 72–74, has convincingly noted, there is a fundamental gulf between Artapanus' view of Moses and that of Philo in that Artapanus emphasizes the congeniality between Egyptian culture and that of the Jews, whereas Philo stresses the difference.

One might ask why, if Moses was so devoted to his Israelite brethren, he fled (ויברח, Exod. 2:15) from Pharaoh rather than stay to help them. Moreover, fleeing does not seem to show courage on the part of Moses. Indeed, the New Testament (Heb. 11:27) makes a point of emphasizing that Moses behaved courageously when he fled and that, indeed, he did not flee because he feared the anger of the Pharaoh. One of the major prerequisites for leadership is persistence. Philo was apparently troubled by this behavior on the part of Moses. Consequently, he took the trouble to remark that when Moses escaped, he at the same time loudly (ποτνιώμενος) implored G-d, on the one hand, to deliver the oppressed from their miserable plight, and, on the other hand, to punish deservedly those who omitted nothing in their abuse and to grant him to see both of these goals (*Mos.* 1.47). G-d, who admired his character, which loved goodness and hated evil, listened to his prayers and, as was fitting for G-d, condemned the Egyptians. Moreover, Philo explains that Moses withdrew (ἀναχωρεῖ, *Leg.* 3.14), using the word found in the LXX's translation (ἀνεχώρησε). He says specifically that for Moses to have fled from the Pharaoh would have been to abandon his warfare with the passions, with which he identifies the Pharaoh, before those pleasures were overcome. Philo says that Moses did not flee from the Pharaoh, since that would indicate that he ran away and did not return. He here draws an analogy between Moses and an athlete who takes an interval to regain his breath so that he may renew the attack later with irresistible power. However, in *Mos.* 1.45 we are not given the allegorical explanation for his withdrawal; rather, in an extra-biblical addition we are given two credible reasons—first, that the Pharaoh was extremely angry with him because his own daughter's son utterly disagreed with him and, second, as already noted, that those in authority poured endless suggestions into the Pharaoh's ears that Moses intended to overthrow him. According to Josephus, as we have noted, in an extensive extra-biblical addition (*A.J.* 2.239–53), the Pharaoh appointed Moses to lead an expedition against the Ethiopians, who had sought to overpower all of Egypt. When he was successful, Moses' enemies among the Egyptians, suspecting that he would start a revolution in Egypt because of his success, convinced the Pharaoh to undertake the murder of Moses.

Philo (*Mos.* 1.149), as we have noted, makes much of the fact that because of the injustices committed in the land and because of Moses' nobility (εὐγένεια) and magnanimity of spirit (φρονήματος μέγεθος) and inborn hatred of evil, he gave up the lordship of Egypt, to which he was destined as the adopted son of the Pharaoh's daughter. Consequently, G-d rewarded him with the leadership of a populous and mightier nation that was destined to be consecrated above all others and that would forever offer prayers on behalf of all mankind so as to be deterred from evil and to participate in good. This reward is clearly intended to reply to the charge that the Jews bear an implacable hatred toward non-Jews, since Jews will forever pray for all humankind. Similarly, it is to answer this charge, as made by Apollonius Molon and Lysimachus (*Ap.* 2.145) and repeated by Tacitus (*Histories* 5.5.1), that Josephus goes out of his way to stress that Jews show compassion for non-Jews.[73]

In sum, by first mentioning the birth and upbringing of Moses and only later the enslavement of the Israelites, Philo puts the spotlight on Moses. Aware of the objection that Moses apparently did nothing to help his fellow Israelites while they were enslaved in Egypt, he explains that Moses was angry and depressed but lacked the power to help them. He did what he could by exhorting the overseers to show moderation and urging the Israelites not to lose hope. Unlike Josephus, Philo does not omit Moses' slaying of the Egyptian overseer but rather defends Moses for taking the law into his own hands. In an unusual departure from the biblical text, Philo apologetically omits mention of the embarrassing incident of the two Hebrews who fought each other. Unlike Artapanus and Josephus, he downplays Moses' military achievements. He is careful to deny that Moses fled from Pharaoh.

b. Moses in Midian

Moses now fled to Arabia, where he stayed with Raguel (that is, Jethro), the chief of the region. It would appear that in antiquity there was a sharp difference of opinion in the evaluation of the personality of Jethro. There were those, notably Demetrius, Artapanus, Ezekiel the tragedian, and Josephus, who elevated him; there were those, notably Philo, who basically denigrated him; there were those, notably in the rabbinic tradition, who were divided in their opinions; and there were those, notably the writers in the Apocrypha and Pseudepigrapha, who ignored him.

Demetrius, a chronographer, who apparently lived in Egypt during the latter half of the third century B.C.E. (so Holladay 1983, 1:51–52), notes, in his summary of Exod. 2:15–21, that Moses fled to Midian, where he was married to Zipporah, the daughter of Jethro (Ἰοθώρ), whom he identifies as the son of Raguel (*ap.* Eus. *PE* 9.29.1). The fact that he then traces the ancestry of Jethro back to Abraham, through the latter's marriage to Keturah, would clearly elevate the status of Jethro. It would also resolve the embarrassing problem of Moses' apparent intermarriage with Zipporah, a Midianite, since it turns out that both Moses and Zipporah are directly descended from Abraham. It is likewise through Abraham's marriage with Keturah that the historian Cleodemus-Malchus, who apparently lived sometime between 200 B.C.E. and 50

B.C.E. (so Holladay 1983, 1:246), proudly reports that a son was born whose daughter was married to the greatest Greek hero, Heracles (*ap.* Josephus, *A.J.* 1.240–41). Moreover, the fact that Jethro is mentioned by Demetrius as the son of Raguel solves the problem of his name in the Book of Exodus, where it is first given in the LXX (the Hebrew text does not give his name at this point), which was clearly Demetrius' source, as Jethro (Ἰοθόρ) (Exod. 2:16) and then as Raguel (Ῥαγουήλ, Hebrew Reuel) (Exod. 2:18). It also solves the problem of the apparent identity with Jethro of Hobab (LXX, Ἰωβάβ), who in Judg. 4:11 is referred to as the father-in-law of Moses, since Demetrius here says that Hobab was the son of Raguel.

Perhaps a century after Demetrius, the historian Artapanus (*ap.* Eus. *PE* 9.27.19)[74] likewise aggrandizes Jethro by referring to him as the chief (ἄρχων) of the region, even though the Bible identifies him merely as "the priest of Midian" (Exod. 2:16).

Ezekiel, the author of the tragedy *The Exodus*, dating from perhaps the second century B.C.E.,[75] considerably enhances the status of Jethro. In one of the fragments (*ap.* Eus. *PE* 9.28.4b), his daughter Zipporah refers to him, as had Artapanus, as chief (ἄρχων) of the state. Far from being merely a priest, he is called both ruler (τύραννος) and general (στρατηλάτης). He not only rules (ἄρχει) but also judges (κρίνει) the people (presumably the latter attribute arises from the fact that it is Jethro who later gives Moses advice as to how to construct a judicial system). Moreover, Ezekiel (*ap.* Eus. *PE* 9.29.4) truly glorifies Jethro by presenting him in the role of interpreter of Moses' dream. This is most remarkable, inasmuch as nowhere in the Bible do we find a non-Jew interpreting a dream for a Jew, but rather the reverse, as in the case of the dreams of the Pharaoh and of Nebuchadnezzar (so Jacobson 1983, 92). The fact, furthermore, that Jethro is able to interpret the dream without any mention of divine help offers a considerable contrast to the methods employed by Joseph and Daniel in the Bible.[76]

Jethro's interpretation in Ezekiel's tragedy that the dream signifies that Moses will judge and lead mankind and will see present, past, and future, is, of course, a tremendous compliment to Moses, but it also glorifies the interpreter as one who is able to perceive this. This portrayal of Jethro as ruler and as interpreter of dreams, in effect, converts him into a kind of biblical Joseph, especially as elaborated by Josephus. The fact that Jethro is portrayed as a military leader converts him into a kind of doublet of Moses, as described in the Bible and especially as elaborated by Josephus. The notion of a priest-ruler is surely reminiscent of the role of the Hasmonean priest-rulers, notably Simon and John Hyrcanus.

The Bible and Philo do not describe the initial impression that Moses made upon Jethro's daughters, whereas, according to the Samaritan tradition (*Molad,* p. 46, ll. 13–14), they expressed amazement at his gracefulness and exclaimed: "This is an angel, or a fiery meteor, or some prophet, or a saint, or a messenger, or a chosen one." Whereas the Bible (Exod. 2:16–17) records in only two verses the incident in which Moses, newly arrived in Midian, drove away the shepherds who prevented Jethro's daughters from drawing water for their sheep, Philo (*Mos.* 1.51–57) develops this in no fewer than seven paragraphs as an example of Moses' tremendous concern for justice. He depicts the shepherds as disdaining the weakness of the girls and as trying to drive them and their flock away. Whereas the biblical text states merely that Moses got up and saved the girls, Philo (*Mos.* 1.54–56) says that Moses, directing all his powers (συντείνας) to rescuing the girls, ran (ἔθει) and, in no uncertain terms, berated the shepherds, who elsewhere (*Mut.* 112) are termed "comrades of envy (φθόνος) and malice (βασκανία, "malignity," "jealousy")." In particular, Moses condemned their injustice, ridiculed them, appealed to G-d's concern for justice (δίκη), declared that he would fight in defense of the girls, warning the shepherds in the strongest and bluntest terms and in highly effective rhetoric, that G-d would punish them if they did not reform their ways (*Mos.* 1.54–56): "Stop this injustice. You think you can take advantage of the loneliness of the place. Are you not ashamed to let your arms and elbows live an idle life? You are masses of long hair and lumps of flesh, not men. The girls are working like youths, and shirk none of their duties, while you young men go daintily like girls. Away with you: give place to those who were here before you, to whom the water belongs. Properly, you should have drawn for them, to make the supply more abundant; instead, you are all agog to take from them what they have provided. Nay, by the heavenly eye of justice, you shall not take it; for that eye sees even what is done in the greatest solitude. In me at least it has appointed a champion whom you did not expect, for I fight to succor these injured maidens, allied to a mighty arm which the rapacious may not see, but you shall feel its invisible power to wound if you do not change your ways." Josephus (*A.J.* 2.260–61) likewise vigorously expands on the charity (εὐποιία) of Moses' beneficent act (εὐεργετηθεῖσαι) and adds that Moses deemed it monstrous (δεινόν) to overlook the injury to the young women and to allow these insolent men's violence to triumph over their rights (δίκαιον), and so he restrained and beat off these arrogant intruders who sought to be greedy.

The Bible does not record the reaction of the shepherds to Moses' deed and statement, but Philo (*Mos.* 1.57), in an editorial-like comment, says that they were filled with fear as if they were listening to some oracular utterance. As he spoke, Moses, according to Philo, in an extra-biblical addition, became inspired and in his ecstasy was transformed into a prophet, so driven was he by this injustice. He was so effective, adds Philo, in chastising the shepherds that, as a result, they became obedient and led the flock of the maidens to the cisterns.

When Jethro asks his daughters how it was that they had returned with such speed (Exod. 2:18), they reply that an Egyptian had saved them from the shepherds. The fact that the daughters of Jethro refer to Moses as an Egyptian rather than as a Hebrew, says Philo (*Mut.* 117), is due to the fact that they could not rise above the world of sense. If so, we may wonder why Moses, who, as Philo has stressed, so utterly denied the senses, agreed to marry one of them. Philo's answer (*Mut.* 120) is that Zipporah was different: Jethro describes her nature as winged (πτηνόν, presumably in allusion to the Hebrew word, צפורה, "bird," from which her name is derived), inspired (θεοφόρητον, "possessed by a god"), and prophetic (προφητικόν). What is striking, however, is that nowhere in the systematic narrative of *Mos.* does Philo mention the actual names of the priest, Jethro, or of the daughter, Zipporah, whom Moses married; presumably, his goal is to keep the focus centered solely on Moses. In the Samaritan *Molad* (p. 47, ll. 8–15), Zipporah, like a flash of fire, exclaims to her father: "O father, this morning the veils opened up, and the mysteries and what was hidden were revealed, along with the interpretation of a dream that I had seen clearly long ago." Thereupon Jethro quickly made Moses his son-in-law.

One of the problems in connection with the life of Moses, as we have noted, is the fact that he married a non-Jewish woman, Zipporah. The Bible is strongly opposed to intermarriage, as we see in the incident of Dinah (Gen. 34), the strict prohibition against taking Canaanite daughters for Israelite sons (Exod. 34:16), the incident of the harlotry with the Midianite women (Num. 25), and the prohibition against intermarrying with the Canaanites (Deut. 7:3). Pseudo-Philo (10.1), apparently aware of this problem and forever concerned with protecting the reputation of Moses, totally omits all reference to Moses' sojourn with Jethro in Midian and to Moses' marriage to Zipporah. Philo

(*Spec.* 3.29) in an unusually strong statement, which may well be drawing upon the experience of the Alexandrian Jewish community, not only repeats the prohibition but also sets forth the consequences of violation of the prohibition, namely that even though you yourself, instructed in the holy laws from your earliest youth, will perhaps continue after intermarriage to abide by them, your children will probably go astray unawares.

And yet, Philo was in a dilemma: how could he oppose intermarriage when Moses himself married a non-Jew? He could have done what Pseudo-Philo did and simply omitted the whole episode, but such an omission would apparently be too obvious. Philo (*Spec.* 3.29) might have been acquainted, in the case of Zimri (Num. 25:6–18), with the tradition (*b. Sanh.* 82a) that Moses upbraided Zimri when the latter openly had relations with the non-Jewish Cozbi, and that Zimri responded by asking Moses who permitted him to marry the non-Jewish Zipporah. He might have resolved the problem by noting that Moses married Zipporah before the revelation of the Torah; but it would have been difficult to assert this in view of Moses' precociousness in separating truth from falsehood at a very early age (*Mos.* 1.24). He might have been acquainted with the tradition that Zipporah had been a pious proselyte long before the revelation at Sinai (*Midr.* cited by *Imre No'am, Balak,* last sentence [see Ginzberg 6:136, n. 791]); and in support of this he might have noted the tradition that her father Jethro was himself a proselyte (*Midr. Exod. Rab.* 1.32) (see Feldman 1998b, 44–45); but Philo, in general, has a negative view of Jethro (see Feldman 1998b, 41–42). He is apparently sensitive to the problem, which he solves (*Mut.* 110), however, by way of allegory, noting that Midian represents the judicial (κριτικόν), justice-dispensing (δικαστικόν) type, which by marriage is akin to the prophetic type.

Significantly, Philo (*Cher.* 40–41) presents Zipporah not as a woman but rather as the personification of virtue and stresses that her name, which, as we have noted, means "bird," refers to her speeding from earth to heaven and contemplating there the nature of things divine and blessed. Moreover, that Zipporah is no ordinary person in Philo's eyes is clear from the fact that, according to Philo's amazing extra-biblical addition (*Cher.* 47), when Moses married Zipporah, he found her pregnant through no mortal. In a divine mystery she is said to have been impregnated by none other than G-d Himself. Indeed, since he refers to Jethro, on the one hand, as the priest of judgment (κρίσις) and justice (δίκη), he is saying, in effect, that Moses, who, as we have seen, represents justice, found a proper match for himself in marrying the daughter of one who represents justice.[77] Moreover, Philo (*Mos.* 1.59) describes her as the most beautiful (καλλιστεύουσα) of Jethro's daughters[78] and hence, we may add, a match for Moses' beauty (*Mos.* 1.15).

On the other hand, Philo (*Gig.* 50) calls attention to the fact that Moses' father-in-law Jethro was amazed at Moses' unwavering and completely consistent character, which is in stark contrast with Jethro's vacillating nature (*Ebr.* 36), which is compared to that of the mythical Proteus. Indeed, the most severe criticism that Philo can make of anyone is that he prefers seeming to being, conceit to truth; and that is precisely the charge that he makes against Jethro, deriving these traits from the very name of Jethro, which he says means "uneven" (περισσός) (*Agr.* 43).[79] Jethro, consequently, stands for variability and inconsistency. Jethro, he says, "values the human above the divine, custom above laws, profane above sacred, mortal above immortal, and, in general, seeming above being" (*Mut.* 104). It is hard to imagine a more devastating attack, coming as it does from one who so admires Plato (*Prob.* 13). Again, he declares that Jethro corresponds to the "commonwealth peopled by a promiscuous horde, who swing to and fro as their idle opinions carry them" (*Ebr.* 36). He bows down to the opinions of the multitude and will undergo any manner of transformation in order to conform with the ever-varying aspirations of human life. To a Platonist such as Philo, this is well nigh the ultimate sin.

This inconsistency in Philo's attitude to Jethro may perhaps be explained by the fact that, on the one hand, Jethro was a Midianite, a member of the people who caused the Israelite youths to sin in the most egregious way (Num. 25:1–9), an act that Philo (*Mos.* 1.295–304) condemns in the strongest terms; but, on the other hand, Philo cannot avoid paying tribute to Jethro for showing hospitality to Moses, a trait so important in the eyes of Philo, especially since the Egyptians, after all that Joseph had done for them, did not display this toward the Israelites.[80] In contrast, the rabbis[81] have a scenario in which, when Zipporah brought Moses to her father and Moses asked to marry her, Jethro threw Moses into a pit in the expectation that he would meet his death there; and Moses survived only because Zipporah had devised a stratagem that saved him.

And yet, unlike Philo, the rabbis were, on the whole, positively inclined toward Jethro, presumably because they found it hard to believe that Moses, the greatest prophet in Israel who had ever lived (Deut. 34:10), would associate with anyone of less than high repute and, in fact, would marry the daughter of an idol-worshipper. Indeed, we hear (*Mek. Beshallah* 1) that there was not an idol on earth that Jethro had not worshipped; and we are told that he permitted his daughter Zipporah to marry Moses only on condition that their first-born son would be raised to worship idols (*Mek. Yitro* 1). In fact, the sheer volume of comments about him in rabbinic literature is a sure indication of his importance for their tradition.[82] But the most important indication of the rabbis' generally positive attitude toward Jethro is that there is even a tradition that Jethro became a convert to Judaism.[83]

Philo (*Sacr.* 50–51), as we have noted, makes much of the fact (Exod. 3:1) that Moses became a shepherd for Jethro. He (*Mos.* 1.60) adds the editorial-like comment that after his marriage to Zipporah, Moses, in taking charge of his father-in-law's sheep, received his first lesson in leadership (ἡγεμονία), since, as Philo says, shepherding is a preliminary exercise (προγυμνασία) in kingship for one who is going to be in charge of the most tame herd of men, just as hunting serves to prepare men for careers as generals. Consequently, as he remarks (*Mos.* 1.61), kings, as a term of the highest honor, are called shepherds of their people.[84] Thus, the management of inferior creatures prepares one for the management of superior creatures, just as initiation into the lesser mysteries must precede initiation into the greater mysteries (*Mos.* 1.62).

Perhaps, on the other hand, Philo, like Josephus (*A.J.* 2.263), felt impelled to defend the fact that the great leader of the Israelites had served as a shepherd because he notes, in particular, the biblical statement (Gen. 46:34) that to the Egyptians every shepherd is an abomination, and that hence in doing so Moses was going against Egyptian tradition.[85] As a shepherd, says Philo, he was doing the great and glorious (λαμπρόν, "radiant," "illustrious") task of drawing the thoughts of the seemingly wise (περισσός) Jethro away from the crowd and tumult of the state to a place where there is no injustice. Moses, says Philo (*Mos.* 1.62), thus received excellent training in becoming a leader through serving as a shepherd in Midian.[86] Indeed, he says, his view, based not on the opinions of the multitude but on his own inquiry into the truth of the matter, is that the only perfect king is one who is skilled in the knowledge of shepherding.

In an extra-biblical remark, Philo (*Mos.* 1.63) says that what characterized Moses as a shepherd is that he was concerned with the benefit of his charges,[87] never shrinking from any duty, but showing an indefatigable and self-motivated eagerness to do what was needed and to exercise his leadership with pure and guileless honesty. His success as a shepherd consequently aroused the envy of other shepherds (*Mos.* 1.64), perhaps a contemporary allusion to the envy toward the Jews in Philo's Egypt, which was apparently an important source of the hatred of the Jews in Philo's and Josephus' own day (see Feldman 1993a, 107–13). Philo himself (*Sacr.* 50), in one of the relatively infrequent instances where he speaks in the first person singular, states that he admires Moses, the guardian of the laws, who regarded the task of being a shepherd as a great and illustrious one.

One might be critical of Moses for not attempting, while he was in exile in Midian, to do something to aid his fellow Israelites. To answer such critics Philo (*Mos.* 1.47) asserts that Moses cried aloud in horror (ποτνιώμενος) to G-d to rescue (ῥύσηται) the oppressed from their helpless plight (ἀμήχανοι . . . συμφοραί) and to punish deservedly those who left no abusive treatment untried and to double the favor by allowing him to see both of these brought to pass. While he was waiting for G-d to accomplish these goals Moses pursued his struggles (ἆθλοι) in virtue, having reason (λογισμός) as his guide to train himself for the best form of life, both theoretical (θεωρητικόν) and practical (πρακτικόν). He toiled always at unraveling the doctrines of philosophy, digesting them easily and entrusting them to his unforgetting memory and impressing them upon his conduct, his goal being truth rather than appearances, his guide being right reason (ὀρθὸς . . . λόγος),[88] the sole source of the virtues (*Mos.* 1.48). Hence, Moses' years in Midian were not, as one would gather from the Bible, a long interlude of seclusion during which he was merely shepherding flocks of sheep: it was a period during which Moses was mastering philosophy and seeking a genuine understanding of the difference between truth and appearance in preparation for his later career as a philosopher-king. One guesses that Philo is here speaking almost autobiographically, since he says elsewhere (*Spec.* 3.1–3) that he had leisure for philosophy and contemplation, but that he was plunged into the great sea of political affairs. Pseudo-Philo, who focuses on G-d's acts in bringing salvation to the Israelites, totally omits Moses' years in Midian.

Once they had arrived in Midian (Exod. 2:15), others might have been eager to live in obscurity or might have sought to win the favor of men of authority (*Mos.* 1.49). Moses, however, says Philo (*Mos.* 1.50), acted like a hotheaded youth (ἐνεανιεύετο) beyond his strength, because he regarded justice as a power that cannot be put down; and, impelled by this justice, he, self-bidden, formed an alliance, as he characteristically did, with those who were weaker.

In an addition to the biblical narrative, Artapanus states that Raguel wished to wage war against the Egyptians in order to return Moses from exile and establish the throne for him. Because, however, Moses regarded the Egyptians as his own people, Moses declined to join in the attempt; instead, Raguel ordered his people to plunder Egypt.[89] Now Chenephres died, being the first person ever to contract elephantiasis, a disease similar to the leprosy (see Holladay 1983, 1:238–39, n. 78), which, it will be recalled, according to Manetho and others, the Israelites were said to have contracted and on account of which they were said to have been expelled. According to Artapanus, this illness befell Chenephres because he had ordered the Jews to be clothed with linen and not to wear woolen clothing in order that they might be marked and consequently harassed.[90]

In sum, Philo expands two biblical verses into seven paragraphs in highlighting the incident in which Moses, in his concern for justice, aided Jethro's daughters. In berating the oppressive shepherds, Moses, according to Philo, was transformed into a prophet. In not mentioning the names of Jethro or of Zipporah, Jethro's daughter whom Moses married, Philo keeps the focus on Moses. He stresses that the fact that Moses became a shepherd for Jethro gave him expert training for his later leadership, since as a shepherd Moses was concerned solely with the welfare of his sheep. His years in Midian were not interludes of seclusion but were spent in mastering philosophy for his later career as a philosopher-king.

c. *The Burning Bush*

Whereas the Bible (Exod. 3:1) states merely that Moses cared for the sheep of Jethro and guided them far into the wilderness, Philo (*Mos.* 1.63–64) expands this considerably by noting that he excelled (ἄριστος) in leading his flocks and in providing for their needs. He never shrank from his duty and showed an indefatigable zeal, even when unbidden, when it was needed, and displayed in his leadership a pure and guileless trust. Consequently, he increased the number of his sheep. As a result, he was envied by the other herdsmen, who did not see a similar growth in the number of their sheep. They regarded it as a matter of luck if the size of their flock remained the same, whereas he regarded the failure to improve every day as a loss, since he was accustomed to see great progress in the quality of fullness of flesh and fatness of the animals and in their fecundity and their healthy mode of life.[91] Indeed, Philo says in an extra-biblical addition (*Mos.* 1.65), it was through his conscientiousness as a shepherd in leading his flock to a place where water and grass were abundant that he came upon the burning bush.

In his version of the burning bush episode, Artapanus (*ap.* Eus. *PE* 9.27.21) says that Moses prayed to G-d that the suffering of the Israelites might be alleviated, when suddenly fire appeared out of the earth, though there was no kindling in the vicinity. Moses was frightened and fled, but a divine voice told him to wage war against Egypt and to lead the Israelites to their ancestral homeland. Moses resolved to do so but first consulted with Aaron.

In the account of the miracle of the burning bush, the Bible (Exod. 3:3) says that Moses thought that he would turn aside to view it since he wondered why the bush was not consumed. Philo (*Mos.* 1.65) does not say that Moses turned aside; rather, he came directly to the place where the bush burned. Nor do we hear that Moses wondered why the bush was not consumed; nor do we hear that G-d called out to Moses and that Moses replied "Here am I." Nor do we hear that G-d told Moses not to come near but to take off his shoes, since the place where he was standing was holy. Nor did G-d have to identify Himself as the G-d of Abraham, Isaac, and Jacob. Nor are we told that Moses hid his face because of his fear of looking directly at G-d. Apparently, Moses was already on such close terms with G-d that all these preliminaries could be dispensed with. In the Bible G-d begins with the statement that He had come to deliver the Israelites from the Egyptians. He starts *in medias res* by urging Moses to assume the mantle of leadership immediately to take the Israelites very soon to a new home. Philo's Moses has too much faith to be frightened by this apparition of the burning bush. In Josephus (*A.J.* 2.267), however, he is frightened by the sight and, in fact, is terrified still more when a voice comes out of the fire; and, in an extra-biblical addition, the voice points out his boldness in coming to a place where no man had previously come because of the presence of G-d and advises him to go far from the flame and to pry no further. There are no such additions in Philo, Moses being on much closer terms with G-d. Indeed, the main difference between Philo's and Josephus' presentation of the burning bush incident is that Philo stresses philosophic issues, whereas Josephus is interested in dramatic effect.

Philo realizes that his sophisticated audience might well be skeptical of an account so contrary to human experience. Indeed, Pseudo-Philo totally omits the whole incident. Whereas the Bible (Exod. 3:2) speaks of an angel of G-d that appeared to Moses in a blaze of fire from amid the bush, Josephus (*A.J.*

2.265) omits mention of the angel, and rather than identifying the voice as that of G-d simply refers to it as a voice; furthermore, he attempts to prepare readers for the incident by admitting that it was an amazing prodigy. Philo paints a fuller picture, presenting it, in effect, as a vision, which makes it more credible to a sophisticated audience, adding that in the midst of the flame was a form of the fairest beauty; and, realizing that a reader would have difficulty imagining this, he admits that the form was unlike any visible object. He is careful, since a reader might well find it difficult to accept this whole scenario, to avoid giving the impression that it was a vision of G-d Himself, and says, rather, that it was most godlike (θεοειδέστατον). And to assure the reader that it was not G-d, he explains that someone might have surmised that it was indeed an image (εἰκών) of G-d; but, he quickly adds, let it be called a messenger (ἄγγελος) which employed the faculty of sight, which is clearer than a voice and which is able to do great things (μεγαλουργηθείσῃ) (*Mos.* 1.66).[92]

The Bible does not explain the significance of the fact that the bush is not consumed. Neither, for that matter, does Josephus (*A.J.* 2.266–67). Though in the essay *Mos.* Philo minimizes allegorical explanations, he (*Mos.* 1.67) felt constrained, as he usually does, to explain the mysterious to the uninitiated. The burning bush, he says, in agreement with the rabbinic tradition,[93] symbolizes the oppressed Israelites, the bramble being a weak plant, but one that will wound if one touches it; the flame represents the oppressors; the angel is a symbol of G-d's providence.

In the Bible (Exod. 3:4) the actual conversation between G-d and Moses begins with the statement that G-d calls out to Moses from amid the bush and says, "Moses, Moses," whereupon Moses replies, "Here I am." G-d then tells him to remove his shoes since this is holy ground, and He identifies Himself as the G-d of Abraham, Isaac, and Jacob, whereupon Moses hides his face, since he is afraid to gaze at G-d. There is none of this in Philo. Rather, realizing that the whole scene would be hard for a critical and skeptical pagan to believe, Philo (*Mos.* 1.69) suggests to the reader that he join him in regarding, in effect imagining, it as all but (μόνον οὐ) a voice proclaiming to those who were suffering: "Do not lose heart; your weakness is your strength. . . . Those who desire to consume you will be your unwilling saviors." He then explains, as the Bible does not, the symbolism: "the fire, the element that destroys, convicts the cruel-hearted. . . The property of flame is to consume, yet it is consumed, like wood. The nature of wood is to be consumed, yet it is manifested as the consumer, as though it were the fire."

In the Bible (Exod. 3:8) G-d tells Moses that He has heard the outcry of the Israelites who are afflicted in Egypt and that He will take them into a good and broad land, the land of the Canaanites, flowing with milk and honey. A similar statement is found a few verses later (Exod. 3:17). The implication is clear: the Israelites are to displace the Canaanites and establish an independent state in the land. In both Philo's and Josephus' versions, however, there is significantly no mention of the Canaanites who are to be displaced and no suggestion of an independent state: the Israelites are merely to go to another unspecified home and settle there (*Mos.* 1.71). Both Philo and Josephus are aware of the charge of dual allegiance[94] and so omit such statements.

In Philo (*Mos.* 1.71) G-d's actual first statement to Moses stresses the importance of leadership: he urges him to take charge of the nation with all speed (σπεύδειν, "to hasten") and to be not merely an assistant (παραίτιος, "accessory"), but a leader (ἡγεμών). Whereas in the Bible (Exod. 3:8) G-d Himself declares that He will rescue the Israelites, the implication being that He alone assumes this responsibility, in Philo (ibid.) He agrees (ὁμολογῶν) that He will take part with (συλλήψεσθαι, "assist") Moses, thus implying that it is Moses who must take the role of leadership.

In the Bible (Exod. 3:10) G-d tells Moses that He is dispatching him to the Pharaoh and that he is to take the Israelites out of Egypt. Josephus, who emphasizes Moses' role as a general, envisages Moses' role as a military one, since, according to him, the voice bids him to act as a general (στρατηγός) and leader (ἡγεμών). Moses' reply (Exod. 3:11) is to indicate his lack of confidence in himself as one who could go to the Pharaoh and lead the Israelites out of Egypt, whereupon G-d assures him that He will be with him. Realizing that his readers would assume that it would be folly for Moses to undertake this task without first consulting the elders of the nation, Philo (ibid.) has G-d immediately direct Moses to take with him the elders of the Israelites and to tell the Pharaoh that G-d had commanded the Israelites to make a three-days' journey outside the boundaries of Egypt and there to sacrifice to Him in accordance with their ancestral rites.

In the Bible (Exod. 3:11), on the other hand, after G-d tells Moses to go to the Pharaoh and before He tells him to consult the elders, Moses' reply is to doubt his ability to do this. Philo (*Mos.* 1.73) omits this self-doubt on the part of Moses at this point, since this would certainly not redound to the credit of a leader. Instead we have G-d telling Moses both to go to the Pharaoh and to take the elders with him. Josephus (*A.J.* 2.269) omits Moses' first question, his humble objection to G-d (Exod. 3:11), which clearly shows his doubt that he can do what G-d bids him to do, "Who am I that I should go to Pharaoh and bring the sons of Israel out of Egypt?" In Philo (*Mos.* 1.74), Moses, the born leader, knows that in any matter involving leadership one must first of all analyze what the problems are that one faces. Therefore, Philo tells us that Moses knew well that the initial and greatest problem was that the Israelites and, for that matter, all others would disbelieve his words.

Hence, what in the Bible is Moses' second question is for Philo's Moses the very first question, namely what is the name of the G-d Who has sent him, since he realized that this would be the first question that the Israelites would ask him. In Josephus (*A.J.* 2.275) the reason why Moses asks for G-d's name is so that he may address Him properly when sacrificing to Him.[95] In Philo, as in the Bible, G-d identifies Himself as the G-d Who Is and as the G-d of the three forefathers—Abraham, who gained wisdom by teaching; Isaac, who gained wisdom by nature; and Jacob, who gained wisdom by practice (*Mos.* 1.76).[96] The goal in each instance, as in the case of Moses by extension, is wisdom. He then indicates to Moses three miracles[97] that he is to perform to verify this. The Bible (Exod. 4:2–5) simply describes the first miracle, the conversion of a staff into a serpent and vice versa. Philo adds drama to the situation: it is not just an ordinary snake: it is the most authoritative (ἡγεμονικώτατον), immensely great (ὑπερμεγέθης), fully grown snake. The Bible says that Moses fled from it. Philo is more detailed and more dramatic: Moses quickly retreats from the creature, and because of his fear is already starting to flee and is recalled by G-d. The Bible (Exod. 4:4) then says that G-d told Moses to stretch out his hand and to grasp the snake's tail, whereupon it once again becomes a staff. Philo is more detailed and more dramatic and presents a more courageous Moses: at G-d's bidding and inspired by Him with courage (θάρσος),[98] he grasps the tail of the snake while it is still wriggling, whereupon the snake stretches itself to its full length before being changed into a staff. Philo adds how Moses felt, namely that he marvels at the double change but is unable to decide which is more astonishing, since both changes have made a profound impression upon him (*Mos.* 1.78).

In the Bible (Exod. 4:6) when Moses expresses doubt that the Israelites will listen to him, G-d tells him to put his hand in his bosom and withdraw it. When he does so, his hand becomes leprous like snow. When he returns his hand to his bosom and withdraws it, the leprosy disappears. In Ezekiel's version (*ap.* Eus. *PE* 9.28.11) the hand becomes like snow, but there is no mention of leprosy. In omitting the reference to leprosy Ezekiel is following the LXX version. The reference to leprosy is likewise omitted in Philo (*Mos.* 1.79) and in Josephus (*A.J.* 2.273), perhaps because in the anti-Jewish version of the Exodus, as, for example, in Manetho (*ap.* Josephus, *Ap.* 1.233), the Israelites were expelled from Egypt because they had been afflicted with leprosy.

Josephus was particularly eager to answer the canard, circulated by Manetho (*ap. Ap.* 1.279), among others, that Moses' appearance was marred by leprosy and that he was, in fact, expelled from Egypt because of the disease. Josephus, in his elaboration, may have sought to counter Manetho's statement (*ap. Ap.* 1.279) that Moses was a leper, as well as Lysimachus' claim (*ap. Ap.* 1.305–11) that the ancestors of the Jews were lepers and diseased people who had been banished from Egypt for that reason.[99]

In Josephus' version there is likewise no mention of leprosy; instead we are told that when Moses drew forth his hand, it was "white, of a color resembling chalk" (*A.J.* 2.273).[100] Josephus points out the inherent contradiction on the part of the anti-Jewish Egyptian writers in, on the one hand, presenting Moses as an Egyptian priest and asserting that he was remarkable and even divine while, on the other hand, claiming that he was expelled because of leprosy (*Ap.* 1.279). Ultimately, Josephus graciously but confidently leaves to the reader the decision as to whether Moses was stricken with leprosy (*A.J.* 3.268). Philo does not have to leave such a decision to the reader, inasmuch as he does not mention the leprosy in the first place.

After mentioning these two miracles, Philo (*Mos.* 1.80) comments on the unique relationship that existed between G-d and Moses when they were alone together, as they were here, Moses being instructed in a one-to-one relationship, namely as teacher to pupil, and while the instruments of the miracles, namely the staff and his hand, were in his own possession. As to the third miracle, turning the water of the Nile into blood, the Bible (Exod. 4:9), as well as Josephus (*A.J.* 2.273), simply states this but does not indicate Moses' reaction. Philo (*Mos.* 1.81), reflecting the great interest and advances in science in his native Alexandria, is apparently concerned with the scientific aspect and its credibility. Consequently, he supplies a non-biblical scientific detail that actually adds to the miracle, namely that not only was the color of the water changed but also its properties. In the Bible (Exod. 4:9) G-d tells Moses that if the Israelites will not believe him even after he performs the first two miracles, he should take water from the river and pour it out on the dry land, and it will become bloody. It is clear from the biblical text that Moses did not rehearse this miracle; and, indeed, Philo (*Mos.* 1.81) remarks that Moses could not rehearse it beforehand, but the amazement that it would cause would be no less.[101] Most importantly, Philo adds Moses' reaction, stressing Moses' faith in the credibility of these miracles because of the truthfulness of the Speaker but also because he had been convinced by the miracles of the staff and the hand.

One major problem remains, namely Moses' attempt to decline the role of leadership (Exod. 4:10–17) on the ground that he had a speech defect and was not eloquent. In the Bible (Exod. 4:10), when G-d tells Moses to lead the Israelites out of Egypt, he modestly replies that he is not a man of words (איש דברים) and that, on the contrary, he is heavy of mouth (כבד פה) and heavy of speech (כבד לשון). Ezekiel (*ap.* Eus. *PE* 9.29.9) remains true to the biblical text. In his version Moses says that he is not a convincing (εὔλογος, "reasonable," "sensible," "articulate") speaker, that, in fact, his speech is too coarse (δύσφραστος, "hard to explain," "speaking with difficulty") and halting (ἰσχνόφωνος, "thin-voiced," "weak-voiced," "having an impediment in one's speech"). That the great leader of a nation should not be eloquent would certainly, to a Greek or Roman, seem to be a defect so great as to invalidate the claim of that person to be the nation's leader.[102] When G-d replies (Exod. 4:12) that He will be with Moses' mouth and will teach him what to say, Moses is apparently not convinced and tells G-d to seek another person as leader.

In the New Testament (Acts 7:32), when Stephen summarizes this incident, he says nothing about Moses' speech defect. Philo (*Mos.* 1.83) is clearly aware of the problem involved in Moses' lack of eloquence (οὐκ εὔλογον); likewise Ezekiel (*ap.* Eus. *PE* 9.29.9) has Moses say that he is not eloquent (οὐκ εὔλογος, where the LXX has ἄλογος). Whereas Josephus (*A.J.* 2.272), quite clearly, for apologetic reasons, omits the biblical references (Exod. 4:10, 6:12) to Moses' speech impediment, Philo, as usual true to the biblical text, asserts that Moses declared that he was feeble of voice and slow of tongue; but he adds two explanations, such as we do not find in the Bible, that will excuse this impediment, namely, that ever since he had heard G-d speaking to him, he was tongue-tied, apparently out of sheer shock,[103] and secondly that he considered human eloquence to be dumbness as compared with G-d's. In defense of Moses, he remarks that Moses, being cautious (εὐλαβής, "discreet," "undertaking prudently"), drew back (ὑπεστέλλετο, "shrank before," "held in undue awe") from immoderate things (τὰ ὑπέρογκα, "excessive things") and judged that things too great were not for him. Whereas in the Bible Moses humbly asks, "Who am I that I should go to Pharaoh and bring the sons of Israel out of Egypt?" (Exod. 3:11), Moses, in Philo's version, goes even further and exhorts (παρεκάλει) G-d to choose another who would easily (εὐμαρῶς, "readily") be able to accomplish each of the things that had been enjoined upon him (*Mos.* 1.83). Far from regarding this as cowardice on Moses' part, Philo looks upon this as modesty, since he says (*Mos.* 1.84) that G-d approved (ἀποδεξάμενος, "received favorably," "accepted") of Moses' modesty (αἰδώς, "reverence," "awe," "sense of honor").

G-d then, in another of Philo's extra-biblical additions, assures Moses that since it is G-d who gives man a mouth, he will become articulate at a sign from Him (*Mos.* 1.84).[104] He then adds, as an afterthought, that if Moses should need an interpreter, he will have one in the person of his brother. This dialogue with G-d would, in the biblical version, appear not to add to Moses' credit; and, indeed, it is in a mood of anger that G-d (Exod. 4:14) tells Moses that his brother Aaron will be his spokesman. Philo is hardly as sharp. In particular, he adds that G-d approved of Moses' modesty. Moreover, He reassures Moses (*Mos.* 1.84): "Therefore, fear not, for at a sign from Me all will become articulate and be brought over to due measure, so that no one will be able to hinder the stream of words from flowing easily and smoothly from a pure fountain." Moreover, it would seem to be significant that though he is frequently referred to as the brother of Moses, Aaron, as we have noted, is actually not mentioned by name even once in the essay *Mos.*, presumably to keep the focus on Moses alone.

In one of Philo's other essays, G-d explains (*Det.* 38) that Moses is not speechless in the sense that we use it of animals, but rather in the sense that refers to the failure to find a fitting instrument in language corresponding to one's understanding of true wisdom, which is the direct opposite of false sophistry. Moses, he says (*Sacr.* 12), sets no value on probabilities but seeks truth in its purity and hence has no desire for eloquence. Moses, he adds (*Her.* 4), pours forth beauty after beauty, not of words but of thoughts. Philo is probably thinking of Socrates' attack on the Sophists for their cleverness of speech. As a result, Moses' inability to speak effectively, far from detracting from Moses' ability as a leader, actually redounds to his credit. Philo thus distinguishes him as a true philosopher-king, as opposed to an opportunistic politician who seeks effect.

Moses says that he will not go to Egypt to engage the Egyptian wise men, as, we might remark, Josephus has Abraham do (*A.J.* 1.161), in conflict with the Egyptian sophists, until he has been fully trained in "the word of utterance" (ὁ προφορικὸς . . . λόγος) (*Det.* 39). Perhaps Philo does not have him do so because he feared that this might appear to be an attempt at proselytism, which would raise a "red flag," so to speak, because of its controversial nature.[105] Philo (*Migr.* 76), however, is self-conscious about the fact that Moses does engage in dialogue with the Egyptians; and he explains that he does so not in order to become acquainted with a greater number of subjects, but, rather, in what appears to be in emulation of Socrates, in order to disprove the Egyptian sophists.

Despite the fact that G-d assures Moses that Aaron will be his spokesman (Exod. 4:14–16) and that it is Aaron who speaks to the elders of the Israelites (Exod. 4:30), in Philo (*Mos.* 1.86), who is apparently concerned not to diminish Moses' role, it is both Moses and Aaron together who address them.

One might wonder why Moses would have agreed to return to Egypt in view of the fact that he had had to escape in order that he should not be put to death after the Pharaoh had heard of his slaying of the Egyptian overseer and in view of the reports that had circulated that Moses was ambitious to seize the throne (*Mos.* 1.45–46). In the Bible, despite G-d's long conversation with Moses at the burning bush (Exod. 3:4–4:17), there is nothing said that would reassure Moses that he could return safely.

In Ezekiel the Tragedian's version (*ap.* Eus. *PE* 9.29.4–5) Moses recounts a dream to his father-in-law, Jethro, in which he sees on the summit of Mount Sinai a man wearing a crown who gave him his sceptre and bade him to sit on the throne, from which Moses beheld the entire earth and the stars. Jethro interprets the dream to signify that Moses will judge and lead humankind. In Philo's version, almost at the very beginning of G-d's speech to Moses (*Mos.* 1.73), G-d tells him that he should not be afraid to return, since, as He informs him, the former king from whom he had fled had died,[106] and that the land is now ruled by one who does not remember any of Moses' actions. Similarly, Josephus (*A.J.* 2.277) adds the extra-biblical remark that it was after Moses had learned that the Pharaoh, in whose reign he had fled, had died, that he decided to return to Egypt.

One means by which Philo, and later Josephus, seek to "improve" upon the biblical narrative is through providing better motivation and through increasing the plausibility of events. In connection with Moses and Jethro, there is an improbability in the biblical text in that Moses asks Jethro for permission to return to Egypt even though he does not yet know (until the following verse) whether those who are seeking to kill him are still alive (Exod. 4:18). In Philo's version G-d at the burning bush has already told Moses (*Mos.* 73) that the Pharaoh from whom he fled is dead.[107]

In the Bible (Exod. 4:18), as well as in Josephus (*A.J.* 2.277), after Moses had decided to depart, he, ever the courteous son-in-law, goes to his father-in-law, Jethro, to ask for permission to leave in order to return to his brethren in Egypt to see how they are faring, whereupon Jethro agrees. In Philo there is no mention of Moses going to Jethro to ask for permission to leave. Rather, we read the statement (*Mos.* 1.85) that immediately after G-d concludes his conversation with Moses, he, the truly pious and faithful leader, knowing how unsafe and, indeed, dangerous it was to contradict G-d so blatantly, picked himself up (ἄρας) and went on the road to Egypt.

One of the most embarrassing biblical passages with regard to Moses as the Israelite leader tells of G-d's attempt (Exod. 4:24–26), because of Moses' failure to circumcise his son, to kill him while he is on his way from Midian to Egypt to undertake his role of leadership. It is, indeed, ironic that his non-Jewish Midianite wife, Zipporah, literally saved his life by circumcising her son. It must have troubled apologists such as Philo and Josephus and surely would have amazed his readers that Moses, the greatest Jew who ever lived (Deut. 34:10) and G-d's chosen messenger to deliver His law, should have been so impious as to disobey so fundamental a precept.[108] Hence, it is not surprising that Philo (*Mos.* 1.85), Pseudo-Philo (10.1), and Josephus (*A.J.* 2.279) omit all reference to this incident. In the case of Philo this is particularly remarkable, inasmuch as he often has references to the same biblical passage in several of his essays. To be sure, Philo rarely omits seemingly embarrassing episodes, but here the very reputation of Moses as a religious leader was at stake, since he might well be accused of being a hypocrite for neglecting so crucial a commandment.

In sum, Philo says that it was through conscientiousness as a shepherd that Moses went to the burning bush. Philo's Moses has too much faith to be frightened. Since a reader might find the whole scene incredible, Philo quickly adds that it was a vision that appeared. Whereas the Bible and Josephus do not explain the fact that the bush was not consumed, Philo explains that it symbolized the oppressed Israelites. Whereas in the Bible G-d declares that He will rescue the Israelites, in Philo He says that He will assist Moses, thus clearly indicating that Moses must assume the role of leader. Philo omits Moses' expression of self-doubt. His Moses is more courageous and has a uniquely close relationship with G-d. Philo is clearly aware of Moses' speech defect, a major flaw for a leader. He explains very convincingly that Moses was tongue-tied out of sheer shock and that he sought beauty of thought rather than of words, as did the Sophists. Philo seldom omits embarrassing episodes, but Moses' failure to circumcise his son was so incriminating that he felt constrained to omit it.

d. Moses' Return to Egypt

In the Bible the respective roles of Moses and Aaron in leading the Israelites to freedom are not clear. According to the biblical text (Exod. 4:27), it is G-d who tells Aaron to meet Moses, whereupon Aaron does so, and Moses relates to Aaron all the words that G-d has spoken to him. Moreover, the biblical text states that Aaron met Moses at the mountain of G-d, whereas Philo (*Mos.* 1.85), who is eager to retain the primary role of Moses, declares that he met him during his journey[109] and thus restricts to Moses the relationship with G-d at the mountain. In Philo the role of Moses is more important, for it is he who meets his brother and persuades him to accompany him (*Mos.* 1.85), though Philo adds that Aaron, due to the watchful working of G-d, was already predisposed to obey. Pseudo-Philo, who focuses on G-d's wondrous acts in rescuing the Israelites, simply lists the ten plagues (10.1) and describes at length (10.2–6) G-d's miracles in effecting the Israelites' crossing of the Sea of Reeds.

A question would naturally arise with regard to the biblical text's statement (Exod. 4:29) that Moses and Aaron gathered all the elders of the Israelites, since it would seem very dangerous to gather Israelite leaders together, inasmuch as such a gathering would be suspected of planning a revolution. Hence, Philo (*Mos.* 1.86), ever concerned about plausibility, adds the phrase ἐν ἀπορρήτῳ ("secretly"). Moreover, there is always the problem whether Aaron is merely the spokesman of Moses or equal to Moses or even the main figure in the liberation of the Israelites. The biblical text (Exod. 4:30) states that Aaron spoke the words that G-d had addressed to Moses; but this clearly reduces Moses' importance, and so Josephus (*A.J.* 2.280) says that it was Moses who recounted the miracles to the elders.[110] Philo (*Mos.* 1.86), whose whole essay, as we have noted, is largely intended (*Mos.* 1.2) to answer those Greek writers who have refused to treat Moses as worthy of memory, says that it was Moses and Aaron together (though Aaron is not mentioned by name) who informed the elders of G-d's words, presumably because it is reasonable to assume that since both were present they joined in addressing the elders.

Again, according to the Bible (Exod. 4:30), after speaking to the elders, Aaron actually performed the signs in the sight of the people. Philo (*Mos.* 1.86) says nothing about Aaron's performing the signs, perhaps because he wished to keep the focus centered on Moses.[111] The Bible (Exod. 4:31) says that the people believed Moses and Aaron, who thereupon went to the Pharaoh (Exod. 5:1), there being no indication that they had any doubts. Philo follows the Bible in this, but Josephus (*A.J.* 2.281) says that when Moses felt assured that the Israelites had been persuaded he went to the Pharaoh, the implication being that he waited until he was sure of their support.

According to Artapanus, in an extra-biblical detail (*ap.* Eus. *PE* 9.27.23; Clement of Alexandria, *Strom.* 1.23.154.2), the Pharaoh imprisoned Moses, but Moses miraculously escaped when the doors of the prison opened of their own accord. Moses went to the Pharaoh, who ordered him to declare the name of the G-d who had sent him. When Moses did so, the Pharaoh fell over speechless; but Moses picked him up, and the Pharaoh came back to life. In a passage reminiscent of the way in which Jesus, according to the *Toledot Yeshu* (see Krauss 1902), managed to perform miracles, the Pharaoh wrote the name on a tablet.

The Pharaoh told Moses to perform some sign for him, whereupon Moses threw out his rod, which was turned into a snake. When everyone was terrified at this sight, Moses picked up the snake, which was turned back into a rod. Moses then struck the Nile River with his rod, whereupon the river overflowed its banks, inundating all of Egypt. It was from that time that the flooding of the Nile began; thus Moses would seem to be responsible, according to Artapanus, for the life-giving gifts of the Nile.

If, indeed, there was a tradition, such as we find in Artapanus (*ap.* Eus. *PE* 9.27.7–11) and in Josephus (*A.J.* 2.238–53), that Moses had served brilliantly as general in a campaign against the much-feared Ethiopians, we may wonder why Philo does not, as Josephus (*A.J.* 2.282) does, remind the Pharaoh of the services that he had given to the Egyptians in that campaign. We may surmise, as we have noted, that Philo, if he did know of this tradition, omits mention of the campaign because he wishes to emphasize Moses' achievement as primarily a political, legislative, and religious leader, rather than as a military leader.

Again, a reader might well wonder why, according to the biblical text (Exod. 5:1), in Moses and Aaron's request to the Pharaoh, it is in the wilderness that the Israelites are to sacrifice. Philo (*Mos.* 1.87), who, as usual, seeks to give a rational explanation for an action where the biblical text is obscure, explains that the reason is that the customs of the Hebrews run counter to the common course of humankind.[112] By offering this explanation, Philo's Moses, as Sills (1992, 694) remarks, recognizes the legitimacy of the Egyptian cult while maintaining the uniqueness of the sacred quality of the Jewish worship. This is in line with Philo's general attitude of showing respect for non-Jewish beliefs, as we see in his adoption (*Mos.* 2.205 and *Spec.* 1.53) of the LXX's version, θεοὺς οὐ κακολογήσεις, of Exod. 22:27 (LXX 22:28), אלקים לא תקלל, "thou shalt not curse gods."[113] As Philo (*Mos.* 2.205) explains, we must refrain from speaking insultingly of the gods of others "lest any of Moses' disciples get into the habit of treating lightly the name 'god' in general, for it is a title worthy of the highest respect and love." If Philo derides the Egyptian religion, it is because, on philosopical grounds, he regards it as atheistic (*Fug.* 180) in valuing earth above heaven and body above soul. He is particularly critical of the Egyptian worship of irrational animals.[114] Again, inasmuch as polytheism is by definition tolerant of various gods, the question might arise why the Pharaoh should have objected to having still another god in the pantheon. Whereas in the Bible the Pharaoh (Exod. 5:2) says "I do not know the L-rd," Philo rationally explains that the Pharaoh could not accept the Israelite G-d because he could not understand a G-d who was discernible only by the mind. What Philo does not say is that the Egyptians could not admit into their pantheon a G-d who denied the authenticity of any other god, since this kind of illiberalism was completely unacceptable throughout pagan antiquity.[115]

When the Pharaoh, in response to the request of Moses and Aaron, ordered the Egyptian overseers to increase their oppression of the Israelites, the Bible (Exod. 5:15) mentions that although the Israelite foremen cried out to the Pharaoh they were treated with disdain; but Philo omits this. Instead, Philo (*Mos.* 1.90) focuses upon Moses and the difficulties that he encountered as a leader. The Bible (Exod. 5:21) says that the Israelite foremen bitterly complained to Moses and Aaron that they had placed a sword in the hands of the Egyptians to murder them.[116] Philo (*Mos.* 1.90) goes even further: it is not just the foremen, but the Israelites generally who are depicted as enraged against Moses and Aaron as deceivers. The Israelites are said to slander them, sometimes secretly, sometimes openly. They accuse them of impiety (ἀσέβεια) in apparently speaking falsely of G-d. In the Bible (Exod. 5:22) Moses responds to the accusations by turning to G-d and complaining why He had done evil to the Israelites and why He had chosen him. He complains that G-d has not rescued the Israelites. In Philo's version Moses does not at this point turn to G-d. Instead, Moses confidently shows the Israelites and, shortly thereafter, the Egyptians the wonders that G-d has taught him to perform. Actually, some of the wonders, according to both the Bible and Philo, were later performed by Aaron, who thus appears to be merely Moses' agent.

Philo omits G-d's reassuring words to Moses. In particular, he omits Moses' demurral, in which he presents the *a fortiori* argument (Exod. 6:12) that if the Israelites have not listened to him how can He expect that the Pharaoh will listen to him, especially since he has a speech defect. Indeed, to have included such a statement would indicate that Moses lacked faith in his mission; and, moreover, it would have called attention to Moses' lack of ability as an orator in a society where eloquence in a leader was a *sine qua non*.

Instead Philo comes directly to the contest between Aaron and the Egyptian magicians in turning a staff into a snake.[117] Here, too, Philo adds picturesque drama to the scene. Whereas the Bible states that Aaron and the Egyptian sorcerers cast down their staves, which turned into snakes, and that Aaron's staff swallowed theirs, Philo adds that Aaron very dramatically waved his staff in a very conspicuous manner before flinging it to the ground, whereupon it immediately turned into a snake (*Mos.* 1.91).[118] In the Bible (Exod. 7:9) G-d instructs Moses to tell Aaron to cast down his staff, whereas in Philo there is no mention of Moses' commanding Aaron. Moreover, in Philo it is neither Moses nor Aaron who produces the miracle: it is, rather, G-d (*Mos.* 1.95) who is responsible for the miracle. Philo also adds the reaction of the onlookers, who were filled with wonder, withdrew in fear, and were at the point of fleeing. He then adds the remarks of the Egyptian magicians, in which they confidently assert that they can produce a similar result, whereupon, indeed, they throw down their staves, which are turned into snakes. Whereas the Bible says simply that the staff of Aaron swallowed theirs, Philo adds drama by describing the multitude of snakes writhing around Aaron's and by noting that Aaron's snake rose high above the rest, widening its chest and opening its mouth, and absorbed the others through the suction of its breath with irresistible force like fishes encircled by a net.

In the Bible (Exod. 7:13), after the Egyptian magicians are able to duplicate Aaron's feat, the Pharaoh remains stubborn. Philo, apparently troubled by the fact that the Egyptians seem to have the same kind of efficacy in magic that Moses and Aaron possess, adds the reaction of the spectators, that the inherent skepticism in every person was refuted by the realization that this was the work of a divine power.[119] The result is that the Egyptians are, to some degree, rehabilitated, whereas it is the Pharaoh who remains utterly stubborn.[120]

It is significant that Philo presents a uniformly derogatory picture of the Egyptian pharaohs. One may guess that his negative view was influenced by the fact that he himself was living in Egypt and was intimately involved in the Jewish community's attempts at refuting the anti-Jewish charges of his Egyptian contemporaries. The fact that Philo does not distinguish among the various pharaohs in his portrayal of them is a further indication of his negative attitude toward them.[121]

In sum, throughout the account of Moses' return to Egypt, Philo keeps the focus on Moses and reduces the role of Aaron. In the negotiations with the Pharaoh, Moses recognizes the legitimacy of the Egyptian cult while maintaining the uniqueness of the Israelites' ways. Whereas the Israelites complain bitterly to Moses that he has, through his negotiations with the Pharaoh, made their life more difficult than ever and whereas, in turn, Moses complains to G-d, Philo's Moses does not turn to G-d, but confidently shows the Israelites the wonders that G-d has taught him to perform.

e. The Plagues

One of the most difficult problems in theodicy is to explain how G-d, on the one hand, says that He Himself will harden the Pharaoh's heart (Exod. 7:3) and, on the other hand, holds the Pharaoh responsible for his actions. Philo, like the later Josephus, systematically avoids this problem by always omitting those biblical statements in which G-d hardens Pharaoh's heart.

In line with his aim to present an apologetic work defending Moses—and no less the Pentateuch, so intimately connected with his name—against his pagan detractors, Philo makes every effort to demonstrate that the Pentateuch is rational. Thus, in connection with the ten plagues inflicted upon the Egyptians, the reader may well ask why G-d, if He is really omnipotent, was apparently so weak that He had to inflict one plague after another when He presumably had the power to bring about the deliverance of the Israelites from slavery through a single action. Philo (*Mos.* 1.96) would appear to answer such critics by stating that the reason that He inflicted ten plagues was that ten is a "complete" (παντέλεια) number (as compared with four, which is only potentially complete), consisting, as it does, of the numbers from one though four added together as well as the ratios of the musical consonances—produced by the intervals of four notes, five notes, an octave, and a double octave, as well as having other geometrical properties (*Opif.* 47–52). Similarly, in his discussion (*Spec.* 2.200) of why the Day of Atonement comes on the tenth day of the month, he remarks that the number ten is called by the learned the all-perfect, so that it sums up fully and perfectly the leading truths of music science. Hence, by implication, ten corresponds to G-d, Who is perfect. This will also explain why the number of commandments given by G-d is ten (*Decal.* 20–31). This also places the plagues on a universal scale, so that they are viewed not as punishment inflicted by a person, but rather by G-d as representative of the whole universe. To be sure, this diminishes the role of Moses himself, but by doing so Philo associates Moses with the forces of the whole universe. This would make a special appeal to Stoics in his audience, since it is so reminiscent of the language of thinkers such as Strabo.[122]

Philo (*Mos.* 1.97) likewise elevates the role of Moses as compared with Aaron in connection with the infliction of the plagues. He notes that the infliction of the three plagues belonging to the denser elements, earth and water, was entrusted by G-d to Aaron. However, he entrusted to Moses the three plagues belonging to air and fire, the two forces most productive of life. The seventh he entrusted to both, and the last three G-d reserved for Himself.

Philo (*Mos.* 1.98–142) enumerates the plagues in the order 1, 2, 3, 7, 8, 9, 6, 4, 5, 10. We may note that Pseudo-Philo (10.1) likewise departs from the biblical order of the plagues and cites them in the order 1, 2, 4, 7, 5, 8, 3, 9, 10, and omits the sixth plague (boils). In Ezekiel the Tragedian (*ap.* Eus. *PE* 9.28.12) boils are in fourth rather than in sixth place and darkness precedes locusts rather than the reverse as in Exodus.[123] Josephus (*A. J.* 2.293), though he indicates that he will enumerate all the plagues, actually eliminates the sixth, boils on cattle. In Psalms 78:44–51 the order is 1, 4, 2, 8, 7, 5, 10; in Psalms 105:28–36 the order is 9, 1, 2, 4, 3, 7, 8, 10. The fact that there are variations in the order and in what is included or omitted and the fact that neither Philo nor other sources that mention the plagues do not state that they have presented the plagues in an order different from that of Exodus indicates that for them such liberty is permissible. In the case of Philo, such a modification is in line with his overall purpose in dealing with the Bible, namely, not to present a paraphrase, but rather to give an analysis. Philo (*Mos.* 1.96–97) justifies his change in this instance by analyzing the elements—earth, water, air, and fire—and the agents—Aaron, Moses, the two together, and G-d—through which the plagues were carried out.[124] He points out a symmetry between these plagues, which were used by G-d to destroy the impious nation of Egypt, and the materials through which G-d created the world.

In connection with the first plague, the Bible (Exod. 7:20–23) says simply that G-d told Moses to warn the Pharaoh that if he persisted in his refusal to allow the Israelites to leave, Moses with his staff would strike the water of the river, which would then change to blood.[125] There is no explanation in the Bible as to why the plagues began with water, but Philo (*Mos.* 1.98), forever seeking to explain things rationally, asserts that since the Egyptians paid special homage to water, which they considered to be the original source of everything in creation, G-d regarded it as fitting that the plagues should start with water.[126]

Philo was apparently troubled by the fact that G-d told Moses to inform the Pharaoh that he (Moses) with his staff would strike the water in the river, which would then turn to blood (Exod. 7:16–17), whereas G-d then instructed Moses (Exod. 7:19) to tell Aaron to take his staff and to stretch out his hand over all the waters of Egypt, which would then be turned to blood. In the next verse we read that Moses and Aaron did as G-d had commanded them and that he held his staff aloft and struck the water of the river, which was then turned to blood. It is not clear who the "he" is, but it would seem to be a reference to Aaron. Nevertheless, there would seem to be a contradiction here, inasmuch as Moses had told the Pharaoh that he would strike the water, whereas G-d had instructed Moses to tell Aaron to take his staff and stretch out his hand over all the waters, which would turn to blood, no mention being made of striking the waters. Moreover, this seems to contradict a previous statement (Exod. 4:9; so also Philo, *Mos.* 1.81) in which G-d tells Moses that if the Israelite elders will not believe him, he (and presumably not Aaron) should take water from the river and pour it on the dry land and the water will become blood.

There is a further contradiction in that Moses had told Aaron (Exod. 7:19–20) to stretch out his hand in order to turn all the waters of Egypt, and not merely the Nile, into blood, whereas we read that when Aaron struck the water in the river the Egyptians could not drink water from the river. To compound the problem, we read (Exod. 7:25) that seven days were completed after G-d struck the river. Furthermore, we are told (Exod. 7:21) that the blood was throughout the land of Egypt, and there is no indication that the waters were not bloody for the Israelites as well. Moreover, we read that after the water was changed to blood, the Egyptian necromancers performed the same act, turning water into blood, as a result of which the Pharaoh remained stubborn in his opposition to the request of Moses and Aaron. The Bible (Exod. 7:25) implies that after seven days the water again became drinkable, though it does not indicate why G-d should have permitted the disaster to abate.

Significantly, Josephus (*A.J.* 2.291) resolves this problem by stating that when Moses went to the Pharaoh he did not mention the water and what he would do to it and how he would achieve this, but rather that he spoke in the most general terms warning the Pharaoh that he would have only himself to blame if he opposed G-d's commands. Moreover, according to Josephus, it is neither Moses nor Aaron who brings on the plague, but rather it is at G-d's command. Philo, however, follows the biblical text as to who brought on the plague; but, in accordance with his general practice of giving reasons for biblical statements, he explains (*Mos.* 1.101) that the Egyptians besought Moses and Aaron to take pity on their perishing, whereupon G-d, whose nature is to show mercy, changed the blood into water fit for drinking.

Additionally, we read in Philo (*Mos.* 1.144) that the river turned to blood for the Egyptians but not for the Israelites. Likewise, Josephus (*A.J.* 2.295) states that the water was bloody only for the Egyptians, whereas for the Israelites it did not change and remained sweet and drinkable.[127] Furthermore, in place of the statement that the Pharaoh persisted in his refusal to permit the Israelites to leave, Josephus (*A.J.* 2.295) says that the Pharaoh, whom he tries to rehabilitate to some degree in the belief that a leader must be obeyed (see Feldman 1993f), being at a loss to explain this astonishing miracle and being fearful for the Egyptians, decided to allow the Israelites to leave,[128] only to change his mind once he saw that the disaster abated. Philo, by omitting the scene in which Moses threatened the Pharaoh, resolves the apparent contradiction between what Moses told the Pharaoh he would do and the fact that it was Aaron who carried out the threat.

As to whether it was Moses or Aaron who brought on the plague, Philo states clearly (*Mos.* 1.99) that it was Aaron who did so. Lest the reader should think that this diminishes the centrality of Moses in the whole story, Philo explains (*Mos.* 1.97), as we have noted, that G-d distributed the punishments so that the first three, which dealt with the denser elements, which go to make up our bodily qualities, namely, earth and water, were assigned to Aaron, whereas the next three, involving air and fire, which are the two most productive of life, were assigned to Moses. As to the statement (Exod. 7:22) that the Egyptian magicians were able to duplicate the feat, Philo, like Josephus, apparently aware that such a statement would detract from the miraculous nature of the plague and from the uniqueness of G-d's achievement, omits it. As to how the Israelites were able to get drinkable water when the waters throughout Egypt had been turned to blood, Philo (*Mos.* 1.144), like Josephus, simply states that when the Israelites wished to draw water from the river, it turned out to be drinkable.

According to the Bible (Exod. 7:25) the plague of blood abated after seven days, but there is no indication that this plague caused the Pharaoh to change his mind. Josephus (*A.J.* 2.295), however, states that the Pharaoh, being at a loss to explain this astonishing thing and being fearful for the Egyptians, now allowed the Israelites to leave, only to change his mind once the plague had abated. Similarly, Artapanus (*ap.* Eus. *PE* 9.27.29) says that the Pharaoh allowed the Israelites to leave after this plague.

Another question that clearly suggests itself is how to explain that Moses, though possessed of true wisdom, seems to know so much that he is able to compete with the sophists of Egypt and their specious fables. The answer, according to the reasonable reply of Philo (*Migr.* 76), is that Moses surely found the researches concerning G-d complete and self-sufficing; but that he became acquainted with the false teaching of the Egyptians only so that he might be able to refute them, just as he became acquainted in his youth with teachers of Egyptian and Chaldean science (*Mos.* 1.23–24) so that he could determine where he might agree and where he might disagree with them.

After the water of the Egyptians was restored to normal following the first plague, there is no indication in the Bible as to the background and reason of the second plague. We hear only (Exod. 7:26) that G-d told Moses to go to the Pharaoh and tell him to allow the Israelites to leave in order to serve Him. Philo (*Mos.* 1.102) fills in the gap by stating that for a short time the Egyptians relaxed their wickedness,[129] but soon returned to their previous cruelty and lawlessness, as if, having been punished once, they would not be subjected to a second punishment. Josephus (*A.J.* 2.296) carefully remarks that the Pharaoh was no longer willing to be wise (σωφρονεῖν, "moderate, reasonable"), the implication being, in accordance with Josephus' tendency to rehabilitate the Pharaoh, that he had previously exercised such wisdom and toleration. Philo, however, omits G-d's instructions to Moses to warn the Pharaoh that if he does not allow the Israelites to leave He will fill the entire country with frogs, since, presumably, such a warning seems to be implied from the parallel with the other plagues. Thereupon, Philo (*Mos.* 1.103) follows the biblical text in stating that G-d commanded Aaron to stretch out his hand over the waters of Egypt, with the result that a multitude of frogs emerged. He adds that because of the omnipresence of the frogs people could neither go out into the streets nor stay indoors. Again, the Bible (Exod. 8:3) notes that the Egyptian magicians did the same through their incantations; but both Philo and Josephus omit this, presumably again because it would detract from the uniqueness of the punishments inflicted by G-d. The Pharaoh then summoned Moses and Aaron and promised to permit the Israelites to leave if they would entreat G-d to remove the frogs. Josephus (*A.J.* 2.299) adds that the Pharaoh permitted them to leave, but that it was rather through fear than through sagacity. Moses and Aaron entreated G-d, and the frogs died; but once relieved, according to the Bible (Exod. 8:8–11), the Pharaoh returned to his stubborn ways.

The next plague, that of gnats,[130] is presented in a mere four verses in the Bible (Exod. 8:12–15). Josephus (*A.J.* 2.300–2) likewise deals with it in three short paragraphs. Philo (*Mos.* 1.106–12), however, always curious as to the particular reasons for events, devotes seven paragraphs to it, discussing, in particular, why G-d chose a very small creature, the gnat, rather than larger animals.[131] On the one hand, he remarks, the gnat is an extremely troublesome creature; but, on the other hand, G-d deliberately chose to admonish the Egyptians rather than to destroy them; and He, the highest and greatest Power, chose not the strongest but the slightest to wreak vengeance on the evil-doers so that they would be forced to cry out, "This is the finger of G-d." Here again, Philo and Josephus omit the biblical statement (Exod. 8:14) that the Egyptian magicians tried in vain to draw forth the gnats. According to the Bible, the magicians then told Pharaoh that "This is the finger of G-d,"[132] but in Philo's version (*Mos.* 1.112) all Egypt was forced to cry aloud, "This is the finger of G-d," signifying, as Philo puts it, that if G-d had put forth His hand, not even the entire habitable world and, indeed, not even the whole universe would be able to stand against it. Again, it is Josephus (*A.J.* 2.301), who, in his concern for the reputation of the Pharaoh, presents a picture of the Pharaoh as dismayed by the calamity and as fearing the destruction of his people and considering the disgrace of such a destruction, and consequently being forced to be reasonable, though, to be sure, only half-way.

As for Philo, in view of the general outcry of the Egyptians, one would expect that the Pharaoh would agree to allow the Israelites to depart; and, indeed, this is precisely, according to Josephus (*A.J.* 2.302), what the Pharaoh does, though he insists that they leave their wives and children as hostages, a demand that angered G-d even more, since it would seem to imply that it was Moses rather than He who was punishing Egypt on the Israelites' behalf. In the Bible (Exod. 8:15), however, the Pharaoh remains stubborn and does not heed the outcry of the magicians. Nevertheless, Philo (*Mos.* 1.113) gives us no indication as to the Pharaoh's reaction to the plague and to the magicians; one assumes that the Pharaoh did not heed the outcry, since Philo proceeds to describe the next set of plagues. According to Josephus (*A.J.* 2.301), however, it is fear of the destruction of his people that leads the Pharaoh to listen to reason (σωφρονεῖν). Again, this creates a certain amount of sympathy for the Pharaoh.

Before describing the plague of hail, the first of the three entrusted to Moses alone, Philo, the Hellenistic scientist, discusses at length (*Mos.* 1.114–17) the peculiarities of the climate of Egypt, his point being that the plagues were particularly suited to take advantage of those conditions. He notes, in particular, that Egypt is almost the only country, apart from those in the southern latitudes, that does not have a winter season;[133] and he conjectures why that should be so. One of his suggestions is that the winter is unneeded in Egypt because the Nile River serves the purpose of rainfall and nature does nothing in vain; indeed, out of opposites it forms the harmony of the universe. Philo (*Mos.* 1.114) seems to have investigated this curious phenomenon, since we find him saying that "some say" that the reason is that Egypt is not far from the torrid zone and that the fiery heat that emanates from that zone warms all its surroundings or that the clouds are used up beforehand by the flooding of the river at the summer solstice. He explains the matter scientifically: the river begins to rise as the summer opens and ceases when it ceases; meanwhile the Etesian winds sweep down opposite to the mouths of the Nile and put a stop to its outflow through them. Furthermore, as the level of the sea rises to a great height through the violence of the winds, extending its huge billows like a long wall, it coops up the river within. Then as the stream that flows from the upland springs, and the other stream that should find its way out but is driven inland by the obstacles that face it, meet each other, prevented from expanding by the banks that compress them on either side, the river naturally rises. Hence the country enjoys springtime in midwinter, whereas with the onset of the plague the parts of the country above Memphis, where the royal palace was, that normally experienced no rainfall at all, now suddenly and most miraculously experienced a complete change, with lightning and thunderbolts running through the hail, their natural antagonist, and yet not melting it or being quenched by it. All of this highlights the miraculous nature of this plague occurring in a country where one would never even imagine the possibility of hail.

When Philo describes (*Mos.* 1.118–19) the plague of hail, he emphasizes how sudden and unexpected it was and the resulting despondency of the inhabitants of Egypt, who concluded, correctly, according to Philo (*Mos.* 1.119), that it was a sign of divine wrath. In the Bible (Exod. 9:13–35), which devotes more verses to this plague than to any other, we read that G-d instructed Moses to tell the Pharaoh that though He could have obliterated the Egyptians totally with a pestilence, He was sending the plagues, one by one, and allowing the Egyptians to endure in order to show His strength and so that His name might be declared throughout the world. He tells him to warn the Pharaoh that He will send a very heavy hail, unprecedented in the history of Egypt, and to gather in the livestock and crops of the field so that they may not be destroyed. Philo has no such warning, but proceeds immediately, with his interest in the scientific aspect of the hail, to describe at length the unusual nature of the hailstorm and the effect that it had upon the Egyptians.

Moreover, the Bible (Exod. 9:26) asserts that the hail did not fall upon Goshen, where the Israelites dwelled; but neither Philo nor Josephus (*A.J.* 2.305) mentions this, perhaps because it might seem incredible to a reader that such a heavy hail should have omitted one small, particular area, though later (*Mos.* 1.143), to be sure, Philo does make the general point that none of the plagues affected the Israelites. Rational scientist that he is, Philo expresses wonder that the same elements in the same place and at the same time brought destruction to one people and safety to the other. Furthermore, the Bible (Exod. 9:27) states that the Pharaoh summoned Moses and Aaron and confessed that he had sinned and that G-d is the Righteous One and that he and his people are the wicked ones; but Philo does not have this admission at all, since he focuses solely on the hail itself as the evidence of G-d's power. Next in the Bible we have the Pharaoh's request to Moses to bring an end to the hailstorm, Moses' statement that he knows that the Pharaoh is still not afraid of G-d, Moses' success in causing the hail to cease, and, nevertheless, the Pharaoh's continued hardness of heart. All of this is omitted by Philo, as well as by Josephus (*A.J.* 2.305), presumably because the Pharaoh's behavior is highly repetitious; and Philo blandly continues on to the next plague.

This next plague, the fifth in Philo's account, the eighth in the Bible (Exod. 10:1–20), is that of a swarm of locusts enveloping all of Egypt. Before bringing on the plague G-d tells Moses to go to the Pharaoh, since He has made his heart and that of his servants stubborn so that He may send these plagues in order that the Israelites may tell their descendants that He had made a mockery of Egypt. Moses and Aaron then go to the Pharaoh and warn him that, if he persists in his intransigence, G-d will send a huge swarm of locusts. This time the Pharaoh's servants complain to the Pharaoh and urge him to allow the Israelites to leave. When the Pharaoh summons Moses and Aaron and asks them who will be included in their entourage, they answer that they will take everyone—men, women, children, and animals. The Pharaoh becomes angry at this reply and says that he will permit only the men to leave, and he drives Moses and Aaron out.[134] G-d tells Moses to bring on the plague, and this he does. Thereupon the Pharaoh summons Moses and Aaron, confesses that he has sinned, and asks them to entreat G-d to remove the locusts. But when Moses does this we read (Exod. 10:20) that G-d hardened the heart of the Pharaoh and that he refused to send out the Israelites.

Whereas the Bible (Exod. 10:13) states that G-d guided an east wind through the land all that day and night and brought on a swarm of locusts, Philo, the scientist, presents a more detailed explanation of the phenomenon (*Mos.* 1.120). A violent south wind, he says, swooped down, gaining force and intensity throughout the day and night. The south wind, he adds, is dry and produces headaches and makes hearing difficult. This causes particular distress, he says, in Egypt, which lies well to the south, where the sun and the planets have their orbits, so that the wind sets in motion the scorching of the sun, which, in turn, burns up everything. Again, Philo (*Mos.* 1.120–21) has omitted G-d's statement that He has made the Pharaoh's heart and that of his servants stubborn, since this presents a serious problem in theodicy, inasmuch as one may immediately ask why G-d can blame the Pharaoh when He Himself admits that He has made him stubborn and why G-d should punish the Egyptians when He Himself has made them recalcitrant. Moreover, Philo omits the warning to the Pharaoh, presumably because the fact that he has not allowed the Israelites to leave is sufficient justification for the infliction of the next plague. Philo does include the complaint of the Pharaoh's magistrates (οἱ ἐν τέλει) to the Pharaoh, who, to be sure, only with difficulty (μόλις) come to the most precise realization of their troubles. Philo adds that the Pharaoh only appeared to agree. Philo, eager to stress the Pharaoh's responsibility for what has happened, adds that after Moses caused the plague to cease, the Pharaoh was sick to death (δυσθανατοῦντος) at the thought of releasing the Israelite people. The Bible (Exod. 10:14) states that after this plague there will never be any such again, but neither Philo nor Josephus (*A.J.* 2.306) is willing to venture such a prediction, since they apparently realize that even such rarities may recur.

The next plague, the sixth mentioned by Philo, that of darkness, is the ninth in the biblical order (Exod. 10:21–29, *Mos.* 1.123–25). In the Bible, Moses, upon instruction from G-d, stretches forth his hand and brings a thick darkness upon Egypt for a three-day period, but light remains in the dwellings of the Israelites. The Pharaoh then summons Moses and agrees to allow the Israelites, including even their children, to depart but insists that they leave their animals behind. Moses, however, asserts that the animals are needed for sacrifices to G-d. The Bible (Exod. 10:27) then states that G-d hardened the Pharaoh's heart and that he refused to allow the Israelites to leave. Thereupon the Pharaoh remarks that the day that Moses will see his face again Moses will die, whereupon Moses replies that, indeed, he will not see the Pharaoh's face again.

In the Bible there is no indication as to why the darkness ceased. Philo, clearly aware that readers will not readily believe that such an unprecedented event as a three-day darkness actually occurred, suggests two possible quasi-scientific explanations, namely, that there was an eclipse of the sun that was more complete than usual or that the stream of rays from the sun was cut off by continuous clouds compressed with great force into masses of unbroken density, and that once there was darkness it seemed like a single night of great length, equivalent to three days and nights (*Mos.* 1.123).[135] He then describes the effects of the darkness upon the people, some of whom did not dare to rise from their beds, while others proceeded with difficulty as though they were blind and could not even bring themselves to speak or to eat. Philo, always concerned with the possible objection of an audience skeptical about such miracles, also explains that the light was obscured by the prevailing storm wind. Aware that a skeptical reader would wonder that in the same country in closely adjoining areas there was light in some areas but not in others, Philo once again omits the biblical statement that in the homes of the Israelites there was light. He also omits the Pharaoh's offer to allow the Israelites to leave but with the proviso, unacceptable to Moses, that they leave their livestock behind. He likewise omits once again the statement that G-d hardened the Pharaoh's heart, as well as the Pharoah's closing remark to Moses warning him that, on the day that he will see Moses again, Moses will die. Nor do we have Moses' reply that the Pharaoh has indeed spoken correctly. On the contrary, Philo adds the extra-biblical statement that Moses felt pity for the Egyptians and besought G-d to restore light. Such a remark greatly enhances the reader's regard for Moses, since it shows that despite all the sufferings that the Israelites had experienced at the hands of the Egyptians, he nevertheless still had feelings of pity for the Egyptians when they were suffering. Consequently, on his own initiative, even before getting the Pharaoh's agreement to release the Israelites, he beseeches G-d on their behalf.[136]

The next plague described by Philo, boils, the seventh in his enumeration, is the sixth in the biblical account (Exod. 9:8–12). It is enumerated in this order since it is the one plague that was entrusted to Moses and Aaron together. According to the biblical account, G-d told Moses and Aaron to take handfuls of furnace soot and to have Moses hurl it heavenward before the Pharaoh's eyes, whereupon it would become dust and would cause boils and blisters to erupt on people and animals throughout Egypt. We read, furthermore, that the Egyptian magicians could not stand before Moses because of the boils. Nevertheless, G-d hardened the heart of the Pharaoh, and he refused to free the Israelites. In Philo (*Mos.* 1.127), as in the Bible, G-d tells Moses and Aaron to take ashes from a furnace, which Moses scatters in the air and which produce boils.[137] However, as with the other plagues, Philo adds a graphic description of the boils themselves, stretching from head to foot, the effect of the boils, and the pain that people felt. Again, as in the case of the plague of darkness, Philo adds that it was through Moses' intercession on behalf of the suffering Egyptians that the boils were alleviated. Philo omits the statement that the Egyptian magicians were unable to stand before Moses because of the boils, presumably because he does not wish to see Moses viewed as a magician in competition with the Egyptian magicians. Philo here, as elsewhere, presumably because of the problem with theodicy, omits the statement that G-d hardened the Pharaoh's heart. Finally, Philo explains that the reason why this plague was entrusted to Moses and Aaron jointly was that the dust came from the earth, the element identified with Aaron, whereas the dust was hurled into the heaven, which was the element identified with Moses.

Philo (*Mos.* 1.130) identifies the eighth plague as dog-flies (κυνόμυια),[138] in accordance with the LXX (Exod. 8:21; Heb. 8:17), whereas the Hebrew text identifies it with a mixture of wild beasts (ערב).[139] According to the Bible (Exod. 8:16), G-d told Moses to get up early in the morning and meet the Pharaoh as he goes out to the water and warn him that if he does not send out the Israelites, G-d will incite against the Egyptians a swarm of wild beasts, but that there will be no such swarm in Goshen. The following day G-d, indeed, does send such a swarm. Thereupon, the Pharaoh summons Moses and Aaron and tells them to bring sacrificial offerings in the land. Moses explains that it is not proper to do so, inasmuch as the Israelites plan to offer an animal that is an Egyptian deity, and the Egyptians will stone the Israelites if they behold this. Hence, says Moses, the Israelites wish to go on a three-day journey into the wilderness in order to sacrifice to G-d. The Pharaoh agrees, but tells him not to go far off. Moses promises to entreat G-d to get the swarm to depart on the following day, but warns the Pharaoh not to mock them by not sending out the Israelites. Moses, indeed, does entreat G-d, Who causes the swarm to depart. However, the Pharaoh hardens his heart and does not send forth the Israelites.

After a comment about the appropriateness of the word "dog-fly" (*Mos.* 1.130), a combination, as he says, of two of the most shameless animals of the land and the air, and of their persistence until they have gotten their fill of flesh and blood, as well as of the audacity of both, Philo remarks about the viciousness of the dog-fly.[140] Philo (*Mos.* 1.131) adds an almost clinical description of how this creature operated, namely that it came with a whirr from a distance, hurled itself like a javelin, and, with a violent onrush, fastened itself on its victim. Always emphasizing that the plagues were sent by G-d, he then proceeds (*Mos.* 1.132) to add another dimension to the plague, namely that it was divinely impelled, "so that its viciousness was doubled, prompted by avidity due not only to nature but to divine providence, which armed the creature and roused it to use its force against the population."

Philo, however, says nothing about Moses' meeting with the Pharaoh or about the Pharaoh's hardening his heart. These omissions may be explained on the ground that they appear to put Moses in a bad light for refusing to accept what would seem to be the compromise offers of the Pharaoh. In other words, Philo (*Mos.* 1.130–32) has none of the details of the biblical account except for the fact that G-d sent a plague of dog-flies. In particular, we may explain the omission by both Philo and Josephus (*A.J.* 2.303) of the offer of the Pharaoh (Exod. 8:21–23) to have the Israelites present sacrifices and of Moses' refusal on the ground that they plan to sacrifice an animal identified with a deity of the Egyptians, since they do not wish to show intolerance and insensitivity to what is sacred to the Egyptians.

The account in the Bible of the fifth plague (Exod. 9:1–7; *Mos.* 1.133), the murrain, states that G-d told Moses to warn the Pharaoh that if he persisted in refusing to allow the Israelites to leave, G-d would on the following day send a murrain, a very severe epidemic, upon the animals of the Egyptians, whereas the Israelite animals would not be affected. G-d does so, yet the Pharaoh's heart becomes stubborn, and he does not send out the Israelites. Josephus totally omits mention of this plague, perhaps because it would seem hard to believe that the Israelites' animals were not affected by it. As Philo, for whom this is the ninth plague, describes it, there is no warning mentioned as having been given to the Pharaoh. He does say, offering a scientific explanation, that the livestock perished as if by an agreed signal on a single day, presaging the destruction that was to follow among humans in the next plague, such as we find in epidemics.

The final plague (Exod. 11:1–10, 12:12–13, 12:29–33, *Mos.* 1.134–39) is the slaying of the first-born by G-d Himself.[141] G-d tells Moses that after this plague the Pharaoh will actually drive the Israelites out of Egypt. Moses then informs the Pharaoh that every first-born,[142] both human and animal, is to die at about midnight, but that the Israelites will not be affected. Then, he declares, all of the Pharaoh's servants will tell him to leave, together with all the Israelites (Exod. 11:8). Moses then, in burning anger, leaves the Pharaoh's presence. G-d tells Moses that the Pharaoh will not listen to him. Indeed, G-d hardens the Pharaoh's heart, and he does not send the Israelites from the land (Exod. 11:10). We are told (Exod. 12:30) that there is not a house where there is no corpse. Thereupon the Pharaoh calls Moses and Aaron and tells them to leave with all the Israelites and their animals and that they should bless him as well (Exod. 12:32). We read, furthermore, that the Egyptians urged that the Israelites should leave with all speed.

The question arises as to the fairness of G-d in killing apparently innocent people and certainly innocent animals. As the biblical text (Exod. 11:4–5: "Thus says the L-rd: About midnight I will go forth in the midst of Egypt, and all the first-born in the land of Egypt shall die") and the Passover Haggadah emphasize, this slaying was done by G-d Himself (Exod. 12:12–13) and not by an angel.[143]

The rabbis were apparently troubled by this seemingly wholesale slaughter, and they have a tradition[144] that when Moses warned the Pharaoh (Exod. 11:4–8) of the forthcoming slaughter of the first-born Egyptians, the latter went to their fathers and said that since everything that Moses had foretold had been fulfilled, the Israelites should be allowed to leave, lest they all die. The fathers, however, replied that it was better that one of every ten should die than that the Israelites should leave. Thereupon, the first-born went to the Pharaoh, seeking to persuade him to let the Israelites leave. However, the Pharaoh not only did not grant their request, but ordered his servants to beat the first-born Egyptians in order to punish them for their presumptuousness. Thereupon, the first-born rose up in battle against their own fathers, and no fewer than six hundred thousand, corresponding to the number of adult Israelite men who later left Egypt, were slain. Moreover, whereas the Pharaoh and his advisers thought that the loss of the first-born would be insignificant, the fact is, according to rabbinic tradition, that G-d's decision was to slay not only the first-born sons, but also the first-born daughters, and not only the first-born of existing marriages, but also of previous illegitimate relationships; and, in view of the immoral lives led by so many of the Egyptians, this was a very considerable number. Finally, again according to rabbinic tradition, G-d decided that the decree should affect not only the first-born, but also the oldest member of every family, whether or not he was the first-born of his parents.[145] Indeed, according to rabbinic tradition (*Midr. Exod. Rab.* 18.2, *Midr. Song of Songs* 1.14), when some of the Egyptians, convinced that Moses' warning would come true, sent their first-born sons to their Israelite neighbors, hoping thus to protect them, the Egyptian first-born were found dead on the following morning. Furthermore, according to the rabbis (*Mek. Bo* 7.7b and 13.13b), in what seems a real assault on justice, not only the first-born of the Egyptians, but also the first-born of other peoples who were then living in Egypt, were slain. Additionally, even the first-born who had died previously were dragged by dogs out of their graves, which were in the houses of the Egyptians. Even the monuments in memory of these first-born were changed to dust and scattered.

In connection with the plague of the first-born, the rabbis were troubled by the infliction of such a punishment on innocent people, some of whom were themselves suffering in prison and should have been viewed sympathetically by those who were similarly suffering. The rabbis have a tradition that explains that the first-born of the slaves deserved to die because they so hated the Israelites that they rejoiced when the Pharaoh decreed their persecution.[146] Moreover, the rabbis also have a tradition that explains why the female slaves who ground corn between mill-stones were slain, namely, because they were said to have declared that they did not regret their own servitude, provided only the Israelites were subjected to similar suffering and because they had actually enslaved the Israelites.[147] The rabbis (*Mek. Bo* 13, 13b) (*ad* Exod. 11:5), clearly troubled by the infliction of punishment on apparently innocent people, remark that the captives were smitten, since if they had not been smitten they would have said that it was their gods who had protected them; but this simply raises the question as to why innocent people should suffer to save the reputation of G-d.

Likewise, the rabbis were troubled that innocent animals, as in the case of the command to exterminate Amalek (1 Sam. 15:3), were punished; and they explain that this was decreed by G-d because the Egyptians worshipped cattle, and they would have attributed their misfortunes to them. Moreover, when He punishes a nation, He punishes its gods (*b. Suk.* 29a), and they cite the verse (Exod. 12:12), "On all the gods of Egypt I will execute judgments." But this again raises the question as to why innocent animals suffer in order to save the reputation of G-d.

Later we are told (Exod. 12:12–13) that G-d Himself will go through the land of Egypt on that night and that He will strike all the first-born as well as the gods of the Egyptians. This is omitted by Philo, as it is by Josephus, presumably because this would contradict the view that both have (Philo, *Mos.* 2.205, *Spec.* 1.53, and *QE* 2.5; and Josephus, *Ap.* 2.237), in accordance with their reading of the LXX's translation of Exod. 22:27, "Thou shalt not revile (κακολογήσεις) gods." As Philo (*Mos.* 2.205) puts it there, "We must refrain from speaking insultingly of these [gods of others], lest any of Moses' disciples get into the habit of treating lightly the name 'god' in general, for it is a title worthy of the highest respect and love." As Josephus puts it there similarly, "Our legislator has expressly forbidden us to deride or blaspheme the gods recognized by others, out of respect for the very word 'G-d.'"

Philo explains the justice of the punishment inflicted on all the first-born by emphasizing that it was not directed to the whole population (*Mos.* 1.134), "since G-d's purpose was not to make a complete desert of the country, but only to teach them a lesson, nor yet of the great majority of the men and women of every age." Likewise, he justifies G-d's action by asserting (*Somn.* 2.266) that the first-born of Egypt were true children of their parents and that they embodied lust, pleasure, grief, fear, injustice, and folly. We may conjecture that since Philo himself was born in Egypt and was a leader of the Alexandrian Jewish community, he was sensitive to the problem of the relations of the Jewish community to the non-Jewish community in Egypt. Consequently, we would expect him to be careful to condemn only those who deserved censure.

As to the death of the first-born, Philo notes that the first-born, all in full health and robust of body, were suddenly slain without apparent cause, and that no household was without calamity (*Mos.* 1.135). When dawn came and the rest of the members of the Egyptian families perceived what had happened, there was a united outcry, the wailing being increased once they realized what had happened to their neighbors, since they realized that in addition to their personal sorrow was added the public sorrow, inasmuch as they had now lost even the hope of consolation, for one could hardly expect to comfort another if he himself needed consolation. Philo adds that they feared that this was the beginning of still greater sorrows, namely the destruction of those who were still alive. In an extra-biblical addition, Philo describes in vivid terms how the mass of the Egyptians, bathed in tears and with rent garments, rushed to the palace and cried out against the Pharaoh. They accused him of being responsible because he had indulged his usual self-will, asserting that none of this would have happened if he had listened to Moses at the beginning, and complaining that it was they who had reaped the rewards of his contentiousness. They furthermore urged one another to drive the Israelites out of the country as soon as possible. Even more, in an extra-biblical addition, they declared, that to detain them for even an hour would bring a dreadful calamity upon them. In Philo's version there is no statement that none of the first-born Israelites died, presumably because it was obvious, inasmuch as G-d Himself carried out the plague. Moses does not warn the Pharaoh, and there is no statement that Moses left in burning anger, presumably because a leader, even under great provocation, must exercise greater self-control. Nor is there any statement that G-d hardened the Pharaoh's heart, presumably because, as we have noted, this would involve a serious problem of theodicy, namely, how to blame the Pharaoh when it was G-d who had actually made him stubborn.

The reader may wonder that the Israelites, witnessing the tremendous suffering of the Egyptians afflicted by the plagues, merely looked on as spectators without offering to help them. Philo (*Mos.* 1.146), indeed, remarks that everyone who witnessed those events could not but have thought that the Israelites were mere spectators; but, he explains, all this was a matter of divine judgment.

Whereas Exod. 12:29–33 presents a detailed and vivid picture of the effect of this plague upon the first-born of the Egyptians, Josephus has a single sentence (*A.J.* 2.313) relating this event: "For on that night the annihilation of the first-born came upon the Egyptians, so that many of those who resided around the palace came together to the Pharaoh to advise him to let the Hebrews go." He says nothing of the annihilation of the first-born of the captives and of the maidservants, let alone of the animals. In particular, he omits the statement (Exod. 12:30) that there was not a house among the Egyptians where there was not someone dead. He has clearly bypassed the problem of the infliction of punishment on apparently innocent people and animals. The statement that many of the Egyptians who resided around the palace went to the Pharaoh to urge him to allow the Israelites to leave is Philo's (*Mos.* 1.139) and Josephus' addition (*A.J.* 2.313), which accords with the rabbinic tradition noted above, intended to cast a good light upon the Egyptians as a people. He seeks to emphasize the good neighborly relations of the Egyptians and the Israelites.

Artapanus (*ap.* Eus., *PE* 9.27.34) remarks that after all these calamities the Pharaoh allowed the Israelites to leave; but, as Holladay (1983, 242 n. 112)[148] points out, Artapanus significantly omits all mention of the plague of the death of the first-born Egyptians.

In order to understand Philo's problems in connection with the plague of the death of the first-born, it may be useful to examine his treatment of similar episodes involving G-d's decision to exterminate whole populations that would appear to be innocent. Thus, a similar problem arises in connection with G-d's decision to exterminate animals in the Flood. Indeed, Philo (*QG* 1.94, 2.9), in commenting on the Flood at the time of Noah, twice raises the question as to what sin the animals had committed that G-d should have deemed it just to obliterate them, except for the pairs taken into the ark. His answer is twofold: Just as when a king is killed in battle his soldiers are also struck down together with him, so also G-d decided that when the human race was destroyed, beasts should be destroyed together with it, as happens also in a plague, during which beasts die with the men with whom they live. Similarly, when the head is cut off, no one blames nature if other parts of the body die with it. Moreover, since animals were created solely for the sake of men and for their service, once G-d had decided that humans should be obliterated, the animals were destroyed together with them. Furthermore, in his usual fashion, Philo gives an allegorical interpretation, namely that man is mind within us, and beast is sense-perception (*QG* 1.94). Once the mind is perverted, that is, when the soul is, so to speak, deluged by streams of passion, the earthly part of the body, that is, sense-perception, perishes together with it, inasmuch as it has no remains of virtue, and the life of evil is death. Indeed, the organs of sight and hearing die when they perceive unjustly.

Similarly, Philo (*Leg.* 3.9), in connection with the wholesale punishment of the Sodomites, cites Abraham's statement to G-d (Gen. 18:23); but it is put not in the form of a question or objection to G-d—"Wilt Thou indeed destroy the righteous with the wicked?"—but rather in the form of an imperative—"Do not destroy the just man together with the impious one, the one that is manifest and known to Thee together with him who shuns and avoids Thee." Abraham here is pleading with G-d, but there is no dialogue, let alone bargaining. The only justice, he insists, is that G-d should be honored. Hence, there is no dispute between Abraham and G-d. He has redefined justice: honoring G-d as He deserves (*Leg.* 3.10). Just as it is impossible to honor parents as they deserve, so it is impossible to honor G-d as He deserves.

Moreover, Philo (*Sacr.* 122) does not mention the actual dialogue between Abraham and G-d in which Abraham endeavors to get G-d to give up His plan to destroy Sodom if even fifty or forty-five or thirty or twenty or ten righteous people are found there. However, Philo does say that if fifty, the number that brings the message of redemption from slavery or any of the numbers down to ten (the number sacred to education), i.e., the perfect number, 1+2+3+4, had been found, the city would have been saved (see Colson and Whitaker 1929, 2:491–92). But, he remarks, no good could balance the vast sum of evil in Sodom that weighed down the scale. And yet, Philo (*Sacr.* 123) adds that one should try to save even those who are most evil, just as a physician will gladly render his service though there is no hope for the patient, lest anyone should think in the event of some unexpected disaster that it is due to the physician's neglect. However, Philo (*Migr.* 122–23) does speak of Abraham the wise as making trial (πεπειραμένος) of G-d's loving-kindness (χρηστότης) among all, in the belief that if some small relic of virtue be preserved, G-d would look with pity on the rest, just as a small spark may be made to blaze. Philo (*Congr.* 109) speaks of the suppliant prayer of wise Abraham when fire was about to consume Sodom; but, as we have noted, he does not speak of an actual dialogue with G-d on the subject. There he equates Sodom with a soul barren of good and blind of reason, again implying that the punishment inflicted by G-d, namely to make the land barren, was appropriate for the crime.[149]

A similar problem of theodicy in connection with the divine destruction of the first-born, including apparently innocent people, arises in connection with the divine commandment to eradicate the seven nations of Canaan. It is striking that Philo, despite the fact that there is hardly a commandment that he does not refer to in one way or another in his numerous essays on passages of the Bible, nowhere at all paraphrases or refers to any of the several biblical passages that mention the commandment to eradicate the seven nations of Canaan, presumably because he felt so strongly that it was wrong to condemn the innocent with the guilty and because he found it inconsistent with his tolerance toward non-Jewish religions (*Spec.* 1.53). Thus, it is significant that when he mentions the occupation of Canaan by the Israelites (*Hypoth.* 6.5), he says that the Bible shows clearly how they established themselves there, but he says nothing at all about how they treated the people whom they conquered. Rather, for him, the supreme penalty of extermination is to be inflicted on Israelites who have abandoned religious observance (*Spec.* 1.54–55). In such cases, according to Philo, the offender is to receive no trial, but to be put to death immediately, in effect by lynching. Apparently, Philo saw a difference between the two cases: the annihilation of the first-born is decreed and carried out by G-d Himself, and G-d's actions are not subject to human scrutiny, whereas the annihilation of the seven nations is to be carried out by the Israelites themselves; and Philo is sensitive to the importance of having good relations with Israel's neighbors. However, Philo (*Hypoth.* 6.5) very frankly tells the reader that in discussing the probable facts of the occupation of the land by the Israelites he thinks that "it is better to go not so much by the historical narrative as by what reason tells us about them [i.e., the Israelites]." He then presents (6.6) two hypotheses and leaves it to the reader to choose between them: "Which alternative do you prefer? Were they still superior in the number of their fighting men, though they had fared so ill to the end, still strong and with weapons in their hand, and did they then take the land by force, defeating the combined Syrians and Phoenicians when fighting in their own [i.e., the Syrians' and Phoenicians'] country? Or shall we suppose that they were unwarlike and feeble, quite few in numbers and destitute of warlike equipment, but won the respect of their opponents who voluntarily surrendered their land to them?" Clearly, Philo preferred the latter explanation, and said, in effect, that their opponents voluntarily surrendered the land.

In sum, in connection with the plagues, the fact that Philo asserts that the infliction of the plagues belonging to the denser elements, earth and water, was entrusted by G-d to Aaron, while He entrusted the plagues belonging to air and fire, the forces most productive of life, to Moses, elevates the status of Moses. Philo makes every effort to explain the plagues scientifically. He omits the biblical statement that G-d hardened the Pharaoh's heart since this raises the question of the justification of G-d's punishment of the Pharaoh and the Egyptians. The fact that Moses felt pity for the Egyptians and besought G-d to restore light to them even before getting the Pharaoh's agreement to release the Israelites creates much sympathy for Moses. There is no statement in Philo that Moses during the final plague left in burning anger, presumably because a leader must exercise greater self-control.

f. The Israelites' Departure from Egypt

There are several questions that scholars have raised in connection with the biblical account of the departure of the Israelites from Egypt: 1) Were the Israelites expelled or did they depart willingly? 2) What was the reason for the departure or expulsion? 3) Did only the Israelites depart or did others join them? 4) Who was the leader or who were the leaders of those who left and by whom was he or they chosen? 5) What goods did the exiles take with them and from whom and how did they get those goods? The Bible's answers to these questions are: 1) The Israelites were not expelled; rather, they sought permission to leave; 2) The reason they sought to leave was that they had been enslaved and had been treated cruelly; 3) A "mixed multitude" joined the Israelites in their departure, but there is no indication as to who these people were; 4) The sole leader was Moses, and he had been chosen by G-d; 5) Before leaving the Israelites borrowed things from the Egyptians.

The earliest extra-biblical account of the departure of the Israelites from Egypt is found in Hecataeus. It is clearly sympathetic to them and their leader Moses, since Hecataeus says (*ap.* Diodorus 40.3.3.1–2) that it is not merely the Jews who were expelled, to whom the Egyptians ascribed their troubles when they were afflicted with a pestilence, but also "many strangers of all sorts dwelling in their midst and practicing different rites of religion and sacrifice."

According to Josephus (*Ap.* 1.279), Manetho asserted that Moses was one of the priests expelled from Heliopolis for leprosy, but he does not indicate that the exiles consisted solely of Israelites. Such a statement could hardly have been reported by Josephus in a polemical work unless the Egyptians had indeed made such a remark.

Pompeius Trogus (*ap.* Just. 36, *Epitoma* 2.12) says that the Egyptians expelled Moses, together with others who were afflicted with leprosy and scabies, but he does not indicate that only Israelites were expelled. He states that Moses was made the leader of the exiles, but he does not indicate by whom. Chaeremon (*ap.* Josephus, *Ap.* 1.289) says that the Egyptians expelled those who were contaminated, but he does not indicate that these were limited to Israelites. Lysimachus (*ap.* Josephus, *Ap.* 1.305),[150] like Manetho and Apion, speaks of the expulsion of the Israelites, who were allegedly afflicted with leprosy and other maladies, although, as Josephus (*Ap.* 1.313) indicates, it is not clear whether it is only the Jews who were so afflicted. Apion (*ap.* Josephus, *Ap.* 2.15) speaks of the expulsion of the lepers under Moses' leadership; but while in the next sentence he speaks of the departure of the Jews, he does not indicate that the exiles consisted solely of Jews. Tacitus (*Histories* 5.3.1) speaks of the expulsion of those who had been afflicted with bodily disfigurement and seems to limit the exiles to Jews; but all the rest in their accounts appear to indicate that others besides Jews were expelled because of leprosy and such ailments, and all agree that their leader was Moses. All this would seem to accord with the biblical statement that among those who joined the Israelites when they left were a mixed multitude (ערב רב) of non-Israelites. Having such a mixed group would certainly add to the difficulties of Moses as a leader.

We may call further attention to the implied compliment in this otherwise anti-Jewish work of Chaeremon, as cited by Josephus (*ap. Ap.* 1.290), that the Jewish leaders at the time of the Exodus were two scribes (γραμματεῖς)—Moses (whose Egyptian name he gives as Tisithen) and another sacred scribe (ἱερογραμματεύς), Joseph (whose Egyptian name he gives as Peteseph). Indeed, the very mention of Moses is a concession, because, as we have noted from Philo (*Mos.* 1.2), in general the envious Greeks did not even deign to speak of him.

The only account outside of the Bible before Philo that mentions the departure of the Israelites and does not refer to it as an expulsion is that by Artapanus (*ap.* Eus. *PE* 9.27.34), who says nothing about the Israelites being afflicted with leprosy, but rather that after the Egyptians had experienced various calamities, the Pharaoh released (ἀπολῦσαι) the Israelites.

Philo (*Mos.* 1.139), apparently aware of the almost unanimous view that the Israelites were expelled, adopts an intermediate position between expulsion by the Egyptians and departure on their own initiative. In an extra-biblical addition, he says that during the plague of the slaughter of the first-born, the Egyptians themselves cried out against the Pharaoh and exhorted each other to expel the Israelites as speedily as possible. The Israelites, he says, were thus driven (ἐλαυνόμενοι) and banished (διωκόμενοι) from the land. However, it was not because of leprosy that they were banished but rather because of pressure from the Egyptians themselves, who had suffered so much on account of the stubbornness of the Pharaoh in refusing to allow them to leave.

Josephus was likewise troubled by the almost unanimous extra-biblical tradition of the expulsion of the Israelites because of their leprosy. Like Philo, he speaks (*A.J.* 2.313) of pressure from the Egyptians themselves upon the Pharaoh, during the plague of the slaughter of the first-born, to allow the Israelites to depart. Far from an expulsion because of alleged leprosy, he states that the Pharaoh then ordered Moses to depart, supposing that once the Israelites were out of the country the suffering of the Egyptians would cease.

One aspect of the Israelites' departure that was particularly troublesome to Jewish commentators was the fact that in one biblical passage G-d tells Moses that before leaving Egypt the Israelites are to ask for jewels and clothing from the Egyptians, "and when you go, you shall not go empty . . . ; thus you shall despoil the Egyptians" (Exod. 3:21–22). Before they actually depart from Egypt, G-d repeats similar instructions to Moses (Exod. 11:2–3). We are informed (Exod. 12:36) that G-d granted the people favor in the eyes of the Egyptians, who granted their request, and so the Israelites "emptied" (וינצלו) Egypt.[151]

This would appear to contradict the Israelites' reputation for honesty and presumably Moses' reputation for integrity, since Moses permitted the Israelites to "borrow" jewelry and clothing from the Egyptians. One might well assume that the Israelites must have practiced deceit in order to obtain these objects, though such theft might perhaps be justified, as we see in the remarks of Jub. (48:18), that the Israelites despoiled the Egyptians in return for the bondage in which they had been forced to serve. Likewise, Ezekiel (*ap.* Eus. *PE* 9.28.12) declares that what the Israelites took was a repayment for what the Egyptians had done to them. Whereas the Bible (Exod. 12:35–36) states that the Israelites requested from the Egyptians silver and gold vessels and garments, that they found favor in the eyes of the Egyptians, and that they thus despoiled the Egyptians, Artapanus has toned down somewhat what the Israelites acquired, limiting it to many drinking vessels, a little clothing, and numerous other treasures.[152] Even Pompeius Trogus (*ap.* Justin 36, *Epitoma* 2.12–13), who is generally friendly to the Jews, states, without comment, that Moses—clearly attaching the full responsibility to Moses—carried off by stealth the sacred vessels of the Egyptians. This remark about the theft of sacred objects might have been made the subject of an attack upon the Israelites because of their having committed such a sacrilegious act, but Pompeius simply reports it and offers not a word of condemnation, such as we find, for example, in Lysimachus (*ap.* Josephus, *Ap.* 1.311), who reports that Jerusalem was called Hierosyla [(town of) temple-robbers] because of the sacrilegious propensities of the Israelites. According to the Bible (Exod. 3:22), G-d tells Moses that He will grant the Israelites favor in the eyes of the Egyptians so that every woman will request silver and gold vessels and garments from her neighbor, and so the Israelites will empty out Egypt. We read (Exod. 12:35–36) that the Israelites succeeded in doing so.

Philo (*Mos.* 1.141) implies that the Israelites, in taking these things from the Egyptians, were accused of being greedy and covetous of what the Egyptians possessed. Philo (*Mos.* 1.140–42) must have been aware of this charge, since he devotes three paragraphs to defending the action of the Israelites, who, he says, were not unmindful of the injustices that had been contrived against them. He then defends their action further by stating that they were, in effect, receiving a bare wage for all the time that they had served (so also in *b. Sanh.* 91a), and that they were retaliating, on a lesser scale, for the very enslavement of their persons.[153] Moreover, he suggests that their action may be viewed as an act of war, a rule of which is that to the victors belong the spoils. Finally, he insists, it was the Egyptians who began the wrongdoing by reducing guests and suppliants to slavery. Consequently, when the Israelites had the opportunity, they avenged themselves without actually taking up arms, shielded by the hand of justice.[154]

Josephus resolves the problem by omitting all reference to this passage; and in his paraphrase (*A.J.* 2.314) of Exod. 12:36, it is not the Israelites who approach the Egyptians, but rather the Egyptians themselves who here take the initiative in honoring the Israelites with gifts. He tries to justify the Israelites' action by saying that the Egyptians honored them with gifts so that they might depart more swiftly[155] or because of the neighborly relations that they had with them. Josephus, the apologist ever concerned to refute the view that the Jews are aggressive troublemakers against those among whom they live, stresses the good relations between Egyptians and Israelites, the clear implication being that it was the Pharaoh whose stubbornness was at fault.

The Talmudic rabbis (*b. Sanh.* 91a), likewise troubled by what would appear to be theft on the part of the departing Israelites, have a similar explanation in the form of a scenario in which the Egyptians bring a lawsuit against the Jews before Alexander the Great, pleading that they should return the gold and silver that they had taken when they left Egypt. An otherwise unknown Gebiha ben Pesisa wins the case for the Jews by demanding that the Egyptians pay them for the toil of 600,000 men whom they had enslaved for 430 years. Moreover, in *b. Ber.* 9b the rabbis emphasize that the Israelites did not want to "borrow" from the Egyptians and were satisfied merely with regaining their freedom; but G-d insisted that they do so in order to fulfill the promise that He had made to Abraham that they would leave Egypt with great substance (Gen. 15:13–14). Obviously, the Israelites had no intention of returning these "gifts."

In sum, the various accounts by non-Jewish writers agree that the Israelites were expelled because they were afflicted with disease, whether leprosy or some other ailment. Philo's view is that they were baished because of pressure from the Egyptians themsleves, who had suffered so much because of Pharoah's stubbornness in refusing to allow them to leave. All agree that they were led by Moses, though one account lists Joseph as a leader also. Most accounts, including the Bible, note that they were joined by many non-Israelite strangers. Having such a motley crew would surely add to the challenge that confronted Moses as a leader. There is no indication in the non-Jewish accounts that Moses had been chosen by G-d or by the Israelites. Since it was Moses who had told the Israelites to borrow items from the Egyptians, he would have to bear responsibility for what appeared to be what Pompeius Trogus referred to as theft. Philo defends the Israelites, remarking that they were merely taking the wages that the Egyptians had withheld from them during the years of enslavement.

g. Moses' Leadership during the Exodus: The Miraculous Crossing of the Sea of Reeds

The Bible (Exod. 12:37–38) simply indicates that the number of those Israelite men who left Egypt was six hundred thousand and that a mixed multitude (ערב רב) went up with them. Philo (*Mos.* 1.147–162), perhaps reflecting the problem of assimilation and intermarriage in the Egyptian Jewry of which he was a leader, uses the occasion to present a long discussion of the qualifications of the leader, Moses. In the first place (*Mos.* 1.147), he expands greatly on the mixed nature of the multitude whom Moses led, the clear implication being that it was extremely difficult to unify such a diverse group. Philo expands on the sheer number of those Israelites who left Egypt under Moses' leadership. The Bible states merely that there were "about six hundred thousand men on foot, besides children." In Philo's version this has become "over six hundred thousand men of military age, while the rest of the multitude, consisting of old men, womenfolk and children, could not easily be counted." The Bible says simply that a mixed multitude went up with them, without specifying what kind of people were included. Philo indicates the greatness of Moses' leadership by specifying that this multitude consisted of mixed (μιγάδες, "mixed pell-mell") people and a crowd of promiscuous people (σύγκλυς, "mob," "rabble," "washed together by the waves") and servants (θεραπεία, "attendant"), a bastard host (νόθος), as it were (ὡσανεί), associated with the true-born (γνήσιοι, "legitimate," "lawfully begotten"). He further explains that the mixed multitude were the children of Egyptian women by Hebrew fathers into whose families they had been added (προσνεμηθέντες), together with those who, reverencing the divine favor shown to the people, had come over (ἐπηλύτης, "incomer," "stranger," "foreigner") to them, and such as were converted (μετεβάλλοντο, "thrown into a different position," "turned around," "changed sides") and brought into a wiser mind by the magnitude and the number of the successive punishments they had undergone because of the stubbornness of the Pharoah.

Philo is saying, in effect, that to be the leader of such a motley crew must have been a challenge of immense proportions, and that only a person such as Moses could have met that challenge. Moreover, Philo takes advantage of this opportunity here to stress his point that Judaism welcomes converts, since he uses the same verb, μεταβάλλω, to refer to those of the mixed multitude who had genuinely converted to Judaism ("brought to a wiser mind") that he employs in his account (*Mos.* 2.44) of the annual festival commemorating the translation of the Pentateuch into Greek, where he expresses his belief that each nation, inspired by the Pentateuch, would renounce (χαίρειν) their ancestral customs and turn (μεταβαλεῖν) to the laws of the Jews alone. Hence, Moses was the leader not only of Jews but also of proselytes, with all the challenge and opportunity that this brought with it.[156]

Elsewhere (*Hypoth.* 6.2) Philo surprisingly states that one may say, if one wishes, that Moses differed not at all from the masses (οἱ πολλοί); but the fact that he was able to bring the whole people in complete safety, despite drought and hunger and ignorance of the way and lack of everything, and to keep them free from internal factions (apparently he discounts Korah's rebellion) and obedient to himself for so many years that they wandered in the wilderness is convincing proof of his ability (see Petit 1976, 137–42).

Pseudo-Philo says nothing about this mixed multitude, his interest being solely in the Israelites. For Josephus the mixed multitude did not constitute a problem, since assimilation and intermarriage were apparently not a problem in the Land of Israel in his own day; hence, he does not mention them at all.

One of the greatest questions about Moses' leadership is why he led the Israelites to Palestine by the long route through the desert rather than by the much shorter and more direct route along the Mediterranean. In the Bible (Exod. 13:17–18) it is G-d who makes the decision not to lead the Israelites by the nearer route through the land of the Philistines because it was near and because He thought that they would want to return to Egypt once they encountered war. Philo (*Mos.* 1.163), presumably because he wondered why it was not Moses who made the decision, arrives at a compromise with the biblical text and states that Moses, whose role as leader he is eager to elevate, made the decision, after receiving the authority that the Israelites willingly gave him and after receiving G-d's consent.

Philo, moreover, supplies another reason, which adds to the stature of Moses as a leader who is concerned with training his people after many years of their having a slave mentality, namely, to test the extent of their loyalty when supplies are not abundant (*Mos.* 1.164).[157] The site of the desert enabled G-d, moreover, by bringing up plenty from nothing, to recall the work of creation (*Mos.* 2.266–67) (see Nikiprowetzky 1989, 103–4). It also served to emphasize the importance for Philo's contemporaries to separate from the degenerate temptations of urban life, as we can see from Philo's praise of the asceticism of the Essenes and the Therapeutae (*Contempl.* 19–20). This offered the Israelites an opportunity for mystic contemplation and thus prepared them for the reception of the Mosaic constitution and way of life. For Pseudo-Philo (10.2) the fact that the Israelites took the much longer route to reach the Land of Israel apparently presents no problem, inasmuch as the Bible indicates that it was G-d's decision to do so; hence, in his piety he sees no reason to mention it. Josephus (*A.J.* 2.322), the military man, offers an additional reason, namely that Moses did not go through the land of the Philistines, though it was much shorter, because the Philistines had a hostile attitude toward the Israelites, owing to an ancient enmity with them.[158]

Moreover, Philo omits the biblical statement (Exod. 13:18) that the Israelites were armed (חֲמֻשִׁים) when they left Egypt, presumably because he followed the LXX version of this verse, which reads that the children of Israel went up out of the land of Egypt in the fifth generation (πέμπτῃ . . . γενεᾷ, a different vocalization of the word חמשים) or, if he did know the Hebrew tradition, because this would seem to be contradicted by the later statement (Exod. 14:9–12) that the Israelites panicked when the Pharaoh approached.[159] However, in his description of the miracle at the Sea of Reeds, Philo (*Mos.* 1.170, 172) asserts that the Israelites, for lack of the necessary weapons, were not ready to defend themselves, inasmuch as their expedition was not for war, but for colonization.

Philo also omits the statement that Moses took the bones of Joseph with him (Exod. 13:19), presumably to keep the focus on Moses alone, though, in another treatise (*Somn.* 2.109), where his focus is not on Moses, he does mention that Moses piously took the bones of Joseph with him when he left Egypt.[160]

A major test of Moses' ability as a leader came as the Israelites traversed a pathless wilderness not long after their exodus from Egypt. The Bible (Exod. 14:1–2) states that G-d told Moses to have the Israelites encamp near the sea. Once they have done so, He tells Moses, the Pharaoh will say that the Israelites are imprisoned in the land. G-d says that He will harden the heart of the Pharaoh and that he will pursue them, whereupon G-d will be glorified through the defeat of the Pharaoh and his army. In Philo (*Mos.* 1.163) it is not G-d who tells the Israelites where to encamp but Moses, who is their military leader. As always, Philo omits the statement that G-d will harden the heart of the Pharaoh, since that, in effect, removes free will from him. Philo (*Mos.* 1.167) enlivens the scene with suspense by adding that the Pharaoh believed that the Israelites had lost their way and that consequently they were traversing a rough and pathless desert and that he was pleased to see that disaster had come upon them, since he thought that they were shut in without any way out. Philo adds that the Pharaoh actually repented that he had allowed the Israelites to leave; and he pursued them, expecting either that they would return to slavery or that he would massacre them. Whereas the Bible (Exod. 14:7) asserts that the Pharoah took with him six hundred elite chariots, Philo

(*Mos.* 1.168) adds that he took with him not only all his cavalry, javelineers, slingers, mounted archers, and his other light-armed troops, but that he expected that he would instill fear in the masses of the Israelites, so that they would prefer to return to slavery. Moreover, Philo states that the Pharaoh gave six hundred outstanding chariots to men of rank so that they might participate in the forthcoming defeat of the Israelites, and that he rushed to attack so as to come upon the Israelites unexpectedly, confident of winning a victory at the first shout (αὐτοβοεί).

Whereas the Bible (Exod. 14:9) does not give the number of the Egyptian forces at the Sea of Reeds, and Josephus (*A.J.* 2.324) gives their number as 600 chariots, 50,000 cavalry, and 200,000 heavily armed footsoldiers, Ezekiel (*ap.* Eus. *PE* 9.29.14) is in accord with the book of Jub. (48:14) in giving the number as one million. According to Ezekiel, the host of men arrayed in battle order was awesome (φρικτός, "to be shuddered at"), with footmen and phalaxes in the middle and leaving passages for the four-horsed chariots to pass through, thus making the achievement of the Israelites in overwhelming them all the greater. He dramatically highlights the difficulties of the Israelites by adding that the men, being unarmed,[161] in trying to care for their young as well as their wives, became exhausted from exertion. In the play an Egyptian messenger asserts that when the Israelites saw the Egyptians, they raised a tearful sound in unison to heaven, whereas the Egyptians were jubilant, fully confident of their numbers and of their armament. Thereupon, divine wonders and incredible sights began to occur. Ezekiel adds that the Egyptians, seeing the waves closing in around them, shouted that they should "flee homeward before the hand of the Most High." However, Philo, apparently realizing that exaggerations would cast doubt on the credibility of his whole narrative, is content to say (*Mos.* 2.248) merely that Pharaoh was accompanied by a not negligible (οὐκ εὐκαταφρόνητος) body of infantry and cavalry.

Philo does, to be sure, build up the drama of the scene by adding that just as the Israelites were preparing to eat their early meal, they heard the loud noise of the Egyptians' approach at full speed. Since they lacked weapons[162] because, as Philo, apologetically, adds (*Mos.* 1.170), their expedition was for colonization rather than for war, they were panic-stricken. By adding this statement Philo attempts to answer those who looked upon the Jews in his own day as aggressive and eager for military expansion of their territory. Furthermore, on the one hand, he adds (*Mos.* 2.247), they could not cross the sea, inasmuch as they lacked boats; and, on the other hand, they did not think it safe to retrace their steps. It is at this point that the Pharaoh, with his huge army of infantry and cavalry, came in hot pursuit, eager to teach them a lesson because they had left Egypt. Philo (*Mos.* 2.249), expanding greatly on the biblical account, paints a vivid picture of the Israelites' despair. Some thought that the most miserable death would be a welcome blessing, while others proposed to throw themselves into the sea rather than to become a laughingstock to their enemies and even went so far as to load themselves with heavy substances so that they might sink more easily.

According to the biblical text (Exod. 14:11–12), the Israelites complained bitterly to Moses that they would have preferred to remain as slaves in Egypt rather than to die in the wilderness. Indeed, Josephus (*A.J.* 2.327) adds that the Israelites actually wished to stone Moses. In Pseudo-Philo (10.2), whose focus is always on G-d and on the faithlessness of the Israelites toward Him, the Israelites challenge not Moses but G-d. "Is it for this," they ask, "that G-d has brought us forth, or are these the covenants that He established with our fathers?" The Israelites (10.3) present three different plans—suicide, return to Egypt, and fighting. Moses, the ideal leader, ignores all these plans (10.4). In the Bible (Exod. 14:15) G-d says to Moses, "Why do you cry to Me? Tell the people of Israel to go forward." In Pseudo-Philo, Moses prays to G-d and has the audacity to tell G-d to think of His reputation.

Philo (*Mos.* 1.170–72) presents their complaint at considerably greater length and with their increased bitterness. Perhaps drawing upon his own experience as a leader of the Alexandrian Jewish community, he generalizes that they acted as people often do in such circumstances. "You enticed this multitude with the hope of liberty," they say to Moses, "and then saddled it with the greater danger which threatens its life. Did you not know our unarmedness, and the bitterness and savage temper of the Egyptians? . . . Can we fly, surrounded as in a net by merciless enemies, pathless deserts, seas impassable to ships? Or, if indeed they are passable, what supply of boats have we to enable us to cross?" Whereas in the Bible (Exod. 14:13–14) Moses answers the people's complaint by telling them not to fear since G-d will battle for them, Philo adds (*Mos.* 1.173) that Moses pardoned them and, in a calm manner, ideal leader that he was, simultaneously, on the one hand, appealed to G-d to save them and, on the other hand, encouraged and comforted those who raised a clamor (καταβοῶντας) by assuring them that when G-d gives help, He needs no weapons. Philo presents a picture of a calm (καθεστώς), Stoic-like Moses, reminiscent of Aeneas (Virgil, *Aen.* 1.198–207), who encourages his men after they have been afflicted by a tremendous storm. He omits completely G-d's statement to Moses (Exod. 14:15–18), which seems to rebuke him for lacking faith, "Why do you cry to Me? Tell the people of Israel to go forward."[163] In effect, what Philo has done is to put G-d's reassuring words into the mouth of Moses, who, he adds (*Mos.* 1.175), calmly discoursed to the people and shortly thereafter became possessed and uttered oracular words of prophecy as to what would happen to the Pharaoh's army. Thus the prophecy of the demise of the Egyptians, which in the Bible is assigned to G-d, is in Philo uttered by the inspired Moses.

The supreme example of Moses'ability to encourage his people and not to despair occurs at the Sea of Reeds. In the Bible Moses' exhortation consists of a mere two verses (Exod. 14:13–14), in which he tells the Israelites that they should stand fast and that G-d will do battle for them. Quite clearly, in the Bible (Exod. 14:15–18) G-d is not satisfied with these words of encouragement, since He rebukes Moses and, as we have stated, says: "Why do you cry to Me? Tell the people of Israel to go forward." There is no such criticism of Moses by G-d in Philo. Moreover, in the Bible (Exod. 14:16) G-d's miraculous intervention comes at His initiative. In a second version of the incident at the Sea of Reeds, Philo (*Mos.* 2.250), seeking to aggrandize the prophetic side of Moses, says that Moses at this point became divinely possessed. Moses starts by expressing empathy for the people, noting the alarm that they must necessarily feel and painting a picture of the terrors that clearly beset them. But then he goes on to encourage them to be courageous (θαρρεῖτε), to stand with unshaken thoughts, and to await G-d's help presently. Finally, speaking as an inspired prophet, he describes a vision that he sees of the dead Egyptians (*Mos.* 2.251–52). We now read that Moses, at G-d's command, struck the sea with his staff and that the waters parted. Thereupon, says Philo, in an extra-biblical addition, Moses, the superlative leader, encouraged his men and bade them to rush ahead. Josephus (*A.J.* 2.334), eager to emphasize Moses' qualities as a general, says that Moses actually led the Israelites into the sea, but in the Bible (Exod. 14:21) we read only that Moses stretched out his hand over the sea, and there is nothing to indicate that he actually led them into the sea.[164]

According to the Bible (Exod. 14:19–20), the angel of G-d came between the Egyptian camp and that of the Israelites. Moses stretched out his hand over the sea, and G-d moved the sea with a strong east wind so as to split the water.[165] Thereupon, the Israelites came within the sea on dry land. The

Pharaoh, his chariots, and horsemen pursued the Israelites. Upon instructions from G-d, Moses again stretched out his hand over the sea, and the water engulfed the Egyptians. In Philo's version (*Mos.* 1.177) the miracle is explained more rationally: a south wind of tremendous violence arose, and, as it rushed down, the sea under it was driven back. The sea, though regularly tidal, was now more so than usual and was swept as into a whirlpool when driven against the shore. Moses did not stretch out his hand, as the biblical text would have it, but, more dramatically, actually smote the sea with his staff, presumably to magnify the role of Moses as a national leader (so Jacobson 1983, 141–44). Pseudo-Philo (10.5), Josephus (*A.J.* 2.338), Ezekiel the Tragedian (*ap.* Eus. *PE* 9.29.14), and the midrashic tradition (*Midr. Deut. Rab.* p. 40 [ed. Liebermann], *Abot R. Nat.* A, chap. 33) likewise state that Moses struck the sea. Apparently, he did so with such force that the staff broke in two. The waters were now divided; and Moses, marvelling and full of joy, encouraged the Israelites to move on. Philo mentions not an angel but, rationalizing, a guiding cloud that turned around and separated the Egyptians from the Israelites. In Pseudo-Philo's version (10.5) there is no rationalization of the miracle; rather, G-d rages at the sea and it dries up. "The streams of water stood up and the depths of the earth became visible, and the foundations of the world were laid bare by the fearful roar of G-d and by the breath of the anger of the L-rd."

Philo paints in vivid detail the confusion that ensued among the Egyptians, overwhelmed by the tides, as they rushed down upon their path as into a ravine (*Mos.* 2.255). Then came a mighty rushing wave flinging their corpses in heaps upon the opposite shore, with not even a torchbearer being left to announce to the people of Egypt the sudden disaster (*Mos.* 1.179). In Pseudo-Philo's version (10.6) the miracle is instantaneous and is all G-d's doing. He dulls the minds of the Egyptians so that they do not know that they are entering the sea. And while the Egyptians are in the sea, G-d commands the sea and instructs Moses to strike the sea again. Instantaneously, the sea returns to its course and covers the Egyptians. Thus the Israelites are able to see with their own eyes their enemies fallen through the power of G-d and not of man. To Philo it is not a battle, but an occasion for Moses to display his supreme gift of leadership and, above all, of prophecy. Josephus (*A.J.* 2.334), the military man, paints the encounter at the Sea of Reeds as a battle, with the Egyptians deferring the battle to the following day only because they were exhausted from the pursuit. In his version Moses addresses G-d when he is about to enter the sea and beseeches Him as an ally, whereas in Philo Moses does not address G-d but rather becomes prophetically possessed.

In the Bible (Exod. 14:16) the miracle comes at G-d's initiative, whereas in Josephus (*A.J.* 2.337) it is Moses who suggests the miracle to G-d, reminding Him that the sea is His and that consequently He can make the deep become dry land. In Philo, to be sure, the miracle does not come at G-d's initiative, but inasmuch as he is particularly interested in stressing Moses' role as a prophet, the idea comes from Moses when he is prophetically inspired. Josephus, but not Philo, has the extra-biblical addition (*A.J.* 2.339) that Moses was the first to step into the sea. Philo (*Mos.* 1.179), followed by Josephus (*A.J.* 2.344), has the extra-biblical addition, that not even a messenger was left of the Egyptians to announce the disaster to the people of Egypt. Josephus (*A.J.* 2.349), but not Philo, adds that on the following day Moses gathered the weapons of the Egyptians that had been carried up by the current, conjecturing that this had occurred through G-d's providence, so that the Israelites should have weapons for future encounters. For Philo, who stresses the power of G-d and the miracles that He performs in aiding the Israelites, such weapons are really irrelevant.

Josephus (*A.J.* 2.347) is very apologletic and self-conscious about the miraculous nature of the whole incident, and he goes out of his way to remark that he has recounted each detail "just as I found it in the sacred books. And let no one wonder at the astonishment of the narrative, if a path of deliverance was found through the sea also for men of old who were unacquainted with wickedness, whether by the will of G-d or by itself." Josephus then offers a parallel account (*A.J.* 2.348) of Alexander the Great's crossing of the Pamphylian Sea, where the sea similarly retired before Alexander's troops (Arrian, *Anabasis* 1.26; Strabo 14.3.9.666–67; Callisthenes, frag. 25; Appian, *Bellum Civile* 2.189; Menander, *ap.* Plutarch, *Alexander* 17). But, even so, he closes with his familiar statement,[166] giving the reader the freedom to decide as it seems best to him.

As to the crossing of the Sea of Reeds, which he refers to as the Red Sea, Artapanus (*ap.* Eus. *PE* 9.27.35–37) is clearly ambivalent. On the one hand, he presents a rationalistic view in the name of those who live in Memphis in Egypt, namely, that Moses, being familiar with the countryside, watched for the ebb tide and then led the Israelites through the dry part of the sea. On the other hand, in the name of those who live in Heliopolis in Egypt, he reports that the Pharaoh rushed upon the Israelites with full force, carrying with him all the sacred animals in order to assure victory. He then presents the biblical view that G-d instructed Moses to strike the sea with his rod and thus to divide it, whereupon Moses touched the water lightly (ἐπιθιγεῖν) with his rod, the stream divided, and the Israelite multitude passed through the dry channel. Artapanus is here attempting to rationalize, referring to the sea as a mere stream (νᾶμα). He also emphasizes Moses' faith in G-d in that Moses does not smite the water, but rather touches it lightly, clearly confident that G-d would care for His people. The Egyptians were consumed not only by the water, but also by the fire that blazed in front of them.

In place of the biblical statement that the pursuing Egyptians were all drowned in the Sea of Reeds, Pompeius Trogus combines the biblical account with a rationalistic interpretation, asserting that in trying to recover these objects by force, the Egyptians were compelled by storms to return home (*ap.* Justin 36, *Epitoma* 2.13).

Finally, the Bible (Exod. 15:1) states that after the Israelites had thus been saved miraculously, Moses and the Israelites sang a song to G-d. Miriam, in turn (Exod. 15:20–21), took her drum and led the women in dancing and singing. Philo himself has two versions of this. In one of them (*Mos.* 1.180) he says that the Israelites set up two choirs, one of men and one of women. Moses and his sister Miriam presided over these choirs and led hymns of thanksgiving to G-d. In the other version (*Mos.* 2.256) it is Moses alone who takes the initiative to organize the Israelites into two choirs, one of men and one of women. He himself leads the men, and it is he who appoints Miriam to lead the women. Moreover, instead of the two choirs being separate, the two choirs join together in singing hymns of thanksgiving to G-d with blending of temperaments and melody in full harmony. Philo thus emphasizes Moses' extraordinary ability to unite the motley crew that he led. It is Moses, moreover, who persuades the tens of thousands of Israelites to sing the same song with their hearts in accord. And, in an extra-biblical touch, Philo (*Mos.* 2.257) paints a picture of Moses the prophet, rejoicing at all this and seeing the people also overjoyed and, moreover, himself no longer able to restrain his delight, leading the singing.

One of the key atttributes of a leader, as we may see in Thucydides' (2.60) portrait of the ideal statesman, Pericles, is the ability to persuade the people. As Aristotle puts it, "Rhetoric is useful because things that are true and things that are just have a natural tendency to prevail over their opposites, so that if the decisions of judges are not what they ought to be, the defeat must be due to the speakers themselves, and they must be blamed accordingly" (*Rhet.* 1.1.1355A21–24). Thus, it is significant that in the Bible (Exod. 15:1), after the Israelites have been saved miraculously by the splitting of the Sea of Reeds, "Moses and the people of Israel sang" a song to the L-rd. Philo (*Mos.* 2.257) adds a significant point when he asserts that it was Moses who *persuaded* so many myriads. This was clearly a tremendous achievement, since, as Philo must have realized from his own experience as a leader of a community, the unity of Moses' people is so crucial. The fact that he managed to get them not merely to sing but to sing the same song with one mind (ὁμογνωμονῆσαι) was clearly another tremendous achievement. Moreover, it was Moses himself who took the lead (κατῆρχε, "began") in the song.[167]

In sum, Philo significantly presents his long discussion of the qualifications of Moses as a leader in the context of Moses' unification of the mixed multitude, whom he refers to as a rabble, clearly a difficult group to control, who had joined the Israelites. Moses emerges as a leader of actual converts to Judaism. He shows his ability in keeping the Israelites free from factionalism. Philo, aware of the question why Moses led the Israelites by the longer route through the desert, insists that the decision was Moses' rather than G-d's and that he sought thereby to separate them from urban temptations and to test their loyalty when supplies were not abundant. It is not G-d but Moses who tells them where to encamp. Philo, in his concern not to cast doubt on the credibility of the narrative, avoids exaggeration of the Egyptian forces at the Sea of Reeds. He is careful to depict the Israelites as not being aggressive and eager for military expansion. He portrays Moses as a Stoic-like leader in facing the complaints of the Israelites. The prophecy of the Egyptians' demise is uttered by an inspired Moses rather than by G-d. The miracles are sent not on G-d's initiative but on Moses'. Philo highlights Moses' ability to unify the people, as we see in his success in getting the Israelites to join harmoniously in song.

h. Moses' Leadership in the Wilderness

Even non-Jewish writers who are viciously anti-Semitic accord grudging respect to Moses as the leader of the Israelites during their long sojourn in the wilderness. According to Lysimachus (*ap.* Josephus, *Ap.* 1.308), the Israelites in the desert fasted and implored their gods to help them. A certain Moses, of whose parentage Lysimachus tells us nothing (unlike Manetho and Chaeremon, Lysimachus does not indicate that Moses was a priest), encouraged them, however, to be courageous and to show good will to no man,[168] to offer not the best but the worst advice, and to destroy the temples and altars of non-Israelites, although, as Josephus (*Ap.* 1.316) remarks, Lysimachus does not indicate what might have been Moses' motive in so doing. When, after great hardships, they reached inhabited country, they destroyed the non-Jewish temples. Finally, they built a city in Judaea called Hierosyla (i.e., town of temple-robbers), although, as Josephus (*Ap.* 1.319) remarks, it would seem strange for the founders of a city to give it a name with the pejorative connotation that Lysimachus attaches to it; and later they changed the name of this city to Hierosolyma.

Josephus (*Ap.* 1.316–18) argues against Lysimachus that it is highly improbable that Moses would have drawn up laws in effect declaring war on the entire rest of the world. We may remark that Lysimachus' claim (*Ap.* 1.310) that the Israelites maltreated the people of the desert and plundered their temples during their sojourn there is contradicted by the biblical narrative. Lysimachus, however, is probably reflecting Moses' statement, frequently repeated (Deut. 7:16, 12:2–3, 20:16–18), in the name of G-d (Deut. 7:1–2), commanding the Israelites, when they enter Canaan, to destroy the Canaanites and their religious objects, though there is no record that the Israelites actually destroyed any pagan religious institutions. But, we must note, even Hecataeus, who, as we have seen, is so generally appreciative of Moses and of his achievements, also notes (*ap.* Diodorus 40.3.4) that Moses introduced an intolerant mode of life.

Even Tacitus, however, the most bitter of disparagers of the Jews, early in the second century bestows some respect on Moses. He is the leader (*Histories* 5.3.1) of those who during a plague that caused bodily disfigurement had been exiled in the desert. He warned them not to hope for help from gods or men, but to trust to themselves. He it was who freed them from their misery by finding water for them (*Histories* 5.3.2). On the seventh day the exiles founded a city, presumably Jerusalem (clearly in contradiction to the Bible), and dedicated a temple. Tacitus (*Histories* 5.3.3) explains the origin of the Sabbath as arising from the fact that the seventh day of their wanderings marked the end of their toils.

Almost immediately after the miraculous victory at the Sea of Reeds, Moses' leadership, according to the Bible, was again tested. This time the Israelites, after journeying for three days, were unable to find water to drink

(Exod. 15:22), only to come to Marah, where the water turned out to be bitter. This again led the people to complain against Moses. Philo, in his contempt for the masses,[169] following in the footsteps of Thucydides' Pericles (2.65.4) and Plato (*R.* 8.557–61), thus elevating the role of Moses in dealing with such a difficult mob, portrays them as grumbling as if nothing good had befallen them up to that point. In an extra-biblical addition, he dramatizes the scene further in stating that they saw springs and ran full of joy to them; but it turned out that they were deceived, since the water was brackish (*Mos.* 1.182). In the Bible the whole incident is related in a mere five verses, but Philo (*Mos.* 1.181–87) elaborates on it greatly. He paints a vivid extra-biblical picture of the dejection of the Israelites and, in particular, of the infants,[170] the sight of whom, as they cried for something to drink, was more than their parents could face without tears (*Mos.* 1.182). Whereas in the Bible (Exod. 15:24) the complaint of the Israelites consists of a single sentence—"What shall we drink?"—Philo expands this with the statement that some of the weaker men (ὀλιγωροτέροι), who were less secure (ἀβέβαιοι) in their piety, then denounced the past events as not having been intended to benefit them but merely to bring them to worse misfortunes. They bitterly add that they would have preferred to die three times at the hands of enemies rather than to die of thirst. To die quickly, they say, is like never dying, whereas to die slowly and painfully is true death.

At this point the biblical account (Exod. 15:25) asserts simply that Moses cried out to G-d, without giving the contents of his supplication. Philo, who is forever amplifying the achievements of Moses, portrays for us in detail (*Mos.* 1.184) a leader who sympathizes with and feels for his people. He reminds G-d very gently that He knows the weakness of His creatures and, in particular, the need for food and drink. Identifying as he always does with the sufferers, Moses asks G-d to pardon the despondent and to bring relief to them, not at some distant time but promptly, since, as he reminds G-d and as he probably realized from his own experience, people are short-sighted in seeking immediate assistance. In the Bible (Exod. 15:25) G-d shows Moses a tree, which he throws into the water, whereupon the water becomes sweet. The Bible does not explain how this occurred, but Philo, always aware that his sophisticated readers might well question such a miracle, rationalizes (*Mos.* 1.185) that possibly the tree had been formed by nature to exercise this virtue or that it had been created on this occasion for that purpose.[171] The Bible (Exod. 15:25) states very simply that the water now became sweet, but Philo expatiates and remarks (*Mos.* 1.186) that the water became so sweet that no one could even guess that it had originally been bitter, since no trace remained of its former brackishness. Significantly, Josephus (*A.J.* 3.2), who frequently emphasizes the military aspect of Moses' leadership (see Feldman 1998a, 401–11), in referring to the march of the Israelites through the wilderness, speaks of Moses as their general (στρατηγός) and of the Israelites as an army (στρατός), whereas the key attribute of Moses, according to Philo, is his ability to empathize with the people.

After the bitter waters of Marah had become sweet, the Israelites journeyed on to Elim (Exod. 16:1).[172] The Bible asserts that in Elim there were twelve springs of water and seventy date palms (Exod. 15:27), with no intimation that there were any problems. Philo (*Mos.* 1.188–90) indicates that Elim was well watered and that the palm trees were luxuriant. Josephus' description (*A.J.* 3.9) of Elim as planted with palm trees that were dwarfed because of lack of water seems to contradict Exod. 15:27, which gives no indication that the trees were disappointing.[173] Here again, though he generally avoids allegorical explanations, Philo (*Mos.* 1.188) realizes that his readers might well ask the significance of the numbers twelve and seventy; and so he explains that twelve signifies the twelve tribes of the Israelites[174] and seventy signifies the seventy elders of the nation (Num. 11:16).[175] The significance of the palm is that it is the noblest of trees and that it has its life-giving principle not buried in its roots, but mounted aloft.

Thereafter the Israelites came to the wilderness of Sin, where they again complained to Moses and Aaron about their lack of food (Exod. 16:2–3). Here likewise Philo (*Mos.* 1.191–95) has greatly expanded the complaint and their despair from one biblical verse (Exod. 16:3) to five paragraphs, but the complaint is directed to Moses alone (*Mos.* 1.196). This again puts the spotlight on Moses and minimizes the role of Aaron. Philo (*Mos.* 1.191–92) says that in addition to their present lack of food, they also despaired of the future. He presents an extensive and vivid portrait of the barrenness of the soil in contrast to the fertility of Egypt. All they had to look forward to was a pathless wilderness. Moses, they grumble, has filled their ears with empty hopes. "Our leader," they say, "promised us happiness; in actual fact, we are the most miserable of men. He buoyed and blew up our hopes with words and then tortured our bellies with hunger, while providing not even minimum nourishment. In the name of colonization he deceived so great a multitude, leading us from an inhabited (οἰκουμένη) to an uninhabited world" (*Mos.* 1.193, 195). The Bible does not record what attitude Moses assumed to these accusations, but Philo (*Mos.* 1.196) shows what a selfless leader Moses was in that he was not indignant at their denunciations of himself so much as he was at their instability of judgment after all the miracles that they had experienced. But Philo immediately adds that Moses forgave them, knowing, as he did, that the multitude is by its nature an insecure thing, thrown into disorder by the circumstances of the moment, which bring about forgetfulness of the past and despondency of the future.[176]

At this point, according to the biblical account (Exod. 16:4), G-d promises Moses that He will send them food from heaven. Moses and Aaron then tell the Israelites that G-d has heard their complaints and that in the morning they will see His glory. Moses then tells them that their complaints are not against him and Aaron, but against G-d. Philo (*Mos.* 1.198), in an extra-biblical addition, adds two reasons why G-d decides to send manna to the Israelites, namely, that He takes pity on them and gives them the manna because He is moved partly by the clemency and benevolence inherent in His nature, but also that He wishes to honor the ruler, Moses, whom He has appointed, and He desires to show them the greatness of Moses' piety.[177] It is this second reason that is particularly typical of Philo's treatment of this whole episode, since his chief motive in retelling the whole narrative is to raise the stature of Moses.

When the people, in their astonishment, ask Moses what the substance was that appeared in the morning, Moses, says Philo (*Mos.* 1.201), possessed by divine inspiration, in his piety explains that the whole world ministers to G-d. To be sure, according to the Bible (Exod. 16:13) and Philo (*Mos.* 1.198), the miracle of the manna is due solely to G-d, but Josephus (*A.J.* 3.26) even further highlights the role of Moses, adding that while Moses raised his hands in prayer, a dew descended and congealed about his hands. In the Bible (Exod. 16:15), when the manna descends, the Israelites are said not to know what it is, whereupon Moses piously tells them that it is the food that G-d has given them to eat. In the account of Philo (*Mos.* 1.200–1), the Israelites ask what the rain is that no one had ever seen before and for what purpose it has come. Moses, ever the teacher to his people and to the scientific world that might very well seek an explanation for this phenomenon, possessed by divine inspiration, as Philo says, offers two analogies: just as air brings water, so it here has brought food; and just as the river of Egypt overflows and waters the fields, so the air has overflowed with this food. Moses then warns the people not to leave over any of the manna until the following morning, but those who do find that it has become infested with worms.[178]

On the sixth day the Israelites receive a double portion, inasmuch as they have to rest on the Sabbath. When Moses tells the Israelites that there will be no manna on the Sabbath, and this turns out to be a true prophecy, they recognize him as a unique prophet (*Mos.* 2.269).[179] This seems to be the main reason why Philo includes this narrative of the manna in Book 2 of *Mos.*, since the main point of that book is to emphasize Moses' quality as a prophet, whereas if the narrative had been put in Book 1, which highlights Moses' quality as a political king, it would have called attention to Moses' ability as a political leader.

Artapanus (*ap.* Eus. *PE* 9.27.37) reports that G-d gave the Israelites food similar in texture to rolled millet having the color of snow (Exod. 16:4–5, 17–24) but does not expand on the further miracles in connection with this manna. Wisdom 16:22 describes it as snow and ice that did not melt. Philo (*Mos.* 1.200), aware that it never snows in the desert, specifically states that it was not snow or ice. In the New Testament (John 6:32–35) the gift of manna is the occasion of a comparison of Jesus with Moses, since Jesus tells his audience that it was not Moses, but G-d, who gave the Israelites bread from heaven, whereas Jesus says that he is the bread of life.

In the Bible (Exod. 16:9), when the Israelites complain further, Moses tells Aaron that he should tell the Israelites that they should approach G-d, since He has heard their complaints. Thereupon Aaron speaks to all the Israelites, and the glory of G-d appears in a cloud. This is followed by G-d's statement to Moses that He has heard their complaints and that they will have meat to eat in the afternoon. This is followed by the descent of the quail. In Philo's version (*Mos.* 1.209) there is no mention at all of the role of Aaron, presumably because Philo, as always, does not want to divert attention from the role of Moses.[180] Also, in the biblical account of the quail in Num. 11: 31–33, the demand for flesh is punished with a plague; but Philo does not mention this, presumably because it seems to contradict the account in Exod. 16:13. Philo (*Mos.* 1.209) adds that with the appearance of the quail the Israelites were well supplied with the means of luxurious living, such as would be found in a rich country. The inclusion of this narrative in Book 1 of *Mos.* illustrates Moses' excellent ability as a ruler to satisfy the basic needs of his people.

The Israelites (Exod. 17:1) now journey to Rephidim, where again they fail to find water and complain against Moses, who rebukes them, "Why do you find fault with me? Why do you put the L-rd to the proof?" (Exod. 17:2). Moses then cries out to G-d, remarking that the people will stone him soon.

He follows G-d's instructions to strike a rock, from which water flows. In his version (*Mos.* 1.210–11) Philo does not mention Moses' rebuke to the people, nor his crying out to G-d, nor the threat to stone Moses.[181] Instead, concerned that his sophisticated readers might disbelieve such a phenomenon, he rationalizes (*Mos.* 1.211), giving two possible scientific explanations, namely that perhaps the rock originally contained a spring and now had its artery severed, or perhaps that the water had been collected in it in hidden channels. To anyone who disbelieves these things,[182] he points out at length that by comparison with the marvelous order that prevails in the universe, such a phenomenon was mere child's play (*Mos.* 1.212–13).

One biblical incident in which both Moses and Aaron are actually criticized by G-d for lack of faith is that at Meribah, where, during a water shortage, Moses and Aaron gather the Israelites, and where Moses, instead of following G-d's instructions to speak to the rock (Num. 20:8), actually smites it with his rod (Num. 20:10). Thereupon G-d, blaming Aaron (whose role in the incident seems unclear) as well as Moses, declares that as punishment neither of them will enter the Promised Land. Such an incident casts aspersions upon the reputation for faith of both Moses and Aaron, and so it is not surprising that Philo and Josephus omit it completely. Indeed, rabbinic tradition (see Ginzberg 1911, 3:319–20) looked upon Moses' hitting the rock instead of speaking to it to bring forth water (Num. 20:2–12) as his greatest sin, since it showed apparent lack of faith.

In sum, even anti-Semitic writers accord Moses respect as a leader of the Israelites in the desert. Philo elaborates on the complaining that the Israelites utter against Moses. He keeps the spotlight on Moses by stressing that their anger was directed to Moses, rather than to Aaron. Moses immediately forgives them in view of their insecurity. One reason why G-d sends the manna is His desire to honor Moses. Philo explains the manna scientifically. The key attribute of Moses is his ability to empathize with the people. In order to save Moses' reputation for faith, Philo omits Moses' disobedience in smiting, rather than speaking to, the rock from which he obtains water.

i. War with the Amalekites

Philo (*Mos.* 1.214), like Josephus (*A.J.* 3.43) after him, paints a picture of the Israelites expecting to find a life of peace and quiet as they were approaching the land in which they hoped to settle. Josephus (*A.J.* 3.40–41) mentions as the motive of the Amalekites in going to war with the Israelites the fear that the latter would pillage them and would gain strength if they were not opposed.[183] Yet, the most remarkable thing about Philo's account is that in his biography of Moses, even though he is clearly referring to the Amalekites and even though the mention of the eradication of Amalek is so important, being found twice in the Pentateuch and even though in the rabbinic tradition it is connected directly with the festival of Purim (Esth. 3:1), Philo does not refer to the Amalekites by name at all, nor does he mention the place where the encounter occurred. Rather, we are told (*Mos.* 1.214), the country was occupied by Phoenicians, presumably a very general reference to the inhabitants of Canaan and certainly not especially to the Amalekites. He implies that there was a general fear in the region and says that the king of the region, fearing a sack, consequently called up the youth of his cities and sought to stop the Israelites, if need be by force of arms.[184] In an addition to the Bible, Philo says that the king noted that his own men were unwearied and fresh for the contest, whereas the Israelites were exhausted with much journeying and famine and drought (*Mos.* 1.215). To Philo the only name that is important is that of Moses, and his sole concern is how Moses was able to meet this and other challenges.

We then read (*Mos.* 1.216), in still another supplement to the biblical account that adds to Moses' qualifications as a leader, that Moses had sent out scouts, from whom he had learned that the enemy was not far distant. According to the Bible (Exod. 17:9), Moses, without any words of how Joshua came to be the general in charge, tells Joshua to choose men and go to battle against Amalek. In Philo, however, as in Josephus (*A.J.* 3.49), he himself takes the lead in mustering his men of military age and plays a more important part in the fight, while naming Joshua to be the general.

Moreover, whereas in the Bible, Moses appears as a weak, old leader hardly able to hold up his hands (Exod. 17:12), according to Philo (*Mos.* 1.216), in an extra-biblical remark, Moses purifies himself according to the customary ritual, very much like soldiers in the Roman army before going out to battle,[185] and proceeds actually to run zealously to the nearby hill to remind G-d of the instances in which He had previously performed miracles and had saved the Israelites and to pray to Him for a victory.[186] Whereas the Bible (Exod. 17:11) and Josephus (*A.J.* 3.53) state simply that when Moses raised his hands the Israelites were stronger, and whereas when he lowered his hands, presumably because he was old and weary, Amalek was stronger, Philo (*Mos.* 1.217), apparently realizing that his sophisticated readers would be hard put to give credence to such a scenario, remarks that Moses' hands were affected in a most marvellous (τερατωδέστατον) way.[187] Thus, the combatants became strong (ἐρρώννυτο) and became more distinguished (ἐπικυδέστερον) for bravery (ἀνδραγαθιζόμενον), apparently inspired by Moses. Philo (ibid.), realizing that a literal interpretation would be hard to believe, then proceeds to explain this phenomenon in a symbolic way, with the hands aloft representing the ethereal and the hands below representing the earthly. He asserts (*Leg.* 3.45, *Prob.* 29) that the hands of a wise man are weighty and immovable; and they are, in fact, steadied by Aaron, whose name, he adds allegorically, indicates the Word, and Hur, whose name indicates Light or Truth.[188] Moreover, Philo omits the biblical statement (Exod. 17:12) that when Moses' hands grew heavy, Aaron and Hur put a stone under him and they supported his hands, one on each side of him, since this would indicate that Moses was old and weak.

Philo (*Mos.* 1.218) justifies the wholesale slaughter that the Israelites inflicted upon the Amalekites by stating that the latter justly suffered the punishment that they had sought to inflict upon the Israelites. Most significantly, Philo (*Mos.* 1.219) omits any mention that G-d told Moses that He would erase the memory of Amalek (Exod. 17:14), or that the Israelites were to wipe out the memory of Amalek (Deut. 25:19) or, as Josephus (*A.J.* 3.60) puts it, that Moses *predicted* that the Amalekites would be utterly annihilated, realizing that this would be nothing less than genocide. Instead, Philo, who is concerned not with political but with philosophical matters and who is not interested in the struggle to overcome the enemies of the Jews and to establish an independent Jewish state in Palestine, presents an allegorical interpretation of the struggle between the Amalekites and the Israelites (*Leg.* 3.186–87), where Israel is equated with mind and the army of the soul and where Amalek is said to be a type of character (*Migr.* 144) who is equated with passion and who hungers after pleasure. Thus, Moses lifting up his hands represents the victory of mind over mortal things.

Similarly, commenting on the birth of Amalek to the concubine of Eliphaz (Gen. 36:12), Philo (*Congr.* 55) remarks that the name "Amalek" means "people licking up" and that it represents the boiling of unreasoning passion that licks up and destroys all that stands in its way. Moreover, the mother of Amalek is the concubine Timna, whose name means "tossing faintness" and signifies the soul's loss of power when it receives from the body the tossing surge driven on by unbridled appetite.

Indeed, whereas Josephus passes over in silence Balaam's prophecy (Num. 24:20) that Amalek is the first among nations, Philo (*Leg.* 3.187), the aristocrat who despises the mob, does refer to it but gives it an allegorical significance, namely, that Amalek is the passion that rules over the promiscuous masses.

What is most remarkable in all this is that Philo has totally omitted the divine injunction to eradicate the Amalekites as a people and instead has equated them with passion or evil. He justifies the wholesale slaughter of the Amalekites in the desert, but he has avoided the problem of the justification of punishing innocent children for the sins of their ancestors. This should not surprise us in view of the long discussion (*Spec.* 3.153–68) in which he stresses the importance of the biblical statement that children should not suffer for the sins of their parents (Deut. 24:16). This is not merely a theoretical matter for Philo, in view of his position as a leader of the Jewish community of Alexandria; and he cites his outrage at a contemporary incident in which children and parents and other relatives of debtors were beaten and tortured by a tax collector and in which some spectators committed suicide in order to avoid such a plight (*Spec.* 3.159–62). He specifically stresses that "our legislator" (*Spec.* 3.167) insisted that children should not suffer for the sins of their parents and, "observing the errors current among other nations, regarded them with aversion as ruinous to the ideal commonwealth."

Philo takes advantage of the opportunity to use the incident of Amalek to preach a much more general lesson, namely, the superiority of mind to passion, one of his favorite themes, as we see, for example, in his comment about Jacob (*Leg.* 3.18) as representing the mind (νοῦς) in training, when he sees passion (πάθος) grovelling low before him. As so often is the case in Philo, he gives an etymology, that of Amalek, to make his point about the character of the person, in this instance as representing "people licking up," that is, the boiling up of passion.

Pseudo-Philo (10.7) says nothing at all about Amalek's attack upon the Israelites as they were going through the wilderness, nor does he say anything about the divine command to eradicate the Amalekites. However, he does regard the Amalekites as the embodiment of wickedness, as we see from the fact that, in an addition to the Bible, he says that it is with the Amalekites that the concubine (Judg. 19:2) had sinned during the period that she had strayed from her man. This, in the eyes of Pseudo-Philo, justifies her terrible fate of being abused by the men of Gibeah that G-d is said to have inflicted upon her (45.3), this being the author's attack on intermarriage with non-Jews, and above all with the Amalekites (see Perrot and Bogaert 1976, 2:45).

Josephus (*A.J.* 3.40–57) has vastly revised, both in additions and subtractions (and much more than he usually does) the account of Amalek's attack upon the Israelites. He emphasizes that the Israelites had done nothing to provoke the battle with the Amalekites. His chief interest is twofold: elevating the role of Moses as a leader and elaborating the military details of Moses' victory over Amalek. He diminishes the miraculous element and explains the victory in rational terms. He has, at least in his paraphrase of the account in the Pentateuch, avoided the most sensitive portion, namely, the command (Exod. 17:14) to wipe out Amalek. Here he speaks neither of G-d's nor of the Israelites' responsibility to wipe out Amalek, but rather has Moses *predict* that the Amalekites will be annihilated (*A.J.* 3.60).

In sum, most strikingly Philo, though clearly referring to the Amalekites, does not refer to them by name in *Mos.*, since to him the only name that is important is that of Moses. The fact that Moses sends out scouts adds to his qualifications as a leader. Moses himself takes the lead in mustering his men and plays a more important role in the fighting. He even runs zealously to a nearby hill. Philo explains the raising and lowering of Moses' hands symbolically. Significantly, realizing that this would be nothing less than genocide, Philo omits mention of G-d's injunction to Moses to erase the memory of Amalek. Since he is not interested in establishing an independent state in Palestine, Philo interprets the struggle between the Israelites and the Amalekites allegorically.

j. The Omission of Jethro's Visit

Next in the Bible (Exod. 18) we hear of the visit to Moses of Jethro, together with Zipporah, Moses' wife whom Moses had sent away, and their two sons. According to the Bible (Exod. 18:9) Jethro rejoiced over all the good that G-d had done for the Israelites, and he offered a sacrifice to G-d (Exod. 18:12). Moses heeded his advice (Exod. 18:13–26) to appoint judges to decide cases of lesser importance.

According to Philo (*Spec.* 4.171, *Leg.* 3.197), Moses adopted Jethro's suggestion of entrusting smaller matters to assistants. What is striking is that in his *Mos.*, which generally follows the Pentateuch chronologically, Philo totally omits this visit, apparently because he thought that, in a quasi-official biography of Moses, inclusion of Jethro's visit to Moses would detract from the authoritativeness of Moses, since Jethro criticized the way in which Moses had been administering justice.[189]

Moreover, whereas in the Bible (Exod. 18:2) it is clear that Moses had been separated from his wife and children, Philo says nothing about this. There is a debate in the rabbinic tradition (*Mek. R. Ish., Amalek* 1 [ed. Horovitz, pp. 190–91]) whether Moses had divorced his wife or had merely sent her away. Josephus (*A.J.* 3.63) asserts that Jethro came alone and welcomed Moses, Zipporah, and their children and says nothing about Moses' separation from Zipporah. Schalit 1944, 1, on *A.J.* 3.63, suggests that Josephus' change is motivated by the fact that in the eyes of the Hellenistic-Roman reader it would have been a defect in Moses' character to depict him as having divorced his wife and sent away his children, especially because of the concern of Augustus and his successors for the strengthening of family life, as reflected in such legislation as the Julian Laws in Augustan Rome of 19 and 18 B.C.E., aimed at the discouragement of childlessness by placing disabilities upon unmarried and childless persons, and the Papian Poppaean Law of 9 C.E. These laws gave precedence to fathers among candidates for public office. The same situation is to be seen in such works as the epigrams of Martial (4.71) and the satires of Juvenal. Philo, in his eagerness to protect the reputation of Moses, similarly avoids all mention of his separation from Zipporah.

What is furthermore remarkable in Philo's portrait of Jethro elsewhere, as we have noted, is that it is almost completely negative.[190] Philo (*Agr.* 43–44), as we have remarked, views Jethro as approving of seeming in preference to being and as welcoming conceit in preference to truth. He regards Moses as the shepherd who leads his flock away from the snares of folly and injustice. Jethro (*Mut.* 104) represents the very opposite of justice, since the great ones of the earth follow his guidance in thinking that it is right to give great justice to the great and little justice to the little.

Moses in his wisdom, says Philo (*Ebr.* 37), recalled the people of the soul (i.e., those who devote themselves to the cultivation of the soul) to piety (εὐσέβειαν) and to honoring G-d and taught them the commandments and the most holy laws. In contrast, Jethro, Moses' father-in-law, only seemed to be wise, did not know the divine blessings, was particularly familiar with human and perishable things, and promulgated laws that contradict the laws of nature.

Indeed, Philo, in treatises other than *Mos.*, completely perverts the biblical account of Jethro's visit to Moses. It is almost as if Philo's text of the Bible ended with the statement, "What you are doing is not good" (Exod. 18:17). According to Philo's version (*Mut.* 104), Jethro suggests to Moses that "he should not teach the only thing worth learning, the ordinances of G-d and the law, but the contracts which men make with each other, which as a rule produce dealings where the partners have no real partnership." In enumerating four classes of children—one who obeys both parents, one who obeys neither, one who obeys only the father (that is, right reason), and one who obeys only the mother (that is, mere variable and unstable convention)—Philo says that the last, which, he explains, symbolizes the one who bows down to the opinions of the masses, is most clearly typified by Jethro (*Ebr.* 35–36). Indeed, Jethro, who in the Bible is depicted as dispensing excellent advice to Moses on how to administer his judicial system (Exod. 18:17–23), is described by Philo as having seven daughters who represent the unreasoning element (*Mut.* 110). Philo undoubtedly has in mind Plato's allegory of the ship (*R.* 6.488A7–89A2) when he condemns Jethro as playing the demagogue (*Ebr.* 37). Instead of welcoming Jethro's statement, "Now I know that the L-rd is greater than all gods" (Exod. 18:11), Philo vehemently condemns Jethro as a blasphemer, first, because the word "now" implies that he had never previously understood the greatness of G-d and, second, because he dares to compare G-d with other gods (*Ebr.* 41–45).

And yet, Philo, as we have noted, is not completely negative in his portrayal of Jethro. We do see a favorable side of Jethro in the gratitude that he exhibits toward Moses for having aided his daughters when they were driven away by some shepherds when they were drawing water at a well. Again, in the treatise *Spec.* 4.173–74, Philo compliments Jethro for having given Moses excellent advice (ἄριστα συνεβούλευσεν) which was useful (συμφέροντα), namely to choose others to adjudicate less important matters, while keeping the greater matters for himself and thus giving himself time to rest. But such favorable comments are few. In accepting the advice given him by Jethro, Moses (*Spec.* 4.175) conveyed the lesson that the ideal ruler should not reject the help of others and should not wear himself out over minor matters, thus neglecting those that are more necessary. As to why Philo presents a positive assessment of Jethro in *Spec.* 4.173–74, we may suggest that the treatise is particularly addressed to wayward Jews; and, in effect, Philo is asserting to these Jews that they should learn a lesson from the non-Jew Jethro. Moreover, as we have noted, in that treatise (1.320) he urges his fellow Jews to go into the marketplace and to spread the knowledge of Judaism among non-Jews.

In any case, the two sides of Jethro may reflect his two names, Jethro having negative associations and Reuel (Raguel), meaning "the shepherding of G-d," having positive associations (*Mut.* 105). A more likely explanation is that

Philo speaks negatively about Jethro in the allegorical treatises, such as *Ebr.*, with their emphasis on philosophical issues deeply influenced by Plato's attack on sophistry, whereas he is more positively disposed toward Jethro in the exegetical treatises, such as *Spec.*, with their emphasis on Judaism as a legal system and where he acknowledges Jethro's advice to Moses in this area.

We may well wonder why Pseudo-Philo in his *LAB* does not mention Jethro at all. Presumably the reason is that Jethro's excellent advice to Moses would detract from the central position that Moses occupies in his narrative. Perhaps this omission may also be explained as arising from Pseudo-Philo's polemic against intermarriage (as seen in Moses' marriage with the Midianite Zipporah in Exod. 2:21 and with the nameless Ethiopian woman in Num. 12:1). We may perceive this polemic, for example, in his extra-biblical statement that Tamar's intent in having relations with Judah was to prevent her being joined with Gentiles (*LAB* 9.5). We see it likewise in his stress on the incident of the Midianite women (and we must not forget that Jethro was a priest of Midian) who led the Israelite youths astray (*LAB* 18.13–14), and in the unique detail that the Levite's concubine of Judg. 19:25 had transgressed against her husband by having relations with foreigners (*LAB* 45.3).

Unlike Philo, the rabbis were, on the whole, positively inclined toward Jethro, presumably because they found it hard to believe that Moses, the greatest prophet in Israel who had ever lived (Deut. 34:10), would associate with anyone of less than high repute and, in fact, would marry the daughter of an idol-worshipper.[191] Moreover, they were less troubled than was Philo by the fact that the great Moses had to accept advice from a pagan priest, since, as we shall see, they have a tradition (*Tan. B, Exod.* 71, *Exod. Rab.* 1.32) that Jethro became a proselyte to Judaism.[192] In fact, the sheer volume of comments about him in rabbinic literature is a sure indication of his importance for their tradition.

The rabbis were apparently troubled by the fact that Jethro was a pagan priest; and, indeed, we find a debate (*Mek., Yitro* 1) as to whether the term *kohen* as applied to him (Exod. 2:16) indicates that he was a priest or, more neutrally, that he was a chief—an appellation that we have already noted in Artapanus and Ezekiel. According to one view, he counselled the Pharoah to throw Israelite baby boys into the Nile River, but later repented (*Midr. Exod. Rab.* 27.6). Another tradition relates that the Pharaoh had three advisers—Balaam, Job, and Jethro; Balaam advised the Pharaoh to cast the Israelite babies into the river, Job was silent, and Jethro fled. Because he refused to join in the scheme, the tradition holds, his descendants were privileged to sit in the Sanhedrin (*b. Sanh.* 106a). It is true that Jethro was viewed by some as an idolater of the worst sort, so much so that we hear that there was not an idol on earth that he had not worshipped (*Mek., Beshallaḥ* 1) and that he permitted his daughter Zipporah to marry Moses only on condition that their first son would be raised to worship idols (*Mek., Yitro* 1). On the other hand, we hear that even before Moses came to Midian, Jethro was excommunicated by his neighbors for giving up his idolatry (*Midr. Exod. Rab.* 1.32).

The tradition is similarly divided in commenting on the reaction of Jethro to the miracles performed by G-d. One view, transmitted by the third-century Rav, is that he actually became a proselyte to Judaism (*Tan. B, Exod.* 71); in fact, according to one view, he became a proselyte even before Moses came to his home (*Midr. Exod. Rab.*1.32). Indeed, he becomes, for the rabbis, the prototype of proselytes (*Mishnat Rabbi Eliezer*, [ed. H. G. Enelow, p. 304]); and the very change of his name from Jether to Jethro ("enlarges") is cited to illustrate G-d's love for proselytes. In striking contrast to Esau, who though born of Israelite parents chose to abandon his ancestral beliefs, Jethro, though born a non-Jew, chose a life of piety (*Midr. Exod. Rab.* 27.2). The fact that Jethro left his very comfortable home in order to meet Moses in the desert shows his sincerity, in the eyes of the rabbis, in the length that he was willing to go in order to become a convert (*Mek., Yitro* 1).[193] The other view, expressed by Rav's contemporary Samuel, is that he felt sympathetic for the sufferings of the Egyptians (*b. Sanh.* 94a), and that he converted to Judaism only after he had heard what had happened to Amalek (*Midr. Exod. Rab.* 7.6).

So highly is Jethro regarded that, according to one tradition, the very Presence (*Shekinah*) of G-d greeted him when he came to visit Moses (*Mek., Yitro* 1)—another indication that Jethro became a convert, inasmuch as the traditional term for conversion is "to be taken under the wings of the Shekinah." One factor in this tradition recognizing Jethro as a proselyte apparently was the concern that a non-Jew should have been responsible for the reorganization of the Jewish judicial system; and, indeed, the rabbis explain that Moses gave credit to Jethro for this even though, in fact, the changes had been commanded by G-d, in order to give merit to Jethro as a convert (*Sifre Num.* 80) and to his descendants and in order to give greatness to Jethro in the eyes of Moses and all Israel (*Sifre Num.* 78; *Mishnat Rabbi Eliezer*, p. 304). Indeed, the fact that Jethro blessed G-d (Exod. 18:10) shows his superiority to Moses and the rest of the Israelites in that they had failed to bless Him before Jethro arrived (ibid.). There is even a view that it was Jethro who was responsible for the revelation of the Torah in its complete form, inasmuch as G-d was afraid, after Jethro had been responsible for the reorganization of the judicial system, that the Israelites might think that it was he who was the source of their whole system of law (*Pesiq. Rb. Kah.* 12.11).

There is likewise a difference of opinion as to the reason for Jethro's departure from Moses. On the one hand, the view is expressed that Moses dismissed Jethro because he did not want him, a non-Jew, to be present at the moment of revelation at Sinai (*Tan. B, Exod.* 75); on the other hand, we have the view justifying Jethro's departure so that he might spread the knowledge of monotheism among his fellow Midianites (*Tan. B, Exod.* 73, *Mek., Yitro* 2). In effect, the contradictory views about Jethro parallel the divergent views of the rabbis with regard to the reception of proselytes; side by side with the prevalent view welcoming them[194] was the view of those such as Rabbi Ḥelbo (*b. Qid.* 70b, *b. Yeb.* 47b, *b. Nid.* 13b), who regarded them as being as injurious to Israel as a scab.

In sum, clearly, Philo shared this ambiguity in his attitude toward Jethro, but in the official biography of Moses, *Mos.*, he goes to the extreme, in his concern not to detract from the centrality of Moses, of omitting even the mention of Jethro's visit to Moses.

k. The Revelation at Sinai

Clearly confused in his geography, Pompeius Trogus (*ap.* Just. 36, *Epitoma* 2.14) states that Moses reached Damascus, his ancestral home, whereupon he took possession of Mount Sinai.

Apion (*ap. Ap.* 2.25) records that Moses ascended a mountain called Sinai, remained there in concealment for forty days, and then descended and gave the Jews their laws. He thus attempted to show that Moses sought to deceive the Israelites by claiming that the laws that he had brought were of divine origin, when actually he himself had composed them. Gager 1972, 124, concludes that Apion, as an official of the Museum, may have been familiar with the LXX, but this remains nothing more than a possibility, because the motif of Moses' stay on the mountain is frequent in the magical papyri; or, alternatively, Apion and other non-Jewish Alexandrian writers may have been familiar with such alleged Graeco-Jewish historians as Artapanus and Eupolemus, or with the tragedy by Ezekiel on the exodus from Egypt. We may respond, however, that Apion knows that Moses was on Mount Sinai for forty days, precisely the length of time that he was there according to the Pentateuch (Exod. 24:18); and this would seem to indicate that he knew the LXX or that, at any rate, he had oral contact with a Jew. Stern 1974, 1:397, suggests that Apion attempted to show that Moses' sojourn on Sinai was part of his plan to deceive the Israelites into thinking that the laws were of divine origin, and that this is in line with the rationalistic criticism of other revelations, such as those of Minos and Lycurgus, as indicated in Strabo (16.2.38–39.762). Unlike the other Alexandrian versions of Moses, which stress his opposition to the Egyptian religion, Apion asserts that it was the basis of his new religious outlook in Jerusalem, and that Moses was, in effect, a plagiarist who had appropriated the doctrines of Egyptian predecessors—perhaps another allusion to Akhenaton, who was so despised that he had become a non-person and whose very name was anathema to the Egyptians.

Arnaldez 1967, commenting on Philo, *Mos.* 2.65, is very surprised that Philo in this treatise does not deal with the most important event in the life of Moses, namely the revelation at Sinai (neither, for that matter, does Ezekiel in the extant fragments of his *Exagoge*). However, Philo (*Mos.* 2.46) says that the Pentateuch consists of two parts, one historical and the other concerned with commands and prohibitions. He then states that in the present treatise on Moses he will deal with the historical side and that he will reserve the other for a later occasion, presumably other treatises. This explains why he omits the account of the revelation of Sinai, which he does, indeed, deal with in his treatises *Decal.*, *Spec.*, and *Virt.* On the other hand, Pseudo-Philo is primarily theological in his orientation; and, unsurprisingly, the revelation at Sinai (11) is a central event in his work.

The Samaritan tradition (*Molad*, p. 65, ll. 2–12) places extraordinary emphasis on the revelation at Sinai and on the miracles associated with it. It claims that Moses fasted 120 days, corresponding to the three times that he was supposedly on Sinai, each time for a period of forty days and forty nights.

Philo realized that his contemporaries associated cities with civilization and culture and learning, and he therefore felt that he had to explain (*Decal.* 2) why Moses chose to promulgate his laws in the seemingly uninspiring atmosphere of the desert. He explains the choice of the desert because most cities are full of countless evils, both acts of impiety toward G-d and wrongdoing between man and man. Moreover, according to Philo, cities are associated with pride and vanity (*Decal.* 3–7), which are the sources of wars, both civil and foreign, and which bring divine things into contempt. In addition (*Decal.* 10–13), those who are about to receive the laws must cleanse themselves of the stains that they have contacted through contact with the promiscuous urban crowds. Indeed, it is better to provide oneself with the rules of life before settling in communities, and it is necessary to establish that the laws are not the invention of man but of G-d. This the Israelites were able to do in the desert, where they received the manna and the quail as a gift of G-d. Finally (15–17), he felt that when they would see the sudden abundance of food and drink through G-d's beneficence in the desert, they would realize that the laws were of divine origin.

This negative attitude toward urban life will also help to explain Philo's admiration for the Therapeutae. It may also be a commentary on Philo's own experience in the huge city of Alexandria. "For every city," he says almost autobiographically (*Contempl.* 19), referring to an apparent attempt to find the leisure to philosophize, "even the best governed, is full of turmoils and disturbances innumerable which no one could endure who has ever been even once under the guidance of wisdom." He may also be referring to the attempt (*Mos.* 2.36–37) of the translators of the Pentateuch into Greek to find peace and tranquillity for their work in seclusion on the island of Pharos.

In the biblical version (Exod. 19:7–8) Moses summons the elders and puts before them all the words that G-d has commanded him. Elsewhere (*Conf.* 58) Philo includes the united response of all the people (Exod. 19:8): "All that the L-rd has spoken we will do." Philo (*Her.* 17), discussing the verse (Exod. 19:19) "Moses spoke and G-d answered him," emphasizes that the verbs have the force of the imperfect tense, that is of continuous action, and hence mean "was speaking" and "was answering," indicating that a steady stream of words came forth from Moses. Similarly, G-d did not teach him (as a completed action) but was answering him always and without interruption. According to the Bible (Exod. 20:19), the Israelites said to Moses, "You speak to us, and we will hear; but let not G-d speak to us, lest we die." Philo (*Her.* 19) deduces from this that wise men take G-d for their guide and teacher, but that the less perfect take the wise man, clearly identified here with Moses. Philo (*Decal.* 18) was confronted with the tremendous question as to whether the laws came directly from G-d or whether they were mediated by Moses: his compromise solution here is that G-d saw fit to deliver some of the laws in His own person alone without employing anyone else, and some through His prophet Moses.

In the Bible (Exod. 28:1), G-d tells Moses to bring near to himself Aaron and his sons to minister as priests to Him without any indication of their qualifications for this office and without any indication that the people should be consulted before making this choice. Furthermore, one of the issues raised by Korah in his later revolt is the fact that Moses proceeded to appoint his brother Aaron as high priest, which would seem to be a case of nepotism. Philo (*Mos.* 2.142–43) addresses himself to all these issues. In the first place, it is Moses and not G-d who makes the selection. Secondly, we are told that he did so on the basis of Aaron's merits. Thirdly, we are told that it is not a case of nepotism, inasmuch as he did not appoint his own sons but was moved, rather, by the piety and holiness that he observed in the merits of Aaron and the latter's sons. Finally, we are informed that the installation was made with the consent of the whole nation.[195]

In sum, some of the opponents of the Jews and perhaps some of Philo's contemporaries, if we may believe that Korah's agreement with this point of view had its followers in Philo's own day, claimed that the Pentateuch was not authored by G-d but by Moses. Philo does not deal in his *Mos.* with the revelation at Sinai because that treatise is a biography of Moses, whereas he wishes to make it clear that the revelation at Sinai was not the work of Moses but rather the word of G-d. Furthermore, when in *Decal.* he does deal with the revelation, Philo, coming from the huge metropolitan area of Alexandria, the leading cultural center of the world in his day, feels constrained to explain to his sophisticated and, one may guess, large urban audience why G-d chose to reveal Himself in the desert rather than in an urban setting, namely to avoid the countless evils of cities.

l. The Golden Calf

Truly a major test of Moses' leadership came when the Israelites built the Golden Calf (Exod. 32:1–6).[196] This is a most embarrassing incident, since there is hardly, from the biblical point of view, a greater sin than idolatry; and one approach that Philo might have taken in dealing with it was simply to omit it, since we find that both the rabbis and Josephus apparently do not feel any qualms about omitting certain biblical passages in their summaries or paraphrases.[197]

Josephus totally omits the account of the Golden Calf in his paraphrase of the Bible in the *Antiquities*[198] not only because it reflects badly upon the Israelites as a people so fickle that they quickly forgot all the miracles that G-d had performed for them, but also because it cast Moses himself in a bad light as a hot-tempered leader and because it was most disgraceful that Aaron, the high priest, should have led the Israelites to and presided over the worst kind of idolatry. Josephus was, we may assume, particularly sensitive to the incident because a leading anti-Semite, Apion (*ap.* Josephus, *Ap.* 2.80, 114, 120), reports similarly that the Jews worshipped an ass's head in the Temple. Moreover, being a priest and very proud of his belonging to the first of the twenty-four courses of priests (*Life* 2), Josephus stresses the high priest Aaron's possession of the four cardinal virtues.[199]

A major reason why Philo includes and indeed emphasizes this incident is that he feels the need to condemn idolatry, since it honors the works of people's hands. "Let no one, then," he says (*Decal.* 76), "who has a soul worship a soulless thing, for it is utterly preposterous (τῶν ἀτόπων, "extraordinary," "paradoxical," "unnatural") that the works of nature [i.e., humans] should turn aside to do service to what human hands have wrought." But the Egyptians, he goes on to say, have gone beyond all other peoples in that, "in addition to wooden and other images, they have advanced to divine honors irrational animals (ζῷα ἄλογα), bulls and rams and goats, and invented for each some fabulous legend of wonder." Indeed, in his attack on polytheism, Philo (*Ebr.* 110) is particularly critical of those who set G-d's honor at naught by deifying that which is mortal; and, as if it were not enough to fashion images of sun and moon, they go to the absurd length of allowing irrational plants and animals to share in the honor that belongs to imperishable things. Moreover, in enumerating here the irrational animals worshipped by the Egyptians, it is significant that the first animals that he mentions are bulls; and the word that Philo uses for the Golden Calf in describing this incident is the Greek word for "bull," ταῦρος, a clear indication that the Israelites were ready to return to the worship of this animal, so crucial in the religion of the Egyptians.

We see this extreme aversion to idolatry in Philo's account of the conversion of Tamar (see Niehoff 2001, 30). There is nothing in the biblical account (Gen. 38:6–30) to indicate that she was an idol-worshipper, but apparently Philo (*Virt.* 220–22) understood her to be such since she was not directly related to the line of Abraham, Isaac, and Jacob. Philo presents her as an example of those women "who unlearnt the errors of their breeding, the ignorance which led them to honor the works of men's hands, and became schooled in the knowledge of the monarchical principle by which the world is governed." In this conversion she is said to be parallel to Abraham himself, in that "she deserted to the camp of piety at the risk of her life," since she came to the realization that the good life meant to be the servant of the one Creator.[200]

Why did Philo include the account of the Golden Calf and, indeed, include it twice in his more or less official biography of Moses (*Mos.* 2.161–73, 270–74) and make reference to it in no fewer than seven of his other treatises: *Sacr.* 130; *Post.* 158–67; *Ebr.* 66–71, 95–110, 121–26; *Migr.* 85; *Her.* 19–20; *Fug.* 90–92; *Spec.* 1.79, 3.124–27? Presumably, the incident is of particular relevance to Philo in stressing the tremendous difference between the Jewish conception of the one G-d and the pagan polytheism and between the rational and the irrational and in praising the tremendous role played by the Levites in extirpating the sinful worshippers of the Golden Calf, whom he, the philosopher, identifies with the mortal enemies of true wisdom, the Sophists.

It is significant that in the Bible this episode comes after the designation of Bezalel and Oholiab as the architects of the Tabernacle (Exod. 31), whereas in Philo (*Mos.* 2.141–60) it comes after the description of the inauguration of the priesthood for the Tabernacle. The Bible does not explain why Aaron and his sons were chosen as priests other than that G-d ordered Moses to do so (Exod. 30:30). Philo (*Mos.* 2.159) presents an extra-biblical explanation of the origin of the role played by the Levites as temple attendants, namely that, since the Israelites were so populous and so pious, it became necessary to have a correspondingly large number of temple attendants to help in the conduct of the religious services. He then adds that the Levites were chosen for this purpose as a reward for their courageous and loyal behavior in fighting idolatry and in upholding the worship of the sole G-d during the incident that follows, namely that of the Golden Calf. Indeed, in an editorial-like remark, Philo declares that they were chosen in a very novel and unusual manner and then proceeds to tell the story of the Golden Calf. Philo (*Mos.* 2.173) clearly approved of this reward, since, as he says, "it was right that those who had voluntarily taken up arms for the honor of G-d and so quickly achieved success should receive the priesthood, and thus be worthily promoted to be His ministers."[201]

As to why Pseudo-Philo (12) includes the account of the Golden Calf, Begg 1996, 592, has insightfully remarked that the story fits in very well with Pseudo-Philo's view throughout his work of Israel's history as marked by the contrast between the people's recurring infidelity and G-d's constant renewal of His promises to His people, while punishing those who deviate from His revealed Law.

The biblical narrative (Exod. 32:1) begins with the statement that the Israelites saw that Moses had delayed in descending from Mount Sinai, whereupon they gathered around Aaron and told him to make for them gods (Pseudo-Philo [12.2] adds, reminiscent of their later demand for a king [1 Sam. 8:5], "as the other nations have"), since they did not know what had become of Moses.[202] There is as yet no indication of condemnation of the Israelites, and it is not until the next day that we read (Exod. 32:2–6) that Aaron told them to bring their rings, which he fashioned into a molten calf, and built an altar upon which he offered sacrifices to the Golden Calf. Whereas in the Bible (Exod. 32:2) Aaron, without making any attempt to calm them down or to deter them, immediately tells them to bring him the women's golden rings, Philo (*Mos.* 2.162, 2.270) does not mention the role of Aaron at all; instead, we are told that it was the Israelites who fashioned a "golden bull" in imitation of the Egyptians. In fact, he does not mention the name of Aaron at all in connection with the whole incident, let alone Moses' rebuke of Aaron for fashioning the Golden Calf. He may well have agreed with those rabbis who attempt to exonerate Aaron by insisting that his very life was threatened by the people and that Aaron agreed to make the Golden Calf only after procrastinating as long as possible by his own delaying tactics (*b. Sanh.* 7a, *Midr. Exod. Rab.* 37.2 and 41.7) and by playing on the piety of the women (*Pirqe R. El.* 45).[203] It is Aaron's love of peace that deterred him from putting to death those who worshipped the Golden Calf (see *Eliyahu Rabbah* 13.63 and 31.157); indeed, unlike Moses, who insisted on applying the law strictly, he is depicted as using every device in order to reconcile litigants (*'Abot R. Nat.* A 12). In fact, it was because of his love of peace that he was chosen to be high priest (*Midr. Exod. Rab.* 37.2); and consequently he becomes the role model for those who prefer peaceful persuasion as the best means of instilling love of the Torah, whence Hillel's dictum: "Be of the disciples of Aaron, loving peace and pursuing peace, loving people and bringing them near to the Torah" (*m. 'Abot* 1:12).

The biblical text (Exod. 32:2) gives no indication that Aaron tried to deter the Israelites. On the contrary, he tells them to bring their gold earrings, and he fashions them into a molten calf. Pseudo-Philo, however, again in defense of Aaron, states that he saw that the people would not heed him. Indeed, he reminded himself of G-d's statement, in connection with the building of the Tower of Babel, that if He did not deter them, they would only venture to do something even worse. Consequently, in his fear,[204] because the people were greatly strengthened, he told them to bring him the earrings of their wives, which they cast into a fire. Philo might have sought to excuse Aaron on similar grounds but apparently decided against it because, we may surmise, he felt that the person who was to be chosen to be the high priest should not have succumbed to such fear; and so he chose the path of silence and omitted the role of Aaron altogether. Strikingly, the LXX text (Exod. 32:4) reads "And he [i.e., Aaron] said, "These are your gods, O Israel," since, according to this reading, not only did Aaron acknowledge the calf to be divine, but he even acknowledged polytheism. This is in contrast to the text in the Hebrew: "And they [i.e., the Israelite masses] said." Moreover, whereas in the Hebrew (Exod. 32:6) it is the people who arise early in the morning to worship the Golden Calf, the LXX has verbs in the singular, indicating that it is Aaron who does so.[205]

In Pseudo-Philo's version (12.3), out came a molten calf, as if it happened by itself, whereas in the Bible (Exod. 32:4) we read that Aaron took the rings from the hands of the people, bound them in a cloth, and himself fashioned them into a molten calf. Indeed, later we read (Exod. 32:24) that Aaron himself threw the earrings into the fire and the calf emerged of itself. Only then (Exod. 32:7) do we find in the biblical narrative that G-d took the initiative to speak to Moses and to tell him that the Israelites had become corrupt in building and sacrificing to a molten calf. However, in Pseudo-Philo (12.3), in the interest of reducing the culpability of Aaron, it is the Israelites who cast the earrings into the fire and who fashioned them into a calf.[206]

On the other hand, Pseudo-Philo (12.2) condemns the Israelites as corrupt even before they come to Aaron. Whereas the Bible depicts the Israelites as being in a state of doubt as to what had happened to Moses, in Pseudo-Philo they are convinced that he has perished. Philo (*Mos.* 2.161), at the very beginning of his account, perhaps reflecting his own experience as a leader with respect to the masses, goes even further in condemning the Israelites as men of insecure (μὴ βέβαιοι) nature. In language reminiscent of Korah's rebellion, they think it a suitable opportunity, as if there were anarchy (ἀναρχία), and forgetting the reverence that they owed to G-d, to rush into impious practices unrestrainedly and to become zealous devotees of Egyptian forgeries (πλάσματα). Indeed, the very word (ἄφετοι) that Philo uses to describe the Israelites' lack of restraint is a word that means "letting loose" and is employed especially with regard to sacred flocks that are free from work and that range at large at pasture[207]—a clear allusion to the fact that they are building and worshipping an animal, namely a calf (bull) that roams at large. When the molten calf emerges, the Israelites, according to the Bible (Exod. 32:4), proclaim that this was the god who had delivered them from Egypt.

The biblical Aaron now built an altar and declared that the following day was to be a festival for G-d, whereupon early the next day the people offered sacrifices, ate, drank, and were merry. Pseudo-Philo says nothing of the altar, the sacrifices, and the merriment.[208]

Philo, who as a leader of the Jewish community in Egypt, must have been aware of the attraction that the Egyptian way of life had for some of the Jews of his own day, in a strong condemnatory tone, makes a point (*Mos.* 2.162) of noting that the Golden Calf (which he terms a bull, ταῦρος) was in imitation of the animal, Apis, which, he notes, is the one held most sacred in Egypt.[209] In effect, Philo is saying that the very people who were delivered from Egypt have succumbed to the worship of the god that the Egyptians worship. We may also suggest that since from the embalmed bull, which was called Osiris-Apis (Diodorus 1.85.4), the cult of Sarapis, which was so popular, especially in Alexandria, was developed during the Hellenistic period, Philo's revulsion may reflect his reaction to the attraction that the Sarapis cult had in his own day. Whereas the biblical narrative gives no reason as to why the Israelites chose to fashion their god in the form of a calf, Philo (*Mos.* 2.161), on a number of occasions in referring to the incident, says that the calf was in imitation of Egyptian animal worship (*Sacr.* 130; *Post.* 158, 165).

As Niehoff 2001, 46, has most appositely noted, the Egyptians are the only ethnic group that Philo places in diametrical opposition to the Jews. They are viewed (*Sacr.* 130) as the personification of body and as the enemies of the Israelites. He refers to the defection as a change of habits (ἐκδιαίτησις), a veritable reversal of life style. The Israelites are no longer mere sinners but utter apostates who have deserted to another way of life. Perhaps Philo is thinking of his nephew, Tiberius Julius Alexander, who, as Josephus (*A.J.* 20.100) puts it, "did not stand by the practices of his people," and of others like him in Alexandria. Though the LXX refers (Exod. 32:4, 8, 19, 20, 24, 35) to the animal worshipped by the Israelites as a golden calf (μόσχος) and though elsewhere (*Post.* 158, 162, 163, 166; *Ebr.* 96, 124; and *Fug.* 90) Philo sometimes refers to the animal as a calf, in what is, in effect, the quasi-official biography of Moses, *Mos.* 2.162 and 2.270, he never speaks of it as a calf but only as a bull (ταῦρος). Indeed, he speaks of the bull as the symbol of the Egyptians (*Ebr.* 95).

It is important to note that Philo does not treat all forms of polytheism in the same fashion. Thus, as Mendelson 1988, 34–38, indicates, in connection with worship there is a hierarchy (*Decal.* 52–81) descending from the more sublime to the ridiculous—astral worship, pantheism, deification of certain elements, idol worship, worship of domesticated animals, and worship of savage animals. On a purely theoretical level, Philo (*Anim.* 77–100), in his debate with his nephew Tiberius Julius Alexander, argues that since animals are not rational, they do not act rationally; hence, he concludes, "to elevate animals to the level of the human race, and to grant equality to unequals is the height of injustice."[210] By this criterion the Egyptians, whom Philo identifies with the gods whom they worshipped (Borgen 1997, 211), are the most debased. Indeed, Philo reduces to absurdity (*Spec.* 1.79) the foolish attachment of the Egyptians to irrational animals, and especially to bulls, and the Israelites' construction of a golden bull in imitation of Egyptian vanity (τῦφος, "delusion," "nonsense," "humbug") attached to irrational animals (ἐπ' ἀλόγοις ζῴοις) (*Spec.* 3.125). He has a particularly strong attack on the Egyptian worship of animals, which he reduces to absurdity, in fact lowering the worshippers to sub-human status (*Decal.* 79–80): "Indeed, strangers, on their first arrival in Egypt before the vanity of the land has gained a lodgement in their minds, are likely to die with laughing at it, while anyone who knows the flavor of right instruction, horrified at this veneration of things so much the reverse of venerable, pities those who render it and regards them with good reason as more miserable than the creatures they honor, as men with souls transformed into the nature of those creatures, so that as they pass before him, they seem beasts in human shape."[211] It is hardly decent, says Philo (*Contempl.* 8), even to mention the gods of the Egyptians, since they "have promoted to divine honors irrational animals, not only of the tame sort but also beasts of the utmost savagery. . . . They render worship to them, the civilized to the uncivilized and untamed, the reasonable to the irrational, the kinsfolk of the G-dhead to ugliness unmatched even by a Thersites [*Iliad* 2.216–19], the rulers and masters to the naturally subservient and slavish."[212] Philo is here, in effect, refuting the claim made by Artapanus (*ap.* Eus. *PE* 9.27.4) that Moses assigned cats, dogs, and ibises as gods to the Egyptians. Elsewhere, to be sure, Philo (*Mos.* 1.23) states that when Moses was young, learned Egyptians instructed him in the regard paid to animals, to which they even paid divine honors; but he quickly adds (*Mos.* 1.24) that Moses sought only for truth, since his mind was incapable of accepting any falsehood.

Philo, significantly, uses the same language with regard to the rebellious son (*Ebr.* 95) that he uses with regard to the worshippers of the Golden Calf, namely that he has made a god of the body, that this god is a god of the vanity most honored among the Egyptians, and that its symbol is the image of the golden bull. Just as the rebellious son in the Bible (Deut. 21:18–21) merits the death penalty, so do the worshippers of the Golden Calf. Significantly, Pseudo-Philo (12.3), who apparently does not have the association with Egypt that Philo has, refers to the animal that the Israelites worship as a calf (*vitulus*) rather than as a bull.

Whereas the Bible briefly states that the Israelites offered burnt offerings and peace offerings and ate, drank, and got up to revel, Philo (*Mos.* 2.162) considerably embellishes the account in strong notes of censure and ridicule, asserting that "they offered sacrifices that were no sacrifices, set up choirs that were no choirs (χοροὶ ἀχόρευτοι), sang hymns that were funeral chants, and, filled with strong drink, were overcome by the twofold intoxication of wine and folly. And so, revelling and carousing the livelong night, and unwary of the future, they lived wedded to their pleasant vices, while justice, the unseen watcher of them and the punishments they deserved, stood ready to strike." The portrait that Philo paints is highly reminiscent of that of the rebellious son (Deut. 21:18–21, *Ebr.* 14–29), particularly the drinking, the reveling and carousing. The disobedient son is depicted as paying contributions, that is, joining a social association or club, where religious activities always played a key role, as they did in the case of the Golden Calf. Borgen, citing this analogy, insightfully suggests that Philo, in his depiction in such similar terms of the Golden Calf incident, is criticizing, by implication, fellow Jews who joined such clubs (see Borgen 1997, 170–71).

In a reprise of this incident, when Philo (*Mos.* 2.270) repeats Moses' exhortations to the Israelites, he recalls their great backsliding from their ancestral traditions and mentions that they had "set up choirs and built altars and brought victims for sacrifice in forgetfulness of the true G-d and to the ruin of the highborn qualities inherited from their forefathers and fostered by piety and holiness." We may call attention to the mention of choirs, since the Levites, who came to Moses' side to slay those who had participated in the worship of the Golden Calf, sang in choirs in the Tabernacle and Temple service; and it is the Levites who will rise up against these carousers and choirs of false worshippers and kill them. Indeed, Philo (*Mos.* 2.271) significantly repeats the mention of the choirs when he declares Moses' utter amazement that the whole people had suddenly been blinded who a few hours before had witnessed G-d's miracles, "on which no eclipse of the sun or of all the starry choir (χορός) can cast a shadow."

At this point the biblical text (Exod. 32:7) declares that it is G-d who told Moses to descend quickly (Deut. 9:12), since the Israelites have become corrupt in that they have made a molten calf for themselves and worshipped it.

He then declares His intention to annihilate the Israelites and to make a nation out of Moses himself. One would hardly expect that Moses, at the summit of the mountain, could hear the commotion far below; but Philo, realizing that a true leader is always concerned with his people, adds (*Mos.* 2.163) that Moses heard the commotion. Still, since the reader might well wonder why, if so, Moses did not descend immediately to halt this most impious of deeds, Philo explains that Moses was in a dilemma between, on the one hand, G-d's love for him and his reluctance to leave his communion with G-d, since he talked with G-d on intimate terms, and, on the other hand, his concern not to disregard the people, now beset by anarchy. Though the noise was seemingly inarticulate, Moses, says Philo, with his extraordinary sensitivity, recognized it for what it was, namely insolence (ὕβρις), and was able to analyze the cause, namely drunkenness, which begets confusion and riot and lawlessness, since intemperance begets satiety, and satiety riot (*Mos.* 2.164). Philo, as a leader of the Jewish community of Egypt and a conservative by nature and very suspicious of the mob, centers his attack on the lawlessness of the Israelites. It was only then that G-d intervened and told him to descend (*Mos.* 2.165), since, He says, the Israelites have run after lawlessness. Even so, lest the reader should think that Moses, the great and patient leader of his people, acted in a fit of temper, Philo (*Mos.* 2.166) says that Moses was actually compelled to believe the incredible deeds of the Israelites, the implication being that Moses at first refused to believe that his people had acted thus.

In the Bible at this point G-d in His anger told Moses that He would annihilate the Israelites and instead would create a great nation out of him (Exod. 32:10), whereupon Moses pleaded with G-d to relent from His anger. Philo (*Mos.* 2.166), while portraying G-d's anger with the Israelites because of their building of the Golden Calf, was apparently troubled by the fact that G-d was ready to condemn the entire nation when only one-half of one percent, three thousand, were put to death as sinners (Exod. 32:28) out of six hundred thousand adult male Israelites. In his reluctance to depict a G-d Who loses His temper and for a single sinful act is ready to annihilate the entire nation of Israel, Philo totally omits G-d's determination to annihilate them, presumably because this would appear to be inconsistent with G-d's promise to Abraham, Isaac, and Jacob that He would give their descendants the Land of Israel.

Pseudo-Philo, who (12.4) strongly reasserts G-d's promise to the Israelites that He will not forsake them, likewise totally omits G-d's angry declaration that He will annihilate the Israelites and start all over again with Moses himself. In Pseudo-Philo's version (12.4) G-d says that in view of their current behavior He knows that when they enter the Land of Israel they will do even greater iniquities. He says, however, that while He will abandon them now, He will ultimately be reconciled with them so that a house may be built among them that will, in turn, be destroyed because they will have sinned against Him.

In Philo's version (*Mos.* 2.166), Moses takes the role of mediator (μεσίτης) and reconciler (διαλλακτής). Indeed, Philo presents Moses as the great intercessor for his people. In describing the ceremony (*Mos.* 2.147) of the installation of the priesthood, Philo had said that Moses ordered a calf and two rams to be brought. The offering of the calf, he says, was to gain remission of sins, "showing that sin is congenital to every created being, even the best, just because they are created; and this sin requires prayers and sacrifices to propitiate the Deity, lest His wrath be roused and visited upon them." Most ironically, it is so shortly after the offering of this calf for the remission of sins at the dedication of the priesthood that the greatest sin in the history of the Israelites, the building of the perversion of the calf, namely the Golden Calf, occurs, and with the consent of the very person at the ceremony who had been inducted as high priest. Surely, it is significant that in describing at such length the incident that follows this dedication Philo says not a word about the role of the high priest, Aaron.

Similarly, it is Pseudo-Philo, whose overall theme, as we see over and over again, notably in the tremendous development of the figure of the judge Kenaz, is the importance of inspired leadership, who develops especially the aspect of Moses as mediator and intercessor. Thus in Moses' pleading with G-d in connection with the sin of the Golden Calf, Pseudo-Philo (12.8–9) develops an elaborate metaphor, in which Moses begs G-d not to be angry with the vine that He Himself has planted.

What disturbed Philo most was that the Israelites, who only a short time previously had excelled every nation in clearness of vision, had suddenly succumbed to the worship of a golden bull (*Mos.* 2.270, *Ebr.* 95, *Spec.* 3.125), in imitation of the very animal held most sacred in the country, Egypt, from which they had fled.

Furthermore, Philo adds (*Mos.* 2.166) that Moses did not leap down (ἀπεπήδησεν) immediately but first made supplication and prayer to G-d, begging Him to forgive the sins of the people. Philo does not, however, present the daring contents of Moses' pleading (Exod. 32:11–13), in which, in effect, Moses asks G-d why His anger should flare up against His own people whom He had just taken out of Egypt. Did He do so, he asks in the Bible, in order to annihilate them? Moses has to recall to G-d His oath to Abraham, Isaac, and Jacob to increase their offspring and to give them the Land of Israel. This reminds one of Abraham's pleading with G-d not to destroy Sodom if there are righteous people left in the city, the implication being that a just G-d would not destroy innocent people. Philo omits this dialogue presumably because it makes it appear that Moses is more merciful than G-d. Furthermore, in the Deuteronomic version of the incident (Deut. 9:20) Moses states that G-d was angry enough with Aaron to have destroyed him, whereupon Moses asserts that he interceded for Aaron. Philo omits this passage altogether, though it does glorify Moses as an intercessor, presumably because it diminishes the stature of Aaron and paints a picture of G-d as less merciful than Moses.

We are then told (Exod. 32:14) that G-d reconsidered and decided not to annihilate the Israelites. This, however, raises the question whether this does not present a G-d who is less than perfect, since a perfect G-d would not have to reconsider.[213] Finally, Philo remarks, Moses descended with mixed emotions, dejection at what his people had done but joy that G-d had accepted his prayers. All this adds to the stature of Moses as a leader devoted to his people.

The biblical text (Exod. 32:15) asserts that Moses descended from the mountain with the two tablets, inscribed by G-d, in his hand. Joshua, we are informed, hearing the shouting of the people, told Moses that the sound of battle was in the camp, whereupon Moses declared that it was the sound of distress. Moses (Exod. 32:19–20) then, in a burst of anger, shattered the tablets that he had brought down, burnt the Golden Calf and ground it to a fine powder, sprinkled it with water, and forced the people to drink it. We may wonder what effect this had upon those who drank it. Such a burst of temper, one would think, is hardly becoming for a leader. Additionally, one may wonder how gold can be burnt, how it can be ground into powder, how one can grind what is already burnt, and how the gold could not have sunk in the water.[214] Moreover, how could Moses have shattered the tablets when they contained the name of G-d Himself? Furthermore, one might well wonder how a man who is eighty years old could have carried two large stone tablets inscribed with the commandments down from a mountain. Moreover, one would have expected a leader to inquire whether there were some who had not joined in building the Golden Calf, whereas in the Bible it is only after his outburst that Moses asks those who are for G-d to join him.

In order to answer these questions we must first ask for whom was Philo intending his treatises, especially the extended accounts in *Mos.* 2.161–73, 270–74. There is perhaps some reason to think, as we can see from the contradictory views that he expresses about such figures as Joseph (see Feldman 1998a, 338–40) and Jethro (see Feldman 1998b, 441–43), that not all the treatises were addressed to the same audience. What is most striking is that Philo in his *Post.* 158–65 does mention and indeed expounds at some length allegorically the biblical statement (Exod. 32:20) that "he [Moses] took the calf which they had made and burnt it with fire and ground it to powder and scattered it upon the water and made the people of Israel drink it." But in the much more extended account in *Mos.* there is not a word about any of these deeds of Moses.

Philo, aware of these considerations, omits (*Mos.* 2.167) the fact that Moses carried down the stone tablets. As to the statement that Moses smashed the tablets when they contained the holy writing of G-d upon them, Philo solves this problem by simply omitting the smashing of the tablets. On the other hand, in Pseudo-Philo's version (12.5), which does mention the smashing of the tablets, we read that Moses looked upon the tablets and saw that they were not written upon[215] and then proceeded to smash them. Pseudo-Philo (12.7) does add the effect that the drinking had, namely that whoever had intended that the calf be made, his tongue was cut off, but whoever had consented because of compulsion of fear, his face shone.[216] Additionally, in an extra-biblical addition, Philo (*Mos.* 2.167) declares that he noticed that not everyone had joined in building the calf and that there were still some who were sound at heart and who cherished a feeling of hatred for evil. Both the Bible (Exod. 32:26) and Philo (*Mos.* 2.168) note Moses' words, namely that if there were some who had not contributed to the building of the Golden Calf and who believed that the works of men's hands are not gods but that there was only one G-d, they should join him; however, Philo not only quotes Moses' words, but he also remarks that the words were few, yet had much significance. We are told that some, whose particular devotion was to the Egyptian life style, rebelled, fearing either the punishment that would be inflicted upon them by Moses or the onslaught of the mob, since, as Philo remarks (*Mos.* 2.169), in an editorial-like comment revealing his distrust of the masses, "The multitude always set upon those who refuse to share their madness."

In his concern to defend Aaron, Philo, like Pseudo-Philo (12.3), totally omits Moses' rebuke of Aaron and Aaron's reply (Exod. 32:21–24), the very portion of the episode that the Mishnah (*Meg.* 4.10) says may be read but not translated in public.[217] In thus defending Aaron, Philo would appear to be in line with rabbinic tradition (*Eliyahu Rabbah* 13.63, 31.157).[218]

When Moses, upon descending, asked those who were on G-d's side to come to him, all his fellow-Levites (Exod. 32:26) gathered around him. Philo (*Mos.* 2.170) has elaborated their zeal considerably. In his version they came running with all speed, "like troops for whom one signal is enough," coming "like racers from the starting-point" (*Mos.* 2.171). Moses then put them to the test, telling each of them to take his sword and to slay "those whose deeds deserve a thousand deaths." Philo (*Spec.* 1.79) elsewhere also praises their championship of piety (εὐσέβεια), which led them to do a truly conspicuous (εὐαγές) deed. Their readiness, we are told, anticipated Moses' exhortations, "for their sentiments had been hostile to the offenders almost from the first moment that they saw their misconduct" (*Mos.* 2.172). In fact, according to Philo's addition (*Mos.* 2.273), the Levites, presumably even before Moses had spoken to them, had for some time been "breathing slaughter against the godless workers of unholiness" but merely were waiting to find a leader who would have the right to tell them when and how to attack. Moses then gave them the order in the strongest possible terms: "Mow them down, holding that to be a truly righteous deed which is done for truth and G-d's honor, a cause which to champion and defend is the lightest of labors." Indeed, they proceeded to slaughter to the number of three thousand, from the youth upwards, including those who but a short while before had been their dearest. Philo then adds (*Mos.* 2.274) that they met no resistance at all and that they were thus accounted the noblest of heroes and awarded the prize most suitable to their action, namely the priesthood.

Apparently, not everyone agreed with this bold act of the Levites, since, as Philo adds (*Mos.* 2.172), as the corpses of the slain lay in the middle of the market-place, the multitude felt pity for them, but they felt wisdom from fear, being terror-stricken at "the still heated and wrathful resolution of the slayers." Moreover, Philo, clearly apologetic, realized, it would seem, that a reader would wonder how the leader of a nation could give the order to these loyal adherents, namely the Levites, to slay not only those who were strangers to them, but even their friends and relations. He explains that Moses gave these orders when he was more than ever possessed by the divine spirit, so that he was changed in both outward appearance and mind (*Mos.* 2.272), and that the deed of the Levites was being done for the sake of truth and G-d's honor (*Mos.* 2.273) and that consequently they were deservedly rewarded with the priesthood.

This exaltation by Philo of the Levites, far beyond the brief statement in the Bible, is in line with his praise of the Levites, who in their cities of refuge receive others as exiles; thus, in effect, they themselves are exiles, having left their families in order to receive an immortal portion (*Sacr.* 129). As Nikiprowetzky (1996, 32–43) has suggested, the Therapeutae, whom Philo praises so highly in *Contempl.* as servants of G-d, have a name that is often associated with the term for suppliants, a term that applies also to the Levites, who are similarly depicted as contemplative philosophers. Philo thus identifies himself, as a philosopher, with the Levites.

We may suggest that Josephus, on the other hand, was particularly sensitive to the attempt of the Levites to attain the status of priests. Thus we may recall that during the procuratorship of Albinus (62–64 C.E.), those Levites who were singers of hymns succeeded in persuading King Agrippa II to convene the Sanhedrin and to grant them permission to wear linen robes on equal terms with the priests (*A.J.* 20.216–18).[219] This, says Josephus, was contrary to the ancestral laws, and he ominously declares that such transgression was bound to make the Jews liable to punishment, presumably by G-d Himself (*A.J.* 20.218). Josephus may have omitted the incident of the Golden Calf from his work not only because of the unflattering image of the Israelites but also because of the role, especially embarrassing to Josephus, the proud priest, played by Aaron, the ancestor of the priests, and because of the heroic action of the Levites, who were the rivals of the priestly class to which he belonged.[220]

Interestingly, Pseudo-Philo (12), who does not omit this incident in his version, says nothing at all about the role of the Levites; but, as Jacobson 1996, 1:484, correctly notes, Pseudo-Philo, throughout his account of this episode, tries vigorously to depict Aaron favorably and to absolve him of guilt. Unlike Josephus, who, as a priest, has a particular reason for seeking to protect the reputation of Aaron, Pseudo-Philo apparently does not; and he does not want to make it appear that he is denigrating Aaron while praising the Levites.

In the Bible, after the Levites have slain the defectors, Moses, the leader who is truly devoted to his people, implores G-d (Exod. 32:31–32) to forgive their sin of building the Golden Calf. Then, amazingly and with utter selflessness, he adds that if G-d will not forgive them He should erase him from His book. Philo quotes no fewer than five other verses (Num. 11:12, 13, 22; Exod. 5:22, 23) in which Moses boldly complains to G-d why He has afflicted the Israelites. Anyone, Philo remarks, would have been afraid to say these or similar words even to a human king, and yet Moses had the courage to declare this to G-d. Philo (*Her.* 19–20) develops this even further. Moses, he says, as the refined (ἀστεῖος) leader, is on such close terms with G-d and is so outspoken that he has the courage to speak out freely (παρρησία) and, what is more, has the confidence to inveigh against (καταβοᾶν) G-d, arising from true conviction (πίστις) and genuine feeling (ἀπὸ γνησίου τοῦ πάθους). Philo (*Her.* 21), aware that his readers might well ask how Moses could have dared to speak thus to G-d, explains that all the wise are friends of G-d and that frankness of speech (παρρησία) is akin to friendship rather than to wilfulness (αὐθαδεία). And yet, in his two accounts which more or less constitute an official biography of Moses, *Mos.*, and which are by far the most comprehensive account of the whole incident of the Golden Calf, there is no mention of G-d's determination to exterminate the Israelites, of G-d's decision to start a new people with Moses, and of Moses' colloquy with G-d succeeding in getting G-d to change His mind. Presumably, the portrayal of G-d being thus angry at all the Israelites without separating the guilty from the innocent and His changing His mind presented considerable theological problems. Pseudo-Philo (12.8–10), on the other hand, who has no problem in defending G-d's ways, has Moses' colloquy with G-d in which he successfully argues that if G-d destroys the Israelites, He will have created the world in vain and He will have no one to glorify Him; and even if He plants another vine (i.e., creates another race), it will not trust Him because He has destroyed the previous race.

Furthermore, Moses is characterized by unselfishness; and he shares his wise spirit (*Gig.* 27) with others, without losing anything of his own understanding (σύνεσις), knowledge (ἐπιστήμη) and wisdom (σοφία). When he, the guardian and intercessor, had propitiated G-d, he, in his devotion to his people, on the one hand, felt joy that G-d had accepted his supplication and, on the other hand, was filled to the point of swelling with anxiety and dejection at the transgression of the multitude (*Mos.* 2.166).

Once G-d has forgiven the Israelites, one would expect that He would immediately direct Moses to obtain another set of tablets. In the account in Deut., after Moses prays to G-d not to destroy the Israelites, G-d apparently forgives them and immediately (10:1) tells him to carve two more stone tablets and to ascend once again on Mount Sinai and have G-d inscribe the same words upon them that appeared in the first set. In the account in Exod. there is a brief interlude in which G-d tells Moses that because the Israelites are stubborn and in constant danger of sinning and of incurring His wrath, He cannot remain in their midst and that He must therefore send His angel instead (Exod. 33:1–3). It is only after this interlude that G-d tells Moses (Exod. 34:1) to prepare two stone tablets that He will inscribe with the words that were on the first tablets. In Deut. 10:4 we read that G-d inscribed the words.[221] Philo, however, totally omits Moses' second ascent to obtain another set of tablets, perhaps because the Bible itself seems to contradict itself, first (Exod. 34:1) declaring that G-d will inscribe the second set of tablets and then (Exod. 34:27–28) stating that G-d told Moses to write on the second tablets and that Moses did so. Presumably, Moses had received full knowledge of the commandments during his first stay and did not need to be reminded of them. Pseudo-Philo (12:10) seems to have a major change in that it is Moses rather than G-d who writes the second set of tablets, since He says, "Write again (*rescribe*) on them the commandments that were on the first ones."[222]

In sum, Philo's account of the Golden Calf incident is an extremely important and excellent indication of his whole approach to the treatment of Moses. In line with the tremendous attempt in the rabbinic tradition, as in Josephus, to absolve Aaron of blame in the making of the Golden Calf, Philo does not even mention the role of Aaron at all, and he omits Moses' rebuke of Aaron. Philo excuses Moses for not descending immediately, upon hearing the commotion attending the building of the Golden Calf, because of his reluctance to leave his communion with G-d. As a leader of the Jewish community in Egypt, Philo centers his attack on the lawlessness of the Israelites and on the fact that the Golden Calf was an imitation of the animal held most sacred in Egypt; indeed, in *Mos.* he refers to it as a bull, reminiscent of the Egyptian Apis, rather than as a calf. He makes much of the fact that the animal chosen was that of the Egyptians, the only nation that Philo places in diametrical opposition to the Jews. In his extreme aversion to idolatry, he is particularly distressed that the Israelites were ready to worship an irrational animal, the work of human hands.

Whereas Josephus, presumably because he found it embarrassing, omits the incident of the Golden Calf, Philo, despite the fact that he aims in *Mos.* to elevate the role of Moses, includes it, noting in particular that on his descent Moses, to his great credit, assumed the role of mediator and reconciler.

Disturbed by the fact that Moses, in a fit of temper, unbecoming to a great leader, smashed the tablets that he was carrying, Philo omits his smashing of the tablets and explains that Moses was actually compelled to believe the incredible deed of the Israelites. Similarly, in his reluctance to depict a G-d Who loses His temper and is ready to annihilate the entire nation of Israel, Philo omits G-d's determination to do so. Clearly troubled by the moral problem in condemning all the Israelites, Philo declares that Moses noticed that not everyone had joined in building the calf.

Philo develops considerably Moses' fiery command to his zealous fellow-Levites to put to death those responsible, including even their dear ones, for the building of the Golden Calf. He makes much of the origin of the Levites as temple attendants as a reward for their behavior in connection with this incident. Philo, aware that readers would wonder how Moses could have been so ruthless as to give such orders, explains that he did so when he was possessed by the divine spirit. Philo praises the courage of Moses in boldly complaining to G-d why He had afflicted the Israelites; but in the most comprehensive account of the episode in *Mos.*, Philo, aware of the theological problem in the biblical portrayal of G-d as being angry at all the Israelites and not separating the guilty from the innocent, makes no mention of G-d's determination to exterminate all the Israelites, of G-d's decision to start a new people with Moses, and of Moses' colloquy with G-d in which Moses is apparently more merciful and in which G-d, Who is supposedly unalterable in His ways, actually changes His mind and forgives the Israelites. Finally, Philo totally omits Moses' second ascent to obtain another set of tablets, perhaps because the Bible seems to contradict itself as to whether G-d or Moses inscribed the tablets.

m. *The Case of the Blasphemer*

The Bible (Lev. 24:10–16) recounts an incident in which a man blasphemed the name of G-d.[223] The account of Moses' reaction to the case of the blasphemer presented Philo with a real problem. How could the great lawgiver be ignorant of the law in this case when he had received the law not long before this? We may well ask why Philo, like Josephus, did not omit the story of the blasphemer, since Moses, in his ignorance, does not appear in a good light (Lev. 24:11–12). And if he did include the episode, why did he not place it in Book 1 of *Mos.* where it would seem to fit chronologically? The answer would appear to be that Philo himself (*Mos.* 2.187) asserts that in Book 1 he had discussed the qualities of Moses as king, lawgiver, and high priest, and that he had left for Book 2 Moses' quality as a prophet of the highest quality. Indeed, Philo (*Mos.* 2.192) cites four instances in the Torah where a divine voice laid down the law in the form of question and answer; the case here of the blasphemer, the individual who gathered wood on the Sabbath (Num. 15:32–36; Philo, *Mos.* 2.213–20), the second offering of the Paschal sacrifice (Num. 9:1–4; Philo, *Mos.* 2.222–32), and the daughters of Zelophehad (Num. 27:1–11; Philo, Mos. 2.234–45). One might think that the fact that in these four cases Moses, the great lawgiver, was apparently at a loss as to how to deal with them would seem to damage Moses' reputation as a lawgiver and leader; but Philo makes clear that there was no precedent in these four cases and hence that Moses had to communicate again directly with G-d. The prophet, says Philo (*Mos.* 2.190), asks questions of G-d about matters on which he has been seeking knowledge, and G-d replies and instructs him. This is precisely what happens in the case of the blasphemer and in the other three cases as well. Moses had to seek out G-d, and in return G-d bestowed upon him a prophecy with a divine ordinance. As Philo (*Mos.* 2.203) says, in a remarkable statement, a new ordinance had to be drawn up because there was no precedent, and "unexpected disorders" required divine intervention and the promulgation of a new law. The offense of the blasphemer is a theological offense, in questioning G-d's very existence. Hence Moses had to use his prophetic faculty in order to be informed by G-d directly.

Philo then apparently recognizes that his non-Jewish audience, with its liberal bent in viewing the many gods and with the precedent of none other than Achilles in Homer (*Il.* 22.15), who addresses Apollo, for example, as the most destructive (ὀλοώτατε) of all the gods, might wonder why one might not feel free to criticize and even use strong language against the gods. Therefore, he explains what it is about this crime that makes it so egregious, namely that refusal to reverence G-d implies refusal to honor parents and country and benefactors. He asks: "What depths of depravity remain for him to reach who besides refusing reverence dares also to revile G-d?" And yet, even reviling is a lesser sin compared with cursing. Such a person is sure to commit some monstrous violation of the moral law. He then asks of the blasphemer: "What other god does he call on to make good the curse, or is it clear that he invokes the help of G-d against Himself?"

Why does Philo expand so greatly the story of the blasphemer? The main point is that the blasphemer is an Egyptian, for if the story is presented merely to give us the punishment to be inflicted upon a blasphemer, why does it not omit narrative details and merely give us the nature of the crime and the punishment to be inflicted upon the offender? The answer seems to be that it is important to identify the offender as an Egyptian. Philo, as a leader of the Jewish community in Alexandria in Egypt, must have been aware of the attraction that the Egyptian way of life had for some of the Jews of his own day. The fact that the blasphemer was the product of a mixed marriage between a Jew and an Egyptian must have recalled for him such products of mixed marriages with Egyptians who accompanied the Israelites in the Exodus from Egypt.

One reason why Philo felt so strongly about the sin of the blasphemer was that he perceived (*Mos.* 2.198) that the blasphemer's refusal to reverence G-d implied refusal to honor parents and country and benefactors. Parents, he says (*Spec.* 2.229–30), are truly benefactors, inasmuch as they brought children out of non-existence and nurtured and educated them; indeed, Philo (*Ebr.* 13–98) has an extraordinarily long discussion justifying the penalty to be meted out to the rebellious son, where he equates the father of such a son with G-d and the mother with G-d's Wisdom.

Philo condemns the culprit, describing him as a bastard (νόθος), the product of a dissimilar (ἀνομοίων) relationship. He then adds that this man had paid no regard (ἠλόγησε) to the ancestral customs of his mother and instead had turned aside (ἀπέκλινεν) to Egyptian impiety and had zealously pursued (ζηλώσας, "desired emulously," "admired") the atheism of that people. He then specifies what this atheism of the Egyptians consisted of, namely that they set up earth as a power to challenge heaven, since they speak of the Nile River, through whose flooding the land is watered, as if it were the counterpart of heaven and hence worthy of being deified. He then adds the circumstances under which the blaspheming occurred, namely that this bastard had quarreled with a Jew and in his anger had lost control over himself and, impelled by Egyptian atheism, with his soul and tongue and all the organism of speech had cursed G-d, Whom even to bless is a privilege not permitted to all, but only to the best. The fact that, as Philo describes it, Moses did not rush to decree the execution of such a man reflects well on Moses' patience and his eagerness to proceed in precise accordance with the law.

It would seem to be embarrassing that Moses, who, after all, had been given a complete code of law by G-d, did not know (Lev. 24:10–12) what penalty to inflict upon the son of the Israelite woman who had blasphemed the name of G-d. The biblical text says merely that the man was brought to Moses and that he was placed under guard so that the punishment might be clarified by G-d. We are then told (Lev. 24:13–16) that G-d declared that the blasphemer was to be put to death by stoning. Since, we later learn (Num. 25:12–13), G-d, through awarding Phinehas with the covenant of peace and the eternal priesthood, approved the zealotry of Phinehas in taking the law into his own hands in putting Zimri to death for having relations with a Midianite woman, one might well wonder why Moses did not show similar zealotry in putting the blasphemer to death. Philo (*Mos.* 2.197–202), apparently disturbed by such a question, adds the extra-biblical comment that Moses was indeed astonished at the madness of the blasphemer. Moreover, filled with noble but desperate courage, he was ready to dismember him with his own hand, but he showed self-control since he was afraid that he would inflict too light a penalty, inasmuch as a human being would not have the strength to devise a well-balanced (ἰσόρροπος) punishment for so great an impiety (*Mos.* 2.197).

Whereas the Bible (Lev. 24:11) declares that they, presumably the Israelites, placed the blasphemer under guard while awaiting G-d's decision, Philo, apparently troubled that it was not Moses who took this initiative, says explicitly that it was Moses who ordered the man to be brought to prison and put in chains (*Mos.* 2.201). Whereas in the Bible we hear nothing of what Moses' own thinking was and what he said to G-d in bringing the case before Him, Philo asserts that, on the one hand, Moses appealed to G-d's mercy and, on the other hand, stressed the impiousness and monstrosity of the man's crime. Again, the reader of the biblical account would be inclined to ask why such a person should be punished by the gruesome method of stoning and why a public spectacle should be made of it through G-d's requirement that all the Israelites were to join in the stoning. Philo, writing in the first person singular, states that he thinks that G-d chose stoning in this case as a suitable punishment for a man who had a hard and stony (λιθίνη) soul and that He wished that all the people should be involved in punishing him, since He knew that they were strongly inclined to kill him; and stoning was the only method which allowed mass participation.

Moreover, it does not speak well for Moses that the Bible says nothing about Moses' attitude in view of the enormity of the blasphemer's crime or about Moses' statement to G-d. In Philo's version, on the other hand, in an extra-biblical comment, Moses implores G-d, to Whose mercy he appeals, to show what should be done to one who, as he describes it, had committed so impious and unholy a crime, so monstrous and unheard-of.

Though this is presented as G-d's decision, Philo (*Mos.* 2.203) adds that a new ordinance was drawn up, presumably by Moses, that whoever curses G-d should be put to death. Philo then addresses Moses, whom he refers to as "all-wise" (πάνσοφε), "who alone hast drunk deep of the untempered wine of wisdom."

The non-Jewish reader might well think that the penalty for cursing G-d is so extreme but that Judaism, with its monotheistic view, would not object to cursing the gods of other nations. Consequently, in a clear answer to those who charge that Jews show disrespect for the religion of others, Jews, says Philo (*Mos.* 2.205), are required to refrain from speaking insultingly of the religions of others, since the very name "god" is a title deserving the highest respect and love.[224] Moreover, Philo (*QE* 2.5) gives three additional reasons why one should not revile the religions of others, namely that praise is better than disparagement, that such an attitude of contempt leads to war, and that refraining from such contempt may lead pagans to speak well of G-d. This is based on the LXX's version of Exod. 22:27, which renders אלקים לא תקלל as θεοὺς οὐ κακολογήσεις, "you shall not curse gods."[225] Indeed, in mentioning the case of the blasphemer, Philo (*Mos.* 2.206), following the LXX, refers to him as blaspheming the L-rd of *gods* and men.[226]

In sum, Philo explains Moses' embarrassing ignorance of what penalty to impose on the man who had blasphemed the name of G-d as due to his fear that he would exact too light a penalty. He stresses that the refusal to reverence G-d implies refusal to honor parents and country and benefactors. The fact that Moses did not rush to execute such an atheist reflects well on his patience and eagerness to observe due process of law. Philo, following the LXX, refers to the blasphemer as cursing the L-rd of gods and men, thus emphasizing that Jews are required to refrain from speaking insultingly of the religions of others.

n. The Second Passover

In the second year after the exodus from Egypt, the Bible (Num. 9:1–3) states that G-d told Moses that the Israelites were to make the paschal offering in its appointed time, that is, the fourteenth day of Nisan. However, there were some who had been contaminated by contact with a human corpse and consequently were not permitted to make the offering on that day. They approached Moses and Aaron (Num. 9:6–7) and asked why they should be discriminated against. Moses was unable to give them an answer and told them to stand by while he put the question to G-d. However, there is no statement as to how Moses felt about their objection. Furthermore, in Josephus' extensive paraphrase of the Bible (*A.J.* 3.294), we read only that this was the first time since the departure from Egypt that Moses offered the paschal sacrifice in the wilderness; and there is no mention at all of the complaint of those who were contaminated and were consequently disqualified from making the offering, let alone G-d's answer. In the Bible we are simply told G-d's answer, namely that such people should make the paschal offering a month later on the fourteenth day and should eat it with matzos and bitter herbs, precisely as the uncontaminated Israelites ate it in the month of Nisan.

Philo (*Mos.* 2.222–32), though it is only tangential to a biography of Moses, has a long discussion of the incident. First of all, he is apparently aware of the question as to why the paschal offering had to be made at this particular time at all. He consequently explains why it is appropriate for the offering to be made at that particular point in the calendar, namely at the time when the corn crops become ripe.

Philo then paints a picture of people who had recently lost relations by death and thus had suffered a double sorrow, since, added to their grief for the dead kinsfolk was the loss that they felt of the pleasure and honor of participating in the paschal offering. Such people, Philo adds, were not even allowed to purify themselves with holy water, since their period of mourning had not yet been completed. It is these people, he says, who came to Moses with their complaint as to why they should be punished rather than pitied. They remark that their fate is worse than that of the dead, since the latter no longer have any perception of their troubles, while they, still being conscious, will be suffering a living death; and very moving is their request that they not fare worse than those who are already dead. Here Philo adds an unforgettable picture of these people who come to Moses, full of gloom and depression, on the one hand still in mourning for their kinsfolk, on the other hand unable to participate in the Passover sacrifice.

Philo (*Mos.* 2.228) then further adds to the biblical narrative a statement that shows so beautifully another side of Moses, namely his feeling of sympathy for those who have suffered; for we are told that Moses, hearing this poignant request and realizing the reasonableness of their claim and the cogency of their reason for absenting themselves from the sacrifice, feels a sympathy with them. Moses, however, in his modesty, is the ideal leader who realizes when he does not know the answer and does not rush to respond. Moreover, he is wise enough to be hesitant to allow his sympathy to dictate his decision when the law, strictly speaking, is at stake; and so we hear that he wavered in his judgment and oscillated as on a balance between pity and justice, on the one hand, and the strict observance of the law, on the other hand. Consequently, he turned to G-d and asked Him to act as judge. G-d answered him, going even beyond the immediate case, that mourning is not an offense, and that as soon as the period of mourning has ended, the mourners should no longer be denied an equal share in the sacred services, and that they should have an opportunity a month after Passover to participate in the Passover sacrifice. G-d, clearly consonant with Moses, adds an extra-biblical law, namely that the same privilege should be granted to those who were unable to participate in Nisan because they were absent in a distant country. We may suggest that in Moses' sympathy for those Jews who had been unable to participate in the Passover sacrifice, he is thinking of his fellow Jews in Egypt, since he equates those who happen to be away on a journey with those who have settled in a foreign land. As he remarks (*Mos.* 2.232), "The same permission also must be given to those who are prevented from joining the whole nation in worship not by mourning but by absence in a distant country. For settlers abroad and inhabitants of other regions are not wrongdoers who deserve to be deprived of equal privileges, particularly if the nation has grown so populous that a single country cannot contain it and has sent out colonies in all directions."[227]

In sum, Philo emphasizes Moses' sympathy for those who had been unable to participate in the eating of the paschal offering at the appointed time because of being contaminated by contact with a corpse. He also stresses Moses' modesty in realizing when he did not know an answer to their complaint.

o. *The Spies*

The first thing that strikes us about the account of Philo (*Mos.* 1.220–36) of the episode of the spies (Num. 13–14) is its brevity. In the Bible the account in the Hebrew comprises 1078 words and in the LXX comprises 1701 words. Philo's version contains 877 words. This gives a ratio of 0.52:1 of Philo to the

LXX.[228] And yet, brief as the paraphrase of the incident of the spies is, there is hardly a passage in which more additions, subtractions, and modifications are made by Philo than in this episode.

It is particularly instructive to compare Philo's treatment of this incident in *Mos.* with his treatment in the five other treatises where he mentions it. The most striking difference is that in *Mos.* there is a straightforward account, in the manner of an historian, without any allegorical interpretations. The five other treatises all focus on allegory. Thus, *Mut.* 121–23 cites the allegorical significance of the change of name of Hoshea to Joshua; *Mut.* 224–27 comments on the allegorical significance of the plucking of a cluster of grapes by the spies; *Mut.* 265 gives an allegorical interpretation of "the L-rd is with us" (Num. 14:9). *Somn.* 2.170–71 remarks on the allegorical significance of the investigations by the spies; *Post.* 60–62 comments on the allegorical significance of the names Hebron, Zoan, Ahiman, Sheshai, and Talmai; *Post.* 122 gives an allegorical interpretation of "the L-rd is with us" (Num. 14:9); *Leg.* 3.175 cites the allegorical interpretation of "let us return to Egypt" (Num. 14:4); and *Migr.* 122–24 gives an allegorical interpretation of G-d's words to Moses "I have pardoned according to your word" (Num. 14:20).

In the Bible (Num. 13:1) there is no indication of the background of the decision to send spies into Canaan. Nor is there any indication of the connection between this decision and what precedes, namely, the punishment inflicted upon Miriam for her criticism of Moses for marrying an Ethiopian woman (Num. 12). In Philo (*Mos.* 1.220–36) the passage comes immediately after the Israelites utterly defeat the Amalekites (Exod. 17:8–16, *Mos.* 1.214–19). It thus offers a reaffirmation of the importance that faith in G-d's assistance has in assuring the future security of the nation.[229]

A good general knows that a most important element in military success consists of obtaining, through reconnaissance, information about the enemy. We read (*Mos.* 1.216), in a supplement to the biblical account that adds to Moses' qualifications as a general, that Moses had sent out scouts, from whom he had learned that the enemy was not far away. We see Moses' ability as a general in the way in which he plans reconnaissance of the land of Canaan, into which he plans to lead the Israelites. In the first place, whereas in the Bible (Num. 13:2) and in Pseudo-Philo (15.1) it is G-d's idea or the Israelites' (Deut. 1:22–23)[230] to send scouts, Philo (*Mos.* 1.220–21),[231] as later Josephus (*A.J.* 3.302), ever seeking to build up the stature of Moses as a military planner, attributes the plan to Moses.[232] One might ask why Moses decided to have twelve scouts rather than an odd number so that if there were disagreements the vote would never be tied. Philo's answer is that the scouting committee should consist of twelve, corresponding to the number of tribes, with one headman from each, so that the nation might achieve unity once they had given their report.[233] Whereas in Josephus (*A.J.* 3.303) it is the Israelites who more democratically choose the twelve scouts, in the Bible (Num. 13:16), Philo (*Mos.* 1.221) and Pseudo-Philo (15.1), it is Moses, who, realizing that a general would not entrust to the masses such an important decision as the choice of the scouts, is said to have chosen them. Consequently, he did not call an assembly of the Israelites. In the Bible (Num. 13:2), as we have noted, G-d does not give any particular reason for sending scouts, nor does He state why He does so at this particular time. Philo (*Mos.* 1.220) explains that since this was already the second year since the Israelites had left Egypt, Moses, on his own, came to this conclusion.

In the Bible (Num. 13:17–20) Moses' instructions to the spies are very brief, consisting of six points: they are to see whether the inhabitants of Canaan are strong or weak, whether they are many or few, whether the land itself is fat or lean, whether they have trees, and what kind of cities they have; and they are to bring back some of the fruit of the land. Josephus (*A.J.* 3.303) omits altogether Moses' instructions to the scouts. Philo's Moses, the consummate planner, speaks at much greater length (*Mos.* 1.222–26). He tells the scouts not only what information he wishes to obtain but why he wishes to obtain those particular kinds of information and how he proposes to counter the number and power of the Canaanites with machines and siege engines. Above all, inspiring commander that he is, he instills in them faith that with the help of G-d they would overcome seemingly invincible forces, as they had been able to do throughout their journey in the desert.

Philo (*Mos.* 1.220) sets forth, as the goals of the mission, to obtain reliable knowledge to replace the mere hearsay and then to calculate what ought to be done.[234] Moreover, very remarkably, Moses tells these twelve leaders of his people that the reason why they should investigate the fertility or infertility of the land is that if it should turn out that the land is poor, it would be foolish to take risks in order to conquer it (*Mos.* 1.224). For the leader of the Israelites to suggest even for a moment that they might not fulfill the divine promise of entering and controlling the Land of Israel just because reconnaissance might indicate that the land is not worth conquering would show tremendous independence on the part of Moses even to the point of a showdown with G-d

Himself. This is not a rubber stamp of G-d. He will use his own judgment as a military planner. Moreover, whereas in the Bible (Num. 13:17–20) and in Philo (*Mos.* 1.222), it is to the scouts that Moses, more democratically, indicates what they are to investigate—the places, the people, and their circumstances—in Josephus (*A.J.* 3.300–2) it is to the entire assembly of the Israelites that Moses indicates the matters to be investigated. Furthermore, whereas Josephus' Moses (*A.J.* 3.300–1) gives an extra-biblical inspiring speech to the entire people reminding them that no nation will be able to stop them and assuring them that the land that G-d has promised them will soon be theirs, Philo's Moses says nothing to the twelve leaders about the Promised Land but rather places matters on a military plane and assures them that their faith in G-d will enable them to overpower their enemies (*Mos.* 1.225).

Philo (*Mos.* 1.220) explains that whereas this was already the second year since the Israelites had left Egypt, Moses, on his own, decided, and without calling an assembly of the Israelites, that it was advisable to investigate the Land of Israel. Philo also explains, as the Bible does not, why Moses has decided to send the scouts now in the spring, namely, that it is in the spring that crops come to their fullness and trees begin to show their natural growth; and hence this is the best time for testing the goodness of the land. Moses (*Mos.* 1.226) then adds the extra-biblical instruction that they should wait until the summer is at its height so as to bring back fruits, presumably in their ripeness, as samples of the wealth of the land.[235]

Whereas the Bible (Num. 13:4–15) gives the names of the scouts, Philo, in *Mos.*, who always seeks to keep the focus on Moses, omits the names of the scouts, even the names of the two dissenters, Joshua and Caleb. In Josephus, Moses presents his plan in a speech to the gathered multitude (*A.J.* 3.300–2), whereas in Philo (*Mos.* 1.220), Moses, discharging his responsibility as a general, without calling an assembly of the Israelites and without consulting anyone, comes to the conclusion that it is advisable to inspect the land in which they propose to settle. Moses remarks that instead of arguing ignorantly, as people generally do, it is preferable to obtain first-hand information and upon that basis to decide on a course of action. It is significant that Philo (*Mos.* 1.306) denominates the Israelites as Moses' army. Like a good general, Moses knows the importance of getting intelligence before engaging in battle; and so, as in a previous case also, in an extra-biblical addition, before the battle with Amalek (*Mos.* 1.216) he learns from his scouts that the enemy is not distant and proceeds to muster his men of military age.

However, this presented Philo and Josephus with a real problem, namely, how, if Moses took the initiative, he could not be held responsible for the failure of the spies' mission.[236] Indeed, one rabbinic tradition presents a scenario in which Moses is persuaded by the Israelites to send spies,[237] thus transferring to the Israelites the responsibility for the failure of the mission.[238] Philo's answer (*Mos.* 1.231) is that the envoys were not of one mind and thus, by implication, that it is they who should be blamed for their disunity and not Moses.

In the Bible (Num. 13:1–2) G-d instructs Moses to send as spies one man from each of the twelve tribes, each of them a leader (נשׂיא) among them. Moses (Num. 13:3) proceeds to select distinguished men, all of them heads of the people. We are given (Num. 13:4–15) the names of those selected from each of the tribes. Philo (*Mos.* 1.221) states that Moses, displaying the excellence of a leader in choosing men carefully for such an important mission, proceeded to choose twelve men, each the chief officer (φύλαρχος) of his tribe, men most esteemed (δοκιμώτατοι, "most notable," "most approved") according to their merit (ἀριστίνδην), the goal being that each of the tribes should be equally represented, so that there should not be any quarreling amongst them and so that the emissaries should report the full truth (ἀψευδεῖν, "not to lie").[239] Neither Philo nor Pseudo-Philo nor Josephus, focusing on Moses, gives us the names of those chosen, including the two who present the minority report,[240] the implication being that it is what they stand for, rather than their identity, that concerns Philo.

After the enumeration of the names of the twelve scouts, the Bible (Num. 13:16) adds that Moses called Hoshea, the son of Nun, Joshua. Philo omits this, though he does mention the change of Sarai's name to Sarah (Gen. 17:15, *Mut.* 61, 77–80) and Abram's name to Abraham (Gen. 17:5, *Mut.* 60–76), and asserts that the change of these names was ridiculed by "a godless and impious fellow."[241]

It is significant that in the Bible (Num. 13:20) Moses tells the spies to take from the fruit of the land of Canaan. This raises the question whether this would not be outright theft. We have already noted how sensitive both Philo and Josephus were to the charge that the Israelites stole from the Egyptians before they left Egypt. We should not be surprised, therefore, that Philo and Josephus, aware of such a charge, do not have Moses thus instruct the spies. Philo (*Mos.* 1.222–26), as we have remarked, has Moses address the spies before the beginning of their mission, but says nothing about bringing back samples of the fruits that they would find in Canaan. Philo (*Mos.* 1.230) does say that they did pluck some of the fruits; but they apparently did so on their own initiative. Josephus (*A.J.* 3.302) has Moses address the assembly of the Israelites and suggests that they send scouts "to mark the richness of the land" but says nothing about actually taking samples of the fruits. To be sure, he does say (*A.J.* 3.304) that the spies brought back some of the products of the land, but it is clear that they did so not because Moses had ordered them to do so but, as with Philo, on their own initiative.

Philo (*Mos.* 1.227–32) devotes much more attention than does the Bible to a description of the actual investigation by the spies. We would naturally wonder what the attitude of the multitude was and what their fears must have been as the spies began their mission. Philo (*Mos.* 1.227) fills in the details, particularly, as he so often does, mentioning the feelings of the people. We are told that the spies had the complete backing of the people as they set out, escorted by the whole multitude; and we are told of the natural fears of the people, since this was, indeed, a dangerous mission, lest they be captured and slain, thus bringing about two misfortunes—the death of these men and the resulting lack of information that was so necessary to guide the Israelites if they were to conquer the enemy. The fact that, according to Philo, in an extra-biblical addition, the whole multitude accompanied the spies would serve to justify the divine punishment meted out to all the Israelites.

We naturally wonder how spies would know where to go in an unfamiliar land, and so Philo (*Mos.* 1.228) adds that they took with themselves scouts and guides. It would make sense that they would first attempt to get a bird's-eye view of the entire country by climbing a high mountain; and this is exactly what Philo (*Mos.* 1.228) tells us they did, namely to ascend the highest of the mountains in the neighborhood in order to survey the country. We are then told what they found in the way of agricultural abundance, namely barley, wheat, and grass. The instructions that they had received, according to Philo, as we have noted, were that they were to investigate whether the land had fruit-producing trees; and they do, indeed, note that the uplands are full of vines and other trees. Though they had not been specifically instructed to see whether the land had sufficient water, they were provident enough to notice that the land was intersected with springs and rivers that gave it an abundance of water. Indeed, they were aware, especially since they had been traveling through an almost waterless desert for so long, how crucial water was to their survival.

In response to their instructions to investigate whether the Canaanite cities were favorably situated and strongly built, they observe (*Mos.* 1.229) that they were, indeed, strongly fortified, owing to both their favorable situation and the solidity of their walls. In response to their instructions to investigate the size and strength of their population, they note that the people of the land were countless in number and of huge stature, though, realizing that their fellow Israelites would raise their eyebrows at such an obvious exaggeration, they remark that they were merely giant-like in their physical superiority in size and strength.

An obvious criticism of the spies is that they did their work too quickly and superficially and were carried away by their first impressions. Philo (*Mos.* 1.230) omits that they spent only forty days on their investigation (Num. 13:25); and, indeed, being an experienced diplomat, he goes out of his way to remark that having noticed these things they stayed on in order to get a more accurate view, since, as he says, "first impressions are treacherous (ὀλισθηρόν, "slippery") and only slowly get the seal of reality" (ἐνσφραγιζόμεναι, "stamped as with a seal").

That the spies used foresight is clear from the fact (*Mos.* 1.230) that when they plucked fruits they were careful to select not those that were at the first stage of hardening, but rather those that were darkening to ripeness, in order that they should be in good condition when they exhibited them to the multitude. Moreover, in what would appear to be a clear effort to show that the spies were aware that their fellow Israelites would wonder whether they were exaggerating in presenting their report, Philo (*Mos.* 1.231) stresses that the spies themselves were amazed by the huge size of the bunches of grapes and the incredible spectacle that they presented. Moreover, the biblical statement (Num. 13:23) that they bore one cluster of grapes on a double pole would seem to be a gross exaggeration; hence, Philo, well aware of such an objection and eager to convince his readers, who, at least in *Mos.*, were for the most part non-Jews,[242] admits that the spectacle of the size of the bunches of grapes was incredible and then proceeds to explain how such huge bunches could have been borne, namely that a fresh pair of youths relieved its predecessors at intervals, since they were wearied by the great weight of the burden. All this care and foresight on the part of the spies, as stressed by Philo, is clearly a tribute to Moses, who had selected them.

Thucydides, notably in his description of the internal dissension at Corcyra (3.80–82), calls attention to its disastrous effect. Similarly, Josephus (*A.J.* 3.302) constantly stresses, both in his portrayal of the revolt of Korah and in his description of the revolutionaries of his own day (see Feldman 1998a,

140–43), how disastrous internal dissension is. Likewise, when Moses addresses the assembly of the Israelites urging them to send spies, he emphasizes that they should all be of one mind (ὁμονοῶμεν). Philo, who, presumably drawing on his own experience as a leader of the Jewish community of Alexandria, must have known how vital it was for his people to be united, says (*Mos.* 1.231) that on vital matters (ἀναγκαῖα, "necessary things") the spies were not of one mind (ὁμοφρονοῦντες). Realizing that in all likelihood the differences of opinion that they later exhibited must have had their antecedents, he specifically notes (*Mos.* 1.232), in an extra-biblical addition, that even during the journey before they returned there were numberless contentions among them, though, he adds, they were of a lighter kind, inasmuch as they did not wish their disputes or conflicting reports to produce dissension (στάσις) in the mass of the people; and it was only after they returned that these disagreements became more severe.[243]

Nonetheless, according to Philo (*Mos.* 1.235), there was unanimity among the spies in extolling the beauty of both the plain and hill country. According to him (*Mos.* 1.233), however, one party, consisting of ten representatives, conveyed their cowardice, exaggerating the fortifications of the cities and their populations, as well as everything (πάντα) else, and consequently created fear in the populace. Philo does not, however, mention that they showed the people the fruits that they had brought back. Nor does he mention that they said that the land was inhabited by giants or that all whom they saw were huge. Nor does he say that they compared themselves with grasshoppers or that they said that the land devours its inhabitants. In short, Philo, apparently realizing that his readers would approach such exaggerations with skepticism, presents a more nuanced majority report so that one can more readily understand why the populace gave it credence.[244] The other party, consisting of two representatives, did the very opposite, conveying their hopefulness and belittling the obstacles, and encouraged the people not to be faint-hearted, assuring them that they would prevail without a fight, since they were so powerful.

According to the Bible (Num. 13:27–29), the majority, while admitting that the land did indeed flow with milk and honey and while exhibiting the huge size of the fruits, stressed the tremendous obstacles that the Israelites would encounter if they attempted to conquer the land, namely, that the people were powerful, that their cities were greatly fortified, that offspring of the giant lived there, that it was inhabited by many tribes, and that the land, as they expressed it, devours its inhabitants. Caleb, however, expressed confidence in the ability of the Israelites to conquer it.[245]

The majority report, as described in the Bible, contradicted itself. On the one hand, we hear (Deut. 1:25) that the spies brought back word to the Israelites that the land that G-d had given them was good, that it flowed with milk and honey (Num. 13:27). On the other hand, as we have noted, they pointed out that the people there were huge and that the Israelites by comparison were like grasshoppers (Num. 13:33). The people turned to complain bitterly against G-d, accusing Him of having taken the Israelites out of Egypt in order to deliver them into the hands of the Amorites (Deut. 1:27). According to the Bible (Num. 14:1), the entire assembly agreed with the majority report. The reaction that followed was that they wept that night, and all of them murmured against Moses and Aaron, all of them expressing regret that they had not died in Egypt or in the wilderness and complaining against G-d, as if pointing out that He had contradicted Himself, in having brought them to the land so as to die there and to have their wives and children taken captive (Num. 14:3); and they expressed the desire to appoint a leader who would take them back to Egypt (Num. 14:1–4). The reaction of Moses and Aaron at this point (Num. 14:5) was to fall upon their faces before the entire congregation. On the other hand, Joshua and Caleb tore their garments (Num. 14:6), as one does when receiving terrible news,[246] and they spoke to the assembly of the people telling them not to fear since G-d was with them.[247]

At this point, according to the Bible (Num. 14:10), the entire assembly wanted to pelt Joshua and Caleb with stones. This, as in the rebellion of Korah (Num. 16–17), was a crucial test of Moses' leadership (see Feldman 1993a, 386–97). There (Num. 16:5–11) Moses stood up to Korah, addressed him and the entire assembly, and fearlessly told him that G-d Himself would choose who should be high priest. Here, however, Moses does not address the congregation either to rebuke them or to encourage them. Instead, we are struck with Moses' silence, perhaps because he felt ambivalent about stifling a majority.[248] Rather, we are told (Num. 14:5) that Moses and Aaron fell on their faces before the entire congregation. Philo (*Mos.* 1.236), however, perhaps reflecting his own experience as a leader and the Platonic-like disdain that he has for the masses, has Moses express indignation at the masses, especially since Moses fears the punishment that G-d might inflict upon them. We are not, nevertheless, informed as to the form of Moses' indignation.

G-d then, in the Bible (Num. 14:26–35), in a supplementary address to Moses and Aaron, spells out His decree that all those twenty years of age and above, except for Caleb and Joshua, will die in the wilderness and that their children will roam in the wilderness for forty years, corresponding to the number of days that the spies spent in investigating the land, after which they will enter the Promised Land. In the pestilence that followed, however (Num. 14:37), the Bible reports explicitly that those who had "brought up an evil report of the land," that is, the ten spies who gave the pessimistic report, perished, while the two who had counselled the people not to be terrified were saved, though it is not clear who else, if any, perished in the plague. Nevertheless, immediately thereafter, according to the Bible, G-d tells Moses that those Israelites who had angered Him through their lack of faith would not see the land that He had sworn to their forefathers, but that Caleb,[249] because he had followed G-d wholeheartedly, would enter the land, and his offspring would possess it.

Philo, nevertheless, omits totally the dialogue between Moses and G-d, in which G-d threatens to annihilate the Israelites and in which Moses pleads with G-d to forgive them.[250] Apparently, Philo was troubled theologically by the fact that G-d did not respect the will of the majority, a principle (Exod. 23:2) at the heart of Jewish law, as we see, for example, in the famous incident (*b. B. Meẓ.* 59b) in which Rabbi Eliezer did not respect such a majority vote and, as a result, was excommunicated.

We may well ask why the ten spies who gave a negative report were punished so severely by G-d when they apparently did the best that they could and presented what seems to be an honest report. Moreover, in a democratic society the majority—in this case ten versus two—should have prevailed, as we see in the traditional exegesis of the scriptural phrase (Exod. 23:2): אחרי רבים ("follow a multitude"), as formulated in the rabbinic dictum (*b. Ber.* 9a): "Where there is a controversy between an individual and the many, the halakah follows the many." Consequently, the rabbis (*b. B. Meẓ.* 59b) insisted that even if a heavenly voice declares that the law is in accordance with the minority, the view of the majority must prevail.[251]

Philo may well have been troubled also by the fact that in the biblical dialogue between Moses and G-d, it is Moses, as also in Pseudo-Philo (15.7), who has to appeal to G-d's sense of mercy and who succeeds in persuading G-d. To say the least, this seems to reflect badly on G-d and appears to indicate that Moses is more merciful than He. Philo and Josephus here, apparently aware of the theological problem, omit the whole passage.

In the episode that follows (Num. 14:40–44), the Israelites, confessing that they had sinned, seek, against the advice of Moses, to make amends by attacking the Amalekites and the Canaanites. However, the Amalekites and the Canaanites inflict a major defeat upon them. In Josephus' version (*A.J.* 4.1–8) the Israelites think that Moses is busily arranging for them to remain without means so that they will always be dependent upon his help, and therefore they seek to prove that even without Moses' zeal they will overcome the enemy. They assert that G-d looked after them not because of His regard for Moses but because of His regard for their ancestors. In effect, they look upon G-d, not Moses, as their general. Philo omits this entire episode, presumably because of the very delicate question raised here by the Israelites, namely, whether the Israelites should look to G-d or to Moses as their general.[252]

In sum, in his view of the episode of the spies, Philo presents Moses as an excellent military planner. It is Moses, rather than G-d, whose idea it is to send scouts, and it is he who selects them. Philo keeps the focus on Moses, omitting the names of the scouts, even of the dissenters. When the Israelites wish to stone the minority representatives, Moses, far from being silent, as in the Bible, fearlessly expresses indignation.

p. The Revolt of Korah

The greatest challenge to the leadership of Moses came from a cousin, Korah (Num. 16:1). We may see a marked contrast between the tremendous attention which Josephus gives to Korah[253] as compared with the relative neglect of Korah in Philo's works (he is mentioned by name only once, *Fug.* 145), presumably because, as we have noted, Philo was not a priest and had no direct ties to the Temple; secondly, because he personally was apparently not subjected to jealousy on the part of his fellow-countrymen; and thirdly, because he strove to keep the focus on Moses. Indeed, in the two extended accounts (*Mos.* 2.174–79, 2.275–87) of the rebellion, Philo not only does not mention Korah by name even once but he does not present the revolt as led by any particular leader. The fact that Korah is mentioned by name only once (*Fug.* 145) in all of the works of Philo would presumably be due to Philo's concern to present the rebellion not as that of a particular person but rather as a conflict of principle between those who know how to govern and those who are merely a rabble.

In the Bible the account of the revolt comes suddenly after the episode of the spies (Num. 13:1–14:39), the incident of the man who violated the Sabbath by gathering wood on that day (Num. 15:32–36), and the commandment with regard to wearing fringes (*zizit*) (Num. 15:37–41) on the corners of garments. Hence, there would seem to be no immediate context. In Josephus (*A.J.* 4.11–66) it comes immediately after the abortive attempt of the Israelites to attack Amalek and the Canaanites against the advice of Moses, and hence the connecting link is the Israelite disobedience toward their great leader. In Philo (*Mos.* 2.174–79 and 2.275–87) the narrative appears twice, each time following the account of the construction of the Golden Calf, the connecting link, apparently, being the fact that some of the Levites who had remained loyal to G-d and to Moses in that episode now rose up against Moses.

In the Bible (Num. 16:3) Korah, Moses' cousin, with his following of 250 men, contends that the whole congregation is holy; and he asks why Moses should have elevated himself above all the rest, since all are equal and holy before G-d. This egalitarian contention is not found in Philo. Josephus (*A.J.* 4.14), in his first mention of Korah, states, in particular, that Korah was envious of Moses, who, he notes, was his fellow tribesman and kinsman. Philo (*Mos.* 2.176, 2.278) is more specific in presenting the extra-biblical addition that Korah's charge against Moses was nepotism, in that he had bestowed the priesthood on his brother and nephews, and deceit in that Moses had falsely claimed that they had been chosen under divine direction.

It is Josephus (*A.J.* 4.14) who introduces Korah to us as one of the Hebrews who was among the most distinguished both in ancestry and in wealth, an able speaker, and most persuasive in dealing with crowds. By building up the personality of Korah, Josephus was no doubt simultaneously aggrandizing the character of the Israelite leader, Moses, whom Korah dared to oppose; and to build up Moses, which was a major aim in the *A.J.*, was crucial for Josephus, inasmuch as a nation was known primarily from the character of its founder (see Feldman 1993a, 233–87). While it is true that the Bible itself gives the names of Korah's father, grandfather, and great-grandfather (Num. 16:1), it does not actually say that Korah's ancestry was distinguished.

The statement that Korah was distinguished in wealth is Josephus' addition; and he specifically adds that Korah was embittered because he felt that he was more deserving than Moses to enjoy the glory of leadership by virtue of the fact that he was wealthier and not inferior in ancestry. Indeed, Josephus mentions Korah's wealth on three other occasions (*A.J.* 4.19, 25, 26). Like Josephus, the rabbis (*b. Pes.* 119a, *b. Sanh.* 110a)[254] stress the immensity of Korah's wealth. Moreover, the statement that Korah was an able speaker and persuasive in addressing crowds is Josephus' addition[255] and is one of the four qualities of the ideal statesman as we see in the speech that Thucydides (2.60.6) ascribes to Pericles. This same quality also serves to associate him with the demagogues whom Thucydides and Plato denounce.[256] Josephus (*A.J.* 4.36) focuses on the fickleness of the tumultuous crowd, swayed by what anyone says, and is probably thinking of the fickleness of the masses that he encountered in Galilee when he was commander of the forces opposing the Romans. Similarly, the rabbis (*Mid. Num. Rab.* 18.1, *Tan. Korah* 2 [ed. Buber, p. 85]) indicate that Korah convinced the Israelites with flattering words, so that all the great men of Israel, including even the members of the Sanhedrin, the supreme court of the Jews, allowed themselves to be persuaded.

The Bible (Num. 16) says nothing about the character and personality of Korah. The rebellion is presented (Num. 16:3) as an egalitarian revolution, whose key objection is that the entire assembly of the Israelites are holy and that Moses and Aaron had no right to exalt themselves over the rest of the people.

Philo, in his two extended references to the revolt (*Mos.* 2.174–79, 275–87) says nothing about Korah's ancestry or his relationship to Moses.[257] Likewise, Pseudo-Philo (16), while he mentions Korah by name five times, says nothing about his background and qualities of leadership. Unlike Josephus and the rabbis, Philo, who, as we have noted, stresses Moses' strongly negative attitude toward wealth, says nothing about Korah's wealth, since this to him is not a major factor. Josephus (*A.J.* 4.14), for whom jealousy is a leitmotif throughout his work (Feldman 1998a, 198–203), especially as directed toward him personally, states that Korah's motive was jealousy. Josephus (*A.J.* 4.14) and the rabbis[258] cite his ability in speaking and persuasion, but Philo, who, as we have noted, explains Moses' supposed speech defect as his disdain for sophistry, says nothing about this. Philo's overriding concern is theological, especially Korah's challenge to the concept of divine revelation.

In the Bible and in Josephus the revolt is an attempt by Korah to displace Aaron; in Philo the revolt, at least initially, is a classic case of *stasis*, that is an attempt by one class, namely the Levites, to gain power over the priests (*Mos.* 2.276–77), whom they vastly outnumbered and whose privileges they sought to wrest from them (*Mos.* 2.174). Philo (*Mos.* 2.277) uniquely makes a special point of noting that the Levites were puffed up with pride at their numerical superiority over the priests, whose small numbers they despised. Philo specifically refers to the priests as superior.

Philo (2.174), quite possibly referring to contemporary events in the community of Alexandria that he headed, remarks that the revolt was due to the strife for precedence and that it is this that is the cause of innumerable troubles to many persons and in many places.

While it is true that Philo's Levites, as in Josephus' account, challenge the selection of Aaron as high priest, they challenge Moses' statement that he had acted under divine direction in choosing his brother as high priest. It is this last point that Philo emphasizes most of all, since his chief concern is theological, and the Levites' objection challenges the very concept of divine revelation. For Philo the contest is between G-d and Korah's impiety (*Mos.* 2.279), between belief and disbelief (*Mos.* 2.280). The issue, in other words, is theological rather than a political contest between two views of government; and more than a personal contest between Moses and Korah is at stake.

One guesses that Philo himself, the aristocrat who was a leader of the Alexandrian Jews, was similarly critical of the possible attempt of the masses to assert their power. As one who looked upon Plato as "most sacred" (*Prob.* 13), it should not be surprising that Philo viewed the ideal form of government as one that was in the hands of a philosopher-king who held a status of unquestioned superiority over his subjects. "In his material substance," he says,[259] "a king is equal to every man, but in the power of his authority and rank he is like the G-d of all, for there is nothing on earth that is higher than he." Elsewhere (*Spec.* 4.46–47) he denounces the view that one should be impressed by the fact that a view is held by many. "Some people," he says, "suppose that what the many think right is lawful and just, though it be the height of lawlessness. But they do not judge well, for it is good to follow nature, and the headlong course of the multitude runs counter to what nature's leading would have us do. So," he adds, alluding, one may surmise, to his own experience with the masses, "if some people collect in groups or crowded assemblages to give trouble, we must not consent to their debasing of the long established and sterling coinage of civic life."

Philo describes the form of government in which the multitude has supreme power as ochlocracy, which he characterizes (*Opif.* 171, *Somn.* 2.287, *Virt.* 180) as the worst of all forms of government, as the very counterfeit of democracy, which is the best of them (*Agr.* 45), and as the offspring of anarchy (*Agr.* 46), where injustice and lawlessness rule (*Conf.* 108). In language similar to that which he uses in his characterization of Korah's revolt, he states that ochlocracy is produced by disorder and covetousness (*Decal.* 155). He describes the pogrom in Alexandria in the year 38 as having been carried on by people who wielded the weapon of mob rule (ὀχλοκρατία, *Flacc.* 65). Indeed, Philo (*Mos.* 2.277), as it were, draws a moral, namely that the revolt of Korah illustrates what happens when subjects attack their rulers "to confound that most excellent promoter of the common weal, order." Likewise, Philo, in his essay *Fug.* 145, emphasizes the philosophic point that Korah had aimed to overthrow order (τάξις), "the most beautiful thing in human life," rather than the political point that Korah had sought to overthrow Moses' commonwealth.

The seriousness of the revolt may be seen from the fact that Korah, in an extra-biblical addition (*Praem.* 75), had actually proceeded to the inmost sanctuary of the tabernacle with the intention of displacing the priests.[260] Moreover, it was not only Korah but also, in an extra-biblical addition (*Mos.* 2.174), the temple attendants who sought to displace the priests, than whom they were far more numerous. Philo uses particularly strong language (*Mos.* 2.277) in attacking the temple attendants as "puffed with pride at their own numerical superiority over the priests." In no uncertain terms, again presumably reflecting the strife between the many and the few, he declares (Fragments, Richter 6.206 [Mangey, 2.651]) that "to give equal things to unequal people is an action of great injustice."[261] The fact, decried by the Emperor Claudius (London Papyrus 1912 [*CPJ* 153], lines 88–92), that the Alexandrian Jews sent two embassies to him, "as if they lived in two cities, a thing that has never been done before," would seem to indicate a similar sharp division within the Jewish community; and there would seem to be good reason to surmise that the second embassy was more militant than that headed by Philo in fighting back against the anti-Semitism in 41.[262] Philo adds that Moses was pained by this lack of trust in him after he had given so much evidence of his good faith (*Mos.* 2.177).

Philo (*Mos.* 2.177) is aware that Moses might be criticized for not attempting to answer Korah's arguments systematically; and thus he defends Moses by remarking that Moses realized the uselessness of explaining his motives since, Philo says, as if it is a truism, it is impossible to change the minds of those who are convinced of their views. Moses is particularly upset by the charge that he has lied, since, as we have remarked that, Philo emphasizes, the virtue of truth is crucial to Moses; and Moses tells Korah's allies, Dathan and Abiram, that the manner of the death of Korah and his followers will prove that they have provoked G-d. In the Bible (Num. 16:31–34) Korah and his assemblage are swallowed up by the earth only after Korah and his followers have brought their firepans before G-d, whereas in Philo, who stresses Moses' greatness as a prophet throughout Book 2 of *Mos.*, it is immediately after the beginning of the conspiracy that Moses is prophetically inspired and predicts that the matter will be judged by the manner in which they will die (Num. 16:30). As part of the prophecy, Moses, in an extra-biblical addition, has a vision of the earth opening up; and as soon as he ceases to speak, the earth does, indeed, open up and they are swallowed (*Mos.* 2.281–82). The speed of the punishment is said (*Mos.* 2.284) to attest to the truth of G-d's pronouncements; and the fundamental parts of the universe itself, namely, heaven and earth, chastise Korah's impiety (*Mos.* 2.285), appropriately enough by the earth swallowing up his adherents and by the heaven raining down fire upon them (*Mos.* 2.286–87).[263] In contrast, Josephus (*A.J.* 4.11–66) seeks to stress, as he does elsewhere so often, the importance of the priesthood and the dangers of jealousy (see Feldman 1993g, 399–426).

Again, when Philo deals with Korah's rebellion in his essay *Praem.* (74), he uses this episode to preach a philosophic sermon on the consequences of unreasonable (ἄλογος) pride (φρόνημα, "presumption," "arrogance," "ambition"). We find a similar moral in Philo's essay *Fug.* (145), where he stresses that the Levites, by aiming to become kings instead of gate-keepers and thus to overthrow the established order of things, not only failed to attain their goal but even lost that which they already had. Indeed, he concludes (*Fug.* 146) by affirming that those who are enamored of things too great for their nature will be convicted of foolishness, "since every effort beyond our strength breaks down through over-violent straining."

The rabbis, like Josephus, emphasize, as a motive for the revolt, Korah's desire for the high priesthood (*Tan. Pequdei* [ed. Buber, 1]). The main point noted by the rabbinic tradition concerning Korah is his attack upon the Torah itself and his attempt to disprove its divine origin (*y. Sanh.* 10.1.27d-28a, *Tan.* [Buber] 4.43b).[264] In this they are akin to Philo, who likewise viewed the revolt in theological terms as an attack on the divine choice of Aaron to be high priest.

Like Philo and the rabbinic tradition, Pseudo-Philo (16.1) does not here mention the confrontation between Korah and Moses, but rather focuses on the conflict between Korah and G-d. He stresses the theological concern, in noting the fact that Korah challenged the concept of divine revelation and the reasonableness of the Torah. However, unlike Philo, Pseudo-Philo does mention Korah by name five times within a single chapter. Thus, at the very beginning of his account (16.1), he, like the rabbis, remarks that G-d commanded Moses concerning the fringes, the passage (Num. 15:37–41) that comes immediately before the account of Korah.[265] In Pseudo-Philo (16.1) the response of Korah is in terms of the unbearability of the law.[266] "Why," he asks, "is an unbearable law imposed upon us in this way?" The conversation then is not between Moses and Korah but between G-d and Korah.

Similarly, Philo, in both of his major accounts of the rebellion (*Mos.* 2.174–79, 2.275–87), not only does not say anything at all about Korah but does not so much as even mention his name, let alone tell us about his genealogy, his wealth, his ability as a speaker and leader, etc. Rather his revolt is presented as a mass movement.

On the other hand, in addition to the inherent dramatic potential of the confrontation between two great leaders, it is Josephus' desire, as it is Philo's, to build up the central personality of the Bible, Moses; but he does so by having his stature rise to even greater heights due to his overcoming so mighty an adversary. Moreover, Josephus seeks to stress the themes of the importance of the priesthood, the dangers of jealousy, and the consequences of political rebellion.

Moses' response to the revolt, according to the Bible (Num. 16:4) is that he fell on his face. Philo (*Mos.* 2.279) was clearly disturbed that Moses did not systematically analyze and refute the charges of Korah. In the Bible (Num. 16:5–11) Moses berates Korah for seeking the priesthood and asks what he has against Aaron. He tells Korah and his adherents to take firepans and to allow G-d to choose who should be the high priest. He explains, defensively, that Moses was distressed (ἀνιαθείς, "grieved," "vexed") and greatly pained (περιαλγήσας) at the accusations (*Mos.* 2.177), especially the charge of falsification. He further explains Moses' failure to refute Korah as due to his nature, namely, that he was very mild (πρᾳότατος, "very gentle," "very meek") and very gentle (ἡμερώτατος, "very civilized"), but that he was spurred on (ἠκονήθη, "goaded on") to justified anger (δικαία ὀργή) and lawful indignation (νόμιμος διαγανάκτησις) by his hatred of evil (*Mos.* 2.279–80).

Inasmuch as, we may suggest, Moses had lost his temper in smashing the tablets when he saw the Golden Calf, Philo (*Praem.* 77) is careful to state that Moses did not lose his temper (ὀργή) here, since he was by nature, he adds, not irascible (ἀόργητος). The Bible (Num. 16:5–11), without describing Moses' feelings, simply states what Moses says to Korah. Korah and his assembly are to take firepans and place fire and incense in them, and G-d will choose who is the holy one. Philo (*Mos.* 2.280) describes Moses' feelings and notes that while he was still seething (ζέων, "boiling") and burning with fire (πεπυρωμένος) arising from his great and lawful indignation, he became inspired (ἐνθουσιᾷ) and was transformed into a prophet. Indeed, the scene is more like that of Elijah against the worshippers of Baal on Mount Carmel.

In the Bible, at the very beginning of the Korah pericope (Num. 16:1), we are told that Korah did not act alone. We are given the names of his confederates—Dathan and Abiram, the sons of Eliab, and On, the son of Peleth,[267] the offspring of Reuben. However, unlike the Bible (Num. 16:1), which merely mentions that Korah had joined with the offspring of Reuben in his revolt, and unlike Josephus (*A.J.* 4.19), who merely presents the argument that the priesthood should have been given by Moses to the tribe of Reuben, the oldest of the tribes, and to Dathan and Abiram, in particular, since they were the oldest of that tribe and the most powerful through abundance of wealth, but who does not actually say that Korah formed an alliance with the tribe of Reuben, Philo (*Mos.* 2.175) broadens the base of the revolt as including more than the Levites. In fact, Philo here, in order to prevent the sedition from being considered merely that of the Levites, states in an extra-biblical addition that they persuaded the tribe of Reuben to join them. In the Bible the Levites have a good case for their revolt in that they were of the same tribe, Levi, as Moses and Aaron; however, by having the Levites join in a coalition with the tribe of Reuben, Philo presents the revolt as a widespread revolt within the Israelite community. In particular, he describes (*Mos.* 2.175) this tribe as having many adherents among the more thoughtless (εἰκαιότεροι, "more rash," "more hasty," "without aim or purpose"), who supposed that they were capable of taking the supremacy as their birthright.

The complaint of Dathan and Abiram, we are told (Num. 16:13–14), is that Moses did not live up to his promise to lead the Israelites to a land flowing with milk and honey but rather had caused them to die in the wilderness and that he seeks to dominate them further. Since this episode occurs shortly after the episode of the spies (Num. 13–14), who had brought back a discouraging report about the prospects of conquering the land of Canaan, we should not be surprised at such a complaint. Moses, we are told (Num. 16:12), sent to summon Dathan and Abiram, but they refused to respond to this summons. Thereupon, Moses, very humbly and apparently swallowing his pride (Josephus [*A.J.* 4.38], says that Moses was shocked by their behavior), followed by the elders of the Israelites, took the initiative to go to Dathan and Abiram, and warned the Israelites that they would perish because of their sins if they did not turn away from the rebels, but to no avail. Indeed, according to the rabbinic tradition (*Moed Q.* 16a), Dathan and Abiram were impertinent and insulting to Moses. According to the Bible (Num. 16:27), Dathan and Abiram went out with their wives, children, and infants. Josephus (*A.J.* 4.39) adds that their servants were around them so that if Moses should bring on some violence, they would defend them.

Philo totally omits mention of the names of Dathan and Abiram (Num. 16:12–15), whose main objection in the Bible is to Moses' attempt to dominate them (Num. 16:13). Moreover, in the Bible Dathan and Abiram attack Moses' integrity, as we can see from Moses' reply (Num. 16:15) that he has not taken even a single donkey of theirs and has not wronged anyone. Philo, however, as we have noted, focuses completely on the rebellion of Korah, which he views as a rebellion against G-d. The net effect, as Philo (*Mos.* 2.284) notes, in an extra-biblical addition, of the sudden destruction of the rebels is to spread the fame (περιβόητον) of Moses' piety as a prophet and the truth of his oracles.

According to the Bible (Num. 16:28), Moses felt it necessary to respond to the charge that it was he, rather than G-d, who was giving directions to the people. Moses is particularly upset by the charge that he has lied, and he tells Korah's allies, Dathan and Abiram, that the manner of the death of Korah and his followers will prove that they have provoked G-d. He consequently tells them that the proof that G-d had not sent him would be manifest from the fact that the rebels died like ordinary men, but that if G-d would create a phenomenon and the earth would swallow the men, together with all that they possessed, this would be proof that it was G-d who was punishing them.

Moses warned the rebels that the earth would swallow them up. Pseudo-Philo (16.4) adds that Korah sent for his three[268] sons, who had not joined him in the plot. The sons insisted that, having received the Law, they intended to follow it. The sons warned Korah of the impending destruction, but he did not heed them.[269] Thereupon the earth swallowed up Korah and his followers, and Korah and his company groaned until the stability of the earth was restored. According to Pseudo-Philo (16.3), when the resurrection of the dead comes about, Korah and his men, who have been enduring in the underworld, will then indeed die. Pseudo-Philo thus aligns himself with the hard-liners in the debate on the ultimate fate of Korah and his men (m. *Sanh.* 10:3). Pseudo-Philo omits the complaint of Korah against Aaron and the instructions that Korah and his assembly should take firepans and place incense upon them and that G-d would indicate whom He had chosen as priests. He also omits the role of Dathan and Abiram as rebels who complain (Num. 16:12–14) that

Moses had not brought them to a land flowing with milk and honey but rather had caused them to die in the wilderness. Through omitting these statements Pseudo-Philo is able to put the stress solely on the theological dispute between Korah and G-d.

Apparently, Philo is troubled by the thought that many innocent people might have been swallowed up. Indeed, Philo is similarly troubled by the divine command (Deut. 25:19) to wipe out the memory of Amalek, which, according to the prophet Samuel, in his instructions to King Saul (1 Sam. 15:3), means that every man, woman, child, and even animal of the Amalekites is to be destroyed, and which raises a tremendous moral question, since we may well ask how such a command, amounting to nothing less than what in modern times has been termed genocide, is to be understood, especially coming from G-d Himself.

There is a seeming contradiction in the Bible concerning the manner in which Korah and his company died. On the one hand, the biblical text states that the earth opened up its mouth and swallowed up all the men that belonged to Korah (Num. 16:32). Three verses later, however, we are told that fire came forth from the L-rd and consumed the 250 men who had offered incense (Num. 16:35), presumably the 250 followers of Korah (16:2). Josephus neatly resolves the problem by asserting that the earth swallowed up Korah's associate, Dathan, and the latter's followers (*A.J.* 4.51–53), whereas Korah's company was consumed by fire (*A.J.* 4.54–56).[270] Whereas in the Bible we are told nothing about the fire that suddenly consumed the 250 followers of Korah, other than that it came forth from the L-rd (Num. 16:36), Josephus, well aware that his readers might find this item hard to believe, disarms them by telling them that the like of this fire had never in the record of history been produced by the hand of man. One guesses that Josephus is suggesting the possibility of a "scientific" explanation for this apparent miracle.[271]

Similarly, in the case of the punishment of Korah and his followers, Philo makes a special point of noting (*Mos.* 2.282) that the earth burst open precisely in that part where the tents of the *wicked* people stood, so that they were borne below in a mass and that the gaping sides closed again when these culprits had been swallowed up.

As to the flame that consumed the 250 men, Philo (*Mos.* 2.283) adds that thunderbolts fell suddenly on the men who had led the sedition and destroyed them in a mass so that no part of their bodies received the tribute of burial. He adds that it was the quick succession of these punishments and their magnitude that clearly established the fame of Moses' godliness and the truth of his pronouncements. Because, apparently, there would seem to be a contradiction between being swallowed up and burned, Philo adds that the work of chastising the impious rebels was shared by earth and heaven, the fundamental parts of the universe, since the culprits had let their wickedness take roots in the earth, while also mounting right up to the ether above. The result, he explains, was the same, whether they were swallowed up or whether they were destroyed by the thunderbolts.

After the rebels had been swallowed up by the earth, the entire assembly of the Israelites complained against Moses and Aaron that they had killed the people of G-d. Thereupon G-d sent a plague (Num. 17:11). Aaron supplied atonement for the people, and the plague was checked after 14,700 had died therefrom. Then G-d instructed Moses to tell each of the tribes to write its name on a staff[272] and to write the name of Aaron on one of the staffs and to place the staffs in the Tent; and the fact that Aaron's staff blossomed was the sign that he had been the one chosen by G-d.[273] Philo (*Mos.* 2.178–86) elaborates on this, noting that the fruits on Aaron's staff were nuts, symbolic of perfect virtue, in that in them seed and edible part are identical.

In sum, for Philo the revolt of Korah is not a personal contest between Moses and Korah; it has a political dimension, reflecting, we are tempted to suggest, Philo's personal involvement in politics as a leader of the Alexandrian Jewish community. Whereas in the Bible and in Josephus the revolt is an attempt by Korah to displace Aaron, in Philo the revolt is a classic case of an attempt by one group, the Levites, to gain power over the priests; and he is particularly critical of the attempt of the masses, for whom he had disdain, to assert their power. Philo's chief concern is theological; and the Levites' objection challenges the very concept of divine revelation. What disturbed Moses most was that the rebels challenged the divine origin of Moses' appointment of Aaron as high priest. In his reaction to Korah's rebellion Philo defends Moses for not attempting to answer Korah's arguments. Philo is troubled by the thought that many innocent people might have been killed when the followers of Korah were swallowed up by the earth; and so he makes a special point of noting that the earth burst open precisely in that part where the tents of the wicked people stood.

q. The War with the Edomites

One striking example of Moses' benevolence (φιλανθρωπία) is to be seen in Moses' dealings with the Edomites (Num. 20:14–21, *Mos.* 1.239–49, *Deus*

142–80).[274] According to the Bible, Moses sent emissaries to the king of Edom, noting that the Edomites were kinsmen of the Israelites (inasmuch as Esau [Edom] was the twin brother of Jacob) and remarking that the Edomites knew all the hardships that the Israelites had endured. The emissaries stated that they were now at the edge of the Edomites' border, and they requested permission to pass through their land, promising not to pass through their fields or vineyards and not to drink their well water. When the king refused, the envoys offered to pay for the water. The king adamantly refused, whereupon the Israelites turned away and took another route.

As Philo (*Mos.* 1.239–49) narrates the incident, he adds that the Israelites thought that the Edomites, being their kinsmen, would actually join with them in war against their neighbors and assist their new settlements in every way or, at any rate, would remain neutral. He notes that the Edomites, like the Israelites, had become a great and populous nation, but had abandoned their ancestral customs and had kept alive their ancient feud. Consequently, the Israelites deemed it fitting for humane (ἥμερος, "civilized," "gentle") natures to show kindness (χαρίζεσθαι, "show favor," "give graciously") in the name of kinship. Moses, says Philo (*Mos.* 1.243), though he might have won an uncontested military victory, nevertheless did not follow this course because of the kinship and instead made the peaceful overtures mentioned in the biblical text. In stressing these peaceful overtures, Philo is, in effect, replying to those who had accused the Jews of his own day as being unduly aggressive. He adds that when the king of the Edomites refused to accept these conditions, the Israelites were angry and were at the point of going to war when Moses, in a speech that is totally extra-biblical and that graphically illustrates his effectiveness in leading his nation along a path of moderation, told them that their indignation was reasonable (εὔλογος, "sensible," "fair") and just (δικαία), since they had offered beneficial (χρηστά, "kind") proposals, whereas the Edomites had replied maliciously. However, the fact that they deserved to be punished for their savagery (ὠμότης, "cruelty") did not justify vengeance (τιμωρία, "retribution"), since the honor of the nation forbade it. Furthermore, Moses added that the Israelites should differentiate their goodness from the Edomites' knavishness (μοχθηρός) by investigating whether some particular persons deserved to be punished and whether that punishment could be properly carried out by the Israelites. It is significant that nowhere in this entire pericope does Philo mention the name of the Edomites, presumably again because he wishes to keep the spotlight on Moses and to generalize that his attitude is that of Jews everywhere and at all times.

Philo (*Mos.* 1.249) then editorializes that the Israelites were prevented from using force against the Edomites by their commander, that is, Moses, who showed two of his beautiful qualities—good sense (φρόνησις, "judgment," "prudence") and kindness (χρηστότης, "goodness of heart"). He showed sagacity (σύνεσις) in guarding against experiencing suffering, and humanity (φιλανθρωπία, "benevolence," "kindliness")[275] in not being willing to take revenge against his kinsmen. Indeed, one senses in these remarks by Moses that Philo is, in effect, preaching to his contemporary fellow Alexandrians that, despite provocations, they should not seek revenge.

Following this incident, in his biography of Moses (*Mos.* 1.254) Philo totally omits any mention of the episode (Num. 21:6–9) in which G-d sent fiery serpents against the Israelites, whereupon the people regarded the serpents as punishments sent by G-d for their speaking against G-d and Moses, and begged Moses to pray to G-d to remove the serpents from them. Thereupon G-d advised Moses to make a fiery serpent and place it on a pole and told him to tell the people that, if anyone was bitten by a serpent, he should stare at the fiery serpent and he would be cured. Inasmuch as *Mos.* is a factual biography, Philo apparently regarded such an incident as straining the bounds of credulity, and so he omitted it here; but in treatises (*Leg.* 2.77–87, *Agr.* 95–99) that present the Bible allegorically, he does not hesitate to include the incident, since he there explains that the serpent represents the principle of self-mastery. Similarly, in the New Testament (John 3:14–15) the incident is understood allegorically as an indication that whoever believes in Jesus may have eternal life.

In sum, in his negotiations with the Edomites, Moses shows special benevolence. He shows his moderation in his response to their refusal to allow the Israelites to pass through the Edomites' land. By not mentioning the Edomites specifically, Philo keeps the spotlight on Moses and signifies that his attitude is that of Jews at all times.

r. The War with Sihon

After his account of the song at the well (Num. 21:17–20), Philo appends a detail that is not found in the Bible, but that adds considerably toward the portrait of Moses as the farsighted commander-in-chief of the Israelites in the wilderness, namely, that he distributed his younger men in the vanguard and rearguard, and placed the old men, the women, and the children in the center so as to be protected on either side.

In his narrative of the incident of the war with Sihon that follows, Philo (*Mos.* 1.258–62) adds touches that emphasize Moses' careful attention to treating other nations fairly and decently in contrast to the way in which the Israelites were treated in return. Thus, the Bible (Num. 21:21) simply states that the Israelites sent emissaries[276] to Sihon asking for permission to pass through his land and promising not to damage anything in it and that Sihon refused. Philo (*Mos.* 1.258) declares, in a reprise of the incident with the Edomites, that Sihon not merely answered the Israelite envoys insolently (πρὸς ὕβριν) who had been sent by Moses, when they came to make their request to pass through his land, but he adds that Sihon would have put them to death, if he had not been prevented by what was the law of nations that was in effect in those times pertaining to embassies. Moreover, whereas the Bible says that Sihon and his entire people (Deut. 2:32) waged war against Israel, Philo adds that he went to war expecting to win an immediate victory. However, Philo adds, he discovered that the Israelites were not untrained or unpracticed fighters, but invincible masters of warfare, who had performed many great feats of bravery and had shown themselves "strong in body, mettlesome in spirit, and lofty in virtue" (*Mos.* 1.259), and through these qualities had captured their enemies with great ease. He remarks, moreover, in an extra-biblical addition, that the Israelites, in their piety, had left the spoils of war untouched so as to dedicate the first prizes to G-d. This is an implied tribute to Moses, their commander-in-chief, for having trained the Israelite soldiers so well.

Having justice on their side, the Israelites, in Philo's extra-biblical comment, showed even greater courage and zeal; and, in a single battle, they turned the entire opposing force to flight and immediately proceeded to annihilate them from the youth upwards (ἡβηδόν)(*Mos.* 1.261), emptied the cities of their inhabitants, and filled them with themselves.[277] According to the summary of the incident in the Book of Deut. (2:34), the Israelites destroyed every populated city, including women and children, and did not leave a single survivor. Likewise, the farmhouses in the country were emptied of their occupants; and others, superior in every respect, took their place.

Philo thus insists that Sihon fully deserved the treatment that he received. One major difference from the Bible is that Philo does not mention that G-d hardened Sihon's heart, just as he omits references to G-d's hardening of the Pharaoh's heart, presumably because this would raise a question as to whether G-d interfered with Sihon's freedom of will. In terms of the treatment of the population of Sihon's land, there are two differences between the biblical account and Philo's version. In the first place, there is in Philo no mention of women and children. In the second place, whereas the Bible speaks of the destruction of the entire population, Philo speaks of the annihilation of the army alone and says that the cities of Sihon were emptied of their inhabitants, but with no indication that the civilian inhabitants were killed. In not mentioning the genocide of Sihon's population, we may surmise that Philo was motivated by a concern to answer the recurring charges, as formulated by such writers as Apollonius Molon and Lysimachus (*ap.* Josephus, *Ap.* 2.145), that Jews had an implacable hatred of non-Jews (see Feldman 1998b, 557–59).

As to the biblical Og (Num. 21:33–35, Deut. 3:1–11), who is coupled with Sihon, Philo does not mention him at all, perhaps because he felt that the Bible's statement that he was nine cubits (approximately 13 1/2 feet) in length and four cubits (approximately six feet) in width would appear to be incredible to sophisticated readers, or perhaps because he felt that the account of Og would, in effect, duplicate that of Sihon, with whom he was closely allied, or perhaps because the military achievements of Moses are less important than his achievements in the five capacities that Philo chooses to emphasize, those of king, philosopher, lawgiver, high priest, and prophet (*Mos.* 2.2).[278]

Elsewhere Philo (*Leg.* 3.225–35) interprets the whole account allegorically. The Bible (Num. 21:27) ascribes the poem about the battle with Sihon to composers of proverbs (המשלים), which the LXX renders as riddlers (αἰνιγματισταί). Whereas in the poem (Num. 21:30) we read that "their [the Amorites'] sovereignty over Heshbon was lost and was removed from [the city of] Dibon, and that we [the Israelites] laid waste to Nophah, which reaches up to Medeba," the LXX, which Philo (*Leg.* 3.225) here follows, has a vastly different rendering: "And their seed shall perish [from] Heshbon to Daibon, and their women (γυναῖκες) have yet kindled (προσεξέκαυσαν) a fire against Moab." Philo notes that "Moab" means "out of a father"; and our father is the mind. Heshbon, the chief city of the Amorites, means "reasonings" (λογισμοί) (*Leg.* 3.226); and "reasonings" are riddles (αἰνίγματα), following the LXX's rendering of the poets as "riddlers." Riddles, he then explains, are full of obscurity (ἀσάφεια, "lack of clarity").

Philo gives an example of a doctor's reasonings, that he will purge the patient, feed him, prescribe medicines, put him on a diet, operate on him, and cauterize him, whereas in the end it is nature that either cures him or brings about his death, thus proving that the doctor's "reasonings" are vain dreams, guesswork in the dark. A second example that he cites (*Leg.* 3.227) is that of a farmer, who sows and plants, sure that he will thus obtain abundant food, whereas a fire or a storm spoils everything. Still other times everything turns out as he had planned, but he himself dies before he can enjoy the fruits of his labors. Philo, the philosopher, concludes (*Leg.* 3.228) that it is best to trust G-d and not our reasonings.

Philo (*Leg.* 3.228) explains that the name Sihon means "corrupting"; and if we trust in our own reasonings, we shall build up the city of Mind that corrupts the truth, and the Mind that corrupts the truth is irrational; that is, in effect, he equates Sihon with the Sophists. Moreover, the god of the Amorites, Chemosh, means "groping," that is, unable to see (*Leg.* 3.231). The word "Amorite," he says, means "the lecturer or sophist of men fond of talking," that is, clever at searching after verbal artifices; and those who transgress the boundary of truth place themselves at the mercy of his quibbling. This is the supreme criticism coming from a Platonist—sophists clever at searching for verbal niceties, while transgressing truth. In a further equation with the Sophists he explains the meaning of Heshbon, the chief city of Sihon, as "quibbling riddles." In a further reference to the Sophists, he explains the meaning of Dihon, another city of Sihon, as "going to law" (δικασμός) (*Leg.* 3.233), "quite appropriately, for probabilities and plausible arguments involve no knowledge concerning truth, but trial and disputation and wrangling conflict and contentiousness and everything of that sort."

Finally, the fire that comes forth from Heshbon is equated with women, that is, the senses, and brings about disaster (*Leg.* 3.234, *Migr.* 99–100), since the senses introduce into themselves from outside a host of mischiefs, from things seen, heard, tasted, and smelled. Thus the fire kindled by the senses adds to mental troubles. Philo notes (*Leg.* 3.234) that at night, when no single one of the senses is actively employed, we entertain strange notions on many diverse topics, since the soul is then in movement and turns in numerous different ways. As an admirer of Plato, committed to the unchanging Forms, he stresses the danger in going in such diverse directions and warns that such variety is sufficient for the corruption of the soul. But as if this internal turmoil were not sufficient, the senses introduce from outside themselves countless mischiefs; and these affect the soul more adversely than the flame kindled in it by the soul itself. These senses, he says (*Migr.* 100), equated, as they are, with women in the biblical poem in the LXX version (Num. 21:30), set the mind on fire in violent and resistless current. As a practical measure, it is best that women, that is the senses in the soul, should be propitiated, for in this way we shall experience a better journey in our lives.

In the Bible (Num. 21:22, also 20:17) we read that the Israelite emissaries tell Sihon they will travel along the king's road (בדרך המלך, ὁδῷ βασιλικῇ) until they pass through his borders. Philo (*Spec.* 4.168) takes the occasion to use this phrase to present the familiar classical theme of the wisdom of following the middle road between excess and deficiency.

Like Philo, Josephus (*A.J.* 4.86–99) insists that the Israelites were justified in their action against Sihon. He asserts that they killed all the inhabitants of Og's (but not Sihon's) cities but, like Philo, says nothing about the women and children, perhaps because he felt that such apparent cruelty would not redound to the credit of the Israelites. He apparently saw a difference between the cases of Amalek and Sihon and Og, remarking (*A.J.* 6.136) that in the former case the Amalekites were everlasting enemies of the Israelites and that in eliminating them they were fulfilling a divine commandment, which, he says, it was dangerous to disobey. Finally, Josephus, always the apologist, like Philo, omits the statement that G-d hardened the spirit of Sihon (Deut. 2:30), presumably because this would indict G-d.

The Samaritan tradition (*Molad*, p. 64, ll. 8–9), which constantly emphasizes the miracles that Moses is said to have performed, asserts that Moses killed Sihon and Og with his prayers so that not one of his people was missing.

In sum, Philo stresses that Moses, in his treatment of Sihon, showed the same consideration that he had demonstrated toward the Edomites. He speaks of the annihilation of the Edomite army alone, with no indication that civilians were killed. He does not even mention the annihilation of Og. Philo emphasizes how carefully Moses had trained the Israelite soldiers to show piety in leaving the spoils of war as prizes for G-d.

s. *Balaam*

That the story of Balaam was of great interest to Philo may be deduced from the extraordinary amount of space that he gives to this narrative (*Mos.* 1.263–99). Thus, whereas the Hebrew (Num. 22:2–24:25) has 142 lines and the LXX has 242 lines, Philo's version has 264 lines. This gives a ratio of 1.86:1 for Philo as compared with the Hebrew and 1.09:1 for Philo as compared with the LXX.[279] This concern with Balaam has already been cited by Colson 1935, 6:xv, who further notes that the story of Balaam has little to do with Moses and seems out of place, certainly when it is presented at such length, in a biography of Moses.

There are several reasons for Philo's interest in the figure of Balaam. In the first place, Philo is very much concerned with the phenomenon of prophecy, since he regarded Moses, as does the Bible, as the greatest of the prophets. Moreover, the biblical prophets had some standing even among pagans, if we may judge from their popularity with the second-century philosophers, such as Numenius of Apamea, the Neo-Pythagorean, who, according to Origen (*Against Celsus* 4.51), quoted not only Moses but also other prophets in many passages in his writings. Furthermore, the fact that Balaam had a great reputation, at least to judge from the rabbinic tradition (*b. B. Bat.* 15b), and in some respects even greater than that of Moses (*Sifre Deut.* last line), meant that Philo had to show that Moses was really superior in prophecy, one of the five areas in which, according to Philo, Moses was supreme (*Mos.* 2.2).

However, Philo was clearly confronted with a dilemma here: if he showed too much regard for Balaam, he would be giving credence to a pagan prophet who had sought to curse Israel; on the other hand, if he downgraded Balaam, he would betray his prejudice against non-Jewish wise men.[280] Nevertheless, as we shall see, unlike Josephus, who gives a relatively unbiased portrayal of Balaam,[281] especially when it is compared with the rabbinic tradition,[282] the New Testament,[283] or the Jewish Scriptures themselves,[284] Philo gives a negative portrait. Most significantly, Josephus shifts the focus from Balaam's personality to the historical, political, and military confrontation between the Israelites and their enemies in Balaam's time. Indeed, to a considerable degree, the Balaam episode, as described by Josephus, functions as a prologue to the war against the Midianites. Furthermore, Josephus employs the prophecies of Balaam to present, in a veiled form to be sure, his own vision of the future of the Jewish people.

Philo, on the other hand, stresses that the very name of Balaam means "empty" (μάταιος, "vain") (*Cher.* 32, *Conf.* 159, and *Migr.* 113). He portrays him as an empty sophist (*Det.* 71), a conglomerate of incompatible and discordant notions (*Det.* 71), a dealer in the vanity of unfounded conjecture and the very antithesis of true prophecy, which, of course, is associated with Moses (*Deus* 181, *Conf.* 159, and *Mut.* 202). In particular, he charges him with conceit (οἴησις) (*Mos.* 1.286), which Philo describes as a great vice (κακὸν μέγα) and discredits his motives, alleging that he was motivated by love of gain (*Migr.* 114). However, in the extended narrative of this incident in his essay *Mos.* (1.263–305), he, remarkably, does not mention the name of Balaam even once, again seeking to keep the focus on Moses, and perhaps motivated by a concern not to offend his non-Jewish audience.

According to the Bible (Num. 22:2–4), Balak, the king of Moab,[285] became frightened because the Israelites were so numerous, and he sought to form an alliance with the Midianites, whereas Philo (*Mos.* 1.263) says that the cause of alarm was the success of the Israelites in the war against Sihon, a victory that clearly redounded to the fame of Moses, the commander of the Israelite army. Philo, moreover, expands the spread of the alarm to all the nations of Asia (ibid.). Whereas in the biblical text there is no indication of the power of Balak, Philo adds that he had brought under his sway a great and populous portion of the East. In view of Balak's power, one would wonder why he did not go to war with the Israelites and why he sought rather to overcome them by cursing them. Philo explains that he gave up before meeting the enemy directly, realizing that in a war his nation would be sacked.[286] Consequently, he turned to augury (οἰωνός) and soothsaying (μαντεία), thinking that he would thus be able to destroy the invincible power of the Israelites.

The Bible goes on to state (Num. 22:5), without indicating what qualifications Balaam possessed for that task, that Balak sent messengers to Balaam[287] to ask him to curse the Israelites. Philo (*Mos.* 1.264) fills in these details. Balaam, he says, was far-famed (περιβόητος) for soothsaying (μαντεία). He had learned (ἐμεμύητο, "had been initiated into the mysteries") all the forms of soothsaying and was especially admired for his skill in augury. Philo then adds example after example of his wondrous skill in prophesying rainstorms in summer, drought and heat in mid-winter, dearth after prosperity and the reverse, rivers flooded and dried up, cures for pestilential diseases and countless others. As a result, his fame kept on spreading everywhere. Such a wondrous prophet would seem to be a match for Moses, whose chief ability was precisely in prophecy (*Mos.* 2.6, 2.69, 2.288–91).

Clearly, Philo, like the later Josephus (see Feldman 1993b, 48–83), was confronted with a dilemma when he came to classify Balaam. On the one hand, if Philo knew the oral tradition—and there is good reason, as we have suggested, to think that he might have known it—he would be aware of the high regard in which that tradition held Balaam as a prophet. Moreover, the fact that Balaam is cited, with virtually no introduction, in an extra-biblical text discovered in 1967, indicates that the name of Balaam was well known to the pagan people to whom the inscription in question (apparently dating from the eighth century B.C.E.) was addressed, so that we may infer that Balaam's prophetic status was a tradition of long standing (see Hackett 1980). On the other hand, Philo, as we can see from his remarks about Balaam, was aware of portrayals of Balaam as the epitome of wickedness.

Against this background, it is only to be expected that Philo would distinguish carefully, in his terminology, between pagan and Jewish prophets. The LXX, we may note, reserves the term προφήτης[288] for those who reveal the divine will, while using the word μάντις and its cognates when referring to heathen soothsayers.[289] Philo, in general, seems to maintain the classical distinction between μάντις and προφήτης (Krämer 1976, 781–96), namely that the former has foresight and knowledge of future events, as Cicero (*De Divinatione* 1.1) puts it (hence this role can continue after the cessation of prophecy, which occurred during the reign of Artaxerxes, according to Josephus' *Ap.* 1.41), whereas the task of the προφήτης is to be the voice of G-d and to declare the knowledge of G-d to those who come for advice (see Feldman 1990, 400–407). The role of the true prophet is that of a mediator, serving both as G-d's spokesman to man and vice versa.

As Krämer 1976, 795, remarks, it is not until the second century C.E., under Christian influence, that the term προφήτης came to denote one who foretells the future. The μάντις, on the other hand, as Rose 1914, 796, notes, was not an inspired prophet but a craftsman (δημιουργός), associated with leeches and carpenters in Homer (*Od.* 17.384). It is significant, then, that Moses is spoken of as a προφήτης, whereas Balaam is denominated a μάντις (*Mos.* 1.276, 1.282 [*bis*], 1.285, 1.305), who seeks omens through birds and voices; and his art is soothsaying (μαντεία, *Mos.* 1.263, 264; μαντικός, 1.264, 1.277, 1.284, 1.285).[290] According to the Bible (Num. 22:38, 23:5, 23:12), Balaam can say only those words that G-d puts into his mouth; but Philo (*Mos.* 1.274) emphasizes that Balaam does not understand what he is saying. Whereas in the Bible (Num. 22:31), after Balaam's donkey speaks, G-d uncovers Balaam's eyes and he sees the angel, Philo, in an extra-biblical remark (*Mos.* 1.272), calls attention to the irony of the fact, as he puts it, that an unreasoning animal showed a power of sight superior to him "who claimed to see not only the world but the world's Maker." Nevertheless, unlike Josephus, who, despite his general tendency to rationalize miracles (see Feldman 1998a, 209–12), retains the miracle of the speaking donkey (*A.J.* 4.109), Philo, clearly aware that his sophisticated readers would find this incredible, says (*Mos.* 1.272) that the animal was evidently terrified by a divine vision that was invisible to Balaam, thus proving Balaam's insensibility.[291]

Philo stresses the difference between a prophet and a soothsayer when he says (*Mos.* 1.277) that when Balaam became possessed by G-d "there fell upon him the truly prophetic spirit which banished utterly from his soul his art of wizardry." Again, there is a contrast between Moses and Balaam in that Moses is G-d's friend and his mind is naturally consonant with that of G-d, whereas G-d must work without the consent of Balaam's mind (*Mos.* 1.274). Likewise, whereas Moses understands what he is prophesying, Balaam (*Mos.* 1.283), when he is possessed, understands nothing (μηδὲν συνιείς); and his reason is, so to speak, roaming.

In short, a major difference between Jews, as epitomized by Moses, and pagans, as epitomized by Balaam, is that the Jews care nothing for augury (οἰωνοί) and all the lore of soothsaying (μαντική), and the Jews trust in the one G-d, who is the ruler of the world (*Mos.* 1.284). Even Balak, in a bitter, extra-biblical remark, says that Balaam in the end came to conceive a great contempt for his own art (τέχνη) (*Mos.* 1.287). And, in an editorial-like comment, Philo cannot restrain himself: "'Why,' we might ask him, 'do you put forth your own personal counsels in opposition to the oracles of G-d?'" (*Mos.* 1.294). Remus (1996, 674) suggests that Philo sees contemporary Balaams as practicing their arts in the streets and marketplaces of Alexandria; and, we may add, such editorial-like comments confirm this suggestion and show Philo as, in effect, preaching to his contemporaries.

The one time that Balaam is referred to as a prophet (*Mos.* 1.266), he is described not as a prophet but as one who talks speciously (ἀστειζόμενος,[292] "talks wittily"), seeking to *pose* as one of the prophets held in high repute (ἐλλόγιμοι προφῆται). In only one other instance (*Mos.* 1.277) do we hear of a prophetic (προφητικός) spirit coming upon Balaam, and that is when, as Philo carefully puts it, the truly prophetic spirit banished his art of soothsaying (ἔντεχνος μαντική), thus stressing the degree to which prophecy is the direct opposite of soothsaying.

When Balak sends his initial envoys to Balaam, hoping to get him to curse the Israelites (Num. 22:7), they go with the fees (קסמים, "magic," "divination," "divining instruments") in their hands. Philo has enlarged upon this and states (*Mos.* 1.266) that they offer him gifts at once and promise others to follow, quite clearly appealing to his greed,[293] in direct and striking contrast with Moses, who, as we recall from the account of the episode of Korah, had made a point of stressing (Num. 16:15) that he had taken not even a single donkey from the people.

In the Bible (Num. 22:5–13), in the initial meeting of the emissaries with Balaam, Balaam's response is that he will give them an answer after G-d has spoken to him. G-d forbids him to go, since the Israelites are blessed, and so Balaam reports to them that G-d has refused to allow him to go with them. Philo's Balaam gives a similar response, but Philo adds (*Mos.* 1.266), significantly, that Balaam, in declining the request of the envoys, was not motivated by any honorable (εὐγενής, "noble-minded," "generous") or sincere (βέβαιος) feelings[294] but rather by a wish to give the impression of being a distinguished prophet who did nothing without the consent of a divine oracle.

Thereupon, Balak sends emissaries of higher rank saying that he is prepared to do whatever Balaam will ask of him; but Balaam replies that even if Balak were to offer him a house full of silver and gold he cannot transgress the word of G-d. In Philo (*Mos.* 1.267), however, when the envoys offer more money and gifts, Balaam, enticed by these, gives the very opposite reply. He, standing in awe of the ambassadors, agrees to curse the Israelites, alleging the divine command dishonestly (οὐκ ἐφ' ὑγιεῖ) as an excuse. In the Bible (Num. 22:20), on the other hand, it is G-d who takes the initiative to come to Balaam at night and tells him that he should go with the envoys but that he should do only what He tells him to do.[295] This raises a question as to why G-d should now change His mind and why He should direct Balaam to accompany the envoys, presumably in order to curse the Israelites.[296] There is no such visit by G-d in Philo; rather, it is Balaam who decides to go; and Philo rationalizes, asserting that Balaam said that clear visions in dreams (without mentioning G-d) impelled him to accompany the envoys.

The Bible (Num. 22:21–22) states that as Balaam accompanied the envoys, G-d became angry because he was going, and an angel stood on the road to impede him. Philo, clearly troubled by the fact that G-d should now become angry when He had previously instructed Balaam to accompany the envoys, omits this and instead states that Balaam, as he was proceeding, was given an unmistakable sign that the mission on which he was going and on which he was indeed exerting (συνέτεινεν, "strive," "strain to the utmost") himself to go would not succeed.

In the Bible (Num. 22:23) Balaam's donkey from the very beginning sees the angel of G-d standing on the road with sword drawn in hand; and this causes the donkey to swerve from the road, whereupon Balaam strikes the donkey to turn it back onto the road. When he continues to strike it, G-d opens the mouth of the donkey and it asks Balaam why he has struck it (Num.

22:28). In Philo's version there is no mention at first of the angel; rather, we are told that the donkey came to a sudden stop, as though someone was pushing it. Philo (*Mos.* 1.272) now rationalizes that it was, as it seemed, a divine vision that the animal had seen. Thus Philo reduces the prophetic claims of Balaam to absurdity, since, he says, the irrational animal proved to have a power of sight superior to that possessed by one who claimed to see not only the world, but also the Creator of the world. Philo omits that the donkey spoke, presumably because sophisticated readers would find it hard to believe this.[297] According to the Bible, G-d then uncovered Balaam's eyes, he saw the angel, and he repented. Philo (*Mos.* 1.273) adds that he discerned the angel not because he was worthy of such a sight but so that he might perceive his own dishonor (ἀτιμία, "disgrace") and nothingness (οὐδένεια, "worthlessness"), whereupon he betook himself to supplications and prayers, seeking forgiveness for a sin committed in error rather than deliberately.

The reader might well be puzzled by the fact that at this point the angel tells Balaam to accompany the envoys, whereas he could and should have told him to return home. But again Philo casts Balaam in a bad light, since, whereas at this point we read (Num. 22:35) that Balaam accompanied the envoys as the angel had told him to do, Philo (*Mos.* 1.274) adds that the angel perceived his dissimulation (εἰρωνεία) when he asked whether he should return home. At this point in the Bible the angel tells Balaam that he should speak whatever he will tell him to say; however, in Philo he sternly says that he will tell him what to say without Balaam's consent. When Balak greets Balaam, the latter asserts that he can say only what G-d puts into his mouth (Num. 22:38); but Philo omits this and instead adds a description of the high feasting with which Balak received him (*Mos.* 1.275). Balak then takes Balaam to a hill where a pillar had been set up that the pagans worshipped (Num. 22:41, *Mos.* 1.276) and from which the Israelite camp was visible. There he consults G-d, who puts an utterance in his mouth. Philo (*Mos.* 1.277) has elaborated this and explains that Balaam became possessed (ἔνθους)[298] and that the prophetic (προφητικός) spirit visited him and banished completely from him the art of soothsaying, since this art and that of true prophecy cannot coexist.[299]

In the Bible (Num. 23:9) when Balaam blesses the Israelites, he refers to them as a nation that dwells in solitude. Philo (*Mos.* 1.278) also does so, but he adds the explanation that because of their peculiar customs the Israelites do not mix with others, in order to avoid departing from their ancestral ways, perhaps an allusion to the corrupting influence of intermarriage in Egypt to which Philo (*Spec.* 3.29) alludes elsewhere.[300] When Balaam blesses, rather than curses, the Israelites, Balak berates him, bitterly remarking (*Mos.* 1.280) that he unconsciously had been deceiving himself in treating Balaam as a friend whereas actually Balaam had been secretly on the side of the enemy and that this was the reason for Balaam's delay in coming to Balak. Philo (*Mos.* 1.283) adds that Balaam was possessed and understood nothing, as the prophetic words were put into his mouth, his reason roaming, as it were. The biblical Balak (Num. 24:10), in his anger, then reminds Balaam that he had called upon him to curse the enemy, whereas Balaam had blessed them three times; but Philo's Balak (*Mos.* 1.285), in his indignation, tells Balaam not to curse or bless, since silence that avoids danger is preferable to words that bring no pleasure.

Nevertheless, Balak persists in importuning Balaam to curse the Israelites. But whereas the biblical Balaam (Num. 23:20), in accordance with G-d's instructions, proceeds to bless the Israelites, Balaam, according to Philo (*Mos.* 1.286), turns out to be even worse than Balak, having been pressed hard (πεπιεσμένος, "weighed down") by a great evil, namely conceit (οἴησις), because of a longing to curse, even if he is prevented by his voice. The biblical Balak then takes Balaam to the summit of a height, where Balaam tells him to offer sacrifices (Num. 23:27–30) and where Balak tells him to curse the Israelites. According to Philo (*Mos.* 1.287), Balaam conceived a great contempt for his art of soothsaying, and so he did not look for omens from birds or voices but realized that the king's aim was not consonant with that of G-d. Thereupon, Balaam, as in the Bible (Num. 24:3–9), so in Philo (*Mos.* 1.288–89), looking upon the Israelites, proceeds once again to bless them.

At this point in the Bible (Num. 24:11–13) an angry Balak tells Balaam to flee, and Balaam defends himself by reminding Balak that he had told Balak's emissaries that he could not transgress the words of G-d, whereas Philo's Balaam continues on (*Mos.* 1.290–91), without the interruption by Balak. Balaam (Num. 24:17) prophesies that a star has issued from Jacob and that a scepter-bearer has risen from Israel. This is interpreted by Philo (*Mos.* 1.290) to be a messianic-like prophecy that some day a man will come forth from the Israelites who will rule over many nations and that his kingdom will be raised on high.[301] That a messianic prophecy is intended seems to be hinted at in the LXX's version of Num. 24:7: "There shall come a man out of his [i.e., Israel's] seed, and he shall rule over many nations; and the kingdom of God shall be exalted, and his kingdom shall be increased."[302] According to the Bible

(Num. 24:18–22), the Israelites will conquer the Moabites, the Edomites, the Amalekites, and the Kenites. Philo, on the other hand, apparently deliberately vague and careful to avoid antagonizing the Romans, who ruled Egypt in his day, does not specify these nations by name, perhaps because he was aware of the later tradition identifying Edom and Amalek with Rome.[303]

Philo (*Mos.* 1.291) closes with the statement that those who bless the Israelites are deserving of being blessed, whereas those who curse them are deserving of being cursed. The Bible (Num. 24:25) concludes this episode by remarking that Balaam and Balak each went his own way. Philo (*Mos.* 1.292), however, adds that Balak, greatly vexed, told Balaam to flee more quickly, lest he be forced to inflict upon him something unexpected (νεώτερον, "newer"). Alluding to Balaam's greed and covetous nature, Philo refers to Balaam as most senseless (ἀνοήτατος, "most unintelligent," "most foolish"), who has robbed himself of wealth and fame, being deranged (φρενοβλαβής, "crazy") and having brought ridicule upon his knowledge.[304]

In sum, Philo devotes much space to the story of Balaam in *Mos.*, despite the fact that it has little to do with Moses, because he felt that he had to show that Moses was superior in prophecy even to Balaam, the greatest of non-Jewish prophets. Remarkably, however, he does not in his *Mos.* mention the name of Balaam even once, thus keeping the focus on Moses. Significantly, he refers to Moses as a προφήτης, whereas Balaam is denominated a μάντις. Unlike Moses, who is visited by G-d, Baalam, according to Philo's rationalization, has visions in dreams. Similarly, it is a divine vision that Balaam's donkey sees; and, indeed, the donkey possesses a power of sight superior to that of Balaam. Moreover, Balaam's greed is contrasted with Moses' utter lack of this vice.

t. The Incident with the Midianite Women and Phinehas

Whereas in the Bible (Num. 25:1–3) there is no mention of Balaam's connection with the episode that follows, namely the harlotry committed by the Israelite youths with the Moabite women, Philo (*Mos.* 1.294), like the rabbinic tradition (*b. Sanh.* 106a), Josephus (*A.J.* 4.129–30), and Pseudo-Philo (18.13), presents this as a plan suggested in strict privacy by Balaam to Balak as the means by which Balak might defend his nation against the Israelites. The Bible (Num. 25:1–3) states with the utmost brevity that the people began to commit harlotry with the daughters of Moab. The latter incited the Israelite youths to attend the feasts of their gods, and the Israelites prostrated themselves to their gods. It is significant that Philo (*Mos.* 1.295–301) devotes 296 words to this episode, whereas the LXX (Num. 25:1–5) has 86 words, a ratio of 3.44:1 of Philo to the LXX. We may conclude that the fact that Philo devotes so much attention to this episode would indicate that though he is directing his *Mos.* primarily to non-Jews, he is also addressing it to those Jews who sought assimilation with Gentiles. According to another essay in Philo (*Virt.* 35), where the role of Balaam is not mentioned at all, it is the Midianites as a whole who sent for the most beautiful of their women and pointed out to them that dangerous as is the unlimited number of the Israelites, even more dangerous is their unanimity and mutual attachment, the source of which is their monotheistic belief. The Midianite women are told that they should not fear the disgrace in the name of harlotry, since they will convert this into immortal renown in that in an unprecedented manner women will have brought a war to a successful conclusion and at no danger to the Midianite men.[305]

According to another version in Philo, whose account (*Mos.* 1.295–99) is even more detailed, Balaam knew that the one way to gain an unquestioned victory over the eternal truths of the Torah and to conquer the Israelites was through putting before them the bait of pleasure, namely, the act of coition (λαγνεία) and licentiousness (ἀκολασία). He told Balak that inasmuch as he had in his land women of outstanding beauty, a man is more easily overcome by this than by anything else. He pointed out that if Balak would permit the most beautiful women to prostitute themselves for hire, they would entice the Israelite youths.

Philo himself (*Mos.* 1.294), in an editorial-like comment, states that in giving Balak this advice, Balaam had convicted himself of the greatest impiety (ἀσέβημα, "sacrilege"); and he addresses him thus: "'Why,' we might ask him, 'do you put forth your own personal counsels in opposition to the oracles of G-d?'" In doing so, he says, Balaam was demonstrating that he was regarding his own counsels as more powerful than the words of G-d. Philo then proceeds to describe Balaam's plan at length (*Mos.* 1.296–99). The Midianite women, Balaam advises, must be instructed not to hand themselves over at once to those who wish to have their beauty, "for titillating coyness arouses the appetites more and inflames the sexual passions. And when they are overpowered by their desires they will submit to do and to suffer anything. To the lover who is in this condition let one of those who are anointing themselves for the hunt wantonly say, 'You are not permitted to enjoy intercourse with me until you give up your ancestral way of life and convert and honor what I honor. Faith in the sincerity of your conversion will be clear to me if you are willing to partake of the same libations and sacrifices that we offer to statues of stone and wood and other images.' Since he has been ensnared by her traps of various kinds, by her beauty and by the cajoling of her small talk, he will refuse her nothing, binding his reason, and wretchedly will minister to her commands and will be enrolled as a slave of passion."[306]

In Josephus' extra-biblical addition (*A.J.* 4.130), Balaam similarly advises Balak to instruct the women that when they see that the Israelite youths have been overpowered by their passions, they should at that point abandon them; and when the youths implore them to remain, they should not agree until they persuade them to give up their ancestral laws and the G-d who established these laws and to worship the gods of the Midianites and the Moabites, and that this will cause G-d to be angry with them.

Josephus' version (*A.J.* 4.129–39) is considerably more romantic than that of Philo in that the women at first surrender to the youths without any conditions; but once they perceive that the latter have been ensnared by passion, they, following Balaam's advice, depart from them. In Philo, perhaps reflecting the instances of surrender to illicit sexual allurements in the contemporary Alexandrian Jewish community, the great sin of the Israelite youths consists of submitting to illicit passion; in Josephus the youths go even further in actually abandoning the Israelite religion. If it were for apologetic reasons, namely, to avoid the charge that Jews are intolerant of other people's religious practices, that Philo and Josephus omit the reference (Exod. 22:19) to the prohibition of sacrifice to foreign gods, we would have expected that they would not have expanded this incident of the fornication of the Israelite youths with the Midianite women. Hence, we may conclude that Philo and Josephus are here addressing their contemporary Jews, who apparently, in some cases, have been attracted to the practices of paganism.

Balak, considering this advice to be not far from the mark, and ignoring the law against adultery and abrogating those against seduction and fornication, as if they had not even been enacted in the first place, permitted the women to have intercourse freely with whomever they wished. They thus deceived the minds of most of the youths.[307] The Bible (Num. 25:3–5) notes that the wrath of G-d flared up against Israel, and that G-d told Moses to hang the leaders of the people in order that He might cease from His anger. Moses then told the Israelite judges that each should kill those of his men who were attached to the Moabite god Baal-Peor. Apparently nothing was done, however, until Phinehas, horrified and angry, displayed the youthfulness befitting an excellent man (*Mos.* 1.301).

For Philo the deed of Phinehas (Num. 25:6–16) in connection with the apostasy of Zimri is of special interest, as we can see from the fact that he deals with it in no fewer than eight of his essays (*Leg.* 3.242, *Post.* 182–85, *Ebr.* 73–76, *Conf.* 57, *Mut.* 108, *Mos.* 1.301–4, *Spec.* 1.56–57, and *Virt.* 41). In four of these (*Leg.* 3.242, *Post.* 183, *Conf.* 57, and *Mut.* 108) Phinehas is extolled as zealous (ζῆλος). The account of Phinehas' deed that is most comprehensive in terms of the narrative is in *Mos.* 1.301–4, and contains 173 words in comparison with the LXX of Num. 25:6–18, which contains 249 words, a ratio of 0.69:1 of Philo to the LXX, and a ratio of Philo to the Hebrew (230 words) of 0.75:1, whereas Josephus (*A.J.* 4.152–55) devotes 178 words to it, a ratio of 0.77:1 of Josephus to the Hebrew. Hence, the episode hardly evokes as much interest as one might expect. Presumably, Josephus found it difficult to extol one who was the prototype of the Zealots, whom he maligns in such strong terms in his *B.J.* (7.268–73). On the other hand, the immediate context, namely the description of the affair of Zimri with the Midianite woman Cozbi (Num. 25:6), is of very great interest, comprising a mere 32 words in the LXX as against an incredible 641 words in Josephus (*A.J.* 4.141–55), giving a ratio of 20.3:1 for Josephus as against the Hebrew. Josephus, it would seem, went all out to stress the terrible danger of intermarriage, on the one hand, but gave much less attention to the hero, Phinehas, who put an end to it. Philo (*Mos.* 1.302) devotes 69 words to the incident, giving a ratio of 2.16:1 for Philo as against the LXX. Why so much less attention than Josephus devotes to it?

What is striking about the passages in Philo dealing with this incident is that in *Mos.* Philo presents a straightforward account, with no mention of an allegorical interpretation, whereas in only two of the other seven treatises mentioning it (*Spec.* 1.56–57, and *Virt.* 41) is the incident not interpreted allegorically.

The Bible (Num. 25:6) reports that an Israelite named Zimri brought a Midianite woman to the actual sight of Moses and the entire Israelite assembly amid the weeping of the Israelites; nevertheless, apparently nothing was done. According to extra-biblical data introduced by Josephus (*A.J.* 4.142–51), Moses, at this point, anxious that matters might become even worse, gathered the people into an assembly. He accused no one by name, hoping that those who were guilty would quietly repent; but Zimri defended his marriage to a foreign wife and, counterattacking, accused Moses of tyrannical behavior. The response of the people was silence. Moses, according to Josephus, unwilling to provoke Zimri further and afraid that many would imitate Zimri's shameless behavior, dissolved the assembly.

Philo (*Mos.* 1.302), however, adds that Phinehas saw the Israelite offering a sacrifice and visiting a harlot, openly and publicly and proudly flaunting his licentiousness. The Bible indicates that Phinehas then stood up from amid the assembly and took a spear and followed the man into his tent and pierced them both, him and his consort into her stomach. Philo adds that he killed them while they still lay together, ripping up her genitals. One guesses that in embellishing this incident Philo may be referring to a contemporary danger of licentiousness in his own community.

A very serious question may be raised as to the justice of the reward (Num. 25:12–13), namely, the covenant of peace and of eternal priesthood, made by G-d to the zealot Phinehas, who, bypassing the rule of law, proceeds to kill Zimri in cold blood for consorting with a Midianite woman (Num. 25:7–13). Indeed, one might well ask why Zimri should be so utterly condemned for the act of marrying a Midianite when Moses had himself married a Midianite woman.

There is no word in the Bible expressing reservations as to the fact that Phinehas had not proceeded through judicial channels, but rather had taken the law into his own hands. On the contrary, Phinehas is, ironically, rewarded with the greatest reward that a person may receive, that of peace, and, since he was a priest, with an eternal priesthood. Moreover, we may ask, even if Zimri is properly punished as an apostate, why should his pagan consort, Cozbi, be put to death when she was simply worshipping the god of her people?

The only other place in the Bible where this event is recalled is Psalm 106:28–31, where Phinehas is praised without limit. There we are told that when the Israelites worshipped Baal-Peor and thus angered G-d with their behavior, and a plague broke out among them, it was Phinehas who arose and executed judgment, and the plague was halted. This passage in Psalms does not use the word "zealot" in connection with Phinehas, nor does it indicate precisely how Phinehas proceeded to perform his deed. It does mention that his act was accounted a righteous deed for all generations forever (ותחשב לו לצדקה לדר ודר עד-עולם), but it does not say explicitly that it was G-d who so regarded it, nor does it mention the twofold reward bestowed by G-d upon Phinehas, though the word עולם does recall the ברית כהנת עולם of the blessing bestowed upon Phinehas in Num. 25:13.

In the Apocryphal Book of Sir. (45:23–24) Phinehas is praised for his zeal (ζηλῶσαι) in the fear of the L-rd and is accounted third in glory (behind only Moses and Aaron) for standing up in brave determination when the other Israelites were in rebellion. Sir. combines the two rewards bestowed upon Phinehas, stating that a covenant of peace was made with him, so that he should be the chief of the sanctuary and of his people, and that he and his posterity should hold the office of the priesthood forever.

Moreover, the second century B.C.E. author of 1 Macc. (2:26) says that Mattathias, in killing the Jew who stepped forward to sacrifice on a heathen altar, cites the precedent of Phinehas in "showing forth his zeal for the Law." This would indicate that he regarded his act as completely legal in bypassing the judicial process. Again, when he is about to die, Mattathias, himself a priest, in addressing and inspiring his sons, urges them to be zealous (ζηλώσατε) for the Law (1 Macc. 2:50) and cites the example of Phinehas, "our father," who, because he was deeply zealous (ἐν τῷ ζηλῶσαι ζῆλος), obtained the covenant of an everlasting priesthood. In neither passage does Mattathias mention the divine reward of a covenant of peace, as if to intimate that peace in and of itself was not a goal to be sought.

Additionally, Hannah, the mother of the seven sons who suffered martyrdom during the persecutions by King Antiochus Epiphanes, in expressing her faith to her sons, recalls that her husband had taught them the Law and the prophets, among the examples from which she mentions the zeal of Phinehas (4 Macc. 18:12), though she does not specifically say that her husband praised Phinehas, as she says he did the example of Daniel (4 Macc. 18:13).

The rabbis generally praise Phinehas for his zeal, since they are most certainly aware that he won divine approval. Indeed, the third-century Rabbi Joḥanan notes that six miracles were performed so that Phinehas might succeed in his act (*b. Sanh.* 82b). Moreover, they portray him, obviously in praise, as arguing with G-d, in a manner reminiscent of Abraham in connection with the Sodomites, for permitting 24,000 to perish in the plague that occurred at this time, presumably because most were innocent; and they likewise, sympathetically, portray him as abused by his fellow Israelites on the ground that his maternal grandfather, Putiel (i.e., Jethro), had also worshipped idols (ibid.). He is even identified, as he is in Pseudo-Philo (48.1), with the prophet Elijah, both of them being known for their zealotry, and is thus regarded as a forerunner of the Messiah (*Tg. Ps.-J.* on Num. 25:12).

Yet, the rabbis do raise some questions about his deed. In the first place, they remark that Moses himself did not act with comparable zeal, and they present a scenario (*b. Sanh.* 82a) in which Zimri asks Moses who permitted him to marry Jethro's daughter, who was similarly a Midianite, whereupon Moses is said to have forgotten the law forbidding intimacy with a heathen woman. Furthermore, *Tg. Ps.-J.* on Num. 25:7 avoids the problem of Phinehas' bypassing the law by translating the words "he rose and left the congregation" as "he arose from his Sanhedrin," clearly implying that he had the approval of the Sanhedrin itself. However, the third-century Rabbi Ḥisda and the third-century Rabbah bar Bar Ḥanah, in the name of his teacher, the renowned Rabbi Joḥanan, assert that if a zealot comes to ask advice whether to take the law into his own hands to put to death one who cohabits with a heathen, even though the Mishnah (*Sanh.* 9:6) permits bypassing the law thus, he is not instructed to do so. What is more, they say that if Zimri had forsaken his mistress and Phinehas had killed him, Phinehas would have been subjected to the death penalty, and that if Zimri had turned upon Phinehas and slain him, he would not have been executed, inasmuch as Phinehas was a pursuer seeking to take his life. They also raise the question whether Phinehas was permitted to act without previously seeking the consent of Moses (*b. Sanh.* 82a). Indeed, the fourth-century Rabbi Judah ben Simeon ben Pazzi (*y. Sanh.* 9:7) goes so far as to say explicitly that Phinehas transgressed the will of the sages.

We may note an apparently similar incident (Num. 15:32–36) in which an Israelite violated the Sabbath by gathering wood thereon, whereupon those who found him doing so did not take the law into their own hands, but placed him in custody until the matter could be clarified as to what should be done to him. Philo, in his treatment of this incident (*Mos.* 2.214), remarks that those who saw him were hardly able to control themselves and, indeed, were minded to kill him. However, in direct contradiction to Phinehas' act in bypassing the law, Philo says, they did not wish to make it appear that they, who were but private citizens, had taken it upon themselves to act as if they were the rulers and to execute judgment without a trial, despite the fact that the offense was so clear and despite the fact that the profanation was that of the most sacred of days, the Sabbath. Therefore, they arrested him and brought him before Moses for judgment, while the whole multitude stood around to listen. Ostensibly, Philo's attitude, in approving the refusal of the people in this case to take the law into their hands, seems to contradict his view in approving of Phinehas' taking the law into his own hands. We may, however, suggest that the case of the violation of the Sabbath was that of a single individual, where there was no immediate threat that the violation would induce others to violate the law, whereas in the case of Phinehas there was such a serious threat that the immorality would infect the Israelite youth generally. Moreover, in the former instance, the Israelites abstained from taking the law into their own hands, according to Philo (*Mos.* 2.214), because for them to shed blood on the Sabbath would have violated the sanctity of that day.[308]

Philo (*Leg.* 3.242), draws a sharp contrast between Joseph, who, lacking the strength to contend with and to conquer pleasure, ran away from it, and Phinehas, who secured his own safety not by flight, but by fighting pleasure. Far from being critical of Phinehas because he did not work through the judicial system, Philo praises him as being zealous for G-d and as securing his own safety not by flight, but by grasping the spear, which he identifies allegorically as the spirit of zeal. The reward that Phinehas receives, peace and everlasting priesthood—"virtues as near of kin as sisters" (*Leg.* 3.242)—is well deserved.

Phinehas (*Post.* 182), in representing allegorically the abhorrence of pleasure, embodies a virtue of the highest order, according to Philo. Philo contrasts him with Onan (*Post.* 180–81), who was interested only in his own self and pleasure. Philo (*Post.* 182) identifies Phinehas as the controller of the inlets and outlets of the body, whose very name means "Mouth-muzzle". Phinehas thus, by reason and intelligence (*Post.* 184), destroyed the creature that hates virtue and loves pleasure (*Post.* 182). The reward of peace, Philo says (*Post.* 183), is particularly appropriate because Phinehas had put an end to the internal war of lusts in the soul; and the reward of the eternal priesthood (ἱερωσύνη) is, in playing upon the sounds of the two words, εἰρήνη and ἱερωσύνη, particularly appropriate because these words recognize the kinship of peace and the priesthood.

In obvious praise, Philo (*Post.* 182) commends Phinehas in superlative terms as, in effect, a philosopher, by equating the spear allegorically with the instrument used for exploring and inquiring into the very nature of all existence and for destroying by reason the creature that hates virtue and loves pleasure. Similarly, in his essay *Mut.* 108, Philo allegorically equates the spear used by Phinehas with the sharp-edged word, "able to probe and explore each thing," so that he pierced passion through the womb, "that it should henceforth bring to birth no plague of G-d's sending." Philo speaks allegorically of the spear that Phinehas employed as a "pit-searcher" (σειρομάστης), used in war to test whether there are pits in the ground, in this case "exploring and inquiring into the nature of all existence."

In view of the fact that Phinehas bypassed the law, it is ironic that Philo (*Post.* 184) praises the priests for maintaining a well-ordered state under good laws and for abolishing wars and factions, including, allegorically, wars that arise in the soul. Before resorting to force, he says, states would do well to prevail upon their citizens to put an end to the disorder that abounds within each one. Surely, this is ironic, inasmuch as Phinehas resorted to force before seeking a peaceful solution.

Philo justifies the manner in which Zimri and Cozbi were slain. Phinehas, he says (*Ebr.* 73), received the strength to pierce Cozbi through her womb "because she believed herself to be the cause of generation, though in reality her [feminine] part is passive rather than active." He derived the strength to pierce Zimri, who represents "the belief which invests the natures that are but the subjects of G-d's action with the dues which belong only to Him Who alone is the cause of all that comes into being."

Philo is clearly aware of the problem of how sanction could be given morally to one who bypassed the law: Phinehas, he admits (*Ebr.* 74), in striking bluntness, must pass for a murderer in the judgment of the multitude, "and be condemned by custom the woman-like" (Philo here regards custom as having less force than divine judgment); but in the eyes of G-d he deserves to be praised beyond reckoning and to receive (so also *Mos.* 1.304) the two great prizes of peace and the priesthood. He deserves these prizes because he preferred "neither wealth nor glory nor honor nor office nor beauty nor strength nor all bodily advantages, nor earth nor heaven, nor the whole world" before the service of G-d (*Ebr.* 75). It would seem ironic that Phinehas should be given the gift of peace when he used violent means, but Philo (*Ebr.* 76) insists that "none could be a man of peace who did not worship in truth and sincerity that Being Who alone is exempt from war and dwells in eternal peace."

Philo (*Conf.* 57) realizes the oxymoron in referring to Phinehas, on the one hand, as "that most warlike reason" and, on the other hand, as one who is given the gift of peace; but he justifies it on the ground that Phinehas waged war against vice and ripped open all created being and had the will to accept the faith that "mortality is full of unfaith" and as one who, like a Platonic philosopher, admired the true reality of the Forms and condemned one who was clinging only to the seeming.

In *Mos.* 1.304 we have another extra-biblical addition, obviously commending Phinehas for his deed, namely, that after he had done his deed, it was Moses himself who sought how to reward him, but that he was forestalled by G-d, who gave Phinehas his twofold reward. Furthermore, whereas the Bible (Num. 31:6) states that Moses sent Phinehas to the army that was to do battle with the Midianites, without indicating his exact capacity, Philo (*Mos.* 1.306) specifies that Moses appointed Phinehas as commander-in-chief (στρατηγός), thus, in effect, making him parallel in rank with Moses himself, and a clear indication that Moses approved of his extra-legal act.

In *Spec.* 1.56 Philo refers to Phinehas as one who acted with admirable courage (τὸ καλὸν τοῦτο τόλμημα). Whereas the Bible (Num. 25:6–7) states that Phinehas saw only the instance of Zimri, Philo, apparently realizing the danger of generalizing from a single case, here says that Phinehas had seen several persons consorting with foreign women. Again, whereas the Bible (Num. 25:14) states merely that Zimri was the head of a father's house belonging to the Simeonites, and presumably was acting alone, Philo (*Spec.* 1.56) speaks of him as the chief ringleader (ἔξαρχος, "leader," "first in rank," καὶ ἡγεμών, "leader," "guide," "authority," "one who does a thing first") of the lawlessness (παρανομίας, "transgression of law"), implying that he, like Korah, was the head of a movement to disobey Jewish law. Moreover, whereas the Bible (Num. 25:6) states merely that Zimri brought the Midianite woman to his family in the sight of Moses and all the Israelites, Philo (*Spec.* 1.56) is more specific in asserting that he openly offered sacrifices to images of wood and stone. Furthermore, whereas the Bible says simply that Phinehas took a spear in his hand and pierced Zimri and Cozbi, Philo (ibid.) delineates Phinehas' mood (ἐνθουσιῶν, "possessed by G-d," "in ecstasy") and adds that he kept back the throng of spectators on either side, who presumably tried to prevent him from proceeding to his murderous mission, and proceeded without any caution (οὐδὲν εὐλαβηθείς). He further adds that the act was committed suddenly (ἐξαίφνης), in the heat (θερμός) of excitement (*Spec.* 1.57). There is additional important justification for the act in that, according to Philo (ibid.) it served as a warning to multitudes who were preparing to make the same apostasy. Finally, he comments (ibid.) on the appropriateness of the reward of peace (though he does not adopt the biblical phrase of "covenant of peace," without necessarily implying that this was to be inherited by his descendants) bestowed upon Phinehas, inasmuch as he had battled for the honor of G-d; and the reward of the priesthood was most suitable to a man of piety, since bondage to G-d is better not only than freedom, but also than kingship.

In *Virt.* 41 Philo adds still another extra-biblical remark, namely that those who had worshipped Baal-Peor would have enticed others also of the less stable kind if G-d had not taken pity on them and lost no time in punishing with death the 24,000 mentioned in the biblical text (Num. 25:9), thus restraining those who were likely to be overwhelmed.

Consequently, we see that in Philo, unlike the rabbinic literature, there is no hint of criticism of Phinehas because he had bypassed the legal system. If he is criticized, it is only by the multitude and by custom. On the contrary, he is praised overwhelmingly; and his deed, the manner in which he acted, and the rewards given him by G-d are completely justified, especially since by his act Phinehas deterred others from apostasizing. Philo has not a word of sympathy for Cozbi, the pagan woman who was simply worshipping the gods of her religious tradition, though elsewhere, as we have noted, Philo (*Mos.* 2.205, *Spec.* 1.53) insists that Jews are forbidden to speak in a derogatory way about the religions of others. Zimri and Cozbi represent passion and seeming, and Phinehas represents sincerity, truth, reason, and intelligence.

The importance of the inclusion of the episode of Phinehas in Philo's *Spec.* is recognized by Seland (1995, 108) as evidence that Phinehas' deed constitutes a legal precedent for such action, which is nothing more or less than lynching. Jean Juster postulates that where Jews in the Diaspora did not have the right to punish someone with death, they resorted to such lynching (Juster 1914, 2:157 n. 2). Citing the passage in *Spec.*, Goodenough (1929, 33) concludes that this was the actual procedure of Jewish courts of Philo's day, though admittedly this is certainly debatable.[309]

Josephus was confronted with a dilemma of the first order in dealing with Phinehas, the priest who was rewarded by G-d with the covenant of a perpetual priesthood. On the one hand, Josephus was extremely proud of being a priest and of belonging to the first of the twenty-four courses of priests, as he makes clear by citing this as the very first point of his autobiography (*Vita* 1–2). As a priest, Josephus, not surprisingly takes pains to defend the choice of Aaron as the first high priest, asserting that he was even more just than Moses himself (*A.J.* 3.190). As for the blots on Aaron's record, notably his participation in the creation of the Golden Calf (Exod. 32) and his criticism of Moses for marrying an Ethiopian woman (Num. 12:1), Josephus conveniently omits them. If, to be sure, Aaron is relatively downgraded, this would seem to be due to Josephus' aim to preserve the primacy of Moses (see Feldman 1996b, 191–92).

The Bible states that after Phinehas' act the plague, which apparently had been raging, was halted. Philo, however, adds that this example by Phinehas inspired others, who, at the command of Moses, massacred without pity those of their friends and kinsfolk who had worshipped idols, thus purging the defilement of the nation. Twenty-four thousand (Num. 25:9) perished; Philo (*Mos.* 1.304) adds that this occurred in one day.[310] Commenting on the statement (Num. 25:5) given by Moses to the judges instructing everyone to kill all those who were attached to Baal-Peor, Philo (*Mos.* 1.303) justifies as most laudable the fact that the Israelites showed no pity even for blood relations, but held that their slayers were free of guilt, though, in his concern for justice, he presents the extra-biblical addition that while they relentlessly punished the actual sinners, they spared those who gave clear proof of their piety. Philo (*Mos.* 1.304), apparently aware that the reader might wonder why it was not Moses, rather than Phinehas, who took action to halt the sacrilege of the Israelite youths and why it was G-d and not Moses who rewarded Phinehas for his brave action, says that when the purging was completed, Moses wanted to reward Phinehas but was anticipated by G-d, who gave Phinehas, as the biblical text (Num. 25:12–13) also indicates, the highest of blessings, peace, together with the eternal possession of the priesthood.[311] Philo explains that these are gifts that no human being can bestow.[312]

One would have thought that it would be Moses who would take the lead in dealing with those Israelites (Num. 25:1–3) who committed harlotry with the Moabite women; and Moses does, indeed, give the order to the Israelite judges to kill those who are guilty; but when Zimri brought a Midianite woman to the very sight of Moses and of the entire assembly of Israelites (Num. 25:6), we hear nothing in the Bible of Moses' response. Rather, it is Phinehas who takes the law into his own hands and dispatches Zimri and Cozbi, the Midianite woman, and receives the divine reward of the covenant of peace and the eternal priesthood (Num. 25:12–13). Whereas in the Bible (Num. 25:5–9) the Israelites, at the command of Moses, kill those who have committed harlotry with the Moabite women, and only afterwards do we hear of the deed of Phinehas in killing Zimri and Cozbi (Num. 25:7–8), in Philo (*Mos.* 1.302) we hear of Phinehas' deed, and only afterwards do we hear that Phinehas' zealous followers copy it at the command of Moses and massacre 24,000. Moreover, whereas the Bible says nothing about Moses' role in getting the Israelites to follow the lead of Phinehas in wiping out those Israelites who had succumbed to licentiousness, Philo's Moses (*Mos.* 1.303) does play such a role, so that we hear that some of those who were zealous for self-control (ἐγκράτεια) and religiosity (θεοσέβεια), at the command of Moses, followed the lead of Phinehas and massacred all their kinsmen and friends who had apostasized.

In sum, it is surely significant that Philo devotes so much space to this episode in *Mos.*, when it actually has little direct connection with the life of Moses. The reason would seem to be that he is directing his essay not only to non-Jews but also to those Jews who sought assimilation with Gentiles. The fact that Moses appointed as general of his army Phinehas, the zealot who killed Zimri and Cozbi without going through legal channels, shows that Moses did approve of such extra-legal action in those circumstances, since he felt that it served as a warning to others. As to why it was Phinehas and not Moses who put an end to this sacrilege and why it was G-d and not Moses who rewarded Phinehas, Philo says that Moses wanted to do so but was anticipated by Phinehas and by G-d.

u. The Choice of a Successor: Joshua

Because one major test of a leader is seen in the ability to select outstanding assistants and successors, Hecataeus pays Moses the supreme compliment of saying (quoted in Diodorus 40.3.4) that he chose men of utmost refinement (χαριέστατοι) and of the greatest potential ability (μάλιστα δυνησόμενοι) to head the entire nation as priests. We may recall that the same word, χαριέστατοι, here used to describe the priests chosen by Moses, is the word used by Aristotle (*EN* 1.5.1095B22) to denote the people of superior refinement and of active disposition who identify happiness with honor, which is, adds Aristotle, the goal of political life. In this crucial decision, selecting the proper priests, Moses parallels the founder of Rome, Romulus, as we see in Dionysius of Halicarnassus (*Ant. Rom.* 2.21).[313]

A leader must realize that he will not live forever and hence must be concerned with the choice of a proper successor who will carry on his work, as the philosophic schools and the Roman principate, for example, learned in choosing successors. In the Bible (Num. 27:15–17) Moses asks G-d to appoint a successor and says merely that this is necessary because sheep should not be without a shepherd.[314] Indeed, Philo (*Post.* 67) says that every flock that has no shepherd over it necessarily meets with great disasters. Philo (*Agr.* 44–46) also explains, clearly having Moses in mind as the ideal shepherd of his flock, that a good shepherd leads his flock away from the snares of thoughtlessness (ἀφροσύνη) and injustice (ἀδικία) and every kind of wickedness (κακία) as well as of mob rule (ὀχλοκρατία), which he denominates as the worst of bad constitutions, and anarchy (ἀναρχία), its mother, and toward the doctrines (δόγματα) of culture (παιδεία) and excellence (ἀρετή). Under mob rule (*Agr.* 45), which is the very opposite of democracy, he says, there are endless clamors (θόρυβοι), disorders (ταραχαί), and civil strife (στάσις). Philo (*Agr.* 47) vehemently declares that we gain nothing from the rule of men who are too good (ἐπιεικεῖς, "reasonable," "fair"), since kindness (χρηστότης) is a quality easy to be despised (εὐκαταφρόνητον).

The Bible (Exod. 2:21–22) states that Jethro gave his daughter Zipporah to Moses as a wife, who gave birth to a son, whom he named Gershom. The Bible says nothing more about the birth of Gershom, but Philo (*Cher.* 47) adds the extra-biblical remark that when he married Zipporah, Moses, without supplication or entreaty, found her pregnant through no mortal. The context of this passage is Philo's contention (*Cher.* 40–41) that in the case of those to whose virtue the Bible testifies—and he names specifically Abraham, Isaac, Jacob, and Moses—these people are not represented as knowing women, since women signify sense-perception, which is rejected by lovers of wisdom. Hence, Philo insists (*Cher.* 42), it is a divine mystery that only the initiated are worthy to understand—that the wives of these key biblical heroes are in reality virtues, and it is G-d Himself who sows seed in them. He proceeds to cite examples of such divine procreation: the pregnancies of Sarah, Rebecca, and Leah, which resulted in the birth of the forefathers of the Israelites. Such divine intervention in the birth of Zipporah's son would thus seem to indicate that the child had a very special role to play, one would presume as successor to his father. And yet, Philo (*Mos.* 1.150), significantly in *Mos.*, does not include this comment, presumably because critical readers would find it hard to believe that a woman could become pregnant in such a fashion. Rather, in an editorial-like comment, Philo adds that Moses did not, like some—he is perhaps thinking of the Ptolemies and contemporary rulers of the Roman principate, Augustus and Tiberius—elevate his sons to great power and designate them as his successors. Instead, he allowed the impartiality (ἀδέκαστον) of reason (λογισμόν) to overcome his affection for his children, his sole goal being to benefit his subjects. Philo notes (*Virt.* 53), in obvious admiration, that Moses did not allow himself to be overcome (ἡττηθείς) by favoritism for kin (εὔνοια συγγενική) and family feeling (πάθος φιλοίκειον), being guided, rather, by reason and by his overwhelming aim to benefit his subjects and subduing his natural affection for his two sons.

Pseudo-Philo (20.5) is aware of the fact that Moses was not jealous when he is told (Num. 11:26) that Eldad and Medad's prophecies. Whereas the Bible does not indicate the contents of their prophecy, Pseudo-Philo states that the prophecy was that Joshua was to succeed Moses as the leader of the Israelites. The reason, we may suggest, why Moses might have been expected to be jealous was that he naturally might have hoped that his sons would succeed him; but apparently his concern was for the welfare of his people, and he was convinced that Joshua would serve best in this role.

The Bible and the rabbinic tradition are amazingly silent about the qualities possessed by Moses' two sons, Gershom and Eliezer.[315] Philo (*Virt.* 53) adds that even if the claims of Moses' own sons were under suspicion, at any rate he had nephews, the sons of Aaron, who were of great excellence and who consequently had been rewarded with the high priesthood. Philo (*Virt.* 54) conjectures that perhaps Moses did not choose them because he did not wish to withdraw them from the service of G-d, or perhaps he did not consider it possible for the same person to do justice to both positions, the high priesthood and the kingship (one thinks of the objection of Eleazar to John Hyrcanus' holding of the positions of both high priest and king [*A.J.* 13.288–92]); or perhaps he did not consider himself qualified to make such an important decision as to select his successor, a task that requires an insight into the inner character of a person that only G-d can judge.

Philo (*Virt.* 55) describes the friendship between Moses and Joshua as having been effected not by the ways in which other friendships are formed but by a passionate, pure, heavenly love (ἔρως), from which all virtue springs. He adds that Joshua had lodged under the same roof (ὁμωρόφιος) and had lived and eaten (ὁμοδίαιτος) with Moses, except for the time that Moses was prophetically inspired (ἐπιθειάσας), receiving divine revelation (χρησμῳδούμενος), and that Joshua had rendered service to him in a way that was always different from that of the masses, so that he was, in effect, all but his lieutenant in government. And yet, Joshua, in his modesty that parallels that by which Moses was distinguished above all other people (Num. 12:3), feared that Moses might have been deceived into thinking that he was a good man when in reality he was not, since the criteria of human judgment are somehow by nature obscure and unreliable. Consequently, Philo says in an extra-biblical addition that Joshua entreated G-d to select the man who would be most suited to lead and who would care for his subjects as a father (*Virt.* 57). This is, of course, ironic, in that Moses, as a father, does not choose his son, but rather a non-blood relative, Joshua.

Moses (*Virt.* 63) explains that he did not choose to be a leader but did so only when G-d repeated His command many times, whereupon he trembled but obeyed. Therefore, he adds that he felt that he should follow this precedent and leave the choice of his successor to G-d without any human participation in the decision.

Philo (*Virt.* 66) states the qualifications of Joshua, namely that he was Moses' disciple (φοιτητής, "one who regularly goes") on the basis of merit (ἀριστίνδην) and that he modeled himself on the character of Moses, which was so worthy of love. He then adds that Moses was not depressed as others might have been because their sons or nephews had not been chosen, but rather was filled with indescribable joy that the nation would have such an excellent leader.

As he is about to die, Moses addresses his successor, Joshua (Deut. 31:7, 23), telling him to be strong and of good courage. Philo (*Virt.* 69) adds Moses' exhortation to Joshua to be strong in his counsels (εὐβουλίαι, "soundness of judgment"), to initiate good plans (γνῶμαι), and to carry out his decisions well with unyielding and formidable (ἐρρώμενοι, "powerful") reasoning (λογισμοί). Moreover, Moses supplied the role model of a leader in that even though Joshua perhaps did not really need such exhortation, still Moses realized how important it was to relate on a personal level; and so he did not conceal his feeling of mutual affection and his patriotism, being stimulated to reveal what he thought would be useful. He did this also because he had been commanded by G-d to exhort his successor thus, who should not fear the burden of ruling. Thus Moses might serve as a model and archetype for all rulers, who might look to him (Moses) as an example, and no one would begrudge his successors good counsels, but would train and weld their souls with instructions and exhortations, which would serve as a source of inspiration to the disheartened.

The Bible (Num. 27:22–23) reports merely that Moses chose Joshua as his successor and placed his hands upon him. In Josephus (*A.J.* 4.165), we are told that before choosing Joshua, Moses had already indoctrinated him with a thorough training in the laws and in divine lore (*A.J.* 4.165). Philo (*Virt.* 52–53) cites Moses' choice of Joshua as his successor as one of the achievements at the end of his life that deserves to be mentioned as proof of his uninterrupted and continuous nobleness of life (συνεχής καὶ ἀδιάστατος καλοκἀγαθία).

It is significant, however, that Philo has no discussion at all in *Mos.* about the choice of a successor to Moses, presumably because he wished to keep the focus solely on Moses. That Philo was aware of this omission from his *Mos.* may be seen from his comment just before his major discussion of this topic in *Virt.* There (*Virt.* 52) he reminds the reader that he has set forth "the actions which he [Moses] performed from his earliest years to old age . . . in two treatises in which I wrote about the life of Moses." He then adds that "there are one or two achievements at the end of his life" that deserve to be mentioned as proof of the nobility of his life. He then proceeds immediately to mention that Moses chose not to bequeath his leadership to his sons. This, then, is, in effect, a postscript to his *Mos.*

In sum, Philo stresses that Moses was so devoted to finding the best possible successor to his leadership that he bypassed his own sons and nephews. Philo depicts the relationship of Moses to his usccessor, Joshua, as one that was derived from a pure, heavenly love; but, in any case, Moses left the choice of a successor to G-d. And when Joshua was chosen, he felt only joy. Philo omits from *Mos.* a discussion of the choice of a successor presumably because he wishes to keep the focus solely on Moses. It is particularly significant that he includes in *Cher.*, which was apparently directed to a Jewish audience, the statement of the divinely originated birth of Moses' son, who would naturally be expected to succeed him, whereas he omits this in *Mos.*, which was directed to a primarily non-Jewish audience.

v. The Battle against Midian

In the Bible (Num. 31:1) G-d tells Moses to take vengeance against the Midianites, presumably because of their role in leading Israelites to immorality and idolatry.[316] Philo (*Mos.* 1.305) spells out the reason for the campaign, namely to avenge the mischief that Balak had plotted and executed. Moreover, a great general knows that before undertaking to avenge some harm inflicted on one's people, one must be sure that internal troubles have ended, that one's people are united, and that those who were treacherous and guilty of treason have perished. Philo, in an extra-biblical addition, states that these conditions had now been met and that, moreover, a suitable opportunity had been found for seeking vengeance. As commander-in-chief, Moses had to decide when and with what troops to go to war and who should serve as soldiers. In the Bible (Num. 31:1–4) it is G-d who tells Moses to take revenge against the Midianites. Philo (*Mos.* 1.305–6) focuses on Moses' role. It is Moses who decides that the internal troubles of the Israelites have ended with the killing of those who have committed harlotry and with the death of those who were suspected of desertion or treachery.

According to the Bible (Num. 31:6), Moses sent Phinehas to the war with the holy vessels and the trumpets for blowing the alarm; but there is no indication that Phinehas was appointed as military commander.[317] Philo explains Moses' choice of Phinehas as commander of the army by saying that Phinehas had already given proof of his courage (*Mos.* 1.306).[318]

Furthermore, whereas the Bible indicates that Moses had asked each of the tribes to supply a thousand men (Num. 31:4), Philo says that Moses himself actually undertakes to select the very best men, as he had chosen the twelve scouts to inspect the Land of Israel (*Mos.* 1.221).[319] Philo (*Mos.* 1.306), in an extra-biblical addition, explaining why Moses asked each of the tribes to contribute a thousand men, depicts Moses as a skilled commander who realizes that it is unwise to employ one's whole army, knowing that over-large multitudes suffer through their unwieldliness, and who understands the advantage of keeping reserves to reinforce those who bear the first brunt of the fighting. Moreover, rather than asking the people to select a thousand from each of the tribes, he himself selects the best of his men of military age from each of the tribes.

In an unusual addition to the biblical text, Philo (*Mos.* 1.306) states that before sending his soldiers off to war against Midian, Moses offered favorable sacrifices. There is no mention in the Bible of such sacrifices, nor is there in Josephus' paraphrase (*A.J.* 4.159). Rather, apparently Philo had been influenced to do so because his primary audience consisted of non-Jews, who would have expected this, since this was the practice of the Greeks and Romans before battle; and Philo has thus cast Moses in the mold of a Greek or Roman general.[320]

We likewise see, in an extra-biblical addition, Moses' ability to encourage his people and his success in inspiring confidence in his men as they prepare to fight against the Midianites (*Mos.* 1.306–9). On the one hand, he uses a logical *a fortiori* argument in telling them that it would be absurd if, after slaying those of their own kinsmen who had violated the law, they should allow the enemy, who was guilty of more severe transgressions, to go free, and similarly, after putting to death those who had learned to do injustice, they spared those who had taught them. But, in addition, he appeals to their idealism, in that, unlike others, their aim is not to acquire power or possessions but only to defend piety, namely, to punish those who have perverted the Israelite youths. The Bible does not explain why the Israelites were so utterly successful, but Philo explains that this was due to the exhortations by Moses that instilled in them courage and confidence. It is these exhortations that so encourage the Israelites to enter the contest with unconquerable spirit (φρονήματα ἀήττητα) and to show their strength (ῥώμη) and daring (τόλμα).

Philo (*Mos.* 1.309) presents a very considerable extra-biblical addition, noting that after slaughtering the Midianites and demolishing their cities and carrying off more prisoners than they could count and a huge amount of booty, the Israelites all returned without any losses, so that any spectator would have supposed that they had returned from a peace-time military review.

The Bible (Num. 31:8) states that the Israelites in this battle killed all the male Midianites, including Balaam, and took captive the Midianite women and children. Moses (Num. 31:14) then expresses his anger at the commanders for allowing the women who have known a man and every male among the young children to live. Philo, realizing that the Israelites in treating the Midianites thus might be accused of undue cruelty, explains that they felt justified because it was the Midianite men who had incited the wicked actions against the Israelites and because it was the women who had led the Israelite youths into licentiousness, and that, in any case, the Israelites showed mercy toward the maidens and young children. In the Bible (Num. 31:17) Moses orders that every male among the Midianite children be killed, but Philo (*Mos.* 1.311) makes a point of saying that the Israelites spared the young boys, perhaps considering that to kill every male child was reminiscent of Pharaoh's cruel orders.[321]

Furthermore, Philo (*Mos.* 1.313) adds that Moses, always careful, as a general must be, to express appreciation for the achievements of his soldiers, praised the general, Phinehas, and the combatants for their exploits and for their unselfishness in not taking the spoil for themselves alone.

In the Bible (Num. 31:19) Moses instructs the soldiers that anyone who has killed a person or who has touched a corpse must purify himself on the third and the seventh day. He does not, however, give a reason for this injunction. Philo (*Mos.* 1.314), consistent with his aim to stress that Jews look upon all human beings as their kin, takes the pains to explain that though the slaughter of enemies is lawful, yet one who kills a person, even if he is justified in doing so in self-defense and under compulsion, is called to account in view of the common kinship of the human race from the very beginning. In presenting this addition to the biblical text, Philo is, it would seem, answering the charge of such writers as Apollonius Molon and Lysimachus (*ap.* Josephus, *Ap.* 2.145) that Jews bear an implacable hatred of non-Jews.

One of the most difficult tasks of a leader is the fair apportionment of prizes. Moses performs this task very beautifully (παγκάλη), as Philo (*Mos.* 1.318) remarks, particularly in the distribution of spoils taken in the war with the Midianites (*Mos.* 1.315–18). The Bible (Num. 31:25–47) simply states how the booty is to be divided between those who fought and the rest of the population, without explaining why the distribution is uneven between the two groups. Philo (*Mos.* 1.315–16) explains why those who had not participated in the fighting should get any portion at all of the booty, namely, as he puts it, because their souls, if not their bodies, had done the fighting (διαγωνισάμενοι). Furthermore, he adds, reserve troops (ἔφεδροι, "those standing nearby") are inferior to the actual fighters not in eagerness (προθυμίαι, "readiness," "willingness") but only in time, since others have anticipated them. He recognized the crucial contribution of the campaigners, who were relatively few in number as compared with the reserve troops, who had remained inactive, by giving half of the spoils to the former, while giving the other half to the reservists, whose spirit he recognized as not being inferior to that of the active campaigners. On the other hand, when it came to the dedication of the firstfruits, the reserves contributed two percent, to be given to the Levites, while the active fighters were asked to give much less, namely, one-fifth of one percent, these to be given to the high priest, presumably as a tribute to them for risking their very lives.[322] Philo's Moses regards approvingly the fact that the tribute of the non-combatants was given to the Levites, while that of the fighters, who had risked both their bodies and their souls and thus had shown perfect (ὁλόκληρος) manly virtue (ἀνδραγαθία), was given to the high priest, while that of the commanders of squadrons was given to G-d Himself, the Leader of all.

In addition, as we learn from the Bible (Num. 31:48–54), the commanders of the soldiers, as a token of gratitude to G-d that they had lost none of their number in the fighting, contributed gold objects that they had taken in the booty. The Bible (Num. 31:54) says simply that Moses and Eleazar the high priest took the gold, but Philo (*Mos.* 1.317), realizing how important it is for a leader to show gratitude to contributors, specifies that Moses honored the piety of the donors and placed the gold in the tabernacle as a memorial of their thankfulness (εὐχαριστία).

In sum, whereas in the Bible it is G-d who takes the initiative to tell Moses to take revenge against the Midianites, in Philo it is Moses who takes the initiative to seek revenge. Philo depicts Moses as a skilled commander who deems it unwise to employ his entire army. Philo's addition that Moses, like any Greek or Roman general, sacrificed before sending off his soldiers to battle is apparently influenced by the fact that non-Jews in his audience would have expected this. Philo attributes the Israelites' success in the war to the confidence that Moses had instilled in the Israelites. In refuting the charge that Jews hate non-Jews, Philo notes that Moses stresses the common kinship of all humans, even including the enemy. Always aware of the charge that the Israelites are merciless, Philo makes a point of adding that the Israelites showed mercy in sparing the young boys and the maidens.

w. The Proposal of Reuben and Gad

One of the most important characteristics of a great leader is that he knows how to admonish his people. The Bible (Num. 32:1) states very simply that the children of Reuben and of Gad[323] had abundant livestock in the land of Jazer and Gilead, which were places suitable for livestock. Philo (*Mos.* 1.319) expands very considerably on this, noting that the land was rich (εὐδαίμων) and deep-soiled (βαθεῖα), and that there was a large plain suitable for growing grain and good for furnishing fodder for cattle, well supplied with water and pastureland and spontaneously producing bounteous herbiage.[324] In the Bible, when the two tribes request permission to settle on the eastern side of the Jordan, Moses, clearly indignant, asks how they can seek to settle there when their brethren will go to battle to win the land west of the Jordan.[325]

Whereas the biblical Moses (Num. 32:6–15) presents a long rebuke to the two tribes in ten verses, Josephus (*A.J.* 4.167–68), in his paraphrase of this incident, devotes a mere two short paragraphs to Moses' address to the two tribes, in which he surmises that it is out of fear of battle with the Canaanites that they had found as a plausible pretext the care of the livestock. He refers to them as most evil (κάκιστοι) and as having contrived a specious (εὐσχήμων, "with an outward show of goodness")[326] pretext for their cowardice, whereas they wished to live luxuriously and without exertion. Philo (*Mos.* 1.321–27), clearly emphasizing the crucial importance of the unity of the Jewish people in working and sacrificing together, as significant in his own day as it was in the time of Moses, has greatly expanded Moses' rebuke to eight paragraphs and uses particularly strong language in condemning the tribes of Reuben and Gad for seeking to remain on the eastern side of the Jordan River rather than joining with the other tribes in conquering the land to the west of the Jordan. "As it is," Moses says (*Mos.* 1.325), "though your own kin supplies you with examples of warning in your fathers who inspected this land, and in the misfortune of them and of those who shared their craven-heartedness (συναπονοηθέντες, 'share in folly'), all of whom perished save two, though you should not let your name be associated with any such as these, so senseless (ὦ κενοὶ φρενῶν, 'empty-minded ones') are you that you follow after (ζηλοῦτε, 'emulate,' 'strive after') cowardice (δειλία) and forget that it will make you an easier prey. And you upset (ὑποσκελίζετε, 'trip up your heels') the ardent resolution (προθυμία, 'readiness,' 'eagerness') of those who are fully disposed (προαιρούμενοι, 'choose deliberately,' 'prefer') to manliness (ἀνδραγαθίζεσθαι, 'act uprightly'), whose spirits (φρονήματα) you paralyze (ἐκλύοντες, 'let loose') and unnerve (παριέντες, 'let fall,' 'disregard')."

However, despite his anger, Philo's Moses, being an experienced and logical administrator, tries to analyze various theories as to why the two tribes should have made such a request (*Mos.* 1.321–22). Were they claiming preference in the distribution of the land and attempting to take their portion before it was due? Were they seeking to avoid participating in the wars that would have to be fought in conquering the Land of Israel and where kings were set to oppose them? As in the Bible (Num. 32:6–15), Philo compares them to the spies who tried to dissuade the Israelites from fighting to reclaim the land, and he emphasizes the lesson to be learnt from what happened to them. In Philo's version (*Mos.* 1.322–27) Moses delivers a long address to them rebuking them for seeking to enjoy an undeserved leisure while their kinsmen, without their help, are saddled with the task of fighting and of undergoing great dangers. He appeals to their sense of justice, noting that it is not right that they should enjoy the blessings of peace while others are suffering countless ills. He stresses the bonds that tie them to the other tribes: ancestry, customs, laws. Why should they display an arrogance such as a ruler might show to his subjects? He cites the truism that wise men do not wait until misfortune strikes them. Justice, he remarks, is wont to move with difficulty, but it eventually overtakes those who run away from it. He promises that when the land has been conquered the prizes will be distributed equally (*Mos.* 1.327).

Philo, apparently uneasy about the undue harshness in Moses' rebuke of the two tribes and his haste in condemning them, emphasizes that when the two tribes of Reuben and Gad expressed their wish to stay on the eastern side of the Jordan and not to cross over into Canaan, Moses, based on official authority, spoke to them without arrogance but rather as a kindly (εὔνους) father out of solicitude for them and with the intention not of casting reproach as such, but rather of bringing them to a better frame of mind.

In an editorial-like comment, Philo (*Mos.* 1.328) says that the two tribes knew that Moses, based upon his authority, did not admonish invidiously (καταλαζονευόμενος) in speaking to them but did so out of concern (προκηδόμενος) for all of them and respect for justice (δικαιοσύνη) and equality (ἰσότης). Moses stresses that his hatred of evil was not intended for moralizing reproach (ὄνειδος σωφρονισμόν) but rather to encourage those to improve who were capable of doing so. The two tribes reply respectfully (*Mos.* 1.328) that they have no intention of leaving the confederacy and of taking their portion before it is due. They declare their obedience to Moses and promise that they will participate fully in crossing the Jordan River and in all the campaigns in the military conquest of the land. All they ask is permission to build houses for their women and children and sheds for the animals lest they lose them at the hands of raiders. Upon hearing this, Moses replies with a kindly look (ἵλεως τὸ βλέμμα, *Mos.* 1.331) and with a gentler voice, granting their request and assuring them that if they, indeed, do join in crossing the Jordan and in being ready to fight if necessary, they will get their share of the apportionment of the land. But whereas in the Bible (Num. 32:23) Moses rather harshly warns them that if they do not live up to their promise they will pay the price for their sin,[327] Philo's *Mos.* omits this warning and stresses a gentler Moses. The two tribes, hearing these promises, were filled, we are told, with joy and courage. Once again Moses has shown the quality of leadership in being stern when he had to be and in being gentle when such an attitude was wiser.

In sum, Philo's *Mos.* emphasizes the importance of the unity of the Israelites, so important for Philo in his leadership of the Jews of his own day, and expands greatly Moses' rebuke to the tribes of Reuben and Gad for not joining the other tribes in conquering the land west of the Jordan. But then

Moses, the experienced administrator, admonishes them as a kindly father and tries to analyze why they had made such a request. Once he hears their explanation, he replies with a gentler voice.

x. The Daughters of Zelophehad

It is embarrassing that Moses (Num. 27:5) is unable to give the daughters of Zelophehad a decision as to whether they are entitled, as they ask, to inherit from their father, who died without male issue, and that instead they must bring their claim before G-d.[328] In the Bible (Num. 27:3–4) the daughters present their claim, noting that their father was not among those who had joined Korah in his rebellion against Moses, and add that he had followed contentedly the quiet life of an ordinary citizen. There is no description of the qualities of character of the maidens, nor is there any particular statement of respect for Moses, whereas in Philo (*Mos.* 2.235) the daughters are characterized as having the modesty (αἰδώς) appropriate for maidens. Furthermore, they introduce their request with a compliment to Moses and, by implication, to the Roman Emperor of Philo's own day, since they say that though they seem to be orphans, in reality they look upon Moses as a father, inasmuch as, they say, a lawful ruler is more akin to his subjects than a biological father. Moreover, Philo adds that in making their request the maidens are not in pursuit of wealth, but rather desire to preserve the name and reputation of their father. Moses, in turn, in an extra-biblical remark, marvels at the prudence (φρόνησις) of the maidens and at their goodwill (εὔνοια) toward their father. Whereas the Bible gives no reason why Moses is unable to reply to their claim, Philo (*Mos.* 2.236) explains that he hesitated because he tended to think that men alone should be entitled to inheritances as a reward for their service in war, whereas since women are exempt from participating in such conflicts they are not entitled to a share in the prizes therefrom. He refers the question to G-d (*Mos.* 2.237), Who alone shows His identification with truth (ἀλήθεια) and justice (δικαιοσύνη) through discerning unerringly the finest differences. G-d, Who is the ruler of men and gods, does not disdain to respond to the petition of the maidens and gives his full approval to them (*Mos.* 2.238) and is gracious enough to judge the women to be worthy of charity (χάρις, "kindness," "goodwill") and kindness (φιλανθρωπία, "benevolence," "humane feeling," "courtesy") (*Mos.* 2.242);[329] but, nevertheless, He does not give them equal status with men in the award of prizes arising from war. In particular,

He strongly attacks those who mock the piteous desolation of orphanhood (*Mos.* 2.240).

In sum, Philo offers a logical reason why Moses was unable to reply to the claim of the daughters of Zelophehad to the inheritance from their father. He graciously replies to them, without demeaning their virtues, for which he expresses a high regard. His explanation is that men alone deserve inheritance because of their service in war. In an important addition, the daughters of Zelophehad introduce their request for a share of the inheritance of their father with a compliment to Moses and, by implication, to the Roman Emperor of Philo's own day, since they say that though they seem to be orphans, in reality they look upon Moses as a father, inasmuch as, they say, a lawful ruler is more akin to his subjects than a biological father.

y. The Death of Moses

(1) The Extraordinary Deaths of Extraordinary Persons

Extraordinary persons, in the Hellenistic and earlier biographical traditions, were expected to experience an extraordinary death. Dionysius of Halicarnassus reports the extraordinary disappearance of Aeneas (*Ant. Rom.* 1.64.4) and Romulus (*Ant. Rom.* 2.56.2), and Philostratus reports the extraordinary death of Apollonius of Tyana (*Apollonius* 8.30–31). That this was a common motif may be seen from the fact that Lucian wrote a parody of it in his *De Morte Peregrini*, in which he describes the flamboyant suicide of a Cynic philosopher named Peregrinus.

There are two parallels in the Bible to the miraculous translation of Moses, those of Enoch (Gen. 5:24; cf. Josephus, *A.J.* 1.85) and Elijah (2 Kings 2:1; cf. Josephus, *A.J.* 9.28). Philo has in his extant writings very few references to the books of the Bible beyond the Pentateuch; and he refers to Elijah only twice (*Deus* 136 and 138), namely, in connection with the incident concerning the widow of Zarephath, but says nothing at all concerning the manner of Elijah's death.

In order to understand how Philo, however, looks upon the extraordinary death of Moses, it is particularly apposite to consider how he views the extraordinary death of the other person, Enoch, who, according to the Pentateuch, experienced such a death. In the first place, one is struck with the amount of interest that Philo has in Enoch, about whom the Bible tells us only the name of his father, Jared, how many years he lived before he fathered

Methuselah, how many years he lived in all, and, the one unusual detail (Gen. 5:24), that he "walked with G-d; and he was not, for G-d took him," which the LXX translates "was well pleasing (εὐηρέστησεν) to G-d, and was not found (εὑρίσκετο), because G-d translated (μετέθηκεν, 'transferred,' 'transposed') him." That Enoch was of particular interest to Philo may be seen from the fact that he is mentioned in no fewer than five of his works. In *Post.* 40 Philo raises the question whether the Enoch who was descended from Cain (Gen. 4:17) was the same as the one descended from Seth (Gen. 5:6–18), and he gives the etymology of the name, "your gift" (*Post.* 41). In deference to his critical audience, however, he understands the "translation" of Enoch as meaning that he had been removed from perishable (φθαρτά) to immortal (ἀθάνατα) status and indicates that Enoch was not unique in this translation, since he says that such a transference is true of all those who have been well pleasing to G-d and who are no longer found (εὑρίσκονται) among the multitude (πολλοί). Philo (*Mut.* 34–38) likewise generalizes in viewing Enoch as representing, allegorically, the *type* of those who are not found, that is, like the wise man who, though actually existing, is hidden from us and shuns our company. It is thus we who are evil and fail to see him. In *Abr.* (17) Philo understands Enoch's transference as turning and changing for the better because it is brought about by the thought of G-d; again Philo applies this to *all* (18, πᾶν) such changes. Such a rare person is said not to have been found because he secludes himself; this is true of all those who are truly repentant (26). The change of abode is representative of all those who repent and who stand above the passions (*Praem.* 16–21) and seek solitude. He again generalizes (*QG* 1.82–86) that the transference of Enoch is typical of those who repent. He explains that the phrase that "he was pleasing to G-d" demonstrates that the souls of all are immortal, "since when they become incorporeal they again become pleasing" (*QG* 1.85). Philo specifically (*QG* 1.86) asks, "What is the meaning of the words, 'And he was not found, for G-d had translated him'?" Again, he applies this not merely to Enoch, but to all worthy and holy men, and he explains that the translation is from a sensible and visible place to an incorporeal and intelligible form. He then compares Enoch's transition to that of the "protoprophet," that is Moses (noting as a point of similarity, that no one knew his burial place), and that of Elijah.[330] It is surely significant that Philo devotes no fewer than five questions in *QG* (1.82–86) to Enoch but mentions the analogy with Moses only once. We may conjecture that he was particularly concerned with the danger of raising Moses to divine status. The fact that even in the case of Enoch he generalizes and says that the translation of Enoch is typical of all who repent is Philo's way of saying that one should not think of Moses' translation to heaven as being unique or even unusual, any more than it was in the case of Enoch.

It is worthwhile to compare Philo's account of the translation of Enoch with that of Josephus (*A.J.* 1.85). Concerning Enoch Josephus says enigmatically that he "returned to the divinity, wherefore they have not recorded his death." Most significantly, he does not repeat the biblical words, that "he walked with G-d" or, in the words of the LXX, that "he was well pleasing to G-d." Apparently, Josephus was concerned that his non-Jewish critical readers would find a disappearance such as is described in the Bible hard to believe, and so he is content to say in the most general terms that "he returned to G-d," which could mean almost anything. Kraft (1978, 256) says that the summary treatment accorded Enoch by Josephus is somewhat startling and may reflect his hesitancy about commenting on eschatological themes. Josephus, he thinks, must have known various extra-biblical traditions about Enoch, since he knew them about so many other biblical figures. Josephus uses the expression "returned to the divinity" in describing the disappearance of Moses when he went to get the tablets of the Law (*A.J.* 3.96) and in describing his death (*A.J.* 4.326). Josephus does not say that G-d took the initiative in translating him but rather that he escaped a normal death and burial.

On the other hand, very striking is the account of Enoch and of his disappearance in Jub. (4:16–25). Jub. presents a tradition that Enoch was the first who learned writing and knowledge and wisdom and wrote down the signs of heaven according to the order of their months and the jubilees. He saw in a vision in his sleep what was and what will be. The angels showed him everything on earth and in the heavens. Finally, he was taken from among humankind and conducted into the Garden of Eden in majesty and honor, and there he writes down the judgment of the world. Similarly, in 1 Enoch 70:3–4 Enoch's abode is in paradise. Likewise, according to rabbinic tradition in *Midr. ha-G.* 1.123 (ed. Margulies, p. 132), Enoch, Moses, and Elijah serve as angels in heaven. All this is absent from Philo and from Josephus.

(2) *Attacks on Biblical Accounts as Myths*

Philo was well acquainted with Greek literature and traditions, and he was aware, probably from his own experience as a leader of the Alexandrian Jewish community, that there were Jews who cherished a dislike of the Jewish ancestral traditions and who went to the length of making it their constant practice to denounce the laws in the Pentateuch and who insisted that what the Jews called "holy books" (ἱεραὶ βίβλοι) also contained myths, precisely the sort that the Jews derided when they heard them related by others. He cites, as an example, Homer's account (*Od.* 11.315, 318) of the story of the Aloeidae's piling Pelion on Ossa on Olympus (*Conf.* 4–5), for which, he says, impious people (ibid. 2, δυσσεβεῖς) declare that Moses substituted the story of the building of the Tower of Babel. He notes a further parallel that these impious people cite with the Greek myth (though he does not cite the precise source) that at one time all the animals had a common language (*Conf.* 6). Quite clearly, as we can see from the contradictory views that he expresses in some essays about such figures as Joseph and Jethro, not all the treatises were addressed to the same audience, and we may conjecture that *Conf.*, with its attack on impious Jews, was addressed to deviant Jews or to elite Jews who knew those who had apostacized.

The one instance where Philo himself (*Praem.* 23) identifies a biblical personality with a non-biblical personality is his identification of Noah with the one whom the Greeks call Deucalion, in whose day, he says, the great deluge took place.[331] We may conjecture that *Praem.*, like *Mos.*, was a warning to deviant Jews, since Philo (*Praem.* 40) speaks of those who deny the existence of G-d and those who "hesitate and fluctuate as though unable to state whether G-d exists or not, as well as those who derive their knowledge of G-d from habit." Likewise, the fact that he lists at length the rewards that are given to the righteous (*Praem.* 79–126), as well as the punishments that are meted out to those who disobey the laws (*Praem.* 127–51), indicates that this discussion is intended as a promise and warning to Jews. In identifying Noah with Deucalion, he is assuring the non-conformist Jews that the events in the Bible, and especially the chronology, are factual. Philo, however, since he had no doubt as to the historicity of the revelation of the Pentateuch (*Sacr.* 79, *Mos.* 2.188), apparently had no doubt as to the historicity of the Flood and consequently saw no need to cite external evidence to support its historicity. Moreover, Philo is not a historian, except incidentally as an apologist for the Jews in his *Flacc.* and *Legat.*, and hence felt no need to buttress his facts concerning the Flood by citing external sources.

Pseudo-Philo is clearly not concerned with the historicity of any of the events of the Bible, since for him there is no doubt that the entire Pentateuch was divinely revealed (11.1–6); and, indeed, as Murphy (1993, 224) has pointed out, G-d is present in every part of his work. He consequently sees no need to cite external evidence to support the historicity of biblical events, and, indeed, he never cites any secular source.

A key to understanding why Josephus has modified the biblical account as he has is the fact that he cites non-Jewish witnesses to the historicity of the Flood (*A.J.* 1.93–95)[332]—an indication, in all probability, that he is seeking the approval of non-Jewish critical readers.[333] However, Josephus does not actually equate Noah with Deucalion of the Greek flood, as, indeed, Philo does (*Praem.* 23). Josephus makes no such equation, presumably because he wished to keep the Pentateuch's words "pure from every unseemly mythology that is found among others" (*A.J.* 1.15). And yet, Josephus is particularly concerned with the credibility of his history. The fact that he is so sharp in his criticism of the Greek historians, whose writings, he says (*Ap.* 1.15), "have no basis of sure knowledge, but merely present the facts as conjectured by individual authors," meant that he himself, seeking a reputation as a critical and careful historian, had to be especially careful with his facts.

That Josephus did identify Noah with the survivor of the Babylonian flood story is clear from his statement (*A.J.* 1.93) that the flood and the ark were mentioned by *all* who have written histories of the barbarians. That he did make this identification is further clear from the passage (*Ap.* 1.130) in which he states that Berosus mentions the ark in which Noah was saved when it landed on a mountain in Armenia. In the passage in question, Berosus refers to Xisuthrus, rather than to Noah, as we see from Syncellus, who here quotes Berosus; but the fact that Josephus relates it as pertaining to Noah shows that he (and presumably his readers) had identified the two. Moreover, to supply proof of the historicity of the Flood, Josephus (*A.J.* 1.93, 20.25) notes that a certain portion of the boat still exists in Armenia and that some people actually remove pieces from the bitumen and use them as talismans. He offers as further proof the fact that at a certain mountain named Minyas remains of the wood of the boat were preserved for a long time.

The rabbinic tradition, having perfect faith in the revelation of everything in the Pentateuch and convinced that everything therein was timeless, is not concerned, as is the critical historian Josephus, with supplying external evidence of the historicity of Noah. Moreover, all the rabbinic works are addressed to Jews who agree with the fundamental presuppositions of the rabbis. Hence, in all rabbinic literature there is never any citation of a non-Jewish work to support any of the historical data found in the Bible.

(3) The Account of Moses' Death according to the Assumption of Moses

In the Ass. Mos. we are told that Satan, after accusing Moses of murdering the Egyptian, acts of his own accord, insisting that he is the lord of matter and that he is entitled to Moses' body (though not his soul) because of the sin of Adam. The author, apparently disturbed by the anthropomorphic thought that G-d buried Moses, uniquely states that G-d commanded the angel Michael to do so (*ap. Acta Synodi Nicaeani* 2.20; *Catena in Epistulam Catholicam*; *Scholion ad Epistulam Judae* 9);[334] and Michael proceeds to refute Satan's arguments.

That Moses was more than human is implied in the Ass. Mos. 11:5–8, where the author indicates that Joshua asks what place will receive Moses, or what will be the monument on his grave (the clear implication being that there will be no such monument), or what human being (the implication being that Moses is more than human) will dare to carry Moses' body from one place to another, since Moses' grave extends in all directions, the entire world being his grave.[335]

(4) Philo's Description of Moses' Last Days

A great leader must be able to encourage his people. The Book of Deut. is, in effect, Moses' last sermon to his people. In the brief passage that parallels it, Philo (*Praem.* 4–6) summarizes Moses' style of leadership as one that educated (συνασκήσας, "trained," "disciplined fully," "helped to practice") the people at once with rather gentle (μαλακώτεραι, "soft," "mild," "tender") guidance (ὑφηγήσεις, "leading," "instructions," "directions") and exhortation (προτροπαί, "encouragement") and, on the other hand (πάλιν, "contrariwise," "in turn"), with more grave (ἐμβριθέστεραι, "more weighty") threats (ἐπανατάσεις) and warnings (νουθεσίαι, "admonitions"). He thus, says Philo, called upon his citizens (πολιτευόμενοι) to show in what they had been educated (ἐπαιδεύθησαν). Whereas Josephus, who had been a general in Galilee in the war against the Romans and who often emphasizes Moses' role as general,[336] has Moses, in his farewell remarks to the Israelites, address them as "fellow-soldiers" (συστρατιῶται, *A.J.* 4.177), Philo, a political leader of the Alexandrian Jewish community, addresses them as, in effect, "fellow-citizens" (πολιτευόμενοι, *Praem.* 4), with the responsibilities of participating in the community. Using the analogy of preparing for a physical contest in sports, Philo says that Moses, through the laws of the Pentateuch, prepared them for the sacred contest in which their sincerity would be tested. The prizes, as in athletic contests, belong to the victors, whereas the losers are tainted with the stigma of defeat more than those who lose in gymnastic contests. Those who lose in athletics can easily rise again, but not so easily those who lose in the contests of life (*Praem.* 6).

The Bible records that before his death Moses characterized each of the twelve tribes and blessed them and predicted their future (Deut. 33). Philo (*Mos.* 2.288–89), like Josephus (*A.J.* 4.320), merely mentions that Moses blessed the tribes without giving the actual content of each of the blessings. He marvels at the appropriateness of the diverse predictions for each of the tribes, though the tribes were so very different from one another, particularly on their descent on their mother's side. Apparently, we may conjecture, this is an allusion to the fact that the Jews of Egypt were quite different from one another in their backgrounds and in their attitude toward life and faith. He adds, inspiring leader that Moses is, that some of these predictions have actually taken place and that the others will inevitably occur (*Mos.* 2.288), "since confidence in the future is assured by fulfillment in the past."

If Moses was so excellent a leader, we may well ask why G-d permitted him merely to view the Promised Land, but not to enter it (Deut. 34:4). Philo (*Migr.* 44–46) is well aware of this objection and notes that some "unconsidering" (ἀπερίσκεπτοι, "thoughtless") people have supposed that G-d said this to demolish (καθαίρεσις, "diminish," "humiliate")[337] the stature of the "all-wise" (πανσόφος) Moses; and we may suggest that perhaps these "unconsidering" people were those who objected to the near deification of Moses. But, in a sharp reply, Philo specifically asserts that it is folly to imagine that ordinary people, that is, the Israelites generally, should take precedence over G-d's friends, among whom, of course, is Moses, in receiving their portion in the Land of Israel; and he explains that the most beautiful (κάλλιστα) things in nature are to be seen (ὁρατά) rather than possessed (κτητά). Since it is not possible, says Philo, to possess things that are located near G-d, all that is possible—and that not for everyone—is to see them.

Philo does not make the point made by Josephus (*A.J.* 4.326), that Moses wrote that he died because he was afraid that people would believe that because of his virtue he had not died, but had gone up directly to G-d.[338] Philo (*Mos.* 2.288), though he speaks cryptically of Moses making the pilgrimage from earth to heaven and of resolving his twofold nature of soul and body into a single unity, "transforming his whole being into mind, pure as the sunlight," which sounds as if he was taken up bodily into heaven like Enoch and Elijah, nevertheless specifically (*Mos.* 2.291) says that Moses wrote about his own death.[339]

Most of all, Philo is impressed that Moses was able to prophesy the account of his own death and to state how he was buried by G-d Himself, and with no one else present. He notes how no one had seen his place of burial and how the Israelites mourned for him for a whole month (*Mos.* 2.291). The statement of Philo here and of Josephus (*A.J.* 4.326), that Moses himself wrote these verses, is similar to the view of the second-century Rabbi Simeon bar Yoḥai, that G-d dictated these verses and that Moses wrote them in tears.

Philo (*Sacr.* 8) insists that Moses died at the command of G-d. Philo, like Josephus, avoids the biblical statement (Deut. 34:6) that no one knows Moses' burial place "to this day," which would imply that the account of Moses' death was written after he had died, a statement that would seem to have confirmed the view of those present-day Bible critics that the Pentateuch was not of divine authorship and that Moses was not the vehicle of its transmission. But whereas Josephus has no statement at all to this effect, Philo (*Mos.* 2.291) avoids the problem by writing from his own viewpoint, rather than quoting the Bible, that until his own day no one had ever seen Moses' burial place.

(5) *Pseudo-Philo's Account of Moses' Death*

Significantly, Pseudo-Philo (19.7), presumably in order not to diminish Moses' stature, does not give the Bible's reason (Num. 20:7–13) why G-d does not permit Moses to enter the Promised Land of Israel, namely, that he had disobeyed instructions to speak to the rock in order to bring water and instead had struck the rock. However, in G-d's farewell to Moses before his death, Pseudo-Philo, in his overwhelming concern with the sin of idolatry, presents a unique reason[340] for Moses' not entering the land, namely, in order that he might be spared seeing the Israelites' worshipping of graven images as they will start to do there.

When Moses approaches death, he predicts, according to Pseudo-Philo (19.3), that the Israelites and their descendants will some day lament that they do not have another leader like Moses who will be a shepherd and a judge and, it would appear above all, an intercessor with G-d when they have sinned. Pseudo-Philo (19.10) gives a cosmic dimension to the death scene, such as is unparalleled in the Bible: G-d shows Moses various unknown and mysterious things—"the place from which the clouds draw up water in order to water the whole earth, and the place from which the river takes its water [that is, the famous question as to the source of the Nile River], and the place in the firmament from which only the Holy Land drinks. He showed him the place from which He rained down manna upon the people, all the way to the paths of paradise." He even showed Moses the measurements of the sanctuary, presumably the Temple in Jerusalem yet to be built (so Jacobson 1996, 1:636–37).

In the actual scene (19.12) depicting Moses' approaching death, Pseudo-Philo adds G-d's statement that the angels will mourn over him.[341] However (ibid.), according to Pseudo-Philo, even the angels were ignorant of his gravesite. In another addition, G-d predicts Moses' resurrection: "I will take you from here and lay you down to sleep with your fathers, and I will give you rest in your resting place and give you peace. All the angels will mourn over you, and the heavenly hosts will grieve. But no angel nor man will know your sepulchre in which you will be buried. You will rest in it until I visit the world. I will raise you up and your fathers from the earth in which you sleep, and you will come together and dwell in the immortal dwelling place that is not subject to time." As the end of the world approaches, time itself will be shortened (19.13). Finally, in a unique addition (19.14), Moses asks G-d to tell him how much time has passed and how much remains before the end of time, whereupon G-d answers that four and a half have passed and two and a half remain (19.15).[342] Indeed, Pseudo-Philo, in an extra-biblical addition (19.16), states that Moses' appearance was changed to a mysteriously "glorious state." He then describes the heavenly funeral procession for Moses as a kind of ascent similar to that of Moses at Sinai: "The angels . . . went before him all together with lightning bolts and torches and arrows." According to Pseudo-Philo (19.16), for the first and only time in the history of the world the hymn of the angels was not sung, whereas according to a Samaritan tradition,[343] the angels sang and rejoiced when Moses died.

Pseudo-Philo, who glorifies Moses so much, makes a special point of adding G-d's blunt statement to Joshua (20.2) stressing that Moses is dead: "Why do you mourn and why do you hope in vain, thinking that Moses yet lives? But you wait in vain, for Moses is dead."[344]

While Moses is not here presented as deified, there is a divine promise of a resurrection and of an immortal dwelling thereafter that is not subject to time. The fact that, according to Pseudo-Philo, Moses makes a special extra-biblical request of G-d, namely, that He reveal to him how much time has passed and how much remains until this resurrection and that G-d gives him a precise answer (19.14–15), would indicate that Moses has such a special relationship with G-d that He will reveal the greatest mystery of all, namely when the *eschaton* will come.

(6) Josephus' Account of Moses' Death

In his account of Moses' death Josephus (*A.J.* 4.326) may be reacting to Sophocles' account[345] of the mysterious disappearance of Oedipus in *Oedipus at Colonus*,[346] that while Moses was still conversing with Eleazar and Joshua, a cloud stood over him and he disappeared into a ravine. Philo lacks such an account, nor does he have a scene such as we find in Josephus (*A.J.* 4.320) of the Israelites bursting into tears, the women beating their breasts, and the children lamenting still more, being too feeble to suppress their grief, which is all the more dramatic, since it takes place after Moses has told the Israelites about his approaching death, but while he is still alive.

In the Bible (Deut. 31:16) it is G-d who tells Moses that he is to die, whereas in Josephus (*A.J.* 4.315) it is Moses who announces to the Israelites his impending death. Later (Deut. 32:48) G-d tells Moses that he is to die that very day, but there is no indication that Moses acknowledges this. In his long address (Deut. 32–33) Moses does not express thanks to G-d, but in Josephus' version he does so (*A.J.* 4.316–18) for His foresight on behalf of the Israelites. The description (*A.J.* 4.320) of the wailing for Moses' approaching death becomes much more graphic in Josephus' version. In the Bible it is only after Moses' death that the Israelites bewail him for thirty days, but there is no description of the wailing itself (Deut. 34:8). Moses' greatness is aggrandized by the fact that the children, we are told, in their lament, understand his virtues and grand achievements to an extent beyond their years and though they have not yet had an opportunity to taste well of his virtue. Perhaps most poignant of all is that Moses himself is reduced to tears when he sees the laments of the people (*A.J.* 4.322).

Josephus (*A.J.* 4.323–24) very emotionally adds that all the Israelites followed Moses to the place where he was going to disappear and that Moses, like the director of an oratorio, signaled with his hand to those who were far off to remain quiet,[347] while urging those who were closer not to make his departure tearful by following him. The populace, in order to show favor to Moses, allow him to depart according to his own wish and restrain themselves, weeping with one another. Josephus (*A.J.* 4.323–26), almost like a lawyer, stresses the point that the Israelites as a group followed Moses to the place where he was going to disappear. They are, therefore, witnesses to the fact that he did die, and they thus combat the view that he did not die at all. Dionysius of Halicarnassus (*Ant. Rom.* 1.64.4; cf. Diogenes Laertius on Empedocles, 8.68) says that Aeneas' body could not be found, and Josephus implies as much with Moses.

(7) The Rabbinic Account of Moses' Death

The rabbis apparently wondered why Moses, the person with whom G-d spoke face to face, should have had to die. Indeed, we find a view (*'Abot R. Nat.*, version B, chap. 25) that G-d told Moses that he had to die only because of the decree against Adam. In fact, even though the Torah (Deut. 34:5) explicitly states that Moses did die, the rabbis (*b. Soṭ.* 13b, *Sifre Deut.* 357, *Midr. Tann.* 224) record an anonymous tradition in the name of "others" that Moses never died and that he continued to minister with G-d. One rabbinic view (*b. Soṭ.* 13b) declares that Moses never died, since in one place we read "So Moses died there" (Deut. 34:5), whereas in another place the same word "there" (שם) is found in the passage "And he [Moses] was there with the L-rd" (Exod. 34:28), whereupon the Talmud comments: "As in the latter passage it means standing and ministering, so also in the former it means standing and ministering."

To counter this view that Moses did not die, the great majority of the rabbis (*b. B. Bat.* 15a, *Men.* 30a, *Soṭ.* 14a), like Philo (*Mos.* 2.291), Pseudo-Philo (19.16), and Josephus (*A.J.* 4.326), stress that Moses did die. Indeed, though we read that the second-century Rabbi Jose denied that Moses ascended to heaven (*b. Suk.* 5a), we also have the view that Moses did go up to G-d (*Tan. Va-era* 19).

The rabbinic tradition (*Sifre Deut.* 305) dwells at length on Moses' attempts to avoid his impending death and to gain permission to enter the Land of Israel and on G-d's refusal to grant this permission and His insistence that he must die. To comfort Moses, G-d is depicted as pointing out to him all the honors that he had received. Realizing that his own efforts were unsuccessful, Moses sought to invoke G-d's mercy through the pleading of others: the Earth, the Heavens, the Sun and Moon, the Stars and Planets, the Hills and Mountains, in particular Mount Sinai, the Rivers, the Deserts, the Great Sea. When these declined to help him, he turned to his disciple Joshua, Aaron's son Eleazar, and Caleb; but Samael, the angel of death, prevented them from praying to G-d. G-d then told Moses that He had made two vows, one that Moses was to die and the other that Israel was to perish, and that Moses was to choose between the two.

Inasmuch as Moses was not permitted to enter the Promised Land because the time had come for Joshua to lead the Israelites, Moses ministered to Joshua. On the seventh day of Adar, when it was decreed that Moses was to die, Moses wrote thirteen scrolls of the Torah. G-d now showed Moses the entire land of Israel and taught him the whole history of the land, from the day of creation to the final day of judgment. He also showed him paradise and hell. Just before his death Moses was permitted to meet the Messiah in heaven, and he saw G-d build a temple in heaven. Moses then blessed the twelve tribes and asked Israel to forgive his sternness toward them. Moses then took a scroll, wrote upon it the ineffable name of G-d, and the book of the song (Deut. 32:1–43), and delivered it to Joshua. When Samael, the angel of death, approached Moses to take his soul from him, he was busy writing the ineffable name of G-d. Moses blinded him with the radiance of his face, but a voice from heaven told Moses to let Samael live since the world is in need of him. In the end Samael was powerless to carry out G-d's mission, and Moses died at the hands of G-d Himself.[348]

One tradition indicates that Moses died only because G-d had decreed that all descendants of Adam must die, whereas another tradition indicates specific ways in which he had sinned (Purvis 1973, 99). Other views are that his death is an atonement for the Israelites' sin with the Golden Calf or that he died in a foreign land so that those who die in the Diaspora may be resurrected through his merits (*Tan. Ve-etḥanan* 5b).

Thereupon G-d revealed Himself to receive Moses' soul. G-d took his soul by kissing him on the mouth. G-d Himself wept for him. Moses' mother, Jochebed, and his student, Joshua, were not sure whether Moses was dead. Samael had not heard that G-d had taken Moses' soul and searched in vain for him. When he died, Adam, Noah, Abraham, Isaac, Jacob, and Joseph claimed to be greater than he, but in each case Moses showed that he was superior to them. He also showed that he surpassed all creation. In the future world he will also be the leader and teacher of the Israelites.[349] In answer to the question as to why the gravesite of Moses is unknown, the Midrash (*Leqaḥ Tov, Berakah* 102) states that this is so that the site may not be converted into a sanctuary where sacrifices would be offered. Origen, presumably basing himself on a rabbinic tradition (so Lowenstamm 1972, 204), asserts that this is so that he might not be worshipped as a god.

The Talmud (*b. B. Bat.* 15a, *b. Men.* 30a) is aware of the question as to how Moses could have written about his own death. One view, that of the second-century Rabbi Judah bar Ilai, or, according to others, the second-century Rabbi Nehemiah, is that the last eight verses of the Torah (Deut. 34:5–12), which give the account of Moses' death and burial, were written by Joshua.

(8) The Samaritan Description of Moses' Death

According to Samaritan tradition, when the time came for Moses to die, he died without his realizing it (*Memar* 5.3). He entered into a cloud and was lifted up as a light. The Samaritan *Memar* 4.12 states that when Moses died, he was gathered with the angels, with whom he had dwelled on Mount Sinai and who, together with the five books of the Torah, the five letters of the name of G-d with which he was clothed there, the sea, the fire, and the cloud, besought G-d that Moses not die. Then Moses himself besought G-d not for himself, but for the congregation of Israel that would now become bereft without his leadership (5.1–2).[350] In his final ascent we find the same imagery of the crown of light, the assembly of the angelic hosts, and the enveloping cloud that we find in his ascent on Mount Sinai (5.2). Moses died without realizing that his life had departed from him (5.3). On this occasion he is said to receive the portion that G-d presented him through Adam. According to the Samaritan work, the *Asatir*, dating from the ninth to the twelfth century, Moses occupies a position in the center of time—26 righteous men before him, 26 princes (some good and some bad) after him. His life is the high point of human history (Purvis 1973, 103).

In summary, extraordinary persons in the Hellenistic Era were expected to experience extraordinary deaths. In deference to his critical audience, however, Philo asserts that the tradition of Enoch's death was not unique, but that such a transference is true of all who have been pleasing to G-d. Josephus has a scene highly reminiscent of the disappearance of Oedipus in Sophocles' *Oedipus at Colonus*. Philo, in one of his treatises, but not in *Mos.*, was sure that there were Jews in his time who, citing parallels between Greek myths and the Tower of Babel and the Flood, attacked what they termed biblical myths. Philo, unlike Josephus, sees no need to cite non-Jewish sources for biblical events, since he has no doubt as to the historicity of the biblical narrative.

Philo, Josephus, and the rabbis, as eager as they were to exalt Moses, were tremendously concerned that he not be worshipped (though there is one rabbinic view that Moses never died and that he continued to minister with G-d), especially since there were precedents for such claims for numerous heroes; and all of these sources, with the exception of one anonymous rabbinic tradition, made a special point of stressing that the fact that Moses wrote in the Pentateuch of his own death was definite evidence that he did die. The Pseudepigraphic Ass. Mos. and the Samaritan traditions, in their exaltation of Moses, come closest to claiming that Moses did not die. The Ass. Mos. and the rabbinic tradition elaborate on Moses' attempts to avoid his impending death. Philo, like Josephus and some of the rabbis, is more conscious than the other sources in anticipating the theory of those critics who claim that Moses could not have written about his own death. To counter the view that the account of Moses' death was written after he died, Philo, rather than quoting the Bible, says that no one until his own day has seen Moses' burial place. Pseudo-Philo and a rabbinic tradition give a cosmic dimension to the death scene and depict the angels as mourning over him; and G-d even tells Moses how much time remains before the end of time, but falls short of actually deifying Moses. The Ass. Mos. and the rabbinic tradition elaborate on Moses' attempts to avoid his impending death.

III. The Virtues of Moses

1. In General

Philo (*Mos.* 2.66) says that Moses happily possessed natural gifts (φύσεως εὐμοιρίᾳ χρησάμενος), and in these philosophy (φιλοσοφία) found good soil. For Philo (*Agr.* 80) Moses represents mind in its perfection. He (*Mos.* 1.154) gives the reader a veritable catalogue of the virtues that Moses constantly exhibited: self-control (ἐγκράτειαι), perseverance (καρτερίαι), temperance (σωφροσύναι), shrewdness (ἀγχίνοιαι), sagacity (συνέσεις), knowledge (ἐπιστῆμαι), laboriousness (πόνοι), endurance of suffering (κακοπάθειαι), contempt for pleasure (ἡδονῶν ὑπεροψίαι), justice (δικαιοσύναι), exhortation to excellence (προτροπαὶ πρὸς τὰ βέλτιστα), lawful censure and punishment of wrongdoers (ψόγοι καὶ κολάσεις ἁμαρτανόντων νόμιμοι), and praise and honor of those doing rightly, again according to law (ἔπαινοι καὶ τιμαὶ κατορθούντων πάλιν σὺν νόμῳ). Elsewhere (*Mos.* 2.9), when he speaks of Moses as legislator, he states that this faculty has four close kinsfolk in particular—love of humanity (φιλάνθρωπον), justice (φιλοδίκαιον), goodness (φιλάγαθον), and hatred of evil (μισοπόνηρον). For Philo (*Mos.* 1.158) Moses represents a well-wrought drawing (γραφὴ εὖ δεδημιουργημένη), an utterly beautiful and godlike work (πάγκαλον καὶ θεοειδές), a model (παράδειγμα) for those wishing to imitate it (*Mos.* 1.159). He thus presents a paradigm of beauty and godliness, a *speculum principis*.[1] No wonder, as Sir. 45:1 says, Moses won favor in the eyes of all.

In his more general essay on the virtues, Philo says (*Virt.* 1) that he has already discussed the virtue of justice (*Spec.* 4.193–238) and that he will now take up the virtues of courage (ἀνδρεία, *Virt.* 1–50), humanity (φιλανθρωπία, *Virt.* 51–174, which is closest akin to piety), repentance (μετάνοια, *Virt.* 175–86), and nobility of birth (εὐγένεια, *Virt.* 187–227).

Philo's Moses (*Mos.* 1.159), alluding to the central Platonic theory of ideas, urges that the mind carry the idea or form (εἶδος) that is perfect (τέλειον) in its excellence (ἀρετή); but if one is not able to reach that level, at least he should have the unambiguous desire to attain that form. Philo (*Mos.* 2.8) says that it is proper for the one who is to obtain excellence as a legislator to possess all the virtues absolutely and completely. And, as he (*Mos.* 2.7) remarks, to have possessed even one of the virtues is to have them all.[2]

That Moses represents the epitome of virtue may be seen, according to Philo (*Mos.* 1.59), from the fact that Jethro gave Moses the most beautiful of his daughters in marriage, thereby attesting to all his nobility and goodness (καλοκἀγαθία) and showing that nobility (καλόν) alone is worthy of love (ἀξιέραστον) and needs no further recommendation. One of the distinct qualities of Moses is that he does not hide anything, and that his nature, being that of a great person (*Mos.* 1.22), is transparent (ἀρίδηλοι, "transparent," "clear," "manifest"). Hence, Jethro was able immediately to recognize his disposition (*Mos.* 1.59) and consequently did not take very long before deciding to give his daughter Zipporah in marriage to Moses. Like the patriarchs, he married not a woman but a virtue (*Cher.* 41), as the very name Zipporah, meaning "bird," indicates, "speeding upwards from earth to heaven and contemplating there the nature of things divine and blessed."

In Philo's eyes (*Sacr.* 8) G-d advanced Moses to stand even higher than Abraham, Isaac, and Jacob, and trained him to soar above species and genus, and stationed him beside Himself. He sent him as a loan to earth and allowed him to dwell there, and appointed him, most remarkably, as god (*Sacr.* 9), placing the body and the mind that rules it in subjection to him.

As for Moses' second marriage, to the Ethiopian woman (Num. 12:1), since it was important for the great man's wife to be the epitome of virtue, Moses himself, says Philo (*Leg.* 2.67), merits the highest praise for marrying the Ethiopian woman, since she represents a trustworthy (δόκιμος), unchangeable (ἄτρεπτος) nature that has been tested by fire (πεπυρωμένη). Indeed, Philo goes so far as to say that G-d Himself arranged the betrothal (ἡρμόσατο) of Moses to the Ethiopian woman. In thus praising the Ethiopian woman in such extraordinary terms, Philo may well be reflecting the attitude of Homer (*Il.* 1.423), who refers to the Ethiopians as blameless; and the admiration for their wisdom, piety, and bravery is expressed by such writers as Diodorus (3.2), Pomponius Mela (3.85), and Seneca (*Hercules Furens* 38–41).[3] He may also be reflecting the positive tradition tracing the Jews back to the time of King Cepheus of Ethiopia (Tacitus, *Histories* 5.2.2) (see Feldman 1996c, 395–97).

The rabbis go further. Indeed, according to the third-century Rab (*b. Sanh.* 98b), the world was created only on account of Moses, presumably so that he might receive the Torah. According to the third-century Raba (*b. Ḥul.* 89a), the world exists only on account of the merit of Moses and Aaron. According to Rab (*b. Meg.* 11a), he was righteous from the very beginning to the very end of his life. According to one rabbinic view, he is described as sinless and as proving that there is death without sin and suffering without iniquity (*b. Shab.* 55b). The last words of the Torah leave no doubt as to Moses' utter uniqueness (Deut. 34:10–12): "And there has not arisen a prophet since in Israel like Moses, whom the L-rd knew face to face, none like him for all the signs and the wonders which the L-rd sent him to do in the land of Egypt, to Pharaoh and to all his servants and to all his land, and for all the mighty power and all the great and terrible deeds which Moses wrought in the sight of all Israel."

In sum, Philo gives a long list of the virtues that Moses constantly exhibited. Philo believed that to be possessed of even one of the virtues was to possess them all. Moses' nature was transparent, and his wife Zipporah was not a woman but a virtue. G-d gave him as a loan to mankind. Moses' Ethiopian wife is likewise praised as an epitome of virtue.

2. Wisdom

If we seek to evaluate Moses' virtues against the backdrop of the virtues generally, as viewed by the Greeks, we would do well, it would seem, to focus on the four (or five)[4] cardinal virtues, the discussion of which forms the basic outline of Plato's most influential work, the *Republic*, a classification which was widely adopted by later philosophers. Indeed, Philo himself (*Leg.* 1.63), in his allegorical discussion of the four rivers of Eden (Gen. 2:10–14), states that the Bible's purpose is to indicate the particular virtues, which are four in number, wisdom, courage, temperance, and justice.

It is striking that the earliest extant pagan author who mentions Moses,[5] Hecataeus of Abdera, who flourished ca. 300 B.C.E., praises him (*ap.* Diod., *Bibliotheca Historica* 40.3.3) in high terms as extraordinary (πολὺ διαφέρων) in practical wisdom (φρόνησις)[6] and courage (ἀνδρεία). In fact, φρόνησις, as we see in Aristotle (*Politics* 3.4.1277A15–17), is the *sine qua non* for a good ruler; and the example par excellence of the person possessing this quality, cited by

Aristotle (*EN* 6.5.1140B8–11), is the great statesman Pericles, because, says Aristotle, men like him "can see what is good for themselves and what is good for men in general; we consider that those who can do this are good at managing households or states." Indeed, this gives Moses a rank among the greatest lawgivers, because similar phraseology is used by Diodorus (1.94.1–5) to describe three Egyptian lawgivers.

In its historical survey showing how past generations were guided by wisdom, the Book of Wisdom, though starting with Adam and the patriarchs, focuses especially on Moses, into whose soul Wisdom (10:16) entered, so that he stood up against terrible kings in wonders and signs. It is Wisdom that prospered the works of the Israelites (11:1–3) "by the hand of a holy prophet," that is Moses, as they journeyed through an uninhabited desert and repelled their foes and relieved their thirst for water. Indeed, when they were beset by a plague of fiery serpents, it was Moses' wisdom that led him to make a brazen serpent to save the people (16:5–6).

In the Pseudepigraphic 2 Bar. 59:7 we read that in addition to the secrets of the universe, including Paradise and Gehenna, that G-d showed to Moses, He gave him the root of wisdom and the riches of understanding and the fount of knowledge, the clear implication being that this was not ordinary but profound and mysterious wisdom, understanding, and knowledge.

In his apology for the Law in Arist., the high priest Eleazar focuses on the wisdom of Moses (139), who, he says, was equipped by G-d with insight into everything, enabling him to survey each detail. In particular, he is praised for his wisdom in creating fences around the Israelites so that they should not mingle with other nations and revere the one true G-d. Moses is credited with ordaining dietary laws (144–47), that only those creatures that are gentle and clean may be eaten. The New Testament (Acts 7:22) likewise refers to Moses as "trained in all the wisdom of the Egyptians."

According to Philo, Moses' prime virtue is his wisdom (*Sacr.* 8); and G-d, we are told, prizes the wise man as the world. He is particularly noteworthy (*Mos.* 2.67) for the honor, which, says Philo, is well becoming the wise (σοφός) and which he bestowed upon G-d, and for the honor that was bestowed upon him by G-d in return.

The status of Moses as the wise man who possesses all the virtues differs from the patriarchs in degree rather than in kind (see Tiede 1972, 120–34). He is higher in that he stands beside G-d Himself (Deut. 5:31, *Sacr.* 8). The fact that Philo (*Praem.* 13–24) applies the imagery of athletic contests in viewing these virtuous men supplies a link with the Cynic and Stoic traditions, where life is similarly viewed as a kind of athletic contest (see Tiede 1972, 108–9).

Moses' wisdom is referred to (*Post.* 78) as self-taught (αὐτοδίδακτος) and requires no other learning (αὐτομαθής). Moses is said to accept from G-d's hands Reason (λόγος) as his betrothed and knowledge, which is the life's companion of the wise.

While he was in exile in Midian awaiting G-d's judgment of the Egyptians (*Mos.* 1.48), Moses was going through the contests of virtue, training himself through elegant reasoning for the best life, both theoretical and practical. He always unrolled the doctrines of philosophy, readily discerning them in his soul and entrusting them to his memory so as not to be forgotten and immediately adapting his own deeds, all of which were praiseworthy. Above all, he aimed not at seeming, but at truth, because the one mark that he set before himself was nature's right reason,[7] which is the beginning and source of virtues.[8]

Philo's Moses studied philosophical doctrines, which he digested with quick understanding, committed them to everlasting memory, and brought his personal conduct in consonance with them, his aim being, in opposition to that of the Sophists, truth rather than mere appearance. He is referred to (*Mos.* 2.204) as "all-wise" (πάνσοφος), "who alone has drunk well the unmixed wine (ἠκρατίσω) of wisdom (σοφία)." Philo (*Congr.* 132) speaks of Moses as the mind of purest quality, the truly goodly (ἀστεῖος, "refined") at his very birth, and contrasts him with Noah, who represents the mind at its lower stage, which is absorbed with the sensible world (*Conf.* 106).

Philo (*Mut.* 104) draws a contrast between Jethro, who is said to value the human above the divine, and Moses, who is referred to as the wise man (σοφός). Moses is also the consummate teacher. Indeed, Moses is presented by Philo (*Ebr.* 38) as the teacher par excellence. In particular, Moses persuaded Jethro to depart from his empty opinions and to follow the truth steadfastly.

Philo (*Decal.* 2–17), who speaks of Moses as being responsible for the laws, regards it as a mark of wisdom, as we have noted, that Moses promulgated his laws in the desert rather than in cities, since cities are full of evils, notably pride and contempt for things divine (one surmises that Philo is thinking of his own great city of Alexandria), and since it is necessary to separate oneself, as one can in the desert, from evil associations, and since it is advisable to provide oneself with rules before settling in cities, and finally, since it is necessary to establish the divine origin of the laws through the miracles that

G-d performed for the Israelites in the desert in providing them with water and food.

Philo (*Mos.* 1.4) refers to the Bible as the wonderful monument of Moses' wisdom (σοφία) that he has left behind. He is particularly commended (*Mos.* 2.204) for his promulgation of the law that one who curses G-d is subject to the death penalty. According to Philo (*Mos.* 2.211–12), Moses showed his wisdom in the laws that he transmitted concerning the way in which festivals were to be observed, not through sports and mimes, but through the love of wisdom (φιλοσοφεῖν).[9] Moses, says Philo (*Mos.* 2.173), by granting the Levites the prize of the priesthood, also showed wisdom (ἐπενόησε) in thus approving their zealous heroism in slaying those who had been responsible for building the Golden Calf. Philo (*Mos.* 2.6, 187), however, realized the limitations of reasoning, as we see in his remark that Moses obtained prophecy through the providence of G-d so that he might discover what he was unable to grasp by reasoning.

Whereas the Bible (Num. 15:32–34) states merely that those who had found the Israelite who was gathering wood on the Sabbath brought him to Moses and Aaron and the entire assembly for judgment, Philo (*Mos.* 2.214–15) adds that they brought him before the ruler, that is Moses, beside whom the priests were seated, while the whole multitude stood around to listen, "for it was the custom, whenever it was possible, especially on the seventh day, to pursue philosophy, with the ruler guiding and teaching what it was necessary to do and to say, while they were advancing and improving their habits of life toward excellence," a practice, says Philo, that has continued until his own day.

One of the attributes connected with wisdom, as we may see in Thucydides' (2.60) portrait of the ideal statesman, Pericles, is the ability to persuade the people. As Aristotle puts it, "Rhetoric is useful because things that are true and things that are just have a natural tendency to prevail over their opposites, so that if the decisions of judges are not what they ought to be, the defeat must be due to the speakers themselves, and they must be blamed accordingly" (*Rhet.* 1.1.1355A21–24).[10]

Indeed, as we have seen, despite Moses' speech defect and despite the fact that according to the Bible it is Aaron who speaks on his behalf to the elders of the nation (Exod. 4:14–16), in Philo (*Mos.* 1.86), who is apparently concerned not to diminish Moses' role, it is both Moses and Aaron together who address them. Furthermore, when he prophesied while still alive the story of his own death (Deut. 34:5), according to Philo (*Mos.* 2.291), Moses did so skilfully (δεξιῶς, "cleverly," "discerningly").[11] Moreover, the New Testament (Acts 7:22), in apparent contradiction to the biblical statement (Exod. 4:10) that Moses was "slow of speech and tongue," says that he was a powerful speaker.

As to the reverse of wisdom, Philo (*Mos.* 2.198), in his comments on what brings a man to curse G-d (Lev. 24:10–16), says that it is endless talking (γλωσσαλγία) and an unbridled mouth (ἀχάλινον στόμα) that bring on lawless (ἔκνομοι) foolishness (ἀφροσύναι).

For Pseudo-Philo Moses is the epitome of wisdom, as we see from the fact that when Joshua takes over the leadership of the Israelites (20.2), G-d tells him, in a scene reminiscent of Eleazar's succession to the high priesthood of Aaron (Num. 20:25–28), in a significant extra-biblical detail, to clothe himself with Moses' garments of wisdom and to gird his loins with Moses' belt of knowledge. Thereupon G-d assures him that he will be changed and become another man. Thus, in typical fashion, Pseudo-Philo emphasizes the mystical power of Moses in being able to transform oneself completely.

Josephus (*A.J.* 1.25), quite surprisingly, looks upon Moses as a profound philosopher, as we see in the statement of Josephus, who is, after all, a historian rather than a philosopher, that whoever examines the reasons for every article in the creed of the Pentateuch would find the inquiry profound and highly philosophical. Josephus stresses that Moses exhibits his wisdom particularly as a lawgiver, just as the constitution that he gave the Israelites is consonant with his reputation for virtue (ἀρετή) (*Ap.* 2.147). We are told as well that Moses gave his people an abundance of good laws, in the belief that this was the best means of displaying his own virtue and of ensuring the lasting welfare of those who had made him their leader (*Ap.* 2.159). Indeed, according to Josephus (*Ap.* 2.168), the wisest of the Greeks, including such celebrated philosophers as Pythagoras, Anaxagoras, Plato, and the Stoics, had learned their conceptions of G-d from principles that Moses had supplied to them. He very proudly states that Plato, in particular, had imitated Moses in ordaining that citizens should study their laws. Indeed, he emphasizes that the laws of the Pentateuch are excellent beyond the standard of human wisdom (*A.J.* 3.323).

In sum, the pagan Hecataeus praises Moses for his practical wisdom, reflecting the view of Aristotle that this is the prime quality of a ruler. The Book of Wisdom focuses on the wisdom of Moses that enabled him to stand up to terrible kings and to journey through an uninhabited desert. *2 Baruch* stresses his mysterious wisdom and understanding. The Letter of Aristeas praises the sound wisdom of his laws. The New Testament refers to him as trained in all the wisdom of the Egyptians. According to Philo, Moses as possessor of wisdom stands beside G-d Himself. Moses showed his wisdom particularly through aiming not at seeming but at truth. The chief monument of his wisdom is to be seen in the laws of the Bible. Yet, he realized the limitations of reasoning. He is also the consummate teacher. He showed wisdom in promulgating the laws in the desert so as to be sundered from evil associations.

For Pseudo-Philo the mystical power of Moses is his ability through wisdom in being able to transform himself completely. For Josephus Moses exhibited his wisdom particularly through the profoundly rational and philosophical laws that he transmitted.

3. Courage

Whereas in the Bible it is Joshua who conquered the Land of Israel, in Hecataeus (*ap.* Diodorus 40.3.3) Moses is said to have taken possession of the land. Indeed, Moses himself is a role model for his people in that, as we have noted, he is said (*ap.* Diodorus 40.3.7) to have led out successful military expeditions against the neighboring tribes.

Manetho (*ap.* Josephus, *Ap.* 1.240) presents Moses as a military master who ordered the Israelites to repair the walls of the city of Heliopolis and to prepare for war against King Amenophis of Egypt. Moses, according to Manetho (*ap.* Josephus, *Ap.* 1.241), is a diplomatic planner who worked together with other priests like himself and who successfully sought an alliance with the shepherds who had been expelled by the previous Pharaoh. In a bold move to form as broad a coalition as possible, he then gathered a multitude of Egyptians and took counsel with their leaders.[12]

Artapanus (*ap.* Eus. *PE* 9.27.7–11) states that after the Pharaoh had appointed Moses as general of a conscripted army of 100,000 farmers, in the hope that Moses would thus be killed, Moses, in a war that lasted ten years, won every battle with distinction. Though the war had been fought against the Ethiopians, the latter now came to love Moses and they, together with the Egyptian priests, adopted from him the practice of circumcision.

Similarly, though less prominently than in Josephus, in Philo (Mos. 1.71), when G-d appears to Moses in the burning bush, He urges him to take charge of the Israelites not as an accessory (παραίτιος) to their liberation, but as the commander (ἡγεμών, "leader"). Philo, in the essay *Mos.*, continues to refer to Moses as the Israelites' commander eleven other times: 1.148, 1.193, 1.198, 1.200, 1.236, 1.243, 1.329, 2.187, 2.215, 2.234, 2.273. But while Philo's Moses certainly serves as commander-in-chief of the Israelites, his chief function is that of being their leader in the broader sense.

Philo (*Mos.* 2.183) finds in the nature of the nut a parable, which he ascribes to Moses, of the practicing soul. The shell of a nut is bitter, and the inner layer surrounding the fruit is very hard, and hence the fruit is not easy to get at. Similarly, the soul must first encounter toil before it attains results. Toil is bitter and hard, yet from it springs goodness. The moral is that one who endures patiently (τλητικῶς, "steadfastly") and bravely (ἀνδρείως, "manfully," "courageously") what is hard to endure (δυσκαρτέρητα) is on his way to blessedness. Indeed, Philo (*Mos.* 2.216) states that on every Sabbath Jews in their synagogues study the four cardinal virtues, including, of course, courage (ἀνδρεία). In the Bible (Exod. 4:27–5:1), after Aaron meets Moses and they gather the elders of the Israelites and tell them what G-d has said to them, we hear that they go to the Pharaoh and ask him to let the Israelites leave to celebrate G-d in the wilderness. There is no indication, however, of their mood when they confront the Pharaoh. Philo (*Mos.* 1.87) adds that once they had met with the elders they were now emboldened (θαρροῦσιν, "of good courage," "confident") to talk with the Pharaoh.

Moreover, Philo (*Her.* 19–20) calls attention to Moses' courage of speech even in addressing G-d. Thus, Moses asks G-d why He has afflicted the Israelites and why He has sent Moses (Exod. 5:22–23). Likewise, Moses shows courage, in connection with the incident of the Golden Calf, in saying to G-d that if He does not forgive the Israelites' sin (Exod. 32:32), He should erase him from His book and, when the Israelites express dissatisfaction with the manna, in asking G-d from what source he is to get meat to feed the people (Num. 11:13, 21–22). Anyone, adds Philo, would have been afraid to speak thus to the king of an earthly kingdom, and yet Moses had the boldness to say these words to G-d.

A crucial element in military success consists of selecting able military leaders. Whereas, according to the Bible (Exod. 17:9), Moses, without any words of how Joshua came to be the general in charge, tells Joshua to choose men and to go to battle against Amalek, in Philo (*Mos.* 1.216), as in Josephus (*A.J.* 3.49), Moses himself assumes the lead in mustering his men of military age and takes a more important part in the fight, while naming Joshua to be the general.

Though Philo places more emphasis on other roles played by Moses, he does realize that a good general knows that a most important element in military success consists of obtaining, through reconnaissance, information about the enemy. Consequently, whereas in the Bible (Num. 13:2) it is G-d's idea to send scouts, Philo, as we have noted, as later Josephus (*A.J.* 3.302), attributes the plan to Moses.

In connection with the contention of the daughters of Zelophehad that they were entitled to obtain the inheritance from their father (Num. 27:1–11), Moses, as we have remarked, though sympathetic to their petition (*Mos.* 2.242), nevertheless, as the general concerned to recognize the sacrifices of his soldiers, does not at first give them equality in inheritances, but rather in recognition of their bravery, he assigns the inheritances to combatants.

As commander-in-chief, Moses had to decide when and with whom to go to war and who should serve as soldiers. In the Bible (Num. 31:1–4) it is G-d who tells Moses to take revenge against the Midianites, and Moses tells the Israelites to supply a thousand soldiers from each tribe. Philo (*Mos.* 1.305–6) focuses on Moses' role. It is he who decides that internal troubles of the Israelites have ended with the killing of those who have committed harlotry and with the death of those who were suspected of desertion or treachery; and, consequently, as we have remarked, he concludes that this is an appropriate time to wage war against Balak.

Pseudo-Philo (9–19) has nothing about Moses' ability as a general either before or during the Exodus. His concern is with Moses the religious leader and the inspiring teacher of the Israelites and his dealings with G-d.

Josephus, perhaps influenced by the fact that he himself had served as a general in Galilee during the war against the Romans, places more influence on Moses' achievements as a general (see Feldman 1998a, 401–11). In a long and striking addition to the biblical text, Josephus (*A.J.* 2.238–53) tells of Moses' incredible exploits on behalf of the Egyptians against the Ethiopians. Indeed, it is striking that whereas in the LXX Moses is never called στρατηγός (general) or even ἡγεμών (leader), in Josephus he is referred to thus fifteen times in *A.J.* (2.241, 268; 3.2, 11, 12, 28, 47, 65, 67, 78, 102, 105; 4.82, 194, 329) and once in the *Ap.* (2.158) by the former term; in addition, the verb στρατηγέω, "to be a field-commander," "to lead an army," is used of him once (*A.J.* 2.243); and the noun στρατηγία, "army command," "office of supreme commander," twice (*A.J.* 2.255, 282). Furthermore, the noun ἡγεμών ("leader," "commander") is applied to him six times (*A.J.* 2.268, 4.11; *Ap.* 1.238, 261; 2.156, 159).[13] Indeed, it is not to him as teacher or legislator that the voice from the burning bush bids Moses to act, but rather as general (στρατηγός) and leader (ἡγεμών) (*A.J.* 2.268). In his final encomium of Moses, Josephus (*A.J.* 4.329) remarks that as a general he had few to equal him. Furthermore, in summarizing Moses' achievements (*Ap.* 2.157–63), Josephus emphasizes that in taking command of the multitudes who left Egypt and in guiding them through a huge desert and in defeating their enemies, Moses proved the best of generals. Not only is Moses presented as a general, but his people are referred to as soldiers. This is especially clear in Moses' exhortation to the Israelites before his death, where he addresses them as "comrades in arms" (συστρατιῶται).

In sum, whereas Manetho, Artapanus, and Josephus stress Moses' ability as a military leader, Philo, though not minimizing Moses' military leadership, particularly in noting the importance of reconnaissance, in selecting the most able generals, and in deciding when to go to war, places less emphasis upon it. Rather, he underlines Moses' courageous endurance of toil and calls attention to Moses' courage of speech in addressing G-d. Pseudo-Philo, on the other hand, emphasizes Moses' role as a religious leader. Josephus greatly emphasizes his role as a general against the Ethiopians and as guide of the masses of Israelites through the desert and in defeating their enemies.

4. Temperance

That Philo feels unusually strongly about the importance of temperance may be seen in the extraordinary list of no fewer than 149 adjectives describing all the terrible qualities that a pleasure-lover will acquire (*Sacr.* 32).

Philo's Moses (*Mos.* 2.183–85) stresses that to attain virtue one must first encounter toil[14] and that he who patiently endures what is hard to bear is on his way to blessedness.

He (*Mos.* 2.185) asserts that the four cardinal virtues—wisdom, courage, temperance, and justice—accompany those who strive after (ζηλοῦσι) a life of austerity (αὐστηρός), hardship (σκληροδίαιτος), self-control (ἐγκράτεια), and patient endurance (καρτερία), together with thrift (εὐτέλεια) and contentment with little (ὀλιγόδεια). It is through these virtues, he adds, that the most authoritative faculty in us, namely reason (λογισμός), advances to sound health (ὑγεῖα ἄνοσος) and bodily vigor (εὐεξία) and overcomes drunkenness, dainty living, sexual indulgence, and insatiable desires, which are the enemies of ready wit. He speaks in the strongest language (*Mos.* 2.184) against those who live luxuriously and whose souls become effeminate. On the other hand, temperance (σωφροσύνη) is one of the cardinal virtues that are studied in synagogues on the Sabbath (*Mos.* 2.216).[15] Philo's great praise for the Therapeutae (*Contempl.*) and the Essenes (*Prob.* 75–91) is based on his admiration for their temperance.

Thus, Moses, following a more severe and more serious rule of life, was a model for his people, so that even the most licentious were converted to a life of continence. He became, in effect, the reasonable and living impersonation of law (*Mos.* 1.162).

Philo (*Mos.* 1.160) notes that if a ruler turns to a life of luxury, his subjects generally allow their appetites for food and sex to go beyond their needs. On the other hand, when a ruler follows a more austere and more severe pattern, even those who are most intemperate change to a pattern of self-control (ἐγκράτεια) and, whether through fear or shame, seek to create the impression that they are zealous to resemble him.

While, as we have noted, Moses practiced the economy and unassuming ways of a private citizen, he was liberal in the truly royal expenditure of those treasures that the ruler may well desire to have in abundance (*Mos.* 1.153). This sounds like a *speculum principis*, as Borgen 1997, 199, remarks; and he, Goodenough 1928, 70, and Meeks 1967, 109–10, call attention to the close parallel description in Diotogenes (*ap.* Stob. 4.7.26) of the way in which a king should behave, namely that the king must excel the rest in virtue, but not on account of his wealth or power or military strength.

After killing the Egyptian, Moses withdraws to Midian, where, Philo (*Leg.* 3.13) says, he is kept waiting to see whether G-d will bestow upon his reasoning faculty a stream sufficient to drown the onrush of the Egyptian king, which he equates with the passions. And, continuing the allegory, Philo says that Moses does not abandon the warfare against the passions until he sees them prostrate and out of action (*Leg.* 3.14).

Moreover, we are told, Moses did not pay attention to the pleasure of sex except for the lawful begetting of childen (*Mos.* 1.28).[16] Indeed, according to Philo (*Mos.* 2.68–69), almost from the time that he entered on his work as a prophet, he disdained having sexual relations, since he regarded it as necessary to be always prepared to receive oracles. He was content with little and scorned the life of luxury. His words and his actions were in complete accord.

Philo (*Conf.* 82), commenting on the biblical explanation of the name of Moses' elder son (Exod. 2:22), Gershom ("for he said, 'I have been a sojourner in a foreign land'"), remarks that Moses was so alienated from his body that never to count it as his own was to give it its due.

In preparation for the divine revelation at Sinai, Moses (Exod. 19:10–23) instructed the Israelites to prepare themselves during a three-day period by purifying themselves and by abstaining from sexual relations, but there is nothing said about Moses' own preparations. Philo (*Mos.* 2.68–69) has filled in this gap by noting that Moses had to be clean in soul as in body by avoiding any passion, by abstaining from all food and drink and from sexual relations. He adds that Moses observed the last for many days, indeed from the very time when he began to prophesy.

The Bible (Exod. 24:18) says that Moses was on Mount Sinai with G-d for forty days and nights and that during that period he did not eat bread or drink water (Exod. 34:28). During this period, Philo (*Leg.* 3.142–43) says, Moses not only renounced the whole belly, but also the feet, that is, the supports of pleasure.[17] Philo (*Mos.* 2.69) says that, when he was there with G-d, Moses had no thought of eating or drinking, doubtless, he adds, because he had the better food of contemplation, through whose heaven-sent inspiration he improved in mind and body and became so strong that those who later saw him could not believe their eyes. During this period (Philo, *Somn.* 1.36), like a being awaiting immortality, Moses heard the perfect harmony of the heavenly bodies going through their movements.

One might wonder why Moses, when he was on Mount Sinai, failed to hear the tumult when the Israelites were building and celebrating the Golden Calf and had to be told by G-d what was happening (Exod. 32:7). Philo (*Mos.* 2.163–64) says that Moses did hear the continuous shouting of the people and analyzed its cause, incontinence (ἀκρασία).

In commenting on Moses' action (Exod. 32:20) in burning the Golden Calf, in grinding it into a fine powder, and giving it to the Israelites to drink, Philo (*Post.* 164) converts this into a plea for extreme asceticism. He says that it signifies the need to burn up one's pleasures by grinding down and dissolving the composition of bodily goods into thin and useless dust, based upon the assumption that from none of them did there ever sprout and bloom that which is truly beautiful any more than from seeds sown upon water.

In the Bible (Num. 11:1–10) we hear of the complaints of the Israelites, and in particular their hunger now as compared to their food in Egypt; but there is no indication that they are gluttons. Philo (*Spec.* 4.126–27), on the other hand, censures them as wantonly self-indulgent gluttons who, though they are in a desert, want to live luxuriously. In the Bible the people cry out to Moses (Num. 11:2), but, according to Philo (*Spec.* 4.127), they not only cry out (κατεβόων), but also accuse (κατηγόρουν) Moses and put him to shame (ἐδυσώπουν) with impudent boldness (ἀναίσχυντον θράσος) and do not cease their rebellion (νεωτερίζοντες) until they have gained their objective. Philo (ibid.) concludes that G-d granted their request for food by sending them quail both to show that everything is possible for G-d and to punish those who had no self-control of their bellies. One would have thought that the people should have been satisfied with the quail, but they merely spur on their lusts more than before (*Spec.* 4.129).

Elsewhere (*Migr.* 155) Philo blames for their insatiable lust the mixed multitude that accompanied the Israelites upon leaving Egypt. He contrasts (*Her.* 79–80) those who look steadfastly for the manna with those who see only the onions and garlic, which give great pain to their eyes. Philo (*Spec.* 4.131) commends as very beautiful (παγκάλως) Moses' advice (Deut. 12:8) not to do what is pleasing in one's own eyes; rather, he says, a person who wishes to become truly excellent should seek to be pleasing to G-d, to the universe, to nature, to the laws, and to wise men, and to deprecate self-love.

When the Israelites, after bypassing the land of the Edomites, complain against G-d and Moses about the lack of food and water, G-d sends fiery serpents that bite many of the people (Num. 21:4–6). Thereupon the people come to Moses to ask him to pray to G-d to remove the serpents. When Moses prays for them, G-d instructs him to make for himself a fiery serpent, so that if anyone has been bitten and looks upon it, they will be cured. Philo (*Leg.* 2.79) emphasizes that the biblical text (Num. 21:8) reads, "Make for yourself a fiery serpent," and explains that Moses made the serpent for no one else but himself, and that this teaches that self-mastery is not possible for every person, but only for the man dear to G-d (θεοφιλής).

At one point Philo (*Deus* 162–65) seems to adopt the Aristotelian view (*EN* 2.6–8.1106B-1109A) of virtue as a mean between two extremes. In fact, he mentions two examples, courage versus rashness and cowardice; and liberality versus stinginess and extravagance, that are also given by Aristotle. Philo cites two other examples, prudence versus knavery and folly; and piety versus superstition and impiety. He cites another example in *Migr.* 147, likewise mentioned by Aristotle (*EN* 2.7.1108A), namely, truthfulness versus boastfulness and humility.

Closely connected with moderation is the quality of modesty, with which Josephus (*A.J.* 6.63) identifies it. This is a peculiarly Jewish virtue, since the pagans tended to frown upon it. Aristotle, for example, is critical of the unduly humble man who, although worthy of good things, robs himself of what he deserves (*EN* 4.4.1125B7–27). Aristotle's charge that the unduly humble man does not know himself is particularly serious, especially since he also says that undue humility is more opposed to pride than is vanity, being both commoner and worse. The Bible (Num. 12:3), on the other hand, states that humility is the virtue most unique with Moses: "Now the man Moses was very meek, more than all men that were on the face of the earth." Philo, in connection with Moses' response to Korah's rebellion, refers to this quality in his remark (*Mos.* 2.279) that though Moses was the mildest (πρᾳότατος) and meekest (ἡμερώτατος) of men, yet he was spurred to righteous anger by his passionate hatred of the evil brought on by Korah. This, however, is the only reference in the extant treatises of Philo to Moses' possession of this virtue of righteous anger (δικαία ὀργή), and he gives no examples where Moses showed this virtue. If we ask why Philo does not have more references to Moses' modesty, we may suggest that he himself, as a leader of the Alexandrian Jewish community, realized that it was important for a leader to assert strongly his power and to instill in his people obedience to that power.

Pseudo-Philo has no reference to Moses' temperance or modesty. His concern is with proper behavior, that is, obedience, and its consequences, and with Moses' dialogue with G-d.

Josephus, like Philo, depicts Moses as a Stoic-like sage. In Josephus' final eulogy for Moses, he is described as having found favor in every way, but chiefly through his command of his passions (τῶν παθῶν αὐτοκράτωρ, *A.J.* 4.328–29); but Josephus does not depict Moses as going to the extreme of sexual abstention, except for begetting children, that we find in Philo. He says (*A.J.* 4.49) that the chief lesson to be learned from the key challenge to Moses' authority, that by Korah, is the necessity of moderation (σωφροσύνη). He affirms that the purpose of the laws that Moses has conveyed to his people is to teach them moderation (*A.J.* 4.184).

In particular, Josephus (*A.J.* 6.63) identifies moderation with modesty, which, as we have noted, the Bible (Num. 12:3) cites as Moses' prime virtue.

He highlights Moses' modesty by citing his readiness to acknowledge the assistance given to him by his father-in-law Jethro (*A.J.* 3.74) and by his recording the prophecies of Balaam, even though he could just as easily have appropriated them for himself (*A.J.* 4.157). But he does not carry his modesty to an extreme, as we see in Josephus' statement (*A.J.* 4.178–79) that through his labors for the public welfare Moses has built a memorial for himself.

In sum, that Philo places an unusual emphasis on temperance as a virtue may be seen in his list of 149 adjectives describing the negative qualities of a pleasure-lover. He stresses that a ruler who exemplifies moderation will have great influence on his subjects. Moses did not pay attention to the pleasure of sex except for begetting children. Philo notes that Moses prepared for the communion with G-d at Sinai by abstaining from eating and drinking and sexual relations; and when he was communing with G-d he likewise abstained from food and drink. His response to the sin of the Israelites' building of the Golden Calf was to plead for extreme asceticism. He censured the gluttony of the Israelites during their sojourn in the desert. When the people continually complained about lack of food and drink, he began with self-mastery. In particular, he upbraided the insatiable lust of the mixed multitude. Closely connected with moderation is Moses' modesty, a peculiarly Jewish virtue. Philo does not stress this virtue unduly, since, as the leader of the Alexandrian Jewish community he realized how important it was for Moses to assert his power. Pseudo-Philo emphasizes Moses' quality of obedience. Josephus, while mentioning Moses' qualities of moderation and modesty, says that he avoided carrying them to an extreme.

5. Justice

The importance of justice for Philo may be seen in the fact that the word "just" (δίκαιος) occurs 281 times in his works, 23 of them in his essay on Moses (*Mos.* 1.24, 31, 45, 50, 55, 102, 142, 244, 260, 274, 279, 302, 314, 315, 323; 2.4, 47, 100, 108, 214, 228, 279 [*bis*]); the word "justice" (δικαιοσύνη) occurs 123 times in his works, 6 times in his essay on Moses (1.154, 328; 2.9, 185, 216, 237); the alternate word for justice (δίκη) occurs 145 times in his works, 13 times in *Mos.* (1.46, 55, 134, 218, 237, 245, 326; 2.53, 99, 162, 200, 202, 206); the word "injustice" (ἀδικία) occurs 70 times, once (2.53) in his essay on Moses; "unjust action" (ἀδίκημα) occurs 110 times, 6 times (1.102, 149, 303; 2.59, 213,

227) in his essay on Moses; "unjust" (ἄδικος) occurs 110 times, 9 times in *Mos.* (1.45, 58, 95, 140, 142, 281, 311; 2.107, 156; and "to do injustice" (ἀδικέω) occurs 139 times, 13 times in his essay on Moses (1.40 [*bis*], 54, 56, 67 [*ter*], 106, 111, 308 [*bis*]; 2.204, 232). Justice, he insists (*Mos.* 2.52–53), is in harmony with the universe and is in agreement with the eternal principles of nature; and those who practice injustice are enemies not of humanity, but of the whole universe. When Moses himself is in doubt as to what judgment to make, as in the case of the one who gathered wood on the Sabbath (Num. 15:32–34), he appproaches the court of justice (δικαστήριον) presided over by G-d, Who knows all before He hears it (*Mos.* 2.217).

Philo (*Mos.* 2.4), in noting that Moses, through G-d's providence, became king, remarks that "it is a king's duty to command what is right and forbid what is wrong. But to command what should be done and to forbid what should not be done is the peculiar function of law; so that it follows at once that the king is a living law, and the law a just king." Philo (*Mos.* 1.162), in a supreme compliment to Moses, says that perhaps, since he was destined to be a legislator, the divine providence which afterwards appointed him as a legislator without his knowledge, caused him long before that time to become a living and reasonable law (νόμος ἔμψυχός τε καὶ λογικός).[18]

Likewise, even though Jethro is presented as a demagogue (*Ebr.* 38) who is concerned only with appearances rather than with reality, Moses, says Philo, had compassion (ἐλεήσας) upon him and pitied (οἰκτισάμενος) him for his great delusion (πλάνος). Philo (*Sacr.* 50) also portrays Moses as leading the thoughts of Jethro, the worldling (περιττοῦ, "the man of superfluity"), away from the tumult of the crowd into the lonely land (ἐρημία, "solitude," "desert") where there is no injustice (ἀδικεῖν).

Moreover, as we have noted, Philo (*Prob.* 29), in commenting on the fact that during the fight with Amalek Moses' hands grew heavy (Exod. 17:12), explains that by this figure the text signifies that Moses' actions were not superficial (ἐπιπολαίως), but firmly based (παγίως ἐρηρεισμέναι), the result of a mind, like a balance, inclining to neither side (ἀρρεπής).

Apparently, Philo was troubled by the question as to why Moses gave the Pharaoh so many opportunities to repent and why he interceded so often with G-d for him. His answer (*Mut.* 128–29) is that this is the meaning of the statement (Exod. 7:1) that Moses was G-d to the Pharaoh, namely in not punishing him summarily, but rather in emulating the merciful power of G-d—since beneficence (εὐεργετεῖν) is the peculiar prerogative (ἴδιον) of G-d—and in acting as a mediator and in showing a generous spirit toward him and in dispensing punishment with more moderation (μετριώτερον) and in a kindlier (φιλανθρωπότερον) spirit. It is this key balance between strict justice and mercy that Moses emulates.

It is presumably embarrassing, as we have noted, that Moses, when confronted by those who are not permitted to partake of the Passover offering on the fourteenth day of Nisan because of contact with the dead, is not able to give them an answer as to the fairness of their being prohibited (Num. 9:4–8). Philo (*Mos.* 2.225–27) further dramatizes this apparent unfairness. He (*Mos.* 2.228), however, adds that Moses, influenced by feelings of pity (ἔλεος) and justice (δίκαια), recognized the cogency of their excuse.

Connected with the virtue of justice is the enormous responsibility to tell the truth. Indeed, a popular definition of justice, as we see from the aged Cephalus in Plato (*R.* 331C), is speaking the truth. That the Greeks realized its importance is to be seen in the fact that Herodotus (1.136) quite obviously admires the fact that Persian boys are carefully instructed to speak the truth and regard it as the most disgraceful thing in the world to tell a lie (1.139), this in contrast to the reputation that the Greeks themselves had, from Odysseus on down, for cleverness in lying and in contrast particularly with the characterization of the Cretans, the proverbial liars of antiquity (Epimenides 1).

From his very birth, says Philo (*Congr.* 132), Moses, being descended on both his father's and his mother's side from the tribe of Levi, had a double link with truth (ἀλήθεια). Truthfulness, he says (*Mos.* 2.177), is the attendant of G-d; reason, he says, is fittingly dutybound to honor truth with complete freedom from falsehood. Furthermore, he says (*Sacr.* 12) that Moses set no value on probabilities and plausibilities, but followed after truth in its purity.

Coupled with justice is the virtue of humanity (φιλανθρωπία, "politeness," "courtesy," "kindness," "generosity"),[19] as we see in Philo (*Mut.* 225; *Mos.* 2.9; *Decal.* 164),[20] just as its Latin equivalent, *humanitas*, is likewise connected with the virtue of justice. Moses, according to Philo, is the paradigm of φιλανθρωπία, to which Philo (*Virt.* 51–174) devotes no fewer than 124 paragraphs. At the beginning of this discussion (*Virt.* 52–55) Philo calls attention to the fact that he has already set forth in the two books of his biography of Moses the actions that Moses performed from his earliest years to old age for the care and protection of every single person. In particular, he calls attention to the fact that when Moses knew that he was about to die, he did not, as we have noted, imitate other kings and commoners who are eager to transmit their power to their sons, but rather, in his φιλανθρωπία, chose a friend, Joshua, as the heir to his leadership. Indeed, Philo has a whole section of his essay *Virt.* (51–174) dealing with this virtue of justice and the way it is incorporated in the various laws of the Pentateuch. In particular, he notes (*Virt.* 54–65) that the supreme example of Moses' personification of this virtue is that he, in his humility, did not take it upon himself to undertake the supreme task of choosing a successor, even though he had sons and nephews who, one would think, should have been considered, but rather entrusted the task to G-d Himself.

Philo (*Abr.* 208) recognizes the close relationship between the nature that is pious (εὐσεβής) and that which is kindly (φιλάνθρωπος); and he concludes that the same person will exhibit both qualities, holiness to G-d and justice (δικαιοσύνη) to men. Philo (*Virt.* 51) speaks of humanity (φιλανθρωπία) as the virtue closest akin to piety, indeed, its sister and twin. He then remarks that he does not know whether anyone else has loved this virtue more than the prophet of the laws (ὁ προφήτης τῶν νόμων), that is, Moses, since he knew that this was the path that led to holiness. Consequently, he set before his followers his own life as a Platonic-like beautiful model (παράδειγμα) and archetype (ἀρχέτυπος) and trained them to follow this quality. Philo (*Virt.* 80) calls attention to Moses' humanity and fellow-feeling (κοινωνία, "communion," "partnership"), qualities that he possessed through natural goodness and through lessons that he had learned from the holy oracles. Moses' possession of this quality of φιλανθρωπία was a case of *imitatio Dei*, since, as Philo (*Virt.* 77) says, the blessings that Moses gave to the tribes just before his death will be fulfilled, inasmuch as we must believe that he who gave them was beloved of G-d (θεοφιλής), and G-d Himself is the lover of men (φιλάνθρωπος).

Moses likewise showed kindness in approaching G-d to ask that He forgive that most terrible of sins, the worship of the Golden Calf (Exod. 32; *Mos.* 2.166). And yet he could be stern, as we see in his orders not to show pity, but to slay those who had engaged in harlotry with the Midianite women (*Mos.* 1.303).

Moses showed φιλανθρωπία in his dealing with the Edomites (Num. 20:14–21, *Mos.* 1.239–49) when they refused to allow the Israelites to pass through their territory, despite the assurances given them by the Israelites. Instead of resorting to force, Moses led the people by another route.

Philo (*Mos.* 2.242) also declares that Moses exhibited the quality of φιλανθρωπία in his treatment of the petition of the daughters of Zelophehad, who sought to gain the inheritance of their father, inasmuch as their father had left no sons (Num. 36:1–12). Moses, he says, awarded the inheritance to them as prizes befitting their uprightness and as being worthy of their goodwill (χάρις, "gratitude," "favor") and kindheartedness (φιλανθρωπία).

Philo cites numerous laws as coming from Moses that show his humanity (φιλανθρωπία): setting free an Israelite slave after six years (*Spec.* 2.79), the sabbatical year (*Spec.* 2.104, *Virt.* 97–98), the jubilee year (*Virt.* 99–100), the prohibition of interest on loans to fellow-Jews (*Virt.* 82–87), the requirement to pay wages to a poor man on the same day (*Virt.* 88), the prohibition of a creditor entering the house of a debtor (*Virt.* 89), ordinances with regard to reapers and grape-pickers (*Virt.* 90–94), equal status to proselytes (*Virt.* 102–4), laws concerning resident aliens (*Virt.* 105–8), treatment of enemies in wartime (*Virt.* 109–15), kindness to animals even of enemies (*Virt.* 116–20), treatment of slaves (*Virt.* 121–24), and concern for trees and plants (*Virt.* 148–60).

Philo makes a point of stressing that Moses was concerned not only with his own Israelites, but also with humankind in general. Moses, as the son of the daughter of the reigning king of Egypt, had expected to obtain the lordship of Egypt. Nevertheless, because of the iniquities committed by the Egyptians and because of his own nobility (εὐγένεια) of soul and magnanimity (μέγεθος) of spirit and inborn hatred of evil, he gave up this expectation. Because of these qualities possessed by Moses, says Philo, G-d thought good to requite him with the kingship of a more populous and mightier nation, namely, the Israelites. He then adds that this nation was destined to be consecrated above all others to offer prayers forever not only on its own behalf, but also on behalf of the human race, that it might be delivered from evil and might participate in what is good. Clearly, in this addition, Philo is refuting those, such as Apollonius Molon and Lysimachus (*ap. Ap.* 2.145), who declared that the Jews bear an implacable hatred toward non-Jews and are interested only in their own welfare. As Philo (*Spec.* 2.163, *Abr.* 98) declares, the Jewish nation is to the whole inhabited world what the priest is to the State. Therefore, he says (*Spec.* 2.167), "It astonishes me to see that some people venture to accuse of inhumanity (ἀπανθρωπία) the nation that has shown so profound a sense of fellowship and goodwill to all men everywhere, by using its prayers and festivals and first-fruit offerings as a means of supplication for the human race in general and of making its homage to the truly existent G-d in the name of those who have evaded the service that it was their duty to give."

Philo's Moses was confronted with the task of estimating the claims of his real and his adoptive parents. Philo (*Mos.* 1.33) is careful to note that while Moses requited his natural parents with good will (εὔνοια) and ardent (ἐκθύμως) affection, he showed gratitude (εὐχαριστίαι) to his adoptive parents for their kind treatment of him. Philo then explains, realizing that the reader might well want to ask how Moses could have shown such gratitude to the Pharaoh when the Pharaoh had treated the Hebrews in so cruel a fashion, that he would have continued to do so throughout his life if he had not found the Pharaoh adopting so impious a course of action.

Pseudo-Philo is not concerned with Moses' exemplification of justice. His focus is on G-d's action and His use of Moses. He is not concerned with the way that non-Jews are treated. He emphasizes G-d's power and sovereignty over the cosmos. He does stress, however, G-d's mercy as necessary for the existence of the human race.

Josephus emphasizes Moses' justice in an addition to the Bible (Exod. 18:13) in which he declares that all who came to Moses thought that only so would they obtain justice, and that even those who lost their cases before him left convinced that it was justice that had determined their fate (*A.J.* 3.66–67). In the rebellion of Dathan and Abiram, when G-d wishes to annihilate the congregation for associating with them, it is Moses who takes the lead to appeal to G-d's sense of justice in stressing that only the sinners deserve to be punished. Moses, Josephus insists (*Ap.* 2.211–13), inculcated into Jews that they must show consideration even for declared enemies. To show that Moses is not prejudiced against non-Jews, he carefully differentiates between the Pharaoh and the Egyptians (*A.J.* 2.315).

In sum, Philo suggests that even before G-d appointed Moses to be a legislator, He caused him to be the personification of a living law, and he stresses that the law's function is to execute justice. It is G-d's balance between justice and mercy that Moses emulates. Moses follows the path of pure truth, a key aspect of justice. Moses is a paradigm of humanity (fellow-feeling), another aspect of justice, which he shows in not selecting his own sons to succeed him. Philo stresses that Moses is concerned not only with his own Israelites but also with all humankind. It was because of the Egyptians' injustices that Moses gave up the lordship of Egypt, to which he was heir apparent.

Pseudo-Philo focuses not on Moses' exemplification of justice but on G-d's power and His use of Moses. Josephus emphasizes Moses' justice even toward the enemies of the Israelites.

6. Piety

The fifth of the cardinal virtues is piety, as we see in Plato (*Protagoras* 330B, 349B) and in the Stoics (*SVF* 3.64.40 and Diogenes Laertius 7.119). Aristotle defines piety as either a part of justice or an accompaniment to it (*De Virtutibus et Vitiis* 55.1250B22–23). Menander of Laodicea (1.17–20) identifies the parts of justice as "piety, fair dealing, and reverence: piety towards the gods, fair dealing towards men, reverence towards the departed." Dionysius of Halicarnassus praises Xenophon for displaying first of all the virtue of piety (*Ant. Rom.* 4.778). Diodorus (1.2.2) in his prologue stresses that if myths about Hades inspire men to piety and justice, "how much more must we suppose history, the interpreter of truth and the source of all philosophy, to be capable of shaping men's characters in honorable ways."[21]

Philo (*Praem.* 53, *Spec.* 4.147) says that the queen of the virtues, the fairest of them all, is piety. Moses, he asserts, the teacher of divine lore, had this virtue in a special degree, and through it he gained, among a multitude of other gifts, four special rewards, namely the offices of king, legislator, prophet, and high priest, the four titles (in addition to that of philosopher) of Moses that form the basic outline of Philo's *Mos.* In faith Moses takes precedence even over Abraham (*Leg.* 3.228): whereas, Philo says, Abraham trusted (ἐπίστευσε) in G-d, and He reckoned it to him as righteousness (Gen. 15:6), Moses refused to place his trust in his own reasonings (see Harrisville 1990, 163). Indeed, says Philo (*Mos.* 2.66), the greatest and most necessary quality required of a priest is piety (εὐσέβεια), and this Moses practiced to an exceptional degree.

Philo ignores the fact that it was Aaron and not Moses who was the priest. But, as Philo (*Mos.* 2.5) stresses, "a king and lawgiver ought to have under his purview not only human but divine things; for without G-d's directing care, the affairs of kings and subjects cannot go aright." Therefore he needed the chief priesthood, so that, fortified with perfect rites and the perfect knowledge of the service of G-d, he might ask "that he and those whom he ruled might receive prevention of evil and participation in good from the gracious Being Who assents to prayers." This is in line with Pythagorean theory, as we find it, for example, in Diotogenes (*ap.* Stob. 4.7.61, cited by Goodenough 1928, 190): "The third duty, that is, worship of the gods, is no less fitting for a king. For the Best must be honored by the best man, and the Governing Principle by one who is a governor." Moses, says Philo (*Mos.* 2.192), was the holiest of men ever yet born. He is depicted by Philo (*Virt.* 67) as the person of supreme faith. In viewing Moses as jointly king[22] and priest,[23] Philo may have been influenced by the fact, which he himself notes (*Mos.* 2.31), that in Judaea the offices of high priest and king were held by the same person at the time when King Ptolemy Philadelphus of Egypt commissioned the translation of the Pentateuch into Greek.[24]

Moses, says Philo (*Mos.* 2.67), came to love G-d and to be loved by Him as have been few others. Inspired by a heaven-sent rapture, Moses honored the Ruler of all, which is the business of the priesthood, and was honored in return.

According to Philo (*Her.* 17), the relationship of G-d to Moses was such that G-d did not talk with him only upon occasion, but that He was continuously talking to him and answering him without interruption. Whereas G-d appeared to other prophets only in a vision, G-d spoke mouth to mouth with Moses and not through riddles (Num. 12:6, *Leg.* 3.103, *Her.* 262).

In his practice of piety, according to Philo (*Mos.* 2.66), Moses made use of his great natural gifts. In these, we may remark, far from finding a conflict between philosophy and piety, Philo states that philosophy found a good soil, which she improved still further by the admirable truths that she brought before his eyes; nor did she cease until she brought the fruits of virtue to perfection in word and deed. Indeed, Philo's Moses, as Völker (1938, 197) remarks, identifies φιλοσοφία and ἀρετή.

It was Goodenough's contention (1935, 180–264) that Moses was the central figure in a Jewish mystery cult that Philo knew and that Philo borrowed thought-patterns and motifs from his Hellenistic environment. Philo, to be sure, does use terms common in the Greek mysteries, such as initiation, illumination, and perfection (see Sandmel 1979, 143–44). He speaks of Moses as a hierophant, the technical term that designated the leader of the pagan mysteries; and he distinguishes between the lesser mysteries (*Abr.* 122) and the greater mysteries (*Leg.* 3.100, *Cher.* 9; *Sacr.* 62). But his use of these terms may be due to the fact that they are part of the common speech of that day and may have no further significance (so Wolfson 1947, 1:46). Even, however, if they have significance, the result would be no worse than to present Philo as a proto-mystic. This would not necessarily constitute a threat to his Judaism and, in fact, might even enrich it if we recall the impact that medieval mysticism had upon Judaism.

As in Philo, so in Pseudo-Philo, Moses is the person of supreme faith. He never questions G-d, as he does in the Bible. Moreover, philosophy is not considered the major factor in his religious outlook.

As to Josephus, at the very beginning of his work (*A.J.* 1.6), he says that the Israelites were trained under Moses in piety and in the other virtues. Once Moses had won their obedience to the dictates of piety, he had no further difficulty in persuading the Israelites of all the rest. In Josephus' version of the incident of the burning bush (*A.J.* 2.270–71) and of the spies (*A.J.* 3.302), as well as the incident of Korah (*A.J.* 4.47), we see Moses' unshakable faith in G-d's providence. Josephus is clearly embarrassed by Moses' failure to circumcise his son (Exod. 4:24), and he significantly omits it totally.

In sum, Philo says that Moses possessed, to a special degree, the queen of the virtues, piety; and it was through piety that he gained the offices of king, legislator, prophet, and high priest. In Moses there was no conflict between philosophy and piety. For Pseudo-Philo philosophy is never considered a factor in his religious outlook. From the very beginning Josephus' Moses trained the Israelites in piety and consequently he had no difficulty in training them in all the remaining virtues.

7. Moses as Lawgiver

The Bible itself (Deut. 1:6–4:40), as Lierman (2002, 100) points out, seems to present a dual function of Moses, on the one hand, as a prophet, as mediator of G-d's commandments and, on the other hand, as legislator possessing the authority to make laws. On the one hand, G-d speaks to the Israelites directly (Deut. 5:6–21), and, on the other hand (Deut. 12–28), Moses speaks to the Israelites directly, whether as the agent of G-d or on his own behalf.

The very Egyptians who maligned Moses apparently regarded him as remarkable (θαυμαστός) and even divine (θεῖος) and as one of their very own priests (*Ap.* 1.279), who, to be sure, had been expelled because of his alleged leprosy. The fact that in the earliest extended mention of Moses by a pagan, that by Hecataeus, he is represented as responsible for all the major institutions of the Jews, including especially those that set them apart from other people, indicates that a tradition had developed, apparently in Alexandria, of upholding the reputation of Moses' greatness.

Hecataeus has such a high opinion of Moses that he even ascribes to him achievements for which, according to the Bible, he was not responsible, notably the division of the Israelites into twelve tribes (so also Philo, *Fug.* 185), the conquest of the Land of Israel, the founding of Jerusalem, the building of the Temple, and the prohibition of infanticide.[25] On this last matter Gager 1972, 34,[26] asks why Hecataeus saw fit to mention a seemingly trivial matter, and he answers that the question of population control had become an important concern of Greek political philosophy. Moreover, Hecataeus contradicts the Bible (Num. 18:24; Deut. 10:9, 12:12, 18:1) in his statement (*ap.* Diod. 40.3.7) that Moses alloted more land to the priests than to private citizens.[27] Moses did so, according to Hecataeus (*ap.* Diod. 40.3.7), so that the priests might, by virtue of receiving more ample revenues, be undistracted and apply themselves constantly to the worship of G-d. This is reminiscent of Plato (*R.* 7.540A-B), where the philosophers, we are told, will, from the age of fifty onward, spend the rest of their lives alternately ruling the ideal state and studying, though spending most of their time in philosophy. Whereas the Pentateuch describes Moses as the vehicle of the laws, since they are of divine origin, Hecataeus declares that Moses actually drew them up and ordered the political institutions and the religious ritual of the Jews.

Though his knowledge of the Bible seems to be vague,[28] Hecataeus has what amounts to almost a verbatim quotation from the Bible in his remark that "at the end of their laws there is even appended the statement: 'These are the words that Moses heard from G-d and declares unto the Jews.' "[29] It is Moses, he declares, who is responsible for the fact that the Jewish way of life differs from that of other peoples. In particular, Hecataeus (*ap.* Diodorus 40.3.4) ascribes to Moses the view forbidding images of the gods, "being of the opinion that G-d is not in human form; rather, the Heaven that surrounds the earth is alone divine and rules the universe." Despite the fact that this view is so vastly different from the predominant Greek point of view, Hecataeus significantly has not a word that is critical of it.

It is clear that Hecataeus looked upon Moses as a philosopher-king in that he ascribes to him, in a non-biblical remark, the division of the Israelites into twelve tribes, explaining that twelve is regarded as the most perfect number and corresponds to the number of months that make up a year (*ap.* Diodorus 40.3.3). This is directly in line with Plato's remark (*Laws* 5.745B–D) that the legislator must divide the ideal city, its citizens, and their property into twelve parts.[30] Indeed, Hecataeus seems to present Moses as the founder of a kind of Utopia such as is described by Euhemerus (Diodorus 5.45.5), as Stern (1974, 1:32)[31] suggests, in which the priest received a double share.

Hecataeus ascribes to Moses not only the commandments but also, in an extra-biblical addition, the reason (*ap.* Diodorus 40.3.7) for such a provision as that which prohibited private citizens from selling their individual plots, namely, lest there be some who for their own advantage should buy them up and by oppressing the poorer classes might bring about a shortage of manpower. This is a great compliment to Moses, inasmuch as the distribution of land was a matter of the greatest concern in antiquity; and rulers such as Kings Agis IV and Cleomenes III of Sparta achieved fame through their plans for the redistribution of land in Sparta in the third century B.C.E. (Plutarch, *Agis* 7.5–8, *Cleomenes* 10–11).

Hecataeus (*ap.* Diodorus 40.3.8) is careful to protect the reputation of Moses by distancing him from the changes in Jewish observance. Moreover, like Plato's philosopher-king in the *Republic*, Moses is praised by Hecataeus (*ap.* Diodorus 40.3.6) for showing foresight (πρόνοια, a key Stoic term) in making provision for warfare and in requiring young men to cultivate "both manliness and steadfastness, and, generally, the endurance of every hardship" (ἀνδρεία τε καὶ καρτερία καὶ τὸ σύνολον ὑπομονὴν πάσης κακοπαθείας; cf. Plato, *R.* 2.375–3.390). Such a description is highly reminiscent of the Lycurgan constitution of Sparta, which was so much praised in antiquity.[32]

Even Hecataeus' statement (40.3.4) that Moses introduced a somewhat unsocial and intolerant mode of life (ἀπάνθρωπόν τινα καὶ μισόξενον βίον) is tempered by the word "somewhat" (τινα).[33] But this would not necessarily be negative, since the same description might be made of the much admired constitution of the Spartans. Moreover, the term ἐξαλλαγμέναι that he uses in referring to the practices of the Jews simply means "different" or "unusual," without any deprecating implication (so Gager 1972, 35), as we see when Diodorus (1.94.1) refers to Egyptian customs and especially (1.27.1) to their marriage practices. Indeed, such expressions are characteristic of ethnographic excursuses. Furthermore, as Trüdinger (1918, 21ff., cited by Gager 1972, 36) has remarked, three themes occur in practically every ethnography: religious laws, including the conception of the deity and the types of sacrifices; unusual customs, especially in connection with marriage; and burial practices. As Gager (1972, 36–37) remarks, it is hardly a coincidence that Hecataeus has these three themes and precisely in this order. Even this attitude of an intolerant mode of life is explained by Hecataeus as arising from the Israelites' experience in being expelled from Egypt. But whereas Strabo (*Geography* 16.2.37.761), who is likewise sympathetic to Moses and to the Jewish theology and way of life, speaks disparagingly of Moses' successors as superstitious and tyrannical, Hecataeus (*ap.* Diodorus 40.3.8) is much more general; he is not critical and says merely that the Jews' traditional practices were later disturbed (ἐκινήθη). We may guess that this attempt to protect the standing of Moses may have been influenced by the potent force that the popular magic of the time attached to the very name of Moses (see Gager 1972, 134–61).

According to Manetho (*ap.* Josephus, *Ap.* 1.239), the first thing that Moses did after he had been appointed leader by the Israelites was to issue a law that the Israelites were to avoid worshipping the gods of the Egyptians while not refraining from any of the animals that the Egyptians regarded as sacred. They were to sacrifice and consume them—a statement to be contrasted with Artapanus' statement (*ap.* Eus. *PE* 9.27.4) that Moses assigned cats, dogs, and ibises as gods. The fact, we may add, that Manetho (*ap.* Josephus, *Ap.* 1.261) declares that Moses instructed the Israelites to have no connection with any save their fellow Jews merely echoes Hecataeus' comment that the Jews are unsocial and hostile to foreigners. Manetho's remark (*ap.* Josephus, *Ap.* 1.240) that Moses framed a great number of laws completely opposed to Egyptian custom may reflect the specific biblical statement that the Israelites are categorically to avoid the practices of the Egyptians (Lev. 18:3).

The historian Diodorus (1.94.1–2), in the first century B.C.E., speaks in praise of Moses as a lawgiver. Others might have thought that Diodorus was disparaging Moses when he cites Moses' claim that he had obtained the laws from G-d, whereas Diodorus clearly implies that they were Moses' own creation. However, the fact that Diodorus, in citing Moses' assertion, parallels it with the similar claims of the greatest of all lawgivers in antiquity, for whom he, like others in antiquity, had the highest regard—Minos of Crete, Lycurgus of Sparta, Zarathustra of the Persians, and Zalmoxis of the Cretans—indicates a similar regard for Moses, the last in his list. It is significant that it is as a lawgiver that Moses is compared thus with several others. Diodorus justifies the device of these lawgivers in claiming that their laws were of divine origin as producing much good among those who believed it. "They did it," he says in obvious admiration, "either because they believed that a conception that would help humanity was marvellous and wholly divine, or because they held that the common crowd would be more likely to obey the laws if their gaze was directed towards the majesty and power of those to whom their laws were ascribed." He actually names the G-d, Iao, from whom Moses declared that he had received his laws, the implication being that all this was merely a device used by Moses to secure compliance with his laws.

Like Diodorus, his contemporary Strabo (*Geographica* 16.2.38–39.762), who was also an older contemporary of Philo, bestows on Moses the highest praise by making him parallel to the revered lawgivers the Cretan Minos and the Spartan Lycurgus, as one who claimed divine sanction for his laws. Strabo clearly views Moses (16.2.39.762) as the actual composer of these laws and, indeed, contrasts him with his successors, who, he says, "with no bad beginning, turned out for the worse." He, moreover, mentions a number of prophets who "were held in so much honor that they were deemed worthy to be kings, on the ground that they promulgated . . . ordinances and amendments from the gods." In particular, he names Teiresias, Amphiaraus, Trophonius, Orpheus, Musaeus, Zalmoxis, Decaeneus, Achaecarus, the Gymnosophists, the Magi, the Chaldeans, the Tyrrhenian nativity-casters, and Moses. Moses, he says (16.2.36.761), achieved a good reputation with the people and organized an excellent form of government, which attracted the people in the surrounding area because of his dealings with them and because of the prospects that he held out for them.[34]

That Pompeius Trogus (*ap.* Justin, *Historiae Philippicae* 36, *Epitoma* 2.15), like Hecataeus, does not view negatively the refusal of Jews to mingle with others[35] may be seen from the fact that he explains the separation of Jews from their neighbors as due to their concern lest they become hateful to the natives for the same reason that led to their expulsion from Egypt, namely their fear of contagious infection. Whereas the Bible indicates that the way of life separating the Israelites from their neighbors was instituted by the revelation at Sinai, Pompeius states that it was only gradually that this way of life became a religious institution. The implication is that Judaism owes its special nature not to the legislation instituted at Sinai, but rather to continuous legislation, whether due to Moses or to others as well.

Pseudo-Longinus (9.9), in the first century C.E., author of the treatise *On the Sublime*, which, next to Aristotle's *Poetics*, is the most important essay on literary criticism emanating from antiquity, refers to the lawgiver (θεσμοθέτης) of the Jews as no chance person (οὐχ ὁ τυχὼν ἀνήρ) (a phrase found also in Strabo [16.2.36.761] with regard to Moses' organization of government), "since he understood and gave expression to the power of divinity as it deserved—when he wrote at the beginning of his laws . . . 'G-d said'—what? 'Let there be light.' And there was. 'Let there be earth.' And there was." This is not an exact quotation but a combination of three verses (Gen. 1:3, 9, 10) that produce a stronger effect. Apparently, Pseudo-Longinus felt that

Moses was sufficiently well known that he did not have to refer to him by name.[36]

Moreover, for Pseudo-Longinus to speak of Moses as a lawgiver was in itself a compliment, putting Moses in a class with Minos and Lycurgus. Pseudo-Longinus includes this passage, together with four others from Homer and a verbal exchange between Alexander the Great and Parmenio, to illustrate his point that the basic ingredient of great writing is not literary style, but rather a great mind. Because this is the last example cited, it would seem to be the climax; and the compliment is all the greater. It is thus clear from the context that Pseudo-Longinus regarded Moses as at least the equal of Homer in matters concerning the gods (so Gager 1972, 57).[37] Furthermore, it is clear from the way that he expresses himself that Pseudo-Longinus was acquainted with more from the Bible than this one quotation. As Stern (1974, 1:362) appositely remarks, it should not surprise us that in Pseudo-Longinus we have a Gentile writer who shows more sympathy for Moses and for the Bible than any other pagan writer, since the first century, in which he lived, was not only the century of such anti-Jewish writers as Apion, Chaeremon, and Seneca, but was also the century marked by an unprecedented diffusion of Jewish ideas and customs among various classes of society (see Feldman 1993a, 201–382).

At the end of the first century, Josephus' contemporary Quintilian (3.7.21), like "Longinus," deems it unnecessary to name Moses but rather refers to him merely as "the founder of the Jewish superstition," the implication being that it was Moses who was responsible for the code of laws constituting the Jewish religion. Likewise, the fourth-century *Historia Augusta*, *Vita Claudii* 25.2.4–5, mentions Moses by name as having lived 125 years, without bothering to introduce him further to the reader, as if he were well known.

Josephus' younger contemporary, Tacitus (*Histories* 5.4.1), like Strabo, views Moses as the actual author of novel legislation. Moses, he says, regarded as profane all that others hold sacred, as a clever political device to secure his authority over the Jews. In this respect Tacitus looks upon Moses as presumably like the universally admired Minos. Lest one regard such alleged deceit as a condemnation of Moses, one will recall that in Plato's ideal state (*R.* 3.414B–415D) the rulers propound a "noble lie" in order to persuade the various classes to accept their status without question.

Likewise, Tacitus' contemporary, Juvenal, regards Moses as the author of legislation and speaks, with obvious exaggeration and disdain, of all the Jewish law that Moses handed down in a secret tome, with no indication that he derived it from G-d or that he served as merely an interpreter of it.

It is because Moses incited the Jews to reject the ancient customs of the Egyptians that the second-century Celsus (*ap.* Origen, *Against Celsus* 3.5) refused to recognize him as one of the wise ancient lawgivers. He views Moses (4.21) as the actual author of the Pentateuch and says that, in particular, his version of the tower of Babel is a corruption of the story of the sons of Aloeus, Otus and Ephialtes, who piled Pelion on Ossa on Olympus[38] and that his version of the destruction of Sodom and Gomorrah by fire is comparable to the story of Phaethon.[39] He (6.28) speaks of Moses as the author of the cosmogony and of the law. Perhaps, he says (6.49), Moses, like the poets of the Old Comedy, wrote these stories about the creation because he understood nothing.

Moreover, whereas in Hellenistic Jewish writers Moses is the author of legislation, in the Apocrypha, Pseudepigrapha, the New Testament, and rabbinic writings, he is the mediator of revelation.

Hafemann (1990, 79–104) has called attention to the fact that whereas the Bible (e.g., 2 Chr. 35:6) highlights Moses' election by G-d to be His prophet-mediator and recipient of the Law, the Apocrypha (e.g., 1 Esdras 1:6) emphasizes Moses as the direct object of G-d's activity. Instead of the reference to Israel as the direct recipient of the "book of the Law of Moses which the L-rd had commanded" (Neh. 8:1), Ezra (1 Esdras 9:39) is told to bring the Law of Moses which had been handed down (παραδοθέντα) by the L-rd. Hence, the implication is that the Law was given not so much through Moses as to Moses.

In the book of Sir. 24:23, Moses is presented as the mediator of G-d's laws, since the Law promulgated for the Israelites by Moses is specified as the book of the convenant of G-d. We see the preeminence of Moses in Sir. 45:1–5, where we read that he was chosen to receive the "Law of life." Again, in Sir. 45:4 we read that G-d chose him above all others for this role because of his loyalty and humility.

Moreover, it is Moses' authority that is central in 2 Macc. His prayer prefigures that of Solomon in the dedication of the Temple (2 Macc. 2:9–10). It is the command of the Law given *by* Moses and his words of consolation that encourage the martyrs (2 Macc. 6:23, 7:6–16, 7:30).

As for the Pseudepigrapha, Moses derives his authority, according to 2 Bar. 59:3–12, from the fact that it was to him that G-d revealed His deepest secrets concerning the Law, the nature of the world, and the end of time. It is Moses who can challenge G-d on the basis of what G-d had previously revealed to him (2 Bar. 3:9), so that for 2 Baruch the word of Moses is the word of G-d (Hafemann 1990, 88).

On the other hand, the Pseudepigraphic Arist. (132) goes much further in making Moses himself the fountainhead of the Law. Moses is the legislator; and he is credited with teaching the unity, the omnipotence, and the omniscience of G-d. Without any indication that he derived it from G-d, he is the one who (131) "laid down the principles of piety and justice and expounded them point by point, not alone by prohibitions but by commandments; and he made clear the discomfitures and visitations that would be inflicted by G-d upon the guilty." In Arist. (139) Moses himself is described as the lawgiver, "equipped by G-d for insight into all things," although, to be sure, the Law itself is said to be of divine origin (4, 31, 313). There (144) we see that the laws are explicitly Moses' laws. Eleazar the high priest says: "Do not accept the exploded idea that it was out of regard for 'mice' and the 'weasel' and other such creatures that Moses ordained these laws with such scrupulous care. Not so, these laws have all been solemnly drawn up for the sake of justice, to promote holy contemplation and the perfection of character."[40] Moreover, Moses (144) ordained the laws as to which winged creatures are permitted and which are forbidden and the reasons for such legislation. When one of the translators in Arist. is asked by King Ptolemy Philadelphus (240) how he might avoid doing anything contrary to law, he replies and wins the king's approval with his reply: "If you know that G-d put the thoughts in the mind of lawgivers for the sake of preserving the lives of men you will become a follower of them." It is clear that the translator has Moses in mind, and it is also clear that the author of the Letter of Aristeas regarded Moses as having been inspired in a general way, but as having used his own mind in devising the details of the laws. What is so surprising, as Hafemann (1990, 87–88) remarks, is the incredible authority vested in Moses: it is not Moses who derives his status from the Law; rather, it is the Law that derives its status from Moses. Moses thus emerges as much more than a mere transmitter of the laws.

The fact that Eupolemus (ap. Eus. *PE* 9.26.1), who apparently flourished in Palestine in the middle of the second century B.C.E., declares that Moses was the first to write down laws gave him tremendous preeminence, since, as Holladay (1983, 1:130, n. 7) points out, there were many candidates for the status of "first lawgiver." The fact that he is cited as the first lawgiver would surely indicate that Moses was more than a mere stenographer. He is also referred to as "lawgiver" by Aristobulus (*ap.* Eus. *PE* 8.10.3), by Cleodemus Malchus (*ap.* Josephus, *A.J.* 1.240), and by Josephus (*Ap.* 1.245).[41]

Gruen 2002, 207–8, expresses surprise that Artapanus, who has a much longer account of Moses than any of the alleged Graeco-Jewish writers prior to Philo and who credits Moses with so many achievements, says nothing about his promulgation of laws for the Israelites. He says that it is most improbable that he was influenced by political or ideological motivation in omitting this aspect of Moses' deeds. He suggests that the unconventional Artapanus was simply asserting his independence of standard interpretations and chose to emphasize the more colorful aspects of Moses' life and achievements. However, if, as we have indicated elsewhere (see Feldman 2006, 125–26), Artapanus was not a Jew at all, he may not have wanted to have Moses bracketed with such lawgivers as Minos and Lycurgus, since a code of law is what constitutes the chief characteristic of a nation and a people.

As to the Dead Sea Scrolls, the Damascus Document (*CD* 6.4–7) views Moses not as a legislator, but as the transmitter and interpreter of G-d's laws.

The name of Moses is mentioned more times (80) in the New Testament than any other figure from the Hebrew Scriptures. The parallels between Moses and Jesus are deliberate and striking. As Allison 1993, 275, puts it: "Both Moses and Jesus were many things, and they occupied several common offices. Moses was the paradigmatic prophet-king, the Messiah's model, a worker of miracles, the giver of Torah, the mediator for Israel, and a suffering servant. And Jesus was similarly a suffering servant, the mediator for Israel, the giver of Torah, a worker of miracles, the Mosaic Messiah, and the eschatological prophet-king."

The New Testament (John 6:32) stresses the role of Moses as G-d's agent, emphasizing that it was not Moses but G-d who gave the Israelites bread, that is, manna, from heaven. As Bovon 1978, 47–65, stresses, Jesus is compared with Moses, "who was in the congregation in the wilderness with the angel who spoke with him at Mount Sinai and with our fathers" (Acts 7:38); that is, he was *among* them as mediator and redactor of the Law, which he gave to the Israelites. To Paul (Gal. 3:19) he is the means through whom the Law was ordained to Israel by angels. It is in this role that Moses is compared with Jesus (Heb. 8:6, 9:15, 12:24), who is regarded as the agent of the new covenant, just as Moses (Heb. 8:5, 9:19–20) was of the old covenant that G-d commanded the Israelites and that Moses ratified by sprinkling with blood both the tabernacle and all the vessels used in worship. According to the New Testament (Acts 7:35), G-d appointed him to be ruler and deliverer of his people, and (Acts 7:38) to receive the Law for the Israelites.

There are some references in the New Testament that seem to indicate that Moses was a lawgiver in his own right and others that seem to point to him as a transmitter.[42] Thus, we read (John 1:17) that the Law was given through Moses, an indication that he was the transmitter of the Law. On the other hand, Moses is presented (Mark 10:5) by Jesus as the one who wrote the Law and not merely as the one who transmitted the Law: "For your hardness of heart he [Moses] wrote you this commandment [to write a certificate of divorce]." Moses is likewise referred to as the author of the Law (Rom. 10:5): "Moses writes that the man who practices the righteousness which is based on the law shall live by it." Again, we read (Rom. 10:19) that Moses says, presumably in his own name (Deut. 32:21): "I will make you jealous of those who are not a nation; with a foolish nation I will make you angry."

On the other hand, where Mark (7:10) says, "Moses said, 'Honor your father and your mother,'" he clearly is referring not to something that Moses added but rather a divine commandment, as we see in the preceding verse. Indeed, in John 9:28 Moses is identified with the Torah itself, since some Pharisees are represented as reviling the man who had been blind, "You are his [Jesus'] disciple, but we are disciples of Moses." We see this equation of Moses with the Torah in the statement (Acts 15:21) that "from early generations Moses has had in every city those who preach him, for he is read every Sabbath in the synagogues." "Those who preach him" would seem to parallel Moses with Jesus. Clearly, it is not Moses but the Torah that is read in the synagogues. Again, Moses is identified with the Torah itself, presumably in the sense that he is the author of the Torah, in Paul's statement (2 Cor. 3:15): "Whenever Moses is read, a veil lies over their [i.e., the Jews'] minds." That Moses is viewed by the New Testament as the equivalent of Judaism may be seen in the reference to circumcision (Acts 15:1) as "the custom of Moses." It would have been more appropriate, it would seem, to refer to circumcision as the custom of Abraham, since it was Abraham who instituted it; indeed, it will be recalled that Moses neglected to circumcise his own son, and it was only his non-Jewish wife, Zipporah, who circumcised the son and thus saved Moses' life (Exod. 4:24–26). Again, Paul (Acts 21:21) is said to have taught all the Jews who are among the Gentiles to forsake Moses, where Moses is clearly equivalent to the Torah. Thus we see that in the New Testament Moses is seen as a metonymy for the Jewish religion (see Gillman 1992, 918–20). This does not, however, mean, as Lierman 2002, 177, would have it, that Moses' role was something like that of the head of the Jewish church. This was certainly not the rabbinic view. Rather it is the Torah, as transmitted by Moses, that guides Judaism.

That Moses is independent of G-d and is identified as a personality in his own right is implied by Jesus' statement (John 5:45) where Moses is equated with the Torah and is parallel to Jesus: "Do not think that I shall accuse you to the Father; it is Moses who accuses you, on whom you set your hope." As for Paul, the fact that when he discusses the Law he says (Gal. 3:19) that it was ordained by angels through an intermediary would indicate that the Law was transmitted through an intermediary, if not by angels then by Moses. Again, Paul sometimes (e.g., Rom. 7:7) speaks of the Law as an independent or hypostatic entity and leaves Moses entirely out of the picture. Yet Moses is presented as a lawgiver in his own right, so much so that Μωυσῆς is repeatedly an abbreviation for ὁ Μωυσέως νόμος (see Jeremias 1967, 4:864). That Paul identifies Moses with the Torah and with Judaism as a whole may be seen from the fact (1 Cor. 10:2) that he speaks of Jews as being baptized into Moses "in the cloud and in the sea," the parallel being that Christians are baptized into Jesus. On the other hand, the fact that Paul compares his role in spreading the Gospel (2 Cor. 3:6) to that of Moses in giving the Law would indicate that he regarded himself as merely an intermediary and that he consequently viewed Moses in a similar vein.

The view of Moses as legislator is frequently found in Philo, more so than any other title. Indeed, the word for legislator, νομοθέτης, occurs sixteen times in the essay *Mos.* (1.1, 1.2, 1.128, 1.162 [*bis*], 2.3, 2.5, 2.6, 2.8, 2.12, 2.45, 2.48, 2.49, 2.187, 2.190, 2.292), once in *Decal.* (176), and seventeen times in the essay *Spec.* (1.9, 1.15, 2.132, 2.239, 2.244, 2.247, 3.22, 3.42, 3.102, 3.151, 3.164, 3.166, 3.167, 4.61, 4.102, 4.120, 4.143); and in every case but two (*Mos.* 2.48, *Decal.* 176) the reference is to Moses or, in a few cases, to other human legislators. Moses is also compared with the legislators of other states: *Mos.* 1.2, 2.12, 2.49; *Decal.* 176; *Spec.* 1.9, 2.244, 2.247, 3.22, 3.164, 3.166, 4.61, 4.102, 4.120.

Philo (*Mos.* 2.2) starts the second book of his biography of Moses by stating that whereas in the first book he had delineated Moses' qualities as king and philosopher, in the second book he will discuss his qualities as lawgiver, priest, and prophet. As legislator, Moses (*Mos.* 2.9), he says, possessed four qualities in particular: love of humanity (τὸ φιλάνθρωπον), love of justice (φιλοδίκαιον), love of goodness (φιλάγαθον), and hatred of evil (μισοπόνηρον). By love of humanity he means that the legislator is expected to produce for public use his thoughts for the general welfare; by justice, to honor equality and to render every man his due; by love of goodness, to approve of things naturally excellent and to supply them without reserve to all who are worthy; and by hatred of evil, to regard the dishonorers of virtue as common enemies of the human race. In his elaboration of these virtues, as Barraclough (1984, 490, n. 668) has noted, Philo has drawn from a cross-section of thought: Platonic (rendering every man his due), Pythagorean (honoring equality), and Stoic (approving the naturally excellent). Moses alone, says Philo (*Mos.* 2.10), grasped all of these together. Possessed of these qualities, Moses composed under G-d's guidance and handed on to his people the laws embodied in the Pentateuch. In these respects Moses is in utter contrast to the Emperor Gaius Caligula, the Egyptian governor Avillius Aulus Flaccus, and the praetorian prefect Aelius Sejanus, all of whom were concerned with themselves rather than with those whom they ruled. These are not, we must stress, the qualities of a stenographer *qua* stenographer; they are the qualities of the author of a system of law.

Moses, Philo (*Mos.* 2.12) insists, was the best of all lawgivers in all countries, better than any among Greeks or barbarians. He states that Moses is unique in that his laws have remained unshaken (*Mos.* 2.15), so that even though over two thousand years have passed since they were promulgated, the Jews "have not changed a single word of what he wrote but would even endure to die a thousand deaths sooner than accept anything contrary to the laws and customs which he had ordained," despite all the changes that the nation has undergone (*Mos.* 2.17).

Philo (*Opif.* 3) remarks that the very beginning of Moses' Law deserves to be admired in the highest degree because it consists of an account of the creation of the world. This, he says, implies that "the world is in harmony with the Law, and the Law with the world, and that the man who observes the Law is constituted thereby a loyal citizen of the world (κοσμοπολίτου), regulating his doings by the purpose and will of Nature, in accordance with which the entire world itself also is administered."

Apparently, there was a dispute among Philo's Jewish contemporaries (*Hypoth.* 9) as to whether the laws that Moses promulgated came from Moses' own reasoning or whether they were derived from a supernatural source. Philo was aware of the debate as to the exact role of Moses in connection with the Law, since at the very beginning of his biography of Moses (*Mos.* 1.1) he states that he proposes to write the life of Moses, "whom some describe as the legislator (νομοθέτης)[43] of the Jews, whereas others refer to him as the interpreter (ἑρμηνεύς) of the laws."[44] From what follows it is clear that Philo in *Mos.* looks upon Moses as primarily a legislator and only secondarily as an interpreter; and yet, Philo himself declines, though he had this opportunity at the very beginning of his essay, to indicate which of these views is correct, whereas in his other treatises Philo quite clearly inclines toward the view that Moses was not a mere transcriber of the laws. In any case, Philo concludes, his countrymen believed that all the laws had ultimately come from G-d. His laws, he insists, truly are of divine origin since they omit nothing that is needful. Yet, Philo (*Mos.* 2.188) makes a point that while everything written in the Scriptures was delivered through Moses, some things were spoken by G-d (*Decal.* 18) with Moses merely as His interpreter, while others are more especially his, having been spoken by Moses in his own person, while possessed by G-d and carried away outside of himself. Nevertheless, there are instances where laws, such as the requirement to restore before sundown the garment that one has given as a pledge (Exod. 22:26–27), which in the Bible are presented as G-d's command, but which Philo (*Somn.* 1.92–93) presents as enacted by Moses as lawgiver. Moreover, there are instances where Philo's Moses gives reasons for commandments where the Pentateuch does not do so. Thus whereas the Bible (Lev. 18:7) prohibits, as a divine commandment, the uncovering of the nakedness of one's mother, Philo (*Fug.* 193) supplies a reason, namely, that it is a great evil to make sins public as though they were the achievements of righteousness.

That Philo looked upon Moses as more than a mere transmitter of the laws may be seen from the fact that the lawgiver, namely Moses, often employs a form of expression that is contrary to the usual practice (*Cher.* 53), the implication being that Moses is responsible for the actual form of expression. Thus Philo (*Leg.* 2.15) particularly admires Moses' ascription to Adam of the fixing of names. He also admires (*Mos.* 2.47–48) Moses' arrangement of material, particularly in that he began his lawbook with the history and only afterwards presented commands and prohibitions, the clear implication being that it is Moses who is responsible for this. Again, according to Philo (*Deus* 52–53), the Lawgiver, as he refers to him here, is an effective teacher in that he uses expressions that serve for a kind of elementary lesson. Similarly, the Therapeutae (*Contempl.* 63) are referred to as disciples (γνώριμοι) of Moses, as if Moses is the head of a school such as that of Hillel or Shammai and is identical with the Torah itself; and we are reminded of John's statement (9:28) that Jews are the disciples of Moses in the same sense as Christians are disciples of Jesus. Moreover, in a rare reference to himself, Philo (*Cher.* 49) refers to Moses, the G-d-beloved (θεοφιλής), as a mystagogue, under whom he was initiated into the greater mysteries, a phrase taken from the Eleusinian Mysteries. If Moses, the keeper (ταμίας, "steward," "controller") and guardian (φύλαξ) of the mysteries of G-d (*Plant.* 26), is thus perceived as a leader of the mysteries, he is clearly more than a mere agent of G-d.

That Philo compared the attitude of other nations toward the Jewish laws and was particularly proud of the respect that these laws had won from other states may be seen in his statement that, impressive as it may be that the Jewish laws have been securely guarded by the Jews through all time, even more marvelous (θαυμασιώτερον) is the fact that the Jewish laws are valued and honored by almost all other peoples. Philo is not content merely to make such a statement. He then offers (*Mos.* 2.18) what he considers to be proof of his assertion, namely, that the Jewish laws are thus honored by others, whereas the most prominent of the Greeks, namely the Athenians and the Spartans, reject the customs and institutions of other peoples, as do the most prominent of the non-Greeks, namely, the Egyptians and the Scythians, in the belief that they will enhance the respect for their own institutions by showing aversion to those of other nations.

Philo (*Hypoth.* 6.8) connects the Jews' reverence for law and their loyal obedience to their religion and justice and piety with their veneration for the man who gave them their laws, since whatever met with his approval also met with their approval. Philo (*Hypoth.* 6.9), amazingly enough, is even ready to consider the possibility that Moses arrived at the laws through his own reasoning. Indeed, he states that whether what Moses told them came from his own reasoning powers or was learnt from some supernatural source, the Israelites held that it all came from G-d, so that after the passage of two thousand years they have not changed a single word of what he wrote.

Philo (*Mos.* 1.162) says that since Moses was destined to be a legislator (νομοθέτης), G-d's providence, without his knowledge, appointed him to be a legislator, so that he became the reasonable and living embodiment of law. On the other hand, Philo (*Mos.* 2.48) declares that it is G-d Who is the Lawgiver and that whoever wishes to observe the laws will accept the duty of following nature and of living in accordance with the ordering of the universe.

To be sure, in *Mos.* 2.48, Philo says that G-d is also and in truth a legislator, the implication being that in point of fact there is also another legislator, and this would, of course, be Moses. Immediately thereafter (*Mos.* 2.49) Philo speaks of other legislators, clearly, by implication, comparing the other legislators with a human legislator, namely, Moses. Indeed, says Philo (*Hypoth.* 6.8), so great was the veneration of the Israelites for Moses that they approved of anything that he had endorsed. In fact, Philo (*Spec.* 4.61; cf. *Conf.* 141) notes that some Greek legislators copied from Moses the law that hearsay is not accepted as evidence (see Colson 1932, 4:556–57).[45]

Philo (*Mos.* 2.49–51) contrasts other legislators, particularly Plato in the *Republic* and the *Laws* (so Colson 1935, 6:472–73, n. b), with Moses (though he does not mention him by name in making the comparison) in terms of ordering what should be done and in terms of penalties for disobedience. In this respect, he says, Moses was unique, in that whereas others (he is thinking particularly of Plato in the *Republic*) first established a state and then framed laws, Moses did the opposite, the implication being that Moses is conceived as the one who actually promulgated the laws. Moses, says Philo (*Mos.* 2.50), thought that to give orders, without first exhorting and gently persuading (παραμυθία), was to act as a tyrant or despot in charge of slaves and that to begin by establishing an ideal man-made state would not satisfy everyone and was beneath the dignity of the laws, which should reflect a world point of view. Instead, he chose to suggest (ὑποτίθεται) and exhort (παρηγορεῖ) rather than to command. His commands are presented with introductions (προοιμίων) and supplementary comments (ἐπιλόγων).

But it is also clear that Philo had not decided between the two views that he mentions (*Mos.* 1.1) are held by various people concerning the role of Moses, namely, whether he was the author of some laws or a mere transmitter of them. Thus he also looks upon him as an interpreter (ἑρμηνεύς) of the laws, prompted by G-d in his utterances with regard to particular laws (*Mos.* 2.188, 191; *Decal.* 175, *Spec.* 2.189, 3.7).[46] But even in these instances Moses has a role that is more creative than that of a mere transcriber. The title of ἑρμηνεύς, moreover, is not restricted to Moses: Aaron is thus referred to (*Mos.* 1.84), as are the translators who produced the LXX (*Mos.* 2.40) and other prophets (*Spec.* 1.65, 4.49), including even the pagan prophet Balaam (*Mos.* 1.277). In any case, however, Moses is presented in Philo, as he is in the Apocrypha and Pseudepigrapha (see Hafemann 1990, 79–104), as a source of religious authority and as a basis of legitimacy that is not explicit in the biblical tradition.

The view of Ginzberg (1928, 6:47, n. 248) and Amir (1973, 1–8) that since the Bible is either from G-d or from man, and since Philo thought that Moses gave the laws he [Philo] should be regarded as a heretic, appears to be one-sided.

In an important statement near the opening of Philo's introductory treatise in the series on the Exposition of the Law, *Opif.* 8, he says that Moses had been instructed in the many and most essential doctrines of nature by means of oracles (χρησμοῖς). This seems to imply that Moses was not a mere scribe. The authority of scripture ultimately derives from G-d Himself, but Moses has been previously instructed as to the method of understanding G-d's words. Philo (*Mos.* 2.188; so also *Spec.* 2.189) says that he is aware that all things written in the sacred books are oracles delivered through Moses. He then, however, proceeds to speak of some that are more especially his. He programmatically states that utterances in the scriptures are all divine, but that some are spoken by G-d in His own Person, with Moses, His prophet, as interpreter (ἑρμηνεύς). In some the revelation comes through question and answer, while in others the utterances are actually spoken by Moses in his own person while he was possessed by G-d and carried out of himself. Elsewhere (*Decal.* 175) Philo asserts that G-d gave in His own Person the pronouncements in which the special laws were summed up, but that He arranged that Moses, whom He filled with the divine spirit, should be the interpreter of the particular laws. He thus presents Moses as a mere interpreter of the divinely-given law (*Mos.* 2.191; *Spec.* 1.65; 3.7, 4.49). And yet, Philo (*Spec.* 4.66) says that "Moses gives us a very instructive command," using the present tense of the verb, as if Moses were still alive in Philo's own day and serving as an active lawgiver. More likely, however, the meaning is that the Law, which is identified with Moses as its transmitter, is still carefully obeyed. Apparently, then, Philo maintained an ambiguous position with regard to whether Moses was the source of the laws or a mere interpreter of G-d's laws.

Philo (*Mos.* 2.46–47) draws a very careful distinction between the portion of the Pentateuch dealing with history and the portion dealing with commands. In the place where he cites the biblical statement (*Spec.* 4.143–48) that one must not add to or subtract from the laws, he makes it clear that this applies only to the laws that are set forth in the Scriptures: "Another most admirable injunction is that nothing should be added (προστιθέναι) or taken away (ἀφαιρεῖν), but all the laws (νόμιμα, "usages," "customs") originally ordained (ὁρισθέντα, "delimited," "determined," "defined") should be kept unaltered (ἀκίνητα, "unmoved"), just as they were." It is clear that Philo is restricting this statement to the biblical laws and has not extended it to the narrative generally, as we can see from the fact that he stresses that the wise legislator (νομοθέτῃ) has omitted nothing that would detract from the complete and precise execution of justice (δικαιοσύνης).

Elsewhere (*Mos.* 2.34), in referring to the translation of the Pentateuch into Greek, Philo says, alluding to the prohibition of making any changes, that the translators reflected how great a task it was to translate (διερμηνεύειν, "interpret," "expound") the laws (νόμους) decreed (θεσπισθέντας, "prophesied") by oracles (χρησμοῖς), where they could not take away (ἀφελεῖν) or add (προσθεῖναι) or change (μεταθεῖναι, "transpose") anything, but had to keep the original form (ἰδέαν, "semblance," "appearance") and shape (τύπον, "form," "pattern," "model"). Hence, it would appear that Philo is stressing the prohibition of altering the laws and is apparently not extending it to modifying the narrative portions of the Pentateuch.

And yet, in discussing the manner in which the translators proceeded, Philo (*Mos.* 2.37) says that the creation of the world is the beginning of the laws (νόμοι), whereas the account of creation has nothing to do with the commandments. Moreover, he says that the translators were possessed (ἐνθουσιῶντες, "inspired," "ecstatic") and that in their prophetic interpretation (προφήτευον), they came out with exactly the same translation. Moreover, he says, the Greek words corresponded literally with the Chaldean (*Mos.* 2.38). Nevertheless, much as he revered the LXX translation, it must be stressed that Philo nowhere asserts that he himself has not added to or subtracted from or modified the biblical text, since his work does not pretend to be a paraphrase of the Pentateuch. Hence, while he promises not to modify the legal portions of the Bible, he apparently reserved for himself the freedom to interpret the narrative portions as he saw fit.

On the other hand, when it comes to law as distinct from philosophy, Philo (*Spec.* 4.61) praises the Greek legislators for copying from the laws of Moses the enactment that hearsay evidence is not acceptable. Indeed, he (*Mos.* 2.44) confidently looks forward to the time when all the nations of the world will throw overboard their ancestral customs and turn to honoring the biblical laws alone.

In particular, Philo (*Spec.* 3.110) speaks of an ordinance prohibiting the exposure of infants and in the strongest language condemns infanticide as "a sacrilegious practice that among many other nations, through their ingrained inhumanity, has come to be regarded with complacence." He (*Virt.* 131–33), similarly, condemns the practice in the strongest language, remarking that "our excellent lawgiver (νομοθέτης) was at pains to insure that even in the case of irrational animals, the offspring should not be separated from their mother so long as it is being suckled," and all the more so human children. The fact that, in this case, Philo goes out of his way to praise Moses as *lawgiver* who showed great foresight (προμήθεια) in watching over (ἐφοράω) his people clearly implies that Moses was not a mere *transmitter* of the laws but played a more active role.

Hindy Najman (2003, 16–19), in a highly original and extremely insightful work, draws a distinction between what she terms "Mosaic Discourse" and the Rewritten Bible. She cites four features of Mosaic Discourse: by expanding older traditions the new text claims authority that those older traditions had; the new text claims the status of Torah; the new text claims to be a recreation of the Sinai experience; the new text claims to be produced by Moses. As examples she cites the Book of Deuteronomy, Jubilees, and the Temple Scroll. There can be no question that Philo links his interpretations to Moses; but Najman (2003, 19) points to a very significant difference between Philo and Mosaic Discourse, namely that he subordinates the Law of Moses to the figure of Moses, whereas the reverse is true in Jubilees and the Temple Scroll. Moreover, Philo does not claim Sinaitic status for his interpretations. Rather, he distinguishes between Mosaic Scripture and his own interpretations. If Philo had wished, he could have found a precedent for a Deuteronomic-type of Mosaic Discourse in the discourses tied to such philosophers as Pythagoras, Socrates, and Aristotle (Najman, 2003, 101). Nevertheless, we must call attention to Philo's own statement (*Mos.* 2.40) that the translation is one and the same both in matter and words as the original text; and the authors of the LXX are to be regarded not as translators but as prophets and priests of the mysteries whose singleness of thought enabled them to go hand in hand with Moses. With this view of the LXX, it would seem, Philo's essays can hardly be regarded as having any originality as Mosaic Discourse. We would add a further major difference between Mosaic Discourse and Philo, namely that in works such as Deuteronomy, Jubilees, and the Temple Scroll the lawgiver presents the law in direct discourse, whereas Philo comments on the law. Moreover, we may add, Mosaic Discourse does not permit divergent views of the same biblical figure, such as we find in Philo's views of Joseph and Jethro. Furthermore, as Najman (2003, 103–4) concedes, the revelation at Sinai is of little importance to Philo in his biography of Moses, who emphasizes, rather, Moses' spiritual transformation (*QE* 2.27–49). Najman (2003, 106) insists that Philo participates in Mosaic Discourse, but with these differences. The differences, however, we may suggest, are too important to be mere differences. Finally, as Najman (2003, 101–2) admits, Philo could not engage in Mosaic Discourse and at the same time accept the authority of the LXX as the perfect word of G-d verbatim.

On the other hand, according to Pseudo-Philo (9.7–8), Moses is merely the instrument of G-d, the intermediary between the Israelites and G-d, Who reveals to him His majesty and statutes and judgments. G-d reveals to Moses the secrets of the cosmos.

The Bible (Deut. 4:2) states that "You shall not add to the word which I command you, nor take from it; that you may keep the commandments of the L-rd your G-d, which I command you." Similarly, the Bible (Deut. 13:1) asserts that "Every word that I command you, you shall be careful to do; you shall not add to it or take from it." It will be recalled that Josephus, in the introduction to his *A.J.* (1.5), seemingly in accordance with these biblical statements, proclaims that his work will embrace the entire ancient history (ἀρχαιολογία) and political constitution of the Jews, translated from the Hebrew records (ἐκ τῶν Ἑβραικῶν μεθηρμηνευμένην γραμμάτων). Again, he promises his readers that he will throughout his work set forth the precise details of the Scriptures (τὰ μὲν οὖν ἀκριβῆ τῶν ἐν ταῖς ἀναγραφαῖς), each in its place, neither adding nor omitting anything (οὐδὲν προσθεὶς οὐδ' αὖ παραλιπών [*A.J.* 1.17]). It would appear that Josephus is promising not to add to or subtract from not merely the commandments of the Scriptures but also the narrative details as well. As is well known, Josephus does not adhere to this promise, and many suggestions have been presented to explain his divergences (see Feldman 1998a, 37–46).

Josephus often refers to Moses as a legislator, indeed no fewer than 79 times: *B.J.* 2.145, 152; 3.376; 5.401; *A.J.* 1.6, 15, 18, 19, 20, 23, 24, 95, 240; 3.180, 187, 213, 266, 267, 268, 273, 286, 287, 317, 320; 4.6, 13, 150, 156, 243, 263, 302, 322, 331; 6.93; 7.338; 8.192, 395; 9.153, 187; 10.59, 63; 11.17, 76, 77, 108, 121, 154; 12.110; 13.74, 79, 297; 17.159; 18.81, 264; 20.44, 115; *Vita* 134; *Ap.* 1.39, 240, 284, 285, 316; 2.25, 145, 154, 156, 161, 165, 169, 170, 173, 175, 209, 218, 237, 257, 279, 286, 290. He is thus compared to other lawgivers, such as Minos, Lycurgus, Solon, and Zaleucus (*A.J.* 1.22; *Ap.* 2.154, 161, 172, 175, 225, 239, 250, 276, 279). Indeed, for Josephus the aspect of Moses' achievement that is most frequently mentioned is that of "our" lawgiver.

Like Diodorus and Strabo, Josephus (*Ap.* 2.154) pays Moses the compliment of comparing him with the most famous of ancient lawgivers. He insists that Moses is the most ancient of all legislators in the records of the world,[47] compared to whom the Spartan Lycurgus, the Athenian Solon, and the Locrian Zaleucus and all others who are so highly esteemed by the Greeks appear to be very recent. Josephus (*Ap.* 2.163), in response to the question as to who of all the great legislators was the most successful, says that we may obtain an answer by comparing the laws that they devised and promulgated with those enacted by others. In his view Moses was superior to other legislators not only because he was the earliest, but also because he ordained Jewish government to be a theocracy (*Ap.* 2.164–65) and not a monarchy or oligarchy and also because he combined in law the two methods of achieving moral conduct—verbal instruction and practice (*Ap.* 2.169).

The very fact, we may suggest, that Josephus summarizes the Mosaic code at such length in a work that is ostensibly a history shows how important Moses as a lawgiver was for Josephus. In large part, Josephus' emphasis upon Moses as a lawgiver is a reply (*Ap.* 2.101, 145) to those opponents of the Jews, such as Apollonius Molon and Lysimachus, who, whether from ignorance or ill will, had maligned Moses as a charlatan and impostor.

Josephus also, like Philo, presents the view that the Torah was believed (δοκοῦσα) to be of divine origin and that Moses was the agent of G-d because of his merit (ἀρετή) (*A.J.* 3.320; cf. 4.13). Josephus makes it clear that when Moses returns from his meeting with G-d on Sinai, he is bringing the laws not of Moses, but of G-d, and that he is merely an interpreter (ἑρμηνεύς) of them (*A.J.* 3.87). Indeed, he says specifically that on Sinai it was G-d who dictated for the Israelites the rules for a blissful life and ordered government (*A.J.* 3.84, 4.193). Yet, on only five occasions do we hear in Josephus of the laws given by G-d through Moses, whereas Josephus speaks of the laws of Moses 23 times. The very fact that Josephus uses the term "lawgiver" (νομοθέτης) 16 times in the first four books of the *Antiquitates* with regard to Moses,[48] usually referring to him merely as "the lawgiver," without explicitly naming him, is an indication that to Josephus Moses was *the* lawgiver par excellence, in the same category as the revered Spartan Lycurgus, the Athenian Solon, and the Roman Numa Pompilius. It was his legislation, according to Josephus, that caused Moses to be ranked higher than his own human nature (*A.J.* 3.320). Moses is said, moreover, to have given the Israelites more than laws; he also bequeathed them a πολιτεία, a constitution comparable to those of the Greek πόλεις (*A.J.* 4.194, 196, 302). Indeed, the Jewish king, Josephus remarks, must concede to the laws the possession of superior wisdom (τὰ πλείονα τοῦ φρονεῖν, *A.J.* 4.224).

According to Josephus (*A.J.* 3.320), though the laws are regarded as G-d's, they apparently were regarded as Moses' laws and made him to be esteemed beyond human nature. That Moses is not merely a transcriber of G-d's laws seems evident from the reference to the wisdom (σοφία) of the lawgiver Moses, in that before prescribing laws for others he first sought (*A.J.* 1.19) to understand the nature of G-d and to imitate this model. Moreover, after mentioning the special provisions in the Pentateuch pertaining to the high priest, Josephus (*A.J.* 3.280) specifically states that Moses transmitted these provisions from G-d as being applicable already in his own lifetime, but that he planned others beforehand (προενόησεν, "perceived before," "foresaw"), presumably on his own initiative, rather than recording what G-d had dictated. In endeavoring to explain this apparent contradiction, Lierman notes that Josephus uses language that almost seems borrowed from Philo.[49] He suggests that this may be due to the unpolished condition of *A.J.*; but the fact that we find a similar inconsistency in Philo would appear to argue that Josephus, like Philo, had ambivalent feelings about the role of Moses. Ultimately, however, Josephus is careful to state that the constitution of the Jews was established by G-d Himself, through the agency of Moses (*A.J.* 3.322). Nevertheless, in typical fashion, he adds that "concerning these matters (i.e., the role of Moses in the conveyance of the Law) each will decide as it seems best to him."[50]

The rabbis are apparently aware of a dispute as to the role of Moses as transmitter or as legislator of the Torah. The dominant position, as we see, for example, in *Tg. Onq.* on Deut. 33:4,[51] is that Moses is the explainer, rather than the author, of the Torah. Again, the usual rabbinic title, "Moses our teacher," indicates that he is the transmitter. According to an anonymous Baraitha (*b. Sanh.* 99a), if someone asserts that the whole Torah is the word of G-d except for a single verse, which he maintains was not uttered by G-d but by Moses himself, such a person is regarded as one who has despised the word of the L-rd and has broken His commandment and whose soul shall be utterly cut off (Num. 15:31). This applies to the Oral Torah as well, as we see from the remark that if a person admits that the whole Torah is from Heaven except for a single point in the oral interpretation of that Torah, such as an *a fortiori* deduction or an exegesis through a similarity of language, he is included among those who have despised the word of G-d. Indeed, the Torah is said to antedate Moses and goes back to G-d Himself, since the third-century Rabbi Joshua ben Levi reports a tradition (*b. Shab.* 88b) that when Moses ascended on high to receive the Torah the angels objected, asking why a mere mortal should be given the Torah that G-d had hidden 974 generations before the creation of the world.

That Moses was merely a transmitter of the Torah, and not utterly unique at that, is clearly implied by the remark of Rabbi Jose (*b. Sanh.* 21b) that if Moses had not preceded him Ezra would have been deemed worthy to receive the Torah. To be sure, one of the rabbis, Abbaye, in the fourth century, asserts that the curses in Deut. (28:15–69) were spoken by Moses of his own accord. Moreover, according to *'Abot R. Nat.* 2.3, *b. Shab.* 87a, *b. Yeb.* 62a, Moses "of his own accord" added a third day [Exod. 19:11] to the prescribed period of sanctification that preceded the revelation at Sinai. The very fact that in a writ of divorce, according to the Mishnah (*Yad.* 4:8), the name of the ruler is to be written together with the name of Moses, rather than with the name of G-d, would indicate that Moses is responsible for this formulation. An interesting Midrash (*Exod. Rab.* 47), moreover, relates that the angels, in their jealousy that Moses and not they had been chosen as G-d's agency to bring the Torah to the Israelites, warned G-d that Moses might write his own ideas into the Torah. One would have expected that G-d's reply would be that He could not imagine that Moses would consider doing such a thing. Instead, G-d's answer is that if Moses were to do so, he could be relied upon not to misrepresent the will of G-d, the implication being that Moses was not a mere transcriber of the Law.

In sum, all the non-Jewish writers who mention Moses unanimously view him as the author and not merely as the transmitter of the Laws and compare him with lawgivers such as Minos and Lycurgus. Hecataeus, in particular, expands on the achievements of Moses as a lawgiver. In the Apocrypha, 1 Esdras implies that the Torah was not given so much through Moses as to Moses. According to the Pseudepigraphic *2 Baruch*, Moses derives his authority from the fact that it was to him that G-d revealed His deepest secrets, so that the word of Moses is the word of G-d. According to the Letter of Aristeas, however, Moses has a more creative role as the fountainhead of the Laws. The Graeco-Jewish writers Eupolemus, Aristobulus, and Cleodemus-Malchus refer to him as the "lawgiver," but Artapanus says nothing at all about his promulgation of the Law. The Dead Sea Scrolls view him as a mere transcriber. The New Testament is ambivalent but overwhelmingly views

Moses as the creative lawgiver. In *Mos.* Philo leaves the question open, but in his other treatises he overwhelmingly sides with those who look upon Moses as the creative lawgiver. The very fact, however, that Philo in *Mos.* compares him with other lawgivers would indicate that Philo himself, who is especially eager to respond to the detractors of Moses' achievements, while aware of the ambiguity, tended to side with those who viewed him as a legislator in his own right. Philo insists that the Laws were of divine origin but states at the same time that some laws were spoken by Moses in his own person while under divine inspiration. And yet, there are instances where Philo's Moses gives reasons for commandments whereas the Torah does not. Pseudo-Philo, always most conservative in his theological views, regards Moses as merely the instrument of G-d. Josephus is ambivalent but regards him primarily as a lawgiver. The rabbis, though divided in their opinions, on the whole are particularly eager to respond to those who would elevate Moses to superhuman status. They overwhelmingly look upon Moses as the mere transmitter rather than as the author of the Torah.

8. Moses as King

Nowhere in the Bible is Moses referred to as a king; but as Porter (1963, 12) remarks, in the ancient Near Eastern world all law, when codified, is necessarily sacral, since it is enacted by the king, a sacral personage, on divine instructions. In fact, however, while it is true that the Torah (Deut. 17:14–20) envisages a time when the Israelites will request a king, it is clear that when, in fact, the Israelites turn to the prophet Samuel (1 Sam. 8:5) and request that he appoint for them a king, we are told that it was wrong in Samuel's eyes to do so; and G-d tells him that in asking for a king the people have rejected Him as king. Nevertheless, the key passage identifying Moses as king, though its meaning has been debated,[52] is Deut. 33:5, which states that "he" was king in Jeshurun, where the context and *Tg. Onq.* and *Tg. Ps.-J.* on the passage suggest that "he" is Moses, and where most of the rabbis understand the passage to indicate that Moses was named king by G-d in order to serve as His regent on earth.

Hecataeus, as we have noted, looks upon Moses as the ruler of the Israelites, the political, military, and religious leader, the source of crucial economic legislation, with, in effect, absolute power. The Jews, he says (*ap.* Diodorus 40.3.5) never have a king, since authority over the Jews is vested in a high priest, who is regarded as superior to his colleagues in wisdom and virtue and who, they believe, acts as a messenger to them of G-d's commandments.

Strabo (16.2.39.762) asserts that in antiquity prophets were held in so much honor that they were deemed worthy to be kings on the ground that they promulgated laws from the gods not only when they were alive, but also when they were dead. He gives a long list of such prophets, starting with Teiresias and ending with Moses, who, he specifically says, was such a person as these.

The Sib. Or. (11.35–40), in the same sentence in which G-d is referred to as a great lord or potentate, also speaks of one who has a name from sandy Egypt, who is thought to have Thebes as his homeland (clearly a reference to Moses), and who is described as a great-spirited king who will rule the Hebrews (see Lierman 2002, 62). Indeed, as Lierman points out (ibid.), kingship is the only attribute here ascribed to Moses.

The tragedian Ezekiel, in an extra-biblical scene (*ap.* Eus. *PE* 9.29.5), speaks of Moses' dream in which a noble man sits on a great throne wearing a crown and holding a great sceptre in his left hand. He gives Moses the royal crown and himself leaves the throne. From the throne Moses beholds the entire world, which does obeisance to him. Whether the dream indicates that Moses is to be viewed as a divine king, it certainly indicates that he is to be viewed as a mighty king. Again, in an extra-biblical addition (*ap.* Eus. *PE* 9.29.16b), Ezekiel describes the appearance of a phoenix.[53] Since he says that it looks like the king of all birds, inasmuch as all the birds follow together behind it, perhaps it symbolizes the leadership of Moses, who is compared to a king.

The New Testament has several passages that parallel Jesus with Moses as king. Two passages (Mark 6:34–44, John 6:1–15) depict the crowd that came to hear Jesus as being like sheep without a shepherd, a simile that we find (e.g., 1 Kings 22:17) in connection with people without royal leadership. Moses in the Pentateuch (as is the later David) is the shepherd par excellence. The miracle about the multiplication of the loaves and fish and the feeding of multitudes, under the inspiration of Jesus, is reminiscent of Moses arranging to give manna to the Israelites in the wilderness. In John 6:15 the concept of Jesus as king is made explicit, in that after the miracle we are told that Jesus, "perceiving that they [the crowd] were about to come and take him by force to make him king, Jesus withdrew again to the hills by himself." Moreover, all four of the Gospels (Matt. 27:37, Mark 15:26, Luke 23:38, and John

19:19) refer to the inscription on the cross denominating Jesus as King of the Jews.

Furthermore, the wicked Hebrew who is striking his fellow Israelites asks Moses (Exod. 2:14) "Who made you a prince (שׂר, LXX ἄρχων, "ruler")[54] and a judge over us?" It is this title of ἄρχων as applied to Moses in this very passage that we find in Stephen's address in Acts 7:35.[55]

Philo organizes his biography of Moses so that the first book of his *Mos.* deals with his capacity as king,[56] and the second book deals with his capacity as lawgiver, high priest, and prophet, the first three being rational faculties and the fourth being necessary so that one may discover what one cannot grasp through reasoning. At the beginning of the second book of his *Mos.*, after briefly summarizing Moses' achievements as narrated in the first book, Philo (*Mos.* 2.2) notes Plato's statement (*R.* 5.473D) that states can make progress in well-being if either kings are philosophers or philosophers are kings and then makes the grand claim that Moses exhibited not only these qualities to an extraordinary degree but also the qualities concerned with legislation, the high priesthood, and prophecy. In each of these functions, says Philo (*Mos.* 2.3), Moses won the highest place. Philo (*Praem.* 54) stresses that though he lacked the gift of speech or possessions or money, he was made a king. The four faculties—king, legislator, priest, and prophet—he insists (*Mos.* 2.7), are harmonious, and intertwined like the four cardinal virtues; and he insists that to have one is to have them all.

Apparently, there was an objection to having all of these functions combined in a single person rather than, presumably, to have checks and balances. One is reminded of the anecdote, related by Josephus (*A.J.* 13.288–92), wherein, when King John Hyrcanus asked the Pharisees to inform him whether he was doing anything wrong, a Pharisee named Eleazar told him to give up the high priesthood and to be content with governing the people.[57] Thus Philo (*Mos.* 2.3–6) deems it necessary to explain why they should be combined. In Philo's view (*Mos.* 1.162), the providence of G-d caused Moses to be the reasonable and living impersonation of law (νόμος ἔμψυχός τε καὶ λογικός), that is, the ideal ruler. Philo[58] then denominates the law as a just king.[59] In using this phrase he is employing the very same language that is employed by his contemporary Musonius Rufus (frag. 8), thus effecting, as Musonius puts it, "good government and harmony, suppressing lawlessness and dissension, a true imitator of Zeus and, like him, father of his people." Colson (1935, 6:xvi) finds it anomalous that Moses the lawgiver should also be the living law, but Richardson (1957, 520) explains that, being the incarnation of the law, Moses could best put it in writing for others and be himself an example of it. Hence, he could both see and converse with G-d and mediate grace to others to live the law.

In contrast, adds Remus (1996, 665, n. 51), to the utter perversion of this ideal of identifying with law, the Roman emperor Gaius Caligula, as Philo (*Legat.* 119) remarks, regarded himself as a law and treated as empty talk the laws laid down by legislators. Moreover, without G-d's directing care, the king cannot succeed; hence he must know the service of G-d and embody it as high priest. Finally, since countless things are wrapped in obscurity, he needs the quality of prophetic insight. Moses, as Calabi (1998, 3–30) has remarked, is at once translator, instrument, mediator, exegete, and interpreter, with emphasis on his role as mediator who transmits to man the word of G-d.

It was because of his virtue (ἀρετή) and his nobility of character (καλοκἀγαθία), according to Philo (*Mos.* 1.148), that G-d bestowed upon Moses the position of king. To be sure, Moses was actually never a king, nor for that matter a high priest, but Philo is presenting him as, in effect, the ideal leader.

At the beginning of Book 1 of *Mos.* (1.1) Philo declares that it is his purpose to write the life of Moses, "whom some describe as the legislator of the Jews, others as the interpreter of the holy laws." He nowhere in this preface refers to Moses as a king.

In closing the first book of his biography of Moses, Philo (*Mos.* 1.334) says: "We have now told the story of Moses' action in his capacity of king." In the next sentence he states that in what follows he will deal with Moses' role as high priest and legislator, "powers which he possessed as the most fitting accompaniments of kingship." And yet, of the 39 occurrences of the word "king" (βασιλεύς) in *Mos.*, 35 refer to foreign kings (mostly the Pharaoh), one (*Mos.* 1.166) refers to G-d as king, two (*Mos.* 1.62) refer to Moses' shepherding as a preparation for kingship, and in only one (*Mos.* 1.158) do we read that Moses was named by G-d to be god and king of the whole nation of the Israelites. Of the eight occurrences of the word for kingship (βασιλεία) prior to *Mos.* 1.334, one (1.60) speaks of shepherding as a preparation for kingship, two (1.148, 149) refer to Moses' appointment to the kingship, and one (1.290) refers to Balaam's prediction of Moses' kingdom. This office was bestowed upon him by G-d as the reward for giving up the kingship of Egypt to which he was heir (*Mos.* 1.148–49). The relative infrequency (in view of the fact that Philo says at the end of Book 1 that he has devoted that book to a discussion of Moses in his capacity as king) of the use of the words βασιλεύς and βασιλεία with reference to Moses in Book 1 may perhaps be explained by the fact that Moses is like a king in his leadership but is not a king in the sense of establishing a dynasty to be bequeathed to his children. Philo (*Mos.* 2.116) remarks, however, that in his dress Moses, with his turban, resembled an Oriental king, though he clearly differentiates him from such rulers. As for the relationship of prophecy and kingship, there is no precedent in Hellenistic kingship; and the connection is to be sought in biblical and post-biblical Judaism (so Meeks 1967, 116).

Goodenough (1935, 182) suggests that Philo's presentation of Moses as the ideal king is for the purpose of appealing to potential gentile proselytes, since his portrait conforms to the Platonic concept of the philosopher-king and to the current Hellenistic ideal of kingship. This would be in line with Philo's conviction that if only the non-Jews would come to know Moses and his legislation (*Mos.* 2.27), they would adopt the Torah as their guide.

Philo (*Mos.* 1.148–49) emphasizes that Moses gave up the lordship of Egypt, to which he was heir as the son of the Pharaoh's daughter, because of the iniquities committed in Egypt and because of his own nobility of soul and magnanimity of spirit and inborn hatred of evil and because he renounced the wealth that would have been his as king of Egypt (*Mos.* 1.155).[60] Consequently, G-d bestowed upon Moses the office of king.

Though, in keeping with the biblical stress on Moses' virtue of modesty (Num. 12:3), Philo does not specifically refer often to Moses' role as king, he certainly in his acts displays the virtues of a king, notably in his negotiations with the Pharaoh, in his successful leadership of the huge number of Israelites in the exodus from Egypt, in his ability to restore confidence to the Israelites when they were panic-stricken at the sight of the pursuing Egyptians, in his patience in dealing with the constant complaints of the Israelites, in his ability to act as a mediator with G-d on behalf of the Israelites, in his planning for the conquest of Canaan, in his military leadership against the Amalekites and others, in his praise for his generals and combatants, in his fair distribution of the spoils of victory, and in his fatherly attitude toward the two tribes that were not co-operating.

As Goodenough (1928, 65) and Meeks (1967, 109–10) have pointed out, Philo's list of Moses' virtues reads like a "mirror for kings," such as we find in a treatise "On Kingship" by the Pythagorean philosopher Diotogenes (*ap.* Stob. 4.7.26). In particular, he asserts that one should be judged worthy to rule not on account of wealth or power or military strength, but because he is given to sharing his possessions. To this Philo (*Mos.* 1.158) has added a philosophic and mystic element, namely, that Moses entered into an understanding of the Platonic Form or archetypal essence of things, so that, in effect, he became a true philosopher-king.

Philo (*Mos.* 2.4) makes much of the relationship between the role of king and that of lawgiver. The king's duty is to command what is right and to forbid what is wrong. This is the function of law; hence the king is a living law (νόμος ἔμψυχος).

Moses is depicted as the ideal ruler since he did not establish a dynasty, but rather judged impartially the merits of his own sons and others, his sole aim being to benefit his subjects. Moreover, one of the four capacities in which Moses is praised as ideal in *Mos.* is as king. Hence, when Philo (*Spec.* 4.186–87) enumerates the qualities that the ideal ruler, who for Philo is clearly Moses, must have, he remarks that he should be like a physician in relation to his subjects (as Plato, *R* 1.342, stresses) and that in so doing he must follow G-d as his model. He concludes by saying (*Spec.* 4.188) that good rulers must imitate (μιμεῖσθαι) these qualities if they have any aspiration to be likened (ἐξομοιώσεως, "made quite like," "assimilated") to G-d.

Moses, the ideal leader, did everything for the sake of others (*Mos.* 1.50, 1.150), always concerned with championing the weaker. He even allowed the incorruptibility of reason to subdue his natural affection for his own children. Thus he did not promote his own sons to potential power but, as a true leader, set before himself a single aim, namely to promote the welfare of his people (*Mos.* 1.150–51).

Moses displayed this quality as a shepherd in the service of Jethro, his father-in-law, since, as Philo remarks (*Mos.* 1.62), the only perfect king is one who is skilled in the knowledge of shepherding, that is, one who has been trained by management of inferior creatures to manage the superior. In speaking thus of the king as a shepherd, Philo is closely paralleled by the language used by Dio Chrysostom,[61] except that Philo adds that shepherding as such is proper training for a king.

Philo (*Mos.* 1.328) also compares Moses as a leader to a very kindly (εὔνους) father, "for they [the tribes] knew that he did not speak with an arrogance founded on official authority, but out of solicitude for them all and out of respect for justice and equality. Moreover, his detestation of evil was never meant to cast reproach but always to bring those capable of improvement to a better kind." In this comparison Philo is likewise paralleled by Dio Chrysostom (*Discourses* 1.37–41); and, in effect, the king must thus imitate Zeus, who is called "father" because of his solicitude and gentleness.

In enumerating the qualities that justified the appointment of Moses as leader of the Israelites, Philo (*Mos.* 1.148) says that he was not like those who thrust themselves into a position of leadership through military means but that he was chosen because of his goodness (ἀρετή) and nobility of conduct (καλοκἀγαθία) and goodwill (εὔνοια) toward all, which he always continued to show. This de-emphasis on Moses' generalship, which is in contrast to the biblical narrative and to Josephus' account (see Feldman 1998a, 401–11), is intended to put the stress on Moses' other virtues. Moreover, his position as leader was bestowed upon him not by humans but by G-d, who loves virtue (φιλάρετος) and goodness (φιλόκαλος), as a reward that he deserved. Philo then adds that Moses, though heir apparent to the throne of Egypt, gave up the lordship of Egypt because of the injustices (ἀδικήματα) committed in the land and because of his nobility (εὐγένεια) of soul and magnanimity of spirit (φρονήματος μέγεθος) and his hatred of evil by nature (μισοπόνηρος φύσει). It is precisely because of his hatred of evil that he was chosen by G-d to deliver the Israelites from evil. Consequently, G-d rewarded him with the kingship of a nation with a greater population and with more power—a nation that was about to be consecrated above all others and that will offer prayers on behalf of the human race so that it may be removed from evil and may participate in the good (*Mos.* 1.149).

Furthermore, whereas the Bible (Num. 31:6) states that Moses sent Phinehas to the army that was to do battle with the Midianites, without indicating his exact capacity, Philo (*Mos.* 1.306) specifies that Moses appointed Phinehas as commander-in-chief (στρατηγός), thus, in effect, emphasizing Phinehas' military leadership rather than his own. Indeed, as Philo says (*Praem.* 54), alluding to Moses' title as king, "he did not become king in the ordinary way by the aid of troops and weapons or the might of ships and infantry and cavalry." All this is added as a background for Moses' escape to the neighboring country of Arabia (*Mos.* 1.47).[62]

In delineating Moses' qualities as a leader, Philo uses phrases, often taken from Thucydides, and, in particular, statements of psychological truisms about people (see Canevet 1986, 189–206). For Philo (*Conf.* 106), Moses is more than the leader of the Israelites. From his very birth he is termed ἀστεῖος, that is, literally, "town-bred," "polite." Philo understands it in a political sense, by virtue of his (Moses') larger citizenship, as cosmopolitan (κοσμοπολίτης), taking the very world (κόσμος) for his township (ἄστυ) and fatherland (πατρίς). This identifies Moses, as we have noted, with the Stoic ideal of the "world-citizen." Elsewhere (*Conf.* 109) Philo identifies the ἀστεῖοι with democracy, which he regards (*Deus* 176) as the best of constitutions.[63]

It is surely significant that having gone to such great lengths in writing two whole books about the life of Moses, Philo ends with a passage that is parallel to Plato's conclusion of the life of Socrates (*Phaedo* 118a): "Such, Echecrates, was the end of our friend—the best man of his time, in our opinion, that we had ever come across, and, in general, the wisest and the most just." Similarly, Philo (*Mos.* 2.292) concludes his work: "Such, as recorded in the Holy Scriptures, was the life and such was the end of Moses, king, lawgiver, high priest, prophet." There is no peroration, no indication that he is to be the model for a messiah, let alone a second G-d.

Moses as king must also necessarily be high priest, since he must supervise divine matters (Philo, *Mos.* 2.5); this is the case in Hellenistic kings generally, as we see in Diotogenes (*ap.* Stob. 4.7.61) (cited by Goodenough 1935, 190). Philo (*Mos.* 2.31), in his account of the translation of the Pentateuch into Greek, states that Ptolemy Philadelphus dispatched envoys to the high priest and king of Judaea, "both offices being held by the same person," though actually there was no king of Judaea at this time, approximately 270 B.C.E., so that we must suppose that Philo was misled by his assumption that such was the norm. Elsewhere (*Virt.* 54) Philo points out, as we have remarked, that Moses did not bequeath his leadership to his sons or nephews perhaps either because he did not think it advisable to withdraw them from the service of G-d or because he considered it impossible for a person to do justice to both offices, the priesthood in service to G-d and the kingship in sovereignty over men.

Meeks (1967, 134–36) is puzzled as to why Josephus never speaks of Moses as king when the idea that Moses was king is well attested in Hebrew and Greek sources and when the functions that Josephus attributes to Moses were so naturally associated with the ideal qualities of Hellenistic kings. If one wonders why Josephus, the protégé of the Roman emperors, should have avoided denominating Moses as king when the Romans were being ruled by emperors with an iron hand at this very time, the answer may be that the Roman emperors during this period and for many years thereafter presented themselves not as kings but as *principes*, "first citizens," and, indeed, kept all the trappings of republican government. In fact, after the expulsion of the last of the early kings, the very word *rex* was anathema to them, as Cicero remarks (*De Republica* 2.30.53). As the protégé of Roman emperors, Josephus may consequently have been sensitive to the use of the word "king."

Moreover, Josephus (*Ap.* 2.164–65) notes of the three forms of government—monarchies, oligarchies, and democracies—Moses was attracted by none of them "but gave to his constitution the form of what—if a forced expression be permitted—may be termed a 'theocracy,' placing all sovereignty and authority in the hands of G-d." We may suggest that Josephus may have felt that the word "king" should be reserved for G-d alone; and if Moses, about whom Josephus was so sensitive that he not be deified as, in effect, he was by the Samaritans, were to be denominated by that term, it would be tantamount to ascribing divinity to him. As noted by Lierman (2002, 63–64), the fact that in the extra-biblical anecdote mentioned by Josephus (*A.J.* 2.233) the Pharaoh sets the crown upon the child Moses' head only to have him trample it underfoot shows that Moses despised the status of royalty.

As to the rabbinic sources, the *Tg. Onq.* and *Ps.-J.* on Deut. 33:5, as we have noted, understand the clause, "And he was king in Israel," as referring to Moses. According to an anonymous rabbinic statement (*b. Zeb.* 102a), Elisheba, the wife of Aaron, had five joys more than other women on the day that the Tabernacle was erected, among them that her brother-in-law, Moses, was a high priest and also a king. Moreover, in *Sifre Deut.* 357, Moses says to G-d, "If I may not enter it [the Land of Israel] as a king, I shall enter it as a commoner." The *Midr. Exod. Rab.* (40.2) has a scenario in which Moses wonders why Bezalel and not he was commissioned to fashion the sacred vessels required for the sanctuary. Thereupon G-d explains to Moses that He had made him a king and that it was not befitting for a king to do anything himself; rather, it was appropriate for him to give orders to others. Again, according to the *Midr. Tan. Beha'aloteka* 15 on Num. 10:2, when G-d instructed Moses to make for himself two trumpets, He did so in order that Moses might be paid the deference due to a sovereign, and He quotes the passage (Deut. 33:5), "He became king."

However, it is surely significant that on Rosh Hashanah, the Jewish New Year, in the extensive prayers in the Amidah of the Additional Service, Moses is referred to four times but always as "Moses Your servant," never as king.[64] The theme of kingship, significantly, is central to those prayers, as seen, for example, in the fact that the precentor of the morning service begins with the word "the King," and the fact that the first of the three major themes in the Additional Service is kingship; but the reference is to G-d, never to Moses. Moreover, the passage (Deut. 33:5), "He became king," which most of the rabbis declare refers to Moses, is cited in the "Kingship" portion of the Amidah as referring to G-d.[65]

According to the Samaritan tradition (*Memar* 1.2, 6.2), however, Moses was crowned and anointed as king when the Torah was given to him, at which time he was made G-d's vice-regent (see Meeks 1967, 234). Indeed, whereas the Bible (Exod. 4:16) has G-d say that He has made Moses a god to Aaron, the Samaritan *Memar* (1.2) speaks of "my (G-d's) second," that is, a "second G-d," reminiscent of Philo's reference to the Logos as "a second G-d" (*QG* 2.62). In fact, Moses is crowned with G-d's name (*Memar* 1.9).

In sum, though Moses is nowhere in the Bible explicitly referred to as king, all law in the ancient Near Eastern world is enacted by a sacral king. Hecataeus, who has so much to say about Moses' achievements as leader of the Israelites specifically does not assign the title of king to him, since he states that the Jews never have a king. Strabo, however, who lists Moses as a prophet, says that prophets are worthy to be kings and clearly implies that Moses deserves such a designation. The *Sibylline Oracles* and Ezekiel the Tragedian seem to imply that Moses was a king. The New Testament parallels Jesus with Moses as a king. Philo says that the office of king was conferred upon Moses as a reward for giving up the kingship of Egypt for which he was the heir. He looks upon Moses as a philosopher-king in the Platonic mold, and as king he is a living law. Yet, Moses is relatively infrequently referred to as king by Philo and never by Josephus, perhaps because the very word "king" was anathema to the Romans, whom both Philo and Josephus were eager not to offend and because, unlike most kings, he did not bequeath his kingship to his sons. The rabbis likewise generally avoid referring to him as a king, since G-d alone is king. The Samaritans have no hesitation at all about referring to Moses as king; and they state that he was crowned king and made G-d's vice-regent when the Torah was given to him.

9. Moses as Sufferer

Moses in the Bible is the epitome of patience while suffering from the accusations at the hands of the Israelites. He is even ready to suffer death (Exod.

32:32), in a kind of vicarious atonement, if G-d refuses to forgive his people's sin in connection with the Golden Calf. The Pseudepigraphic Ass. Mos. (3.11) stresses that Moses suffered for forty years on behalf of his people in the desert. Stephen in the New Testament (Acts 7:39) likewise refers to Moses' suffering, noting that the Israelites had refused to obey him and had thrust him aside. The New Testament (Heb. 11:24–25) also refers to Moses' suffering in that when he was grown up he refused to be called the son of the Pharaoh's daughter, but chose instead "to share ill-treatment with the people of G-d rather than to enjoy the fleeting pleasures of sin."

Philo (*Mos.* 1.149–54) asserts that Moses chose to endure toil and hardships with his fellow Israelites and to set before himself one essential aim, namely, to benefit his subjects rather than to enjoy the material wealth and power that would have been his as heir apparent to the throne of Egypt.

Pseudo-Philo also takes note of the suffering undergone by Moses at the hands of the Israelites. At the Sea of Reeds, they bitterly and sarcastically cry out to Moses: "Are these the covenants that He [G-d] established with our fathers, saying, 'To your seed will I give the land which you inhabit'? Now let Him do with us whatever is pleasing in His eyes" (102).

Josephus remarks that there are two respects in which Moses excelled—namely, in grandeur of intellect and in contempt of toils (πόνων καταφρονήσει) (*A.J.* 2.229). Josephus, always ready to criticize the fickle masses, stresses the constant criticism and the threat of rebellion that Moses underwent during the sojourn in the desert. Thus, after the spies came back with their pessimistic report, the Bible (Num. 14:10) declares merely that all the congregation desired to stone Moses and Aaron. Josephus (*A.J.* 3.307) states that the people loaded Moses and Aaron with abuse, pouring vituperations (βλασφημιῶν) upon them and plotting to stone them and to return to Egypt. Again, when Moses tells them not to fight the Canaanites, the Israelites proceed to accuse and suspect him of scheming to keep them without resources in order that they may always stand in need of his aid (*A.J.* 4.1). They refer to Moses as a tyrant (*A.J.* 4.3). They assemble in disorderly fashion and with tumult and uproar (*A.J.* 4.22–23, 36). When confronted with the revolution led by Dathan and Abiram, Moses remarks that though he could have secured a life of ease, he had chosen to share the tribulations of his people (*A.J.* 4.42).

In rabbinic tradition (*Midr. Exod. Rab.* 1.31 on 2:10) the suffering that the Messiah will undergo while staying in the hated city of Rome is compared to that which Moses underwent while he grew up in the court of Pharaoh.

In sum, Philo, Pseudo-Philo, and Josephus all emphasize the suffering that Moses underwent at the hands of the Israelites. Philo's and Josephus' Moses, even more than the biblical Moses, chose to suffer hardships with his fellow Israelites, his constant concern being the welfare of his subjects rather than his own profit. Josephus, perhaps reflecting his own personal experiences, is particularly bitter about the way that the fickle masses treated Moses.

10. Moses as Priest and Theologian

To be sure, Moses was not a high priest, but it was axiomatic in antiquity for the king to supervise divine as well as human matters, as we see, for example, in the case of the Roman kings, notably Romulus and Numa Pompilius. The biblical basis for ascribing the priesthood to Moses was Psalm 99:6: "Moses and Aaron were among the priests." Moreover, by implication, since Moses, as a Levite, was the one who inaugurated his brother Aaron as high priest, the priesthood was really his.

Among alleged Graeco-Jewish writers, Artapanus states that Moses divided the state into thirty-six nomes and assigned to each of the nomes the god to be worshipped; among those gods, though it is hard to believe that a Jew could make such a statement, were cats, dogs, and ibises (*ap.* Eus. *PE* 9.27.4). Moses set aside land exclusively for the use of the priests, to whom he assigned the sacred writings.[66] According to Artapanus (9.27.5), he did all these things in order to keep the monarchy stable for Chenephres, the son-in-law of the Pharaoh Palmanothes, since prior to this time the masses had been unruly, alternately installing and deposing rulers. Consequently, he was loved by the masses and was deemed worthy of honor equal to the gods (ἰσόθεος) by the priests (9.27.6).

So wise was Moses that, according to Artapanus (*ap.* Eus. *PE* 9.27.6), he was called Hermes because of his ability to interpret the sacred writings.[67] To a pagan, this identification with the god Hermes would have signified a particular gift in the skill of communication with strangers, which was especially the province of Hermes, and in the art of interpretation (ἑρμηνεία). Such an identification is most striking because, as is well known, according to the Bible (Exod. 4:10), Moses had a speech impediment.[68]

The fact that Hermes was associated by the Hellenized Egyptians with Thothmosis (cf. Diod. 1.16.1–2) and the fact that the second part of the name

Thothmosis is so similar to Moses aided further the equation of Moses with the god Hermes. The fact that Thothmosis, the god of intelligence, was particularly associated with the ibis, which played such a key role in Moses' triumph over the Ethiopians, may have bolstered the association with Moses. In thus elevating the status of Moses, Artapanus may be countering the derogatory statements about Moses in Manetho's history.

Among non-Jewish writers, because one major test of a leader is seen in the ability to select outstanding assistants and successors, Hecataeus pays Moses the supreme compliment of saying (quoted in Diod. 40.3.4) that he chose men of utmost refinement (χαριέστατοι) and of the greatest potential ability (μάλιστα δυνησόμενοι) to head the entire nation as priests. We may recall that the same word, χαριέστατοι, here used to describe the priests chosen by Moses, is the word used by Aristotle (*EN* 1.5.1095B22) to denote the people of superior refinement and of active disposition who identify happiness with honor, which is, adds Aristotle, the end of the political life. In this crucial decision, selecting the proper priests, Moses parallels the founder of Rome, Romulus, as we see in Dionysius of Halicarnassus (*Ant. Rom.* 2.21).[69]

That Hecataeus was impressed with the form of government adopted by Moses is clear from his statement (quoted in Diod. 40.3.5), as we have noted, that, according to the Mosaic code, the authority over the people is regularly vested in a priest regarded as superior to his colleagues in wisdom and virtue, and that this priest is called the high priest. The compliment is all the greater when we realize that in the time of Hecataeus, to judge from the pages of Josephus, the high priest was far from being necessarily superior to his colleagues in wisdom and virtue. It is also all the greater when we realize that the high priest was, during the period of the Second Temple (538 B.C.E.–70 C.E.), regularly chosen not on the basis of ability, as Hecataeus would have it, but rather in direct succession from father to son.

One would think that, in view of the general contempt that the Greeks had for undue credulity, Hecataeus would make some remark of criticism when he declares (40.3.6) that the Jews are so docile that they fall to the ground and do reverence to the high priest when he expounds the commandments; but so great is his regard for the high priest as a kind of philosopher-king that he writes no such word of criticism.

Manetho (*ap. Ap.* 1.238, 250, 265) identifies Moses with an Egyptian priest from Heliopolis named Osarsiph, who, he says, gave the Israelites a constitution and a code of laws. According to Manetho (*ap. Ap.* 1.239), the first thing that Moses did after he had been appointed leader by the Israelites was to issue a law that the Israelites were to avoid worshipping the gods of the Egyptians while not refraining from any of the animals that the Egyptians regarded as sacred, but should sacrifice and consume them, a statement to be contrasted with Artapanus' statement (*ap.* Eus. *PE* 9.27.4) above that Moses assigned cats, dogs, and ibises as gods.

Furthermore, Moses' reputation was enhanced by Manetho's reference to him (*ap. Ap.* 1.235) as one of the learned (λόγιοι, "erudite") priests, especially because the word λόγιοι implies not only erudition, but also skill and eloquence in words, an attribute much prized among the Greeks. That Manetho's description of Moses as an Egyptian priest (*ap. Ap.* 1.250) is not anti-Jewish is clear from the fact that Strabo, who is not hostile to Jews as such (see Stern 1974, 1:263–64), describes Moses (16.2.35.760) as one of the priests of lower Egypt who left the country because of his disaffection with Egyptian animal worship. That, moreover, the identification of Moses as a priest does not in itself prove animosity toward Moses may be seen from the fact that other writers who are favorably disposed toward the Jews—Pompeius Trogus (*ap.* Justin, *Historiae Philippicae* 36, *Epitoma* 2.16) and Artapanus (*ap.* Eus. *PE* 9.27.4, 6)—likewise identify him thus. Moreover, Manetho's identification (*Ap.* 1.238) of Moses as one of the priests of Heliopolis adds considerable status to his person, especially because, as we learn from Strabo (17.1.29.806), both Plato and the famed mathematician and astronomer Eudoxus spent time there with the priests. Moreover, the Egyptian priests were said to possess esoteric knowledge; and Herodotus, for example, as he shows throughout the second book of his *Histories*, was very much impressed with this wisdom.

Strabo,[70] in the first century B.C.E., like Manetho (*ap. Ap.* 1.250) before him and like Chaeremon (*ap. Ap.* 1.290) after him, describes Moses as an Egyptian priest (*Geographica* 16.2.35.760). Significantly, whereas almost all of the pagan sources declare that the Israelites were lepers and were thus expelled from Egypt, Strabo (16.2.35.760) asserts that Moses left because he was displeased with the state of affairs in Egypt, in particular with the Egyptian worship of images of animals, and was likewise critical, following in the path of the philosopher Xenophanes, of the Greek worship of anthropomorphic gods. Moses, he says, held to the belief that G-d benefits those who live righteously, but not those who live otherwise. Moses, we are then told, persuaded not a few thoughtful (εὐγνώμονες) men, who were worshippers of the Divine Being, and, as in Hecataeus' version, led them to Jerusalem. He established a

Temple (whereas, according to the Bible, it was Solomon who did so) for sacrifices and promised the people a kind of worship that would not oppress them with extravagant expenses or divine obsessions.

Strabo pays Moses the supreme compliment of remaking him in the image of his own (Strabo's) Stoic conceptions and ideals (so Bar-Kochva 1996, 213), ascribing to him (16.2.35.761) a view of G-d, very similar to that which Hecataeus (*ap.* Diod. 40.3.4) ascribes to Moses, as "the one thing alone that encompasses us all and encompasses land and sea—the thing that we call heaven, or universe, or the nature of all that exists." But whereas Hecataeus says that the heaven that surrounds the earth is alone divine and rules the universe, Strabo equates it with the universe and with all of nature. Moreover, Strabo's G-d encompasses not only land, as in Hecataeus, but also the sea and all humanity. Both emphasize the unity of G-d and oppose the belief in anthropomorphic deities.

It signifies the high regard that the ancients had for Moses that Strabo (16.2.36–37.761) draws a distinction between, on the one hand, Moses, whom he admires, and the latter's successors, who, he says, at first acted righteously and piously, and, on the other hand, the superstitious men who were later appointed as priests and tyrannical rulers (presumably an allusion to the Hasmonean kings).[71] It is owing to this superstition, he says, that the Jews adopted the practice of abstaining from flesh,[72] as they did in Strabo's own day, as well as the practice of circumcision and excision of females[73] and other such observances. Elsewhere (16.2.39.762) Strabo repeats this contrast between the prophet-king Moses and his successors, "who, with no bad beginning, turned out for the worse."

Pompeius Trogus (*ap.* Justin, *Historiae Philippicae* 36, *Epitoma* 2.16) clearly implies that Moses was high priest before Aaron, since he says that "after Moyses, his son Arruas [i.e., Aaron] was made priest to supervise the Egyptian rites."

Apion (*ap. Ap.* 2.10), the most notorious anti-Jewish writer of the first century, says that he has heard from the elders (πρεσβύτεροι) of the Egyptians that Moses was a native of Heliopolis.[74] He thus follows the tradition, noted above, of Manetho, who had described Moses as a priest of Heliopolis. His assertion that he had heard it from old people aims to emphasize the antiquity of the tradition. Apion declares (*ap. Ap.* 2.10) that Moses, being pledged to his ancestral customs, erected prayer-houses (προσευχαί, the usual word for synagogues in the Hellenistic period), open to the air, facing to the east, and that in place of obelisks he set up pillars. This statement, in and of itself, is certainly not anti-Jewish.

The fact that the second-century Numenius (*ap.* Eus. *PE* 9.8.2) refers to Moses as "a man who was most powerful in prayer to G-d" is surely a great tribute. Apparently, to judge from Origen (*Against Celsus* 4.51), Numenius quoted Moses and the prophets in many passages in his writings and gave them no improbable allegorical interpretations. In his praise of Jewish theology he says (*ap.* Lydus, *De Mensibus* 4.53) that the power of the Jewish G-d is not to be shared with any other, that He is the father of all the gods, and that any other god is unworthy of having a share in his cult.

The New Testament (Heb. 3:1–6) parallels Jesus with Moses as high priest: "Therefore, holy brethren, who share in a heavenly call, consider Jesus, the apostle and high priest of our confession. He was faithful to Him who appointed him, just as Moses also was faithful in G-d's house. Yet Jesus has been counted worthy of as much more glory than Moses, as the builder of a house has more honor than the house. (For every house is built by someone, but the builder of all things is G-d.) Now Moses was faithful in all G-d's house as a servant, to testify to the things that were to be spoken later, but Christ was faithful over G-d's house as a son."

Philo was troubled by the fact that in the case of Hellenistic kings generally, as we note in Diotogenes (*ap.* Stob. 4.7.61) (cited by Goodenough 1935, 190), as well as in Rome, as we see from the days of Romulus and Numa Pompilius, a king was expected to be in charge of the priestly establishment (*Mos.* 2.5), and yet he was not the high priest. According to Philo (*Mos.* 2.71), while Moses was staying with G-d atop Mount Sinai, he was being instructed in all the mysteries of his priestly duties. Indeed, Philo remarks (*Mos.* 2.75) that it was fitting that the construction of the sanctuary should be entrusted "to him who was truly high priest." Moreover, one of Moses' most important duties was to select as priests the most suitable persons, so that they might learn how to perform the holy rites (*Mos.* 2.141). Indeed, we learn (*Mos.* 2.153) that Moses spent seven days initiating his nephews and Aaron and acting as their guide in the sacred mysteries.

Moses is, however, more than a high priest. He achieved a position nearer to pure being than any other person, since he was able, through his asceticism, to divest himself of all bodily things, and thus he could enter into the darkness where G-d was (*Mos.* 1.158), into the archetypal essence of existing things. According to Philo (*Mos.* 2.68–69), in order to qualify as a priest, Moses had to purify himself of all the calls of a mortal nature, food and drink, and sexual intercourse.[75] As for food and drink, he abstained from them for forty consecutive days because he had better food, namely that of contemplation, so that those who saw him afterwards could not believe their eyes. Despite his abstinence from food and drink, Moses' countenance was far more beautiful than it had been when he ascended Mount Sinai. Moreover, as Meeks (1967, 124) insightfully remarks, the striking thing about Philo's description of Moses' translation in his death is that it parallels exactly his description of Moses' ascent upon Sinai, leaving the mortal realm to enter the incorporeal realm. This is mystical ecstasy.

Pseudo-Philo, like the Bible, says that Moses did everything that G-d commanded him to do. He (51.6) quotes the passage from Psalms 99:6 that links Moses, Aaron, and Samuel as priests, and notes (19.3) that after Moses' death, the Israelites will have no one like him who will make atonement for their sins.

Josephus was clearly in a quandary with regard to Moses' status as a priest, since, on the one hand, he certainly did not want to diminish Moses' high standing and, on the other hand, as a direct descendant of Aaron, he did not want to diminish Aaron's standing. Thus he says (*A.J.* 3.212) that Moses devoted himself exclusively to the veneration of G-d. It was he (*A.J.* 3.197) who purified both the Tabernacle and the priests, and it was he who offered sacrifices in the Tabernacle (*A.J.* 3.204).

According to the third-century Rab (*b. Zeb.* 101b), who cites "It was Moses' portion of the ram of consecration" (Lev. 8:29), Moses, during the seven days of the consecration of the Tabernacle, was a high priest and received a share of the holy sacrifices, just as we find also, as we have noted, in Philo. Others (*b. Zeb.* 102a) maintain that Moses remained a priest for the rest of his life.

According to Samaritan tradition (*Memar* 5.3), when Moses ascended Mount Sinai, he rose from human to angelic status. He washed in the trough of the angels and ate their bread (4.6). His very flesh became angelic (6.3). He learned at a synagogue among angels, sat on a great throne, and wrote what G-d had taught him (4.6). He was inducted into the priesthood of the heavenly sanctuary (4.6) and became a priest of the mysteries.

In sum, as king, in accordance with the prevailing practice among Hellenistic kings and Roman rulers, Moses was expected to be in charge of organizing the priestly establishment; and yet, it was his brother Aaron who was high priest. Hence, we find that Hecataeus lauds Moses' wisdom in organizing the high priesthood and in selecting the lower priests. He pays Moses a tremendous compliment in equating him with Hermes, who excelled in the art of communication. Even the Egyptian priest Manetho refers to Moses himself as a learned Egyptian priest. Strabo lauds his pantheistic view of G-d as equated with all of nature. He contrasts Moses, whom he admires, with Moses' superstitious priestly successors. Pompeius Trogus says that Moses was high priest before Aaron. Numenius highly praises Moses' view of G-d. The New Testament parallels Jesus with Moses as high priest. In Philo's view Moses as king had to supervise all divine matters and was instructed in all the mysteries of his priestly duties by G-d Himself, so that he was truly high priest. Through his asceticism (he abstained from food and drink and sexual relations for forty days when he was getting the Torah) he was able to come closer to true being than any other human. According to the rabbinic tradition, Moses was a high priest during the consecration of the Tabernacle and remained a priest for the rest of his life.

11. Moses as Prophet

That Moses is regarded by G-d not only as a prophet,[76] but as a unique prophet, may be deduced from G-d's angry words to Miriam and Aaron when they spoke against Moses for marrying a Cushite woman. G-d tells them (Num. 12:6–8) that if there should be ordinary prophets among the Israelites, He would make Himself known to them in a vision or in a dream, but that His relation to Moses is different, in that He speaks with him mouth to mouth in a clear vision and not in riddles. The Bible (Deut. 34:10) emphasizes the utter uniqueness of Moses as a prophet, who knew no peer in this respect: "And there has not arisen a prophet since in Israel like Moses, whom the L-rd knew face to face."

Even in the eyes of some pagans, notably Strabo (*Geography* 16.2.39.762), Moses was a prophet, as we have noted, who, together with some famous pagan prophets, was held in so much honor that he was deemed worthy to be a king. Moses, says Strabo (ibid.), in obvious admiration, was a prophet (μάντις) like—and the list is an international "Who's Who" of ancient prophets, scientists, philosophers, and musicians—Teiresias, Amphiaraus, Trophonius, Orpheus, Musaeus, Zalmoxis, Decaeneus, Achaecarus, the Gymnosophists, the Magi, the necromancers, the dish-diviners, the water-diviners, the Chaldeans, and the Tyrrhenian nativity-casters. He is thus in the tradition of prophet-kings described by Herodotus (4.94–95), Plato (*Leges* 1.632D), and Polybius (10.2.1ff.). The fact that Moses is the last to be named and that his name is added in a special sentence would appear to indicate his special status in this list.[77] Apparently, Moses was part of the canon of ancient wise men, so that his omission from Celsus' list is noted as remarkable by Origen (*Against Celsus* 1.16). Moses is, however, listed by Strabo not with the lawgivers Minos and Lycurgus but with the prophets and religious leaders (16.2.39.762).

Numenius, than whom there is no pagan who is more laudatory of Moses,[78] refers to Moses as *the* prophet who, basing himself on the statement (Gen. 1:2) that the spirit of G-d is carried above the water, concluded that the souls rest on the water that is divinely animated (*ap.* Porphyry, *De Antro Nympharum* 10).

This view of the uniqueness of Moses as a prophet is found throughout the Apocrypha and the Pseudepigrapha. We have in Sir. 45:5 a portrayal of Moses as a prophetic mediator of G-d's teachings to the Israelites: "He [G-d] allowed him [Moses] to hear His voice, and led him into the dark cloud, and gave him the commandments face to face, the law of life and knowledge, so that he might teach Jacob the covenant, and Israel His decrees."

In the book of Wisdom (7:22–23) twenty-one attributes of Wisdom are enumerated. These have their parallel in *Sifre* for *Haazinu* 306: "For I will proclaim the name of the L-rd" (Deut. 32:3), from which we learn that, counting from the beginning of chapter 32 of Deut., there are twenty-one words. Moses is said to have learned this from the ministering angels, who mentioned the name of the L-rd after the threefold קדוש ("holy") (Isa. 6:3), whereupon Moses said: "It is enough that I be in somewhat less than seven, like the ministering angels," since seven times three is twenty-one. Here we see that Moses had a special relationship to G-d comparable to that of the angels, in that the angels taught him the name of G-d after the threefold unique expression of G-d's holiness.[79]

In the book of Wisdom (10:16) Wisdom personified is described as having entered into the soul of the servant of the L-rd, that is, Moses, and stood up against terrible kings (i.e., the Pharaoh) in wonders and signs. In an allusion to Moses' speech defect (Exod. 4:10), Wisdom (10:21) is said to have opened the mouths of those who were mute and made the tongues of infants clear. It is Wisdom who prospered the works of the Israelites through the hand of a holy prophet, i.e., Moses.

Moreover, it is Moses' authority that is central in 2 Macc. It is his prayer that prefigures that of Solomon in the dedication of the Temple (2 Macc. 2:9–10). It is the command of the law given by Moses and his words of consolation that encourage the martyrs (2 Macc. 6:23, 7:6–16, 7:30).

In the book of 2 Esdr. 7:57 (127)–59 (129) the angel instructs Ezra to view life as a contest, as Moses teaches, "Choose life and live" (Deut. 30:19), in which one must accept suffering in defeat and rewards in victory. However, the angel adds, neither did the Israelites believe him, nor the prophets after him, nor when the angel spoke to them. Hence, there will be no sorrow at their destruction, whereas there will be joy for those who have believed. Thus we see that Moses is specifically compared with the prophets after him, and that those who believed him experienced joy and those who did not experienced destruction. Moreover, in 2 Esdr. 14:5 G-d tells Ezra that he had told Moses many wonderful things, had shown him the secrets of the times, and had disclosed to him the end of the times, but that he had to keep those secrets to himself.

In the Pseudepigraphic Ass. Mos., which is usually identified with the Testament of Moses and which seems to date from the first part of the first century,[80] the key point in the depiction of Moses is his role as a prophet, as we find in the very beginning of the work (1:5), with its reference to the book of the prophecy that was given by Moses in the Book of Deut. Moses is portrayed (1:14) as having been planned by G-d from the very creation of the world so that he might be the mediator of G-d's covenant with Israel. Moses (11:16) is referred to as the divine prophet for the world (*per orbem terrarum*), the perfect teacher for this generation (*consummatum in saeculo doctorem*). But he is more (3:13), since he is depicted as having been able to predict the future of the Jewish people, events which, according to the Ass. Mos., have come true up to the expulsion of the Jews to the land of the East, that is, Babylonia. He is said to have predicted as well the fact that the Jews would be in captivity there for 77 years (3:14). He is the great messenger who, as in the Bible (Num. 12:7–8), can look directly at the omnipotent Ruler of the world.

As Moses' death approaches and he is clearly under divine inspiration, he says that he will reveal to his successor, Joshua, the purpose of G-d's creation. Moses (3:11) is then described as having prophesied the future history of the Israelites, including the conquest of the Kingdom of Israel, the exile of the inhabitants of the Kingdom of Judah, the apostasy of Hellenizing Jews in the time of Antiochus Epiphanes, the rise of the Hasmoneans and of Herod—prophecies that have now, says the author, been fulfilled. The mention (3:11) of Moses' sufferings in Egypt, at the Sea of Reeds, and during the forty-year sojourn in the desert adds to his authority as a prophet.[81] Moses then describes the vengeance meted out by G-d for the death of a mysterious figure named Taxo (9:1)[82] and his sons and the final redemption of Israel, so that all the people will mount the eagle sent by G-d and will be exalted to heaven, where they will live among the stars (10:1–10). In short, Moses as such is not the central figure in the work, as he is in Philo's essay on Moses; rather, the revelation of the future history of Israel by Moses as prophet is the chief interest of the author (see Tiede 1973, 86–92).

As in the Ass. Mos., so also in 2 Bar. (84:5), Moses is presented as predicting that the time will come when the Israelites will forsake the Law. But in 2 Bar. (59:5–11) Moses is presented as a true confidant of G-d Himself, who is shown the ultimate secrets of the universe: "the measures of the fire, also the depths of the abyss and the weight of the winds and number of the drops of rain, and the suppression of anger, and the multitude of longsuffering, and the truth of judgment, . . . and the height of the air and the greatness of Paradise and the consummation of the ages and the beginning of the day of judgment and the number of the offerings and the earths which have not yet come and the mouth of Gehenna and the station of vengeance and the place of faith and the region of hope and the likeness of future torment and the multitude of innumerable angels and the flaming hosts and the splendor of the lightnings and the voice of the thunders and the orders of the chiefs of the angels and the treasuries of light and the changes of the times and the investigations of the Law."

Moses derives the authority to be shown the ultimate secrets of the universe, according to 2 Bar. 59:3–12, from the fact that it was to him that G-d revealed His deepest secrets concerning the law, the nature of the world, and the end of time. It is Moses who can challenge G-d on the basis of what G-d had previously revealed to him (2 Bar. 3:9), so that for 2 Bar. the word of Moses is the word of G-d (Hafemann 1990, 88).

As to Graeco-Jewish writers, the Jewish philosopher Aristobulus, who lived in the second century B.C.E., wrote exegetical works, all lost except for fragments, on the Pentateuch, that employed, like Philo after him, allegorical methods of interpretation. Aristobulus remarks (*ap.* Eus. *PE* 8.10.4) that those who have keen intellectual powers are amazed at Moses' wisdom and divine spirit (θεῖον πνεῦμα), on account of which he has also been proclaimed a prophet.

In the Dead Sea Scrolls Moses is viewed as the *Urprophet*, the first in the series, and superior to all who follow (so Schnackenburg 1959, 632). Whereas the other prophets did not understand the mysteries conveyed to them, Moses is unique in that Moses understood them, inasmuch as G-d spoke to him mouth to mouth. The Israelites, in fear of G-d's presence at Mount Sinai, asked Moses to mediate between them and G-d (4Q377.2.ii) (cited by Falk 2000a, 576–77). He is the one who foresees the sins and punishment of the Israelites until the end of days. Moses is the "man of G-d"; he is the great intercessor. In his Torah are the hidden things that only Moses understands. In an extra-biblical remark, he is called by G-d His "anointed one" (Apocryphon of Moses C [4Q377.2.ii]). He is the "man of G-d" who knows the highest of knowledge and whose voice is heard in G-d's council (Apocryphon of Joshua 4Q378.3.26). He is covered by a cloud, and G-d speaks through him as through an angel (4Q377.2.ii). The Teacher of Righteousness mentioned in the Scrolls is modeled after Moses; but Moses is portrayed, as he is in Philo and in rabbinic literature, as Israel's ideal king (see Falk 2000, 577). Nevertheless, it is surely significant that the Temple Scroll, to a greater or lesser degree, seems to be a new Torah given without the mediation of Moses or a rewritten Torah in which the author goes out of his way to eliminate every mention of Moses and to portray G-d as speaking in the first person. The net result is the downgrading of the importance of Moses (see Falk 2000, 578). According to this document, the sect would appear to represent a new post-Mosaic era in which G-d communicates directly with the adherents of the sect.

In the New Testament Moses is the prophet who predicted that Jesus would be the Messiah (Luke 24:27 and parallels) and that Jesus would suffer[83] and rise from the dead (Acts 26:23). Moreover, Moses is presented as a prototype for Jesus as a prophet in the statement in Acts 3:22–23: "Moses said, 'The L-rd G-d will raise up for you a prophet from your brethren as he raised me up. You shall listen to him in whatever he tells you. And it shall be that every soul that does not listen to that prophet shall be destroyed from the people' (Deut. 18:15–16, 19)." There may well be significance in the fact that the text in Acts says that "Moses said" rather than that "Scripture said," in that it indicates that the parallel between Moses and Jesus is due to Moses himself. Moses is likewise presented, in a parallel with Jesus (Acts 7:25–29), as the prophet who was rejected by his own people.

To Philo Moses is the archprophet (ἀρχιπροφήτης, *Mut.* 103, 125; *Somn.* 2.189; *QG* 4.8) and the most perfect of the prophets (ὁ τελειότατος τῶν προφητῶν, *Decal.* 175) and even "the prophet word" (ὁ προφήτης λόγος, *Congr.* 170; *Migr.* 151). In his *Mos.* (2.3), Philo enumerates the attributes of Moses as king, lawgiver, high priest, and prophet; and it would seem that these four functions are presented in an ascending order of importance, even though the office of king occupies approximately half of the book. Philo (*Mos.* 2.187) defines a prophet as one who declares by inspiration (προφητεία) what cannot be apprehended by reason (λογισμός).

Philo then proceeds, apparently reflecting his own life (Levison 1995a, 280–306), to describe three types of divine utterances: those spoken by G-d in His own Person with the prophet as interpreter, those in which the prophet asks questions of G-d and G-d replies, and those spoken by Moses in his own person when possessed by G-d (ἐπιθειάσας, "calling upon in the name of G-d") and carried away (κατασχεθείς, "possessed") out of himself. Of the first type, which Winston (1989, 50) denominates as "hermeneutical prophecy," Philo notes that interpretation and prophecy are not the same thing. Here the individual is not rendered passive, and his reason does not surrender to inspiration. At Sinai, receiving the ten commandments, Moses was this type of prophet in a manner very similar to Socrates' δαιμόνιον (Plut., *De Genio Socratis* 568Dff.). As described by Hecht (1981, 149), hermeneutical prophecy is "the activation of man's higher mind, is intuitive intellect, by means of which he grasps the fundamental principles of universal being viewed as a unified whole." This is similar to Maimonides' description of prophecy (*Guide for the Perplexed* 2.37) as that which comes only to a superior person who has perfected his character, disciplined his imaginative faculties, and fully developed his rational mind. Prophecy, in this sense, is seen as the culmination of schooling and moral discipline, combined with natural endowment, attainment rather than a sudden inspiration. This is the path by which the great philosopher becomes a great prophet (so Silver 1982, 246–47). It is only in the second and third cases, which Philo describes together (*Mos.* 2.191) and which Hecht denominates "ecstatic prophecy,"[84] that the prophet is truly a prophet and is merely a passive medium of a divine message (*Spec.* 4.49).

According to Winston (1989, 49–67; 2002, 118–21), Philo invokes the ecstatic possession only to explain the ability of Moses to predict the future, whereas when Moses is analyzing the present he uses his rational faculty. Levison (1994, 89), however, notes that when Moses (*Mos.* 2.274) makes his announcement of the Sabbath, which is not predictive of the future but is an analysis of the present, Philo specifically says that he was guided not so much by surmise (ἐστοχάσατο, "guessing") as by G-d-sent inspiration (θεοφορηθείς). Moses, as a prophet of the highest quality, is of the third type, whereby G-d gave him His own power of foreknowledge, so as to be able to reveal future events or, we may add, to confirm his rational analysis. The distinctive characteristic of Moses as a prophet, according to Philo (*Mos.* 2.188–91) was that he remained wholly rational while he was inspired. Thus Moses (*Mos.* 2.263–65) was able to predict the arrival of the Sabbath through rational conjecture (εἰκασία) while he was inspired (Levison 1995b, 198). This would be in line with the analysis of Burkhardt (1988), that the two types of prophecy are not mutually exclusive but that even ecstatic prophecy takes into account the prophet who speaks, and that Moses' role in the transmission of Scripture cannot be detached from his own personality. This is in direct contrast to Balaam's method of prophecy, whereby an inspiring angelic spirit (*Mos.* 1.274, 277) displaced Balaam's rational faculties and used his vocal organs to produce a prophetic utterance, in a manner reminiscent of the description in the δαίμονες in Plato (*Symposium* 202E) and in Plutarch (*De Defectu Oraculorum* 418C–D) (Levison 1995b, 190–92) and described by Philo (*Gig.* 6–18) (see Winston 1983, 197–200).

As a prophetic priest (*Mos.* 2.74) Moses saw with the soul's eye the Platonic-like immaterial forms of the material objects of the Tabernacle that was to be constructed.

While it is true that Philo (*Mos.* 1.21) does say that Moses anticipated the instruction of his teachers so that "his seemed to be a case of recollection (ἀνάμνησις) rather than of learning (μάθησις)," Wolfson (1947, 2:9) correctly emphasizes the word "seemed," and consequently notes that Philo differs from Plato's epistemology in that Moses' knowledge was the result of prophetic inspiration. Prophecy, in the case of Moses, thus takes the place of recollection. It is in this sense that we can understand Philo's statement (*QG* 4.140) that "the sacred scriptures are not monuments of knowledge and vision but are the divine commands and divine words," that is, they are based on prophetic revelation. Since countless things are obscure to even the most gifted mortal, Moses necessarily obtained prophecy so that "through divine providence he might discover what by reasoning he could not grasp" (*Mos.* 2.6).

Philo also stresses the insoluable link between prophet and lawgiver. As he says (*Mut.* 125), the chief of the prophets, that is, Moses, has many names. In particular, "when he interprets and teaches the oracles vouchsafed to him he is called Moses. . . . To enact fresh laws for the benefit of those to whom they would apply is the task of one [that is, Moses] whose hands are ever in touch with divine things, . . . one who has received from Him a great gift, the power of language to express prophet-like the holy laws." There is likewise an indissoluble link between prophet and priest, as we see in the passage (*Mos.* 2.76) in which he discusses Moses' qualities as priest and in which he adds, "So the shape of the model was stamped upon the mind of the prophet."

In this respect, Philo is following the pattern of the LXX, which reserves the term προφήτης for those who reveal the divine will, while using the word μάντις and its cognates when referring to heathen soothsayers. Philo thus sees a basic difference between Minos, the Cretan lawgiver who was guided by the oracles of Zeus (Plato, *Laws* 1.624A), but who actually authored the laws, and Moses, a prophet who revealed the laws authored by G-d. Thus Philo does not apply the term προφήτης to Balaam, but rather speaks of him as a soothsayer (μάντις) who with his mock wisdom defaced the stamp of heaven-sent prophecy (*Mut.* 203). He thus refers to Balaam's widespread fame for soothsaying (μαντείᾳ).

To Pseudo-Philo Moses is so close to G-d that G-d shows him the land of Israel and all that is in it and the source from which He rained down manna upon the Israelites. Moses then has the audacity to ask him (19.15) how much time has passed in history and how much still remains. G-d actually fulfills his request and tells him that four and a half (presumably thousand years) have passed and that two and a half (presumably thousand years) remain.[85]

Similarly, Josephus never applies the word προφήτης to Balaam or, for that matter, to himself.[86] In this respect Philo and Josephus parallel pagan usage, which restricted the use of the term προφήτης to a religious sphere, where it designates one who speaks in the name of a god (as in the etymology from πρό + φημί), declaring the divine will and counsel in the oracle. Historical seers and prophets who are not recipients of the oracles—the biblical parallel would be those acting without G-d's direction—are called not προφῆται, but χρησμολόγοι ("expounders of oracles," "soothsayers") or the like. But since Josephus wishes, on the whole, to restrict his use of the word προφήτης to those who qualify as prophets according to the Bible, he applies such terms as μάντις to post-biblical Jews, notably Judas the Essene (*B.J.* 1.79; *A.J.* 13.312, 313) and even himself (*B.J.* 4.625) (see Feldman 1998b, 113–16).

Indeed, Josephus highlights the role of Moses as a prophet, twice identifying him as a prophet when the biblical text does not (*A.J.* 2.327 vs. Exod.

14:13; *A.J.* 4.320 vs. Deut. 33:1). Though he realized that to recount all of the plagues might be boring for his readers, Josephus nonetheless does so in order to show that Moses erred in none of his predictions (*A.J.* 2.293). In summarizing Moses' greatness, Josephus (*A.J.* 4.329) says that "as a prophet he knew no peer, so that in whatever he said one seemed, when he spoke, to be listening to G-d." In Moses' final address to the people, we are told, he predicted future events, "in accordance with which all has come and is coming to pass, the seer having in no whit strayed from the truth" (*A.J.* 4.303).[87] In fact, according to Josephus (*A.J.* 4.165, 311), in choosing a successor Moses found in Joshua one who possessed qualities as a prophet and as a general.

The rabbis, as we have noted, were ambivalent in their attitude toward Moses, especially since the Samaritans had elevated Moses to such a degree as to convert their Judaism into a kind of Mosaism and since some of the Christians in their interpretation of Judaism had elevated their messiah to divine status. The rabbis, of course, are aware of the biblical statement (Deut. 34:10) that "there has not arisen a prophet since in Israel like Moses, whom the L-rd knew face to face." Moreover, the vision that Moses had was clear and distinct, whereas the other prophets saw only dimly. Furthermore, they were not conscious of their prophecies when they made them, whereas Moses was. In addition, Moses received his revelations directly from G-d, whereas the other prophets received them through an angel. Only Moses received his prophecies in Hebrew, whereas the other prophets received theirs in Aramaic. Finally, Moses was the only one who uttered original prophecies, whereas the other prophets merely confirmed Moses' prophecies. The rabbis note (*Sifre Deut.* 306) that Moses was "the greatest of the wise, the greatest of the great, and the father of prophets."

And yet, there is even a view that he was not unique as a Jewish prophet, since G-d is said to have spoken to Isaiah mouth to mouth, as He did to Moses (*Pesiq. Rabbati* 4.3), and, indeed, we have the statement paralleling Moses and Isaiah as the greatest of the prophets (*Midr. Deut. Rab.* 2.4) (cited by Ginzberg 1928, 6:44–45, n. 242). So also the *Tg. Ps.-J.* and *Tg. Neof.* on Deut. 32:1 parallel Moses and Isaiah as prophets. Moreover, they are quick to add that in no way was Balaam inferior to Moses either in wisdom or in the gift of prophecy. In fact, they assert that in some ways Balaam was superior to Moses (*Sifre Deut.* end), in that whereas Moses did not know who spoke with him, Balaam did know; whereas Moses did not know when G-d would speak with him until He addressed him, Balaam did know; and whereas Moses did not speak with G-d until he had stood up, Balaam spoke with Him as he was falling.[88]

Perhaps because the Samaritans have only the written Torah and not the oral Torah, their religion focuses on the figure of Moses to a greater degree than it does in Judaism. Whereas none of the Jewish sources assign a specific date to his birthday, the Samaritans celebrate his birthday on the fifteenth of Nisan; this celebration of his birthday is connected with the Samaritan doctrine of Moses as the Light of the world (see Purvis 1973, 108). In any case, for the Samaritans Moses is not only a great prophet: he is the prophet *par excellence*. He is described as "exalted man, L-rd of all the world"; "the crown of humanity who was sent as savior of Israel"; "man of G-d"; "the bringer of the Law"; the one to whom G-d gave "knowledge of secret things"; the one who was "vested" with the name of G-d; the one who on Sinai "entered into the unseen world"; "the father of wonders, the storehouse of miracles, the lord of covenants, the light of the two worlds"; "the speaker at creation"; "our lord" (cited by Hall 1993, 234). When he was born the heavens declared that everything that was hidden in the universe would be shown to him (*Molad*, p. 29, ll. 10–11). Paeans of praise of Moses by Fire, Darkness, the Cloud of Glory and Fog followed. The Samaritan *Molad* (p. 63, ll. 2–3), enumerating ten miracles that he performed, asserts that the light of the sun was eclipsed by the power of his light. In particular, the Samaritans stress his role as the supreme prophet: "the great prophet Moses"; "the faithful prophet"; "the prophet who was entrusted" (with the Torah, with secrets, with "the unseen"); "the true prophet"; "the righteous prophet"; "the treasure of prophethood"; "master of the prophets"; "seal of the prophets."[89]

Whereas the Jews had Joshua as a successor to Moses, the Samaritans cannot conceive the possibility of a successor: "Who can compare with Moses, the prophet, the like of whom has not arisen and never will arise? Let us, therefore, not listen to anyone but him, for it is death to disobey him and judgement too to bring it to nought. Who can succeed him?" (*Memar* 4.10).[90] The *Memar* (2.10) lists seven extraordinary things: the light, Sabbath, Mount Gerizim, Adam, the two stone tablets, the great prophet Moses, and Israel. What is remarkable about this list, as Meeks (1967, 222) remarks, is that Adam and Moses are the only people in this list. Moses is apparently regarded as the new Adam. Indeed, whereas no one formulated a Jewish creed before Maimonides in the twelfth century and whereas that creed never attained official status, the Samaritan creed,[91] as stated in the fourth-century Samaritan work

Memar (4.8), places the belief in Moses side by side with the belief in G-d: "Let us believe in Him and in Moses His prophet." Indeed, the same work states: "He who believes in him [Moses] believes in his L-rd." In some ways the role of Moses among the Samaritans parallels that of Jesus in Christianity and that of Mohammed in Islam. Indeed, according to Macdonald, it was Christian influence that helps to explain the Samaritan belief in Moses. This belief, to be sure, is based on the biblical statement (Exod. 14:31) that the Israelites at the Sea of Reeds, seeing what G-d had inflicted upon the Egyptians, "believed in the L-rd and in His servant Moses"; but this does not state that the one who believes in Moses *ipso facto* believes in G-d. In particular, Macdonald cites John 14:1: "Believe in G-d, believe also in me."[92]

The *Memar* (1.9) goes so far as to have G-d say to Moses, "Were it not for your prophethood I would not have revealed Myself, and My voice would not have been heard as long as the world lasts." In other words, if not for Moses, there would have been no revelation of the Torah. To the Samaritans (*Memar* 1.9), Moses is *the* apostle of G-d.

There is, however, another tradition among the Samaritans that appears to challenge the unique position of Moses, and that is the tremendous regard for Joseph. Thus we find the statement in *Memar* 4.12: "There is none like Joseph the king, and there is none like Moses the prophet. Each of them possesses high status; Moses possessed the prophethood, Joseph possessed the Goodly Mount. There is none greater than either of them."

In sum, the Bible emphasizes Moses' uniqueness as a prophet whom G-d knew face to face, and the Apocrypha and Pseudepigrapha stress his uniqueness. Even non-Jewish writers such as Strabo and Numenius exalt his greatness as a prophet. In the Dead Sea Scrolls he is the great intercessor, but the Temple Scroll is presented as a new Torah independent of Moses. The New Testament depicts Moses as a prophet parallel to Jesus. In Philo he is the great philosopher who became a great prophet. Moses invokes ecstatic prophecy only to explain the future, whereas in analyzing the present he uses his rational faculty. Philo stresses the link between Moses as prophet and as lawgiver. As a prophet Moses was not rendered passive, and his reason did not surrender to inspiration. Josephus says that when Moses spoke, one seemed to be listening to G-d. The rabbis, perhaps in response to the claims of the Samaritans, are, amazingly enough, ambivalent, paralleling Isaiah with Moses and even declaring that in some respects Moses was inferior to Balaam as a prophet. The Samaritans are the most extreme in their claims for Moses, regarding him as the lord of the world and even stating that a belief in Moses is a belief in G-d.

12. The Reference to a Prophet like Moses

According to the Bible (Deut. 18:15, 18:18) Moses tells the Israelites that G-d promises to send another prophet like Moses. In the New Testament in Mark 6:15 and 8:28 we hear that some people identify Jesus as the resurrected John the Baptist, some identify him as the prophet Elijah, and others apparently disagree and assert that he "is a prophet like one of the prophets of old." This would seem to refer to a class of prophets of an era earlier than that of Elijah. The only notable prophet earlier than Elijah was Moses. Jesus' disciple Peter (Mark 8:28–29) identifies Jesus as the Messiah, but it is clear that Peter disagrees with those who identify Jesus as a prophet. The distinction between prophet and messiah is clear also from the questions (John 1:19–21, 25) put to John the Baptist as to whether he was the Messiah, Elijah, or the prophet, and from John's denial to all of these questions. The distinction is likewise clear in the statement (John 7:40–41) of some people that Jesus was the Messiah and of others that he was a prophet. There is, however, a passage (John 6:14–15) that indicates that in the view of Jesus' followers the prophet of Deut. 18:15, 18 was the Messiah.

In the New Testament Peter (Acts 3:22, in contrast to the statement in Mark 8:28–29), cites Deut. 18:15, 18 in identifying the prophet of that passage with Jesus. The New Testament (Rev. 11:6) clearly refers to these two passages in its claim that the prophets will have power to turn water into blood and to smite the earth with every plague as often as they desire. The reference to the power to bring about plagues is definitely reminiscent of Moses' ability to do so.

Philo does not refer to either Deut. 18:15 or 18:18 in *Mos.*, perhaps because he sought to emphasize the utter uniqueness of Moses as a prophet; but in *Spec.* (1.65) he predicts that a prophet possessed by G-d will suddenly appear. He does not say, as the Bible does, that the prophet will be like Moses; and the statement that he will *suddenly* appear is not in the Bible. Moreover, the reference is not, most likely, to a specific later prophet, such as Isaiah or Jeremiah, since, if he intended this, Philo would most probably have said that "prophets" will appear, since he cites passages from several prophets, namely,

Isaiah (*Somn.* 2.172), Jeremiah (*Fug.* 197–205), Hosea (*Plant.* 138, *Mut.* 139), and Zechariah (*Conf.* 62).

Pseudo-Philo (19.3) perhaps alludes to Deut. 18:15 and 18:18 when Moses, in his farewell speech to the Israelites, tells them that they and their descendants will lament the day of his death and will say in their hearts, "Who will give us another shepherd like Moses or such a judge to the sons of Israel to make atonement always for our sins and to be answered on behalf of our iniquities?" There is a similar scene in Pseudo-Philo 24.6, where the Israelites lament the death of Moses' successor, Joshua: "Who will go and tell the righteous Moses that we have had a leader like him for forty years?" But neither of these passages in Pseudo-Philo alludes to the passages in Deut. 18:15 and 18:18, a crucial difference being that neither of them alludes to a prophet, which is the key element in the passages in Deut. Moreover, the passage in Pseudo-Philo 24.6 says that the leader has already come in the person of Joshua; and surely Joshua is not the prophet promised in Deut.

Josephus (*A.J.* 20.97; cf. Acts 5:36) mentions an impostor named Theudas who asserts that he is a prophet and who acts like a messiah in that he appeals to the masses to take up their possessions and to follow him to the Jordan River, where he claims that at his command the river will miraculously provide them with easy passage. The fact that the procurator Fadus sent a squadron of cavalry, who cut off Theudas' head and killed many of his followers and took many prisoners, would indicate that Theudas' followers looked upon him as a kind of messiah, and that Fadus regarded him as a dangerous political revolutionary. Similarly, Josephus (*A.J.* 20.169–72, *B.J.* 2.261–63; cf. Acts 21:38) mentions an Egyptian who likewise claims to be a prophet, who appeals to the masses, and who asserts that at his command Jerusalem's walls would miraculously fall down. Thereupon, Felix fell upon the Egyptian and his followers, killing many and taking many prisoners.

The Samaritan tradition (*ap.* Eus. *Theophania* 4.35)[93] regards Deut. 18:15, 18, as referring to the Messiah; but, as Jeremias (1967, 4:858) remarks, this does not necessarily imply that the rabbinic tradition so regarded it, inasmuch as the Samaritans' canon was restricted to the Pentateuch and hence did not look to Isaiah and the other prophets for references to the Messiah.

Meeks (1967, 189), Allison (1993, 74), and Lierman (2002, 57–58) make much of Deut. 18:15 in their effort to show that some first-century Jews, as well as the Samaritans, regarded this verse as promising a succession of prophetic rulers of Israel, beginning with Moses, and continuing with Joshua, the judges, Samuel, Saul, David, Isaiah, and Jeremiah. We may guess that the determined effort, as we shall see, on the part of some rabbis to downgrade the uniqueness of Moses may be part of their counterattack to the spread of Christianity.

In sum, whereas the Samaritan tradition regards Deut. 18:15 and 18 as referring to the forthcoming appearance of a prophet who will be a messiah and who will be like Moses, and whereas the New Testament identifies the passages as predicting the coming of Jesus as resembling Moses and as the Messiah, Philo in *Mos.* nowhere refers to these passages. In *Spec.* he refers to the forthcoming sudden appearance of a prophet, but he does not say that he will resemble Moses, let alone that he will be a messiah. Some of the rabbis deemphasize the uniqueness of Moses as part of the counterattack against Christianity.

13. Moses as Mediator

Tiede (1973, 88) asserts that the term "mediator" ("arbiter," μεσίτης) with reference to Moses' role is not to be found in the biblical account of Moses. As intercessor, Moses is, however, apparently not unique. The prophet Samuel is compared to Moses in his role as the preeminent intercessor. Both appeared at crucial times in Israel's history—Moses as the leader in deliverance from Egyptian bondage and Samuel in the transition from theocracy with judges to monarchy with kings. Hence, it is not surprising that they are juxtaposed in Jer. (15:1) and Psalms (99:6).

In the Pseudepigraphic Ass. Mos. (11.17), we find that Moses, the great messenger, prayed on behalf of his people every hour of the day and night and constantly reminded G-d of the covenant with the forefathers. When Joshua expresses his fear as to how the Israelites will fare under his leadership since they will have no advocate to offer prayers to G-d on their behalf, Moses reasssures Joshua that his intercessions on behalf of the Israelites will not end with his death, since G-d prepared him, even before the creation of the world (Ass. Mos. 1.14), to be the mediator of the covenant (Ass. Mos. 1.17)that He had planned to establish with Israel[94] and appointed him to intercede on their behalf. However, the view that Moses is to be the intercessor for sinners at the last judgment is rejected by 2 Esdras 7:102–11.

Moses is the mediator, however, not only for Israel. He is the divine prophet for the whole world, the perfect teacher for this earth (Ass. Mos. 11.16). It is to him that G-d has revealed all the secrets of time (2 Esdras. 14:5).

Philo also presents Moses as the great intercessor for his people. In describing the ceremony (*Mos.* 2.147) of the installation of the priesthood, Philo says that Moses ordered a calf and two rams to be brought. The offering of the calf, he says, was to gain remission of sins, "showing that sin is congenital to every created being, even the best, just because they are created; and this sin requires prayers and sacrifices to propitiate the Deity, lest His wrath be roused and visited upon them." When, as so often was the case, the Israelites, instead of being grateful for all the miracles that G-d had performed for them, complained to Moses about the lack of food and water, it was Moses (*Mos.* 1.184) who interceded with supplications to G-d, knowing full well the weakness of humans.

Pseudo-Philo, whose overall theme, as we see over and over again, notably in the tremendous development of the figure of the judge Kenaz, is the importance of inspired leadership, develops especially the aspect of Moses as mediator and intercessor. Thus in Moses' pleading with G-d in connection with the sin of the Golden Calf, Pseudo-Philo (12.8–9) develops an elaborate metaphor, in which Moses begs G-d not to be angry with the vine that He Himself has planted. Again, when Moses (19.2–3) bids farewell to his people before his death, he predicts that they will forsake the words that he had established for them and that G-d will punish them. Then, he says, the Israelites and their descendants will say in their heart, "Who will give us another shepherd like Moses or such a judge to the sons of Israel to make atonement always for our sins and to be answered on behalf of our iniquities?" Remarking on this, Murphy (1993, 90) says, "It is noteworthy that the leader desired is neither royal nor military but is called a 'judge' and an intercessor." In his final address to his people, instead of, as in the Bible (Deut. 33:6–24), blessing each of the twelve tribes, Moses (19.8) intercedes with G-d on their behalf: "And now I beg, may your mercy toward your people and your pity toward your portion, L-rd, be firm; may your long-suffering be directed toward your place upon the chosen nation, because you love them beyond all others."

In the Bible Moses predicts (Deut. 32:15–35) that the Israelites will anger G-d with their transgressions and will be punished; but Pseudo-Philo (19.9) recalls G-d's giving the Law to the Israelites, and closes, as mediator for them, with a fervent plea to G-d for mercy toward the Israelites: "For who is the man who has not sinned against you? And unless your patience abides, how will your portion be secure, unless you be merciful to them? Who will yet be born without sin?" And finally, with a intercessory plea full of pity: "Chastise them for a time, but not in anger." Indeed, in another extra-biblical addition (19.11), G-d assures Moses that when He will be angry He will recall Moses' staff, which will be an eternal reminder to Him that He is to show mercy toward the Israelites.

In rabbinic literature it is Moses who begged G-d for mercy on behalf of those who had sinned in worshipping the Golden Calf (Exod. 32:32; *b. Soṭ.* 14a) and even asked G-d to erase him from His book if He refused to forgive them.

In sum, Philo presents Moses as the intercessor for his people. Likewise, in the Pseudepigrapha, we read that even before the creation of the world G-d prepared Moses to be the intercessor on behalf of Israel and indeed of the whole world. Pseudo-Philo especially develops the aspect of Moses as mediator and intercessor, notably in connection with the sin of the Golden Calf. In his farewell to the Israelites, Moses (Pseudo-Philo 19.3) asks rhetorically who will give them another intercessor who will make atonement for their sins and will find an answer on behalf of their iniquities. Likewise, the rabbis stress Moses' intervention on behalf of his people even when they committed the egregious sin of worshipping the Golden Calf.

14. Moses as Philosopher and Inventor

If, as was especially true in antiquity, the reputation of a people rose or fell with the reputation of its founder or lawgiver, the fact that the historian Eupolemus (*ap.* Clement of Alexandria, *Strom.* 1.23.153.4; Eus. *PE* 9.26.1),[95] in the second century B.C.E., declared that Moses was the first wise man (σοφός) and that he was the founder of philosophy was the supreme compliment to the Jewish people. In particular, he notes that Moses gave the alphabet to the Jews, who in turn taught it to the Phoenicians, who thereafter transmitted it to the Greeks. Only if we compare the simplicity of this alphabet with the complexity of the syllabic script of Linear B previously employed by the Greeks can we appreciate the tremendous importance of this revolutionary innovation.[96] Moreover, the letters of the alphabet, as instruments of mystery and magic, were regarded as powerful; and knowledge of the letters was regarded as a divine gift (see Dornseiff 1922).

In contrast to Apollonius Molon's contention (*ap.* Josephus, *Ap.* 2.148) that the Jews had contributed no useful invention to civilization, Artapanus (*ap.* Eus. *PE* 9.27.4), in the second century B.C.E., gives a veritable catalogue of Moses' inventions: ships, machines for lifting stones, Egyptian weapons, devices for drawing water and for fighting, and philosophy.[97] He is thus made comparable to Joseph (*ap.* Eus. *PE* 9.23.3) and such pagan heroic figures as Ninus, Semiramis, Sesostris, Isis, and Osiris. Artapanus thus answers the charge that the Jews are parochial; on the contrary, Moses turns out to be the father of all civilization, including, above all, philosophy, which the Greeks prized so greatly.[98]

The fact that, according to Artapanus (*ap.* Eus. *PE* 9.27.3–4),[99] Moses was called Musaeus[100] by the Greeks and was a teacher of Orpheus would raise the stature of Moses considerably, inasmuch as Orpheus was said to be the founder of extraordinarily popular mysteries, and Musaeus was said to have been his son or teacher or student. The close association of both with music (as was Moses),[101] which played an enormously important role among the ancients, as we can see from the education of the guardians in Plato (*R.* 3.398C–402D, 530C–31C),[102] meant that Moses was raised tremendously in public esteem. One recalls Socrates' remark (Plato, *Apology* 41A6–8), after he has been condemned to death, that if death is a journey to another world he should welcome death, for "What would not a man give if he might converse with Orpheus and Musaeus and Hesiod and Homer?"

A compliment paid by Apion (*ap. Ap.* 2.11) to Moses, by implication at least, is that he was a scientist,[103] inasmuch as he is said to have set up a model of a boat to serve as a sundial.[104] In view of the Hellenistic emphasis on science,[105] to impute such knowledge to Moses is a distinct compliment. The source of this statement that Moses devised a sundial may be the tradition, based on statements, such as we have noted are found in Artapanus (ap. Eus. *PE* 9.27.4), that Moses bestowed on humanity many useful contributions through his inventions. Here the anti-Jewish Apion ascribes to Moses inventiveness in astronomy and chronography, which the Egyptians admired so much, and thus implicitly admits the baselessness of his own charge (*ap. Ap.* 2.135) that the Jews have not produced any geniuses, inventors in arts and crafts, or eminent sages. In view of the fact that the early Greek philosophers, notably Thales, are depicted as well versed in science, especially astronomy (one of the subjects of higher education in Plato's ideal state, *R.* 7.528B–530B), and in view of the Hellenistic emphasis on science, and especially astronomy—a field of which the Egyptians had supposedly been ignorant prior to

Moses and which was to become the most popular of the four branches of mathematics in Hellenistic times (Marrou 1956, 182)—to atribute such knowledge to Moses enhanced his status.

In the second half of the second century C.E., admiration for Moses reached its height in the remark of the Neo-Pythagorean and Middle Platonist (see Dillon 1977, 361–79) Numenius of Apamea, who writes (*ap.* Clement of Alexandria, *Strom.* 1.22.150.4). "For what is Plato but Moses speaking in Attic Greek?" The popularity of this dictum may be seen from the fact that it is quoted in no fewer than four other places (Eus. *PE* 9.6.9, 11.10.14; Theodoret, *Graecarum Affectionum Curatio* 2.114; Suda, *s.v.* Νομήνιος)[106] in extant literature. In view of the tremendous reputation enjoyed by Plato and in view of the revival, in modified form, of his teachings in the guise of Neo-Platonism, of which Numenius was a major forerunner, this is a tremendous compliment. So positive is Numenius' view of Moses and of Judaism that it has actually been suggested that Numenius himself was a Jew (so Bigg 1913, 300, n. 1).[107] But for someone to be identified as a Neo-Pythagorean and yet to be also a Jew would be a remarkable and unparalleled combination.

The second-century philosopher Celsus wrote an attack on Christianity, *Alīthīs Logos* (*True Doctrine*), significant portions of which survive in Origen's third-century reply, *Against Celsus*. Whereas Eupolemus (*ap.* Clement, *Strom.* 1.23.153.4; Eus. *PE* 9.26.1) and Artapanus (*ap.* Eus. *PE* 9.27.4) had spoken of Moses as the first wise man and the founder of philosophy, Origen (1.16) expresses wonder that Celsus did not include Moses in his list of wise men. The fact, says Gager (1972, 96), that the names of Musaeus and Orpheus appear in the list of ancient sages of both Celsus and Strabo (16.2.39.762) arouses the suspicion that Celsus did not merely fail to include Moses, but rather consciously removed him from the list. Celsus presents Moses as the originator of monotheism (1.23–24), and he refers disparagingly to Moses' followers as goatherds and shepherds (1.23), people of the lowest class. Moses, he says (1.26, 5.41), taught his followers to worship angels and to practice sorcery.[108] Consequently, he remarks, the Jews worshipped the heaven and the angels in it, but they rejected the worship of the heavenly bodies (5.6). Moses, says Celsus (1.21), borrowed from the wisdom and true doctrine of other nations and distinguished men.

Though the eminent second-century physician and philosopher Galen is critical of Moses for framing his laws without offering proofs,[109] there is no venom in this criticism; and it simply confirms the view of Moses as a divinely inspired lawgiver. That Galen did have regard for Moses as a philosopher is clear from his comment (*De Usu Partium* 11.14) that Moses' way of treating Nature is superior to that of Epicurus, though inferior to that of Plato. In particular, he commends and agrees with Moses' doctrine of the demiurge as the origin of every created being.

We see, then, that there is a long tradition looking upon Moses as a major philosopher who influenced Greek philosophers. Philo's predecessor, the philosopher Aristobulus, states that among those who admire Moses are the philosophers, who apparently included adherents of Aristotelian philosophy, in the study of which Aristobulus is said to have participated (*ap.* Eus. *PE* 8.9.38). Among these philosophers is Pythagoras (*ap.* Clement of Alexandria, *Strom.* 1.22.150, 5.14.99.3; Eus. *PE* 9.6.8, 13.12.1, 13.13.21), who is said to have borrowed much from Jewish traditions and to have incorporated them into his own doctrinal system, a view that is also found in Hermippus (*ap.* Josephus, *Ap.* 1.162–65) and Antonius Diogenes (*ap.* Porphyry, *Vita Pythagorae* 11). Moreover, Plato, according to Aristobulus (*ap.* Clement of Alexandria, *Strom.* 1.22.150.1, 5.14.99.3; Eus. *PE* 9.6.6, 13.12.1, 13.13.21), followed the tradition of the Mosaic law and worked through all its details, since, he claims, there had been translations of the Pentateuch before the LXX.

At the very beginning of Book 2 of *Mos.*, Philo (*Mos.* 2.2) notes that it has been said, "not without good reason, that states can make progress in well-being only if either kings are philosophers or philosophers are kings." This phrase, of course, comes from Philo's favorite, Plato (*R.* 5.473D). It is these two faculties—the kingly and the philosophical—that Philo claims to have set forth in Book 1 of his treatise, so that he may now concentrate in Book 2 on Moses' capacity as lawgiver, high priest, and prophet.

Philo himself was confronted with a dilemma in dealing with the relationship of Moses to Greek philosophy. On the one hand, he notes (*Mos.* 1.21) that Moses received an outstanding education in the liberal arts, including the philosophy conveyed in symbols, and sciences, including astronomy and astrology, from teachers summoned from Egypt and Greece. According to Philo (*QG* 4.152), Heraclitus stole his theory of opposites from Moses "like a thief." And yet, on the other hand, Philo insists on dissociating Moses from whatever falsehood he found in the teachings of the philosophers. If he finds similarities between the Torah and Greek philosophy, it is not that he wants to form a synthesis between them, but rather that he wishes to emphasize the greater antiquity of the biblical writings and of Moses himself. Thus,

Heraclitus' theory, he says (*Her.* 214), had been discovered long before him by Moses (see Wolfson 1:141–42). Again, Philo insists (*Mut.* 167–68) that one need not turn to the nameless Greek philosophers for the view that virtue is a state of happy feeling, inasmuch as the same idea had been expressed earlier in the teachings of Moses (Exod. 4:14). Philo does not, however, mention anything about Moses being the inventor or discoverer of the arts of civilization, despite his statement (*Mos.* 1.21–24) that Moses was educated by Egyptian and Greek tutors in such subjects as mathematics and astronomy.

Pseudo-Philo, who focuses on Moses as a dynamic leader, lawgiver, and mystagogue, says nothing about Moses as a philosopher or inventor.

That Josephus looked upon Moses as a profound philosopher is to be inferred from his statement that anyone who examines the reasons for every article in the creed transmitted by Moses would find the inquiry profound and highly philosophical (φιλόσοφος). Josephus clearly implies that the profound symbolism attached to the tabernacle and to the vestments of the high priests originated with Moses (*A.J.* 3.179–87) and that it illustrated his wisdom (*A.J.* 1.187). Indeed, according to Josephus, the wisest of the Greeks, including such celebrated philosophers as Pythagoras, Anaxagoras, Plato, and the Stoics, had learned their conceptions of G-d from principles that Moses supplied to them (*Ap.* 2.168). Plato, in particular, the most influential of all philosophers during the Hellenistic period (Hadas 1958, 1–13; 1959, 72–82), he notes, imitated Moses in ordaining that citizens should study the laws of the Israelites and in prohibiting foreigners from mixing with citizens (*Ap.* 2.257).

The rabbis, reflecting their opposition to the study of "Greek wisdom" (*b. B. Qam.* 82b, *Soṭ.* 49b), say nothing about Moses as philosopher or inventor.

In sum, since the reputation of a people rested on the reputation of its founder or lawgiver, we are not surprised that such historians as Eupolemus stressed that Moses was the founder of philosophy and inventor of the alphabet. Even some non-Jewish writers, notably Numenius, acknowledged his status as a philosopher, though Philo, like Josephus, still felt impelled to answer the charge that the Jews had produced no eminent thinkers by emphasizing the achievements of Moses. Philo proudly looked upon him as a philosopher akin to Plato's philosopher-king. And yet, Philo was confronted with a dilemma. On the one hand, in an extensive extra-biblical addition, he speaks of Moses as having been taught the liberal arts, including philosophy, by Greek teachers; and he proudly notes that the Greek philosophers and legislators borrowed from Moses. Yet, he is careful to emphasize that Moses, in his education, dissociated himself from whatever falsehoods he found in Greek philosophy, and, unlike Artapanus, he and Pseudo-Philo say nothing about Moses as the inventor of the arts of civilization. Rather, he wishes to stress the greater antiquity of the Bible and of Moses. Josephus views Moses as a profound philosopher from whom leading Greek thinkers derived their views.

15. Moses as Performer of Miracles

The Bible notes numerous miracles performed by Moses but always as G-d's agent. This is succinctly summarized in Psalms 105:26–27: "He [G-d] sent Moses His servant, and Aaron whom He had chosen. They wrought His signs among them, and miracles in the land of Ham."

According to the Bible (Exod. 7:9), when the Pharaoh told Moses to perform some sign for him, Moses threw out his rod, which was turned into a snake. When, according to Artapanus (*ap*. Eus. *PE* 9.27.27), everyone was terrified at this sight, Moses picked up the snake, which was turned back into a rod. Moses then struck the Nile River with his rod, whereupon the river overflowed its banks, inundating all of Egypt. It was from that time that the flooding of the Nile began; thus Moses would seem to be responsible, according to Artapanus, for Egypt being the gift of the Nile. When the stagnant waters began to smell and the animals in the river perished and people began to die of thirst, the Pharaoh promised to release the Israelites within a month if Moses would restore the river to its banks. Again Moses struck the river with his rod and the water subsided. The Pharaoh summoned the priests of Memphis and threatened to kill them unless they performed some marvelous deed. Thereupon they made a serpent and changed the color of the river. Moses then raised up winged creatures[110] and all the Egyptians broke out in body sores, which even the physicians were unable to cure. Artapanus then states that Moses produced hail and earthquakes throughout the night.[111] He adds the extra-biblical remark that at that time all of the houses and most of the temples collapsed.[112] It is important to note that in Artapanus there is no indication that the miracles were performed by Moses as the agent of G-d. Rather, the miracles are of his doing.

Unlike his beloved Plato, who declares (*Timaeus* 41B) that the laws that G-d implanted into the world when He created it will never be changed (see

Wolfson 1947, 1:348), Philo (*Deus* 87) insists that G-d reserves for Himself the right to change nature. He thus accepts the historicity of all the miracles mentioned in the Scriptures, including certain of the plagues brought on by Moses in Egypt. At the time of the crisis of confidence when the Israelites were beset by the huge forces of the Pharaoh before the crossing of the Sea of Reeds, Moses (*Mos.* 1.174) encourages his people: "Why are you quick to trust in the specious and plausible and that only? . . . What is impossible to all created being is possible to Him only." In Philo it is G-d who is responsible for the miracles of the ten plagues (*Mos.* 1.97), with Moses acting merely as His agent.

To be sure, however, Philo in *Mos.* is aware that scientific thinkers in his audience, who, as we have suggested, consisted primarily of non-Jews (see Goodenough 1935, 180–98), might find it hard to accept the concept of miracles that violate the laws of nature. Thus, in explaining how Moses had managed to sweeten the bitter waters of Marah (Exod. 15:22–25) through throwing into the spring a tree that G-d showed to Moses, Philo (*Mos.* 1.185) gives the reader a choice of believing either that the tree possibly had been formed by nature to exercise a virtue that had up until that time remained unknown, or that possibly it had been created on this occasion for the service that it was destined to perform. In giving the reader such a choice, one is reminded of the remark found frequently[113] in Josephus when he mentions miracles, of giving the reader a choice as to whether to accept them literally. Sometimes, as in the case when Moses smote the rock and brought forth water (Exod. 17:6), Philo suggests an allegorical interpretation, namely that the rock refers to G-d, from whom all that exists comes forth as showers (*Somn.* 2.221–22) (Wolfson 1947, 1:352–53). But the allegorical interpretation does not deny the validity of the act as understood literally. In several cases Philo presents a rational explanation, as, for example, in mentioning the miracle of the crossing of the Sea of Reeds, where he (*Mos.* 1.176–79) explains that the sea was driven back as into a chasm or a whirlpool, when propelled against the shore (see Goodenough 1935, 187). As to the manna, Philo (*Mos.* 1.202) explains that just as the air can bring forth rain, so might it produce food. If Moses does perform miracles, it is to get the Israelites to believe in him (Exod. 4:1–8; *Mos.* 1.76–84). Philo emphasizes the amazement that Moses felt (*Mos.* 1.78, 81), which is precisely what he expected his reading audience to feel.

As Murphy (1993, 223) correctly notes, G-d is the most important character in Pseudo-Philo. Hence, it should not surprise us that when Pseudo-Philo mentions miracles, it is G-d who works all the miracles, and Moses and Aaron are merely His agents. Thus when Amram (9.6) decides not to destroy the baby with which his wife is pregnant, G-d remarks that because Amram's decision has pleased Him, He will do signs and wonders, such as He has not done for anyone else, through the child who will be born. It is G-d who gives Moses the power to perform miracles with his staff, and it is G-d who recalls the staff when the Israelites sin (19.11). Thus, in connection with the miracle of drowning the Egyptians in the Sea of Reeds, in Pseudo-Philo, in an extra-biblical addition (10.6), it is G-d who performs the miracle directly. It is He, we are told, who actually dulled the minds of the Egyptians so that they did not know that they were entering the sea, and it is G-d Himself who commanded the sea.

In dealing with miracles, Josephus was clearly in a dilemma.[114] On the one hand, as a believing Jew, he could hardly deny the centrality of such miracles as the plagues in Egypt, the crossing of the Sea of Reeds, and the revelation at Sinai. On the other hand, he hardly wished to expose himself to ridicule for being credulous. He insisted that Moses wrote nothing that was unreasonable, and that everything in Scripture was in keeping with the nature of the universe (*A.J.* 1.24).

Miracles actually presented less of a problem for Josephus, however, than one might have thought, inasmuch as the Stoics, the dominant philosophical school in Rome in Josephus' day, did allow for divine intervention in the world (see Dionysius of Halicarnassus, *Ant. Rom.* 2.68.1–2). Nevertheless, Josephus frequently (for example, *A.J.* 1.108, 3.81, 3.322, 4.158, 10.281, 17.354; cf. 3.268, 8.262, 19.108, and *B.J.* 5.257) employs the time-honored formula, found not merely in Dionysius of Halicarnassus, Lucian, and Pliny, but also earlier in Herodotus and Thucydides,[115] allowing the reader to make up his own mind. This formula, as Delling (1957–58, 291–309) and MacRae (1965, 136–42) have remarked, is more an expression of courtesy to his pagan readers than a confession of his doubt about the veracity of these accounts.

On the whole, however, Josephus tends to downgrade miracles, as we see especially when we compare, for example, his depiction of Abraham and Moses as talented generals with the rabbinic portraits of these leaders as prevailing because of G-d's miraculous assistance.[116]

We can see the delicacy with which Josephus approaches the subject of miracles in his description of the incident of the burning bush. The Bible states that an angel of the L-rd appeared to Moses in a flame of fire out of the midst of a thorn-bush (Exodus 3:2). Josephus realizes that his skeptical, largely pagan, audience would have difficulty accepting the idea that an angel appeared thus and might even ridicule the incident. He, therefore, introduces the incident by admitting that it was an amazing prodigy (*A.J.* 2.265). He then omits completely the role of the angel and describes in more exact detail the appearance of the blazing bush. That he decries miracles may be seen from the fact that he introduces an extra-biblical addition (*A.J.* 2.320) that it was the Pharaoh's annoyance that the exodus had occurred through the jugglery of Moses that led him to set out after the Israelites. Philo is not tempted to have such an addition because he has an important place for miracles in his narrative.

As for the miracle of the crossing of the Sea of Reeds, Josephus notes the parallel to this marvelous event in the parting of the Pamphylian Sea before the troops of Alexander the Great (*A.J.* 2.347–48); Philo sees no need for such parallels.[117]

The rabbis were ambivalent about miracles. On the one hand, they never express any doubt about the miracles mentioned in the Bible. They explain these miracles as part of nature in the sense that they were provided for when G-d created the world. In fact the Mishnah (*'Abot* 5:6) enumerates ten miracles that were arranged by G-d on the eve of the Sabbath of creation at twilight: the mouth of the earth (Num. 16:30, i.e., whereby Korah and his followers were swallowed up); the mouth of the well (Num. 21:16–18, i.e., which accompanied the Israelites as they proceeded through the wilderness); the mouth of the donkey (Num. 22:28, i.e., that spoke to Balaam); the rainbow (Gen. 9:13–17, that G-d sent to Noah as an eternal covenant); the manna (Exod. 16:4, that G-d sent to the Israelites in the wilderness); the rod (Exod. 4:17, with which Moses performs miracles before the Pharaoh); the shamir (Exod. 20:25, a worm with which the Israelites were enabled to cut stones when building the sanctuary, since ordinary tools were forbidden to be used); the text (Exod. 24:12) of the Ten Commandments that G-d wrote; the writing itself on the tablets by G-d; and the tablets themselves (Exod. 32:16, which were the work of G-d). On the other hand, whereas Rabbi Eliezer (*b. B. Mez* 59b) tries to support his halakic view by citing various miracles that will prove that he was correct, Rabbi Joshua ben Hananiah and the majority of the rabbis refuse to accept such evidence, since they insist that the Torah is not in heaven. Moreover, whereas the rabbis acknowledge that miracles have occurred in the past, those miracles, they assert (*Ber.* 20a), occurred because the people were willing to sacrifice their very lives for the sake of the sanctity of G-d's name. Yet, the rabbis emphasize the miracles that occur in ordinary life (*Midr. Exod. Rab.* 24.1). Nevertheless, one must not rely upon miracles (*Pes.* 64b).

In sum, unlike Artapanus, according to whom, Moses performed the miracles connected with the plagues on his own initiative, Pseudo-Philo elaborates on the role of G-d in performing miracles. Unlike Josephus, who generally tones down miracles, Philo insists that G-d reserves the right for Himself to change nature. Furthermore, it is G-d who is fully responsible for the miracles, with Moses acting merely as His agent, though Philo gives the reader a choice as to how to interpret the miracles. And yet, in deference to his sophisticated audience, Philo often seeks to explain miracles scientifically or allegorically. If Moses does perform miracles, it is to get the Israelites to believe in him. Josephus regularly gives the reader a choice as to how to understand miracles. The rabbis are ambivalent about miracles: on the one hand, they are part of nature; on the other hand, one must not rely upon them.

16. Moses as Magician

The Torah (Deut. 18:10–11, Lev. 19:26, 20:6) seems to be clear in its strong condemnation of various kinds of magic—prediction of the future by various signs, soothsaying, augury, divining, fortune-telling; sorcery, casting spells; and raising the spirits of the dead. They were regarded as an abomination, and a sorceress was not permitted to live (Exod. 22:17). The very fact that these activities are condemned in such strong language indicates that these activities were widely practiced in the milieu in which the Israelites found themselves. There is a distinct difference between the magic performed by the Egyptians with their secret arts and the miracles performed by Moses and Aaron at the command of G-d.

That the practice of magic was by no means eliminated is evident from the fact that we hear (2 Macc. 12:40) of Maccabean warriors who wore amulets under their shirts. Ben Sira (*ap. b. Sanh.* 100b) is quoted as saying that a daughter is a vain treasure to her father, since there is the fear that when she grows old she may engage in witchcraft. In the book of Tobit (3:8) we read of Asmodeus, the evil demon, who is alleged to have killed seven husbands of Sarah, the daughter of Raguel, and (6:7–9) of magical cures.

In Artapanus, in particular, Moses is depicted as possessing magical power. Thus we read (*ap.* Eus. *PE* 9.27.23) that when he was imprisoned by the Pharaoh, all the doors of the prison opened of their own accord. Again, when the Pharaoh ordered Moses to declare the name of the god who had sent him, Moses spoke into the Pharaoh's ear and the Pharaoh fell over speechless (*ap.* Eus. *PE* 9.27.24–25), whereupon Moses picked him up and he was revived. Again, after Moses had written the name on a tablet and one of the Egyptian priests showed contempt for what was written there, the priest died in a convulsion (*ap.* Eus. *PE* 9.27.26). Tiede (1972, 170–71) has noted Artapanus' fascination with the magical properties of Moses' rod, which he mentions no fewer than nine times in ten paragraphs (*ap.* Eus. *PE* 9.27.27–36), always in reference to a miraculous occurrence.

Indeed, Moses had been depicted as a mere magician, as we see in Pliny (*Natural History* 30.11) and Apuleius (*Apology* 90), and as one who had deceived the Jews through his sorcery, as we see in Celsus (*ap.* Origen, *Against Celsus* 1.23, 1.45, 5.41). In this Moses had been anticipated by Joseph, according to Pompeius Trogus (*ap.* Justin, *Historiae Philippicae* 36, *Epitoma* 2.7), who even refers to Moses as Joseph's son, apparently because he shared this skill in magic. This view had been extended to the Jews generally, as we see in Poseidonius (*ap.* Strabo 16.2.43.764), Celsus (*ap.* Origen, *Against Celsus* 1.22, 1.26, 4.33), and Lucian (*Gout* 173). The fact that the Jews were connected with Egypt through the stories of Joseph and Moses and their enslavement there underscored their association with magic, inasmuch as the Egyptians had a reputation of excelling in magical arts. Indeed, according to the second-century Numenius (*ap.* Eus. *PE* 9.8.1–2), Jannes and Jambres, Egyptian sacred scribes who are mentioned in the *Damascus Document* (*Zadokite Fragments*, lines 17ff.), in the New Testament (2 Tim. 3:8), and in rabbinic literature (*Tg. Ps.-J.* on Num. 22:22; *Yalqut* Exod. 168, 176, and *Tan.* 19) and who were judged to be inferior to none in magic, were chosen by the Egyptian people to stand up to Musaeus (i.e., Moses),[118] the Jewish leader.[119]

Egyptian magic and esoteric wisdom were acknowledged throughout the Mediterranean world as unmatched. In Egyptian painting and sculpture of the Middle Kingdom the staff is the sign of power to perform magic. That Moses, with his Egyptian origins, performing his miracles with a staff, was famous as a magician[120] may be seen in the reference to a branch of magic derived from Moses, Jannes, Lotapes, and the Jews (Pliny, *Natural History* 30.11). Similarly, Apuleius (*Apology* 90) mentions Moses, "whom you know," in a list of famous magicians. Apparently, both Pliny and Apuleius go back to the same tradition, inasmuch as Pliny lists Moses, Jannes, Lotapes, and the Jews as living many thousand years after Zoroaster; and Apuleius mentions Zoroaster as the figure whose time marks the beginning of magic. It is possible that Apuleius, who by his own admission (*Apology* 91) took these names from very famous writers (one would guess that one of these was Pliny the Elder, who has the names of six of the eight magicians mentioned by Apuleius) in public libraries, is simply trying to impress his audience with his erudition; but it is more likely that the phrase "whom you know" is to be taken at face value, since it applies only to Moses. This reputation may well have its origin in the feats of magic ascribed to Moses in the Bible and is in accord with the reputation that the Jews generally had as magicians, as we see, for example, in Pompeius Trogus (*ap.* Justin, *Historiae Philippicae* 36, *Epitoma* 2.7), who remarks that the biblical Joseph, when carried into Egypt, made himself, by his shrewdness, master of the arts of magic. Poseidonius (*ap.* Strabo, *Geographica* 16.2.43.764) speaks of the Jews as sorcerers who pretend to use incantations in extracting asphalt. Likewise, Lucian (*Alexander Pseudopropheta* 13) mentions a Jew who dazed his audience by bringing in Apollo and Asclepius.

According to Celsus, Moses acquired a reputation for divine power (ὄνομα δαιμόνιον), presumably a reference to his alleged magical powers. Perhaps this is Celsus' reply to the claim of such apologists as Josephus (*Ap.* 1.162–65) that such great thinkers as Pythagoras had borrowed their doctrines from the Jews. We meet the familiar theme of Moses the magician in Origen's report (1.45) of a conversation that he had with some Jews in Egypt in which he asked them how they countered the charge of the Egyptians who rejected Moses "as a sorcerer who seemed to have performed his great deeds by magic." Significantly, we are told (3.5), the Egyptians "do not deny entirely the powerful miracles done by Moses, but claim that they were done by sorcery and not by divine power."

That Moses had achieved a reputation for wisdom even among those who were critical of him is clear also from Celsus (*ap.* Origen, *Against Celsus* 1.21), who admits that Moses accepted wise and true doctrines and educated his people with them, and that he, moreover, became famous for his divine power, that is, presumably, through magic and sorcery.[121]

In addition to being known among the intelligentsia such as Pseudo-Longinus and Quintilian, Moses also had a popular audience as a magician. This aspect of Moses is celebrated, as we have noted, in the works of Pliny,

Apuleius, Numenius, and Celsus. That Moses' renown as a magician extended beyond the intelligentsia to the masses may be seen in the surviving papyri. In particular, he was said to be the author of several magical books and charms; thus *PMG* 13, dating from the third or fourth century, bears the title "Holy Book called the Monad or Eighth Book of Moses on the Sacred Name" (lines 343–44 and 1077). In the magical papyri, which are syncretistic in nature, and in astrological and alchemical treatises, the name of Moses appears frequently as a figure of great authority and as the supposed author of these texts (see Gager 1972, 134–61). In particular, Moses makes known to initiates the various names of G-d and their mystic significances. We note that the title of *PMG* (ed. K. Preisendanz) 13 is the *Eighth Book of Moses Concerning the Great Name.* In a third-century Demotic magical papyrus (Griffith and Thompson 1904, verso, col. 12, lines 6–8) the speaker asks the gods to awaken a longing between a man and a woman like that of G-d for Moses. Among the magical papyri we find a work entitled *The Key of Moses.* We find the same title in the *Corpus Hermeticum*, and this would appear to indicate a rivalry between Moses and Hermes.[122] Another work, *The Secret Moon Book of Moses*, contains some magical words and an appeal to the moon goddess. Still another treatise, *The Diadem of Moses*, contains magical charms, making the user invisible and securing the love of a woman. A work entitled *The Diplosis of Moses* contains a recipe for producing gold from base metals. The Jews had a reputation for knowing the secrets of alchemy, a founder of which was the celebrated Maria the Jewess (see Patai 1994, 60–91). There are also some amulets and a phylactery containing the name of Moses (cited by Gager 1972, 155–58).

As Remus (1996, 665–80) has noted, Philo's denigrating portrayal of Balaam as a mercenary technician stands in sharp contrast to that of Moses, the true prophet, the philosopher-king, priest, thaumaturge, and mystagogue. Philo, himself coming from Egypt, must have been aware of the close association with magic alleged of Moses and of the Jews. Indeed, according to Josephus (*Ap.* 2.145), Apollonius Molon, Lysimachus, and others had maligned Moses as a sorcerer (γόης). Similarly, Philo (*Hypoth.* 6.2–3) says that there were people who abused Moses by calling him a sorcerer (γόης). Finally, Philo (*Spec.* 1.60, 3.93) is well aware of and reiterates the strong biblical prohibition (Exod. 22:17, Lev. 19:31, Lev. 20:6, Deut. 18:10–11) of divination and such magical arts. Hence, by setting forth the techniques of Balaam in such graphic detail, Philo effectively contrasted him with the purity of Moses the prophet.

Tiede (1972, 171) notes that Philo follows the biblical text in stating that it was Aaron who threw down his rod before the Pharaoh, turning it into a serpent (*Mos.* 1.91). Aaron turned the river into blood when he struck it with his rod (*Mos.* 1.99), brought forth a multitude of frogs with his rod (*Mos.* 1.103), and brought forth a stream of lice with his rod (*Mos.* 1.107). Nevertheless, Tiede notes that in Artapanus (*ap.* Eus. *PE* 9.27.27–32), it is Moses who performs all of these acts with his rod. Likewise, in Ezekiel (*ap.* Eus. *PE* 9.28.12) and in Pseudo-Philo (19.11) (see Jacobson 1996, 1:638–639), it is Moses who performs all of these acts.

If we ask why there are no references to Moses as a magician in the voluminous works of Philo, Tiede (1972, 170) suggests that Philo would have regarded such a portrayal as alien to his portrait of Moses as wise man, lawgiver, and prophet. We may also recall that Roman laws prohibited the possession of magical books;[123] and Philo, as a leader of Egyptian Jewry, especially in his embassy to Gaius Caligula, was very conscious of the charge of dual loyalty spread by anti-Semites.[124] If we may judge from Apuleius' *Apology*, in which Apuleius defended himself against the charge of magic, a mention of Moses' apparent deeds of magic would have aroused considerable criticism, at least on the part of intellectuals and the government.

Exorcising of demons was the sign of special power in a wise man, if we may judge from the example of the famous philosopher Apollonius of Tyana, who successfully exorcised a demon from a boy (*ap.* Philostratus, *Life of Apollonius of Tyana* 4.20). Lucian, who flourished not long after Josephus, mentions a Syrian from Palestine,[125] who, he claims, was known to everyone and who, for a large fee, was alleged to have restored to health, through exorcism of foreign spirits, people who were possessed (*Philopseudeis* 16). Hence, Josephus was on sure ground in his extra-biblical portrayal of Solomon as skilled in exorcising demons (*A.J.* 8.45–49). Thus, he says, Solomon's understanding and wisdom (σύνεσις καὶ σοφία) were revealed.

The Mishnah (*Sanh.* 7:7, 11) reiterates the strong revulsion against soothsaying and sorcery that we find in the Pentateuch. In particular, it takes a strong stand against magical cures as being the ways of the Amorites (*Shab.* 6:10) and goes so far as to say (*Sanh.* 10:1) that one who whispers a magical formula over a wound has lost his share in the world to come. Apparently, however, the practice of magic was a real problem, since we find that members of the Sanhedrin were obliged to study magic (*b. Sanh.* 17a) in order to determine whether an alleged practitioner of magic was liable to the death penalty. The rabbinic tradition (e.g., *Tg. Ps.-J.* on Exod. 2:21), in an addition to the biblical text, associates Moses with magic in the report that when Moses was thrown into a pit by Reuel, he noticed the staff that had been created at twilight on the eve of the first Sabbath of creation on which was engraved the name of G-d with which he was to work wonders in Egypt (see Maher 1996, 91–93).

In sum, despite the strong prohibition of all types of magic in the Torah and in the rabbinic tradition, it was apparently widely practiced. Several non-Jewish writers, notably Pliny and Apuleius, list Moses as a famous magician, and his name appears frequently in the magical papyri; and according to Philo, there were people who abused Moses by calling him a sorcerer. The Egyptians had a reputation for skill in magic, and the Jews were said to be more than a match for them. Moses himself is said to be the author of several books of magic. There are no references to Moses as a magician in any of Philo's works; presumably such a reference would have been viewed negatively both by intellectuals and the government.

17. Moses as Messiah and the Return of Moses

Klausner (1955, 18) regards the traditions about Moses, the savior of Israel, and the Exodus as the source of the messianic idea. Just as Moses brought forth the Israelites from their first captivity, so will the Messiah bring forth the Israelites from their current captivity (so Strack and Billerbeck 1922, 1:68–69).

One of the Dead Sea Scrolls (Testament of Levi 8:14–15) refers to the Messiah as king, priest, and prophet, precisely the three functions that are ascribed to Moses in Philo's *Mos.*, Book 2. Another of the Dead Sea Scrolls, Apocryphon of Moses C, dating from the Herodian period in the first century B.C.E., eulogizes Moses as G-d's "anointed one," that is, Messiah, and states that G-d speaks through his mouth "as an angel" (see Falk 2000b, 1:581); but since kings were also anointed, the reference may be to Moses as king.

There is a scene in the New Testament (Mark 9:4–5) in which Peter, James, and John are with Jesus; and Elijah and Moses appear to them and talk to Jesus, whereupon a cloud overshadows them and a voice comes out of the cloud saying, "This is my beloved son; listen to him." Peter says to Jesus, clearly implying that he expected the return of Moses and Elijah, "Let us make three booths, one for you and one for Moses and one for Elijah." However, immediately after this scene, when Jesus' disciples ask him why the scribes say that first (that is, before the Messiah) Elijah must come, he replies that Elijah has already come, "and they did to him whatever they pleased" (Mark 9:11–13). There is a passage in John (5:45) in which Jesus is reported to have said to his followers that it is Moses who accuses them "on whom you set your hope," the implication being that Jesus' followers expect Moses to intercede for them in the last judgment, but that he will be a witness against them.

When his followers (John 6:30) ask Jesus what sign he can give them so that they may believe him, they say that their fathers ate the manna in the wilderness, implying that Jesus might do the same as Moses in giving them this same sign. Jesus rejects the comparison and asserts that it was not Moses, but G-d, who gave them the manna. One would suspect, as Jeremias (1967, 4:856) suggests, that alongside the early Christian expectation (Ethiopian Enoch 90:31, 4 Ezra 6:26) that Enoch and Elijah would appear as forerunners of the Messiah, there was another tradition that Moses and Elijah would be the two precursors.

Nevertheless, in all the extant works of Philo there is no clear mention of a personal messiah (so Wolfson 1947, 2:413–14), let alone of Moses, whether during his lifetime or returning after his death, as messiah. To be sure, Wolfson does cite two passages in Philo that may possibly refer to a messiah. The first (*Praem.* 95) refers to the LXX version of Balaam's prophecy (Num. 24:7): "There shall come forth a man out of his [Israel's] seed, and he shall rule over many nations; and the kingdom of Gog shall be exalted, and his kingdom shall be increased." The Hebrew version of this passage clearly does not refer to a messiah: "Water shall flow from his buckets, and his seed shall be in many waters. His king shall be higher than Agag, and his kingdom shall be exalted." Interpreting this verse, Philo (*Praem.* 95) says that "leading his host to war, he [the man] shall subdue great and populous nations, because G-d has sent to his aid the reinforcement which befits the godly, and that is dauntless courage of soul and all-powerful strength of body, either of which strikes fear into the enemy; and the two if united are quite irresistible." "He promises," he adds, "to marshal against them, to their shame and perdition, swarms of wasps (σφηκῶν) to fight in the van of the godly, who will win not only a permanent and bloodless victory in the war but also a sovereignty which none can contest, bringing to its subjects the benefit that will accrue from the affection or fear or respect which they feel."

Nor does Philo have a scene, such as we find in Pseudo-Philo (19.12), in which G-d tells Moses: "You will rest in it [your sepulchre] until I visit the world. I will raise you up and your fathers from the earth in which you sleep, and you will come together and dwell in the immortal dwelling place that is not subject to time." While Moses is not here presented as deified, there is a divine promise of a resurrection and of an immortal dwelling thereafter that is not subject to time. The fact that, according to Pseudo-Philo, Moses makes a special extra-biblical request of G-d, namely that He reveal to him how much time has passed and how much remains until this resurrection and that G-d gives him a precise answer (19.14–15) would indicate that Moses has such a special relationship with G-d that He will reveal the greatest mystery of all, namely when the *eschaton* will come.

There is a rabbinic tradition, to be sure recorded a century after Philo in the *Tg. Ps-J.* and *Tg. Yer.*, on this passage, of which Philo might have been aware, that this refers to a personal messiah, but Philo does not use the word "messiah" and does not identify him as Moses. According to Philo, as we have seen, G-d promises to marshal against the enemy swarms of wasps (σμήνη σφηκῶν). If the reference were to the resurrected Moses, one would guess that the promise would be not to send, as Philo adds here (*Praem.* 96), swarms of wasps but rather, in reminiscence of the plagues of which Moses was the agent against the Egyptians, swarms of frogs or lice or wild beasts (dog-flies according to the LXX) or locusts.[126] Though the man appears to be an eschatological ruler, the fact that this leader brings swarms of wasps may, however, be a reference to Moses, inasmuch as (Exod. 23:28) G-d tells Moses that He will send wasps before him, which shall drive out the Hivvites, Canaanites, and Hittites before him. This seems to be the implication of Philo's explanation (*QE* 2.24).

The fact, pointed out by Borgen (1992, 352), that Philo (*Mos.* 1.290), in citing the page from Balaam's prophecy (Num. 24:7), adds the word ποτε ("one day") in noting that this event will occur at some time in the future would appear to distinguish the universal reign, under the universal role of the Israelites, foretold in the prophecy, from the present conflict with Balak. For Philo the central idea is the eschatological role of the Jewish nation, rather than of Moses, as the head of all nations. These eschatological blessings are conditional upon the observance by the Israelites of the commandments in the Torah.

A second possible reference in Philo to a messiah (*Praem.* 165) states that those who are scattered throughout the world will come to the appointed place guided by a vision more divine than is compatible with its being of the nature of man, invisible to others but manifest only to those who were saved. The fact, however, that this speaks of these returnees as being led by a vision rather than as being guided by a person would argue against their being directed by a personal messiah, let alone Moses.[127] There is another possible reference (*Spec.* 1.65), noted by Jeremias (1967, 4:857, n. 114), to the appearance of a prophet who will be truly under the control of divine inspiration. But this passage does not mention the return of a prophet, and it nowhere mentions Moses by name. The fact that it speaks of the sudden appearance of *a* prophet and yet does not mention the name of the *greatest* prophet would appear to be an indication that the reference is not to the reappearance of Moses.

The future state of souls and the end of the world are of considerable interest to Pseudo-Philo, as we see in a number of passages cited by James 1917, 34–36.[128] Klausner 1955, 367, adds a number of others (15.5, 25.7, 44.4, and 60.3). None of these, however, refers to a person of messianic type who will bring about the changes that a messianic figure is supposed to effect. The word "anointed" (*Christus*) occurs four times (51.6, 57.3, 59.2, and 59.4) and only in connection with anointed kings. Moses plays a role in connection with the end of the world (e.g., 19.7). It is surprising that in a work that shows eschatological interest there is no reference to the Messiah. To be sure, Winter 1962, 795, has noted the occurrence of the striking expression *sanctus christus* ("the holy one, the anointed," 59.2), which has a parallel in the Dead Sea Scrolls (*CD* 6.1); but the passage clearly refers to David and has no apparent messianic significance.

There is reason to think, despite the efforts of de Jonge 1966, 132–48; Neusner 1987, 265–82; Horsley 1992, 4:791–97, and others, that expectation of a messianic figure, whether or not he was called by the name "messiah," was widespread among Jews. In particular, Josephus (*B.J.* 6.312) says that what more than all else incited the Jews to war against the Romans in 66 was "an ambiguous oracle, likewise found in their sacred scriptures, to the effect that at that time, one from their country would become ruler of the world."[129] However, nowhere in Josephus do we find Moses identified with the Messiah, despite the fact that the concept of the Messiah was widespread.

Nor do we find Moses identified with the Messiah in rabbinic literature. On the contrary, the Messiah is compared with Moses, and we learn (*Midr. Ps.* 21.179) that the rays that will emanate from the countenance of the Messiah will have a greater luster than those of Moses and Joshua. According to the Midrash (*Tan.* [ed. Buber] 1.139), the Messiah is greater than the three patriarchs, more exalted than Moses, and superior to the angels (see Ginzberg

1928, 6:142, n. 836).[130] The fact that the Messiah, according to rabbinic midrash, is more exalted than Moses clearly indicates that Moses himself is not the Messiah. Similarly, the rabbis (*Midr. Eccl. Rab.* 1.28 on 1:9) compare and distinguish Moses, the first redeemer, who with his wife and sons rode on an ass, from the last redeemer, the Messiah, who will ride on an ass (Zech. 9:9).[131]

The rabbinic tradition speaks of Moses as continuing his activity as the teacher of Israel (*Exod. Rab.* 2.6) and again leading the Israelites, arisen from their graves, in the desert into the promised land (*Exod. Rab.* 2.4); but this is not a messiah who leads the living. That Moses is not to be the Messiah can be deduced from the fact that the rabbis envisage a time when Moses will come from the desert and the Messiah will come from Rome. Clearly, these are two separate events (*Pirqe R. El.* 48 and *Tg. Yer.* Exod. 24:10), and Moses is distinguished from the Messiah.

There is, however, a reference to the return of Moses in rabbinic literature (*Midr. Deut. Rab.* 3.17): "One day when I cause the prophet Elijah to come, you [Moses and Elijah] shall both come together" (cited by Jeremias 1967, 4:855, n. 96). To this may be added another tradition (*Tg. Yer.* Deut. 33:20, *Aggadat Bereshit* 67.133) that in the time to come Moses will lead Israel back to the Holy Land. We likewise read (*Midr. Deut. Rab.* end and 3, end) that G-d promised Moses to send him and Elijah at the end of days as precursors of the Messiah.[132] There is also a tradition (*Beit Hamidrash* [ed. Jellinek] 6.Introduction 22, *Midr. Tannaim* 216, *Sifre Deut.* 352, *Midr. Gen. Rab.* 56.10) that on the day of his death Moses was permitted by G-d to ascend to heaven and was shown the reward that awaited him there, as well as the future generally. In fact, we are told (*'Abot R. Nat.* 12, version A) that Moses' place in the world to come has been awaiting him since the days of Creation. In heaven he has an interview with the Messiah, who tells him that G-d Himself will build the Temple on earth (see Ginzberg 1928, 6:152, n. 905). Clearly, this differentiates Moses from the Messiah.

We find an association of Moses and the Messiah in a rabbinic comment (*Tg. Yer. 2* Exod. 15:18) that Moses will lead the wilderness generation of the Israelites at the head of a cloud, that the Messiah will come out of Rome and will lead the Diaspora Jews at the head of a cloud, and that G-d will lead between them both. Here, too, there is a clear differentiation of Moses from the Messiah.

There is, moreover, a midrashic tradition (*Tan. Vayikra* [Vienna, 1863] 133b, *Tan. Vayikra* [ed. Buber] 6.3a, *Mid. Deut. Rab.* 9.5 on 31:14) that Moses will return "at the head of all in the future world when the righteous come to receive their reward" (cited by Jeremias 1967, 4:856, n. 106). There is a similar reference in the *Tg. Neof.* (Exod. 12:2) to the return of Moses together with the coming of the Messiah.

The Samaritan *Memar* (4.10) declares that at the end of time there will be a "day of vengeance," at which time the *Taheb* ("the Restorer" or "the Returning One"), who is described as both prophet and king, will come and the Samaritans will be resurrected (*Memar* 5.3). The *Taheb,* who is a kind of messiah, is analogous with Moses and, in fact, in the *Memar* is identified as Moses.[133] This belief is based on the promise given in the last of the Ten Commandments according to the Samaritan text of the Pentateuch and on Deut. 18:15 and 18, according to which tradition a prophet like Moses will come out of the tribe of Levi, from which Moses was born, and that he will discover the hidden vessels of the Samaritan temple. It is Moses' intercession that will, at that time, bring about the salvation of the dead.

Meeks (1967, 247–48) calls attention to an incident reported by Josephus (*A.J.* 18.85–87) about a scoundrel who told the Samaritans to accompany him to Mount Gerizim, their sacred mountain. He assured them that on their arrival he would show them the sacred vessels that were buried there, where Moses, he said, had deposited them.[134] Before they could ascend, the procurator, Pontius Pilate, apparently fearing a revolution, sent his troops, who proceeded to kill a number of the Samaritans and take many prisoners.

In sum, though the expectation of a messiah was widespread among the Jews, there is no clear reference in all the extant works of Philo to a personal messiah, let alone of Moses as the Messiah; and in rabbinic literature there is a clear differentiation between Moses and the Messiah. There is no passage, or even a hint in Philo, in Pseudo-Philo, or in Josephus, as there is in the New Testament, rabbinic and Samaritan literature, that Moses will some day return in the future world. In the Samaritan tradition the *Taheb,* who is a kind of messiah, is identified as Moses.

18. The Divinity of Moses

(a) The Term "G-d" as Applied to Humans in the Hellenistic and Roman Periods

That the word θεῖος was used in the more general sense of "godlike" or "more than human" as an epithet of honor may be seen in its numerous occurrences in Homer with reference to warriors, such as Odysseus, born of human mothers and fathers (e.g., *Il.* 2.335, *Od.* 1.65, etc.), human kings as holding their office from Zeus (e.g., *Od.* 4.621, etc.), human heralds as being under the special protection of Zeus (e.g., *Il.* 4.192, 10.315), and bards as singing under divine inspiration (e.g., *Od.* 1.336, etc.), or with reference to a superlative degree of excellence (e.g., *Od.*, 2.341, etc.). Likewise, Pindar (*Pythian Odes* 6.38) refers thus to the human Antilochus, the brave son of Nestor who bought with his own life the rescue of his father; Aeschylus (*Agamemnon* 1548) refers thus to the human king Agamemnon; Plato (*R.* 1.331E) refers thus to the poet Simonides; and Aristotle (*EN* 7.1145A29) notes that when the Spartans admire anyone highly they call him "godlike." Aristotle (*Politics* 1284A3–11) says that if there should be a person, or more than one, whose virtue is so preeminent that he is beyond comparison with others, such a person may truly be deemed a god among men; but this would seem to indicate that he is to be regarded as supreme among men rather than that he is no longer a man.

Nevertheless, it is understandable that Jews would make a particular effort to be sure that a human being should not be worshipped as a god. This was particularly necessary in view of the frequency among the Greeks of the apotheosis of heroes, such as Heracles (cf. Diod. 4.38.3–5, 39.1–2), and Asclepius.[135] Even after death the hero was thought to have power to bring good fortune. Founders of cities were objects of religious devotion, as we see in Pausanias (10.4.10).[136] Moreover, stories were told of Alexander the Great's attempt to throw himself into the Euphrates River so that it would be thought that he had passed directly to the gods.

In sum, though the term "divine" was often used in a more general sense of "godlike," still, in view of the apotheosis of heroes among the Greeks, the Jews were particularly concerned that a human being should not be worshipped as a god.

(b) The Attitude of the Apocrypha and the Pseudepigrapha to the Divinity of Moses

The Apocrypha and the Pseudepigrapha are likewise concerned with defining the status of Moses vis-à-vis G-d. Sir. (45:1) has a tremendous tribute to Moses as a man of faith who won favor in the eyes of all the Israelites, though, we may recall, in the Bible in addition to the great revolt of Korah, Daṭhan, and Abiram, the Israelites were once actually on the point of stoning Moses. Again, whereas the Bible (Exod. 4:16) states that Aaron will speak for Moses to the Israelites and that Moses will be to him as G-d, and whereas, furthermore (Exod. 7:1), G-d tells Moses that He will make him as G-d to Pharaoh, Sir. (45:2), on the basis of Exod. 7:1, declares, according to the Hebrew text, that G-d magnified him as a god. Moreover, according to the Greek text, G-d made him similar (ὁμοίωσεν) in glory to the angels, made him great to the terror of his enemies, and showed him part of His glory. But similar does not mean the same as, and the phrase "part of His glory" indicates that Moses is inferior to G-d.

Despite the fact that the *argumentum ex silentio* is never conclusive, Tiede (1972, 91) asks whether there may be significance in the fact that though the Ass. Mos. focuses on chapters 33 and 34 of Deut. there are two statements that appear in those chapters that are noticeably absent in Ass. Mos., namely the reference to Moses as the man of G-d (ἄνθρωπος θεοῦ, Deut. 33:1) and the special qualifications of Moses as a prophet whom G-d had known face to face, as evidenced by all the signs and wonders that G-d sent him to perform in Egypt.

In sum, according to Sir., G-d made Moses *similar* in glory to the angels, with the implication that he is inferior to G-d Himself. The Ass. Mos., apparently significantly, though focusing on the last two chapters of Deut., omits the biblical reference to Moses as the man of G-d.

(c) The Deification of Moses according to (Generally Regarded) Graeco-Jewish Writers

In telling the story of when Moses with his rod raised up frogs, locusts, and fleas,[137] Artapanus (*ap.* Eus. *PE* 9.27.32) adds that it was for this reason that the Egyptians set up a rod in every temple. He says that they do the same with Isis because the earth is Isis, and it produces these wonders when it is struck with a rod. The holy status of the rod and the equation with Isis are thus an indication that Moses was revered as a god (see Barclay 1996, 129).

The fragment known as Pseudo-Orpheus, consisting of forty-six lines of hexameter verse and generally regarded as being of Jewish authorship, claims, in one version, to be cited by the second-century B.C.E. philosopher Aristobulus; but actually, it seems to date from the third century C.E. It is in the form of an address by Orpheus to his son Musaeus (*ap.* Pseudo-Justin, *Cohortatio ad Graecos* 15, l. 3; *ap.* Eus. *PE* 13.12.5, l. 3; Cyril of Alexandria, *Contra Iulianum* 1.35, l. 3), whom he refers to as the child of the light-bearing Moon. Musaeus, it will be recalled, is identified as Moses by Artapanus (*ap.* Eus. *PE* 9.27.3) and Numenius (*ap.* Eus. *PE* 9.8.2), and is indeed referred to by Artapanus as the teacher of Orpheus. But whereas in Hecataeus of Abdera (*ap.* Diod. 1.96.2) Orpheus transmits to the Greeks the esoteric wisdom that he has gained from his travels in Egypt, in Pseudo-Orpheus he transmits it to Moses.

There is one obscure passage in Pseudo-Orpheus (Recension C, ll. 21–30) (Holladay 1996, 4:194–95), which states that "around him a cloud has been fixed remaining in my way; and it stands tenfold for other men, for no one among mortals could see the ruler of men, except a certain person, a unique figure, by descent an offshoot of the Chaldean race; for he was expert in following the sun's course and the movement of the spheres around the earth, as it rotates in a circle regularly, all on their respective axes." It would seem that the reference to the Chaldean is to Abraham, who achieved fame for his knowledge of astronomy and astrology;[138] but Holladay (1996, 4:182) notes that similar language is used by Philo (*Mos.* 1.5), who speaks of Moses as a Chaldean. The reference to the cloud would seem to be to Moses, and it recalls the account of the giving of the Torah on Sinai, accompanied by clouds, thunder, lightning, and smoke. Moreover, the word "tenfold" (δεκάπτυχον) may refer to the Decalogue (so Holladay 1996, 4:207). Orpheus is thus the recipient of divine revelation, which he transmits to other men. In the passage that follows (ll. 31–40), Moses seems to be elevated to divine status: "And the winds he drives around both air and stream of water. And he brings forth a flame of mighty fire. He, indeed, is firmly established hereafter over the vast heaven on a golden throne, and earth stands under his feet. . . . In every way he himself is heavenly, and on earth brings all things to completion, since he controls their beginning, as well as their middle and end." The passage (ll. 41–44) that follows definitely refers to Moses' exposure as a baby in the reeds of the Nile: "As a word of the ancients, as one born in the undergrowth proclaimed having received G-d's teaching in statements on the two-tablet law. . . . On high he rules over everything in order." Holladay (1996, 4:51) concludes that during the time between Clement and Eusebius the poem underwent additional expansion by editors who added these Moses passages in order to glorify Moses. He notes that the vision in the dream of Moses in Ezekiel the Tragedian (*ap.* Eus. *PE* 9.29.4–6) bears a remarkable resemblance to the portrayal of Moses here in Recension C.

The interpretation of a scene in Ezekiel's *Exagoge* (*ap.* Eus. *PE* 9.29.5) is much debated (see Holladay 1989, 2:441–42, n. 73). According to Ezekiel, Moses, in dialogue with his father-in-law, reports a dream that on the summit of Mount Sinai there was a great throne extending up to heaven on which there sat a noble man (φὼς γενναῖος) wearing a crown and holding a great sceptre in his left hand, while with his right hand he beckoned to Moses. In the dream Moses beheld the entire earth; moreover, a host of stars fell on its knees before him like a squadron of soldiers, and he numbered them all. The dream is interpreted by Moses' father-in-law (*ap.* Eus. *PE* 9.29.6) as an indication from G-d that Moses will judge and lead humankind as he beholds the whole inhabited earth, both things beneath and above heaven, and that he will see things past, present, and future, and in effect will be a great prophet.[139] There are similar scenes in Jewish apocalyptic literature, where Enoch (see especially 3 Enoch) or Moses ascends to a throne; but 3 Enoch dates from a period (sixth or seventh century, though it contains much traditional material that is considerably older) (so Alexander 1992, 2:522) much later than that of Philo; and none of the possible parallels between Ezekiel and Philo (see Jacobson 1983, 38–39) include the motif of Moses' exaltation to divine status. According to van der Horst (1983, 21–29; 1984a, 364–69), the scene bears a striking similarity to *merkavah* mysticism, especially 3 Enoch. Van der Horst (1983, 24–25) notes a number of impressive parallels: G-d makes a throne for Enoch that is similar to the throne of glory, G-d's own throne (3 Enoch 10:1); G-d gives him a garment of glory and a royal crown (12:1–3); G-d makes him ruler over all kingdoms and heavenly beings (10:3); all the angels fall prostrate when Enoch sits on his throne (14:1–5); G-d reveals to him all the secrets of heaven and earth (10:5); G-d calls him the lesser G-d (12:5). Van der Horst views the noble man in Ezekiel's vision as G-d and Moses as G-d's vice-regent who is to be elevated to divine status. Van der Horst comes to this conclusion because in Ezekiel there is only one throne, G-d's, and Moses is requested to sit on it, all alone.

If, as most scholars agree (see Jacobson 1983, 10–13; Holladay 1989, 2:308–12), Ezekiel's play dates from the second century B.C.E., this might support the view of a pre-Christian exaltation of Moses. But this dating rests heavily on the assumption that when Eusebius cites Ezekiel, he is actually quoting Alexander Polyhistor, who lived in the first century B.C.E., and that therefore Ezekiel must have lived earlier than this. Nevertheless, as Van de Water (2000, 61–64) points out, Eusebius makes no mention of the name of Alexander Polyhistor where he actually cites from Ezekiel. Moreover, it would seem remarkable that neither Philo nor Josephus mentions Ezekiel or his work (so Van de Water 2000, 60), though, as Jacobson (1983, 38) notes, Philo never mentions any Jewish sources aside from the Bible.

Runia (1988, 48–75) has raised the interesting question as to how Philo, if he had seen the performance of Ezekiel's tragedy, *The Exodus*, might have reacted to the scene (*ap.* Eus. *PE* 9.29.5) in which Moses recounts this dream. Holladay (1989, 2:442) suggests that the dream and its interpretation sketch the eventual fall of the Pharaoh and the consequent rise of Moses; but the mention of the person on the throne beholding the stars of heaven and earth seems to indicate a more than human king, and Goodenough (1935, 290) uses this passage to support his view that Moses was the central figure in a Jewish mystery religion influenced by Orphism. The parallels in rabbinic tradition (see Van de Water 2000, 66–68) date from a latter period and suggest that the Moses-exaltation motif arose in response to Christian exegesis that sought to replace Moses with Jesus.

According to Jacobson (1981, 272–93), however, there is no mystical influence in *Exagoge*, and Moses is not being groomed for divine status. In his view Ezekiel's account is actually a polemic against the idea of Moses' deification. It would seem strange for G-d to be referred to as a man, especially, we may add, since the word φώς in Homer's *Il.* (17.98) refers to a mortal who fights against a god, and again in Aeschylus (*Prometheus Bound* 549) refers, quite strikingly as here with reference to a dream, to the helplessness, feeble as a dream, that fetters the blind tribes of men (φῶτες), sharply contrasting man with the gods. Again (Euripides, *Bacchae* 542), King Pentheus, in his opposition to the god Dionysus, is referred to as inhuman (οὐ φὼς βρότειος, "not a mortal man").

The key point in Jacobson's interpretation is that in the many other stories of heavenly ascension by Moses, none reports his ascension as a dream (Jacobson 1981, 277). In fact, in the Bible itself (Num. 12:6–8) G-d Himself declares that with all other prophets He makes Himself known in a dream. "Not so," he adds, "with my servant Moses; he is entrusted with all my house. With him I speak mouth to mouth, clearly, and not in dark speech, and he beholds the form of the L-rd." Hence, Jacobson concludes, Ezekiel, in presenting the ascension in the form of a dream, has deliberately chosen to portray the "ascension" as an imaginary event. This, then, is Ezekiel's polemic against the idea of Moses' divinization. To be sure, van der Horst 1984a, 366, argues that only the Jewish part of Ezekiel's audience might have caught the subtle reference to the passage in Numbers, whereas the non-Jewish public would not have perceived this, since the play draws its biblical material only from the first fifteen chapters of Exodus. To this we may reply that there is good reason to believe that Ezekiel was writing for both, as Jacobson 1983, 17 et passim, has pointed out.[140] It is reasonable to believe that the Jews would have known the passage in Numbers, but, in any case, the author of the play surely knew the passage and, indeed, seems to allude to a number of passages outside the first fifteen chapters of Exodus.

Most likely, as Bauckham 1999, 55–57, has suggested, Raguel takes the dream, like most symbolic dreams in Jewish literature, as figurative. Moses in the dream sees, as one would from G-d's throne, the three parts of the cosmos—the earth, the seas, and the heavens. Raguel interprets this to mean that Moses, as prophet, will see the three divisions of time—past, present, and future. In the dream Moses has sovereignty over the stars; Raguel interprets this to mean that Moses will govern mortals, that is, he will be king over Israel. Similarly, Joseph (Gen. 37:9) dreams that the sun, moon, and stars bowed down to him. The interpretation of the dream is that his parents and brothers will bow down to him.

However, perhaps the best explanation of this scene is that the man with the crown upon his head is the Pharaoh, who regards himself as a god, as the Egyptian kings always did; and the reference is to the fact that Moses was raised in the palace of Pharaoh to be his successor. Indeed, as Philo (*Mos.* 1.32) states, Moses, being the adopted son of the king's daughter, was expected to be the successor to the Pharaoh and was regularly called the young king (νέος βασιλεύς). The scene would be parallel to that (Josephus, *A.J.* 2.233–34)[141] in which the Pharaoh placed his crown upon the infant Moses' head only to have Moses throw it down upon the ground and trample upon it, which was interpreted by an Egyptian sacred scribe as an evil omen for the kingdom (see Jacobson 1983, 91). Raguel is, in effect, interpreting the biblical passage (Exod. 7:1): "See, I make you as G-d to Pharaoh." The dream depicts Moses as G-d in his sovereignty over the universe, but this is a metaphor for Moses' rule over Israel.

That, however, there is no indication of a forthcoming apotheosis of Moses seems to be indicated by the fact that when, in Ezekiel's version of the burning bush incident (*ap.* Eus. *PE* 9.29.8), G-d speaks to Moses, He tells him that "you cannot see My face, since you are mortal (θνητός)."

In sum, Artapanus appears to indicate that the Egyptians revered the miracle-working Moses as a god comparable to Isis. According to Pseudo-Orpheus, Orpheus transmitted his wisdom to Moses. Moses is further glorified in Pseudo-Orpheus' statement that Moses is in every way heavenly, with the earth at his feet. According to a dream mentioned in Ezekiel's *Exagoge*, Moses, like G-d, beholds things beneath and above heaven. But it may well be that Ezekiel's portrayal is intended to counter the idea of Moses' divinization, since all this is in the form of a dream, through which G-d says that He makes Himself known to prophets other than Moses, and since elsewhere G-d refers to Moses as mortal.

(d) The Alleged Deification of Moses in the Dead Sea Scrolls

Fletcher-Louis (1996, 247–51) has interpreted a fragmentary text of the Dead Sea Scrolls (4Q374) as referring to the deification of Moses. The text (ll. 6–10) reads: "[And] He made him as G-d to the mighty ones and a cause of reeling to Pharaoh [clearly a paraphrase of Exod. 7:1]. [And] they melted and their hearts trembled and their inward parts dissolved. [But] he had compassion upon. . . . And when he caused his face to shine upon them for healing, they strengthened [their] hearts again, and knowledge. . . . And though no one had known you, they melted and trembled. They staggered at the s[ound of]. . . . to them. . . . for deliverance." In her preliminary commentary on this text, Carol Newsom (1992, 40–52) understands line 6 to refer to G-d making Moses as G-d to the Israelites. As Fletcher-Louis understands it, Moses is here presented as the divine warrior. He finds evidence of Moses' deification in his shining face, which in the Midrash (*Pesiq. Rb. Kah.* 32 on Deut. 33:1) also has this effect.[142] The shining face is that of Moses; but whereas in the Bible (Exod. 34:29–35), when Moses descends from Mount Sinai with his face shining, the Israelites are afraid to approach him, here Moses strengthens their hearts; and this is similar to Josephus' interpretation (*A.J.* 3.82–83), according to which Moses, upon his appearance, rids the people of their anxiety. Moreover, the fragment speaks of G-d making Moses *as*, that is like, G-d: this would imply that he was not actually G-d. There is, furthermore, a parallel between his power to the powerful ones and his show of power to the Pharaoh. Hence, it would seem, this Dead Sea fragment is no proof of Moses' divinity.

Lierman (2002, 165–70) has called our attention to another Dead Sea fragment, 4Q545 (Visions of Amram^{c}ar), which speaks of an individual named Malachiyah, "who will be G-d and called an angel of G-d." This may be a reference to Moses (it may, of course, be to Aaron), whose name, to be sure, does not appear as such in the fragmentary text, which does state that Amram addressed both of his sons. Another line in the text reads: "And an angel of G-d you will be called," but does not specify who is being addressed. Pseudo-Philo (9.16) says that Moses' mother called him Melchiel. Clement of Alexandria (*Strom.* 1.23) says that according to the initiates, Moses, after his assumption, was called Melchi. Malachiyah does seem close to Melciel, where *yah* is another name for G-d, *el.*

If, indeed, the reference is to Moses' angelization, this may be parallel to the statement in the Greek version of Sir. 45:2 that G-d "made him [i.e., Moses] equal in glory to the holy ones" [i.e., the angels]. So also in Samaritan thought he is said to have attained angelic status (see Fossum 1985, 123); and, indeed, in *Memar* he is said to dwell among the angels (see Lierman 2002, 171).

In sum, the references in the Dead Sea Scrolls are fragmentary and inconclusive; at best they refer to Moses as similar to G-d and as angelic. They do not refer to Moses as being G-d.

(e) The Association of Moses with Divinity in the New Testament

In Acts 6:11 we read that the charge has been made against Stephen that he had been heard to speak blasphemous words against Moses and G-d. Blasphemy is normally understood to mean a contemptuous or profane act or utterance concerning G-d.

We see a similar close association of Moses and G-d in Num. 21:6–7, where G-d sends fiery serpents against the Israelites, whereupon they confess that "We have sinned, for we have spoken against the L-rd and against you"; but this is not blasphemy, which is an act derogatory to and contemptuous of G-d's power and which is a very special form of sinning.

In sum, there would seem to be an explicit reference in the New Testament paralleling Moses and G-d in that Stephen is accused of uttering blasphemies against Moses and G-d.

(f) Philo's View of the Alleged Divinity of Moses

Philo himself, though he uses the word θεῖος 555 times, employs it only once (*Virt.* 177) with reference to a human when he says that absolute sinlessness (μηδὲν συνόλως ἁμαρτεῖν) is proper (ἴδιον) to G-d or perhaps (τάχα) also to a divine man (θείου ἀνδρός); but he is speaking here in theoretical terms and is not necessarily referring to Moses. The word τάχα connotes any contingency from a probability to a bare possibility. That Philo is here, however, thinking of Moses as possibly a divine man seems to be indicated by the fact that in the sentence that immediately follows this statement he speaks of Moses as initiating people into his mysteries. If Philo really intended to have us believe that Moses was divine, here was the opportunity to say so clearly. But on such matters as divinity surely one does not speak of "perhaps" or "possibly." The fact that Philo does indicates that Moses is not divine.

It would also appear that Philo is here referring to Moses[143] since in the passage just before this (*Virt.* 175) he speaks of the most holy (ἱερώτατος) Moses, who loved virtue (φιλάρετος) and loved goodness (φιλόκαλος) and, above all, loved his fellow men (φιλάνθρωπος), and who urged everyone to become zealous for piety (εὐσέβεια) and justice (δικαιοσύνη) and who offered membership in the best commonwealth to those who repented. Indeed, Goodenough (1935, 232–33) says that the reference must be to Moses. Philo says that although Moses was only a single individual, in power he was equal to a whole nation (*Virt.* 185). He notes, as an analogy, the pilot who is equal to the whole crew and the general who is equal to all his soldiers (*Virt.* 186). Moreover, in the passage immediately after the sentence containing the phrase "divine man," Philo says, referring to those who convert from sin to a blameless life, "And therefore," presumably as a consequence of the previous sentence, "when he [i.e., Moses] calls together such people and initiates them into his mysteries," he exhorts them to embrace truth. Furthermore, though Moses is not G-d, he seems to have existed before he was born, since we read (Philo, *Sacr.* 9) that G-d sent him as a loan. Among biblical figures there is a hierarchy of excellence, proceeding from Enosh, the man of hope (*Abr.* 7–16), to Enoch, the man of repentance and improvement (*Abr.* 17–26), to Noah, the man of justice, who was perfect in his generation (Gen. 6:9), but not absolutely perfect (*Abr.* 27–47), to Abraham, Isaac, and Jacob, who are wise men who are symbols of virtue acquired respectively by teaching, nature, and practice (*Abr.* 52).[144] Each of this last triad, he adds, married not women, but virtues (*Cher.* 41). A clue to the fact that Philo is thinking not of Moses as divine, but of Moses as a philosopher who has grasped the essence of things through knowledge of the Forms, is indicated by Philo's statement (*Virt.* 178) that invites people "to rise in rebellion against the mythical fables impressed on their tender souls from their earliest years by parents and nurses and tutors and the multitude of other familiars, who have caused them to go endlessly astray in their search for the knowledge of the best." This is precisely what Plato in the *Republic* says is the goal of education, namely to get people to forget what their parents and teachers have tried endlessly to impregnate in them and through their own efforts to discern the true knowledge of the Forms through dialectic. Moreover, the fact that Philo deemphasizes Moses' role as a miracle worker and often attempts to explain miracles scientifically or allegorically (see Tiede 1972, 134–37) would likewise indicate that he did not regard Moses as divine, since the ability to perform miracles is a key attribute of G-d.

Elsewhere (*Leg.* 3.134) Philo speaks of Moses as being perfect (τέλειος) and as going so far as to cut off all passions everywhere. As to whether Moses was sinless, Philo, on the one hand, says (*Leg.* 3.135) that unlike others who acquire virtue by toil and thus fall short of full achievement, Moses received virtue easily and without toil from the hands of G-d. On the other hand, he says (*Mos.* 2.147) that sin is congenital to every created being, even the best, just because they are created; and this sin requires prayers and sacrifices to propitiate G-d.

Indeed, as Wolfson (1947, 1:451, n. 85) has noted, there are conflicting views in rabbinic literature as to whether the patriarchs—Abraham, Isaac, and Jacob—did or did not sin. Moses specifically (*b. Yoma* 86b) is spoken of as having sinned and as begging that his sins be recorded, whereas elsewhere (*b. Shab.* 55b), according to another tradition, he and Aaron are spoken of as having fulfilled the whole Torah and nevertheless as having died though they were without sin. In fact, rabbinic tradition (*b. Shab.* 55b) records that there were four others—Benjamin the son of Jacob, Amram the father of Moses, Jesse the father of David, and Caleb the son of David—who were sinless and who died only because the serpent caused Adam and Eve to sin. The significant point is that Moses is not included in this list.

It would seem to be embarrassing that Moses, who is so G-d-like and who, after all, had been given a complete code of law by G-d, did not know (Lev. 24:10–12) what penalty to inflict upon the son of the Israelite woman who had blasphemed the name of G-d.

The one great blot on Moses' reputation for piety is the incident (Num. 20:7–12) in which, when the Israelites once again lacked water and complained bitterly to Moses, G-d commanded Moses and Aaron to speak to the rock in order to bring forth water, whereas Moses did not speak to the rock, but struck it with his staff. Philo says nothing about G-d's anger with Moses and Aaron and the punishment that He promised to inflict upon them. Clearly, Philo could not conceive of so godlike a person as Moses committing so egregious a sin.

Philo is understandably reluctant to speak of Moses as divine (θεῖος), especially since this term was used of deified emperors, as we see in the reference to the divine Augustus (θεῖος Σεβαστός) in Claudius' edict as quoted by Josephus (*A.J.* 19.289). Philo was particularly sensitive to such a view because he headed a delegation seeking to reverse Caligula's attempt to seek the Jews to acknowledge his divinity. In his *Legat.* 85, Philo condemns Caligula's claim to divinity—an assertion in obvious contrast to that of Moses, who insisted that worship is reserved only for G-d. The Jews, Philo says (*Legat.* 117–18), are unique in their opposition to Caligula's claim, an opposition based upon the principle that a human being cannot become G-d, since a human is mortal. Jews, he explains (ibid.), are accustomed "to accept death as willingly as if it were immortality, to save them from submitting to the destruction of any of their ancestral traditions, even the smallest." Caligula's attempt, however, is the greatest possible challenge to the ancestral traditions of the Jews, since it makes the created and corruptible nature of humanity to appear uncreated and incorruptible "by a deification which our nation judged to be the most grievous impiety, since sooner could G-d change into a man than a man into G-d." Moreover, he adds in further vehement language, it includes "the supremely evil vices of infidelity and ingratitude to the Benefactor of the whole world, who through His power bestows blessings poured in unstinted abundance on every part of the All." Moreover, as Najman 2003, 97, n. 54, remarks, the Jews were not alone in objecting to apotheosis, since we have Seneca's satire, *Apocolocyntosis*, ridiculing the Emperor Claudius' attempt at apotheosis. Having subscribed to this view in such unambiguous language, Philo could hardly have thought of Moses, the great role model of the Jews, as anything but mortal.

One of the biblical passages that is most troublesome from a theological point of view is that in which G-d says to Moses (Exod. 7:1): "See, I make you as G-d (אלקים, LXX θεόν) to Pharaoh; and Aaron your brother shall be your prophet." It is true that the word here translated as "G-d" could mean "master" or "powerful," but the fact that Aaron is designated as his prophet would seem to indicate that the meaning is really "G-d." Fletcher-Louis (1996, 242),[145] basing himself on Philo's citation of this passage (*Leg.* 1.40, *Sacr.* 9, *Mut.* 19), concludes that it is "well known that . . . Philo deified Moses." Amir (1973, 4) insists that Philo is not at all offended by the statement that Moses is called G-d, since for Philo something divine must be incorporated in Moses' personality in order to understand the Pentateuch as coming from his hand. Philo, however, is aware of the problem and resolves it by interpreting allegorically that the word "G-d" refers to the mind (*Migr.* 81, 84; cf. *Prob.* 43–44), which is, so to speak, the G-d of the unreasoning part. Elsewhere (*Mut.* 128, *Det.* 162) he explains that Moses is a god as compared with the Pharaoh in the sense that he is wise as compared with a fool, just as a counterfeit coin is not a genuine coin (see Helleman 1990, 68). He emphasizes the same point in his comment (*Mut.* 181) on the question as to why Abraham showed a breath of unbelief when once he believed. He explains this questioning by noting that a human being is not G-d and that he can attain merely the image of G-d's excellence.[146]

But Philo himself (*Det.* 161) makes it clear that when G-d (Exod. 7:1) declares to Moses that "I make you as G-d to Pharaoh," "he did not become such in reality but only in a manner of speaking" (μὴ πρὸς ἀλήθειαν, δόξῃ δὲ μόνον). The fact that Philo (*Mos.* 1.158) interprets the biblical verse (Exod. 7:1) "See I make you as G-d to Pharaoh" to mean that G-d appointed Moses to be both G-d and king, implying that the role of king was one aspect of G-d, leads Meeks (1967, 192–95) to note a similar connection in the rabbinic tradition (*Tanḥuma* [ed. Buber] 4.51–52), and he concludes that this connection is older than Philo.

However, in his discussions (*Sacr.* 8–10, *Mut.* 125–29) of Exodus 7:1 ("I am giving you as a god to Pharaoh"), Philo explains that Moses had control of his passions, that is, he had divine ruling power (βασιλικὴ δύναμις); hence, Moses is like G-d in that he reflects divine virtue. But even Moses was limited in his understanding of G-d (*Det.* 159–62); he says of G-d, "only as best he may in human speech." It is G-d Who says, "I am He that is" (Exod. 3:14) (see Helleman 1990, 67–70). Only G-d, says Philo (*Mut.* 183–84), possesses a single nature, whereas man's excellences are mixed.

Still further, Philo (*Mut.* 129) asserts that Moses is compared to G-d in that he is like a merciful mediator making intercession on the Pharaoh's behalf.[147] Moses is thus one step higher than the three patriarchs, Abraham, Isaac, and Jacob, who represent the virtue acquired, respectively, by teaching, nature, and practice, and who are referred to as G-d-lovers (φιλοθέους) and G-d-beloved (θεοφιλεῖς); and G-d is, consequently, known as the G-d of Abraham, the G-d of Isaac, and the G-d of Jacob (*Abr.* 50–52) (see Tiede 1972, 109–12).

Indeed, Philo (*Som.* 2.234) calls Moses the perfect (τέλειον) man, *neither G-d nor man*, on the borderline between the uncreated and the perishing form of being. He is different from those who preceded him (*Post.* 173), in that they are in the circle outside the holy places of G-d, like one seeking initiation into the mysteries, whereas he is spending his time in the inner sanctuary as a hierophant.

On the other hand, at one point, when Philo is discussing the qualifications of Moses to be the leader of the Israelites, he remarks (*Mos.* 1.158) that the joy of his partnership with the Father and Maker of all was also magnified by his being deemed worthy to be addressed in the same way (προσρήσεως τῆς αὐτῆς). Philo then actually and explicitly says that Moses was named god and king of the whole nation and entered into the darkness where G-d was, so that he beheld what ordinary mortals do not see; hence we must conclude that Moses is no ordinary mortal. Indeed, Moses in the Bible is depicted as having a very special relationship to G-d so that he is even referred to as "man of G-d" (Deut. 33:1, Josh. 14:6, Ezra 3:2, Ps. 90:1).

In *QE* 2.29 Philo, commenting on Exodus 24:2, "Moses alone shall come near to the L-rd, but the others shall not come near," remarks that the statement that Moses alone shall go up is said "most naturally" (φυσιώτατα), "for when the prophetic mind becomes divinely inspired and filled with G-d, it becomes like the monad, not being at all mixed with any of those things associated with duality. But he [i.e., Moses] who is resolved into the nature of unity is said to come near to G-d in a kind of family relation, for having given up and left behind all mortal kinds, he is changed into the divine, so that such men become akin to G-d and truly divine" (cited by Holladay 1977, 160–61). This is very similar to Philo's statement (*Mos.* 2.288) that when it came time for Moses to leave his mortal life for immortality, he was summoned by G-d, "Who resolved his twofold nature of soul and body into a single unity (εἰς μονάδος ἀνεστοιχείου φύσιν, "resolved the matter into the nature of a single element"), transforming his whole being into mind."

However, the fact that Philo says that when a prophet becomes inspired he becomes *like* a monad indicates that he is not a monad but only similar to a monad. In such a state he comes *near* to G-d. That he is *truly* divine indicates that he is not *actually* divine, since he is only *akin* to G-d. When a person dies, his matter is dissolved and he becomes all mind and thus is immortal, but there is no indication that he actually becomes G-d. Commenting on the verse (Exod. 24:12) "The L-rd said to Moses, 'Come up to Me on the mountain, and wait there,'" Philo (*QE* 2.40) says that this signifies that the holy soul is divinized[148] by ascending to a region above the heavens. "And beyond the world there is no place but G-d. . . . But those who do not return from the holy and divine city, to which they have migrated, have G-d as their chief leader in the migration." Again, the divinization that is spoken of here cannot refer to one's becoming G-d, since the passage refers to G-d as a separate entity, namely, as the *leader* in the migration. Rather, Philo is speaking here of the divinization of the soul, not of Moses himself.[149] Elsewhere Philo (*QG* 1.86) compares the translation of Moses, "for no one knew his burial-place," to that of Enoch and Elijah. He describes this as a movement "from a sensible and visible place to an incorporeal and intelligible form." This is Philo's way of describing the immortality of the soul; there is no indication that the soul becomes identified with G-d.

If Moses is not regarded by Philo as G-d, he is, nevertheless, spoken of by Philo as a friend of G-d. The biblical passage (Exod. 33:11, Deut. 34:10) reads that "the L-rd used to speak to Moses face to face, as a man speaks to his friend." Philo (*Mos.* 1.156) elaborates: "If, according to the proverb,[150] the possessions of friends are in common, and the prophet [i.e., Moses] has been called a friend of G-d, according to what follows, he would share His possessions, so far as is necessary," and would, in effect, be a world citizen. Moses speaks with frankness to G-d; and Philo (*Her.* 21) explains that since frankness of speech is akin to friendship, Moses is called the friend of G-d. Furthermore, Philo states (*Prob.* 44), though Moses was not deemed worthy of divine rank in his own right—here Philo clearly says that Moses is not to be regarded as G-d—that he was bound to be happy (εὐδαιμονεῖν) because he had G-d as his friend.[151] One is reminded that the title "friend" was bestowed by the emperor upon those who were nearest and dearest; thus it was bestowed by Caligula on Agrippa (*Legat.* 268, *Flacc.* 40).[152] As the friend of G-d, Moses (*Mos.* 1.155–57) was judged by G-d to be worthy to be a partner in His possessions and to be rewarded by being given the greatest and most perfect wealth so that all the elements should obey him and change their natural properties and submit to his command.[153] This explains why Moses was able to perform miracles (see Blackburn 1991, 68–69).

Furthermore, since Philo also stresses that Moses was human, we must note, as Helleman (1990, 60–61) does, that in commenting on the verse in G-d's covenant with Noah (Gen. 9:6) that "in the image of G-d He made man," Philo (*QG* 2.62) makes the remarkable statement that nothing mortal can be made in the likeness of G-d but only in that of the second G-d, that is, the Logos. Moses, as a mortal, would, then, not only not be G-d but would be further removed from G-d, being an image of an image.

Philo (*Ebr.* 94, *Mos.* 1.1) refers to Moses as most perfect (τελειότατος) of men and most perfect of the prophets (*Decal.* 175, τοῦ τελειοτάτου τῶν προφητῶν). Josephus (*A.J.* 3.180), in vehemently refuting the canard that Jews slight the divinity whom the pagans profess to venerate, maintains that if one looks at the construction of the tabernacle in the wilderness and the vessels used in the sacrificial system, he will discover that every one of these objects symbolically represents the universe and that "our lawgiver was a man of G-d (θεῖος ἀνήρ) and that the slanders that we hear from the others are unfounded."[154]

The mind of the wise man, says Philo (*Somn.* 2.229), is actually superior to men but less than G-d. Indeed, the good man is on the borderline between divinity and humanity. The high priest (*Somn.* 2.188–89) is less than G-d but superior to man. He is not a G-d because that name is assigned to Moses, who is called the G-d of Pharaoh (Exod. 7:1).

By contrast, the elevation of Moses to divine status seems to be implied in Philo, who remarks that Moses' associates, struck by his total asceticism and by the fact that he was so utterly unlike all men, pondered whether he was human or divine or a mixture of both (*Mos.* 1.27; cf. 2.291).

In the Bible (Exod. 25:8–9) G-d tells Moses that the Israelites are to make a sanctuary for Him like everything that He will show him concerning the form of the tabernacle.[155] Later (Exod. 31:2) G-d tells Moses that He has appointed Bezalel as the architect of the tabernacle to be constructed in the wilderness, and that He has endowed him and Oholiab with the wisdom to do all the work. Philo (*Leg.* 3.95) adds the extra-biblical remark that G-d made this appointment despite the fact that Bezalel had done no work that would have qualified him for such a task. Elsewhere (*Somn.* 1.206) Philo explains that whereas Bezalel was the chief builder, it was Moses who built the patterns, which, in effect, we may suggest, were Platonic-like Forms or Ideas.

Philo (*Mos.* 2.71, 74) explains that it was G-d Himself who set forth to Moses, while the latter was with Him on Mount Sinai, the principles of the construction of this tabernacle, that is, as Philo says, the immaterial forms of the material objects of the Tent about to be made.[156] Consequently, if Moses was not actually G-d, he was second to G-d, at least from a Platonic point of view, in that he built the Forms or Ideas of the tabernacle in the wilderness. Moses, says Philo (*Leg.* 3.102), is the artificer of the archetypes, whereas Bezalel is the artificer merely of the copies of these, since Moses' instructor is G-d Himself (Exod. 25:40), whereas Bezalel is instructed by Moses. With reference to the way in which he adorned the ark (*QE* 2.54), he is termed "the divine (and) holy Moses."

Moses, according to Philo (*Gig.* 54), is the one who has learned the secrets of the most holy mysteries (τελεταί) and who has become the hierophant and teacher of the divine secret rites (ὄργια), which he will teach to those whose ears have been purified. He is the one (*Mut.* 7) who entered into the darkness (Exod. 20:18), which Philo interprets to mean invisible and incorporeal existence, whereupon he searched everywhere in his desire to see G-d clearly. To be sure, Moses is referred to in the Bible (Deut. 33.1) as a man of G-d, which Philo (*Mut.* 125) says refers to Moses as praying and blessing the people.

We note the extraordinary description of Moses (*Mos.* 1.155) as a partner (κοινωνός) of G-d who was honored "by being deemed worthy to bear the same title. For he was named god and king of the whole nation, and entered, we are told, into the darkness where G-d was. . . . Thus he beheld what is hidden from the sight of mortal nature" (*Mos.* 1.158). This relationship between Moses and G-d, as Borgen (1997, 201) has remarked, is also used for persons who are partners of emperors, such as was true with Gaius Caligula and his cousin, Tiberius Gemellus (*Legat.* 23, 25, 28). According to Philo, Moses, as partner of G-d (*Mos.* 1.158), entered into the darkness where G-d was, "that is, into the unseen, invisible, incorporeal, and archetypal essence of existing things." Here Philo is combining the LXX's (Exod. 20:21) reference to the darkness where G-d was with the Platonic archetype or form. Elsewhere (*Mut.* 7) Philo states that Moses, the explorer of nature that lies beyond our vision, entered into darkness, that is the invisible and incorporeal existence of G-d, and searched everywhere in order to see Him clearly but was unsuccessful in his quest. However, Philo (*Post.* 14–15) remarks that the quest is not really in vain, in that Moses came to the realization that G-d is apprehensible by no one (see Wolfson 1947, 2:110–26).

Runia (1988, 49–75) objects that Philo depicts Moses not as G-d's cosmic vice-regent but rather as a Platonic-like philosopher-king and a Stoic-like citizen of the world (*Mos.* 1.157). In disagreeing with Runia, Borgen (1997, 203) notes that Philo goes so far as to say that G-d sent Moses as a loan to the earthly sphere and appointed him as G-d, subjecting the bodily region to him (*Sacr.* 9). In effect, Philo implies a contrast between Moses as the legitimate G-d-like king, the living and reasonable law (*Mos.* 1.162), and the Emperor Gaius Caligula as the counterfeit G-d, who regarded himself as the law but practiced lawlessness (*Legat.* 119) (so Meeks 1976, 43–67).

Nevertheless, in his portrayal of Moses, Philo, like Josephus, must have been faced with a number of problems. On the one hand, the Bible itself indicates that since Moses' time there had not arisen a prophet equal to him (Deut. 34:10).[157] However, Philo, like Josephus and the rabbis, must have been concerned that the figure of Moses should not be aggrandized to the point of deification. Philo, like Josephus, was, we may conjecture, especially careful not to do so because the Samaritans, the bitter enemies of the Jews in Philo's time, had built up the figure of Moses to the point where their religion was almost a Mosaism (MacDonald 1960, 149–62). We may also guess that he was reacting against the near deification of Moses as a "man of G-d" and as the most perfect of men (*Mos.* 1.1).[158]

Since, says Philo, a ruler is a model for his people, who emulate their leader, Moses, he says, in effect, by becoming the reasonable and living impersonation of law and by adopting a more severe and more serious rule of life, converted even the licentious to continence. Inasmuch as, according to the Bible (Exod. 7:1), G-d appointed Moses to be G-d to the Pharaoh, Philo remarks (*Sacr.* 9) that G-d is not susceptible to addition or diminution, and consequently no one knows Moses' grave (Deut. 34:6), for no human being has the power to perceive the passing of a perfect soul to G-d.

In sum, Philo carefully avoids referring to Moses as G-d by explaining the biblical passage Exod. 7:1 allegorically. He refers to Moses as the perfect man but, though he refers to Moses as "divine man," he insists that he was neither G-d nor man. The fact that he says that Moses came near to G-d indicates that he was not actually divine. Rather he was a friend and partner of G-d. Philo was reluctant to speak of Moses as divine, since this term was used of deified emperors. He was also reacting against the Samaritan near-deification of Moses.

(g) The Alleged Deification of Moses in Pseudo-Philo

Pseudo-Philo (19.16) would seem to be clearly combatting the view that Moses was deified, inasmuch as he says that Moses died and that G-d buried him as He had promised and that the angels mourned his death. However, there is a question as to the meaning of the Latin text: *mutata est effigies eius in gloria.* Does it mean that his appearance became glorious, or is *in gloria* the equivalent of *in gloriam*, that is, "his appearance was changed to a glorious state"? Or does it mean "in a glorious way"? Would "glorious state" imply divinity?

Moreover, at the end of this paragraph (19.16) there is an enigmatic statement that G-d buried Moses with His own hands in a high place *in lumine totius orbis.* Ginzberg (1928, 6:151–52, n. 904) understands this phrase as parallel to one in Ass. Mos. 1.15: "I am now going in the presence of all the people to meet with my fathers." That is to say, Pseudo-Philo meant that Moses did die and that G-d buried him in public. The sentiment would seem to be similar to that of Josephus (*A.J.* 4.326) in which Josephus seeks to combat the view that Moses had become deified. But, we may respond, if so, how, if Moses was buried in the open presence of all the Israelites, could the Bible (Deut. 34:6) assert that no one knows Moses' place of burial "until this day?" Hence, Jacobson (1996, 2:657–58) argues that *in lumine* is probably the common use of *in* plus the ablative for *in* plus the accusative. The meaning would then be that Moses became "a light for the entire world." Israel is so designated (Isaiah 42:6), as is Jesus (John 8:12), and as are Jesus' disciples (Matthew 5:14); Adam is so designated (*y. Shab.* 2.5b) as is Rabbi Johanan ben Zakkai (*'Abot R. Nat.* 25a) (see Jacobson 1996, 2:657–58). This would not necessarily mean that Moses was deified; rather, it might mean only that Moses' face continued to glow even after his death.[159]

Pseudo-Philo's reference to the death of Moses is unclear, but he does say that Moses died, and he is apparently thus combatting the view that Moses was deified.

(h) *Josephus' View of Moses' Alleged Divinity*

Josephus (*Ap.* 1.279) comments, though he does not give his source, that the Egyptians wished to regard Moses as remarkable (θαυμαστός), and even divine (θεῖος), and actually sought to claim him as one of their own. He clearly felt a need to counter this claim.

Josephus notes that Moses was held in such great admiration for his virtues and his charismatic ability to inspire faith in all his utterances that his words are alive to this day (*A.J.* 3.317). He remarks that Moses' legislation, being believed to come from G-d, has caused him to be ranked higher than his own human nature (*A.J.* 3.320). Even a pagan such as Celsus (*ap.* Origen, *Contra Celsum* 1.21) says that Moses acquired a reputation for divine power, presumably through his abilities as a magician. But in the very passages where Josephus refers to Moses as so inspiring and as ranking higher than his own nature he is careful to refer to him as a man (ἀνήρ) (*A.J.* 3.317, 320). He omits G-d's statements that Moses was to be to Aaron as G-d (Exod. 4:16) and that G-d was making him as G-d to Pharaoh (Exod. 7:1). He is careful to dispel the view held by some that when Moses tarried on Mount Sinai for forty days it was because he had been taken back to the divinity (*A.J.* 3.95–96). If he refers to Moses, as he does, as a "man of G-d" (θεῖος ἀνήρ) (*A.J.* 3.180), it is not to assert Moses' divinity but rather to refute those enemies of the Jews who had charged them with slighting the divinity whom they themselves professed to venerate (*A.J.* 3.179). That Josephus has no intention of asserting here that Moses was actually divine is clear from the proof that he gives of Moses being a "man of G-d," namely that the construction of the tabernacle and the appearance of the vestments and vessels of the priests show his concern for piety.

Josephus is explicit in stressing that Moses died and in refuting the notion that he was somehow elevated to divine status (*A.J.* 4.326).[160] Thus, whereas the Bible says simply that Moses died in the land of Moab (Deut. 34:5), Josephus explains why Scripture mentions this, stressing that Moses "has written of himself in the sacred books that he died, for fear lest they [the Israelites] should venture to say that by reason of his surpassing virtue he had gone back to the D-ity" (*A.J.* 4.326). Very significantly, Josephus does not include the biblical remarks that G-d Himself had buried Moses and that no one knows to this day where he is buried (Deut. 34:6), presumably because he realized that his skeptical readers might have considerable difficulty accepting such statements (see Tabor 1989, 237) and perhaps because the latter statement might indicate that the Torah was written after the time of Moses. He also attempts, more or less naturalistically, to give further details of Moses' disappearance, noting that while Moses was bidding farewell to Eleazar the high priest and Joshua his successor, a cloud suddenly descended upon him and he disappeared into a ravine. Such an account might well have reminded Gentile readers of the traditional version of the deaths of the two founders of the Romans, Aeneas and Romulus, as described by Dionysius of Halicarnassus, for example (Thackeray 1929, 57). In the case of Aeneas, Dionysius says that his body could nowhere be found, and some conjectured that he had been translated to the gods (*Ant. Rom.* 1.64.4). As to Romulus, he remarks that "the more mythical writers[161] say that as he was holding an assembly in the camp darkness descended upon him from a clear sky and he disappeared, and they believe that he was caught up by his father Ares" (*Ant. Rom.* 2.56.2). Josephus would thus seem to be underscoring the difference, to some degree, between Moses and these Roman forefathers in the way their lives ended.

To be sure, in Josephus' account of Moses' ascent on Mount Sinai, he hints that Moses ate heavenly food (*A.J.* 3.99), inasmuch as, whereas the biblical narrative states that Moses neither ate bread nor drank water during the forty days that he was on the mountain (Exod. 34:28), Josephus says that he tasted no food of the kinds designated for men (*A.J.* 3.99). The implication, according to Meeks (1967, 141), is that Moses partook of heavenly food, that is, that he drank nectar and ate ambrosia; but we may suggest that Josephus' concern was that his skeptical readers would wonder how a human being could subsist without any food or drink at all for forty days.

In particular, we may note that to the biblical account of Moses' death (Deut. 34:1–6) Josephus has added lamenting people, a walk to the mountain, companions on Moses' final walk, and "disappearance" (*A.J.* 4.323–26), details which are found in no other post-biblical source, though those sources recount Moses' last hours in far greater detail than does the Bible. Josephus may also be reacting to Sophocles' account of the mysterious disappearance of *Oedipus in Oedipus* at Colonus, which bears a striking resemblance to that of Moses in his presentation.[162]

In sum, though Josephus asserts that Moses' divinely given legislation caused him to be ranked higher than his own human nature, he is careful to refer to him as a man. Josephus is explicit in stressing that Moses died. He omits, however, the biblical statements that G-d buried Moses and that no one knows the place of his burial "to this day." Yet, Josephus' description of the death of Moses is strikingly similar to that of the disappearance of Aeneas and Romulus, who were deified.

(i) *The Divinity of Moses in the Rabbinic Tradition*

Meeks (1968, 355), noting that the Bible (Exod. 7:1) states that G-d told Moses that He had made him as G-d to Pharaoh, asks whence Philo came to connect this with Moses' kingship, and asks whence Philo derived the extra-biblical mystic ascent of Moses into heaven. In reply, Meeks points to a rabbinic tradition (*Tan.* 4.51–52 [ed. Solomon Buber]) that interprets the verse "He became a king in Jeshurun" (Deut. 33:5) to mean not that G-d became king over the Israelites but that G-d made Moses king, and that just as G-d the King is greeted with trumpets, so Moses will also be greeted. As to Moses' ascent to heaven, Meeks points to the rabbinic tradition (*Pesiq. Rabbati* 32.198b) that, commenting on the verse (Deut. 33:1) that refers to Moses as the "man of G-d," states that when he ascended on high he was a man, but that when he descended below he was "G-d."

Indeed, according to one rabbinic tradition Moses did not die but rather continued to guide the people from above (*b. Soṭ.* 13b, *Sifre Deut.* 357, *Midr. Tannaim* 224). See Ginzberg (1928, 6:163–64, n. 452). The *Palaea Historia* (Vassiliev

1893, 257–58; see Flusser 1971, 72), recounts a tradition that when Moses died alone on the mountain, Samael the devil tried to bring his body down to the people so that they might worship him as a god. G-d then commanded the archangel Michael to take Moses' body away. Samael objected and they quarreled, whereupon Michael was vexed and rebuked the devil.

And yet, perhaps in response to the divinization of Jesus in Christianity and the quasi-divinization of Moses in the Samaritan tradition, the rabbis insisted that Moses was human and had human failings (see Jacobs 1971, 393–95). To make sure that Moses, after his death, would not be worshipped, the *Midr. Lekaḥ Tov* on Deut. 34:6 states that the reason why the grave of Moses was concealed was so that the Israelites should not turn it into a sanctuary and so that the non-Jews should not turn it into a place of idolatrous worship.

Moreover, the Mishnah (*Rosh Ha-Sh.* 3:8), commenting on the verse (Exod. 17:11) "Whenever Moses held up his hand, Israel prevailed; and whenever he lowered his hand, Amalek prevailed," clearly diminishes Moses' status by asking, "Now do Moses' hands make war or stop it?" and explains, "So long as the Israelites would set their eyes upward and submit their hearts to their Father in heaven, they would grow stronger, and if not, they fell." Again, when the Israelites built and were worshipping the Golden Calf, G-d told Moses, who was then with G-d obtaining the Torah, to go down. The second-century Rabbi Eleazar (*b. Ber.* 32a) explains that G-d rebuked Moses: "Descend from your greatness. Have I at all given to you greatness save for the sake of Israel? And now that Israel has sinned, why do I want you?" Thereupon Moses is said to have had no strength to speak.

Moreover, according to the second-century Rabbi Jose (*b. Sanh.* 21b), Moses was really not unique, in that if Moses had not preceded Ezra, Ezra would have been worthy of receiving the Torah. Finally, Moses is criticized for his quick temper (*b. Pes.* 66b) when he was angry with the commanders of his army (Num. 31:14), whereupon, according to the third-century Resh Laqish, Moses forgot his own Torah. That Moses is not omniscient in his own Torah may be seen from the scenario in which, when Moses went up on Mount Sinai to receive the Torah, he is shown Rabbi Akiva expounding the Torah, but he is not able to follow Rabbi Akiva's discourse. The rabbis also stress Moses' sin of striking the rock (Num. 20:11) when he had been told to speak to the rock (*Sifre Deut.* 26, *Midr. Num. Rabbah* 19.12).

Moreover, even the quality of humility, which is Moses' supreme virtue according to the Bible (Num. 12:3), is questioned by the rabbis (*'Abot R. Nat.*

9, p. 41 [ed. Schechter]), who ask, "Was he perhaps more meek than the ministering angels? The verse (Num. 12:3) says, 'More so than all men': more than men, it is said, but not more than the generations of old? The verse says (*ibid.*), 'Upon the face of the earth': more than his own generation, it is said, but not more than the generations of old."

Goldin (1953, 278–79) calls attention to a dispute between Rabbi Yose the Galilean and Rabbi Akiva (*'Abot R. Nat.* 1 [ed. Schechter]) which centered on whether the figure of Moses might be magnified beyond human proportions. According to Rabbi Yose, when Moses received the Torah at Sinai the cloud sent by G-d covered him for six days in order to purify him. According to Rabbi Akiva, the cloud covered the mountain but not Moses, and on the seventh day G-d called out to Moses as an honor to Moses. According to him, honoring is a special distinction but not the same thing as an extraordinary purification, which borders on receiving a superhuman role. Moreover, there is a tradition (*Mek. Pisḥa* 1 [ed. Lauterbach, 1.13], *Sifra* [ed. Weiss, 4a], *Yalkut* Exod. 187) (cited by Goldin 1953, 279, n. 6) that definitely deflates the stature of Moses, namely, that there was a period of some 38 years during which G-d did not speak with Moses while he was leading the Israelites in the desert, since He was angry with the Israelites.

Surely the fact that in the Haggadah that is recited at the Passover Seder the name of Moses, who most certainly would appear to be the hero of the whole narrative of the liberation of the Israelites from slavery in Egypt, appears only once would indicate the fear of the rabbis that if they had given more attention to Moses this might lead to his being regarded as divine and G-d's role would be diminished.[163] Moreover, in the central prayer in Judaism, the *Amidah*, consisting of nineteen benedictions, there is mention of Abraham, Isaac, Jacob, and David but no mention at all of Moses. Furthermore, the opening of the *Amidah* addresses G-d as the G-d of Abraham, Isaac, and Jacob, all of whom lived before the revelation at Sinai, and does not address G-d as the G-d of Moses. Presumably, the rabbis, who are responsible for these prayers, wished to stress that Israel has been redeemed and will be redeemed by G-d alone. Perhaps this is intended to counter the way in which Christians pray to G-d through Jesus.

Moreover, despite their admiration for Moses, the rabbis (*b. Ber.* 3b) make a point of remarking that he was not omniscient. Thus some of them note that Moses did not know the exact time of midnight, and they supply proof from the fact that Moses quotes G-d as saying (Exod. 11:4) that at *about* midnight He would go out in the midst of Egypt. G-d, they say, could not have been in doubt as to when He would go; hence, it must be that it was Moses who was in doubt.

In sum, the rabbis are somewhat ambivalent with regard to the divinization of Moses. On the one hand, they say that he was a man when he ascended on high but that he was G-d when he descended. Indeed, according to one tradition, he guided the Israelites from above even after his death. Yet, they emphasize that the reason why his grave was concealed was so that it should not be made into a sanctuary. The fact that Moses might be worshipped may have influenced the rabbis to omit mention of Moses from the central prayer of Judaism, the *Amidah*.

(j) The Alleged Divinity of Moses in the Samaritan Tradition

As we have noted, Moses has a unique position in the Samaritan creed. Indeed, as Purvis (1973, 93) remarks, in many respects his role corresponds to that of Jesus in Christianity and of Mohammed in Islam. There can be no doubt that in the Samaritan tradition, as in the rabbinic tradition, Moses is regarded as being preeminent among the prophets and as the preeminent mediator between G-d and men (see Meeks 1967, 220–21).

But the Samaritans go beyond this in their view of Moses. The *Molad* (Arabic version, p. 15, l. 3), which is read by Samaritans on every festive occasion, compiled by unknown authors in the early Middle Ages but apparently containing more ancient traditions, and reedited in an Arabic version by Ismạil ibn Badr ibn Abu ̣lAziz al-Rumayḥi (Stenhouse 1993, 159), actually equates the light that G-d created on the first day of creation with Moses. It does so through the form of exegesis that the rabbis[164] refer to as *gezerah shavah* thus: according to the Bible (Exod. 2:2), Jochebed, Moses' mother, saw him (Moses), that he was good; similarly, in the account of creation (Gen. 1:4), G-d saw the light, that it was good. Since both light and Moses are referred to as good, therefore the light was Moses, and the world was created for his sake. Hence, Moses is the creation of G-d, in the same way that the Christians viewed Jesus as the creation of G-d. Moses, in effect, is thus like the Logos that G-d created and is thus a second G-d. Moses, according to this passage in *Molad*, was thus created before all the creatures of creation, including Adam; and all the lights, great and small, derive their light from his light. This light was transmitted to every prophet and saint in accordance with the degree of his constancy, until it was incarnated in the person of Moses. The supreme moment of revelation came when G-d revealed the Torah to Moses, whom the *Molad* (p. 16, l. 12) refers to as "the exalted, the perfect, the perfected." The fact that he is referred to as "the pattern" would appear to equate him with the equivalent of a Platonic form. Moses is thus the beginning and end of all prophecy. By this light Moses knew what was hidden under symbols and enigmas. The rabbis (*b. Soṭ.* 12a) also draw an analogy between the mention of light in Genesis 1:4 and Exodus 2:2, but, most significantly, they do not go so far as to identify the light with Moses; rather, they say, when Moses was born the whole house was filled with light.

That Moses is the apostle of G-d (*Memar* 1.9) would seem to be nothing more than what is stated in the Bible (Exod. 3:13, 4:28), namely that he had been sent by G-d. But for the Samaritans he is more than G-d's messenger. After the statement that Moses is the true prophet sent by G-d we read (*Memar* 4.8): "Blessed are they who believe in him. Let us love him and keep his commandments, that our L-rd may love us and send us deliverance." There is an ambiguity in that "him" might refer to Moses or to G-d; but, as Meeks (1967, 227, n. 2) remarks, it is more likely, in view of the sentence immediately preceding, which speaks of Moses as the true prophet sent by G-d, that "him" refers to Moses in light of the Samaritan doctrine (*Memar* 4.7) that to believe in Moses is to believe in G-d. Indeed, according to the *Memar* (ibid.), if one believes in Moses one will be safe from all wrath in the final Day of Vengeance.

That the Samaritans have a belief in the divinization of Moses would seem to be implied by the portrayal of Moses as vested with the name of G-d and as dwelling in the mysteries and as crowned with light (*Memar* 2.12). The Samaritan tradition describes him as clothed in a robe of light, as we find the Messiah is to be. We read (ibid.) that the True One, that is, G-d, was revealed to Moses, that G-d gave him His handwriting, and that G-d made him drink from ten glorious fountains. Indeed, Moses' ascent of Mount Sinai is viewed as an enthronement in heaven. There he is said to have been entrusted with secrets from G-d that ensured life for humans. A Samaritan hymn[165] describes Moses' coronation in heaven, hidden in a cloud, clothed in a garment in which no king is able to be clothed, and his face emitting a beam of light. Moses is described as a second G-d and as the G-d of the lower world (*Memar* 1.2). Commenting on G-d's statement that He has made Moses a god to Pharaoh (Exod. 7:1), the *Memar* states that He has vested him with G-d's name. As Meeks (1967, 235–36) concludes, the fact that Moses receives the name "G-d" is equivalent to becoming the divine king on earth. In the Samaritan tradition (*Molad* [p. 39, ll. 2–3]) the angels proclaim that Moses is the master of the human race and the defender of the true religion (*Molad* [p. 40, l. 3]).

The Samaritan tradition (*Memar* 2.12) likewise stresses the significance of the fact that the biblical statement (Exod. 7:1) in which G-d tells Moses that He has made him as G-d to Pharaoh employs the word אלקים for G-d, the name by which G-d revealed Himself to Moses and the name by which Moses is known as "the man of G-d" (איש האלקים) (Deut. 33:1). Furthermore, as Meeks (1968, 361–62)[166] points out, the radiant skin of Moses' face as he descended from Mount Sinai (Exod. 34:29) is identified as a crown of light, signifying divinity in some sense in rabbinic and Samaritan tradition. Indeed, Meeks suggests that the stories of Moses' heavenly enthronement may have laid the foundation for an eschatological ideology. He notes that in the apocalyptic genre the ascension of the prophet in whose name the book is written is an almost invariable introduction to the description of the secrets that he saw (Meeks 1968, 366–67). In effect, as Meeks (1967, 110–11; and 1968, 354–59)[167] has suggested, Moses attains an intermediate status as G-d's vicegerent between G-d and the rest of men.

In the Bible (Exod. 33:18), when Moses asks G-d to show him His glory, G-d declines and tells him that He will show favor when He chooses to show favor. In the Samaritan tradition (*Molad* [p. 54, ll. 8–14]) He explains to Moses all the secrets of creation.

The Samaritans looked upon Moses as the most perfect of men, without any blemish at all, whether physical or moral, a priest among angels, one for whose sake the very world had been created (see Gaster 1927, 75). Far from being the amanuensis that he seems to be in the rabbinic tradition, Moses is termed by the Samaritans the light of knowledge and understanding, whose ascent to Mount Sinai is said to have taken him to the very heart of heaven (see MacDonald 1960, 153–54). In addition to the laws intended for ordinary mankind he received esoteric knowledge to be transmitted solely to men of deep spiritual insight. It is Moses who, on G-d's behalf or acting as spokesman for G-d, pronounced the creative words, "Let there be light." He, unlike all other creatures, is said to have been in existence prior to the initial creation process; and, indeed, like the Jesus of the Fourth Gospel, he was created in order to function as G-d's creative agent. He is the great intercessor, and only through him can prayer be accepted.

Moreover, for the Samaritans Moses is the Taheb ("Restorer"), the expected Messiah-like eschatological figure who will bring about a golden age and will pray for the guilty and save them. The Samaritans alone give prominence to the title "man of G-d" for Moses; and, indeed, their depiction of Moses is highly reminiscent of the New Testament's description of Jesus as the first begotten being, whose preexistent bodiless state subsequently takes on matter. Moses is a second G-d, G-d's vice-regent upon earth (*Memar* 1.2), whose very name includes the title "Elokim" (G-d) (*Memar* 5.4), so that he who believes in him believes in his L-rd (*Memar* 4.7). See Holladay 1977 101, n. 344, who cites the Samaritan *Memar* 6.6. So prominent is Moses for the Samaritans that we hear that an unnamed man was able to gather a large following by promising that he would show them the sacred implements buried on Mount Gerizim by Moses (*A.J.* 18.85). What is particularly striking in this connection is that Moses could not possibly have buried the vessels there, inasmuch as he never entered the Land of Israel, as Meeks (1967, 248) remarks. Indeed, this exaltation of Moses, as MacDonald 1960, 149–62, has remarked, is a unique Samaritan doctrine, without parallel in Jewish, Christian, or Moslem belief.

In sum, the Samaritan tradition goes beyond the rabbis and actually equates the light that G-d created on the first day of creation with Moses, who thus emerges as a second G-d, as a Platonic Form, and as the G-d of the lower world. He dwells in the mysteries, that is, in heaven, and is crowned with light. G-d explains to him all the secrets of creation. In the light of the tremendous antagonism between the Samaritans and the Jews throughout the Hellenistic and Roman periods, it would appear that Philo, Pseudo-Philo, Josephus, and the rabbis all seek to distance themselves from the extreme Samaritan position with regard to Moses. In the case of Philo, who has such a high admiration for the LXX (*Mos.* 2.25–44), the fact that there were quarrels (Josephus, *A.J.* 12.10) between the Jews and the Samaritans from the beginning of the Ptolemies and that the two parties appealed to Ptolemy Philadelphus to establish their superiority over the other as the true Scriptures (see Hadas 1951, 67–68; Jellicoe 1968, 63–64) might well have influenced Philo to express more strongly his opposition to the divinization of Moses.

IV. Conclusion

Moses is the one figure in the Jewish tradition who was well known to the non-Jewish world, as we can see from the relatively large number of references to him in non-Jewish literature. The fact that the author of Pseudo-Longinus' *On the Sublime* does not even need to identify "the lawgiver of the Jews" would indicate that the reader was expected to know who he was. However, Philo is aware that Moses has been misunderstood and insufficiently appreciated by non-Jews. Philo was confronted with added problems in defending the reputation of Moses, namely, that the Bible itself presents data about him that would appear to be less than complimentary, and that some of the practices that he transmitted were viewed as misanthropic by even those who viewed the Jews favorably.

The fact that a leader of these attacks on Moses was an outstanding Homeric scholar and intellectual, Apion, meant that Philo had the crucial task of refuting these charges, even though he does not mention Apion by name. He thus undertakes a mission, notably in his quasi-official biography of Moses, *De Vita Mosis*, the first known biography of Moses that has come down to us, to correct these misunderstandings. He is particularly concerned to do so because Moses was born in Egypt, where Philo was a leader of the Jewish community. In this essay, which as a biography merits comparison with Plutarch's lives, in that a major goal is to present to his readers a person on which they may model their lives, he mentions almost no other biblical figures by name, so as to focus almost completely on Moses. Indeed, amazingly enough, he does not, in this essay, extensive as it is, mention by name Moses' father Amram, his mother Jochebed, his sister Miriam, his brother Aaron, his adoptive mother the Egyptian princess, his father-in-law Jethro, and his major rival Korah. Unlike most of his other essays, including his biographies of Abraham and Joseph, which focus so heavily on allegorical and symbolic explanations, this essay introduces symbolism only in such instances as Philo's explanation of the tabernacle and of the vestments of the high priest.

That *Mos.* was intended primarily for a non-Jewish audience seems likely from Philo's statement that he hopes to bring the story of Moses to the attention of those who deserve not to be ignorant of it. The fact that the biography has a considerable digression, which is not directly relevant to the account of the life of Moses, relating the story of the translation of the Pentateuch into Greek, indicates that a major goal of the essay is to call attention to the annual celebration of the completion of this translation and to the contents of the Pentateuch as promulgated through Moses. Just as that translation was done because a non-Jewish king was interested in having this greatest of Jewish works for his library, so according to Philo, Jews and non-Jews continue every year, by assembling to commemorate this event, to manifest their admiration for this work and for the great lawgiver who transmitted it. Philo proudly states that these celebrations occur in the presence of Jews and "multitudes of others," that is, non-Jews, in the confidence that the non-Jews will abandon their peculiar ways and "turn to honoring our laws alone." Another indication that he is addressing non-Jews is that he digresses to compare the laws of Moses with all the other laws that have ever arisen among the Greeks and barbarians in all other countries.

In view of the apparent eagerness with which Jews welcomed non-Jews to Judaism during this period, one of the goals of an essay such as *Mos.* may very well have been to call the attention of non-Jews to the greatness of the code of law issued by the Jews' great lawgiver. In a society that placed a tremendous weight on antiquity, Philo stresses that Moses was the most ancient of lawgivers. In an era when mystery cults were attracting many, he declares that Moses himself saw elements of a mysticism in Judaism.

Philo presents, in effect, an aretalogy, similar to that of mythical divine and heroic figures, glorifying the birth, education, and virtues of Moses. In an encomium a writer was permitted, by the standards of ancient rhetoric and by the precedent of biographies in both the Isocratean and Aristotelian schools, to take certain liberties that one would not be permitted to take in a general history. However, unlike his other essays, including his biographies of Abraham and Joseph, Philo in *Mos.* almost completely avoids allegory except where a literal interpretation would puzzle the reader. Moreover, unlike Josephus, who in the introduction to his *A.J.* (1.17) declares that he has not added to or subtracted from anything in the scriptural account, Philo restricts this to the legal portions of the Pentateuch. He declares that he will adhere to what is written in the Bible, complemented by what he has heard from the elders, that is the oral tradition, apparently that which was known in Palestine. In addition, Philo is forever careful to explain in a scientific way those portions of the

Bible, particularly miracles, that would appear to be incredible to his skeptical intelligent readers.

Book 1 of *Mos.* is a factual history, Plutarchian in style, while Book 2 is a biography, Suetonian in style, systematically ordered and concentrating on Moses' virtues.

Philo is aware that Moses was compared with several other lawgivers, such as Lycurgus, in antiquity; and he insists that Moses is, indeed, unique among them, in that his laws have remained unshaken. He is even ready to consider the possibility (*Hypoth.* 6.9) that Moses arrived at these laws by his own reasoning, but asserts that the Israelites claim that he derived them from G-d. In any case, he views Moses as primarily a legislator and only secondarily as an interpreter of the laws. He stresses that these laws are honored by almost all other peoples. Throughout his work Philo has in mind a comparison with the greatest and most influential political treatise of the Greeks, Plato's *Republic*; and he stresses that whereas in this work Plato first described an ideal state and then prescribed the laws to govern that state, Moses started by exhorting the Israelites and then codifying the constitution to govern them.

In dealing with the Bible Philo's purpose is to present not a paraphrase but rather an analysis. Thus he presents the plagues inflicted upon the Egyptians in an order different from that in the Bible. His reclassified order takes into account his analysis of the elements—earth, water, air, and fire—and the agents—Aaron, Moses, the two together, and G-d—through whom the plagues were carried out.

In the relatively few places where Philo makes changes in the biblical narrative, he does so to respond to logical objections that readers might make. Thus, the reader might well wonder why the Pharaoh would enslave the Israelites and then order that male babies should be put to death, since a slave owner would normally be interested in increasing the number of his slaves; and if he were interested in decreasing their number he would accomplish his goal more readily by putting female babies to death. Hence, Philo rearranges the order: first the Pharaoh orders the male babies to be put to death, and then he enslaves the Israelites. Again, the Bible finds the cause of the Pharaoh's edict in his fear that the Israelites would join the enemies of the Egyptians and leave the country. But, as Philo must have realized, getting rid of such people would not be such a terrible thing from an Egyptian point of view. Rather, as Philo puts it, the fear was that the Israelites would join with the enemies of the Egyptians and try to overthrow their regime.

A good example of the difference in the way that Philo and Josephus deal with a troublesome biblical passage is their treatment of the fact that the Pharaoh appointed two Israelite women to carry out his decree to drown the male babies of the Israelites. The reader might well ask how two women could carry out such a huge task in view of the tremendous population of the Israelites. Moreover, why would the Pharaoh entrust this task to Israelites rather than to Egyptians? Josephus solves this problem by stating that the task was entrusted to two Egyptian women. Philo, aware that his readers, like Pseudo-Longinus, might well consult the LXX, says nothing about this at all in *Mos.*

A good example of the different ways in which Philo, Pseudo-Philo, Josephus, and the Samaritans deal with a tradition is their treatment of the view, found in Pseudo-Philo (9.7), according to which G-d expresses pleasure with Amram's decision to resume having sexual relations with his wife and, placing the focus solely on G-d, predicts that He, G-d, will perform signs and wonders through him. In Josephus' version (*A.J.* 2.216) G-d appears to Amram in a dream and, placing the focus on Moses, declares that the child to be born to him will deliver the Israelites from slavery and that he, Moses, will be remembered forever not only by Israelites, but also by non-Israelites. In the Samaritan tradition, when the time was approaching for Moses to be born, an Egyptian astrologer predicts that Amram will become the father of a famous child who will bring about the destruction of Egypt and will rescue the Israelites. Philo, though agreeing with Josephus' point of view in aggrandizing Moses' achievements, apparently felt that his sophisticated readers would have difficulty accepting a vision in which G-d appeared to Amram, and so he does not mention this tradition at all and proceeds to tell the story as it is found in the Pentateuch.

A clue to the difference in approach of Philo, the Samaritans, and the rabbis is in their treatment of the tradition that Israelite women had multiple births. The Samaritan view is that the Israelites had two or three or even four children at one time. The rabbis declare that they bore as many as six or twelve or even sixty or seventy children at one time. Philo, who specifically says that he had access to one of the traditions of "the elders of the nation," says nothing about this and instead focuses on the one child, Moses.

Unlike the rabbinic and Samaritan traditions, Philo, like the tragedian Ezekiel, minimizes or rationalizes the miraculous elements in connection with Moses' birth. In deference to his sophisticated non-Jewish audience he makes relatively few references to G-d in interpreting coincidences, as, for example, the fact that the Pharaoh's daughter just happened to be at the river when Moses was floating in the basket; or he presents an explanation as his own opinion, in effect inviting the reader to draw his own conclusion. Where the Bible has the Egyptian princess, rather improbably, deriving the name of Moses from Hebrew, Philo has her derive the name from the Egyptian word for "water."

In line with Plato's view in the *Republic* that a philosopher-king should, if at all possible, be handsome, Philo describes Moses as very beautiful both at birth and as an adult when he descended from Mount Sinai. He avoids, however, such comments as that of the rabbis comparing his beauty to that of an angel, or that of the Samaritan tradition that the sun was eclipsed by his light, or that of Josephus that people left aside their serious affairs in order to view him.

The greatest changes from the biblical narrative are to be found in Philo's account of Moses' education. The reason for this, we may suggest, is that education meant so much to Philo himself. Moses is said to have had Egyptian teachers in mathematics, music, philosophy, and even to have been taught the regard for animals that the Egyptians had. Most remarkably, teachers were imported from Greece to teach him the liberal arts, the very curriculum that Plato prescribes for the higher education of the philosopher-kings in his *Republic*—notably grammar, geometry, astronomy, rhetoric, and music—and which, most likely, reflects Philo's own education. Moreover, in an allusion to Plato's theory of recollection, Moses is said to have given the impression of recalling what he had not yet been taught. His precociousness was such that he seemed to devise problems that were difficult to understand.

Where Philo does add to the biblical narrative he does so to paint psychological portraits, perhaps under the influence of the tragedians, notably Euripides, with whose works he was so well acquainted. He realized that a sensitive reader would wonder how Moses balanced his feelings toward his biological parents with his feelings toward his adoptive family. Whereas the Bible and Josephus are silent, Philo, keenly aware of human issues, comments that he showed profound affection toward the former and gratitude toward the latter.

Josephus omits the account of Moses' slaying of the Egyptian overseer, since he is apparently embarrassed by the idea that Moses took the law into his own hands. Philo, however, who seeks, wherever possible, to adhere to the biblical text, includes it, but justifies it by stressing that the Egyptian had persecuted the Hebrews to the point of death. However, like Josephus, he omits the account of the two Israelites fighting, presumably since such an account would not redound to the credit of the Israelites. During this period, despite the fact that Moses was heir to enormous wealth and to the very rulership of Egypt, he is said to have maintained his deep devotion to the culture of his kinsmen. In answer to the apparent objection as to why Moses did not do more to help his brethren, Philo stresses that Moses did what he could, especially in helping the morale of the Israelites.

Though one of the characteristics of a great hero is often that he is wealthy, Moses, despite the fact that he possessed enormous wealth as heir apparent to the throne of Egypt, was not extravagant in dress or food and was concerned only with the welfare of his people. Since Philo himself was a member of an extremely wealthy family, such a statement presumably reflects his attitude toward the proper use of wealth.

A good example of the difference between Philo's treatment of the same incident in *Mos.* and in his other treatises may be seen in the way he deals with Moses' escape from Egypt to Midian. Philo realized the problem of explaining how Moses could have abandoned his fellow Israelites who were suffering so much. In *Leg.* 3.14 Philo explains allegorically that his conflict with the Pharaoh was not with the Pharaoh, but with the passions, and that he did not flee, but rather withdrew temporarily like an athlete to regain his breath so as to renew the attack later with greater power. In *Mos.* 1.45, on the other hand, Philo does not mention the allegorical explanation at all, but rather presents two extra-biblical (and, under the circumstances, highly credible) factors that led Moses to leave Egypt, namely the Pharaoh's anger that his own daughter's son utterly disagreed with him and the malicious suggestions from every side that Moses intended to seize the sovereignty from the Pharoah.

Philo stresses that during the long interval that Moses was in Midian, he was mastering philosophy. Philo expands greatly the biblical account of Moses' aid, in his ecstatic concern for justice, to the daughters of Jethro. In not mentioning by name Jethro or Zipporah, Jethro's daughter and Moses' wife, he keeps the focus on Moses alone. As a shepherd taking care of Jethro's flock Moses is said to have received lessons in leadership.

As to the incident of the burning bush, Moses had too much faith to be frightened by it. However, realizing that his audience might be skeptical of the miracle, Philo states that Moses saw not an image of G-d, but a G-dlike vision. As for the miracle that the bush was not consumed, Philo, in a rare resort to allegory in *Mos.*, in agreement with rabbinic tradition, asserts that the burning bush symbolized the oppressed Israelites. Moreover, whereas in the Bible G-d says that He will rescue the Israelites, in Philo's version G-d says that He will take part with Moses, clearly implying that Moses is to be the leader. Indeed, Philo, always concerned to present Moses as the ideal leader, omits Moses' self-doubt.

As a sign to convince the Israelites that he supported Moses, G-d tells Moses that he should put his hand into his bosom and that it would become leprous, whereupon he should do so again and his hand would be restored. Philo, like Josephus, is apparently aware of the charge that Moses was a leper; and so he states merely that when he put his hand into his bosom it became whiter than snow. As to Moses' attempt to decline the role of leadership because of his speech defect, Philo, realizing that in antiquity eloquence of speech was regarded as a prerequisite for leadership, offers two extra-biblical explanations: that Moses was speechless, apparently out of sheer shock, since he heard G-d speaking to him, and that he considered human eloquence to be dumbness and false sophistry as compared with G-d's.

One of the most embarrassing incidents is Moses' life is his failure to circumcise his son; but the apologetic Philo, like Josephus, omits this episode.

In explaining Moses' request to the Pharaoh that the Israelites be permitted to go into the wilderness to offer their sacrifices, Philo says that Moses states that the customs of the Israelites run counter to those of other people; he thus recognizes the legitimacy of the Egyptian cult while maintaining the uniqueness of the sacred quality of Jewish worship. Inasmuch as it would indicate a lack of faith in his mission, Philo significantly omits Moses' argument that if the Israelies have not listened to him, how can G-d expect that the Pharaoh will listen to him, in view of his speech defect.

Moses' stature is heightened by the fact that G-d entrusts to Aaron the three plagues belonging to the denser elements, whereas He entrusts to Moses the three plagues belonging to air and fire, the forces most productive of life. Philo makes every effort to explain the plagues scientifically. As to how Moses knew so much that he was able to compete with the Egyptian magicians, Philo explains that he did so merely in order to refute them. There is no statement in Philo that Moses during the final plague left in burning anger, presumably because a leader must exercise greater self-control. Moreover, Philo (*Mos.* 1.140–42) must have been aware of the charge that in borrowing from the

Egyptians, with no apparent intention to repay the loan, the Israelites had been instructed by Moses to steal. Consequently, he defends their action by asserting that they were retaliating for their enslavement. Josephus, typically, in contrast, omits reference to this charge.

Philo, sensitive to his relations with non-Jews, omits the commandment to eradicate the seven nations of Canaan, presumably because he felt so strongly that it was wrong to condemn the innocent with the guilty and because he found it inconsistent with his tolerance toward non-Jewish religions (*Spec.* 1.53).

In his dealings with the Pharaoh, Moses emulates the merciful power of G-d. Moreover, it is Moses, rather than G-d, who takes the initiative in decision-making. In a work intended primarily for non-Jews, in order to answer the charges of those who sought to malign Moses, Philo presents Moses as a role model reminiscent of Plato's philosopher-king and Thucydides' ideal statesman, Pericles, with undoubted ability as a general, but with less emphasis on this quality and more on his ability to inspire a difficult and rebellious motley multitude.

In elaborating on the qualifications of Moses as a leader, Philo expands on the sheer number of the Israelites and on Moses' ability to unite such a motley crew, a "bastard host," that included the mixed multitude, and on his skill in persuasion. Since some of them were proselytes, he emerges as a leader of actual converts to Judaism. He shows his ability in keeping the Israelites free from factionalism. In the Bible (Exod. 13:17–18) it is G-d who makes the decision not to lead the Israelites by the nearer route through the land of the Philistines, whereas Philo, always concerned to elevate the role of Moses as leader, says that it was Moses who made the decision, after democratically receiving the Israelites' and G-d's consent. Philo then explains why Moses led the Israelites by a roundabout route to Canaan, namely to test their loyalty and to separate the Israelites from the temptations of urban life, perhaps an allusion to contemporary conditions in Alexandria.

It is not G-d but Moses who tells the Israelites where to encamp. Philo, perhaps drawing upon his own experience as a leader of the Alexandrian Jewish community, stresses the Stoic-like patience of Moses by expanding on the bitterness with which the difficult, grumbling, despairing Israelites complained during the sojourn. Philo amplifies Moses' ability to understand the weakness of his people and to sympathize with them. One reason why G-d sends the manna is His desire to honor Moses.

Philo, in effect, puts G-d's reassuring words into the mouth of Moses at the Sea of Reeds; and it is Moses, rather than G-d, who prophesies the annihilation of the Pharaoh's army. For Pseudo-Philo, the miracle is all G-d's doing. To Philo it is an occasion for Moses to display his supreme gift of leadership and, above all, of prophecy. The miracles are sent not on G-d's, but on Moses', initiative. Josephus, the military man, paints the encounter as a battle. Josephus' Moses beseeches G-d as an ally; Philo's Moses does not address G-d, but rather becomes prophetically possessed.

Moses' greatest sin, according to rabbinic tradition, was in smiting the rock at Meribah instead of speaking to it, as G-d had instructed him (Num. 20:8). As punishment he was not permitted by G-d to enter Canaan. Such an incident casts aspersions on Moses' reputation for faith. Consequently, as closely as Philo usually adheres to the biblical text, he omits this completely.

Significantly, Philo refers to the Israelites as Moses' army. Moses himself takes the lead in mustering his men of military age and plays a more important part in the fight against Amalek. What is most striking is that although the battle with Amalek was the key battle during the sojourn in the wilderness, Philo never mentions the name of Amalek at all, so important is it for him to keep the focus on Moses. In place of the weak, old leader who is hardly able to hold up his hands (Exod. 17:12), Philo's Moses is more vigorous and runs to the task of organizing his people militarily, though, in general, he places much less stress than does Josephus on Moses' military ability.

Philo omits in *Mos.* Jethro's advice to Moses with regard to organization since it would seem to detract from Moses' administrative ability. He omits in *Mos.*, where he centers on the personality and achievements of Moses, an account of the revelation at Sinai, which was the work of G-d. He answers the charge of nepotism in Moses' appointment of Aaron as high priest by stressing that Moses did not appoint his own sons to that position.

An instructive example of Philo's handling of a biblical episode that presented problems to him may be seen in how he views the incident of the Golden Calf, as compared with the treatment by Pseudo-Philo and Josephus. The Bible (Exod. 32:19–20) states that when Moses came down with the tablets at Mount Sinai and found the Israelites worshipping the Golden Calf, he shattered the tablets, ground the Golden Calf to a fine powder, sprinkled it with water, and forced the people to drink it. Josephus, apparently because he found the incident embarrassing, omits it; but Philo, who, as we have noted, generally remains close to the biblical narrative, includes it. However, because he keeps stressing Moses' self-control, he found such a burst of temper unbecoming for a leader. A very significant point is that Philo, as a leader of the Jewish community in Egypt, uses this incident, in effect, to condemn Jews of his own day who were attracted to the Egyptian way of life. Whereas in some other treatises he refers to the animal as a calf, in *Mos.* he terms it a bull (ταῦρος), which, he says, was in imitation of the animal, Apis, that is the one held most sacred in Egypt.

As to G-d's determination to exterminate the Israelites and to start a new people with Moses, and as to Moses' colloquy with G-d succeeding in getting G-d to change His mind, this is embarrassing because it depicts G-d as being less merciful than Moses in not separating the guilty from the innocent. Indeed, His changing His mind presented considerable theological problems. It is actually reminiscent of Abraham's argument with G-d in connection with the wickedness of the Sodomites. In his essay *Quis rerum divinarum heres sit* Philo says that Moses was on such close terms with G-d that he could afford to be frank with Him. However, in *Mos.*, in what is, in effect, an official biography of Moses, he omits all these embarrassing details.

In the case of the blasphemer, Philo is aware that the reader may wonder why Moses did not even know what penalty to inflict upon him. In apparent reply, Philo explains that Moses was afraid that he would inflict too light a penalty, inasmuch as a human being would not have the strength to devise a well-balanced punishment for so great an impiety. Moses is depicted as one who did not rush to judgment, who proceeded in precise accordance with the law, and who always appealed to G-d's mercy.

In his account of those who complained to Moses that they had been unable to offer the paschal lamb because they had been contaminated through contact with a corpse, Philo shows effectively another side of Moses, namely his feeling of sympathy for those who have suffered. Moses, in his modesty, is the ideal leader who realizes when he does not know the answer and does not rush to give an answer.

Whereas in the Bible it is G-d's or the Israelites' idea to send scouts into Canaan for reconnaissance purposes, Philo adds to Moses' ability as a commander by stating that the initiative came from Moses; and he shows how excellent a planner Moses is by having him give much fuller instructions to them. The care and foresight on the part of the spies, as stressed by Philo, is clearly a tribute to Moses, who had selected them. Philo, who, as the leader of the Jewish community of Alexandria, must have known how vital it was for his people to be united, stresses how important it was that the spies should be of one mind. Moreover, to keep the focus on Moses, Philo omits the names of the scouts, even (in *Mos.*) those of the two dissenters, Caleb and Joshua. When the Israelites wish to stone the minority representatives, Moses, far from being silent, as in the Bible, fearlessly expresses indignation. Significantly, in the five other treatises in which Philo mentions this episode he focuses in every case on its allegorical significance, which is not mentioned at all in *Mos.*, which concentrates on a straightforward, factual presentation.

Philo gives less attention to the revolt of Korah than does Josephus because the contest was primarily between Korah and Aaron, with whom Josephus as a priest especially identified, rather than between Korah and Moses. It is Moses' mildness and gentleness, even in the face of Korah's revolt, that Philo emphasizes. Moses is upset by the charge that he has lied, since the virtue of truth is so crucial to him. Philo realizes that Moses might be criticized for not attempting to answer Korah systematically, but he explains that Moses did not do so because, as a pragmatic leader, he was aware that it is impossible to change the minds of those who are convinced of their views. Philo's Moses is, however, especially concerned to answer Korah's accusation of nepotism and his challenge to divine revelation. Unlike his treatment of the rebellion in his *Praem.* 74, where he uses this episode to preach a philosophic sermon on the consequences of unreasonable pride and ambition, Philo focuses on the political contest, thus reflecting Philo's personal involvement in politics as a leader of the Alexandrian Jewish community.

In an apparent answer to the charge that Jews are unduly aggressive, Philo stresses that Moses made peaceful overtures to his kinsmen the Edomites, though he might have won a military victory over them; and when the Edomites reply maliciously, he urges the Israelites not to seek vengeance. Significantly, Philo nowhere in this entire pericope mentions the name of the Edomites, thus keeping the spotlight on Moses and inviting the reader to generalize that Philo's attitude is that of Jews at all times.

It is typical and extremely significant that Philo in *Mos.* omits all mention of the episode in which G-d sent fiery serpents against the Israelites. Moses, we are told, in accordance with G-d's advice, made a fiery serpent and told the people that they would be cured if they would stare at the serpent. Quite clearly in his apologetic biography of Moses, Philo realized that his predominantly non-Jewish literate audience would look upon such an incident as incredible, and so he omitted it here; but in other treatises (*Leg.* 2.77–87 and

Agr. 95–99), that are intended for a Jewish audience and that present the Bible allegorically, he explains that the serpent represents the principle of self-mastery.

In his account of the war against Sihon, Philo emphasizes Moses' fair treatment of other nations. Moreover, in an extra-biblical detail, he highlights Moses' ability as a commander in the way he positions his people. Furthermore, aware that the biblical statement that the Israelites, presumably at the direction of Moses, committed genocide in annihilating the men, women, and children of Sihon, he defends Moses by stating that they killed only the soldiers.

It is most striking that Philo develops his portrait of Balaam as a soothsayer and mercenary technician at unusual length even though it has litle direct connection with Moses. He does so in order to contrast him strongly with Moses, the true prophet, the philosopher-king, the priest, the thaumaturge, and the mystagogue. Unlike Josephus, who presents a relatively unbiased portrait of Balaam, Philo, like the Bible itself, the New Testament, and the rabbinic tradition, presents a strongly negative portrait. Because he apparently realized that his sophisticated readers would consider a speaking donkey as incredible, he omits this altogether and mentions only the donkey's unusual power of sight. Amazingly enough, however, Philo does not mention the name of Balaam even once in *Mos.*, thus keeping the focus on Moses.

As to why Moses did not take the initiative to reward Phinehas for killing the Israelite who had relations with a Moabite, Philo adds that actually Moses sought to reward Phinehas for his zealotry, but that he was anticipated by G-d. Moreover, whereas the Bible says nothing about Moses' role in getting the Israelites to follow Phinehas' zealous lead, Philo does present the extra-biblical addition that Moses did play such a role. Philo is careful, however, to add that they, presumably upon instructions from Moses, the epitome of justice, restricted the punishment to the actual sinners, while sparing those who gave clear proof of their piety.

In *Mos.* Philo does not discuss Moses' choice of a successor, but in *Virt.* he reminds the reader that he had forgotten to do so and that now he wishes to add something. What he proceeds to state is that Moses would have been expected to groom his sons to succeed him, but that he did not even consider this possibility, since he sought as his successor the one who was most qualified. Leaving the choice of a successor to G-d, he was not influenced by family feeling and, indeed, rejoiced in the choice of Joshua. It is particularly significant that he includes in *Virt.*, which is apparently directed to a Jewish audience, the statement that the birth of Moses' son, who would naturally be expected to succeed him, was divinely originated, whereas he omits this in the non-Jewish-directed *Mos.*

Whereas in the Bible it is G-d who tells Moses to take revenge against the Midianites, Philo asserts that it was Moses who decided that the Israelites were now united and that the time was ripe for the campaign against the Midianites. In the campaign Philo's Moses is a skilled leader who realizes that one should not deploy one's entire army, but that he should keep some troops in reserve. In an unusual addition to the biblical text, Philo (*Mos.* 1.306) states that Moses, before sending his soldiers off to war against Midian, offered favorable sacrifices. There is no mention in the Bible of such sacrifices, nor is there in Josephus' paraphrase (*A.J.* 4.159). Rather, apparently, Philo has been influenced to do so because his primary audience consisted of non-Jews, who would have expected this, since this was the practice of the Greeks and Romans before battle; and Philo has thus cast Moses in the mold of a Greek or Roman leader. Philo explains that the reason for the Israelites' success was that Moses instilled in them courage and confidence. Philo also comments on how wisely and fairly Moses distributed the booty taken in war.

Philo realizes the importance of unity, and thus his Moses rebukes at much greater length the tribes of Reuben and Gad for seeking to remain east of the Jordan when the other tribes were fighting to secure land west of the Jordan. But, even so, Moses, acting as a kindly father, does not allow his anger to interfere with his analysis of the possible reasons why these tribes should have made such a request.

In his farewell address to the Israelites, Philo's Moses, though he is denominated their commander-in-chief, addresses them as fellow citizens, in contrast to Josephus' Moses, who addresses them as fellow soldiers.

Philo, Josephus, and the rabbis, as eager as they were to exalt Moses, were tremendously concerned that he not be worshipped (though there is one rabbinic view that Moses never died), especially since there were precedents for such claims for numerous heroes; and all of the rabbis, with the exception of one anonymous rabbinic tradition, made a special point of stressing that the fact that Moses wrote in the Pentateuch of his own death was definite evidence that he did die. The Pseudepigraphic Ass. Mos. and the Samaritan traditions, in their exaltation of Moses, come closest to claiming that Moses did not die.

Philo's Moses represents the epitome of the four cardinal virtues—wisdom (his prime virtue, seen particularly in the laws that he transmitted, though he realized the limitations of reasoning), courage (the key to which is patient endurance and his fearlessness in confronting G-d), temperance (marked by strong opposition to the luxurious living that he had seen in the Pharaoh's court, by a disdain for sexual relations, and by self-mastery and modesty), and justice (which is in harmony with the very universe, which embodies maintaining a balance between strict justice and mercy, which embodies telling the truth, and which is integrally connected with the virtue of humanity toward the entire human race, though balanced with the ability, when necessary, to be stern), as well as an additional virtue, piety, the queen of them all—which he attained through leading a life of austerity and self-restraint and with which he saw no conflict with philosophy. To attain these virtues Moses first had to encounter toil.

On the all-important question as to whether Moses was the mere transmitter of G-d's laws or was a creative lawgiver in his own right, the non-Jewish writers who refer to Moses are unanimous in viewing him as the latter. The Dead Sea Scrolls and the overwhelming majority of the rabbinic tradition view him as a mere transcriber. The New Testament and Philo in his treatises other than *Mos.* overwhelmingly view Moses as the creative lawgiver. In *Mos.* Philo leaves the question open, but the fact that he compares Moses with other legislators indicates that he tends to side with those who look upon Moses as the creative lawgiver.

Though one of the four capacities in which Philo in *Mos.* praises Moses is as a king, he is careful not to stress this too much, perhaps because the word "king" was avoided by the Romans, including, in particular, the Roman emperors themselves. In this respect Philo differs from the New Testament, which parallels Jesus with Moses as king.

Philo stresses the sufferings that Moses, in his concern for his subjects, underwent at the hands of his fellow Israelites.

Since the ancients regarded it as axiomatic that a king would be the chief priest of his nation, it is not surprising that Moses is thus depicted by Jewish and non-Jewish sources alike. Philo, however, goes further and describes Moses as being instructed in all the mysteries by G-d Himself.

Furthermore, he is the highest kind of prophet, namely one who speaks in his own person when possessed by G-d, but who is not merely passive. Philo says that G-d gave Moses His own power of prediction. He stresses the connection between Moses as prophet and lawgiver. However, in contrast to the Christian tradition that identified Jesus as the prophet predicted in Deut. 18:15 and 18 who would be like Moses and in contrast to the Samaritan tradition that claims that these passages refer to a forthcoming messiah like Moses, Philo nowhere refers to these passages, perhaps to emphasize the utter uniqueness of Moses.

Whereas the Apocrypha, Pseudepigrapha, and the New Testament stress Moses' role as the mediator of revelation, Philo and Josephus do not develop this theme to the extent that we find it in Pseudo-Philo or in rabbinic literature, perhaps because they wished to stress Moses' role as a creative lawgiver in his own right.

Whereas historians such as Eupolemus insisted that Moses was the founder of philosophy, and writers such as Artapanus stressed his many inventions, Philo, like Josephus, felt that in stressing the achievements of Moses as a philosopher-king he could answer the charge that the Jews had produced no eminent thinkers. He says nothing, however, about Moses' inventions, since he stresses his achievements as the oldest and greatest legislator.

Unlike Artapanus, who depicts Moses as performing miracles on his own initiative, Philo and Josephus clearly indicate that he did so as an agent of G-d. Pseudo-Philo even elaborates on the role of G-d in performing miracles. Unlike Josephus, who generally tones down miracles, Philo broadens the framework of the natural order; and thus the biblical miracles are to be seen within the laws of nature. Like Josephus, he gives the reader a choice as to how to interpret the miracles. In deference to his sophisticated audience he often seeks to explain miracles scientifically, that is, naturally, or allegorically.

Despite the prohibition of black magic in the Torah and in the rabbinic tradition, it was apparently widely practiced, especially in Egypt; and Moses himself, to judge from the magical papyri, was famous as a magician. Philo has no references to Moses as a magician, presumably because such a practice would have been strongly opposed by both intellectuals and the government.

There is no indication in Philo, as there is in the New Testament, rabbinic and Samaritan literature, that Moses will some day return in the future world.

As to the divinity of Moses, Philo strongly objects to the view that a human being can be deified, but he does follow Plato in saying that one should seek the goal of becoming as godlike as possible. To be sure, he calls Moses perfect, but he is also ambivalent in insisting that no human being can be sinless. He refers to him as second to G-d, as a friend of G-d, as co-ruler with G-d, and as a philosopher who knows the true Forms, but he reacts against the near-deification of Moses by the Samaritan tradition and the Romans' deification of their emperors.

Pseudo-Philo, though he views Moses as having an intimate knowledge of G-d's ultimate secrets, nevertheless clearly states that Moses died and that G-d buried him, though it is unclear whether he states that Moses was changed to a glorious state.

Josephus is particularly careful to refer to Moses as a human. He stresses that the reason why the Bible states that he died was to refute the notion of his divinity. Yet, his account of Moses' death is very similar to the disappearance of Aeneas and Romulus and to the disappearance of Oedipus.

As to the Apocrypha, Ecclesiasticus, on the one hand, says that G-d magnified Moses as a god; but the fact that it represents Moses as similar to the angels would indicate that he was not an angel. The Ass. Mos. omits reference to Moses as the man of G-d.

A Dead Sea fragment speaks of G-d as making Moses as G-d to the Pharaoh, implying that he was not actually G-d.

The one work that seems to refer to Moses as parallel to G-d is the New Testament, which refers to blasphemies against Moses and G-d.

According to a dream mentioned in Ezekiel's *Exagoge*, Moses, like G-d, beholds things beneath and above heaven. But it may well be that Ezekiel's portrayal is intended to counter the idea of Moses' divinization, since all this is in the form of a dream, through which G-d says that He makes Himself known to prophets other than Moses, and since elsewhere G-d refers to Moses as mortal.

In the Samaritan tradition Moses is a second G-d, G-d's vice-regent upon earth. He uniquely was in existence before the creation of the world. It is to him that G-d revealed all His mysteries. In the light of the tremendous antagonism between the Samaritans and the Jews throughout the Hellenistic and Roman periods, it would appear that Philo, Pseudo-Philo, Josephus, and the rabbis all seek to distance themselves from the extreme Samaritan position with regard to Moses. In the case of Philo, who has such a high admiration for the LXX (*Mos.* 2.25–44), the fact that there were quarrels (Josephus, *A.J.* 12.10) between the Jews and the Samaritans from the beginning of the Ptolemies and that the two parties appealed to Ptolemy Philadelphus to establish their Scriptures as superior to the other (see Hadas 1951, 67–68; Jellicoe 1968, 63–64) might well have influenced Philo to express more strongly his opposition to the divinization of Moses.

The rabbis, on the other hand, assert that Moses was a man when he ascended on high, but that he was as G-d when he descended. Yet, they emphasize that the Bible states that no one knows the place of his burial, in order that he should not be worshipped. Likewise, the omission of Moses from the central prayer of Judaism, the *Amidah,* is intended to warn Jews not to view Moses as more than human.

In conclusion, to appreciate the special character of Philo's portrayal of Moses, it is particularly useful to compare him with the depiction that we find in Pseudo-Philo, Josephus, Artapanus, rabbinic literature, and the Samaritan tradition. Philo's Moses is the Jewish equivalent of Plato's philosopher-king, the greatest of lawgivers, more than a mere transcriber of G-d's decrees, the model high priest, and the prophet who had a unique relationship with G-d. He is also a military leader and planner, but that is not his chief greatness. Pseudo-Philo's Moses is G-d-intoxicated, and Moses' most important role is as intercessor with G-d, who is the sole focus of attention. Josephus' Moses is modeled on Thucydides' portrait of Pericles; he has self-control and has a special ability to speak to and control a crowd, and, above all, as Josephus fancied himself, is an extraordinary general. Artapanus' Moses excels as a general against the much-feared Ethiopians, but he is also an extremely versatile inventor, is able miraculously to escape from prison, and was deemed worthy of divine honor by the priests. The rabbis differ as to whether he was a mere transmitter of the laws or whether he was also creative. They are particularly fearful lest he be worshipped, and so they greatly diminish his role in the liturgy, particularly in opposition to the central role that he plays in the Samaritan religion, where he is practically equated with G-d Himself and where his miracles are emphasized even more than they are in the Bible itself.

As to Philo's portrait of Moses, there is a definite difference between the way he is viewed in *Mos.* and the way he is presented in Philo's other treatises. *Mos.* is intended primarily for non-Jews in order to answer the misunderstandings, disparagement, and maligning of Moses. Philo is particularly eager in this treatise to point out to non-Jews the excellence of Judaism in the hope that they will want to adopt the Jewish way of life, but he is sensitive to non-Jewish sensibilities. Philo, in this treatise, with very few exceptions, avoids allegory and philosophizing. Unlike Josephus, he remains true to the biblical narrative, again with very few exceptions. He makes a special appeal to intellectuals, omitting some data that intellectuals may regard as incredible, answering objections to seemingly illogical passages, and, in other cases, offering readers the choice of deciding for themselves how to accept difficult data. He presents Moses as a philosopher-king, in effect, a Jewish answer to Plato's *Republic*, particularly in his presentation of Moses' education. In his treatment of miracles he presents scientific explanations on a number of occasions. Despite the popular view in Jewish and non-Jewish circles of Moses as a magician, Philo avoids this role. As a leader of the Jewish community of Egypt, Philo feels a particular kinship with Moses, who is a native son of Egypt and the forerunner of the current Jewish population of the country. He thus focuses particularly on Moses, mentioning by name very few others. He stresses Moses' role as a creative lawgiver and not merely as a transcriber of G-d's law. He places less emphasis on G-d's role and diminishes Moses' role as a general. Finally, much as he admires Moses, he objects strongly to the view of Moses as divine.

Notes

I. General Considerations

1. Likewise in the second half of the second century, Numenius (*ap.* Eus. *PE* 11.18.14) sees no need to inform the reader that it is Moses of whom he is speaking when he refers to the Lawgiver (νομοθέτης) as one who plants and distributes and transplants for people the germs that have been previously deposited from a higher source. Similarly, the *Scriptores Historiae Augustae* (*Divus Claudius* 2.4), dating perhaps from the fourth century, mentions Moses by name as living 125 years, without bothering to introduce him further to the reader, as if he were well known.

2. We find a similar charge in Josephus (*Ap.* 1.204), who ascribes the omission of reference to the Jews in some historians as due not to ignorance but to envy (φθόνος) or to some other disingenuous (οὐχ ὑγιής, "unhealthy," "unsound") reason (*Ap.* 1.213) On envy as a conventional motif noted and refuted in encomiastic literature, see Stuart 1928, 55–56, 92–93, cited by Robbins 1947, 47, n. 4.

3. Some of Apion's glosses on Homer have been found in a papyrus fragment (P. Rylands 1.26) dating from the first century C.E.; moreover, a few first-century scholia on Homer's *Od.* (P. Lit. London 30; British Museum inv. 271) mention his name among other commentators. It is not surprising, therefore, that Apion was apparently Philo's counterpart as a leader of the Alexandrian non-Jews, since he was a member of the three-man delegation sent by the Alexandrians to the Emperor Gaius Caligula (Josephus, *A.J.* 18.257). See further Feldman 1987–88, 238–39.

4. Quintilian's use of the word *superstition* would indicate that he apparently felt that Judaism had gone beyond the usual bounds of religion.

5. Moses is also termed most perfect (τελειότατος) elsewhere by Philo (*Ebr.* 94). Similarly, one current of rabbinic tradition spoke of Moses as "very much above all the men that were upon the face of the earth" (*Sifre Num. Beha'aloteka* on Num. 12:3). Cf. *Midr. Tannaim* 2.186 (ed. David Hoffmann) on Deut. 34:10: "There has not arisen a prophet since in Israel like Moses," cited by Ginzberg 1928, 6:46, n. 245. See also the citations given by Ginzberg 1925, 5:398, n. 47, who remarks that rabbinic tradition declared that the angels had conversed with G-d about the fate of Moses. In contrast to this view, some of the rabbis (*Sifre Num.* 101) held that the three patriarchs—Abraham, Isaac, and Jacob—surpassed Moses in meekness.

6. See Hengel 1974, 1:70: "Only with Philo and Josephus do we meet an apologetic deliberately aimed at outsiders."

7. Cicero, *Brutus* 316; Plutarch, *Cicero* 4; *Caesar* 3.

8. Some scholars, for example, Freudenthal 1874, 1:29, and Reinach 1895, 65, n. 2, have suggested that the notion of a female lawgiver had originated in the history of the Sibyls. Indeed, in the first century B.C.E., Alexander Polyhistor (*ap.* Eus., *Chronica* 1, dependent on Sib. Or. 3.97ff., cited by Josephus, *A.J.* 1.118) cites a Sibyl as referring to the Tower of Babel. In fact, as Gruen 1998, 289, has noted, the authority of the Sibyls had spread through much of the Greek world, and we hear in the second-century Pausanias (10.12.9) of a Hebrew woman named Sabbe who is identified by some as a Babylonian or an Egyptian Sibyl. However, the Sibyls, we may note, were not lawgivers but prophetesses. We may here suggest, as a parallel, the passage in Juvenal (6.544–45) that speaks of the interpreter of the laws of Jerusalem, the great priestess of the tree (perhaps an allusion to the grove of Numa Pompilius, where he had been instructed by the nymph Egeria, and which had now become a gathering-place for begging Jewesses), "the faithful messenger of the decrees of the sky" (an allusion to the fact that the Jews worshipped only the divinity of the sky [*caeli numen*], as Juvenal put it elsewhere [14.97]). Heinemann 1935, 360, has described the tradition as malevolent and cites as parallels the transformation of the name Cleomenes to Cleomene in Aristophanes' *Clouds* (680) and Chrysippus to Chrysippa in Cicero's *De Natura Deorum* (1.34.93).

9. Moses is thus identified by Artapanus (*ap.* Eus. *PE* 9.27.3); and his name is spelled thus by Numenius (*ap.* Eus. *PE* 9.8.2).

10. On the dispute as to whether the anti-Jewish passages ascribed to Manetho by Josephus are really by Manetho, see Feldman 1996c, 178, n. 2 and 184, n. 14. Indeed, there is reason to separate Manetho, who is not anti-Jewish and, moreover, never speaks of the Israelites as such, from Pseudo-Manetho, who is.

11. We may wonder, although admittedly the *argumentum ex silentio* is hardly conclusive, why Philo, who writes at such length apologetically about Moses in his *Mos.* and is particularly concerned to answer the charge of Jew-baiters, does not repeat the story of Moses' Ethiopian campaign, which would have served to answer so many of their contentions, particularly the alleged disloyalty of Jews to their government. Perhaps one answer may be that Philo sought to emphasize, especially in his treatises directed to Jews, Moses' role as a lawgiver.

12. Freudenthal (1874, 169–73), Bloch (1879), Ginzberg (1925, 5:409–10, n. 80), Rappaport (1930, 25–32), Heinemann (1935, 372), and Maher (1996, 86–87) argue that Josephus knew the work of Artapanus and was influenced by him. Both Freudenthal and Rappaport focus on Josephus' account of Moses' Ethiopian campaign; but as Sterling 1992, 269–77, points out, there are numerous differences in detail and no verbal parallels. In particular, Artapanus omits the crucial story of Moses' marriage to the Ethiopian princess. Halévy 1927, 115, endeavors to explain this omission by asserting that he did so for apologetic reasons, inasmuch as he did not want to have Moses figure in a love story; but in view of the fact that Artapanus does attribute to Moses such un-Jewish conceptions as the worship of cats, dogs, and ibises (*ap.* Eus. *PE* 9.27.4), we

may assume that he was seeking to impress his pagan audience, who certainly would have appreciated such a love story as that of Moses and Tharbis. Moreover, he attributes to Moses the foundation of Meroe, so named from Merris, Moses' adoptive mother, whereas Josephus (*A.J.* 2.249) says that Meroe drew its name from the sister of Cambyses. Josephus surely had ample opportunity to mention Artapanus, particularly in his apologetic treatise, *Ap.*

13. Freudenthal 1874, 173, on the basis of the identical spelling of Moses as Μουσαῖος in Artapanus (*ap.* Eus. *PE* 9.27.3) and the second-century Numenius (*ap.* Eus. *PE* 9.8.2), suggests that Numenius was acquainted with Artapanus; but the point of Artapanus' mention of Musaeus is to indicate that Moses-Musaeus became the teacher of Orpheus, who, indeed, is associated with Musaeus either as his teacher or his pupil; and Numenius makes no such association.

14. The list includes such luminaries as Schwartz (1895, 1306); Willrich (1900, 111–17); Friedländer (1903, 112–14); Hengel (1974, 1:90–91); and Fraser (1972, 1:704–6).

15. There are indications that even anti-Jewish writers such as Apion admitted that the Jews were an ancient people. See Feldman 1987–88, 199–206.

16. So also Eupolemus (*ap.* Eus. *PE* 9.26.1).

17. For a number of excellent suggestions analyzing Lysimachus, I am indebted to two unpublished essays by my student, Burns (2000, 2002).

18. Apion (*ap. Ap.* 2.16) dates Bocchoris as ruling 1700 years before his time. This is in sharp contradiction to the date of the king of the twenty-fourth dynasty, being approximately a thousand years earlier than that date.

19. Tacitus (*Histories* 5.3.1) likewise places the Exodus in the reign of King Bocchoris and similarly states that Bocchoris approached the oracle of Ammon seeking a remedy for the plague. As Stern 1974, 1:385, remarks, Bocchoris' connection with the Jews may be explained by the Egyptian tradition that dated the Prophecy of the Lamb concerning the rule of foreigners over Egypt to his reign.

20. It appears clear, as Burns 2002, 14, points out, that Apion and later Tacitus chose to promote Lysimachus' version of the Exodus rather than that of Manetho.

21. Stern 1984, 3:38–41, finds insurmountable difficulties in accepting the authenticity of this statement in Pseudo-Justin. In particular, he finds it hard to understand how Jewish-Hellenistic (notably Josephus) and Christian apologists prior to the *Cohortatio,* who took so much trouble to find ancient evidence to support the antiquity of the Jews, should have had to wait until the second half of the third century to quote the evidence of Hellanicus and Philochorus. We may note, however, that Origen (*Contra Celsum* 4.21), attacks the second-century Celsus for not noticing the evidence of Moses' antiquity. The statement of the sixth-century John Malalas (*Chronographia*), who couples Thallus with Castor, Polybius, and Herodotus as the wisest of the historians, is likewise of dubious value.

22. Georgi 1986, 182, concludes that both Jews and Gentiles are being addressed throughout Philo's works.

23. Such is the conclusion also of Robbins 1947, 47. An indication that Philo's *Mos.* was read by non-Jews may be seen in the third-century romance the *Aethiopica* (9.9) of Heliodorus, who echoes *Mos.* 2.195, cited by Nock 1933, 286.

24. For an extensive critical survey of the history of scholarship on aretalogies and, in particular, the definition of aretalogy, see Smith 1971, 174–99. See the most recent treatment by Najman 2003, 89–91, who cites (89, n. 34) selected bibliography.

25. Sigal 1984, 171, offers, as a further objection to categorizing Philo's biography as an aretalogy, the fact that Philo nowhere uses or alludes to the term ἀρετή in connection with Moses. But Philo (*Mos.* 1.48) does say that while Moses, after fleeing from Egypt, was in Midian, he was "carrying out the exercises of virtue (ἀρετή) with an admirable trainer, the reason within him, under whose discipline he labored to fit himself for life in its highest forms, the theoretical and the practical."

26. Shuler calls attention to Stuart 1928, Momigliano 1971a, and Cox 1983.

27. On the development of the genre of biography, see Feldman 2005, 209–12.

28. Moreover, there are three specific instances, as noted here by Helmbold and O'Neil, where Plutarch's *Lycurgus* seems to have drawn upon Isocrates: 4.5, on Lycurgus' visit to the Egyptians, from whom he derived the separation of the military from the other classes of society; 16.6, on Lycurgus' decision that boys should learn only enough of reading and writing to serve their turn; and 17.3, on the practice of having boys steal whatever food they can.

29. Momigliano 1971a, 106, is, however, reluctant to see a direct influence of Aristotelian philosophy on the growth of Greek biography in the Hellenistic period.

30. On the distinction among history, biography, and encomium, see Wardman 1974, 10–18.

31. However, in Momigliano's work (1971a) presenting a systematic history of the genre of biography from its beginnings to the Roman period, there is no mention of Philo as a biographer.

32. Significantly, Josephus, in *A.J.*, which is an historical work, does include (*A.J.* 3.180–87) in one place an analysis of the symbolism of the Tabernacle and its vessels and the vestments of the priests. That this is a special case we may perceive from Josephus' introductory comment (*A.J.* 3.179), before this passage, that he seeks, with this discussion of the symbolism to answer the charge of the anti-Semites that Jews belittle the Divinity that they themselves have made up their minds to reverence. See, for example, the charge of Manetho (*ap.* Josephus, *Ap.* 1.239) that Osarsiph (i.e., Moses), by his first law, ordained that the Israelites should not worship the gods. In contrast, Philo's biographies of Abraham and Joseph are really moral or religious essays, so that Joseph, for example, becomes political virtue incarnate (see Arnaldez et al. 1967, 12).

33. *Midrash Ha-Gadol* 2.25 and many other parallels. See Ginzberg 1925, 5:416, n. 115.

34. On this passage, see Wolfson 1947, 1:190–92. A similar distinction between written and unwritten laws is to be found in Philo (*Hypoth.* 7.6).

35. For examples, see Cohen 1995, 33–71.

36. Runia 2001, 248, concludes that Philo's language here is the clearest indication in *Opif.* that Philo, in presenting his exegesis, draws on earlier traditions.

37. See Feldman 1998a, 335–73, especially 338–40.

38. However, Schorr (1991) argues that Philo's etymologies are derived from midrashim and prove his knowledge of Hebrew; but the fact that onomastica have been found shows that Philo may have derived his knowledge of names therefrom and that he did not necessarily derive it through a knowledge of Hebrew. This, indeed, is the conclusion of Grabbe 1988, 119–21. Since, in most cases, Philo gives only one etymology for a given name, it is most likely that he had a single source, probably a list of some sort. Moreover, as Grabbe 1988, 54–55, has pointed out, Philonic etymologies differ basically from those of the rabbis in that the latter are generally plays on words or are etiological or are related to events within the lifetime of the persons involved, whereas Philo's are the means for further exegesis.

39. For further examples of Philo's parallels with rabbinic midrash, see Treitel (1915, 85–113); Stein (1931); and a number of articles in Hebrew by Belkin: 1951, 1–52; 1957–58, 25–92; 1958–59, 1–60; 1960a, 1–74; and 1960b, 1–68, as well as his book (1989). Belkin's methodology has been challenged by Werblowsky 1959, 25–44, 113–35; but it is defended by Cohen 1992, 100–5; 1995, 4–8, who points out that Belkin does not seek to prove that there was a direct relationship between Philo and rabbinic midrashim but rather that there was a living midrashic tradition that contained these ideas and that both Philo and the rabbis drew upon this material.

40. Other instances where Philo parallels midrashic tradition are his symbolic interpretation of the burning bush (*Mos.* 1.67; cf. *Midr. Exod. Rab.* 2.5; see Kugel 1997, 301–2); the role of the four elements—earth, water, air, and fire—in performing the ten plagues (*Mos.* 1.96; cf. *Midr. Exod. Rab.* 12.4, 15.27; see Ginzberg 1925, 5:426, n. 170); and the significance of the palm tree at Elim (*Mos.* 1.189; cf. *Midr. Gen. Rab.* 40.6; see Ginzberg 1928, 6:15, nn. 87–88). See Geljon 2002, 12.

II. The Life of Moses

1. Examples are numerous: Isocrates' *Evagoras* (12–19, 22), Xenophon' *Cyropaedia* (1.2.1–4.15), Plato's *Menexenus* (237A), Aristotle's *Rhetorica* (1.9.33.1367B), Plutarch's *Lives*, and Suetonius' *De Vita Caesarum* (see Remus 1996, 676, n. 52, and Talbert 1980, 133–34). In particular, we may note in Suetonius discussions of the ancestry of the emperors Claudius (1–2), Nero (1–6), and Vespasian (1–2).

2. Indeed, the Greeks made a virtue of good birth in and of itself. Thus in Homer, when Glaucus meets Diomedes, they first exchange genealogies (*Il.* 6.123–231).

Herodotus (7.204 and 8.131) makes a special point of tracing the individual genealogies of King Leonidas and Leotychides back twenty generations, naming all their ancestors going back to Heracles. He similarly traces the genealogy of Theras of Sparta (4.147), Laius of Thebes (5.59), Aristodemus of Sparta (6.52), and the Persians Abrocomes and Hyperanthes (7.224). Moreover, Antigone in Sophocles' play (*Antigone* 38) is described as well-born by nature (εὐγενὴς πέφυκας). We see the same emphasis in Aristotle's description of the great-souled man (μεγαλόψυχος) as well-born (εὐγενής) (*EN* 4.3.1124A21–22). When Aristotle considers the gifts of fortune by which human character is affected, his first topic of discussion is good birth (*Rhet.* 2.15.1390B11–30). The well-born will look down, he says, even on those who are as good as their own ancestors. When Cornelius Nepos (*Epaminondas* 1) begins his life of Epaminondas, he speaks of his family and only then goes on to discuss his education and his personal qualities. Similarly, we may note the genealogies of famous heroes in the following: Plutarch, *Theseus* 3; *Fabius Maximus* 1; *Brutus* 1–2; *Pyrrhus* 1; *Lycurgus* 1; Philostratus, *Life of Apollonius* 1.4; *Historia Augusta*, *Hadrian* 1.1–2; and *Antoninus Pius* 1.1–7 (see Talbert 1980, 135). Even so, the Egyptians, if we may judge from Plato (*Timaeus* 22B), had sneered at the genealogies of the Greeks as being little better than nursery tales. We can also see the importance of genealogy in Josephus' contemporary Tacitus (*Agricola* 4). And we should note the importance given to genealogies of Jesus in the Gospels of Matthew (1:2–16) and Luke (3:23–28). Furthermore, that the hero or heroine should be of lofty birth is one of the characteristic features of Hellenistic novels. See Schmeling 1980, 21, who notes that genealogy would be the first thing in a Hellenistic author's mind as he begins his novel, and remarks that this is true for Xenophon of Ephesus' Habrocomes and Anthia in *Ephesiaca*, as well as for the tale of Cupid and Psyche in Apuleius' *Metamorphoses* (4.28) and for the novel of Apollonius of Tyre by an anonymous author (cf. Goethals 1959, 1ff.).

Perhaps because Josephus himself was so proud of his ancestry, being descended from the first of the twenty-four courses of the priests, as well as (on his mother's side) from the Hasmoneans (*Vita* 1–8), he frequently adds such details when they are not found explicitly in the Bible. Thus, Josephus tells us that Abraham was the tenth generation after Noah (Scripture simply enumerates his ancestors) and adds to his antiquity by remarking that he was born 992 years after the flood (*A.J.* 1.148). He thereby increases by some 701 years the interval between the flood and the birth of Abraham. Josephus would thus seem to be answering such detractors of the Jews as Apollonius Molon (*ap.* Eus. *PE* 9.19.2–3), who had declared that Abraham was born only three generations after Noah. In an extra-biblical addition, Abraham's servant Eliezer commends Rebekah for her good birth (εὐγενείας) and goodness of heart (*A.J.* 1.247). When Jacob first meets Rachel, he gives his genealogy at some length (*A.J.* 1.288–90). In explaining why Jacob loved Joseph more than his brothers, Josephus adds the extra-biblical explanation that he did so because of the beauty of person that he owed not only to his excellence of character but also to his good birth (εὐγένεια), that is, the fact that his mother Rachel was exceptionally beautiful (*A.J.* 2.9). Again, Amram,

Moses' father, is described as of noble birth (εὖ γεγονώς) (*A.J.* 2.210), whereas the Bible simply describes him as "a man from the house of Levi" (Exod. 2:1). Korah also is described as being among the most eminent of the Hebrews by reason both of his birth (γένος) and of his riches (*A.J.* 4.14). Moses speaks of the nobility of birth of his brother Aaron as not being the factor that justifies the bestowal of the high priesthood upon him (*A.J.* 4.26), the implication being that others might think so.

3. See the passages cited by Borgen et al. 2000, s. v. Ἑβραϊκός, Ἑβραῖος, Χαλδαϊκός, Χαλδαῖος, Χαλδαϊστί; and the note by Earp 1962, 10:298–99.

4. According to Philo (*Abr.* 82), the name "Abram" signifies one who is called an astrologer and meteorologist. When he leaves Chaldea, Abram is told (*Abr.* 71) to dismiss "the rangers of the heavens and the science of Chaldea."

5. So also in rabbinic tradition (*Sifre Num.* 67, *Midr. Exod. Rab.* 1.8).

6. Thackeray 1930, 4:264, n. a, remarks that the sentence stating that Moses was the seventh generation after Abraham and enumerating these seven generations has been rejected by some editors as an interruption of the narrative and suggests that it may be a postscript of the author; but in view of Josephus' emphasis elsewhere on genealogy, as we have noted, the greater likelihood is that it is authentic.

7. *Pesiq. Rb. Kah.* 23.10 states that every seventh generation is dearest and cites the fact that Moses was the seventh generation from Abraham. Gaster 1927, 74, notes that Moses' position in the seventh generation from Abraham is a distinct feature of Samaritan chronology.

8. For an exhaustive study of rabbinic traditions concerning Moses' birth, see Bloch 1955, 93–170.

9. Josephus (*A.J.* 2.205–6) adds an additional factor that brought on this decree, namely that a certain Egyptian sacred scribe had predicted the birth of an Israelite who would humble the rule of the Egyptians. This, in effect, shifts much of the blame to the scribe rather than to the Pharaoh. Pseudo-Philo (9.1) adds that the Egyptians proposed to keep the Israelite females so that they might give them to their slaves as wives and then raise the children as slaves. For rabbinic parallels with regard to the birth of Moses, see Bloch 1955, 102–18.

10. So also *Pirqe R. El.* 48. Cf. *Mek. R. Shim.* 1, which connects the murder of the sons with the enslavement: "After drowning their sons in water they also immured them in the construction work."

11. On Philo's extremely negative image of the Egyptians, with its corollary that Jews should live in Egypt in a merely physical sense, while ideologically sundering themselves off radically from the Egyptians, see Niehoff's amply illustrated and comprehensive analysis (2001, 45–74).

12. See *Conf.* 88, *Fug.* 124, *Migr.* 160, *Ebr.* 208, *Abr.* 103, *Ios.* 151.

13. Pseudo-Philo (9.2), however, reports a meeting of the Israelite elders and their resolve not to have children; but he says that Amram, in his faith that G-d would not abandon the Israelites, disagreed with this decision (9.4). Pseudo-Philo (9.7) then remarks that G-d, who is always his central focus, was pleased with Amram's resolve

and declares that through the child who is to be born from Amram, He will perform wonders for the Israelites. G-d then promises (9.8) that He will kindle His lamp, presumably divine wisdom, to reside in him, that He will show him His house that no one has hitherto seen, and that He will kindle an eternal light for him. G-d then claims to have thought of Moses when He set the limit of human life at 120 years. Pseudo-Philo (9.10) next reports a dream that Miriam had in which she is instructed by the spirit of G-d to tell her parents that a child will be born to them who will be cast into the water and that through him the water will be dried up; but her parents do not believe her. In Josephus (*A.J.* 2.211–17) it is not Miriam who has a prophecy in a vision but Amram, Moses' father; and it is G-d Himself who appears to him and who prophesies to him that the child to be born will be remembered forever not only among the Hebrews but also among foreigners.

14. Josephus (*A.J.* 2.210–17) adds an extra-biblical account that when Jochebed was pregnant with Moses, G-d appeared to her husband Amram and assured him that He would reward their piety and that the child to be born would deliver the Hebrews from slavery. Josephus (*A.J.* 2.218) adds, moreover, that Jochebed did not feel any violent pain while she gave birth to Moses. The rabbinic tradition (*b. Soṭ.* 12a, *Midr. Exod. Rab.* 1.20) goes so far as to say that Jochebed gave birth without any pain—a proof, according to the second-century Rabbi Judah bar Ilai, that righteous women are not included in the decree pronounced upon Eve (Gen. 3:16).

15. See *Mek. Bo* 12.13a and *Beshallaḥ* 24a and parallels cited by Ginzberg 1925, 5:391, n. 4.

16. When the time was approaching for Moses to be born, an Egyptian astrologer (Samaritan *Molad* p. 21, l. 14–p. 22, p. 23, l. 9) predicted that Amram would within forty days become the father of a famous offspring who would bring about the destruction of Egypt and would rescue the Israelites. The Pharaoh ordered that the Israelite men be separated from their wives for forty days. However, after nineteen days Amram managed to have relations with Jochebed.

17. This similarity of motif in Matt. 2:1–18 is noted by Bloch 1879, 66–67, and others. Another parallel may be cited in connection with the birth of Augustus (Suetonius, *Augustus* 94.5). A portent had warned the Roman people a few months before the birth of Augustus that Nature was making ready to provide them with a king. This caused the Senate such consternation that they issued a decree that forbade the rearing of any male child for a whole year. However, a group of senators whose wives were pregnant prevented the decree from being officially filed in the Treasury and thus becoming law, since each of them hoped that the prophesied king would be his own son.

18. There is also a rabbinic tradition (*Midr. Exod. Rab.* 1.19, *b. B. Bat.* 120a) that whereas Jochebed was 130 years old when she gave birth to Moses, "the marks of youth came back to her, her flesh was again smooth, the wrinkles were straightened out, and her beauty returned." Though, as we have noted, Philo was acquainted with

some oral traditions akin to those of the rabbis, he generally avoids miraculous details such these.

19. According to the Samaritan *Molad* (p. 23, ll. 14–15), Jochebed was 135 years old.

20. So also Heb. 11:23.

21. Ezekiel was almost certainly Jewish, though perhaps a Samaritan, but Eus. (*PE* 9.1.1–4) apparently regarded him as a non-Jew (see Jacobson 1983, 5, 14–15, and Holladay 1989, 302–3 and 320, nn. 4–5).

22. Josephus (*A.J.* 2.219) similarly explains why Amram felt that he could no longer hide the child, i.e., lest he perish with the child, having himself fallen under the wrath of the king; and so he entrusted the preservation of the child to G-d Himself.

23. Reinhartz 1992, 51, n. 32, notes that Philo here (*Mos.* 1.11) puts into the mouths of Moses' parents the self-accusation as to why they had not cast Moses away as soon as he was born and thus have saved him from further suffering. In defense of casting a newborn child away they state that a child who has not survived to enjoy a gentle nurture is not generally reckoned as a human being, the implication being that the infanticide in such a case is not generally regarded as murder. She remarks that the view expressed here contradicts Philo's comment (*Spec.* 3.117–18) that a child is considered a full human being at the moment of birth, and that, therefore, infanticide is murder, "since the displeasure of the law is not concerned with ages." She explains the discrepancy between this passage and that in *Mos.* 1.11 by suggesting that this may be indicative of a wider debate concerning the point at which a child becomes a full human being. However, the passage in *Spec.* is extremely clear in its utter condemnation of such infanticide; and the explanation of the discrepancy would appear to be that Philo in *Mos.* does not say that Jewish law generally regards such an exposed child as not qualifying as a human being; rather, he says that οἱ πολλοί, that is, the masses, think so. Clearly, Moses' parents did not agree with this view of the masses.

24. Josephus, *A.J.* 1.108, 2.348, 3.81, 3.268, 3.322, 4.158, 8.262, 10.281, 17.354, 19.108; *B.J.* 5.257.

25. Syncellus (1.227) cites two names, Thermouthis and Pharie. Artapanus (*ap.* Eus. *PE* 9.27.3) refers to her as Merris. In 1 Chr. 4:18 and in the Talmud (*b. Meg.* 13a) her name is given as Bithiah.

26. The princess' childlessness, not mentioned in the Bible, is also referred to in Josephus (*A.J.* 2.232) and Artapanus (*ap.* Eus. *PE* 9.27.3).

27. Van der Horst 1984a, 362, points out that whereas the LXX reads that the princess saw that the baby was a Hebrew, Ezekiel and Philo state that she knew that he was a Hebrew.

28. So also the rabbinic tradition (*b. Soṭ.* 12b) asserts that at first the infant Moses was given to all the Egyptian women, but that Moses refused to nurse from them. A similar remarkable utterance is found in the Samaritan *Book of Asatir* (9.13), which

declares that Moses would drink only of "undefiled" milk, the implication being that he had refused the milk of Egyptian nurses.

29. Josephus (*A.J.* 2.228), like Philo, says that the Egyptians call water *mōu;* but he adds a second element to the name, noting that the Egyptians call those who have been saveud *esēs.* This agrees with a Coptic etymology: *mōu,* "water," *ouaiṣi,* "save." Goodenough 1958, 9:223, n.196, suggests that Philo and Josephus reflect an account that originated in Hellenistic Egypt, and that this etymology was substituted by readers of the LXX, who also spoke Coptic, since the original Hebrew etymology became meaningless in Greek translation. The name may have an Egyptian origin: *mw,* "water," *ḥsy,* "exalted," which is transcribed in papyri as ἑσιῆς, hence the Greek spelling of Moses' name, Μωυσῆς. See Griffiths 1953, 225–26. In actuality, however, the name apparently comes from the Egyptian verb *msy,* "to give birth," and frequently appears as "Mose" with the name of a god, for example, Tuthmosis ("Toth is born") and Rameses ("Re is born"). According to the Bible (Exod. 2:10) and Philo, Pharaoh's daughter alone gave Moses his name, whereas Josephus (*A.J.* 2.228) says that the Egyptians conferred the name upon Moses.

30. See Grabbe 1988, 188–89, who remarks that it is not clear that the derivation from ψηλάφημα is meant to be an actual etymology. As Grabbe indicates elsewhere (119–20), it is likely that Philo did not know Hebrew but had an onomastical list which he consulted when he had the need.

31. E.g., note Philo's explanation (*Hypoth.* 11.14) as to why the Essenes, whom he admires so much, are opposed to marriage, namely "because a wife is a selfish creature, excessively jealous and an adept at beguiling the morals of her husband and seducing him by her continued impostures."

32. See Perrot 1967, 481–518, who has collected the haggadic materials relating to the childhood of Noah, Abraham, Isaac, Moses, Samson, Samuel, and Elijah. Thus we hear, for example, that Abraham in his third year recognized that all the idols of his father were naught and destroyed them (*Midr. Gen. Rab.* 38, *Tg. Ps.-J.* on Gen. 11:28).

33. One may note the examples, cited by Talbert 1980, 135, in Plutarch's *Theseus* (6.4), *Solon* (2), *Themistocles* (2.1), *Dion* (4.2), *Alexander* (5.1), *Romulus* (8), and *Cicero* (2.2); Quintus Curtius' *History of Alexander* (1); Philostratus' *Life of Apollonius of Tyana* (1.7.11); Pseudo-Callisthenes' *Alexander Romance*; 1 Enoch 106:11 (where Noah blesses G-d while still in the hands of a midwife); and Jub. 11–12 (Abraham as a child prodigy). See Usener 1912, 4:127–28, and Bieler 1936, 1:34–38. The former cites the examples of Evangelos of Miletus (Conon, *Narrationes* 44), Amphoteros and Akarnan the sons of Alkmaion (Apollodorus, *Bibliotheca* 1.7.4). Cf. Luke 2:40, 52, where we are told that the child Jesus "grew and became strong, filled with wisdom; and the favor of G-d was upon him. . . . And Jesus increased in wisdom and in stature and in favor with G-d and man." See Lévy 1927, 141, n. 4.

34. Cf. Josephus (*A.J.* 2.230), who adds that when Moses had attained the age of three—presumably, this was after he had completed the standard nursing period of two years (cf. *m. Ned.* 2:1 and *b. Ket.* 60a)—G-d gave him wondrous increase of his

stature. In the rabbinic tradition we are told that since Exod. 2:6 says not that the infant but that the lad was crying, the child, though an infant, had a lad's voice (*Tan. Exod.* 8.9, p. 213). Furthermore, we hear that when he was only three months old, he prophesied and declared that he was destined to receive the law amid flames of fire (*Midr. Deut. Rab.* 11.10). Again, when Moses was but five years old, he appeared as though he were eleven years of age (cf. *Yal.* 165 [ed. Heyman, p. 28]). Indeed, the rabbis, as did the New Testament, speculate about the supernatural circumstances of both Moses' conception and delivery. Daube 1965, 5–9, goes so far as to speculate that the Passover Haggadah interpreted Exod. 2:25 ("And G-d saw the people of Israel, and G-d knew (*yada'*) their condition") in a sexual sense, in that *yada'* means both "to know" and "to have sexual relations with," thereby attributing divine fatherhood to Moses in a manner reminiscent of Christian attribution of divine fatherhood to Jesus. See Allison 1993, 146–47. On rabbinic and New Testament parallels to the early date of Moses' weaning, see Allison 1993, 150.

35. The *Midr. Exod. Rab.* 1.27 also reports his unusual growth. Indeed, he is said to have grown to a height of ten cubits, that is fifteen feet (*b. Bek.* 44a).

36. Moses' upbringing in Egypt is paralleled in the New Testament (Matt. 2:14–15) in Jesus' being taken to Egypt so as to escape Herod's decree to destroy the male childen of the Hebrews. When the angel appears to Joseph (Matt. 2:20) and tells him to return to the land of Israel, he tells him that all who sought the child's life are dead, just as Moses returns to Egypt from Midian when he is informed by G-d (Exod. 4:19) that all those who had sought to kill him had died.

37. The rabbinic tradition (*Midr. Exod. Rab.* 1.26 and *Midr. Deut. Rab.* 11.10) similarly tells how Moses took the crown from the Pharaoh's head and threw it down. Flusser 1971, 63–67, notes a similar narrative in a Byzantine work, *Palaea Historica*, dating from not before the ninth century. There it is Moses who takes the Pharaoh's crown (as in the rabbinic tradition) and tramples upon it. Consequently, one of the noblemen who advise the Pharaoh suggests that gold and a burning torch (rather than an onyx stone and a burning coal, as in the rabbinic tradition) be placed before Moses, whereupon Moses chooses the torch and puts it into his mouth, which is the cause of his speech defect (Exod. 4:10). As to precocity, such a picture is reminiscent of that of the ten-year-old future Persian king Cyrus, whose parentage was discovered through an incident that occurred while he was playing with the village boys, during which he ordered one of them to be beaten because he had disobeyed his command (Herodotus 1.114–16). Likewise, we may note that Josephus develops the theme of the precocity of Solomon (*A.J.* 8.2, 211) and of Josiah (*A.J.* 10.50) (see Feldman 1993e, 115–16). With respect to such qualities, Josephus seems to have molded his biblical heroes in his own image (or vice versa), since he cites his own precocity, noting that while still a mere youth, about fourteen years of age, he won universal applause for his love of letters, and that the chief priests and the leading men of Jerusalem used to come to him constantly for precise information with regard to the laws (*Vita* 9).

38. Similarly, in his portrait of Isaac, Philo (*Cher.* 8) remarks that Isaac's heart was not in the pursuit of childish sports (παιδιαί) but of those that are divine. In contrast, according to Josephus (*A.J.* 2.230), Moses clearly showed his mature superiority in his childish amusements. To be sure, Nodet 1990, vol. 1, adopts, in his commentary ad loc., the reading παιδείαις with several manuscripts (OMSPAL) in place of παιδιαῖς, the word that Philo uses and the reading of a single manuscript (R) that has been adopted by all other editors, including Niese, Naber, and Thackeray. If Nodet is right, the meaning would be that Moses showed his maturer excellence in his educational activities rather than in his childish games. But the sixth-century Latin version ascribed to Cassiodorus, reading *infantia*, clearly favors the reading adopted by the other editors, as does the context, which speaks of Moses' extraordinary precocity in his early years.

39. Cf. Philo, *Abr.* 6: "They [the forefathers, notably Enosh, Enoch, Abraham, Isaac, and Jacob] were not scholars or pupils of others, nor did they learn under teachers what was right to say or do: they listened to no voice (αὐτήκοοι, "hearing oneself," "self-acquired") or instruction but their own (αὐτομαθεῖς, "self-taught"): they gladly accepted conformity with nature, holding that nature itself was, as indeed it is, the most venerable of statutes, and thus their whole life was one of happy obedience to law. They committed no guilty action of their own free will or purpose, and where chance led them wrong they besought G-d's mercy and propitiated Him with prayers and supplications, and thus secured a perfect life guided aright in both fields, both in their premeditated actions and in such as were not of freely-willed purpose." Similarly, Melchisedek's priesthood, says Philo (*Congr.* 99), was self-taught (αὐτομαθὴς καὶ αὐτοδίδακτος) (cited by Robbins 1947, 54–55). On Moses' precocity compare the statement (Luke 2:46–47) that when Jesus was twelve his parents "found him in the Temple, sitting among the teachers, listening to them and asking them questions; and all who heard him were amazed at his understanding and his answers."

40. Cf. Plato's theory, propounded in the *Meno* 81C-D: "The soul, then, as being immortal, and having been born again many times, and having seen all things that exist, whether in this world or in the world below, has knowledge of them all; and it is no wonder that she should be able to call to remembrance all that she ever knew about virtue, and about everything; for as all nature is akin, and the soul has learned all things, there is no difficulty in her eliciting, or as men say learning, out of a single recollection all the rest, if a man is strenuous and does not faint; for all enquiry and all learning is but recollection" (trans. Benjamin Jowett). Plato's theory is that one possesses perfect knowledge of the Forms in the womb before one's birth and that through skillful questioning this knowledge can be brought out. See also Plato's *Phaedo* 72A-78B and *Theaetetus* 150D.

41. See *Sacr.* 6. Isaac is referred to as αὐτομαθής no fewer than 34 times and as αὐτοδίδακτος no fewer than seven times. See Earp 1962, 10:326, nn. a–b.

42. According to Artapanus (*ap.* Eus. *PE* 9.27.3–4), Moses was called Musaios by the Greeks. This Musaios was a legendary Greek poet who is said to have been a pupil

of Orpheus, though Artapanus speaks of him here as being a teacher of Orpheus, the great legendary musician. A collection of oracles and poems connected with Orphism was attributed to him. The second-century Neopythagorean Numenius of Apamea (*ap.* Eus. *PE* 9.8.2) also refers to Moses as Musaios. Clement of Alexandria (*Strom.* 1.23.413) adds medicine to the list of subjects in which Moses was instructed.

43. Cf. Acts 7:22: "Moses was instructed in all the wisdom of the Egyptians."

44. In the *Republic* the order is arithmetic, geometry, astronomy, and music. Philo has omitted astronomy, which he says was taught to Moses by Chaldeans and Egyptians. This reflects the well-founded belief that it was the Chaldeans and the Egyptians who pioneered in the field of astronomy and that the Greeks learned from them. On the encyclical studies in Philo, see Mendelson 1982, 1–46, especially 4–5.

45. So also Chadwick 1967, 137, n. 2. Cf. *Cher.* 105, where Philo speaks, though not in the first person, of grammar, geometry, and music; and *QE* 2.103, where he speaks of arithmetic, geometry, and music in that order. Indeed, Plato (*Laws* 2.656D–657A) remarks that the Egyptian chants were said to have been composed by the goddess Isis and that because of their sacred character they had not changed in thousands of years. Because (*Laws* 7.799A) in Egypt the hymns and dances were consecrated to the gods, anyone who offered any other hymns or dances was subject to suits of impiety (ibid.). Plato (*Laws* 7.819A) also praises the Egyptians for devising pleasant and amusing arithmetical games in teaching chidlren. Philo (*Somn.* 1.205) says that he admires the lover of wisdom in that when the latter sees a multitude of different things he weaves them together. He then elaborates on the actual educational program of his own day, explaining the contents of grammar, arithmetic, geometry, music, rhetoric and philosophy—precisely the topics that he says constituted Moses' education (*Mos.* 1.23): "For instance, he takes from the 'grammar' taught to children the two first subjects, writing and reading; from the more advanced 'grammar' acquaintance with the poets and a learning of ancient history; from arithmetic and geometry absolute accuracy in matters which require a making of calculations and noting of proportion; from music rhythms and metres and melodies enharmonic, chromatic, diatonic, conjunct too and disjunct; from rhetoric come conception, expression, arrangement, treatment, memory, delivery; from philosophy everything that has been omitted in the items given already, and other things that constitute the whole life of men,—and from these combined he frames a single work gay and bright to a degree, blending wide learning with readiness to learn still more."

46. As Ginzberg 1925, 5:402, n. 67, points out, a similar description of Moses' education is to be found in Clement of Alexandria, *Strom.* 1.23.155, which, he suggests, is very likely taken from Philo. Eusebius (*PE* 9.28.3) quotes from a speech of Moses in the *Exagoge* of Ezekiel the Tragedian, where Moses says that as a child he received a royal upbringing (τροφαὶ βασιλικαί) and education (παιδεύματα); but he does not give details.

47. Mansfeld 1988, 77, notes that Chaeremon, a notorious defamer of the Jews (see Josephus, *Ap.* 1.288–303) was a Stoic who interpreted Egyptian religion in terms

of Greek philosophy, just as Philo did for the Jewish religion, and that Philo may have been familiar with Chaeremon's views, since he here (*Mos.* 1.23) speaks of Egyptian philosophy as being conveyed in symbols, as displayed in the so-called "holy letters," one of Chaeremon's favorite themes. Cf. van der Horst 1984b. Most recently Sterling 1993, 103–5, noting general similarities between Chaeremon and Philo, concludes that these point to the presence in first-century Alexandria of Egyptian priests and Jewish exegetes using Stoic and Platonic philosophy in seeking an accommodation between their ancestral traditions and Greek thought.

48. According to Eupolemus (*ap.* Eus. *PE* 9.26.1), Moses was the first wise man and gave the alphabet to the Jews, who in turn gave it to the Phoenicians, who in turn gave it to the Greeks; and he was the first to write down laws. According to Artapanus (*ap.* Eus. *PE* 9.27.4), he was the first philosopher. Spencer (1685) draws upon the statement of Philo (*Mos.* 1.23) that the Egyptians instructed Moses in the philosophy conveyed in symbols, as displayed in the so-called holy inscriptions; and he theorizes that the ritual laws of the Hebrews have an Egyptian origin. See Assmann 1997, 55–90, especially 56 and 72–73. Spencer understands the symbols mentioned by Philo to be the hieroglyphic writing, which, he says, was the secret code by which the Egyptian priests transmitted their wisdom to the initiated.

49. So also *Post.* 165; *Spec.* 1.79; *Contempl.* 8–9; and *Legat.* 139, 163–66.

50. Robbins 1947, 55–56, notes the possibility of two separate schools of astrology and cites Cumont 1937, 14.

51. See Ginzberg 1925, 5:405, n. 73. So also the Samaritan *Molad* (p. 45, l. 12).

52. Bieler 1936, 35, notes that these are the three possibilities in Aristotle's definition of the θεῖος ἀνήρ. As one who was apparently regarded as heir apparent to the throne of Egypt, Moses might well have been regarded as divine or as destined for divinity. According to Artapanus (*ap.* Eus. *PE* 9.27.6), Moses was so loved by the masses because of the wonderful things that he did for them that he was deemed worthy of divine honor by the priests and was called Hermes because of his ability to interpret the sacred writings. See Goodenough 1928, 43–102.

53. Philo is here perhaps thinking of those Jews such as Dositheos the son of Drimylos, who in the third century B.C.E. "altered his customs and abandoned his ancestral beliefs" (3 Macc. 1:3); or Jason the high priest, who in the second century B.C.E. sought to convert his countrymen to the Greek way of life (2 Macc. 4:10); or his own nephew, Tiberius Julius Alexander, who in the first century C.E. "did not remain faithful to his ancestral customs" (Josephus, *A.J.* 20.100). On the various degrees of assimilation, acculturation, accommodation, and apostasy among contemporary Jews in Egypt before, during, and after Philo's lifetime, see Barclay 1996, 103–24.

54. Tiberius Julius Alexander was born ca. 14–16 C.E. As a young man, he entered Roman military service; and in 42 he was appointed *epistrategos* of the Thebaid in Egypt, a position that probably entailed defection from Jewish practices. Philo led the Alexandrian Jewish delegation to the Emperor Gaius Caligula in 40. We do not know the date of his death, but it is sometimes conjectured (e.g., by Amir 1971, 409) that he

lived until about the year 50. We do not know when Tiberius Julius Alexander's defection from Judaism occurred, but it would seem possible and perhaps even likely that it occurred during Philo's lifetime. We do not know the date when Philo composed *Mos.*

55. Heb. 11:24–25 reflects Moses' dilemma: "By faith Moses, when he was grown up, refused to be called the son of Pharaoh's daughter, choosing rather to share ill-treatment with the people of G-d than to enjoy the fleeting pleasures of sin."

56. So also Iamblichus (*Life of Pythagoras* 10) says that when Pythagoras was seen, he turned everyone around to view him.

57. Justin's date is problematic, but a date in the third or fourth century C.E. (so Stern 1974, 1:332) seems likely. One must approach the fragment with caution not only because it has come down to us by second hand and is several centuries removed from the original, but also because Justin himself indicates that he has been selective and subjective in the choice of material. "I have selected," he says, "what is most fitting for learning and omitted what is not agreeable to the joy of learning or essential to the contents."

58. This is perhaps an allusion to Moses' great concern (Exod. 13:19) to carry out Joseph's wish to be buried in the land of Israel.

59. Gager 1972, 50, cites this as evidence that Pompeius or his source was familiar with Jewish sources, noting that the Bible (Exod. 2:2) describes the newly born Moses as beautiful. But in view of Pompeius' egregious errors in making Moses the son of Joseph and in making Arruas (presumably Aaron) the son rather than the brother of Moses (presumably he had heard that Aaron was subordinate to Moses), it seems more likely that he had no direct knowledge of the LXX. Moreover, the fact that Pompeius refers to Aaron as both high priest and king is an indication that he did not consult the Bible directly but rather was influenced by the fact that just before his own time the Hasmonean rulers were both high priests and kings.

60. So also Stephen in Acts 7:20 refers to Moses' charming (ἀστεῖος) appearance. Similarly, Heb. 11:23. In *Abr.* 103 ἀστεῖος is opposed to φαῦλος ("mean," "common," "bad"). In *Fug.* 18 it is opposed to μοχθηρός ("wretched," "inferior," "knavish").

61. As the baby grew, according to the Samaritan *Molad* (p. 2, l. 10), even the sun was eclipsed by his light. After the ark containing the infant Moses had been placed in the Nile, the waters of the river, according to the Samaritan tradition (*Molad* [p. 25, l. 16]), stopped flowing and actually spoke, expressing their appreciation of Moses. According to the *Molad* (p. 26, l. 13), the Pharaoh's daughter had originally intended to kill him, but her soul longed for sanctification.

62. Josephus also states (*A.J.* 2.231) that no one was so indifferent to the beauty of the young Moses that on beholding him, he was not astonished at his handsomeness. Indeed, Josephus continues, many people who happened to meet him as he was being borne along the road turned back at the sight of him and left aside their serious affairs and used their time to view him. Other references to Moses' beauty may be found in Acts 7:20 and Heb. 11:23. See Cohen 1993, 40, n. 23. So also the rabbinic tra-

dition *Midr. Exod. Rab.* 1.26: "Because he was handsome everyone would take him out in their eagerness to see him." Indeed, according to the midrashic tradition (*Tan. Exod.* 8 [p. 213]), such was Moses' beauty that the Pharaoh's daughter did not allow him to leave the palace, since whoever saw him could not detach himself from the sight. In Josephus (*A.J.* 2.232) he is actually described by the Pharaoh's daughter as divine in appearance. In fact, the rabbis (*Pirqe R. El.* 48.21) compare Moses' beauty to that of an angel. One is reminded of the story that Herodotus (1.112) tells of how the wife of a cowherd who had been ordered to slay the infant Cyrus was so moved by the size and beauty of the child that she reared it as her own to replace the child whom she had borne dead.

63. The term appears to have been originated by Diogenes the Cynic, who, when asked whence he came, is said to have replied, "I am a citizen of the world" (κοσμοπολίτης, Diogenes Laertius 6.63). The term became a leading Stoic concept (*SVF* 1.262).

64. See Claudius' edict (Josephus, *A.J.* 19.280–85) and his letter to the Alexandrians (*CPJ* 153). Gruen 2002, 79–83, argues that in both the edict and in the letter Claudius merely affirmed freedom for the Jews to practice their religious rights, and that it is Josephus in his version who refers to Jewish political rights. We may suggest, however, that the statement in the papyrus (lines 88–91) in which Claudius expresses his indignation that the Jews have sent two embassies may be a clue to the fact that there was a difference of opinion among the Alexandrian Jews as to the goal of their delegation. One goal was that their religious rites should be reaffirmed, but another goal sharply differed from this and insisted that, in addition, the delegation should insist on equal political rights. Claudius adopted the view of the first delegation, but this does not mean that the second delegation did not aim at political rights.

65. Ginzberg 1910, 2:277, and 1925, 5:404–5, n. 70, cites the rabbinic tradition (*Midr. Exod. Rab.* 1.27, *Tan. Exod.* 9, *Midr. Lev. Rab.* 37.2) that Moses, in his sympathy for the suffering Israelites, actually worked in their place, an act that the Pharaoh interpreted as an indication that Moses was doing this in order to get the Israelites to carry out his orders. He even managed to get the Pharaoh to allow the Israelites to rest on the Sabbath, convincing him that the Israelite slaves would perish from overwork if they toiled ceaselessly (*Midr. Exod. Rab.* 1.28, *Yashar Shemot* 133a, *Shibbole ha-Leket* 55–56). According to the midrashic tradition (*Mek. Shirah* 1.34b, *Midr. Tannaim* 96, *Midr. Exod. Rab.* 30.4), Moses endangered his life for the sake of the Israelites, and consequently he was rewarded by the fact that G-d speaks of "the Torah of Moses" and of Israel as "the people of Moses."

66. Ginzberg 1925, 5:405, n. 72, cites a similar motif that Azariah dei Rossi, *Meor 'Enayim* 4.4, quotes from an unidentified work by Origen, that on the Sabbath Moses showed the Israelites the book of Job in order to emphasize that the suffering of the righteous is only temporary and eventually makes room for joy.

67. On the comparison of Moses with a physician, see Philo, *Deus* 67: "So then the lawgiver, thereby being now approved as the best of physicians for the distempers

and maladies of the soul, set before himself one task and purpose, to make a radical excision of the diseases of the mind and leave no root to sprout again into sickness which defies cure."

68. See Ginzberg 1925, 5:405, n. 73, and Holladay 1989, 2:425–26, n. 41. The Midrash (*Exod. Rab.* 1.28, *Lev. Rab.* 32.4–5, *Yashar Shemot* 133b, *Dibre ha-Yamim* 4, and parallels) has an account of an Israelite officer named Dathan, who served under an Egyptian taskmaster, who dishonored Dathan's wife. When the Egyptian sought to kill Dathan, Moses happened to pass by. At first he waited to see whether someone would avenge the outrage. When no one came, he consulted the angels, who agreed that the Egyptian deserved to die, whereupon Moses pronounced the name of G-d and the Egyptian died immediately.

69. The one scenario where the rabbinic tradition criticizes Moses' slaying of the Egyptian is at the time when Moses pleads with G-d for mercy as his death is approaching. There (*Petirat Moshe* 1.118–19, cited by Ginzberg 1928, 6:149, n. 891), G-d reminds Moses that He had not counselled him to slay the Egyptian, whereupon Moses counters with the argument that since G-d did slay all the first-born of the Egyptians, why should he die on account of one single Egyptian whom he had slain, whereupon G-d retorts: "Are you my equal?"

70. According to the midrashic tradition (*Midr. Exod. Rab.* 1.29–31 and parallels cited by Ginzberg 1925, 5:405–6, n. 75), the two Israelites were Dathan and Abiram, who later, together with Korah, rebelled against Moses (Num. 16:1, 24–27); and it is they who told the Pharaoh that Moses was not the son of his daughter, whereupon the Pharaoh issued an order that Moses be executed.

71. Josephus (*A.J.* 2.255) does say that the Pharaoh was ready to undertake the murder of Moses; but he does not indicate why, though presumably the reason was that he resented Moses' murder of the Egyptian, an event that Josephus does not mention at all.

72. Another example where Philo departs from the biblical text for apologetic reasons is his omission of Joseph's slander of his brothers (Gen. 37:2), though he refers to this verse itself on four occasions (*Deus* 119, *Agr.* 55, *Sobr.* 12, *Ios.* 5).

73. Thus, in an extra-biblical addition, Joseph sells grain to all people and not merely to native Egyptians (*A.J.* 2.94, 101). Again, in an extra-biblical remark very similar to that of Philo, Solomon, in dedicating the Temple, asks that G-d grant the prayers not only of Jews but also of non-Jews (*A.J.* 8.116–17).

74. Artapanus' date is apparently somewhere between the middle of the third and the middle of the second century B.C.E. See Holladay 1983, 1:189–90.

75. This is the conclusion of the most exhaustive treatment of this playwright, Jacobson 1983, 5–13, as well as of the most recent extensive discussion, that by Holladay 1989, 2:308–12.

76. Jacobson 1983, 37–38, notes several narrative details in which Josephus is reminiscent of Ezekiel and concludes that he was familiar with the latter's play. Though the *argumentum ex silentio* is never conclusive, it seems surprising, if Josephus

did know the work of Ezekiel, that he does not mention Moses' dream and the interpretation by Jethro, especially in view of Josephus' great interest in dreams. See Gnuse 1996.

77. Josephus (*A.J.* 2.263) says that Jetho actually adopted Moses as his son, but there is no such statement in the Bible.

78. Ginzberg 1928, 6:90, n. 488, cites numerous rabbinic passages in which Zipporah is identified as the Cushite woman whom Moses married (Num. 12:1) and who is described as distinguished for her beauty and piety.

79. This is the most common epithet applied to Jethro. Its meaning is "superfluous," "over-wise." Colson and Whitaker 1929, 2: ad loc., translate it as "worldling" in *Sacr.* 50 and as "worldly-wise" in *Gig.* 50; Colson and Whitaker 1930, 3: ad loc., translate it as "uneven" in *Agr.* 43; Colson and Whitaker 1934, 5: ad loc., render it as "superfluous" in *Mut.* 103.

80. On Philo's ambivalent attitude toward Jethro, see Feldman 1998b, 41–43.

81. *Va-Yosha'* 43, *Yashar Shemot* 138b, 140–41, *Dibre ha-Yamim* 7, cited by Ginzberg 1925, 5:412, n. 96.

82. On the rabbinic attitude toward Jethro, see Feldman 1998b, 43–46.

83. See *Tan. B, Exod.* 71, *Midr. Exod. Rab.* 1.32, *Mishnat R. Eliezer* p. 304 (ed. H. G. Enelow), *Sifre Num.* 78. See Feldman 1998b, 44–45.

84. On shepherding as preparation for a career of leadership, see Philo (*Ios.* 2). It is also found frequently in the rabbinic tradition (*Midr. Exod. Rab.* 2.2–3, *Tan. Buber* 2.6, *Midr. Psalms* 78.357, cited by Ginzberg 1925, 5:414, n. 109).

85. Moreover, according to the rabbis (*b. Sanh.* 25b), shepherds were disqualified as judges or witnesses in Palestine, presumably because they sometimes grazed their flocks on the private property of others.

86. On Moses as shepherd, see Josephus (*A.J.* 2.263–64) and Pseudo-Philo (19.3, 9). Cf. the depiction of Jesus as shepherd: Matt. 2:6, 25:32, 26:31, cited by Allison 1993, 214, n. 174.

87. Cf. Plato, *R.* 1.342E: "No ruler of any kind, insofar as he is a ruler, considers and prescribes for his own advantage, but for that of the ruled, the subject of his skill." Philo (*Ios.* 2) remarks that "the order of poets [he is thinking particularly of such a passage as Homer, *Il.* 1.263] often speaks of kings as shepherds of peoples, for success in shepherding will produce the best king, since through the charge of flocks which deserve less thought and care he has been taught the charge of the noblest flock of living creatures—mankind." Ginzberg 1925, 5:414, n. 109, notes that in rabbinic literature Moses is often called the "faithful shepherd."

88. The term is found in Plato, Aristotle, the Cynics, and the Stoics. See Goodenough 1935, 54–55.

89. There is some question as to the meaning of Artapanus' Greek here. For alternate translations, see Holladay 1983, 1:238, n. 77.

90. The allusion would seem to be to the biblical prohibition (Lev. 19:19, Deut. 22:11) of wearing *sha'atnez*, cloth combining wool and linen.

91. The rabbinic tradition (*Pirqe R. El.* 40, *Midr. ha-Gadol* 2.23) states that during the forty years that Moses served as a shepherd for Jethro's flocks, they were incredibly fertile, and not a single sheep was attacked by wild beasts.

92. Robbins 1947, 68, notes that Plato (*R.* 6.507C) also regarded the power of seeing as the most priceless of the senses; and he notes that Philo elsewhere (*Conf.* 141, *Abr.* 150, and *Somn.* 1.129) likewise has a higher estimate of sight than of hearing.

93. A similar explanation of the symbolic significance of the bush is found in the rabbinic tradition (*Midr. ha-Gadol* 2.25 and parallels cited by Ginzberg 1925, 5:416, n. 115). Philo's symbolic interpretation of the burning bush is parallel to *Midr. Exod. Rab.* 2.5; see Kugel 1997, 301–2.

94. See, e.g., Apion's charge (Josephus, *Ap.* 2.38).

95. The rabbinic tradition (*Pirqe R. El.* 40) reports that Moses asked G-d to tell him His name so that he might call upon Him by name and so that He might give him a favorable hearing.

96. These three methods of gaining wisdom are found in Aristotle (*EN* 2.1103A15). They appear frequently in Philo: *Mut.* 12, *Sacr.* 5–6, *Abr.* 52.

97. On Philo's views concerning miracles, see *Mos.* 1.212–13, where he argues that the greatest miracles are to be found in G-d's creation, but, because they are so familiar, they are held of little account. For a comprehensive analysis of Philo's view of miracles, see Wolfson 1947, 1:347–56, 424–32.

98. So also in Josephus (*A.J.* 2.274), G-d, both before and after showing Moses the three miracles, exhorts him to be courageous (θαρρεῖν), the verbal form corresponding to Philo's noun (θάρσος).

99. This canard is repeated by Nicarchus (*ap.* Photius, *Lexicon*, *s.v.* ἄλφα) in the first century C.E., by Ptolemy Chennos (*ap.* Photius, *Lexicon* 190) in the early second century C.E., and by Helladius (*ap.* Photius, *Lexicon* 190) in the early fourth century C.E. There we learn that Moses the legislator was called ἄλφα by the Jews because he had much dull-white leprosy (ἀλφοί) on his body. Inasmuch as Moses is nowhere else called ἄλφα in the extant literature, Heinemann 1935, 361, and Gager 1972, 130–31, have suggested that the source of this tradition is the Alexandrian anti-Jewish version of the Exodus. As we can see from Ptolemy, such puns in connection with letters of the alphabet were common; thus, a certain Satyrus was called *zeta* because of his inquisitiveness (ζητέω). From the fact that the LXX, Philo, and Josephus (*A.J.* 2.273) on Exod. 4:6 omit the statement that Moses' hand was leprous, and from Photius' reference to Nicarchus' statement as nonsense and to Helladius' as a lie, we may infer that a pun was intended to express hostility toward the Jews. And yet, we may suggest that Moses was indeed called *alpha* by the Jews themselves because he was regarded as the greatest prophet, just as in the Book of Revelation (1:8) Jesus, presumably as the new Moses, is spoken of as the Alpha and the Omega. Jacobson 1999, 626–27, suggests that the Jews thought of Moses as their teacher par excellence and hence referred to him as Alpha from the Aramaic root for the verb "to teach."

Josephus points out the inherent contradiction on the part of the anti-Jewish Egyptian writers in, on the one hand, presenting Moses as an Egyptian priest and asserting that he was remarkable (θαυμαστός) and even divine (θεῖος), and, on the other hand, claiming that he was expelled because of leprosy (*Ap.* 1.279). Josephus, recalling this charge of leprosy (*A.J.* 3.265), refutes it by remarking that if it were true, Moses would not have issued to his own humiliation statutes banishing lepers, especially since there are nations that honor lepers (*A.J.* 3.266–68). In fact, in a significant change, according to Josephus, Moses banished lepers not merely from the camp, as the Bible has it (Lev. 13:46, 14:3), but also from the city (*A.J.* 3.261, *Ap.* 1.281), the implication being that there were no lepers in Jerusalem in Josephus' own day (see Hata 1987, 190). Furthermore, Josephus deliberately omits the lengthy discussion of the symptoms of leprosy found in the Bible, inasmuch as this would presumably indicate to the reader that the malady was common among Jews. Ultimately, Josephus graciously but confidently leaves the decision to the reader (*A.J.* 3.268). However, just as Plato had declared that a philosopher-king should, if at all possible, be handsome (*R.* 7.535A11–12), so Josephus remarks that Moses legislated that even the slightest mutilation was reason enough for disqualification from the priesthood and that a priest who during the course of his service met with such an accident was to be deprived of his position (*Ap.* 1.284). Josephus then asks whether it is likely that Moses would have enacted such a stringent law if he himself had been affected by such an affliction (*Ap.* 1.285).

100. Similarly, the LXX avoids the mention of leprosy and declares that Moses' hand became as snow.

101. In Josephus (*A.J.* 2.273) Moses actually does take some water and pours it on the ground, whereupon it becomes bloody.

102. Cf., e.g., Thucydides on Themistocles (1.138.3) and Pericles (2.60.6).

103. So also *Midr. ha-Gadol* 3.33 and 86, as noted by Ginzberg 1925, 5:422, n. 140. Another version as to how Moses acquired a speech defect is that when, according to the midrashic tradition (*Exod. Rabbah* 1.26), the infant Moses took the Pharaoh's crown and placed it upon his head, the Pharaoh, terrified, called for his wise men, who advised him, by placing before Moses an onyx stone and a coal of fire, to test whether the child really wanted to assume the sovereignty. If the child should grasp the onyx, it would be a sign that he was ambitious for the rulership and should be slain. In this test Moses actually stretched forth his hand to grasp the onyx, but the angel Gabriel, according to the Midrash, guided his hand toward the hot coal, which burnt his hand, whereupon he lifted up his hand to his mouth and burnt part of his lips and tongue.

104. Cf. Luke 21:15: "For I will give you a mouth and wisdom, which none of your adversaries will be able to withstand or contradict."

105. Elsewhere (*Migr.* 76), however, Philo says that Moses does investigate specious arguments for the sake of getting the better of the sophists in Egypt.

106. Cf. Exod. 4:19: "And the L-rd said to Moses in Midian: 'Go back to Egypt; for all the men who were seeking your life are dead.'"

107. In Josephus (*A.J.* 2.277) we read that after he had learned that the Pharaoh in whose reign he had fled had died, he asked Raguel (Jethro) for permission to leave.

108. There is a rabbinic tradition that the reason why the son was uncircumcised was that Moses' father-in-law, Jethro, had stipulated, when he consented to the marriage of his daughter to Moses, that the first son of their union should be brought up as a gentile (*Mek. Yitro* 1.58a).

109. Josephus (*A.J.* 2.279) states that Aaron met Moses when Moses came near the border of Egypt.

110. In establishing the importance of Moses, Josephus systematically downgrades the role of Aaron as Moses' spokesman. Thus, when, at the beginning of his mission, Moses first consolidates his backing among his own people, Exod. 5:1 states that he and Aaron then went to see the Pharaoh; in Josephus (*A.J.* 2.281) Moses betakes himself alone after he is assured of the allegiance of the Israelites, of their agreement to follow his orders, and of their love of liberty. It is Moses, rather than Aaron, who performs miracles with his rod in the presence of the Pharaoh (Exod. 7:10 vs. *A.J.* 2.284, 287); and Moses' achievement is all the more impressive because, according to Josephus' addition, the king had ridiculed him. Whereas Exod. 7:19 says that it was Aaron who with his staff produced the plague of blood, Josephus, though he generally avoids imputing miracles to G-d, says that the plague was produced at G-d's command and leaves the human agent unidentified (*A.J.* 2.294). Likewise, in Exod. 8:2 and 8:13 it is Aaron who brings on the plagues of frogs and lice, whereas in Josephus it is G-d who produces them (*A.J.* 2.296, 300).

111. In Josephus (*A.J.* 2.280) it is Moses alone who recounts the miracles and who then actually performs them.

112. In Josephus (*A.J.* 2.282) Moses reminds Pharaoh of the help that he had given the Egyptians when they were humiliated by the Ethiopians and asserts that he had received no just recompense despite the fact that he had put himself in danger.

113. So also Josephus, *A.J.* 4.207 and *Ap.* 2.237. In the latter passage Josephus similarly explains that "our legislator has expressly forbidden us to deride or blaspheme the gods recognized by others, out of respect for the very word 'G-d.'"

114. See *Decal.* 79, *Post.* 165, *Legat.* 139, *Spec.* 1.79, *Mos.* 1.93, cited by Wolfson 1947, 1:23.

115. On alleged Jewish illiberalism, see Feldman 1993a, 125–31.

116. In Josephus' version (*A.J.* 2.290) it is Moses alone whom the Israelites hold accountable for the increased severity of their labors.

117. In the rabbinic tradition (*b. Men.* 85a, *Midr. Exod. Rab.* 9.6–7) the Egyptian magicians, Jannes and Jambres, since Egypt was famous as a land that had great magicians, deride Moses for performing such simple magical tricks before Pharaoh.

118. Josephus (*A.J.* 2.287), who is ever concerned to focus particularly on Moses as the leader who took the Israelites out of Egypt, says that it was Moses, rather than Aaron (Exod. 7:10), who performed the miracle with his rod in the presence of the Pharaoh. His rod, after making the circuit of the Egyptians' rods, which merely looked like pythons, then proceeded to devour them all.

119. Josephus (*A.J.* 2.286) is likewise aware of the problem that the Egyptian magicians were able to duplicate the conversion of a staff into a snake. Moses tells Pharaoh that he does not disparage the wisdom of the Egyptians but that his feats far excel theirs as things divine differ from things human, and that he will show that his miracles are manifest not through jugglery and deception but through G-d's providence and power.

120. Josephus (*A.J.* 2.284) the Pharaoh, in his indignation, calls Moses a rogue who had formerly fled from the slavery among the Egyptians and who now had brought about his return through deceit and had undertaken to intimidate him by juggleries and magical arts.

121. The most general and most severe condemnation of the pharaohs may be seen in Philo's equation of the Pharaoh with materialism and in his portrayal of the Pharaoh rejoicing in buildings constructed from brick (*Conf.* 88). He is enamored of "what is material and female" and knows not the First Cause (*Leg.* 3.243). Indeed, "when this mind becomes enamored of the body, its efforts are expended on three things which it deems most worthy of its care and trouble—bread, meat, and drink" (*Ios.* 151). For Philo, who calls Plato "most sacred" (*Prob.* 13), the strongest criticism of the Pharaoh is that he is the mind that is king of the body, namely Egypt (*Conf.* 88, *Fug.* 124, *Migr.* 160, *Ebr.* 208, *Abr.* 103, *Ios.* 151), as well as the body in each of us (*Ios.* 151). He is weak-willed and incontinent (*Ebr.* 210). Such people are irrational and lifeless, and should consequently be shunned (*Fug.* 126). Moreover, it is he whom the passions follow as their leader (*Leg.* 3.13). He is identified with the senses and with the search for pleasure and love of the self (*Somn.* 2.215, 2.219, 2.277, *Mut.* 171, 173, *Leg.* 3.212, *Post.* 115); indeed, the Pharaoh crowns his self-love with madness (Cher. 74), thinking that his constitution is more than human (*Post.* 115). He opposes "what training and education establish for our dealings with the world of creation, and thus he will work universal confusion."

Again, one sees the Platonist in Philo bitterly criticizing the Pharaoh as one who, in body and soul alike, is the subject of movement and turning and change (*Somn.* 2.219). Things created and perishable seem to him bright and shining, so that he dwells in night and profound darkness (*Ebr.* 209). He "cannot receive the vision of timeless values, for the eyes of the soul, whereby alone incorporeal natures are apprehended, are blinded in him" (*Sacr.* 69). In this respect he is identified with the land of Egypt (*Leg.* 3.212), just as he is contrasted with Judaism's paternal and truly real wealth (*Mut.* 173). The love of pleasure, with which he is identified, is devoid of all the chief necessities, namely temperance, modesty, self-restraint, justice, and every virtue; "for no two things can be more hostile to each other than virtue is to pleasure" (*Ios.* 153).

He is the epitome of senselessness and wine-frenzy and ceaseless life-long intoxication and incontinence (*Somn.* 2.200–201). In a word, he is the very antithesis of Moses.

Over and over again Philo presents the etymology (a clearly wrong one, the correct derivation being from the Egyptian term for "the Great House") of the Pharaoh as derived from the word meaning "scattering," in the sense, according to Philo, that he made scattering and undoing of continence his business (*Somn.* 2.211). Indeed, he is the scatterer of all things noble and of pious thoughts and deeds (*Leg.* 3.12, 3.236, 3.243, *Sacr.* 69, *Det.* 95, *Her.* 60). His tyranny, rife with lawlessness and cruelty, is impossible to escape (*Her.* 60). Like an actor in a play, he "assumes a counterfeited fellowship, the licentious with chastity, the profligate with self-control, the unjust with justice, and in his desire to earn a good repute with the multitude invites virtue to join him" (*Abr.* 103). He is at once boastful (*Ebr.* 111) and stiff-necked (*Somn.* 2.184).

Indeed, the Pharaoh is steeped in greed, is licentious and unjust, priding himself on his impiety, of which he is the crowning example (*Mut.* 19), since he dared to say "I know not the L-rd" (Exod. 5:2) (*Somn.* 2.182). In fact, in saying "I know not the L-rd," he is asserting that even if there is a G-d He is not known to us (*Ebr.* 19). Over and over again he is described as godless (*Leg.* 3.13, 3.212, *Sacr.* 69); indeed, he is the very antithesis of G-d, since he is the mind that usurps His place (*Somn.* 2.183). He is "disobedient to the commandments which law and custom regularly prescribe in these matters; but rebellion or strife-stirrer is the name for him who turns aside to their direct opposite, impiety, and becomes a leader in godlessness" (*Ebr.* 5.18).

Indeed, he is the archetype of the foolish man (*Det.* 161–62, *Mut.* 128, 175, *Conf.* 29–30) and the wicked man (*Somn.* 2.237, *Leg.* 3.212). In fact, in surveying all the numerous references to the Pharaoh in Philo one finds not a single positive trait nor any mitigating circumstances. Undoubtedly, Philo has been influenced in this regard by the long and bitter history of hostility to the Jews in Egypt, starting with Manetho in the third century B.C.E. and culminating in his own day in the vicious remarks of Apion as cited in Josephus' essay, *Ap.* Most of all, perhaps, he has been influenced by the terrible suffering of his fellow Alexandrian Jews in the pogrom of the year 38, which he himself reports in such graphic colors in his essays *Flacc.* 41–85 and *Legat.* 120–31. Compare this with Josephus' nuanced view of the pharaohs. See Feldman 1993f, 49–63. Josephus (*A.J.* 2.281) evincees a certain amount of understanding for the Pharaoh's position, since we are told in an extra-biblical addition that he had only recently been promoted to the throne. One might be reminded of a similar understanding that one might feel for Zeus in Aeschylus' *Prometheus Bound* (312), where, we are told, he, too, is new to the throne and presumably should be given a greater opportunity to establish his rule more firmly.

122. Cf., e.g., Strabo 16.2.35.761, who praises Moses for teaching that "G-d is the one thing alone that encompasses us all and encompasses land and sea—the thing which we call heaven, or universe, or the nature of all that exists."

123. On the order and description of the plagues in Ezekiel, see Jacobson 1996, 1:114–21.

124. Robbins 1947, 75, notes that Philo's classification of the plagues according to the four elements—air, fire, water, and earth—follows his architectonic scheme of physics (*Her.* 134–40): cold (air), hot (fire), wet (water), and dry (earth), and remarks that this is basically Stoic. Cf. the biography of Zeno by Diogenes Laertius (7.137).

125. The meaning, as Ladouceur (1983, 18–38) indicates, basing himself on the usage in medical writers, is not "stained with blood" as if Josephus were attempting to rationalize the plague but rather, as Galen (8.379, 17 [2].692) and Rufus (*De Renum et Vesicae Affectionibus* 5.2) use it, "changed to blood," a meaning confirmed by the LXX's translation (Exod. 7:20) of the plague.

126. Ginzberg 1925, 5:427, n. 172, cites the dictum (*b. Sanh.* 90a) of "measure for measure" ascribed to an anonymous Tanna: "In all the measures [of punishment or reward] taken by the Holy One, blessed be He, the Divine act befits the [human] deed"; and *b. Soṭ.* 11a: "They were cooked in the very same pot in which they cooked." The rabbinic tradition (*Mek. Amalek* 2, 55a; *Mek. Beshallaḥ* 6.32; *t. Soṭ.* 3.13, *Sifre Num.* 106), as well as Wisdom (11:5), consequently, maintains that each plague corresponds to a crime committed by the Egyptians against the Israelites. Thus, because the Egyptians forced the Israelites to draw water for them and also hindered them from the use of the ritual baths, G-d changed their water to blood.

127. *Midr. Deut. Rab.* 3.8 likewise reports that the water was undrinkable for the Egyptians alone. It states that when the Egyptians and the Israelites went to the Nile to drink water, the Egyptians drank blood and the Israelites drank water. Exod. 8:22 makes the distinction between the effect of the plagues upon the Israelites as contrasted with their effect upon the Egyptians in connection with the fourth plague and specifically mentions that the land of Goshen was not affected.

128. The statement that the Pharaoh allowed the Israelites to leave after this plague is an addition found also in Artapanus (*ap.* Eus. *PE* 9.27.29).

129. Josephus (*A.J.* 2.296) also remarks that the Pharaoh was no longer (οὐκέτι) willing to be wise (σωφρονεῖν, "moderate," "temperate," "reasonable"), the implication being that he had previously exercised such wisdom and moderation.

130. As Ginzberg 1925, 5:429, n. 183, notes, it is the unanimous opinion of the rabbis that this plague was one of lice. See, e.g., *Midr. Exod. Rab.* 10.2, 6–7 and 15.10; *Tan. Va-era* 14; *Midr. ha-Gadol* 2.62; *Seder Eliyahu Rab.* 7.41. Josephus (*A.J.* 2.300) also identifies them as lice (φθεῖρες).

131. Robbins 1947, 76, cites Wisdom 11:17: "For Thy all-powerful hand, that created the world out of formless matter, lacked not means to send upon them a multitude of bears or fierce lions, or new-created wild beasts, full of rage, unknown before, either breathing out a blast of fiery breath, or blowing out roarings of smoke, or flashing dreadful sparks from their eyes."

132. Commenting on this verse in the Talmud (*b. Sanh.* 67b), the third-century Rabbi Eleazar ben Pedat explains that the reason why the Egyptian magicians were not able to reproduce the plague of the lice (gnats) was that a magician cannot pro-

duce a creature less than a barley corn in size. As for the first two plagues, according to the rabbis (*Midr. Exod. Rab.* 10.7 and 11.2), all they succeeded in doing was to produce an optical illusion upon the Pharaoh.

133. Josephus (*A.J.* 2.305) also notes that the hail was not similar to that which comes down among others in the season of winter. The midrashic tradition (*Midr. Exod. Rab.* 12.3) notes that the hail was such as had never occurred in Egypt nor even in the rest of the whole world.

134. Josephus (*A.J.* 2.307), who, in his regard for authority as such, is eager to prevent the full blame from being placed upon the Pharaoh, offers an extra-biblical explanation as to why the Pharaoh ordered the Israelites to leave their herds behind, namely that the Egyptians had lost their own.

135. Unlike Philo, Josephus (*A.J.* 2.308) does not resort to rationalization here. See Moehring 1973, 376–83.

136. Whereas in the Bible it is the Pharaoh who summons Moses, in Josephus (*A.J.* 2.309) we read that the darkness dispersed after three days and nights without any indication as to why it ended. Instead, whereas in the Bible the Pharaoh agrees to allow the Israelites to depart, provided that they leave their livestock behind, in Josephus (*A.J.* 2.309) we read specifically that the Pharaoh did not repent and that it is Moses who went to the Pharaoh and warned him that he would not be relieved of suffering until he allowed the Israelites to leave. Thereupon, in an extra-biblical addition, the Pharaoh threatened to cut off Moses' head if he should come again, whereupon Moses said that he would no longer speak about these matters to the Pharaoh but that the Pharaoh himself, together with the foremost of the Egyptians, would implore the Israelites to depart.

137. In Josephus (*A.J.* 2.304) there is no mention of G-d's instructions to Moses and Aaron. Rather, it is G-d Himself who brings about the boils.

138. So also Ezekiel the Tragedian (*ap.* Eus. *PE* 9.28.12). *Midr. Exod. Rab.* 11.2–3 likewise views the plague as consisting of stinging flies and describes the sun and the moon as being darkened by them.

139. Pseudo-Philo (10.1) renders it *pammixia*, "all mixture." Aquila (*ap.* Jerome, *Epistula* 106.85) uses almost the same word, πάμμικτον. Wis. 11:17–18 may perhaps be alluding to this plague when it states that G-d did not lack the means to send a multitude of bears and fierce lions, as well as newly created wild beasts.

140. Note that the word "Cynic" is derived from the Greek word for dog (κύων, κυνός). The Cynics were so called because of their uncouth and aggressive manners and their alleged shamelessness. Diogenes, the Cynic philosopher, on being asked what he had done to be called a dog, is said to have replied (Diogenes Laertius 6.60): "I fawn on those who give me anything, I yelp at those who refuse, and I set my teeth in rascals."

141. As Ginzberg 1925, 5:433–34, n. 213, points out, the rabbis emphasize greatly that it was G-d Himself who directly accomplished the slaying of the first-

born (*Mek. Bo* 7.7b, 13.13b, *Midr. Tannaim* 173, Passover Haggadah), although in later literature we find the view that the slaying was done by an angel.

142. The Pharaoh himself, being the first-born, was the only one who escaped death on that night (*Mek. Bo* 13.73).

143. The rabbis (*Mek. R. Shim.* 52) present a scenario in which ninety million angels, some of hail and some of flames, appear ready to carry out the annihilation, but G-d restrains them, since He insists on carrying out this decree Himself.

144. *Pesiq. Rb. Kah.* 7.65a, *Pesiq. Rabbati* 17.88a, *Midr. Psalms* 136.520, *Tan. B.* 2.51–52, *Midr. Va-Yosha'* (ed. Jellinek, *Bet Ha-Midrash*, 1) 50–51, *Dibre Ha-Yamim* (ed. Jellinek, *Bet Ha-Midrash*, 2) 10, cited by Ginzberg 1925, 5:433, n. 211.

145. *Pesiq. Rb. Kah.* 7.64b, *Pesiq. Rabbati* 17.87b and 197b, *Tan. B.* 2.52, *Dibre Hayamim* 10, *Midr. Exod. Rab.* 18.3, *Midr. Psalms* 78.355 and 105.452, cited by Ginzberg 1925, 5:433, n. 212.

146. *Mek. Bo* 13, 13b; *Mek. R. Shim.* 23–24, cited by Ginzberg 1925, 5:434, n. 218.

147. *Pesiq. Rb. Kah.* 7.65b, *Pesiq. Rabbati* 17.88b, *Midr. Exod. Rab.* 18.10, cited by Ginzberg 1925, 5:434, n. 219.

148. Holladay suggests that the omission of the plague of the first-born may be due to Alexander Polyhistor, upon whom Artapanus is dependent for his account.

149. Philo, obviously concerned with the question as to how G-d could have destroyed all the people of Sodom rather than merely those people who were proven to be wicked, emphasizes (*Conf.* 27–28), basing himself on the biblical text (Gen. 19:4), that all the people of Sodom from every quarter converged on the house where Lot was extending hospitality to his guests, and that all the people of Sodom, both young and old, surrounded the house. He adds that they ran round and round the house, which he equates with the soul, and thus brought dishonor and ruin on those sacred thoughts, that is the angels, that were its guests and guardians, and that none of the inhabitants of Sodom was opposed to this unjust act. Philo (*Fug.* 144) adds that the Sodomites, blind in understanding and madly bent on bringing shame upon the sacred and undefiled words, that is the angels, ran all around the house and left no stone unturned in order to carry out their unnatural and unholy lust.

150. Burns 2000, 16, asks why Lysimachus chose to compose a new version of the Exodus rather than to adopt that which had already been established by Manetho. He suggests that he did so because Manetho's account had obvious internal inconsistencies and that it was unclear, and so he created an account more consistent with history and less subject to refutation by apologists such as the later Josephus. In point of fact, Lysimachus' account in Josephus' version is, indeed, less subject to refutation than are the accounts of Manetho and Chaeremon. Josephus is able to point out only the sheer *unlikelihood* of Lysimachus' account; Josephus can offer comments only on Lysimachus' vagueness and improbability.

151. Rabbinic tradition (*b. Ber.* 9b) cites a dispute as to whether the Israelites took what they acquired against the will of the Egyptians or against their own will. According to rabbinic tradition (*b. Ber.* 9a–b), G-d told Moses to tell the Israelites to bor-

row gold and silver vessels so that Abraham might not say that G-d fulfilled for the Israelites the first half of the verse (Gen. 15:14) "I will bring judgment on the nation which they serve" but that He did not fulfill for them the rest of the verse "and afterward they shall come out with great possessions."

152. In the Bible (Gen. 15:13–14) G-d promises Abraham that the Israelites will leave Egypt with great substance. In another biblical passage (Exod. 3:21–22) G-d tells Moses that before leaving Egypt the Israelites are to ask for jewels and clothing from the Egyptians, "and when you go, you shall not go empty . . . ; thus you shall despoil the Egyptians." Before they actually depart from Egypt G-d repeats similar instructions to Moses (Exod. 11:2–3) to tell the Israelites "that they ask, every man of his neighbor and every woman of her neighbor, jewelry of silver and gold." We are then told that G-d gave the people favor in the sight of the Egyptians. Philo (*Mos.* 1.141) is clearly defensive about this action on the part of the Israelites. "They did this," he explains, "not in avarice, or, as their accusers might say, in covetousness of what belonged to others. No, indeed. In the first place, they were but receiving a bare wage for all their time of service; secondly, they were retaliating, not on an equal but on a lesser scale, for their enslavement." Josephus (*A.J.* 2.314) goes even further in minimizing the responsibility of the Israelites. In his version it is not the Israelites who approach the Egyptians but rather the Egyptians themselves who take the initiative in honoring the Israelites with gifts, some in order to speed their departure, others to show their neighborly feelings toward old acquaintances.

153. So also Jub. 48:18 states that the Israelites took the vessels and garments from the Egyptians in return for the bondage in which they had forced them to serve.

154. In *b. Ber.* 9b we read that according to one view the Israelites took the things against the will of the Egyptians, whereas another view is that the Egyptians gave it to them even though the Israelites did not want them.

155. Nodet (1990, ad loc.) notes that the view that the Egyptians sought to have the Israelites depart more swiftly corresponds to the LXX's translation (Exod. 12:39) that the Egyptians actively cast out the Israelites, whereas the Hebrew text reads גרשו, "they were cast out."

156. On Philo's favorable attitude toward conversion of non-Jews to Judaism, see Feldman 1993a, 295–96.

157. Josephus (*A.J.* 2.323) adds other reasons why Moses did not lead the Israelites in a more direct route to Canaan, namely, because the Philistines had a hostile attitude toward the Israelites due to an ancient enmity with them and because G-d had commanded him to lead the people to Mount Sinai in order to do sacifices there. Rabbinic tradition likewise mentions the Philistine menace (*Midr. Exod. Rab.* 20:11, *Mek. R. Ish. Beshallaḥ* intro. on Exod. 13:17 [ed. Horovitz, p. 76], *Tg. Ps.-J.* ad loc.). Rabbinic tradition (*Mek. R. Ish. Beshallaḥ* 23b, *Mek. R. Shim.* 38, *Midr. Exod. Rab.* 20.11–17, as cited by Ginzberg 1928, 6:2, n. 8) presents numerous additional reasons why the Israelites took the roundabout route: G-d wanted them to go to Sinai first and receive the Torah; the time, divinely appointed, for the Gentiles to occupy Canaan had not yet

elapsed; if they had come to Canaan quickly, they would have devoted themselves to cultivating the land, whereas in the desert they had plenty of opportunity to study the Torah, since G-d provided for their needs; when the Canaanites heard that the Israelites were headed to their country, they burnt the crops, whereas when the Israelites did not arrive immediately, the Canaanites had an opportunity to repair the damage; the many miracles performed for the Israelites in the wilderness infused fear into the Canaanites, so that when the Israelites finally did come into Canaan they had a much easier time. Josephus (*A.J.* 2.315) says, in contradiction to the biblical statement that the Israelites took a longer, roundabout way, that they departed by a shortened route.

158. As Nodet 1990, ad loc., remarks, the ancient enmity between the Philistines and the Israelites is an anchronism. However, rabbinic tradition (*Midr. Exod. Rab.* 20.11, *Mek. R. Ish. Beshallaḥ*, intro. on Exod. 13:17 [ed. Horovitz, p. 76], *Tg. Ps.-J.* ad loc.) likewise mentions the Philistine menace.

159. Demetrius (*ap.* Eus. *PE* 9.29.16) asks how the Israelites managed to obtain weapons in the wilderness, inasmuch as they had departed unarmed from Egypt. Similarly, Ezekiel the Tragedian (*ap.* Eus. *PE* 9.29.14) asserts that the Israelites were all unarmed for fighting. Josephus (*A.J.* 2.321) also explicitly declares that the Israelites were unarmed. One of the paintings in the synagogue in Dura Europos depicts the Israelites as armed (see the painting [Goodenough 1953, 1: plate xiv, fig. 330] and the discussion by Goodenough [1958, 10:118–19]). According to the midrashic tradition (*Mek. R. Ish. Beshallaḥ* intro. [ed. Horovitz, p. 77] and *Mek. R. Shim.* 38 [ed. Epstein, p. 45]), as well as according to Pseudo-Philo 14.1, forty-nine fiftieths of the Israelites perished in Egypt.

160. According to the Bible (Exod. 13:21), G-d Himself guided the Israelites in a pillar of cloud; but Philo, apparently concerned about such an anthropomorphism, tones it down by suggesting (*Mos.* 1.166) that perhaps (τάχα) enclosed within the cloud was one of G-d's lieutenants, an unseen angel. So also the rabbinic tradition (*Mek. Beshallaḥ* 5.31a–b, *Mek. R. Shim.* 49–50).

161. This is in contrast with the Hebrew text (Exod. 13:18), which states that the Israelites were armed (חמשים) when they left Egypt. The LXX reads πέμπτη (a fifth), that is, that a fifth of the Israelites left Egypt. Ezekiel adds drama to the scene: when the Egyptians saw the Israelites they raised a tearful sound to heaven to their ancestral deity. He then describes the divine wonders. In particular, the wheels of the Egyptians' chariots refused to turn.

162. Demetrius (*ap.* Eus. *PE* 9.29.16) explains that those Israelites who did not drown appropriated the weapons of those who did drown. Josephus (*A.J.* 2.349) likewise explains the later source of the Israelites' weapons as coming from the arms that they gathered from the Egyptians who had been drowned in the Sea of Reeds.

163. So also Josephus (*A.J.* 2.329–33) has no rebuking of Moses by G-d.

164. According to a rabbinic tradition (*b. Soṭ.* 37a, *Mek. R. Ish. Beshallaḥ* 5 [ed. Horovitz, pp. 106–7]), it was Naḥshon, the son of Amminadab, the chieftain of the tribe of Judah (Num. 2:3), who was the first who descended into the sea; according to

another version all the tribes were eager to obey Moses' command and competed among themselves as to who should be the first, whereupon the tribe of Benjamin jumped in first; but the tribe of Judah, eager to be first themselves, attacked them with stones (*b. Soṭ.* 36b–37a).

165. Josephus, surprisingly, in view of his tendency to rationalize and to explain miracles in naturalistic terms, omits the method by which the sea became dry land, namely through the strong east wind that blew all that night. Even though generally Josephus downgrades or rationalizes miracles whereas the Bible declares that it took all that night for G-d to drive back the sea (Exod. 14:21), in Josephus (*A.J.* 2.338) we are told that the miracle was instantaneous and that the sea recoiled at Moses' very stroke. Jacobson (1983, 37–38) cites a number of parallels between Josephus' account of the crossing of the Sea of Reeds and that of Ezekiel, notably that Moses struck the sea with his staff (Josephus, *A.J.* 2.338; Ezekiel, *ap.* Eus. *PE* 9.29.14).

166. Cf. *A.J.* 1.108, 3.81, 3.268, 3.322, 4.158, 8.262, 10.281, 17.354, 19.108; *B.J* 5.257.

167. In the New Testament (Rev. 15:3) the song of Jesus, the Lamb, is compared with the song of Moses after crossing the Sea of Reeds, where just as Moses was the liberator of the Israelites from sin, so is Jesus regarded as the liberator from sin.

168. Cf. Apion's statement (*ap. Ap.* 2.121) that Jews swear by their G-d to show no good will to any foreigner, above all, to the Greeks. Cf. the statement of Tacitus (*Histories* 5.5.1), that toward every other people the Jews feel only hate and enmity (*adversus omnes alios hostile odium*). Cf. the statement of Juvenal 14.103, that Jews are forbidden to point out the way to any not worshipping according to their rites.

169. So also Josephus (*A.J.* 3.5), who refers to the Israelites as a rabble of children and of women.

170. Josephus (*A.J.* 3.6), like Philo, speaks of poor women supplicating Moses on behalf of their infants.

171. Josephus (*A.J.* 3.7), likewise troubled by the credibility of such a miracle, says that Moses took the end of a stick that had been flung downwards at his feet, split it in the middle, and threw it into the well. He then ordered those who stood in the prime of life to draw water, stating that what remained after the greater part had been emptied beforehand would be drinkable. Philo similarly (*Mos.* 1.211) presents two rationalized explanations of how Moses was able to bring forth water from a rock.

172. Josephus (*A.J.* 3.9–12) says that the palms were hardly growing because of lack of water and that from the springs nothing wet oozed through. The Israelites kept accusing Moses, saying that they were suffering because of him, and they actually pressed forward to stone him. While they were complaining and even holding stones in their hands with the intention of hurling them upon him, Moses bravely went into their midst and began to still their anger, reminding them of the miracles that G-d had performed on their behalf and pointing out why they should not despair and suggesting that this was G-d's way of testing them (*A.J.* 3.13–20). Moses, in Josephus' version, states that he was not so much afraid for his own safety if they should stone him, but

rather for them, since they would thus be passing sentence against G-d. Moses asks G-d to pardon the people, inasmuch as those who experience misfortune are by nature grumbling. Moses then tells the people that G-d had promised to deliver them from their present difficulties. Apparently, Josephus has conflated what happened at Elim with what happened at Sin.

173. The rabbinic tradition (*Mek. R. Ish. Vayasa'* 1 [ed. Horovitz, pp. 158–59]), unlike Josephus, speaks of Elim as rich in water.

174. Philo (*Fug.* 184), commenting on this passage, finds further significance in twelve as a perfect number, corresponding to the number of hours of the day and of the night, as well as the twelve months of the year and the twelve signs of the zodiac.

175. Philo (*Fug.* 186) finds further significance in seventy as the number of calves offered as sacrifices at the Feast of Tabernacles.

176. Cf. Thucydides (2.65.4), who points out the truism that the way of the multitude is fickle, as seen by the fine that the Athenians, in their anger at the terrible losses that had befallen them during the great plague, imposed upon their great leader, Pericles, only to reverse themselves shortly thereafter and to choose him again as general. Josephus also stresses that mankind is by nature morose and censorious (*A.J.* 3.23). See Feldman 1998a, 145–47.

177. Philo (*Migr.* 121–22), as noted by Vermes 1969, 261–62, likwise attributes the descent of the manna to the intervention of Moses, as the reference to the ceaseless downpour of rain and snow seems to indicate. So also Pseudo-Philo (20.8), Josephus (*A.J.* 3.31), and the rabbis (*b. Ta'an.* 9a) declare that the manna descended due to the merit of Moses.

178. Josephus (*A.J.* 3.31), but not Philo, rationalizes so as to have it appear that the manna was not so exceptional, since he notes that in his own day the entire region of Arabia was watered by a rain similar to that which the Israelites experienced in the days of Moses.

179. Josephus (*A.J.* 3.26), realizing that the people would be reluctant to eat a food that they had previously never seen, has Moses take the role of leader in tasting it first.

180. Aaron likewise plays no role in Josephus' version (*A.J.* 3.24).

181. Likewise, Josephus (*A.J.* 3.33–34) omits Moses' rebuke and the threat to stone Moses. He adds that Moses shunned the impetuosity of the multitude for a little while. He also adds (*A.J.* 3.37) that the people became dismayed that, having been exhausted by both the thirst and the march, they should have to smite the rock. Finally, he adds (*A.J.* 3.38) that a writing in the Temple reveals that G-d foretold to Moses that water would thus issue forth from the rock.

182. Cf. the phrase, frequently found in Josephus (*A.J.* 1.108) and parallels, that "concerning such matters let each one judge as is pleasing to him."

183. Josephus (*A.J.* 3.40) adds that the Amalekites claimed that the Israelites were lying in ambush for them.

184. Josephus (*A.J.* 3.40) and the rabbinic tradition (*Mek. R. Ish. Amalek* 1 [ed. Horovitz, p. 176] and *Mek. R Shim.* 81 [ed. Epstein, p. 119]), but not Philo, assert that the Amalekites also urged on other nations against the Israelites.

185. See Fowler 1911, 96, 215–16, cited by Robbins 1947, 93, n. 2. There is no such ritual in biblical or rabbinic Judaism.

186. Josephus (*A.J.* 3.44–47) adds that Moses spoke to the Israelites, calming them, reminding them that their army was great and lacked no weapons or supplies, exhorting them to take courage and to listen to him, their general, and to trust in G-d's decree. He also adds (*A.J.* 3.48) that the Israelites urged Moses to lead them at once against the enemy. He likewise adds (*A.J.* 3.50) that Moses stayed awake all night instructing Joshua how to arrange the camp. Furthermore, he encouraged Joshua, as well as the most worthy of the Israelites, individually.

187. Josephus (*A.J.* 3.54–57) adds that the Israelites inflicted a crushing blow upon the Amalekites, that all of them would have perished had not the night intervened, and that the Israelites captured great quantities of wealth. He also adds (*A.J.* 3.59) that Moses gave honors to those who distinguished themselves and that he praised Joshua in particular.

188. The Mishnah (*Rosh Ha-Sh.* 3:8) likewise declines to interpret literally the effect of the raising and lowering of Moses' hands and instead, like Philo, chooses to understand the effect in a spiritual sense: "Now do Moses' hands make war or stop it? But the purpose is to say this to you: so long as the Israelites would set their eyes upward and submit their hearts to their Father in heaven, they would grow stronger. And if not, they fell."

189. In the Bible (Exod. 18:17) Jethro comes right out with his criticism: "What you are doing is not good." Such a criticism must have been disconcerting for Philo, especially since there is no indication in the biblical text that Jethro took Moses aside so as to avoid embarrassing him in the presence of the Israelites. In Josephus' version Jethro shows real sensitivity so as to avoid embarrassing Moses. When he sees the way in which Moses administers affairs, he holds his peace at the moment (*A.J.* 3.67). Josephus (*A.J.* 3.73), in an extra-biblical addition, commends Moses for not claiming as his own the advice given to him by Jethro. According to the rabbinic tradition (*Sifre Num.* 80 [ed. Horovitz, p. 77]), G-d caused Moses to forget in order to give Jethro an opportunity to attain fame.

190. Baskin 1983, 62, notes only the unfavorable comments about Jethro in Philo; she neglects to cite *Spec.* 4.173–74, which, in contrast to the official biography of Moses in *Mos.*, speaks of the excellent (ἄριστα) and useful (συμφέροντα) advice given to Moses by Jethro.

191. On the rabbinic attitude toward Jethro, see Bamberger 1939, 182–91, and Baskin 1983, 47–61.

192. On Jethro's alleged conversion to Judaism, see Feldman 1998b, 44–45.

193. Baskin 1983, 74, after surveying the evidence with regard to the treatment of Jethro in the writings of the Church Fathers, concludes that, aside from Aphraates

and Cyril of Alexandria, Jethro remains a virtual nonentity in Christian exegesis. We may suggest that one reason for this neglect was that the Fathers may have been aware of the rabbinic tradition that Jethro became a proselyte to Mosaic Judaism, a type of Judaism which Christianity claimed to supersede.

194. See especially Bamberger 1939 and Braude 1940.

195. Josephus, himself a priest, and undoubtedly sensitive to the charge that those who are priests have no other qualifications than the mere fact of their birth, is careful to remark (*A.J.* 3.188) that Aaron's virtue (ἀρετή) rendered him more deserving than all others to obtain this dignity. Josephus (ibid.) also states that Moses convened the multitude and described in detail Aaron's merit and good will and the dangers that he (Aaron) had undergone on their behalf, whereupon they gave witness to all his words and showed their enthusiasm with regard to him. In Josephus, however, it is G-d and not Moses (ibid.) who chooses Aaron. Moreover, he does not make the point that Moses did not advance his own sons to positions of power, perhaps because, if he had noted this, it might have been regarded as a criticism of the Roman emperor Vespasian for choosing his son Titus as his successor.

196. According to Josephus (*A.J.* 3.95–98), when Moses was delayed in returning from his meeting with G-d on Mount Sinai, the Israelites were troubled by the thought that Moses might have perished, while others believed that he had returned to the Divinity. According to one rabbinic tradition (*Tan.* 13 [ed. Buber, p. 113]), some believed that they had seen the body of Moses.

197. On rabbinic sanction for not reading or translating certain passages of the Bible in the synagogue see Feldman 1998a, 72–73. Of the three passages from the Pentateuch that are listed in the Talmud that are to be read but not translated, namely, the affair of Reuben and Bilhah, the second portion of the incident of the Golden Calf, and the blessing of the congregation by the priests, all are omitted by both Philo and Josephus; and Pseudo-Philo (12.2–3) omits the affair of Reuben and Bilhah and the blessing of the congregation by the priests, but does mention the Golden Calf incident and alone cites the role of Aaron and attempts to explain his action. It would seem that in the case of the incident of the Golden Calf, a unique compromise was reached by Philo, namely, that the first portion of the account was included but that the second portion, in which Aaron explained his action, was not translated. In the Gemara the point is made that one might think that the first account of the Golden Calf should not have been read and translated out of respect for the Israelites; consequently, we are told, there is no objection to including it because the sin was followed by atonement. The Gemara offers no explanation as to why the second account was not translated; but inasmuch as this portion deals with Aaron's role in the affair, the rabbis may have been concerned with protecting the reputation of Aaron (see Feldman 1998b, 56–57), inasmuch as the final verse (Exod. 32:25) in this second account condemns Aaron in the strongest terms, since it states that Aaron had "exposed the Israelites to disgrace among those who rise up against them." This freedom in not translating certain biblical passages reminds one of the rabbinic passage (*Meg.* 9a–b)

that lists thirteen places (other versions of this passage list as many as eighteen) (see Tov 1984, 65–89), where the translators of the LXX deliberately made certain changes in their translation of the Torah, presumably to avoid embarrassment or ambiguity; and it seems quite clear from the context of *Meg.* 9a–b that the rabbis approved of these changes, since they state that it was under divine inspiration that all the translators, though placed in seventy-two separate rooms, arrived at exactly the same translation including all the changes from the meaning of the original Hebrew text. Significantly, eventually, to judge from *Soferim* 1.7, the rabbis had a change of heart and compared the translation to the building of the Golden Calf.

198. For a list of similar embarrassing episodes omitted by Josephus, see Feldman 1998a, 37–38. Interestingly, Josephus is in accord with the Mishnah in omitting the incident of Reuben and Bilhah, the second account of the Golden Calf, and the blessing of the priests, though he does not omit the incidents of David and Bathsheba and Amnon and Tamar. Moreover, the rabbis (ibid.) expressly declare that the incident of Judah and Tamar (Gen. 38) and the first account of the Golden Calf (Exod. 32:1–20) are both read and translated, whereas Josephus omits both. In the Gemara on the above passages, the rabbis add to the list of passages that are to be read and translated the account of creation (Gen. 1), the story of Lot and his daughters (Gen. 19:31–38), the curses and blessings promised to Israel (Lev. 26 and Deut. 27), the story of the concubine in Gibeah (Judg. 19–20), the passage from Ezekiel (16:1) about Jerusalem's abominations, and the rest of the incident of Amnon and Tamar (2 Sam. 13:2–22) (*Meg.* 25a–b); Josephus has all of these but does not actually enumerate the blessings amd curses and omits the passage from Ezekiel (as he does most prophetic passages). From this we can see that the rabbis did take the liberty to omit the translation or even the very reading of certain passages; and from the comments of the Gemara on the list we can readily deduce that there were disputes among the rabbis as to how to deal with specific passages. Here, too, Josephus and the rabbis appear to be drawing upon a common tradition.

199. See Feldman 1998b, 55–73.

200. Not surprisingly, since idolatry is also a major theme in Pseudo-Philo's work, this episode (12.2–10) is given major importance, inasmuch as it calls attention to G-d's faithfulness to His promises and to Moses' qualities as a leader. See Begg 1996, 577–94. If we ask why Pseudo-Philo includes it, whereas Josephus omits it, the answer would appear to be that Pseudo-Philo is writing for a Jewish audience, as seen by the fact that he constantly assumes that his readers are familiar with the Bible and with Jewish tradition in general. Thus he warns this audience of what happens when Jews do not abide by the covenant with G-d, while reassuring them that G-d will never completely abandon the Jewish people, no matter how much they suffer. Indeed, Pseudo-Philo even goes so far as to insert the theme of idolatry as the root of all evil where it is not found in the biblical text, since idolatry is the extreme example of faithlessness to G-d and His law. See Murphy 1988, 275–87; Murphy 1993, 13; and Jacobson 1996, 1:241–46.

201. So also Philo, *Spec.* 3.127.

202. According to the rabbinic tradition (*Tg. Ps.-J.* on Exod. 32:1 and *b. Shab.* 89a), we hear that the people suspected that Moses had died.

203. See Kaunfer 1988, 87–93. The great medieval Jewish commentators—Rashi, Abraham Ibn Ezra, Nachmanides, Gersonides, and Isaac Arama—all seek to exculpate Aaron and even seek to make him something of a hero. See Fox 1993, 87–102. Isaac Arama concludes that the episode comes to teach us that not even the most exalted community or the most exalted individual can hope to escape sin, but that the gates of repentance are open to all. Aaron apparently chooses the path of silence, however, presumably because he was not convinced that pious Jews would accept such excuses.

204. Kugel 1998, 718, commenting on the verse (Exod. 32:5) "When Aaron saw this, he built an altar before it [the Golden Calf]," perceptively notes that by an interesting coincidence the same Hebrew letters (וירא) translated as "saw" could be read as if they spelled "was afraid." Indeed, as Jacobson 1996, 1:486, notes, *Tg. Ps.-J.*, *Tg. Neof.* and *Frg. Tg.* on this verse (cf. *Midr. Exod. Rab.* 41.7) state that Aaron saw Hur [who had been killed by the masses, *Lev. Rab.* 10.3] before it and was afraid. See Smolar and Aberbach 1968, 109–11, on the rabbinic attempts to vindicate Aaron, notably by calling attention to his attempt to deter the Israelites from their plan by getting the people to make heavy sacrifices of golden earrings (*Tan. Ki Tisa* 19) and by other devices to gain time, such as insisting on building the altar himself (*Midr. Exod. Rab.* 41.7, *Lev. Rab.* 10.3).

205. For a close grammatical analysis of the LXX's version of the Golden Calf episode, see Wevers 1993, 115–27.

206. On Pseudo-Philo's attempt here to exculpate Aaron, see Begg 1996, 580.

207. So in Aeschylus, *Prometheus* 666; Plato, *Critias* 119D; Plato, *Protagoras* 320A; Plato, *R.* 6.498C; Isocrates 5.127; Callimachus, *Hymn to Delos* 36.

208. On Pseudo-Philo's treatment of the Golden Calf episode, see Begg 1996, 577–94.

209. Ginzberg 1928, 52, n. 271, who is unaware that the identification of the bull with Apis comes from Philo, notes that this identification is frequently mentioned by early Christian writers, notably *Apostolic Constitution* 6.20 and Lactantius, *Divinae Institutiones* 4.10, but is unknown in early rabbinic literature.

210. See Borgen 1997, 231, who asserts that Philo draws his arguments here from Stoic philosophers from Chrysippus to Poseidonius.

211. On this ridiculing of the Egyptian zoolatry, see Niehoff 2001, 45–74.

212. For further denunciation of Egyptian worship of animals, see *Legat.* 139, 163–66; also Josephus, *Ap.* 1.224–25; 2.66, 81, 86–88, 139. For pagan critiques of Egyptian animal worship, see Cicero, *De Natura Deorum* 1.36.101; Strabo 16.2.35; Plutarch, *Isis and Osiris* 71; Juvenal 15.1–13; Athenaeus 7.299–300; Lucian, *Deorum Concilium* 10.11, *Imagines* 11, *Juppiter Confutatus* 42, cited by Holladay 1983, 1:234, n. 51.

213. Similarly, Philo (*Deus* 21–22, *QG* 1.93) is troubled by the fact that G-d, Who is perfect and presumably unchanging, should have changed His mind and repented that He had created mortals (Gen. 6:6). In an unusually sharp attack he says that those who as much as hint (αἰνίττεσθαι) that G-d repented that He had created humans when He beheld their impiety and that this was the reason why He wished to destroy the whole human race are careless inquirers (ἀνεξετάστων), using the word employed by Plato (*Apology* 38a) in referring to the life that is unexamined as not worth living. He even goes so far as to say that those who hold such a view make the sins of the people who lived during the era of the Flood seem light and trivial compared with the vastness of their own godlessness. He asks what greater impiety there could be than to suppose that the Unchangeable changes; and he notes that even among men there are some—he is presumably referring to the Stoic doctrine of the constancy of the Sages (see Stobaeus [*SVF* 3.48], cited by Colson 1930, 3:483)—who, because of their study of philosophy in all its purity, do not change with changing circumstances. He explains (*Deus* 33–34) the biblical verse (Gen. 6:6) "G-d had it in His mind (וינחם) that He had made men upon the earth and He bethought (ויתעצב) Him" to mean that the former clause refers to thought quiescent in the mind, while the latter clause refers to thought brought to an issue. The oldest manuscripts of the LXX (Gen. 6:6) have that G-d "was angry" (ἐνθυμέομαι, "took to heart," "was concerned"); other manuscripts read "pondered," presumably to avoid this problem. The meaning, he says, is that G-d was concerned or reflected on the reason why He had made man, and, in particular, on the twofold impulse that characterizes man—toward wickedness and virtue.

214. See Frankel 1994, 330–31, who cites the attempts made by such medieval commentators as Ibn Ezra and Abravanel (who assert that it was the pedestal on which the calf stood that was burnt) and Nachmanides (who assumes that the gold was charred and then ground) to solve these problems. In apparent despair to explain the account rationally, Nachmanides concludes that it was a miracle. Lowenstamm 1967, 481–90; 1975, 330–43, points to a very similar description in Ugaritic literature, where Anat is said to have burnt Mot in fire, ground him, and strewed him in the field and whose flesh was eaten by birds or, in a parallel text, whose flesh was scattered on water. According to this view, both the biblical and the Ugaritic descriptions are literary stereotypes used to depict total annihilation. Begg 1985, 208–51, cites many other Near Eastern parallels. Frankel suggests that the proper parallel is the ordeal of the *sotah*, the woman suspected by her husband of adultery (Num. 5:11–31) who is forced to drink the bitter waters in which the scroll in which the curses uttered by the priest have been inscribed and whose stomach becomes distended only if she is guilty. However, in response to Frankel, we must note that there is no indication of a test; rather, it is clear (Num. 32:20) that all the Israelites drank of the water in which the powdered calf had been immersed, and the clear implication is that all the Israelites were deservedly punished.

215. Similarly, as Jacobson 1996, 1:490, notes, in the midrashic tradition (*'Abot R. Nat.* [version A] 2.11) and *Midr. ha-Gadol* on Exod. 32:19, we read that Moses first looked upon the tablets and that when he noticed that the writing had vanished, he proceeded to smash them. *Tg. Ps.-J.* on Exod. 32:19 states that the writing on the tablets flew off and ascended to heaven.

216. Somewhat similarly, the anonymous rabbis explain to the second-century Rabbi Jose that the effect of the drinking was similar to that of the test done to the *sotah*, the woman suspected of adultery (Num. 5:11–31), namely that if she was guilty, her stomach would distend and collapse but that if she was innocent, nothing would happen to her.

217. Indeed, Philo's effort to exculpate Aaron raises the question whether Philo himself may have been a priest. To be sure, Jerome (*De Viris Illustribus* 11) says that Philo was of priestly descent; and Schwartz 1984, 170, differing with the skepticism of Foster 1976–77, 26–29, and the majority of other scholars, concludes that Jerome's statement should likely be believed, since it is not written the way a legend would be written nor exploited as one. He argues that Philo extols priests and is particularly well informed about the Temple and the sacrificial cult. In particular, we may add that in the one instance where Philo (*Prov.* 2.64) reports that he went to the Temple in Jerusalem, he says that he went to offer up prayers and sacrifices (εὐχόμενός τε καὶ θύσων), though, as Schwartz (162) notes, these terms often mean simply "to worship." It is remarkable that Philo mentions an incident, namely the large number of pigeons that he saw in Ascalon, on his way to the Temple, but says nothing about his arrival in Jerusalem, what he did there, and his emotional reaction to his visit to such a sacred site. To be sure, he does not say that this was his only pilgrimage to Jerusalem, but neither does he say that he has been there before. If we may judge from his autobiographical statement (*Spec.* 3.1–6), Philo can express himself with great passion about his personal deep love of philosophy and can lament in poignant tones the way he has been forced to participate in community affairs. We would consequently expect a burst of passion when he describes his pilgrimage to the holy Temple in Jerusalem; but there is no such language in *Prov.* 2.64 or anywhere else in his extant works. It is surprising that Josephus, who mentions Philo (*A.J.* 18.259–60) and other members of his distinguished family, such as his brother Alexander the alabarch (*B.J.* 5.205; *A.J.* 18.159–60, 259; 19.276–77; 20.100) and his nephew Tiberius Julius Alexander (*B.J.* 2.220, 223, 309, 492–98; 4.616–18; 5.45, 205, 510; 6.237, 242; *A.J.* 20.100, 102–3), says nothing about their priestly family. We may also express surprise that Eusebius (*PE* 8.14.398), who has much to say about Philo and who is our source for the fragments of *Prov.*, says not a word about his being a priest; and Jerome, who is the first who denominates him a priest, does not cite Eusebius or anyone else as a source for his information. If, indeed, he were a priest, it would seem surprising that one as wealthy and voluminous as Philo should mention only a single visit to the Temple in Jerusalem. Finally, the sixteenth-century Azariah dei Rossi, who cites Philo extremely often and

who holds him in high regard and who is very well acquainted with the Church Fathers, never mentions in his *Meor Enayim* the tradition that he was a priest.

218. Mandelbaum 1990, 207–23, convincingly shows that attempts to defend the actions of Aaron and of the Israelites are conspicuous by their almost total absence in tannaitic traditions, that is, during the first two centuries, whereas in the amoraic period thereafter we find a strong apologetic for the main characters of the episode, both Aaron and the Israelites. We may suggest that an important factor in the change in the rabbinic view may well have been, as Smolar and Aberbach 1968, 91–116, have pointed out, the rabbis' need to answer Christian polemics, which utilized the episode as evidence that G-d had severed His covenant with the Jewish people. Prior to the third century the threat of Christianity was not particularly great; but it was during the third and fourth centuries, when Christianity became the state religion, that the need for apologetics was urgent.

219. On Josephus' apparent reaction against the Levites and his favoritism toward priests, see Feldman 1998a, 61–62.

220. On the background of this dispute see Feldman 1965, 504–5, n. b; Vogelstein 1889; and Meyer 1938, 721–28, especially 727.

221. As Feldman 1971, xcvii, indicates, the Codex Vaticanus and many other manuscripts of the LXX on Deut. 10:2 disagree with the Hebrew in having G-d tell Moses, "Thou shalt write."

222. Lieberman 1950, 80–81, notes that the rabbis are divided on the question as to who wrote on the second tablets. The majority (*t. B. Qam.* 7.358.1ff. and *Midr. Deut. Rab.* 3.17) declare that it was G-d Who did so. Pseudo-Philo is in accord with the minority (*Midr. Exod. Rab.* 47.9), who state that it was Moses who wrote upon them.

223. According to the midrashic tradition (*Midr. Lev. Rab.* 33.4–5 and *Midr. Num. Rab.* 9.14), the blasphemer was the son of Shelomith, a Danite woman, and an Egyptian who had sexually violated her. When the Danites refused to enroll him in their tribe, inasmuch as paternal descent is the determining factor, he blasphemed the name of G-d that he had heard at Mount Sinai and cursed Moses.

224. It is only in Philo and Josephus (*A.J.* 4.207 and *Ap.* 2.237), as van der Horst 1993, 5, remarks, that we find this reason for not reviling the religions of others. Van der Horst suggests that Philo sees the prohibition in these terms as a means of attracting non-Jews to a belief in the G-d of Israel.

225. So also Philo (*Spec.* 1.53) and Josephus (*A.J.* 4.207 and *Ap.* 2.237). Philo (*Post.* 2) has no tolerance for the Egyptian religion because he regards it as being atheistic from a philosophical point of view, since it valued earth (including their deification of animals and the Nile River) above heaven. See Wolfson 1947, 1:30–32. Niehoff 2001, 45, insightfully notes that Philo's criticism of the Egyptians played a key role in his construction of Jewish identity.

226. So also *Spec.* 1.307 and 2.165. Cf. Homer's frequent reference to Zeus as father of gods and men (e.g., *Il.* 1.544) As Wolfson 1947, 1:38–39 and 173, notes, Philo

(*Prob.* 140) similarly refers to the Furies as the "venerable goddesses" and also uses stereotyped epithets that in Greek literature are used with reference to pagan deities.

227. So noted by Mendelson 1988, 65.

228. For comparative purposes, for the episode of the binding of Isaac in the LXX (Gen. 22:1–9, 458 words), the ratio of Philo (*Abr.* 167–77, 486 words) is 1.06:1; for the episode of Moses' campaign against the Midianites (Num. 31), there are 1179 words in the LXX, whereas Philo's version (*Mos.* 1.305–18) contains 835 words, a ratio of 0.71:1 to the LXX. For the episode of Dinah (Gen. 34), there are 753 words in the LXX, whereas Philo's version (*Migr.* 223–25) contains 205 words, a ratio of 0.27:1. The ratio for Philo's other account (*Mut.* 193–200, which contains 460 words) against the LXX is 0.61:1. For the episode of Phinehas and Zimri (Num. 25:6–15), there are 219 words in the LXX, wheras Philo's version (*Mos.* 1.301–4) contains 173 words, a ratio of 0.79:1 to the LXX.

229. In Pseudo-Philo (15) it comes after the census of the people (Num. 1) and, in what seems to be something taken from the narrative of the spies, G-d's decision to put to death forty-nine fiftieths of the multitude because they lacked faith in Him (14.4). In what seems to be something derived from the episode of the spies, he notes that the mourning and lamenting by the people in the desert lasted two years. Again, this juxtaposition emphasizes the importance of having faith in G-d and of the terrible price paid for lack of faith in Him. In Josephus (*A.J.* 3.300–16) it comes immediately after the Israelites complain about lack of food and the appearance of the quail (*A.J.* 3.295–99). This juxtaposition emphasizes the degree to which the Israelites needlessly complain, whereas faith in G-d fully guarantees their future.

230. Ginzberg 1928, 6:92, n. 503, remarks that the rabbis recognized the problem of the contradiction between these two passages and attempted to reconcile them.

231. See also *Midr. Num. Rab.* 16.8 and the parallels cited by Ginzberg 1928, 6:92, n. 503.

232. Ginzberg 1928, 6:92, n. 503, notes the apparent contradiction between Num. 13:1–2, in which it is G-d who directs Moses to send the scouts into Canaan, and Deut. 1:22–23, in which it is the Israelites who suggest this to Moses. He notes that Josephus and Philo ignore Num. 13:1–2. Like a good general, Moses seeks to obtain a good idea of the country through a firsthand report. Instead of having the Israelites argue among themselves in their usual way, he wants to obtain a report of the country by firsthand information.

233. So also Josephus (*A.J.* 3.302): "Let us all be of one mind."

234. Josephus (*A.J.* 3.302) sets forth, as the goal of the mission, to find out the excellence of the land and the amount of power that the inhabitants have. Pseudo-Philo does not mention any instructions at all, as if they were not to use their minds in answering any specific questions but rather simply to have complete confidence in G-d and to report what they saw, with the implicit understanding that G-d would take care of everything.

235. Moses in Josephus (*A.J.* 3.302) proposes that the scouts investigate the excellence of the land and the amount of power that the inhabitants have. But, more important, he adds what is not found in the biblical instructions, namely that they should be united (an aim, according to Philo also [*Mos.* 1.221]) and, above all, that they should honor G-d, "Who is our helper and ally in all matters." This, we may say, prepares us to justify what G-d does to the majority of spies, who give up hope of conquering the Canaanites; for if, indeed, they had recalled all that G-d had done for them in inflicting the Egyptians with the ten plagues, in enabling the Israelites to leave Egypt, in splitting the Sea of Reeds and defeating the Egyptians, in giving them the means to survive in the totally barren desert by feeding them with manna and quail, and in giving them the power to defeat the Amalekites utterly, they should have had faith that G-d would enable them to fulfill the promise that He had given the Israelites to lead them into the Promised Land.

236. Josephus saves Moses from this criticism by having him exhort the multitude to be of one mind (ὁμονοῶμεν, *A.J.* 3.302).

237. See *Midr. Tannaim* 11 and other midrashic passages cited by Ginzberg 1928, 6:92, n. 502.

238. Pseudo-Philo (15.1) does not give any reason for the decision to send spies other than it was so commanded by G-d to Moses. This fits in with his emphasis on the centrality of G-d's actions. As Murphy 1993, 77, remarks, Pseudo-Philo's leaders are good not when they devise their own plans but when they follow G-d's will.

239. Pseudo-Philo (15.1) does not specify that the spies are to be one from each of the tribes, nor does he indicate what qualities they are to have, as if to say that the only important point is that they should have faith in G-d.

240. Philo does not present the names of Caleb and Joshua here but only when he discusses the significance of the change of their names (*Mut.* 121–24). In the case of Josephus, the omission of the names should not surprise us, inasmuch as he declares (*A.J.* 1.176–77) that he is inclined to omit, because of their strangeness to a Greek ear, the names of the seventy descendants of Jacob who went down to Egypt (*A.J.* 1.176–77); but he ends up citing the names, only to refute those opponents of the Jews who had contended that the Jews were of Egyptian rather than of Mesopotamian origin. On the other hand, Josephus omits the names of the families that returned to Jerusalem from Babylonian captivity (Ezra 2:2–61, 1 Esdras 5:4–38, *A.J.* 11.68), the names of those Jews who sent away their foreign wives at the request of Ezra (Ezra 10:18–44, 1 Esdras 9:18–35, *A.J.* 11.152), the names of King Ahasuerus' seven chamberlains (Esth. 1:10, *A.J.* 11.190), the names of his seven counsellors (Esth. 1:14, *A.J.* 11.192), and those of Haman's ten sons (Esth. 9:7–9, *A.J.* 11.289).

241. Josephus omits this last point about ridicule, as he does the changes of name of Abram to Abraham and of Sarai to Sarah, though he does have the change of Jacob's name to Israel (*A.J.* 1.333). To the Greeks, the addition of an alpha to the name of Abram (Gen. 17:5) would seem difficult to comprehend, as Philo's efforts (*Mut.* 66–76) to explain the matter make clear (so Sandmel 1956, 66, n. 277). Moreover,

Josephus may well have been sensitive to the scoffing, noted by Philo (*Mut.* 60–62), of those who ridiculed the change of name of Abram to Abraham. Hence, Josephus simply omits this change of names completely. For similar reasons, as appears from Philo's strained efforts to explain the change of Sarai's name to Sarah (Gen. 17:15, Philo, *Mut.* 77–80), Josephus omits her change of name also. Josephus' retention of the change of name of Jacob to Israel (*A.J.* 1.333) perhaps results from his wish to aggrandize the reputation of the Jewish people. Josephus (*A.J.* 2.91) retains the change of name of Joseph to Zaphenath-Paneah ("he who explains what is hidden") because this is the name given to him by the Egyptian king. Those appointed to high positions were customarily given names reflecting their newly gained importance, and hence this is a tribute to Joseph.

242. Philo expresses the aim of seeking to answer the misrepresentation of Moses by non-Jews, since, as he remarks at the very beginning of *Mos.* (1.2), "Greek men of letters have refused to treat him as worthy of memory."

243. Unlike Philo, Josephus (*A.J.* 3.303) mentions the biblical statement that they had completed the whole task within a mere forty days and thus emphasizes the superficiality of their observations. However, influenced by the beauty of the fruits of the land, the multitude, being unsophisticated, were at first aroused to war. Pseudo-Philo (15.1–2) presents both the majority and minority reports in the most sharply divergent tones.

244. We may note that similarly, in other places in his reworking of the biblical narrative, Josephus also avoids undue exaggeration and the grotesque, which might have provoked the ridicule of a later satirist such as Lucian. Thus, for example, whereas the Bible (Judg. 16:9) reports that Samson "broke the bowstrings as a string of tow is broken when it touches the fire," Josephus avoids this gross exaggeration, and his Samson simply bursts the shoots asunder (*A.J.* 5.310). Pseudo-Philo (15.4), while not mentioning that the Israelites wept or that they had expressed regret that they had not died in Egypt or in the wilderness, does remark that the people did, in effect, say that G-d had contradicted Himself, on the one hand saying that He would convey the Israelites to a land flowing with milk and honey and, on the other hand, bringing them up that they should fall by the sword and their wives be captured. Pseudo-Philo (15.5) omits the murmuring of the people against Moses and Aaron. He also omits the determination of the people to appoint a leader to replace Moses and to lead them back to Egypt. Apparently, Pseudo-Philo wishes to emphasize that the rebellion of the populace was not against Moses but against G-d Himself; and hence this will justify the punishment inflicted by G-d upon the people.

245. Josephus, though he definitely did not agree with the majority report of the spies, nevertheless, apparently felt that to include such exaggerations would invalidate the credibility of his own account; and he completely omits these statements.

246. Thus in the Bible Reuben (Gen. 37:29) tears his garments when he finds Joseph missing, and Jacob does likewise (Gen. 37:34) when he sees Joseph's blood-stained garment.

247. In Josephus' version the spies start by presenting a more positive report (*A.J.* 3.304): they refer to the beauty (εὐπρέπεια, "splendid appearance") of the fruits and add greatly to the praise of the land by mentioning the abundance of blessings (τὸ πλῆθος τῶν ἀγαθῶν) that the land had. The fact that Josephus, in an extra-biblical addition, gives the impression that the report of the scouts was self-contradictory, in that the beauty of the fruits and the many blessings that they reported that the land possessed roused the multitude to war, would seem to indicate that the people, being unsophisticated, were positively impressed, at least at first, by the report and that they interpreted it as favoring an attack on the Canaanites. However, whereas the biblical account of the report states that the Canaanites were powerful and that their cities were very greatly fortified and that the scouts had seen there "the offspring of the giant," but does not indicate the mood with which they made these statements, Josephus actually says that the scouts terrified (φοβοῦντες) the multitude and were much more specific in indicating what frightened them, namely that the rivers were impossible (ἀδύνατοι) to cross because of their size and depth, the mountains were impossible (ἀμήχανα) for travelers to climb, and the cities were mighty with ramparts and with the strength of surrounding walls (*A.J.* 3.304).

248. At this point it is G-d Who appears in the Tabernacle to the congregation (Num. 14:10). He then speaks to Moses and, in exasperation, declares that He will annihilate the people and will make Moses himself into a greater and more powerful nation than they. This does seem like a case of G-d losing His temper, and one wonders how just it is for G-d to wipe out the entire people without exception instead of restricting Himself to those who sought to stone Joshua and Caleb, since, we may assume, not all the people were present in the assembly that sought to stone Joshua and Caleb. Moses then successfully argues that if G-d does so, the nations of the world will say that G-d destroyed the Israelites because He lacked the power to bring them into the land. He then appeals to G-d's quality of mercifulness (Gen. 14:13–19); and G-d is apparently convinced by Moses' plea to forgive the Israelites (Num. 14:20).

249. At this point G-d mentions Caleb alone because it was he who (Num. 13:30) silenced the people toward Moses.

250. In Josephus' version (*A.J.* 3.310), however, Moses and Aaron, in an extra-biblical addition, instead of panicking, show their compassion for the people, their ability to analyze the cause of this depression, and their own true leadership by supplicating G-d to rid them of their ignorance and to calm their spirits.

251. The question might well be raised whether G-d was justified in deciding that the entire multitude should be condemned to die in the desert when all that they had done was to accept the majority report of a committee, whether appointed by G-d, Moses, or themselves. A clue to the answer may be seen in the fact that whereas the Bible (Num. 14:1) says that upon receiving the report of the majority of the scouts, the people wept, Josephus (*A.J.* 3.306) says that they wept, together with their wives and children. In the biblical version, G-d angrily protests that the Israelites do not have faith in Him despite all the miracles that He has performed for them (Num.

14:11). Josephus (*A.J.* 3.306) is more sarcastic in stating that the people acted as though G-d had helped them not at all with action but had only promised them with words.

252. On Josephus' interpretation of the episode of the spies, see Feldman 2001, 22–41.

253. For Korah the ratio of Josephus (*A.J.* 4.11–66: 198 lines) to the Hebrew text (Num. 16:1–35: 58 lines) is 3.41:1.

254. Cf. also *Midr. Gen. Rab.* 50.11, *Midr. Exod. Rab.* 31.3, *Midr. Lev. Rab.* 5.3, *Midr. Num. Rab.* 10.3, 18.13, 22.7, *Midr. Eccl. Rab.* 5.12, *Midr. Esth. Rab.* 7.4, and other parallels cited by Rappaport 1930, 124, n. 17a.

255. Josephus (*A.J.* 4.20) portrays him as a typical demagogue who wishes to seem to care for the common good but, in fact, is manipulating to have the honor transferred by the multitude to himself.

256. See Feldman 1998b, 97–109. As a proud priest, Josephus is particularly sensitive to the attempt of a Levite such a Korah to usurp the privileges of the priests, an issue which was very much alive in Josephus' own day. The revolt is further presented by Josephus as an object lesson in the terrible effects of jealousy, a theme that appears so frequently throughout Josephus' works. In particular, Korah's jealousy of Moses is paralleled in Josephus' own life by that of his archrival, John of Gischala, toward him. Above all, the rebellion highlights the terrible consequences of sedition, another theme that pervades Josephus' works, especially under the influence of his experiences in the revolt against the Romans. Whereas Korah in the Bible bases his appeal on theological and egalitarian grounds, Josephus' Korah focuses on political and legal issues. See Feldman 1998b, 97–109.

257. The very first statement in the Bible (Num. 16:1) about Korah refers to his distinguished ancestry and his relationship to Moses. So also in Josephus (*A.J.* 4.14, 19).

258. *Midr. Num. Rab.* 18.1 and *Tan. Korah* 2 (ed. Buber, p. 85).

259. Fragments (Richter 6.235–36; Mangey 2.673).

260. Josephus (*A.J.* 4.12) says that this was a rebellion such as has occurred among neither Greeks nor barbarians. He (*A.J.* 4.12) and the rabbis (*Midr. Num. Rab.* 18.4) say that the Israelites threatened to stone Moses.

261. Cited by Wolfson 1947, 2:389.

262. This is the conclusion of Tcherikover in Tcherikover, Fuks, and Stern 1960, 2:50–53.

263. In contrast, in Josephus' version (*A.J.* 4.51) the event is more scientifically presented as an earthquake, which he then proceeds to compare dramatically to a wave tossed by the violence of the wind.

264. In Pseudo-Philo (25.13) the tribe of Benjamin confesses to Kenaz a similar doubt that the Torah is of divine origin and a belief that it was authored by Moses himself.

265. Similarly, the rabbis (*Tg. Ps.-J.* on Num. 16:2) connect Korah's rebellion with the law on fringes.

266. Jacobson (1996, 1:553) calls attention to the passage in the New Testament (Matt. 23:5) attacking the insincerity of the Pharisees in doing all their deeds so as to be seen by men, for example, making their fringes long. Jacobson (1:554) remarks that the rabbis do not cite any objection to the law on the grounds that it is unbearable. Rather, it is mocked as being silly and illogical. He remarks that in the rabbinic tradition there are other laws that attribute Korah's revolt to their unbearability, for example, the obligatory gifts to the priests that are imposed even upon the poor.

267. Josephus (*A.J.* 4.19) refers to On as Palaos, presumably the name of his father. The Bible (Exod. 6:14) refers to Pallu as the second son of Reuben. Chronologically, Palaos here cannot be Pallu, the son of Reuben, who lived much earlier. The Bible (Num. 16:1) mentions On only once, and in later references mentions only Dathan and Abiram among the Reubenites who were involved in the rebellion. According to the tradition preserved by the third-century Rav (*b. Sanh.* 109b), On was saved by his wife, who convinced him to leave the rebellious forces when she argued that it would make no difference to On whether Moses or Korah were the master. Thereupon, though he had sworn to join the conspiracy, she intoxicated him with wine, while she herself stood at the entrance to his house with loosened hair so that those who came to summon him saw her and retreated.

268. The manuscripts read "seven," but as Jacobson 1996, 1:563, remarks, Exod. 6:24 mentions three sons of Korah.

269. Jacobson 1996, 1:563, notes that Pseudo-Philo's exoneration of the sons of Korah is based on the fact that in Num. 26:11 we are told specifically that the sons of Korah did not die. Moreover, there are frequent references in the book of Psalms to the sons of Korah as having some role in the Temple service. Finally, like Pseudo-Philo, midrashim (*Lekaḥ Tov* on Num. 16:33) assert that Korah's sons did not participate in the rebellion.

270. Rabbinic tradition, bound by adherence to the biblical text, generally asserts that Korah was swallowed up by the earth. See Feldman 2000a, 347, n. 138.

271. As Thackeray (1930, 4:503, n. e on *A.J.* 4.55) remarks, Josephus' description is based on and, in fact, is intended to outdo that of the Plataean bonfire as described by Thucydides (2.77). Josephus' description also contains an implied allusion to the eruption of Mount Vesuvius in the year 79, which Josephus mentions elsewhere (*A.J.* 20.144), and which is described so graphically by Josephus' younger contemporary, Pliny the Younger (*Epistles* 6.16).

272. Josephus' concern to protect the primacy of Moses may be seen in the fact that whereas in the Bible G-d instructs Moses to tell the Israelites to inscribe each man's name upon his rod and to write Aaron's name upon the rod of Levi (Num. 17:17), Josephus, apparently aware that this would give greater prominence to Aaron

than to Moses, who no less than Aaron came from the tribe of Levi, states that Aaron took the initiative to write the name "Levite" upon his staff.

273. In Josephus (*A.J.* 4.63) it is Moses rather than G-d who takes the initiative in convening an assembly of the Israelites and in telling them to bring their staffs to the tabernacle.

274. Pseudo-Philo omits discussion of this passage altogether.

275. On φιλανθρωπία as a key Jewish virtue, see Feldman 1998a, 116–17.

276. Cf. Deut. 20:10: "When you draw near to a city to fight against it, offer terms of peace to it." Philo (*Spec.* 4.221) notes how the law advises behavior toward rebels who show an inclination to peace: "And if their [the Israelites'] opponents repent of their rebellious conduct and give way and show an inclination to peace, the others must accept and welcome the treaty, for peace, even if it involves great sacrifices, is more advantageous than war." Elsewhere (*Virt.* 109) he notes what he terms the charitable (χρηστά, "kind") and very merciful (μεστὰ ἡμερότητος, "full of gentleness") regulations with regard to the treatment of enemies in wartime: "They must not, he declares, be yet regarded as enemies, even if they are at the gates or stationed beside the walls in full array and planting their engines, until envoys have been sent with invitations to peace, so that if they yield they may obtain the supreme boon of friendship, but if they refuse to listen and continue their opposition, you may, with justice to reinforce you, advance to defend yourselves in the hope of victory."

277. According to the one sentence that Pseudo-Philo (18.1) devotes to the episode of Sihon and Og, it is Moses who smote (*interfecit*) them and then apportioned all their land to his people. However, as Jacobson 1996, 1:575, remarks, this is not to be taken any more literally than the statement at the beginning of 19.1 that Moses smote (*occidit*) the nations, that is, presumably the Midianites.

278. Josephus (*A.J.* 4.96–99), whose biblical paraphrase is more systematic than that of Philo, does mention the attack by and the defeat of Og, perhaps because, despite the apparent exaggeration of Og's size in the Bible and consequent problem of credibility of the narrative, Josephus himself was proud of his own generalship in Galilee during the war against the Romans and because he constantly, for apologetic reasons, seeks to emphasize the military prowess and bravery of the Jews.

279. This contrasts with a ratio of 2.21:1 for Josephus (*A.J.* 4.102–58) as compared with the Hebrew and 1.39:1 for Josephus as compared with the LXX. On the reasons for Josephus' extraordinary interest in Balaam, see Feldman 1998b, 111.

280. On Josephus' similar concern not to downgrade non-Jews and to show tolerance and respect toward them, see Feldman 1998b, 557–58.

281. Vermes 1973, 174, remarks that Josephus plays down Balaam's wickedness slightly by imputing all of Balaam's wrongdoing to his desire to please Balak. Apart from this specific slant, he shows the same general bias toward Balaam that is exhibited in the rest of the Palestinian tradition and in the New Testament. It is our argument (Feldman 1993b, 48–83) that Josephus' positive changes are much more substan-

tial. Interestingly, the portrayal by Pseudo-Philo (18.3) is even more favorable to Balaam (perhaps because Balaam, at least at first, accepted the direction of G-d) than is Josephus, as Baskin 1983, 99, has noted. Origen (*PG* 12.683D) is surprisingly evenhanded, blaming him for inspiring idolatry and immorality but praising him when the word of G-d is placed in his mouth. See Braverman 1974, 41–50. The chief reason, however, why Balaam is viewed more positively in patristic literature is that he was regarded as prophesying the coming of Jesus.

282. To be sure, the rabbis (*Sifre Deut.* 357.2 [ed. Finkelstein, p. 430]), commenting on the verse that there has not arisen a prophet in Israel equal to Moses (Deut. 34:10), assert that among the nations such a prophet did arise, namely Balaam. In fact, the rabbis were ready to grant (*Sifre Deut.* 357.2) that in some respects Balaam was actually superior to Moses; that is, Moses did not know who spoke with him, whereas Balaam did know; moreover, Moses did not know when G-d would speak with him until he was actually addressed by G-d, whereas Balaam knew in advance (*Sifre Deut.* 357.2). The reason, say the rabbis, why G-d raised Balaam to such heights was so that the Gentiles would not be able to say that if they had had a prophet of the stature of Moses they would have accepted the Torah (*Seder Eliyahu Rab.* 26, ed. Freedman, p. 142). Indeed, an anonymous rabbinic tradition regarded the Balaam episode as so important that, with its statement that Moses wrote his own book and the portion of Balaam (*b. B. Bat.* 14b), it singles it out as a separate book distinct from the rest of the Torah. But even those rabbinic passages which acknowledge his greatness as a prophet denigrate Balaam for his greed, envy, immorality, and bestiality (cf. *b. Sanh.* 105a, where he is said to have committed bestiality with his ass) and depict him as liable to all four of the modes of capital punishment (*b. Sanh.* 106b). He is known as Balaam the Wicked (*b. Sanh.* 105b) and, indeed, is looked upon as the very epitome of wickedness because of his skill in being able to gauge the exact moment when G-d becomes angry (*b. Sanh.* 106b). He is, thus, worse than any of those who are denied a portion in the world to come (*m. Sanh.* 10:2). His greatest wickedness consisted of his seeking to strike at the very heart of the religion of the Israelites by cursing them that they should have no synagogues or schools (*b. Sanh.* 105b). Indeed, he is identified as one of Pharaoh's counsellors who advised him to cast into the Nile River the newborn male children of the Israelites (*b. Sanh.* 106a). The Mishnah berates him for his evil eye, his haughty spirit, and his proud soul (*m. 'Abot* 5:19). Though he was at first an interpreter of dreams and then a prophet, he sank to the level of sorcerer (*Tan. B* 4.134). There are even those who find a veiled reference to Jesus in the passage which states that a *min* (heretic) asked Rabbi Ḥanina how old Balaam was [when he died], whereupon he replied that since, according to the Psalm (55:24), "Bloody and deceitful men shall not live out half their days," it follows that Balaam was 33 or 34 years (since a normal lifetime is seventy years), whereupon the *min* stated that he had seen Balaam's Chronicle in which he read that Balaam the lame was 33 years old when Phinehas the Robber put him to death (*b. Sanh.* 106b). The theory, however, that Ba-

laam is Jesus, that the Chronicle is the Gospel, and that Phinehas is Pilate has been generally rejected, though Jesus also was 33 years old when he died. See, for example, Ginzberg 1928, 6:123–24, n. 722, and Klausner 1925, 32–35.

283. Cf., e.g., 2 Pet. 2:15: "Forsaking the right way, they [the heretics] have gone astray; they have followed the way of Balaam, the son of Beor, who loved gain from wrongdoing, but was rebuked for his own transgression; a dumb ass spoke with human voice and restrained the prophet's madness." The same theme of Balaam's unholy search for gain is to be found in Jude 1:11: "Woe to them [i.e., false teachers], for they walk in the way of Cain and abandon themselves for the sake of gain to Balaam's error." Finally, in the seer's vision of Jesus in Rev. 2:14 there is a bitter reference to Balaam as the one who inspired the Israelites to perform the cardinal sins of idolatry and immorality.

284. When Balaam appears after the scene in Num. 22–24 in which he is the central figure, he is depicted in negative tones. Thus in Deut. 23:5 we read that G-d would not listen to Balaam but, instead, turned his curse into a blessing. Almost exactly the same statement is found in Josh. 24:10 and in Neh. 13:2.

285. Though Philo narrates the episode of Balaam and Balak at length (*Mos.* 1.263–99), he nowhere mentions the country, Moab, where Balak was king, though elsewhere (*Somn.* 1.89) he does refer to the licentious intercourse with the women of Moab. He also identifies the women as Midianites (*Virt.* 34–41). The biblical text (Num. 25:1) speaks of the harlotry with Moabite women, but a few verses later (Num. 25:6) mentions a Midianite woman with whom an Israelite had relations. Josephus (*A.J.* 1.102) states that Balak had an ancestral friendship and alliance with the Midianites. According to *Tg. Yer.* on Num. 22:4, Moab and Midian formed a confederate state, with a Moabite and Midianite alternating as king. *Tg. Ps.-J.* on Num. 22:4 states that the Moabites and Midianites formed a single people and had a single king. It appears that there was confusion between the two. Philo avoids this here by not mentioning the land where Balak was king.

286. According to Josephus (*A.J.* 4.103), Balak decided not to go to war with the Israelites because the latter had had outstanding successes and were even bolder now that they had experienced misfortune.

287. Though elsewhere (*Cher.* 32, *Det.* 71, *Conf.* 66, 159, *Deus* 181, *Migr.* 113, *Mut.* 202) he does mention Balaam by name, here, strangely enough, despite the length of the passage, Philo does not mention his name even once, perhaps to emphasize that in prophecy, which is the most important of Moses' attributes according to Philo (*Mos.* 2.6, 2.69, 2.288–91), Balaam is not even worth mentioning as compared with Moses.

288. Rendtorff 1976, 812, remarks that in the LXX נביא is always translated by προφήτης. Προφήτης is also the translation in a few instances for רואה (1 Chr. 26:28, 2 Chr. 16:7, 10) and חוזה (2 Chr. 19:2, 29:30, 35:15).

289. One reason perhaps why Philo and Josephus avoid using the term μάντις for biblical prophets is that the word is associated with the words μαίνομαι, "to be mad," and μανία, "madness."

290. Balaam comes from a place called Pethor (Num. 22:5), which means "interpreting dreams." Pseudo-Philo (18.2) refers to him as an interpreter of dreams (*interpretem somniorum*), as do *Tg. Ps.-J.* (on Num. 22:5), and *Midr. Num. Rab.* 20.7. Origen questions whether Balaam was a prophet (*Commentary on John* 28.12 [*PG* 14.707]). He concludes that Balaam was not a prophet, inasmuch as his prophecies were involuntary and shortlived and inasmuch as he is referred to in the LXX only as a soothsayer (μάντις).

291. In *Cher.* 35 Philo does refer to the donkey as speaking, but he interprets it allegorically. Cf. *Deus* 181–82.

292. Colson 1935, 6:414, in the Loeb version on *Mos.* 1.266, seems to prefer Cohn's emendation, ἀκκιζόμενος, that is, "feigning reluctance."

293. Cf. 2 Pet. 2:15: "Balaam, the son of Beor, who loved gain from wrongdoing." From Josephus (*A.J.* 4.118) we learn that Balaam received liberal gifts for his services.

294. So also the rabbinic tradition (*Midr. Num. Rab.* 20 and *Tan. Balak* 9 [ed. Buber, p. 136]), as well as in the *Second Samaritan Chronicle* 3.

295. Josephus (*A.J.* 4.107), in an extra-biblical addition, not only does not blame Balaam but even seems to castigate G-d, since we are told that Balaam did not realize that G-d had deluded him in giving him this order. So also in the rabbinic tradition (*Midr. Num. Rab.* 20.9, 20.11) it is G-d who leads Balaam astray by directing him to accede to the request of the envoys.

296. The rabbis resolve this contradiction by insisting that since Balaam wanted to act wickedly he was permitted to do so, inasmuch as "a man is divinely assisted in treading the path he desires" (*Midr. Num. Rab.* 20.12). Josephus (*A.J.* 4.107) resolves the problem by having G-d express indignation that Balaam should have tempted Him and by having Balaam misunderstand G-d's sarcasm in permitting him to go with the envoys: it was all a ruse on G-d's part.

297. Pseudo-Philo (18.9), also, though mentioning the donkey, says nothing to indicate that it spoke. Josephus might have omitted the incident, as he did several other episodes in the Bible, but he chose (*A.J.* 4.109) to include it. Instead, only at the very end of the whole episode of Balaam and not, rather, in direct connection with the donkey episode do we meet the familiar words of Josephus: "On this narrative readers are free to think what they please" (*A.J.* 4.158). We may guess that Josephus was not deterred from including the narrative of the speaking donkey because his audience was probably familiar with the account of Achilles' horse, Xanthos, which likewise speaks after being unfairly accused by his master (Homer, *Il.*, 19.408–17). And just as Balaam's donkey speaks, according to Josephus (*A.J.* 4.109), because G-d willed it, so Xanthos is said to have spoken because the goddess Hera gave him speech. Both narratives clearly acknowledge that human speech is not natural for animals. Philo's audience, we may assume, was likewise acquainted with the parallel in Homer, but Philo seems to be better acquainted than is Josephus with scientific evidence, in this case that animals do not speak.

298. Josephus' description of Balaam (*A.J.* 4.118) as one who is no longer his own master (οὐκ ὢν ἐν ἑαυτῷ) is reminiscent of the Platonic concept of ecstatic possession (*Phaedrus* 245A), whereby the god enters, for example, into the Pythian priestess at Delphi and uses her vocal organs as if they were his own (Plato, *Laws* 672B). Cf. Philo (*QG.* 3.9), who similarly defines the ecstasy of prophets as a state when the mind is divinely possessed and becomes filled with G-d, so that it is no longer within itself, inasmuch as it receives the divine spirit to dwell within it. See Levison 1997, 29–42.

299. Josephus (*A.J.* 4.113) says that Balaam saw the signs of an inflexible destiny (ἄτροπον).

300. The biblical Balaam narrative was a real challenge for Josephus, inasmuch as Balaam was a non-Jew, and Josephus was aware of the charge that Jews hated non-Jews. Josephus (*A.J.* 4.114), aware of the misanthropy charge, avoids presenting the Israelites as sundered off from all other peoples and instead speaks of the *excellence* of the Israelites as compared with other peoples. His Balaam asserts that G-d has given the Israelites the potential to become the *happiest* of all peoples.

301. According to Josephus (*A.J.* 4.125), Balaam "predicted what sufferings would befall kings and what would befall the most distinguished cities, of which it happened that some had not yet begun to be inhabited, and some things that have happened to people in previous times, through land and sea, within my memory. From all the things that have attained the kind of end which he predicted, one might draw conclusions as to what should also occur in the future." Presumably, the cities would include Jerusalem, which was not established as the capital of the Israelite state until hundreds of years later by David. If Balaam foretells the calamities that will befall kings and cities of the highest celebrity, Josephus keeps this prophecy cryptic enough so that gentile readers will not necessarily connect it with Rome, just as he has a similarly cryptic prophecy in connection with the interpretation of Nebuchadnezzar's dream in his pericope of Daniel (*A.J.* 10.210). Cf. the ambiguous oracle, which Josephus says (*B.J.* 6.312) was found in the sacred scriptures of the Jews, to the effect that someone from their country would become ruler of the world. This oracle seems to be reflected in Tacitus' comment (*Histories* 5.13.2): "The majority [of the Jews] firmly believed that their ancient priestly writings contained the prophecy that this was the very time when the East should grow strong and that men starting from Judea should possess the world." Similarly, Suetonius (*Vespasian* 4.5) reports that "There had spread over all the Orient an old and established belief that it was fated at that time [when Vespasian became emperor] for men coming from Judea to rule the world."

302. In any case, the passage was interpreted messianically shortly after the time of Josephus in reference to Bar Kochba (*y. Ta'an.* 69d) by Rabbi Akiva. Such a messianic understanding was apparently avoided by Josephus because of his subservience to the Romans.

303. On the equation of Esau and Edom with Rome, see Feldman 1998a, 322–24. On the equation of Amalek and Rome, see Feldman 2000b, 284–88. Moreover, as one who had participated in the war against the Romans and who had come to

the conclusion that resistance to Rome was futile and that Rome was divinely destined to rule the world, Josephus constantly seeks to prevail upon his compatriots to give up their dream of national independence. We may see an instance of this concern where Josephus avoids terminology suggestive of an independent state (Num. 23:21) in Balaam's remark that G-d has granted untold blessings to the Israelites and has vouchsafed to them His own providence as their perpetual ally (σύμμαχος) and guide (ἡγεμών) (*A.J.* 4.114). This rendering is clearly not merely an equivalent for the biblical concept of covenant but actually a replacement for it. See Attridge 1976, 79–80. As Josephus' Balaam puts matters, the Israelites are thus to be happy (εὐδαίμων, *A.J.* 4.114) rather than to dominate the world. It is their fame—rather than, it would seem, their sheer force—that will fill the whole earth, as we see in another of Josephus' extra-biblical additions (*A.J.* 4.115). In particular, we may note that in place of the Bible's picture comparing the Israelites to lions that do not lie down until they have eaten their prey and drunk their blood (Num. 23:24), Josephus avoids such sanguinary particulars and speaks only of the land that the Israelites will occupy (*A.J.* 4.115–16). Indeed, Josephus clearly shifts the focus from the land of Israel to the Diaspora when he has Balaam declare that whereas now the Israelites are circumscribed by the land of Canaan, the habitable world (ἡ οἰκουμένη), that is the Diaspora, lies before them as an everlasting habitation (*A.J.* 4.116).

304. In Josephus' version (*A.J.* 4.126) Balak expresses his fury by summarily dismissing Balaam, granting him no reward.

305. In the Bible (Num. 25:1) and in Philo's *Mos.* (1.300) the women are Moabites; but it is a Midianite woman whom Phinehas kills (Num. 25:8) and it is against the Midianites (Num. 31:1–2) that the Israelites take vengeance. Colson 1939, 8:444, suggests that since Balak is described by Philo as having brought under his sway a great and populous part of the East, Balak may have been king of both Midian and Moab. According to Josephus (*A.J.* 4.102), Balak, as king of the Moabites, had an ancestral friendship and alliance with the Midianites.

306. According to Pseudo-Philo (18.13–14), Balaam, presenting advice on how to overcome the Hebrews through licentiousness, said to Balak: "Pick out beautiful women who are among us and in Midian, and station them naked and adorned with gold and precious stones before them. When they see them and lie with them, they will sin against their L-rd and fall into your hands; for otherwise you cannot overcome them." Josephus' version (*A.J.* 4.129–30) of Balaam's advice is very similar to that found in Philo, namely to send the Moabite women who are most beautiful and most appealing to the Israelite camp and to order them to have relations with the young Israelites who request it. When they see that the young men have been overpowered by their passions, they are to abandon them, and when they implore them to return, they should not agree until they give up their ancestral religion. Robbins 1947, 104, n. 3, persuasively suggests that Balaam's advice in Josephus depends on Philo's presentation. A similar account is found in the rabbinic tradition. Thus the third-century Rabbi Abba bar Kahana (*b. Sanh.* 106a) presents the following scenario: "He [Balaam] said

thus to him [Balak]: 'The G-d of these [Israelites] hates lewdness, and they are very partial to linen [i.e., linen was worn by the wealthy and noble]. Come, and I will advise you. Erect for them tents enclosed by hangings, in which place harlots, old women without, young women within, to sell them linen garments.' . . . And when an Israelite ate, drank, and was merry, and issued forth for a stroll in the market place, the old woman would say to him, 'Do you desire linen garments?' The old woman offered it at its current value, but the young one for less. This happened two or three times. After that she would say to him, 'You are now like one of the family; sit down and choose for yourself.' Gourds of Ammonite wine lay near her, and at that time Ammonite and heathen wine had not yet been forbidden. Said she to him, 'Would you like to drink a glass of wine?' Having drunk, [his passion] was inflamed, and he exclaimed to her, 'Yield to me!' Thereupon she brought forth an idol from her bosom and said to him, 'Worship this!' 'But I am a Jew,' he protested. 'What does that concern you?' she rejoined; 'nothing is required but that you should uncover yourself'—while he did not know that such was its worship. 'Nay,' [said she], 'I will not leave you before you have denied the Torah of Moses your teacher.'" (Soncino translation). Cf. also *Midr. Num. Rab.* 20.23 and 22.4. The connection of Balaam with this incident is, as noted by Jacobson 1996, 1:608, built by the rabbis on the fact that this incident (Num. 25) occurred immediately after Balaam's last words to Balak and on the reference to Balaam in Moses' words to the Israelites in Num. 31:16: "Behold, these [Midianites] caused the people of Israel, by the counsel of Balaam, to act treacherously against the L-rd in the matter of Peor [Num. 25:3–5], and so the plague came among the congregation of the L-rd."

307. In Josephus' version (*A.J.* 4.140) the lawlessness of the young men soon pervaded the entire army, and a sedition far worse than that of Korah (which Josephus [*A.J.* 4.12] had already described as without parallel among Greeks or barbarians) and a danger of total destruction of their particular practices came upon the Israelites.

308. See Seland 1995, 23–24, who concludes that it is not appropriate to use this passage as indicating Philo's opposition to lynching.

309. Heinemann 1932, 224–25, insists that Philo is presenting only a theoretical, not a practical, law and that *Mos.* 2.213–15, in which Philo mentions that when some people observed a man picking wood on the Sabbath they did not kill him immediately but brought him before Moses and the priests, shows that Philo did not approve of lynching; but Heinemann, 228, admits that in the case of idolatry such lynching was regarded as justified. Seland 1995, 103–36, in a long and careful analysis of the passage in *Spec.*, concludes that Philo used this passage as the legitimating example from the Torah, and that the formula, ἀναγέγραπταί τις ἐν τοῖς νόμοις ("someone is recorded in the laws"), with which Philo introduces his discussion of the episode (*Spec.* 1.56), indicates that he regarded this as the actual law in practice.

310. The order of events in Num. 25:1–8 is that first the Israelite men acted immorally with the Moabite women, then a plague afflicted the Israelites, then Phinehas killed the Israelite who openly had relations with the Midianite woman, then the

plague was stayed. In Philo, as in Pseudo-Philo 47.1 and Josephus (*A.J.* 4.155), the plague takes place after Phinehas' deed.

311. In *Post.* 183, *Ebr.* 74–75, and *Conf.* 57, Philo interprets allegorically the rewards bestowed upon Phinehas: peace symbolizes the end of the intestine war of lusts in the soul, and it is associated with the priesthood because in name (ἱερωσύνη) and in fact it is akin to peace (εἰρήνη).

312. According to a rabbinic tradition (*Tan.* 4.29 [ed. Buber, p. 148]), the fact that it was Phinehas and not Moses who reacted to the provocation of Zimri resulted in the punishment inflicted upon Moses of having his burial place remain unknown (cf. Deut. 34:6).

313. The importance of the appointment of priests may likewise be seen in the fact that, according to Livy (1.20.1), the first act of Numa Pompilius, Romulus' successor as king, after establishing the calendar, was his appointment of priests.

314. Pseudo-Philo does not paraphrase this episode.

315. The only reference in the rabbinic literature to these sons of Moses is to the tradition (*Midr. Num. Rab.* 15.19, *Tan. B* 4.57, *Tan. Beha'aloteka* 12, *Sifre Num.* 96, *Sifre Zuta* 202–3, *Tg. Yer.* Num. 11:28, cited by Ginzberg 1925, 6:89, n. 483) that identifies Gershom, Moses' elder son, as the youth (Num. 11:27) who heard the prophecy of Eldad and Medad (Num. 11:26–29) and who rushed to his father and told him. In the Bible (Num. 11:28) when the news of the prophecy reaches Moses, it is Joshua who speaks up and tells Moses to incarcerate Eldad and Medad. According to the rabbinic tradition (*b. Sanh.* 17a), the prophecy of Eldad and Medad was that Moses would die and that Joshua would bring the Israelites into the Land of Israel. We may guess that what concerned Gershom, though the rabbinic tradition does not say it explicitly, was that Joshua and not he, the elder son of Moses, was predicted to be Moses' successor. We may guess that what concerned Joshua was that he, in his modesty, realized how far inferior he was to Moses.

316. Pseudo-Philo does not paraphrase this episode.

317. The rabbinic tradition (*Sifre Num.* 157), like Philo, states that Moses appointed Phinehas as commander-in-chief of the army.

318. Phinehas is also named as commander-in-chief according to several sources in the rabbinic tradition. See *Midr. Aggada* Numbers 31:9, *Sifre Num.* 157, and *Pirqe R. El.* 47, cited by Ginzberg 1928, 6:145, n. 860.

319. In Josephus (*A.J.* 3.303), as in the Bible, the tribes of the Israelites select the twelve scouts.

320. To be sure, Josephus is also writing primarily for a Greek or Roman audience; but he is a very knowledgeable and proud priest and adheres to the traditions of the Bible in priestly matters. Hence he omits these sacrifices, since the Bible omits them.

321. Whereas, according to the Hebrew text (Num. 31:17), Moses ordered the Israelites to kill every male among the young children, the LXX omits the young children.

322. Josephus (*A.J.* 4.164) equalizes the portions given to the priests and to the Levites.

323. Philo nowhere mentions the identity of the two tribes and is content to refer to them simply (*Mos.* 1.320) as the two cattle-breeding tribes. He omits completely the biblical reference (Num. 32:33, Deut. 3:13) to the fact that the half-tribe of Manasseh was associated with them, but he is perhaps influenced by the omission of Manasseh in Num. 32:1. Josephus (*A.J.* 4.166) does mention the half-tribe of Manasseh.

324. Pseudo-Philo does not paraphrase this episode.

325. According to Josephus (*A.J.* 4.167), Moses excoriates them in strong terms as most evil (κάκιστοι) and as having contrived a specious (alternate reading: ἀσχήμονα, "shameful," "unseemly") pretext for their cowardice, whereas they wished to live luxuriously and without exertion, although all had striven hard to acquire the land that was claimed by them.

326. This is the reading of the *editio princeps.* The manuscripts read ἀσχήμονα ("shameful," "unseemly").

327. Rabbi Meir in the *m. Qid.* 3:4 cites the biblical language here as the classic formulation of a condition, that is, "Any condition which is not stated as is the condition of the sons of Gad and the sons of Reuben [that is, in both the positive and negative formulations], is no condition."

328. According to Josephus (*A.J.* 4.174), it was the principal men of the tribe of Manasseh who approached Moses and inquired whether the inheritance of Zelophehad should belong to his daughters. Whereas in the Bible Moses is unable to decide their case and presents it to G-d, Who decides in their favor (Num. 27:5), Josephus omits this scene altogether, perhaps because it would demean Moses' ability as a judge. Rabbinic tradition, as noted by Nodet 1995, 43, n. 5, is divided: on the one hand (*Tg. Yer.* on Lev. 24:12), Moses is congratulated because of his humility in admitting that he did not know the answer; on the other hand (*Midr. Song of Songs Rab.* 1.10), the rabbis note the juxtaposition of Num. 27:7, where G-d declares that the daughters are right, with Num. 27:12, where G-d commands Moses to ascend the mountain of Abarim, implying that the day of his death is approaching. Num. 36:1–12, in which Moses states that the inheritance must remain within the tribe, appears to contradict Num. 27:7–8, which says that daughters inherit when there are no sons, without the qualification that they do so only if they marry within the tribe. Josephus has the scene, based on Num. 36:1–12, in which the chiefs of the tribe of Manasseh inquire *de novo* about the inheritance of Zelophehad, who had left no sons. However, whereas in Num. 36:1–4 the chiefs of the families of the sons of Joseph come to Moses to complain about his decision—pointing out that when the Jubilee occurs, their inheritance will be added to the tribe into which they have married—here in Josephus there is an inquiry but no reference to a previous decision by Moses and no complaint. Josephus' Moses does not hesitate to give his answer without consulting G-d, as he does in

Num. 27:5; he tells the daughters that if they marry within their tribe, they will carry the inheritance with them, but if they do not, the inheritance is to remain in their father's tribe. Josephus omits the statement (Num. 36:6) that the daughters are free to marry whomever they think best but that they should marry within the tribe of their father; nevertheless, if they do not, the inheritance is not to be transferred from one tribe to another (Num. 36:9). Nodet (ad loc.) remarks that Josephus' synthesis of the two passages is logical, since he generalizes from the particular case of the daughters of Zelophehad in placing it after the distribution of the Amorite land. Pseudo-Philo does not paraphrase this episode.

329. Elsewhere (*Spec.* 2.124), to be sure, Philo makes the general statement, without qualification, that just as in nature men take precedence over women, so should it be when it comes to inheritances.

330. Elsewhere in Jewish tradition there is a difference of opinion as to Enoch. On the one hand, Ben Sira (44:16, 49:14–16) emphasizes that he had to die; and some of the rabbis (*Midr. Gen. Rab.* 25.1) describe him as fluctuating between sin and repentance, whereupon G-d removed him so that he should not fall again into sin. On the other hand, the Pseudepigraphic 1 and 2 Enoch describe him as ascending to heaven during his lifetime. The New Testament (Heb. 11:5) is explicit in stating that Enoch did not die: "By faith Enoch was taken up so that he should not see death; and he was not found, because G-d had taken him." For an exhaustive analysis of the relationship of the traditions about Enoch to the origins and early development of Jewish apocalyptic literature, see VanderKam (1984), who contends that the Enoch tradition did not hesitate to borrow literary devices and themes from non-Jewish writings and traditions that were popular in the Hellenistic world, particularly prophecies after the event.

331. To be sure, Philo (*De Somniis* 1.58) seems to equate Terah with Socrates; but he equates, rather, the characteristic of being concerned with one's own self.

332. On the similarity between Josephus' language with regard to the Flood and the language of Berosus, Apollodorus, Lucian, and Plutarch with regard to the Greek flood, see Feldman 1988, 44–47.

333. The word for "ark" used by Josephus, λάρναξ, is the word used by classical writers in referring to Deucalion's ark (e.g., Apollodorus 1.7.2; Lucian, *De Syria Dea* 12), rather than the word κιβωτός used in the LXX (Gen. 6:14ff.) and in Philo (*De Plantatione* 43). Josephus apparently adopted the word directly from Nicolaus of Damascus, whom he quotes (*Ant.* 1.94–95)—even to the point of giving the number of the book (96) where the passage occurs in Nicolaus' history—as saying that many refugees found safety on a certain mountain in Armenia at the time of the Flood, including a man, transported in an ark, "who would be the one of whom Moses, the lawgiver of the Jews, wrote" (*A.J.* 1.95). One factor that led Josephus to select his word for Noah's ark may have been his desire to use a word different from that which he uses for the Ark of the Covenant. That Josephus' choice of the word for Noah's

ark is significant is to be seen from the fact that when the same word "ark" (תבה) occurs in the Bible (Exod. 2:3) for the container where Moses' mother placed him when he was an infant, whereas the LXX renders it by the word θῖβις (presumably derived from the Hebrew), Josephus, perhaps because he wished to use a unique word for Moses' ark, does not use the word that he had used for Noah's ark, but instead employs the word πλέγμα ("plaited basket") (*A.J.* 2.224), even though λάρναξ would appear to be the appropriate word for a basket in which a baby is exposed, to judge from Simonides (37.1), Apollonius of Rhodes (1.622), and Diodorus Siculus (5.62).

334. Cited by Lowenstamm 1972, 216, nn. 60–61.

335. Cf. Thucydides 2.43.3: "For the whole world is the sepulchre of famous men, and it is not the epitaph upon monuments set up in their own land that alone commemorates them, but also in lands not their own there abides in each breast an unwritten memorial of them, planted in the heart rather than graven on stone."

336. Cf. Josephus' brief closing encomium for Moses (*A.J.* 4.329): "If, as a general he was in elite company, as a prophet he had no peer, so that in whatever he said he seemed, when he spoke, to be listening to G-d."

337. Whitaker 1932, 4:156, n. a, cites Mangey's comment on this word: "referring to the death of."

338. Cf. *A.J.* 1.85, where Josephus says of Enoch, using the same phrase, that he had returned to the Divinity. Herrmann 1970, 125, and Fornaro 1979, 431–46, suggest that Josephus is here responding to the Church of Jerusalem's narrative of the ascension of Jesus.

339. Josephus (*A.J.* 4.320) describes the weeping by the populace on the imminent death of Moses. He even adds (*A.J.* 4.322) that Moses himself, who had always been persuaded that one ought not to be dejected when the end was forthcoming, since one suffered this in accordance with the will of G-d and by a law of nature, was overcome by weeping when he saw how the people were affected.

340. See the comment on this passage in Feldman 1971, ciii. Jacobson 1996, 1:623, suggests as a partial parallel the midrashic tradition (*Sifre Num.* 91 and parallels) that Moses desired to die (Exod. 32:32, Num. 11:15) before witnessing the corruption of the Israelites. But there it is Moses' desire, whereas here it is G-d's decision.

341. So also *Sifre Deut.* 355 (ed. Finkelstein, p. 418) and *'Abot R. Nat.* 25b (end), cited by Jacobson 1996, 2:641.

342. For attempts to explain these mysterious figures, see Feldman 1971, cv, and Jacobson 1996, 2:651–52.

343. *Death of Moses*, in Gaster 1927, 319.

344. Pseudo-Philo may here be responding to a tradition such as we find in a later midrash (Jellinek 1853, 1:129) in which Joshua looked for Moses after he had already died.

345. This is particularly significant, inasmuch as Josephus is definitely indebted to Sophocles elsewhere. See Feldman 1998c, 62–74. It is also just possible that Jose-

phus is reacting against the Christian tradition of the apotheosis of Jesus (Luke 24; Acts 1). See Fornaro 1979, 431–60, and Paul 1985, 473–80. Jacobson 1983, 89–97, interprets the scene (verses 68–89) in the play by Ezekiel in which Moses says that he dreamt about a great throne on top of Mount Sinai on which a noble man (i.e., G-d) was seated with a crown and a sceptre, which he gave to Moses, as a polemic against the notion of the apotheosis of Moses, inasmuch as Ezekiel chose to portray his ascension as an imaginary event. However, inasmuch as even the Epicureans gave credence to dreams, the import of such a dream would intimate the divinization of Moses. If this were really a polemic against the apotheosis of Moses, Ezekiel should have had the noble man explicitly declare that while Moses is destined to be recognized as a king he should realize that he is mortal.

346. To the biblical account of Moses' death (Deut. 34:1–6) Josephus has added lamenting people, a walk to the mountain, companions on Moses' final walk, and "disappearance," details which are found in no other post-biblical source, though those sources recount Moses' last hours in far greater detail than does the Bible. See Jacobson 1993. And yet, it is precisely these details that are found in Sophocles' *Oedipus at Colonus.* On the parallels between Josephus' account of the death of Moses and Sophocles' account of the death of Oedipus in his *Oedipus at Colonus,* see Feldman 2000a, 474, n. 1125.

347. Cf. Socrates' words to his disciples in Plato's *Phaedo* (117D7–E1), as he faces his final moment.

348. For a comprehensive survey of the rabbinic accounts of Moses' death, see Kushelevsky 1995.

349. For the sources, see Ginzberg 1911, 3:417–81, and 1928, 6:146–68, nn. 870–966.

350. On these traditions, see Purvis 1973, 93–117.

III. The Virtues of Moses

1. Goodenough 1928, 70, quotes a parallel in a fragment of the treatise *On Kingship* by the Pythagorean Diotogenes (*ap.* Stobaeus 4.7.26), according to whom the king "must excel in virtue and on that account be judged worthy to rule, but not on account of his wealth, or power, or military strength. For the first of these qualities he has in common with all sorts of people, the second with irrational animals, and the third with tyrants, while virtue alone is peculiar to good men. So that what king is self-controlled in pleasure, given to sharing his possessions, and is prudent and powerful in virtue, that man will be a king in very truth."

2. As Arnaldez et al. 1967, 196, remark, this is a theme running throughout classical antiquity. As representative citations they note Plato, *Protagoras* 329C; Cicero, *De Officiis* 2.10.35; Diogenes Laertius 7.125; and *SVF* 3.295–304.

3. See Snowden 1970, 144–47, and 1983, 46 and passim. But while mythology idealizes the Ethiopians, we must, on the other hand, in all fairness, note that the Greeks and Romans did not always admire blackness, as we can see in Philodemus' use of Andromeda as an example of a woman loved despite her race.

4. On piety as the fifth of the cardinal virtues, see Plato, *Protagoras* 349B.

5. To be sure, the third-century Pseudo-Justin, *Cohortatio ad Gentiles* 9, states that Hellanicus, who lived in the fifth century B.C.E., and Philochorus, who lived in the fourth to third centuries B.C.E., mention Moses as a very ancient (σφόδρα ἀρχαῖος) and old (παλαιός) leader of the Jews. However, as Stern (1984, 3:39) has remarked, Josephus (*Ap.* 1.16), who appears to have searched high and low for references to the Jews in Greek authors, mentions Hellanicus but does not refer to the passage citing Moses. Similarly, Clement of Alexandria (*Strom.* 1.15.72.2) in the early third century knows of Hellanicus but not of this passage. Indeed, it would seem remarkable that it is not until the third century that we find this reference to Hellanicus and Philochorus in Pseudo-Justin as mentioning Moses.

6. Plato had equated wisdom (σοφία, *R.* 4.428B) with prudence (φρόνησις, *Laws* 1.631C), whereas Aristotle defines wisdom as dealing with things divine (*Metaphysics* 1.2.983A6–7) and prudence as dealing with things human (*EN* 6.5.1140A24–B30), as noted by Wolfson (1947, 2:211–12). The Stoics (Sextus Empiricus, *Adversus Physicos* 1.13) define wisdom as combining the Aristotelian definitions of wisdom and prudence. Philo, apparently realizing the tremendous prestige of Plato, Aristotle, and the Stoics, combines all three in his definition of wisdom, while claiming at the same time that this wisdom was embodied in the Pentateuch (*Leg.* 3.46).

7. The same phrase, ὁ τῆς φύσεως ὀρθὸς λόγος ("the right reason of nature"), occurs in Philo (*Ios.* 31). On "correct reason" as the foundation of all ethical dealings, see Völker 1938, 208.

8. So also Philo (*Praem.* 11). "The hope of happiness incites also the devotees of virtue to study wisdom, believing that thus they will be able to discern the nature of all that exists and to act in accordance with nature and so bring to their fullness the best types of life, the contemplative and the practical, which necessarily make their possessor a happy man."

9. Cf. the dispute, recorded in the Talmud, as to how a festival should be observed. According to Rabbi Eliezer, one should either eat and drink or sit and study. According to Rabbi Joshua ben Ḥananiah, one should devote half of it to eating and drinking, and half of it to study (*b. Pes.* 68b). Or, as Rabbi Joshua puts it elsewhere (*b. Beẓah* 15b), "Divide it, half of it for the L-rd, and half of it for yourselves."

10. According to Josephus, Abraham's power of persuasion is seen particularly in his ability to convince the Egyptians on any subject which he undertook to teach (*A.J.* 1.167). As to Moses, it is nothing short of amazing that Josephus is able to praise his extraordinary ability in addressing a crowd (*A.J.* 3.13, 4.328), despite the fact that the Bible declares that he had a speech impediment (Exod. 6:12). Likewise, Joshua is termed highly gifted in speech (*A.J.* 3.49) and supremely skilled in expounding his

ideas clearly to the multitude (*A.J.* 5.118). Again, Nehemiah, before approaching the king for permission to go to Jerusalem, prays to G-d to give his words some measure of grace and persuasion (*A.J.* 11.165).

11. To be sure, Colson 1935, 6: ad loc., remarks that this is a rather strange use and cites the suggested emendation, διεξιών ("going through," "passing through," "going through in detail") of Mangey. In all the other instances (*Mos.* 1.270, 1.294, 2.78, 2.150, 2.151) where the word δεξιός appears in *Mos.*, and in the one instance (*Mos.* 2.151) where the word δεξιότητος occurs, the reference is to cleverness.

12. So also Abraham was remodeled to accentuate his ability as a general. See Feldman 1984b, 43–49.

13. We should likewise note, as Meeks 1967, 134, remarks, that in the Hellenistic world στρατηγός also designated a provincial governor.

14. On the importance of toil, according to Philo, see Völker 1938, 229–33.

15. On Philo's concern with the struggle against the passions, see Völker 1938, 263.

16. That Moses abstained from intercourse with his wife, "considering it fitting always to keep himself ready for the oracles" is also found in *'Abot R. Nat.* p. 10 (ed. Schechter) and *Midr. Deut. Rab.* 11.10: "From the day when he received a revelation, he did not go in to his wife." Cited by Meeks 1967, 128, n. 6.

17. Josephus (*A.J.* 3.99) says that during the forty days and nights that Moses was with G-d on Mount Sinai, he tasted no food of the kinds designated for humans, hinting that Moses had heavenly food and drink. See Meeks 1967, 141.

18. Goodenough 1928, 65, cites a parallel from Diotogenes (*ap.* Stobaeus 4.7.61): "The most just man would be king, and the most lawful would be most just. For without justice no one would be king, and without law [there would be no] justice. For justice is in the law, and the law is the source of justice. But the king is animate law or is a legal ruler. So for this reason he is most just and most lawful."

19. For a survey of the usage of this term, see Lorenz 1914 and Luck 1974, 9:109–10. For a popular survey, see van Veldhuizen 1985, 215–24.

20. See the discussion by Wolfson 1947, 2:218–20, especially the passage in Macrobius, *Commentarius ex Cicerone in Somnium Scipionis* 1.8. In general, see Spicq 1958, 169–91, and 1978, 2:922–27; and Le Déaut 1964, 255–94. See especially Winston 1984, 391–400, who notes the kinship in Philo of φιλανθρωπία with both justice and piety (*Virt.* 51); but it is to piety that he gives the chief place (*Spec.* 4.9). See also the other passages cited by Winston 1984, 395, n. 77.

21. Downing 1980, 64, n. 8, is correct in noting that Attridge 1976, 183, is wrong, at least in the cases of Dionysius and Diodorus, in denying that the Greek historians placed a stress on piety similar to that found in Josephus. In particular, Downing, 52–53, notes that Dionysius (*Ant. Rom.* 2.68 et passim) hoped to reassert a trust in divine providence. He remarks that repentance, so frequently found in Josephus' additions in the Bible, is also stressed by Dionysius, and that the use of the term in reference to G-d as an ally, which is so common in Josephus, in the sense of divine grace

and human responsibility, was perhaps borrowed from Dionysius (*Ant. Rom.* 6.63). The importance of piety, particularly for the Romans, may be seen in the fact that the key quality of Aeneas in Virgil's great national poem is *pietas.*

22. This is, according to Jewish tradition, based upon the verse (Deut. 33:5): "And he was king in Jeshurun." According to one rabbinic view (*Midr. Exod. Rab.* 40.2), Moses was appointed by G-d; according to another rabbinic view (*Midr. Tannaim* on Deut. 33:5, p. 213), he was elected by the seventy elders.

23. This is based, according to tradition, upon the verse (Psalm 99:6): "Moses and Aaron were among His priests." According to one rabbinic tradition, Moses was invested with the priesthood only during the seven days of the consecration of Aaron; but according to another view, he continued to serve as a priest throughout his life.

24. Actually, Judaea was not ruled by a king until the Hasmoneans gained control over a century later. More likely, Philo was thinking of the practice of Hellenistic kings who also served as priests.

25. As Gager 1972, 34, remarks, there is no specific prohibition of infanticide in the Bible. As he notes, Strabo (17.2.5.824) remarks that one of the customs most zealously observed among the Egyptians is that they rear every child that is born. Strabo then adds that this is also customary among the Jews, who are, he says, Egyptians in origin. Tacitus (*Histories* 5.5.3) likewise notes that the Jews regard it as a crime to kill any child.

26. Gager notes that Aristotle frequently discusses the matter of population control. In particular, Aristotle, *Politics* 1335B19–26, speaks of the exposure of children in these terms.

27. Philo (*Spec.* 1.131) is clearly aware of the biblical provision, as we see from his statement that the priests were not allotted land, and that instead it is G-d who is their inheritance.

28. Stern 1974, 1:21, concludes that Hecataeus used a Jewish source, which, it seems, was an oral one. Bar-Kochva 1996, 26–28, distinguishes between Hecataeus' facts, on the one hand, which, he says, except for one or two, are based on Jewish tradition and history and which, he thinks, were certainly provided by Egyptian Jews, probably of priestly descent, and, on the other hand, the explanations of those facts which were provided by Hecataeus himself and are typically Greek.

29. This statement is not quite what is found at the end of the book of Deut. in the Pentateuch, but it is similar to the statement at the end of the book of Lev. (27:34): "These are the commandments which the L-rd commanded Moses for the people of Israel on Mount Sinai"; and at the end of the book of Num. (36:13): "These are the commandments and the ordinances which the L-rd commanded by Moses to the people of Israel in the plains of Moab by the Jordan at Jericho."

30. Likewise, Herodotus (1.145, 148) comments on the recurrence of the number twelve in noting the number of settlements established by the Ionians in Asia. Similarly, Aristotle (frag. 385 [Rose]) speaks of a division into twelve parts correspond-

ing to the twelve months of the year. Philo (*Fug.* 184) is also aware of the connection of the number twelve with astronomy, which was regarded as the queen of the sciences in Hellenistic times (see Marrou 1956, 182), and remarks that twelve is a perfect number, as attested by the number of constellations in the zodiac, the number of the months, and the number of hours in the day. Specifically, like Hecataeus, he connects Moses (*Fug.* 185) with the number twelve, noting that Moses celebrates this number in several places, telling us, as had Hecataeus, of twelve tribes, and adding that Moses directed that twelve loaves be set forth on the table in the Tabernacle and bade the Israelites weave twelve stones on the "oracle" of the high priest's garment.

31. Another possibility suggested by Stern is that Hecataeus may reflect the actual economic conditions prevailing in Judaea in the Hellenistic period.

32. Cf. Polybius 6.48.3–4, cited by Stern 1974, 1:32.

33. Consequently, Schäfer 1997, 17, is not convinced that there is an overall pro-Jewish attitude in Hecataeus' version of the Exodus tradition.

34. Presumably, this is a reference to a peaceful conversion of the neighboring tribes to Judaism.

35. Cf. Hecataeus, *ap.* Diodorus 40.3.4.

36. Cf. Quintilian (3.7.21), who likewise refers to Moses, without mentioning him by name, as "the author of the Jewish superstition."

37. Some scholars, such as Ziegler 1915, 572–603, have argued that the citation from Gen. breaks the train of Pseudo-Longinus' thought and that the parallels with Jewish thought and vocabularly could not possibly stem from him. Russell 1964, 93, argues that the fact that Pseudo-Longinus quotes Gen. rather freely is an indication of non-Jewish authorship, since Jewish and Christian authors quote the Bible more precisely; but Josephus and now the Dead Sea Scrolls have shown that Jewish authors often take considerable liberties in quoting from the Bible. Moreover, Mutschmann 1917, 161–200, has correctly noted that the passage in question is very much in place and is, indeed, the climax of Pseudo-Longinus' argument. Norden (1955) has suggested that Pseudo-Longinus was a pagan Greek author who knew and used Jewish writings, especially those of Philo. In particular, he notes that Pseudo-Longinus' use of χωρεῖν with the accusative, which is rare in pagan literature, occurs twenty-five times in Philo. The fact that the author of the treatise declares himself (12.4) to be a Greek would probably indicate that he was not a Jew, since Jews, even so deeply imbued with Greek culture as was Philo, do not refer to themselves thus. Mommsen (1885, 5:494); von Christ (1905, 788); and Sedgwick (1948, 198–99) have called him a Hellenized Jew. Goold 1961, 177, says that he belonged to the same environment that produced Philo and that he is in some sense a Jew. Gager 1972, 63, plausibly states that because the line of demarcation between Greeks with Jewish sympathies and Hellenized Jews was extremely vague in cultural, philosophical, and religious matters, we cannot draw any convincing conclusion in the matter.

38. Homer, *Il.* 5.385ff., *Od.* 11.305ff.; Philo, *Conf.* 4–5.

39. Hesiod, *Theogony* 987; Ovid, *Metamorphoses* 1.751–79.

40.. See Hafemann 1990, 87, who notes that here Moses does not derive his status from the law, but rather that the law derives its status from Moses.

41. For citations in other authors—Jewish, Christian, and pagan—who refer to Moses as lawgiver, see Allison 1993, 232, n. 223.

42. See a systematic consideration of the evidence in Lierman 2002, 119–40.

43. So also *y. Soṭ.* 6.1, cited by Ginzberg 1928, 6:47, n. 248.

44. Calabi 1998, 6–9, raises the question whether Moses, according to Philo, is an interpreter or even an exegete, and asks whether if Moses is viewed as an exegete, it can be hypothesized that Philo intends to claim an autonomous role for Moses with respect to G-d, in which case Moses' role is to be regarded not as a transcriber of words dictated by G-d but rather as an interpreter similar to that of a Targum. She concludes, however, that this is not Philo's reading of the Bible, which repeatedly is attributed to G-d in the first person.

45. Similarly, in rabbinic procedure in capital cases (*m. Sanh.* 4:5) hearsay evidence is strictly forbidden. But Philo is probably thinking of the parallel in Greek law, as mentioned in Demosthenes, *Contra Eubuliden*, p. 1300, among others.

46. On the much-debated question as to whether Philo knew the Pentateuch in the original Hebrew see especially the evidence for a negative verdict supplied by Nikiprowetzsky 1977, 50–96, and Grabbe 1988, 119–20. Already in the sixteenth century, the learned Italian rabbi, Azariah dei Rossi (*Me'or Enayim* 1.5) comes categorically to the conclusion that Philo was ignorant of both Hebrew and Aramaic and that his only source for the knowledge of the Bible was the LXX. For a valiant attempt to present the opposing point of view, see Schur 1991. Kahn 1996, 53*–58* without offering convincing evidence, goes so far as to argue that Philo had some understanding of the Bible in Hebrew and was actually capable of holding discussions with Hebrew-speaking rabbis in Judea and in the Diaspora.

47. On the importance of establishing the antiquity of the Jews as one major factor in their attractiveness to non-Jews, see Feldman 1993a, 177–200.

48. In addition, Moses is the subject of the verb νομοθετέω three times (*A.J.* 3.266, 268, 317); and the noun νομοθεσία is applied to him twice (*A.J.* 3.287, 320).

49. See Lierman 2002, 111, who cites the statement of Thackeray 1930, 4:xiii, that there are places where Josephus shows dependence on Philo. Feldman 1998a, 52–54, cites a number of parallels between Philo's treatises and Josephus.

50. See *A.J.* 1.108, 2.348, 3.81, 3.268, 4.158, 8.262, 10.281, 17.354, 19.108; *B.J.* 5.257.

51. So noted by Lierman 2002, 112–13.

52. See the discussion by Meeks 1967, 186–96.

53. For a discussion as to why Ezekiel included this episode, see Jacobson 1983, 158–64.

54. Rofé 1988, 170, notes that in the LXX of the Pentateuch whenever a king of Israel is mentioned, apart from four instances in Gen., his title is ἄρχων.

55. To speak of Moses as ἄρχων, as Lierman 2002, 73, points out, rather than as βασιλεύς does not downgrade his rank, any more than it does that of David or of the Messiah.

56. This is presumably based on Deut. 33:5: "He became king in Jeshurun." From the context it would appear that the "he" refers to Moses, but the Hebrew commentators differ as to whether it refers to G-d or Moses. See Wolfson 1947, 2:16, n. 40.

57. When John Hyrcanus asked Eleazar why he should give up the high priesthood, he replied that he had heard from his elders that Hyrcanus' mother was a captive during the reign of Antiochus Epiphanes, a fact, if true, that would disqualify Hyrcanus from being the high priest. The story turned out to be false; and when one of Hyrcanus' close friends named Jonathan, who belonged to the school of the Sadducees, who held views in opposition to those of the Pharisees, said that Eleazar had spoken with the approval of the Pharisees, Hyrcanus asked the Pharisees what penalty should be inflicted upon Eleazar. When the Pharisees, in accordance with their general policy of leniency in such matters, replied that Eleazar deserved stripes and chains, Hyrcanus, in his anger with the Pharisees, joined the Sadducees. A similar story is found in the Talmud (*b. Qid.* 66a), where the king is Alexander Jannaeus, the person who objected to the king holding both offices is Judah the son of Gedidiah, and the Sadducee is Eleazar the son of Po'irah. Of course, in this incident the objection is not necessarily to the king's holding of both offices but rather to his disqualification for one of these offices, that of high priest.

58. See Philo, *Abr.* 5, and the extensive discussion of this concept in the Hellenistic world in Goodenough 1928, 55–104.

59. Cf. Plato, *Symposium* 196C: "Where there is voluntary agreement, there, as the laws that are the lords of the city say, is justice." Cf. Philo, *Det.* 141: "Rulers are living tables on which laws are inscribed."

60. This theme, that Moses refused to take advantage of the fact that he was the son of the Pharaoh's daughter but rather chose to share ill-treatment with the Israelites, is likewise sounded in the New Testament (Heb. 11:24–25).

61. Dio Chrysostom, *Discourses* 1.12, 2.6, 3.40–41, 4.43–45, cited by Cukrowski 1994, 155, n. 233.

62. According to the version of Artapanus (*ap.* Eus. *PE* 9.27.4–18), Moses did many things to keep the monarchy stable for Chenephres, who was married to the Pharaoh's daughter. This led the masses to love Moses. When Chenephres saw the fame of Moses, he became jealous and sought to kill him on some reasonable pretext, sending him, for example, with few troops to fight the Ethiopians. When Moses proved to be successful, Chenephres formed a plot, to be carried out by a certain Chanethothes, to assassinate him. When Moses decided to flee to Arabia, Chanethothes lay in wait in order to kill him. When he saw Moses approaching, he drew his dagger, but Moses drew his own sword and killed Chanethothes.

63. On this view of democracy, see Colson and Whitaker 1930, 3:489. As Wolfson 1947, 2:386–93, points out, Philo's endorsement of democracy as the best form of

government is not at variance with Plato's condemnation of democracy (*R.* 8.555–64), since Plato's democracy stands for the distribution of things equally regardless of merit, whereas Philo's democracy is proportional, in accordance with the principle that each person enjoys what is justly due to him (*Spec.* 4.72, 237).

64. The Mish. (*Rosh Ha-Sh.* 4:5–6), codified ca. 200 C.E., actually mentions the number of biblical verses to be recited in each of the three sections (dealing, respectively, with the themes of kingship, remembrance, and the shofar) of the Additional Service as something well established.

65. The context reads: "And it is said: 'He gazes at no iniquity in Jacob and sees no evil schemes in Israel; The L-rd his G-d is with him, and the affection of the King is in him' [Num. 23:21]. And it is said: 'And He became a King in Jeshurun when the leaders of the people assembled, the tribes of Israel together' [Deut. 33:5]."

66. Cf. Philo (*Mos.* 1.23), who declares that learned Egyptians instructed Moses in the philosophy conveyed in symbols, as displayed in the so-called holy inscriptions (presumably hieroglyphics).

67. Elsewhere (Plato, *Phaedrus* 274–75) Hermes Thoth is said to be the inventor of writing, which, he told the Egyptians, would make them wiser and would give them better memories. Cf. the statement of Diodorus (1.94.1) that the first to use written laws was Mneves, an Egyptian, who claimed that Hermes had given the laws to him with the assurance that they would be the cause of great blessings.

68. A further compliment may be seen in the sheer popularity of Hermes (he is, for example, the pagan god most often referred to in the Talmudic tractate *'Abod. Zar.*). He is a trickster (see Brown 1947, 66–101) and was said, according to the *Homeric Hymn to Hermes*, to have stolen, shortly after his birth, the cattle of Apollo and to be able to transform himself into a mist and thus to penetrate a keyhole that has been *hermetically* sealed. He was said to have been able to steal the god Ares out of the brazen pot where Otus and Ephialtes had imprisoned him. His gift to Pandora is described as "lies and deceitful words and a stealthy disposition." As the god of commerce and communication who can cross all boundaries, symbols of his cult were placed in such diverse places as mountain tops, rural waysides, state boundaries, city streets, doorways and courtyards of houses, gymnasia and libraries, and graves. A lucky find was called ἕρμαιον, a gift of Hermes. He carried a magic wand, and was the protector of enterprise of all sorts and the inventor of various arts, including religious ritual. Because he possessed this magic wand, he was said to be able to make dreams come true; and this wand became the symbol of a golden age of peace and plenty. As a master of the magic art of seduction, he was the patron god of marriage. As a rural deity he was a friend of shepherds, and as an urban deity he was a friend of merchants. Indeed, he is the one god, as we can see from Aristophanes' *Plutus* (admittedly a satirical setting), who was still receiving sacrifices when all the others were being starved out. Moreover, his invention of the lyre made him a general patron of literature, so that in Petronius' *Satyricon*, for example, the wandering scholars are said to be under his special protection. He is also the inventor of the rustic pipe, as well as the art of making fire with

firesticks. He is presented as the perfect young gentleman, the ideal ephebe, the flower of physical and mental culture. He is the patron god of heralds, the ceremonial chief of protocol, a highly paid craft in antiquity. Finally, he is the psychopomp, who accompanies the dead in their journey to the Lower World.

69. The importance of the appointment of priests may likewise be seen in the fact that, according to Livy (1.20.1), the first act of Numa Pompilius, Romulus' successor as king, after establishing the calendar, was his appointment of priests.

70. As Gager 1972, 38, notes, Strabo's remarks about Moses have been widely, though not unanimously, attributed to Poseidonius. See especially Gager's note 40. The latest writer on Strabo's ethnographic excursus on the Jews, Bar-Kochva (1996) concludes that it was taken from Poseidonius and that it is a consistent adaptation following Hecataeus step-by-step.

71. Tacitus (*Histories* 5.5.1) similarly, we may note, though generally very critical of the Jews, distinguishes between the Jewish observance of the Sabbath, which, he says, is upheld by its antiquity, and all other customs, which were introduced at a later period. Among these other customs, Tacitus notes particularly the practice whereby proselytes contribute two drachmas annually (a reflection, presumably, of Tacitus' bitterness at the success of the Jews in winning proselytes), the xenophobic separation of the Jews, and their refusal to set up statues of the emperor. This tradition of a distinction between Moses' legislation and that of a later era, we may remark, was still alive as late as the fourth century, for we read in Julian (*Contra Galilaeos* 238C) that although Moses taught the Israelites to worship one G-d, he added, "Thou shalt not revile gods" (so in the LXX version of Exodus 22:27, in Philo's *QE* 2.5 and *Spec.* 1.53, and in Josephus' *Ap.* 2.237); later generations, he says, had the shamelessness and audacity to insult other religions.

72. Presumably, the reference is to the Jewish abstention from pork.

73. Elsewhere Strabo (17.2.5.824) notes that the Egyptians, as well as the Jews, circumcise males and excise females; but, so far as we know, excision of females was never practiced among Jews.

74. Because Heliopolis was the city of the sun-god, whence the name, perhaps such a tradition is an oblique reference to the connection of Moses with Aton, the sun-god of the hated religious rebel Akhenaton, whose henotheism Moses may have been thought to have borrowed, as Freud in his *Moses and Monotheism* was later to suggest. Moreover, inasmuch as a Jewish temple had been established at Leontopolis in the district of Heliopolis (which was the nome that was the center for the worship of the cult of the sun-god Re) in the second century B.C.E. by Onias IV (*B.J.* 1.33, 7.421–36; *A.J.* 12.388, 13.62–73, 13.285, 20.236), this connection may have seemed more credible.

75. On Moses' sexual abstinence, cf. *'Abot R. Nat.* A2, *Midr. Deut. Rab.* 11.10, *Midr. Song of Songs Rab.* 4.4.

76. For a summary of Moses as prophet, as viewed in *Mos.*, see Starobinski-Safran 1978, 67–80. Lierman 2002, 21–39, very briefly summarizes the portrayal of

Moses as a prophet in the Hebrew Scriptures, the Apocrypha, Pseudepigrapha, pagan writers, Philo, Josephus, Samaritan literature, rabbinic literature, and the New Testament.

77. Stern 1974, 1:266, on the ground that Strabo's account of the exodus contradicts considerably the account in the Bible, opposes the view that Strabo's source was a Hellenized Jew who was not particularly loyal to Scripture. He thinks that it is best to look for a pagan philosophical source.

78. See especially Numenius, *De Bono* (*ap.* Eus. *PE* 9.8.2), who refers to Moses as Musaeus (the teacher or student of Orpheus), "who led forth the Jews, a man who was most powerful in prayer to G-d," as well as the statement found several times among Christian writers (e.g., Clement of Alexandria, *Strom.* 1.22.150.4): "For what is Plato but Moses speaking in Attic?"

79. David Winston (*per litt.*) calls my attention to the fact that there is only a partial parallel between Wisdom and *Sifre Haazinu* here, namely in the number 21; and even here the author of Wisdom might just as well have been influenced by Neopythagorean number symbolism. In any case, the angelic relationship is found in *Sifre* but not in Wisdom; and what is especially significant is that the attributes are borrowed largely from Greek philosophy. See Winston 1979, 178–79, on Wisdom 7:22b–24.

80. See Collins 1973, 15–32, and Tromp 1993, 116–17. However, Nickelsburg 1973, 33–37, has argued for a second-century B.C.E. date during the persecution by Antiochus Epiphanes.

81. We find a similar picture of the suffering prophet in Josephus (*A.J.* 3.298), who, when he is abused shamefully by the Israelites during the sojourn in the desert because they lack food, responds, "G-d and I, though being insulted by you, will not cease our exertions on your behalf."

82. On the many attempts, none of them satisfactory, to identify Taxo, see Tromp 1993, 124–28.

83. Jeremias 1967, 4:865, is surprised that Luke says that Moses predicted that Jesus would suffer, inasmuch as there is no passage in the Pentateuch that might be so interpreted. He suggests that perhaps the reference is to Deut. 18:15, 18, which predicts the coming of a prophet like Moses, and that since Moses suffered, so would this later prophet.

84. For an extensive survey of the scholarship on the subject of ecstatic inspiration in Philo, see Burkhardt 1988, 7–72.

85. On the meaning of this cryptic phrase and suggested emendations, see Jacobson 1996, 2:651–52. On rabbinic parallels to Moses as a prophet of future history, see *Sifre Deut.* 357 and other rabbinic passages cited by Ginzberg 1928, 6:151, n. 902.

86. Josephus uses the terms μάντις, μαντεία, μαντεῖον, and μαντεύομαι with reference to pagan prophecies (particularly those derived from dreams), for example, of the Egyptian seers (*A.J.* 2.241; *Ap.* 1.236, 256, 257, 258 [2], 267, 306), Balaam (*A.J.* 4.104 [2], 112, 157), the Witch of Endor (*A.J.* 6.330, 331, 338), the Babylonian sooth-

sayers (*A.J.* 10.195), a seer in Alexander the Great's army (*Ap.* 1.203, 204), the Emperor Tiberius (*A.J.* 18.217, 223), the Delphic Oracle (*Ap.* 2.162), and soothsayers in general (*A.J.* 6.327, 331, 17.345; *B.J.* 2.112).

87. This statement, that Moses' final song contains a prediction of events to come, agrees with rabbinic tradition; see *Sifre Deut.* 307–33, *Midr. Tannaim* 192-204, and *Tg. Yer.* ad loc., cited by Ginzberg 1928, 6:155, n. 920.

88. Cf. *Midr. Tannaim* (end) and other parallel passages cited by Ginzberg 1928, 6:125, n. 727.

89. For references, see Meeks 1967, 220–21.

90. To be sure, the fourteenth-century Samaritan Book of Josh. declares that G-d commanded Moses to deliver to his successor, Joshua, "information of the profound secret."

91. On the historical development of the Samaritan creed, see Macdonald 1964, 49–55, and Bowman 1958, 302–10.

92. Meeks 1967, 239, suggests that a closer parallel is John 5:46: "If you believed in Moses, you would believe in me." He asserts that the statement in *Memar* is actually a close paraphrase of Exod. 14:31: "They believed in the L-rd and in His servant Moses." He notes another parallel in *Mek.* on Exod. 14:31: "If you say they believed in Moses, is it not implied by *Kal vaḥomer* [*a fortiori*] that they believed in G-d?"

93. See also the other references cited by Jeremias 1967, 4:858, n. 126.

94. Presumably, as Priest 1983, 922, suggests, the author, consistent with his thorough determinism, is here stating that Moses' role had been decreed from the beginning of the world.

95. There is a real question as to whether Eupolemus, of whom we have only fragments, was Jewish at all. See Feldman 1998a, 74–77.

96. On the degree to which the introduction of the alphabet into Greece was indeed revolutionary, see Harris 1989, 45–47, 331.

97. This catalogue is paralleled by similar claims for numerous pagan heroes. See Holladay 1983, 1:232–33, n. 46. Moses is also termed the first wise man (σοφός) by Eupolemus (*ap.* Clement of Alexandria, *Strom* 1.23.153.4; *ap.* Eus. *PE* 9.26.1).

98. On the trend in Artapanus and other alleged Graeco-Jewish writers to bolster Jewish self-esteem by asserting the cultural ascendancy of the Jews, see Gruen 1997, 72–88.

99. Most scholars—notably Freudenthal 1874–75, 143–53; Willrich 1900, 111–17; Schürer 1909, 3:477–80; Sterling 1992, 167–86; and Gruen 1998, 155–60—regard Artapanus as a Jew (see Holladay 1983, 1:195, n. 8a). However, Eusebius (*PE* 9.18.1, 9.23.1–4, 9.27.1–37) and Clement of Alexandria (*Strom.* 1.23.154.2–3), who cite him at length, nowhere mention that he was a Jew. Philo never mentions him at all. Likewise, Josephus never mentions him; and while there are some parallels with his account of Moses as general in Ethiopia, there are considerable differences as well. It seems hard to believe that a Jew, however liberal he might have been, could have stated, as Arta-

panus (Eus. *PE* 9.27.4) says, that in the time of Joseph the Israelites built temples in Athos and Heliopolis (*ap.* Eus. *PE* 9.23.4), that Moses became the teacher of Orpheus, that he established the worship of cats, dogs, and ibises (9.27.4, 9, 12), and that he was deemed worthy of divine honor by the priests and was called Hermes because of his ability to interpret the sacred writings (9.27.6). If he was Jewish and presumably acquainted with the Bible, it is hard to understand how he could have said (9.27.20) that the Pharaoh Chenephres died because he had ordered the Jews to be clothed with linen and not to wear woolen clothing, and that he did this so that once they were so marked they could be harassed by him, whereas the Bible prohibits wearing cloth that *combines* wool and linen (Lev. 19:19, Deut. 22:11). For a systematic refutation of the view that Artapanus was a Jew, see now Jacobson 2006.

100. Moses is also called Musaeus by Numenius (*ap.* Eus. *PE* 9.8.2), as we have noted above.

101. According to Josephus (*A.J.* 2.346), it was in hexameter verse that Moses composed his song on the occasion of the miraculous crossing of the Sea of Reeds, as well as his final song (*A.J.* 4.303) before his death.

102. One is also reminded of Socrates' dream (Plato, *Phaedo* 60E6–7), just before his death, telling him to cultivate and make music, whereupon, even though he was convinced that philosophy, which he had pursued throughout his life, was the noblest and best music, he composed a hymn in honor of Apollo and versified some fables of Aesop.

103. Josephus has similarly enhanced his portrait of Abraham by presenting him (*A.J.* 1.167), in an extra-biblical detail, as a mathematician and astronomer who taught these sciences to the famed Egyptians, who in turn taught them to the Greeks.

104. We may also note the importance attached to time-reckoning by the pre-Socratics, since we are told (Pliny, *Natural History* 2.187) that it was Anaximenes who first showed a horologium, what the Spartans call a σκιοθήρικον (sundial); cf. Strabo 25.4; Cleomedes 1.8; Plutarch, *Marcellus* 19; Diogenes Laertius 2.1; Ptolemy, *Geography* 1.22; Vitruvius 1.6.6. See Becker 1873, 317–21. That such an invention would have been especially appreciated by the Romans is apparent from the fact that according to Pliny (*Natural History* 7.60) there was no sundial in Rome until eleven years before the war with Pyrrhus (ca. 293 B.C.E.). The water glass (clepsydra, solarium, or gnomon) was, according to Athenaeus (4.174), invented by Ctesibios about the year 145 B.C.E. during the reign of Ptolemy Euergetes II, although Pliny (7.69) declares that the first water glass was set up by Scipio Nasica in Rome in 158 B.C.E. Its importance to the Romans is indicated by Pliny's remark (36.73) that a magnificent horologium, a gnomon in the shape of an obelisk, was erected by Augustus in the Campus Martius, whereupon Pliny complains that eventually it became incorrect in its keeping of time. Here may be the source of Moses' sundial. An obelisk was made to serve as a sundial, and somebody centuries later attributed the device to Moses, as so many of the tall isolated ancient columns in Transjordan and southern Syria are now said to have been

built by "Pharaoh." Elsewhere, the eighth-century Byzantine Christian Georgius Syncellus (*Ecloge Chronographia*, ed. Alden A. Mosshammer [Leipzig, 1984] 377) asserts that Abraham instructed the Egyptians in calendar reckoning and that the Greeks derived this art from them. Here the anti-Jewish Apion ascribes to Moses inventiveness in astronomy and chronography, which the Egyptians admired so much, and thus implicitly admits the baselessness of his own charge (*ap.* Josephus, *Ap.* 2.135) that the Jews have not produced any geniuses, inventors in arts and crafts, or eminent sages.

105. See Marrou 1956, 176–85, and Feldman 1968, 154–56.

106. The Suda actually accuses Plato of plagiarizing his views of G-d and creation from the works of Moses; but the statement, as simply construed, seems to indicate merely that their teachings are similar.

107. Gager 1972, 68, raises the question whether a Jew could have written that G-d was the father of all the gods (*ap.* Lydus, *De Mensibus* 4.53) and that Jannes and Jambres could have matched Moses in a contest of magic (*ap.* Eus. *PE* 9.18.1). But, we may remark, the comparison with other gods implicit in the statement that G-d is the father of all the gods is reminiscent of the statement (1 Chr. 15:25) that G-d is awesome above all gods. As to the contest in magic between Jannes and Jambres, on the one hand, and Moses, on the other hand, a Pseudepigraphic book entitled Jannes and Jambres, of which only fragments survive, presents them as continuously opposing Moses with their magic. Gager himself concludes that preconceived notions of what constituted orthodoxy in post-exilic Judaism are of little help in such matters.

108. Moses is likewise denominated a sorcerer (γόης) by Apollonius Molon and Lysimachus (*ap.* Josephus, *Ap.* 2.145).

109. The passage, preserved only in Arabic, is from Galen's *On Hippocrates' Anatomy*; see Walzer 1949, 10–11, 18–23.

110. Presumably a reference to the fourth biblical plague (Exod. 8:16–28), ערב (mixture of wild beasts), which the LXX (Exod. 8:20–32) renders as "dog-fly." Whereas Artapanus says that Moses raised up the winged creatures, in the Bible it is G-d Himself (Exod. 8:17) who does so.

111. The Bible does not speak of earthquakes, but the reference may be to the ninth plague, darkness (Exod. 10:21–29), as suggested by Holladay 1983, 1:242, n. 110.

112. Holladay 1983, 1:242, n. 111, suggests that the basis for this statement may be Num. 33:4, which states that as the Egyptians were burying their first-born, G-d inflicted punishments on their gods.

113. *A.J.* 1.108, 2.348, 3.268, 3.322, 4.158, 8.262, 10.281, 17.354, 19.108; *B.J.* 5.257.

114. On Josephus' treatment of miracles, see Delling 1957–58, 291–309; MacRae 1965, 127–47; Moehring 1973, 376–83; Betz 1974, 23–44; and Feldman 1998a, 209–12.

115. Dionysius of Halicarnassus, *Ant. Rom.* 1.48.1, 1.48.4, 2.40.3, 2.74.5, 3.36.5; Lucian, *Quomodo Historia Conscribenda Sit* 10; Pliny, *Natural History* 9.18; Herodotus, 2.123, 5.45; Thucydides, 6.2.1.

116. Thus the prediction that the angel will return and that Sarah will bear a son "according to this season of life," that is a year from then (Gen. 18:10), is toned down in Josephus, who states merely that one of the angels will return some day in the future (*A.J.* 1.197). Then, when the birth takes place, Josephus says simply that it occurred during the following year (*A.J.* 1.214). Again, the scene of the ram being caught in the thicket by its horns may have seemed grotesque and too much of a miracle for a rationalizing Greek intellectual (Gen. 22:13). Hence, Josephus omits it and says merely that G-d brought the ram from obscurity into view, implying that it had always been there. Josephus does not state explicitly, as does the Bible, that Abraham offered the ram in place of his son (Gen. 22:13), presumably because he wished to avoid the theological implication that it was a substitute for the sins of man.

117. We may discern the deemphasis on miracles in Josephus' version of Gideon in the omission of Gideon's challenge to the angel to produce miracles comparable to those that the Israelites' ancestors had experienced (Judg. 6:13 vs. *A.J.* 5.214), as well as the omission of a request for signs to prove that it is really G-d Who has spoken to Gideon (Judg. 6:17–18). Josephus likewise omits the double miracle of the fleece of wool on the threshing floor which develops dew upon it while all the ground around it is dry, as well as vice versa (Judg. 6:36–40 vs. *A.J.* 5.215). Josephus, much as he might have liked to exaggerate Samson's exploits in order to build up his stature as a hero, is careful to omit miraculous and magical elements. Whereas the Bible declares that Samson broke the bowstrings binding him, "as a string of tow snaps when it touches the fire" (Judg. 16:9), Josephus' account omits the miraculous element, and we are left with the statement that he burst the shoots asunder (*A.J.* 5.310). The Bible remarks that Samson snapped the ropes off his arms as if they were a thread (Judg. 16:12), but Josephus states merely that Delilah's ploy met with no success (*A.J.* 5.311). That, in the popular mind, Elijah's dominant association was with miracles may be seen in the Gospels, where, immediately after the miracles that Jesus and his followers performed, notably in casting out devils and in healing the sick, he is identified as Elijah (Mark 6:15). Nevertheless, Josephus tones down the miracle of the feeding of Elijah by the ravens. A skeptical pagan might well be astonished to read the biblical statement that G-d commanded the ravens to feed Elijah (1 Kings 17:2-4) and might well wonder whether G-d gives commands to birds; hence in Josephus' version we are told, what is much easier to believe, merely that the ravens brought food to him every day, presumably of their own accord (*A.J.* 8.319). Even the extent of the miracle is toned down in that the Bible is very specific in stating exactly what the ravens brought to Elijah, namely bread and meat, and how often they came, namely in the morning and in the evening, whereas Josephus, who is generally more specific than the Bible, is apparently deliberately more vague in stating that the ravens brought him food every day, without indicating what they brought and exactly when they came. Josephus rationalizes the seemingly impossible statement that the fire of G-d licked up the water in the trench in the contest on Mount Carmel by explaining that when

the fire consumed the altar the water went up as steam (1 Kings 18:38 vs. *A.J.* 8.342). Josephus does not attempt to eliminate or play down the miraculous fire from heaven (Begg 1993, 188); but if he does not do so, it is because his readers were ready to accept such prodigies, as we can see from the pages of Livy, Plutarch, and Suetonius.

Likewise, Josephus makes more credible the account of the rain that miraculously descended upon the land after the contest between Elijah and the priests of Baal. In the biblical version Elijah tells Ahab to go up to eat and drink since the sound of the rushing of rain is already present, even though actually there is no sign of rain at all (1 Kings 18:41). Josephus is more cautious and declares not that the rain is already present but rather that the rain will come in a little while (μετ᾽ ὀλίγον) (*A.J.* 8.343). When Elijah sends his servant to see whether the rain is coming, the latter is told merely to look toward the sea (1 Kings 18:43). The Josephan Elijah is more detailed and more scientific; he tells his servant precisely what to look for, namely to discern whether a cloud is rising in any direction, inasmuch as until then the sky had been clear (*A.J.* 8.344). When Elijah flees from Jezebel, an angel, according to the Bible, visits him and supplies him with food for forty days and nights (1 Kings 19:8); Josephus, omitting the miraculous element (*A.J.* 8.349), says nothing about an angel but rather that Elijah found food and water after someone had awakened him (*A.J.* 8.349); and he does not indicate how long he was sustained by this food. Moreover, he has totally omitted the spectacular miracle whereby Elijah struck the Jordan River with his mantle and was able to get the water to part so that he and Elisha could cross it (2 Kings 2:8 vs. *A.J.* 9.28). In accordance with his rationalizing tendency, Josephus says nothing about the spectacular miracle of Elijah going up in a whirlwind in a chariot of fire into heaven (2 Kings 1:11–12); instead, in a passage, highly reminiscent of the scene at the end of Sophocles' *Oedipus at Colonus* (1655–60), we are told merely that he disappeared from among men, and that to this day no one knows his end (*A.J.* 9.28) (see Feldman 1994a, 74–81). Josephus explains by natural means the miracle performed by Elisha in curing the waters of Jericho (2 Kings 2:19–23 vs. *B.J.* 4.462–64). He totally omits this miracle from *A.J.*, where his readership apparently consisted primarily of non-Jews, and inserts it in *B.J.*, where his readership, at least originally, since the work was composed in Aramaic (*B.J.* 1.3), consisted of Jews. (Apparently, those who helped Josephus [*Ap.* 1.50] with the translation into Greek did not tamper with the content of the actual text.) Surely the most amazing miracle performed by Elisha is the revival of the dead child of the Shunammite woman (2 Kings 4:34); Josephus omits the entire incident (see Feldman 1994b, 20–24). To be sure, Josephus does not omit the comparable miracle of Elijah's revival of the widow's son (*A.J.* 8.325–27), but, as we have noted, he tones down several other miracles attributed to Elijah.

In Josephus' account of the miracle by which Daniel's three companions emerged unscathed after having been cast into a fiery furnace (*A.J.* 10.214), we may readily see changes that Josephus has introduced for the sake of his audience. Whereas the Bible states that Nebuchadnezzar ordered that the furnace be heated seven times more than usual (Dan. 3:19), Josephus, realizing that this kind of exaggeration would probably be viewed as incredible, simply omits it. Likewise, Josephus, though he is generally aware of Apocryphal books, totally omits the "Prayer of the Three Youths," which puts the spotlight so brightly upon the miracle. In explanation of their rescue, Josephus says that they were saved by divine providence (πρόνοια), employing a term that was a favorite of the Stoics, who undoubtedly constituted a large portion of his pagan audience. Finally, Josephus rationalizes the miracle, explaining that G-d, presumably through the vegetarian diet that they had followed, had made their bodies too strong to be consumed by the fire (*A.J.* 10.215). In contrast, we may note, Josephus' apparent contemporary, Pseudo-Philo, in his *LAB*, in describing the similar scene (6.17) where Abraham was cast into a furnace, actually exaggerates the miracle by describing a great earthquake and fire which gushed forth from the furnace consuming all those who stood round about, so that no fewer than 83,500 were burnt to death on that day.

Josephus' inclusion of the miracle of Jonah's remaining alive for three days in the belly of the big fish (Jonah 1:17) would likewise seem to be an exception to this tendency of Josephus to downgrade miracles; but even here a careful reading of Josephus' text shows that Josephus presents it as a Herodotean-like story (λόγος, *A.J.* 9.213) which he does not necessarily endorse. Moreover, he omits the statement that G-d spoke to the fish that had swallowed Jonah (Jonah 2:10) (see Feldman 1952d, 14–16).

If we ask why Josephus did include the story of Balaam's speaking ass, we may suggest that it was because his audience was familiar with the account of Achilles' horse, Xanthos, which likewise speaks after being unfairly accused by his master (Homer, *Il.* 19.408–17). And, in any case, at the end of the whole episode of Balaam we have Josephus' familiar disclaimer: "On this narrative readers are free to think what they please" (*A.J.* 4.158).

118. For the identification, see Artapanus, *ap.* Eus. *PE* 9.27.3.

119. The contest is also mentioned in 2 Tim. 3:8, *b. Men.* 85a, and *Tg. Yer.* on Exod. 7:11. See Pietersma 1992, 3:638–40, and 1994. A parallel but not identical tradition is found in Yohanah and his brother in the *Damascus Document* (*CD* 5.17b–19, 4Q266 3.2.6–8 [13–15], 4Q267 2.1–3, 6Q15 3.1–2). See Pietersma 2000, 2:1000–1.

120. On the fame of Moses as a magician, see Graf 1997, 6–8; and Gager 1972, 134–61.

121. See Celsus, *ap.* Origen, *Against Celsus* 5.41–42.

122. We recall that according to Artapanus (*ap.* Eus. *PE* 9.27.6), Moses was called Hermes because of his ability to interpret the sacred writings.

123. See Paulus, *Sententiae* 5.23.18, who states that not only the profession of magic but also the knowledge of it are prohibited, and that if such books are found in someone's possession, that person's possessions are confiscated, the books themselves are publicly burned, and the person himself is subjected to capital punishment. See Graf 1997, 236–37, n. 9.

124. Cf. Apion's charge (*ap.* Philo, *Legat.* 115–17) that the Jews were unpatriotic because they did not bow down to the Roman emperor.

125. It seems likely that the allusion here is to a Jew, since we find the same phrase, *Palaestino . . . Syro*, in Ovid (*Ars Amatoria* 1.416), where the reference is definitely to a Jew, since the passage refers to the Sabbath which he observes. See Stern 1980, 2:221, n. 4.

126. Wolfson 1947, 2:414, suggests that there may be a parallel between the aid, namely, "dauntless courage of soul and all-powerful strength (ἰσχύς) of body," which G-d will instill in the man's troops, and the spirit of counsel and might (ἰσχύς) in the description of the Messiah in Isaiah (11:2); but there is little similarity aside from the one word, ἰσχύς.

127. Colson 1939, 8:418, in his comment on this passage, suggests that the reference is to a belief that the second deliverance of the nation will be guided, as was the first, by a cloud, in which there was a divine vision flashing rays of fire.

128. James 1917 lists 3.10, 19.4, 19.7, 19.12–13, 21.9, 23.6, 23.13, 26.12, 28.10, 32.17, 33.2–5, 38.4, 48.1, 51.5, and 62.9.

129. The fact that Josephus declares that this, more than anything else, drove the Jews to war would indicate that it was a strongly and widely held belief. That it was, indeed, widely held seems indicated by the fact that a similar prediction is mentioned by Tacitus (*Histories* 5.13.2), who states that the majority (*pluribus*) were persuaded that "their ancient priestly writings contained the prophecy that this was the very time when the East should grow strong and that men coming from Judaea should possess the world." Similar evidence, as we have noted, that such a belief was widely held is to be found in Suetonius (*Vespasian* 4.5), who reports that "there had spread over all the Orient an old and established belief, that it was fated at that time for men coming from Judaea to rule the world." Menahem, the leader of the Sicarii, who appeared in the Temple dressed in royal robes (*B.J.* 2.444), certainly gives the appearance of a messiah-like figure, as does the Jew from Egypt who, with 30,000 followers, proposed to overpower the Roman garrison in Jerusalem (*B.J.* 2.261–63).

130. One possible reference, cited by Jeremias 1967, 4:857, n. 110, to Moses as Messiah is to be found in Sib. Or. 5.256–59: "But one will come again from heaven, an outstanding man whose hands he spread out on the fruitful wood, the best of the Hebrews who once caused the sun to stand still." But, we may remark, the one who caused the sun to stand still is Joshua, not Moses; and it would seem that this is a Christian interpolation, where the reference is to Jesus, whose Hebrew name was Joshua. A Jew would not say that Joshua was the best of the Hebrews, but a Christian might well say that Jesus (Joshua) was the best of the Hebrews.

131. Mentioned by Jeremias 1967, 4:860–63, who cites many additional parallels.

132. A similar coupling of Moses and Elijah as forerunners of the Messiah is found in *Sifre Deut.* 355 and *Midr. Tannaim* 219, cited by Ginzberg 1928, 6:167, n. 966.

133. See the discussion by Meeks 1967, 250–54.

134. On this incident, see Gaster 1925, 90–91, who finds here a reference to the Samaritan doctrine of the Taheb.

135. See Lucian (*Cynicus* 13), where Heracles is called a divine man (θεῖος ἀνήρ). Cf. Pfister 1909–12 and Farnell 1921.

136. See Welles 1955, 157, and Talbert 1975, 428. Likewise, it was told of the philosopher Empedocles that after an evening party he disappeared and was nowhere to be found, and that one of those present at the party claimed to have heard a voice from heaven declaring that he was now a god (Heracleides of Pontus, *ap.* Diogenes Laertius [8.68]). Apollonius of Tyana is depicted as a god-like man (θεῖος ἀνήρ), whose divinity is manifest in his wisdom and virtue (*ap.* Philostratus, *Life of Apollonius of Tyana* 1.2, 2.17, 2.40, 5.24, 7.21, 7.38, 8.5, 8.7). Again, when speaking of the death of Apollonius, Philostratus adds (8.29), "if he did actually die," and then declares that no one ventured to dispute that he was immortal. Furthermore, a certain senator named Numerius Atticus swore that he had seen Augustus after his death ascend to heaven like Romulus and Proculus (*ap.* Suetonius, *Augustus* 94.4). Indeed, the motif of the apotheosis of rulers and philosophers became so widespread that it became the subject of satire in Seneca's *Apocolocyntosis* and in Lucian's *Deorum Concilium* and *De Morte Peregrini.*

137. The second (Exod. 7:26–8:11, LXX 8:1–15), the eighth (Exod. 10:1–20, LXX 10:1–20), and the third plague (Exod. 8:12–15, LXX 8:16–19). This differs from the biblical order of the plagues. In Philo, (*Mos.* 1.99) the order of the plagues is blood (1), frogs (2), fleas (lice) (3), hail (4, seventh in Exod. 9:22–35), locusts (5, eighth in Exod. 10:1–20), darkness (6, ninth in Exod. 10:21–29), boils (7, sixth in Exod. 9:8–12), dog-fly (Hebrew: mixture of wild beasts) (8, fourth in Exod. 8:20–30), murrain (9, fifth in Exod. 9:1–7), death of first-born (10, tenth in Exod. 12:29–36). Whereas Artapanus here says that Moses brought on the plagues of the frogs, locusts, and fleas with his rod, in the Bible it is Aaron who brings on the plague of the frogs (Exod. 8:2) and the plague of the fleas (Exod. 8:13) by stretching out his hand with his staff, whereas Moses brings on the plague of the locusts by stretching out his staff (Exod. 10:13).

138. See Pseudo-Eupolemus (*ap.* Eus. *PE* 9.17.4, 9.17.8, 9.18.2), Artapanus (*ap.* Eus. *PE* 9.18.1), Vettius Valens (*Anthologiae* 2.28), and Firmicus Maternus (*Mathesis* 4, Prooemium 5; 4.17.2).

139. Cf. Gruen 1998, 134: "The vast dominion that Moses beholds from his lofty vantage point extends in time rather than in space. The symbolism connotes the prophetic powers that he could now exercise."

140. For a list of scholars who believe that Ezekiel was writing for a non-Jewish audience, see Jacobson 1983, 181, n. 1. For a list of scholars who believe that he was writing for a Jewish audience, as well as for a list of scholars who believe that he was writing for both, see Jacobson 1983, 181, n. 2.

141. Cf. a similar scene in *Midr. Exod. Rab.* 1.26; *Sefer Hayashar* (ed. Dan, p. 289).

142. The shift from the third person singular in lines 6–7 and the second person in line 8 remains a problem, as both Newson and Fletcher-Louis recognize. One solu-

tion is to say that there are some words missing. Another, suggested by Fletcher-Louis (250), is that the fluidity between the second and third person is itself indicative of the extent to which Moses has become merged with the divinity. Fletcher-Louis asks whether it is Moses or G-d whom the Israelites fail to recognize. He suggests that "if Moses now possesses something of the glory of the one G-d, then in a sense it can be said that they have missed the presence of both."

143. Holladay 1977, 176, says that the "divine man" here must remain anonymous.

144. Graf 1976, 115–16, notes that Philo's view, that it is the possession of ἀρεταί, moral virtues, by a wise man that qualifies a man as divine, is in accord with the Stoic conceptual framework.

145. Fletcher-Louis here asserts that a proof-text that Philo regarded Moses as divine may be seen in *Sacr.* 8–10, where, he claims, Philo explicitly joins together Exod. 7:1 with Moses' ascent on Sinai to receive the Torah (Deut. 5:28). But while Philo does cite Deut. 5:28 in *Sacr.* 8 and Exod. 7:1 in *Sacr.* 9, he does not bring them together. In the first passage he indicates that Moses is one of the *others* whom G-d has trained to soar above their species; but the fact that he is one of the others indicates that he is not unique, let alone divine. In the second passage Philo asserts that Moses is *as* G-d to Pharaoh but not that he is G-d.

146. In a recent discussion of Exod. 7:1, Kügler 2000, 234, concludes that from Philo's understanding of Exod. 7:1 we may deduce that Moses was G-d's representative on earth and that the boundaries between G-d and humanity were not eradicated.

147. Borgen 1997, 203, cites *Sacr.* 9, where Philo says that G-d sent Moses as a loan to the earthly sphere and suffered him to dwell therein, appointing him as "G-d." But Philo here understands "G-d" in a figurative sense, since he explains that G-d placed all the bodily region and the mind that rules it in subjection to him. However, Moses' entry into the darkness where G-d is does not indicate that he is actually divine. Moreover, it is clear that Philo did not regard Moses as divine, since immediately after the passage, *Sacr.* 9, in which Philo says that G-d appointed Moses as god, we read (*Sacr.* 10) that G-d is not susceptible of addition or diminution, clearly implying that G-d does not have the power to give up divinity to someone else. "And therefore," he adds, "no one is said to know his grave," a clear indication that Moses died, and hence could not have been G-d.

148. Aucher translates the Armenian here by the Latin *deificari.*

149. For Jacobson 1981, 290, n. 13, the non-mystical character of Ezekiel is to be contrasted with Philo's account (*QE* 2.40) of Moses' divinization (Exod. 24:12) "to a region above the heavens" beyond this world, where there is no place but G-d, in his ascent on Mount Sinai.

150. The proverb that Philo cites is also quoted by Diogenes Laertius (6.72) in his life of Diogenes the Cynic and is consonant with the Stoic view of the sage as the possessor of all.

151. Other references in Philo to Moses as a friend of G-d are to be found in *Ebr.* 95 and *Somn.* 1.193–94, 1.231–32.

152. Tiede 1972, 125, n. 43, cites a similar concept, attributed by Diogenes Laertius (6.72) to Diogenes the Cynic: "All things belong to the gods. The gods are friends of the wise, and friends share all property in common; therefore, all things are the property of the wise."

153. On Moses as G-d's friend, see also Jub. 21.15, 20; Sib. Or. 2.245; and Pseudo-Philo 23.9, 24.3, 25.3, 25.5, 32.8, 33.4, 35.3.

154. As Georgi 1986, 126, notes, Josephus proves the divine quality of Moses by noting the cosmic character of the laws given by him, the implication being that he is not actually divine. The nature of the lawgiver was thus able to capture the order of the process of nature and thereby the will of G-d as expressed in G-d's works. That Josephus has no intention of asserting Moses' divinity is clear from the proof that he gives of Moses being a "man of G-d," namely that the construction of the tabernacle and the appearance of the vestments and vessels of the priests show his concern for piety. See Georgi, 204, n. 304. Elsewhere Josephus (*A.J.* 10.35) refers to the prophet Isaiah as acknowledged to be divine (θεῖος) and marvelously possessed of truth. Again, after King Solomon, in the dispute between the two harlots about their infants, discovers the real mother, he is regarded by the multitude as possessed of a divine (θεῖα) understanding (*A.J.* 8.34). Likewise Daniel, through the auspiciousness of his predictions, wins the esteem of the multitude for his nature especially endowed by G-d (θειότης, *A.J.* 10.268). Josephus himself (*Ap.* 1.279), in his refutation of Manetho, notes that the Egyptians regard Moses as remarkable (θαυμαστός) and divine (θεῖος) and wish to claim him as one of their own; but the fact that he asserts this as an Egyptian claim indicates that he does not identify with it. In answer to the question as to why Josephus refers to Moses as θεῖος ἀνήρ (*Ant.* 3.180), rather than as ἄνθρωπος θεοῦ, Holladay 1977, 89–100, suggests that perhaps he did so because of his anti-Samaritan sentiments, since the Samaritans identified Moses as the man of G-d. For Josephus, he states, the word θεῖος here shades off into ἱερός or ἅγιος or εὐσεβής and does not mean divine in the most literal sense, as we may see from his recasting of other biblical personalities. Bieler 1936, 2:33–36, notes that the characteristics of Philo's Moses closely parallel those of the typical Hellenistic "divine man." But there is, he says, a major difference in that Philo does not stress the aspect of Moses as a miracle worker.

155. Josephus (*A.J.* 3.137), in an unparalleled addition to the Bible, says that Moses actually saw the Cherubim adhering to the throne of G-d.

156. In Josephus (*A.J.* 3.104), however, it is Moses, not G-d, who appoints the construction supervisors for the tabernacle, in accordance with the instruction of G-d; and he says (*A.J.* 3.107) that Moses, in accordance with G-d's direction, instructed them in all the details. Josephus further diminishes the supernatural element in the choice of the architects by adding the extra-biblical detail that the multitude also

would have selected them if the authority had been in their power. The third-century Rabbi Isaac (*b. Ber.* 36a), citing Exod. 35:30, referring to G-d's choice of Bezalel, remarks that we must not appoint a leader over a community without first consulting it. He cites a tradition that G-d asked Moses whether he considered Bezalel suitable to be the architect of the tabernacle, whereupon Moses said that if G-d considered him suitable, surely he also should, whereupon G-d told him to consult the people of Israel. When Moses did so, their reply was that if G-d and Moses considered him suitable, surely they should too.

157. Maimonides, in his classic formulation of the thirteen principles of Jewish faith (Commentary on the Mishnah, *Sanhedrin*, introduction to chapter 10) in the twelfth century, includes the belief that Moses was the greatest of the prophets as one of those fundamentals. Nevertheless, the rabbis found it possible to relate the entire story of the Exodus in the lengthy narrative compiled for the Passover seder while mentioning the name of Moses only once, and that only because his name is included in a biblical verse that they quote there.

158. Similarly, one current of rabbinic tradition spoke of Moses as "very much above all the men that were upon the face of the earth" (*Sifre Bamidbar Beha'aloteka* on Num. 12:3). Cf. *Midr. Tannaim* 2.186 (ed. David Hoffmann) on Deut. 32:3: "Moses, than whom there has not been one greater in the world." See also the citations given by Ginzberg 1925, 5:398, n. 47, who remarks that rabbinic tradition declared that the angels had conversed with G-d about the fate of Moses.

159. Cf. 3 Enoch 15B5, where we read that the skin of Moses' face shone from one end of the world to the other. Cf. also *Pesiqta Rabbati* 21.102a, where we read that opening Moses' grave even a bit would reveal a dazzling light sufficient to overwhelm the world (cited by Jacobson 1996, 2:658).

160. Similarly, Pseudo-Philo (19.16) and the Ass. Mos. (1.15) affirm that Moses' death took place in public and that G-d buried him.

161. One of these is Ovid, who describes a scene in which Jupiter fulfills his promise to lift up Romulus to heaven (*Metamorphoses* 14.805–85). Cf. Ovid, *Fasti* 2.481–509 and Livy 1.16.

162. This is particularly significant, inasmuch as Josephus is definitely indebted to Sophocles elsewhere. It is also just possible that Josephus is reacting against the Christian tradition of the apotheosis of Jesus (Luke 24; Acts 1). See Fornaro 1979, 431–60; and Paul 1975, 473–80. Begg 1990, 692, objects that in the end Josephus negates the whole impression of Moses' disappearance with his closing affirmation that in reality Moses did not "return to the divinity" but simply died. This does not, however, detract from the point that prior to this "correction" Josephus has described the disappearance of Moses in terms closely parallel to those used by Sophocles. There are several other touches in Josephus' extra-biblical modifications of the account of Solomon that indicate that he had Oedipus in mind. See Feldman 1998a, 174–75.

163. Another significant fact is that although we know the names of thousands of rabbis who lived during the Talmudic period we find that only one, Moses ben Aẓri (*b. B. Bat.* 174b, *ʿArak.* 23a), bore the name of Moses; and he is presented in an unfavorable light, since he was unwilling to give his son-in-law, Rabbi Huna, the cash dowry stipulated in his daughter's wedding contract. To be sure, the name of Abram (Abraham) is found only once, namely, Abram of Hozae (*b. Git.* 50a).

164. As expounded by Rabbi Ishmael (*Sifra*, introduction, 5).

165. The sixth hymn of the Durran cycle by Amram Darah, cited by Cowley (1909, 1:40–41).

166. Meeks calls attention to Philo's description of the mad Roman emperor Caligula dressed as the sun-god Apollo, his head encircled with garlands of the rays of the sun.

167. Himmelfarb 1993, 48–49, 70–71, cited by Borgen 1997, 202, suggests that Philo, in this description of the ascent of Moses, has given perhaps the most extended treatment in Jewish or Christian literature of the divination of a human being.

Bibliography

Alexander, Philip S., 1992. "Enoch, Third Book of." In *ABD* 2:522–26.

Allen, Edgar L., 1955–56. "Jesus and Moses in the New Testament." *ET* 67:104–6.

Allison, Dale C., Jr., 1993. *The New Moses: A Matthean Typology*. Minneapolis: Fortress Press.

Amir, Yehoshua, 1971. "Philo Judaeus." *EJ* 13:409–15.

Amir, Yehoshua, 1973. "Philo and the Bible." *SPA* 2:1–8.

Amir, Yehoshua, 1988. "Authority and Interpretation of Scripture in the Writings of Philo." In *Mikra: Text, Translation, Reading and Interpretation of the Hebrew Bible in Ancient Judaism and Early Christianity*, ed. Martin J. Mulder, 421–53. Assen: Van Gorcum.

Arnaldez, Roger; Mondésert, Claude; Pouilloux, Jean; and Savinel, Pierre, eds., 1967. *Les Oeuvres de Philon d'Alexandrie: De Vita Mosis I-II*. Paris: Editions du Cerf.

Assmann, Jan, 1997. *Moses the Egyptian: The Memory of Egypt in Western Monotheism*. Cambridge, Mass.: Harvard University Press.

Attridge, Harold W., 1976. *The Interpretation of Biblical History in the Antiquitates Judaicae of Flavius Josephus*. Missoula: Scholars Press.

Badke, William B., 1988. "Baptised into Moses—Baptised into Christ: A Study in Doctrinal Development." *EQ* 88.1:23–29.

Balch, David L., 1982. "Two Apologetic Encomia: Dionysius on Rome and Josephus on the Jews." *JSJ* 12:102–22.

Bamberger, Bernard J., 1939. *Proselytism in the Talmudic Period*. Cincinnati: Hebrew Union College Press.

Barclay, John M. G., 1996. *Jews in the Mediterranean Diaspora: From Alexander to Trajan (323 BCE-117 CE)*. Edinburgh: Clark.

Bar-Kochva, Bezalel, 1996. *Pseudo-Hecataeus, On the Jews: Legitimizing the Jewish Diaspora*. Berkeley: University of California Press.

Barraclough, Ray, 1984. "Philo's Politics, Roman Rule and Hellenistic Judaism," *ANRW* 2.21.1:417–553. Berlin: de Gruyter.

Barrett, Charles K., 1962. *From First Adam to Last: A Study in Pauline Theology*. New York: Scribner's.

Baskin, Judith R., 1983. *Pharaoh's Counsellors: Job, Jethro, and Balaam in Rabbinic and Patristic Tradition*. Chico, California: Scholars Press.

Bauckham, Richard, 1999. "The Throne of G-d and the Worship of Jesus." In *The Jewish Roots of Christological Monotheism: Papers from the St. Andrews Conference on the*

Historical Origins of the Worship of Jesus, ed. Carey C. Newman, James R. Davila, Gladys S. Lewis, 43–69. Leiden: Brill.

Becker, Wilhelm A., 1873. *Gallus; or Roman Scenes of the Time of Augustus*, tr. Frederick Metcalfe, 4th ed. London: Longmans, Green; Parker.

Begg, Christopher T., 1985. "The Destruction of the Calf (Exodus 32,20/Deut 9,21)." In *Das Deuteronomium. Entstehung, Gestalt und Botschaft*, ed. Norbert Lohfink, 208–51. Leuven: University Press.

Begg, Christopher T., 1990. "Josephus' Portrayal of the Disappearances of Enoch, Elijah, and Moses: Some Observations." *JBL* 109:691–93.

Begg, Christopher T., 1996. "The Golden Calf Episode according to Pseudo-Philo." In *Studies in the Book of Exodus: Redaction, Reception, Interpretation*, ed. Marc Vervenne, 577–94. Leuven: University Press.

Belkin, Samuel, 1940. *Philo and the Oral Law*. Cambridge, Mass.: Harvard University Press.

Belkin, Samuel, 1951. "Midrash Tadshe or Midrash of Rabbi Pinehas ben Ya'ir" [Hebrew]. *Horeb* 11:1–52.

Belkin, Samuel, 1957–58. "The Midrash ha-Ne'elam of the Zohar and Its Sources in Ancient Alexandrian Literature" [Hebrew]. *Sura* 3:25–92.

Belkin, Samuel, 1958–59. "Philo and the Midrashic Tradition of Palestine" [Hebrew]. *Horeb* 13:1–60.

Belkin, Samuel, 1960a. "Philo of Alexandria's Questions and Answers on Genesis and Exodus" [Hebrew]. *Horeb* 14–15:1–74.

Belkin, Samuel, 1960b. "The Philonic Exposition of the Torah in the Light of the Ancient Rabbinic Midrashim" [Hebrew]. *Sura* 4:1–68.

Belkin, Samuel, 1989. *The Midrash of Philo—The Oldest Recorded Midrash Written in Alexandria by Philo before the Formulation of Tannaitic Literature*, vol. 1, ed. Elazar Hurvitz. New York: Yeshiva University Press.

Bentzen, Aage, 1955. *King and Messiah*. London: Lutterworth.

Betz, Otto, 1974. "Das Problem des Wunders Bei Flavius Josephus im Vergleich zum Wunderproblem bei den Rabbinen und im Johannes-evangelium." In *Josephus-Studien: Untersuchungen zu Josephus, dem antiken Judentum und das Neuen Testamen, Otto Michel zum 70. Geburtstag gewidmet*, ed. Otto Betz, Klaus Haacker, Martin Hengel, 23–44. Göttingen: Vandenhoeck & Ruprecht.

Bieler, Ludwig, 1935–36. *ΘΕΙΟΣ ΑΝΗΡ. Das Bild des 'Göttlichen Menschen' in Spätantike und Frühchristentum*, 2 vols. Wien: Höfels.

Bigg, Charles, 1913. *The Christian Platonists of Alexandria*. Oxford: Clarendon Press.

Bilde, Per, 1988. *Flavius Josephus between Jerusalem and Rome: His Life, His Works, and Their Importance*. Sheffield: Sheffield Academic Press.

Birnbaum, Ellen, 1996. *The Place of Judaism in Philo's Thought: Israel, Jews, and Proselytes*. Atlanta: Scholars Press.

Blackburn, Barry, 1991. *Theios Anēr and the Markan Miracle Traditions: A Critique of the Theios Anēr Concept as an Interpretive Background of the Miracle Traditions Used by Mark*. Tübingen: Mohr.

Bloch, Heinrich, 1879. *Die Quellen des Josephus in seiner Archäologie*. Leipzig: Teubner.

Bloch, Renée, 1955. "Quelques Aspects de la Figure de Moise dans la Tradition Rabbinique." In *Moise: L'Homme de l'Alliance*, ed. Géza Vermès, 102–18. Paris: Desclée.

Boismard, Marie-Émile, 1993. *Moses or Jesus: An Essay in Johannine Christology*. Leuven: Peeters Press.

Borgen, Peder, 1965. *Bread from Heaven: An Exegetical Study of the Concept of Manna in the Gospel of John and the Writings of Philo*. Leiden: Brill.

Borgen, Peder, 1984. "Philo of Alexandria. A Critical and Synthetical Survey of Research since World War II." *ANRW* 2.21.1.2:98–154. Berlin: de Gruyter.

Borgen, Peder, 1992. "'There Shall Come Forth a Man': Reflections on Messianic Ideas in Philo." In *The Messiah*, ed. James H. Charlesworth, 341–61. Minneapolis: Fortress Press.

Borgen, Peder, 1997. *Philo of Alexandria, an Exegete for His Time*. Leiden: Brill.

Borgen, Peder; Fuglseth, Käre; and Skarsten, Roald, eds., 2000. *The Philo Index*. Grand Rapids: Eerdmans.

Botte, Bernard, 1954. "La vie de Moise par Philon." *CS* 8:173–80.

Bovon, François, 1978. "La Figure de Moise dans l'oeuvre de Luc." In *La figure de Moise: Ecriture et relectures*, ed. Robert Martin-Achard et al., 47–65 (Publications de la Faculté de Theologie de l'Université de Genève, no. 1). Geneva: Labor et Fides.

Bowman, John, 1958. "Samaritan Studies." *BJRL* 40:302–10.

Braude, William G., 1940. *Jewish Proselyting in the First Five Centuries of the Common Era: The Age of the Tannaim and Amoraim*. Providence: Brown University Press.

Braun, Martin, 1938. *History and Romance in Graeco-Oriental Literature*. Oxford: Blackwell.

Braverman, Jay, 1974. "Balaam in Rabbinic and Early Christian Traditions." In *Joshua Finkel Festschrift*, ed. Sidney B. Hoenig and Leon D. Stitskin, 41–50. New York: Yeshiva University Press.

Brown, Norman O., 1947. *Hermes the Thief: The Evolution of a Myth*. Madison: University of Wisconsin Press.

Burkhardt, Helmut, 1988. *Die Inspiration heiliger Schriften bei Philo von Alexandrien*. Giessen, Basel: Brunnen.

Burns, Joshua, 2000. "Contra Josephum in Lysimacho" [unpublished paper]. New York: Yeshiva University, Department of Classics.

Burns, Joshua, 2002. "Identifying Josephus' Lysimachus" [unpublished paper]. New York: New York University, Department of Classics.

Calabi, Francesca, 1998. *The Language and the Law of G-d: Interpretation and Politics in Philo of Alexandria*. Atlanta: Scholars Press.

Canevet, Mariette, 1986. "Remarques sur l'Utilisation du Genre Littéraire Historique par Philon d'Alexandrie dans la *Vita Mosis*, ou Moise Général en Chef-Prophète." *RSR* 60:189–206.

Cazelles, Henri, et al., 1955. *Moise: L'Homme de l'Alliance*. Paris: Desclée.

Chadwick, Henry, 1967. "Philo and the Beginnings of Christian Thought." In *The Cambridge History of Later Greek and Early Medieval Philosophy*, ed. Arthur H. Armstrong, 137–92. Cambridge: Cambridge University Press.

Chancey, Mark A., 2002. *The Myth of a Gentile Galilee.* Cambridge: Cambridge University Press.

von Christ, Wilhelm, 1905. *Geschichte der griechischen Literatur bis auf die Zeit Justinians*, 4th ed. München: Beck.

Coats, George W., 1988. *Moses: Heroic Man, Man of G-d.* Sheffield: Sheffield Academic Press.

Cohen, Jonathan, 1993. *The Origins and Evolution of the Moses Nativity Story.* Leiden: Brill.

Cohen, Naomi G., 1992. Review of Samuel Belkin, *The Midrash of Philo—The Oldest Recorded Midrash Written in Alexandria by Philo before the Formulation of Tannaitic Literature*, vol. 1, ed. Elazar Hurvitz. New York: Yeshiva University Press, 1989. In *JSJ* 23 (1992): 100–105.

Cohen, Naomi G., 1995. *Philo Judaeus: His Universe of Discourse.* Frankfurt am Main: Lang.

Cohn, Leopold, trans. and ed., 1909. *Die Werke Philos von Alexandria.* Breslau: Marcus.

Collins, John J., 1973. "The Date and Provenance of the Testament of Moses." In *Studies on the Testament of Moses: Seminar Papers*, ed. George W. E. Nickelsburg, 15–32 (Septuagint and Cognate Studies, 4). Cambridge, Mass.: Society of Biblical Literature.

Colson, Francis H., and Whitaker, George H., trans. and eds., 1929–62. *Philo*, 10 vols. (Loeb Classical Library). London: Heinemann.

Connor, W. Robert, 1967. "History without Heroes: Theopompus' Treatment of Philip of Macedon," *GRBS* 8:133–54.

Cowley, Arthur E., ed., 1909. *The Samaritan Liturgy.* Oxford: Clarendon Press.

Cox, Patricia, 1983. *Biography in Late Antiquity.* Berkeley: University of California Press.

Crown, Alan D.; Pummer, Reinhard; and Tal, Abraham, eds., 1993. *A Companion to Samaritan Studies.* Tübingen: Mohr-Siebeck.

Cudworth, Ralph, 1678. *The True Intellectual System of the Universe.* London: Royston.

Cukrowski, Kenneth L., 1994. "Pagan Polemic and Lukan Apologetic: The Function of Acts 20:17–38." Ph.D. diss., Yale University.

Cumont, Franz, 1937. *L'Égypte des Astrologues.* Bruxelles: La Fondation Égyptologique Reine Élisabeth.

D'Angelo, Mary Rose, 1979. *Moses in the Letter to the Hebrews.* Missoula: Scholars Press.

Daube, David, 1965. *The New Testament and Rabbinic Judaism.* London: University of London.

Delling, Gerhard, 1957–58. "Josephus und das Wunderbare." *NT* 2:291–309.

Dexinger, Ferdinand, 1993. "Moses." In *A Companion to Samaritan Studies*, ed. Alan D. Crown, Reinhard Pummer, and Abraham Tal, 160–62. Tübingen: Mohr-Siebeck.

Dexinger, Ferdinand, 1998. "Die Moses-Terminologie in Tibat Marqe—Einige Beobachtungen." *FJB* 25:51–62.

Dihle, Albrecht, 1956. *Studien zur griechischen Biographie.* Göttingen: Vandenhoeck & Ruprecht.

Dillon, John, 1977. "Numenius of Apamea," in his *The Middle Platonists, 80 B.C. to A.D. 220,* 361–79. Ithaca: Cornell University Press.

Donaldson, Terry L., 1981. "Moses Typology and the Sectarian Nature of Early Christian Anti-Judaism: A Study in Acts 7." *JSNT* 12:27–52

Dornseiff, Franz, 1922. *Das Alphabet in Mystik und Magic.* Leipzig: Teubner.

Downing, F. Gerald, 1980. "Redaction Criticism: Josephus' *Antiquities* and the Synoptic Gospels." *JSNT* 8:46–65; 9:29–48.

Droge, Arthur J., 1989. *Homer or Moses? Early Christian Interpretations of the History of Culture.* Tübingen: Mohr.

Earp, J. W., 1962. *Philo,* vol. 10: Index (Loeb Classical Library). London: Heinemann.

Falk, Daniel K., 2000a. "Moses." In *Encyclopedia of the Dead Sea Scrolls,* ed. Lawrence H. Schiffman and James C. VanderKam, 576–77. Oxford: University Press.

Falk, Daniel K., 2000b. "Moses, Texts of." In *Encyclopedia of the Dead Sea Scrolls,* ed. Lawrence H. Schiffman and James C. VanderKam, 577–81. Oxford: University Press.

Farnell, Lewis, 1921. *Greek Hero Cults and Ideas of Immortality.* Oxford: Clarendon.

Feldman, Louis H., 1963. *Scholarship on Philo and Josephus (1937–1962).* New York: Yeshiva University Press.

Feldman, Louis H., 1965. *Josephus,* vol. 9 (Loeb Classical Library). London: Heinemann.

Feldman, Louis H., 1968. "Abraham the Greek Philosopher in Josephus." *TAPA* 99:143–56.

Feldman, Louis H., 1971. Prolegomenon to reissue of M. R. James, *The Biblical Antiquities of Philo,* vii–clxix. New York: Ktav.

Feldman, Louis H., 1984a. *Josephus and Modern Scholarship (1937–1980).* Berlin: de Gruyter.

Feldman, Louis H., 1984b. "Abraham the General in Josephus." In *Nourished with Peace: Studies in Hellenistic Judaism in Memory of Samuel Sandmel,* ed. Frederick E. Greenspahn et al., 43–49. Chico, California: Scholars Press.

Feldman, Louis H., 1986. *Josephus: A Supplementary Bibliography.* New York: Garland.

Feldman, Louis H., 1987–88. "Pro-Jewish Intimations in Anti-Jewish Remarks Cited in Josephus' *Against Apion.*" *JQR* 78:187–251.

Feldman, Louis H., 1988. "Josephus' Portrait of Noah and Its Parallels in Philo, Pseudo-Philo's *Biblical Antiquities,* and Rabbinic Midrashim." *PAAJR* 55:31–57.

Feldman, Louis H., 1991–92, 1992–93. "Josephus' Portrait of Moses." *JQR* 82:285–328; 83:7–50, 301–30.

Feldman, Louis H., 1992a. "Josephus' Portrait of Ahab." *ETL* 68:368–84.

Feldman, Louis H., 1992b. "Josephus' Portrait of Nehemiah." *JJS* 43:187–202.

Feldman, Louis H., 1993a. *Jew and Gentile in the Ancient World: Attitudes and Interactions from Alexander to Justinian.* Princeton: Princeton University Press.

Feldman, Louis H., 1993b. "Josephus' Portrait of Balaam." *SPA* 5:48–83.

Feldman, Louis H., 1993c. "Josephus' Portrait of Ezra." *VT* 43:190–214.

Feldman, Louis H., 1993d. "Josephus' Portrait of Jeroboam." *AUSS* 31:29–51.

Feldman, Louis H., 1993e. "Josephus' Portrait of Josiah." *LS* 18:110–30.

Feldman, Louis H., 1993f. "Josephus' Portrait of the Pharaohs." *SC* 6:49–63.

Feldman, Louis H., 1993g. "Josephus' Portrait of Korah." *OTE* 6:399–426.

Feldman, Louis H., 1996a. "The Jews as Viewed by Plutarch." In Louis H. Feldman, *Studies in Hellenistic Judaism*, 529–52. Leiden: Brill.

Feldman, Louis H., 1996b. "Josephus' Portrait of Aaron." In *Classical Studies in Honor of David Sohlberg*, ed. Ranon Katzoff, Yaakov Petroff, and David Schaps, 167–92. Ramat Gan: Bar-Ilan University Press.

Feldman, Louis H., 1996c. "Pro-Jewish Intimations in Tacitus' Account of Jewish Origins." In Louis H. Feldman, *Studies in Hellenistic Judaism*, 377–407. Leiden: Brill.

Feldman, Louis H., 1998a. *Josephus's Interpretation of the Bible*. Berkeley: University of California Press.

Feldman, Louis H., 1998b. *Studies in Josephus' Rewritten Bible*. Leiden: Brill.

Feldman, Louis H., 1998c. "The Influence of the Greek Tragedians on Josephus." In *The Howard Gilman International Conferences, I: Hellenic and Jewish Arts: Interaction, Tradition and Renewal*, ed. Asher Ovadiah, 51–80. Tel Aviv: Ramot.

Feldman, Louis H., 2000a. *Flavius Josephus, Judean Antiquities 1–4: Translation and Commentary*, vol. 3. Leiden: Brill.

Feldman, Louis H., 2000b. "Rabbinic Insights on the Decline and Forthcoming Fall of the Roman Empire." *JSJ* 31:275–97.

Feldman, Louis H., 2001. "Josephus on the Spies (Num. 13–14)." *Internationales Josephus-Kolloquium Paris 2001*. *MJS* 12:22–41.

Feldman, Louis H., 2001–2002. "The Reshaping of Biblical Narrative in the Hellenistic Period: A Review Essay." *IJCT* 8:60–79.

Feldman, Louis H., 2005. "Parallel Lives of Two Lawgivers: Josephus' Moses and Plutarch's Lycurgus." In *Flavius Josephus and Flavian Rome*, ed. Jonathan Edmondson, Steve Mason, and James Rives, 209–42. Oxford: Oxford University Press.

Feldman, Louis H. 2006. *Judaism and Hellenism Reconsidered*. Leiden: Brill.

Fischer, Ulrich, 1978. *Eschatologie und Jenseitserwartung in hellenistischen Diasporajudentum*. Berlin: de Gruyter.

Fisk, Bruce N., 2001. *Do You Not Remember? Scripture, Story and Exegesis in the Rewritten Bible of Pseudo-Philo*. Sheffield: Sheffield Academic Press.

Fletcher-Louis, Crispin, 1996. "4Q374: A Discourse on the Sinai Tradition: The Deification of Moses and Early Christology." *DSD* 3.1:236–52.

Flusser, David, 1971. "Palaea Historica: An Unknown Source of Biblical Legends." *SH* 22:48–79.

Fornaro, Pierpaolo, 1979. "Il cristianesimo oggetto di polemica indiretta in Flavio Giuseppe (*Ant. Jud.*, IV 326)." *RSC* 27:431–46.

Fossum, Jarl E., 1985. *The Name of G-d and the Angel of the L-rd: Samaritan and Jewish Concepts of Intermediation and the Origin of Gnosticism*. Tübingen: Mohr.

Foster, S. S., 1976–77. "A Note on the 'Note' of J. Schwartz." *SP* 4:25–32.

Fowler, William Warde, 1911. *The Religious Experience of the Roman People*. London: Macmillan.

Fox, Marvin, 1993. "R. Isaac Arama's Philosophical Exegesis of the Golden Calf Episode." In *Minḥah le-Naḥum: Biblical and Other Studies Presented to Nahum M. Sarna in Honour of His 70th Birthday*, ed. Marc Brettler and Michael Fishbane, 87–102. *JSOT Supplement Series* 154.

Frankel, David, 1994, "The Destruction of the Golden Calf: A New Solution." *VT* 44:330–39.

Fraser, Peter M., 1972. *Ptolemaic Alexandria*, vol. 1. Oxford: Clarendon Press.

Freudenthal, Jacob, 1874–75. *Hellenistische Studien: Alexander Polyhistor und die von ihm erhaltenen Reste jüdischer und samaritanischer Geschichtswerke*, vols. 1 and 2. Breslau: Grass, Barth.

Friedländer, Moritz, 1903. *Geschichte der jüdischen Apologetik*. Zurich: Schmidt.

Fritz, Volkmar, 1970. *Israel in der Wüste. Traditionsgeschichtliche Untersuchung der Wüstenüberlieferung des Jahwisten*. Marburg: Elwert.

Fröhlich, Ida, 1980. "Historiographie et aggada dans le Liber Antiquitatum Biblicarum du Pseudo-Philon." *AAASH* 28:353–409.

Gager, John G., 1972. *Moses in Graeco-Roman Paganism*. Nashville: Abingdon.

Gaster, Moses, 1925. *The Samaritans: Their History, Doctrines and Literature*. London: Schweich Lectures for 1923.

Gaster, Moses, 1927. *The Asatir: The Samaritan Book of the 'Secrets of Moses' together with the Pitron or Samaritan Commentary and the Samaritan Story of the Death of Moses*. Oriental Translation Fund, n.s., vol. 26. London: Royal Asiatic Society.

Geljon, Albert C., 2002. *Philonic Exegesis in Gregory of Nyssa's De Vita Moysis*. Providence: Brown Judaica Studies.

Georgi, Dieter, 1986. *The Opponents of Paul in Second Corinthians*, rev. ed. Philadelphia: Fortress.

Gillman, Florence M., 1992. "Moses: New Testament." In *ABD* 4:918–20.

Ginzberg, Louis, 1909–38. *The Legends of the Jews*, vols. 1–7. Philadelphia: Jewish Publication Society.

Glasson, T. Francis, 1963. *Moses in the Fourth Gospel*. Naperville: Allenson.

Gnuse, Robert K., 1996. *Dreams and Dream Reports in the Writings of Josephus: A Traditio-Historical Analysis*. Leiden: Brill.

Goethals, Thomas R., 1959. "The Aethiopica of Heliodorus: A Critical Study." Ph.D. diss., Columbia University, New York.

Goldin, Judah, 1953. "The First Chapter of *Abot de Rabbi Nathan*." In *Mordecai M. Kaplan Jubilee Volume*, ed. Moshe Davis, 263–80. New York: Jewish Theological Seminary.

Goodenough, Erwin R., 1928. "The Political Philosophy of Hellenistic Kingship." *YCS* 1:55–104.

Goodenough, Erwin R., 1929. *The Jurisprudence of the Jewish Courts: Legal Administration by the Jews under the Early Roman Empire as Described by Philo Judaeus.* New Haven: Yale University Press.

Goodenough, Erwin R., 1933. "Philo's Exposition of the Law and His *De Vita Mosis*." *HTR* 26:109–25.

Goodenough, Erwin R., 1935. *By Light, Light: The Mystic Gospel of Hellenistic Judaism.* New Haven: Yale University Press.

Goodenough, Erwin R., 1940. *An Introduction to Philo Judaeus.* New Haven: Yale University Press.

Goodenough, Erwin R., 1953–68. *Jewish Symbols in the Greco-Roman Period,* 13 vols. Princeton: Princeton University Press.

Goodhart, Howard L., and Goodenough, Erwin R., 1938. *General Bibliography of Philo* in *The Politics of Philo Judaeus: Practice and Theory,* 125–348. New Haven: Yale University Press.

Goodman, Martin, 1994. *Mission and Conversion: Proselytizing in the Religious History of the Roman Empire.* Oxford: Clarendon Press.

Goold, George P., 1961. "A Greek Professorial Circle at Rome." *TAPA* 92:168–92.

Grabbe, Lester L., 1988. *Etymology in Early Jewish Interpretation: The Hebrew Names in Philo.* Atlanta: Scholars Press.

Graf, Fritz, 1997. *Magic in the Ancient World.* Cambridge, Mass.: Harvard University Press.

Graf, Mary Ruth, 1976. "The Hellenization of Moses." Ph.D. diss., Hebrew Union College, Cincinnati.

Griffith, Francis L., and Thompson, Herbert, eds., 1904. *The Demotic Magical Papyrus of London and Leiden.* London: Grevel.

Griffiths, John G., 1953. "The Egyptian Derivation of the Name Moses." *JNES* 12:225–31.

Gruen, Erich S., 1997. "Fact and Fiction: Jewish Legends in a Hellenistic Context." In *Hellenistic Constructs: Essays in Culture, History, and Historiography,* ed. Paul Cartledge, Peter Garnsey, and Erich Gruen, 72–88. Berkeley: University of California Press, 1997.

Gruen, Erich S., 1998. *Heritage and Hellenism: The Reinvention of Jewish Tradition.* Berkeley: University of California Press.

Gruen, Erich S., 2002. *Diaspora: Jews amidst Greeks and Romans.* Cambridge, Mass.: Harvard University Press.

Hackett, Jo Ann, 1980. *The Balaam Text from Deir 'Alla.* Chico: Scholars Press.

Hadas, Moses, ed. and trans., 1951. *Aristeas to Philocrates (Letter of Aristeas).* New York: Harper

Hadas, Moses, 1958. "Plato in Hellenistic Fusion," *JHI* 19:3–13.

Hadas, Moses, 1959. *Hellenistic Culture: Fusion and Diffusion.* New York: Columbia University Press.

Hadas, Moses, and Smith, Morton, 1965. *Heroes and Gods: Spiritual Biographies in Antiquity.* New York: Harper.

Hafemann, Scott J., 1990. "Moses in the Apocrypha and Pseudepigrapha: A Survey." *JSP* 7:79–104.

Halévy, Meyer A., 1927. *Moise dans l'histoire et dans la légende*. Paris: Rieder.

Hall, Bruce, 1993. "Theology of the Samaritans." In *A Companion to Samaritan Studies*, ed. Alan D. Crown, Reinhard Pummer, and Abraham Tal, 233–35. Tübingen: Mohr-Siebeck.

Harrington, Daniel J., ed., 1976. *Pseudo-Philon Les Antiquités Bibliques*, vol. 1. Paris: Editions du Cerf.

Harris, William V., 1989. *Ancient Literacy*. Cambridge, Mass.: Harvard University Press.

Harrisville, Roy A., 1990. "In the Footsteps of Abraham: The Figure of Abraham in the Epistles of Saint Paul." Ph.D. diss., Union Theological Seminary in Virginia, Richmond.

Hata, Gohei, 1987. "The Story of Moses Interpreted within the Context of Anti-Semitism." In *Josephus, Judaism, and Christianity*, ed. Louis H. Feldman and Gohei Hata, 180–97. Detroit: Wayne State University Press.

Hecht, Richard D., 1981. "Scripture and Commentary in Philo." In *Society of Biblical Literature 1981 Seminar Papers*, ed. Kent H. Richards, 129–64. Chico: Scholars Press.

Heinemann, Isaak, 1927. "Die Lehre vom ungechriebenen Gesetz im jüdischen Schrifttum," *HUCA* 4:152–59.

Heinemann, Isaak, 1932. *Philons griechische und jüdische Bildung: Kulturvergleichende Untersuchungen zu Philons Darstellung der jüdischen Gesetze*. Breslau: Schatzky.

Heinemann, Isaak, 1935. "Moses." *RE* 31:359–75.

Heinemann, Isaak, 1939–40. "Josephus' Method in the Presentation of Jewish Antiquities" [Hebrew]. *Zion* 5:180–203.

Helleman, Wendy E., 1990. "Philo of Alexandria on Deification and Assimilation to G-d." *SPA* 2:51–71.

Helmbold, William C., and O'Neill, Eugene N., 1959. *Plutarch's Quotations*. Baltimore: American Philological Association.

Hengel, Martin, 1974. *Judaism and Hellenism: Studies in Their Encounter in Palestine during the Early Hellenistic Period*, 2 vols. Philadelphia: Fortress.

Hengel, Martin, 1989. *The Zealots: Investigations into the Jewish Freedom Movement in the Period from Herod I until 70 A.D.* Edinburgh: Clark.

Herrmann, Léon, 1970. *Chrestos: Témoignages paiens et juifs sur le christianisme du premier siècle*. Bruxelles: Latomus: Revue des Études latines.

Himmelfarb, Martha, 1993. *Ascent to Heaven in Jewish and Christian Apocalypses*. New York: Oxford University Press.

Hirzel, Rudolf, 1900. "L'Ἄγραφος νόμος." *Abhandlungen der philologisch-historischen Classe der Königlich Sächsischen Gesellschaft der Wissenschaften* 20.1.

Holladay, Carl R., 1977. *Theios Aner in Hellenistic Judaism*. Missoula: Scholars Press.

Holladay, Carl R., 1983. *Fragments from Hellenistic Jewish Authors*, vol. 1: *Historians*. Chico: Scholars Press.

Holladay, Carl R., 1989. *Fragments from Hellenistic Jewish Authors*, vol. 2: *Poets*. Atlanta: Scholars Press.

Holladay, Carl R., 1995. *Fragments from Hellenistic Jewish Authors*, vol. 3: *Aristobulus*. Atlanta: Scholars Press.

Holladay, Carl R., 1996. *Fragments from Hellenistic Jewish Authors*, vol. 4: *Orphica*. Atlanta: Scholars Press.

Horsley, Richard A., 1992. "Messianic Movements in Judaism." In *ABD* 4:791–97.

van der Horst, Pieter W., 1983. "Moses' Throne Vision in Ezekiel the Dramatist." *JJS* 34:21–29.

van der Horst, Pieter W., 1984a. "Some Notes on the *Exagoge* of Ezekiel," *Mnemosyne* 37:354–75.

van der Horst, Pieter W., 1984b. *Chaeremon: Egyptian Priest and Stoic Philosopher*. Leiden: Brill.

van der Horst, Pieter W., 1993. "'Thou Shalt Not Revile the Gods': The LXX Translation of Ex. 22.28 (27), Its Background and Influence." *SPA* 5:1–8.

Jacobs, Louis, 1971. "Moses: Rabbinic View." *EJ* 12:393–95.

Jacobson, Howard, 1981. "Mysticism and Apocalyptic in Ezechiel's *Exagoge*." *ICS* 6:272–93.

Jacobson, Howard, 1983. *The Exagoge of Ezekiel*. Cambridge: Cambridge University Press.

Jacobson, Howard, 1993. "Josephus on the Death of Moses." In *Tria Lustra: Essays and Notes Presented to John Pinsent*, ed. H. D. Jocelyn and Helena Hunt. Liverpool Classical Papers, no. 3. Liverpool: *Liverpool Classical Monthly*.

Jacobson, Howard, 1996. *A Commentary on Pseudo-Philo's Liber Antiquitatum Biblicarum*, 2 vols. Leiden: Brill.

Jacobson, Howard, 1999. "Moses as Alpha," *JTS* 50: 626–27.

Jacobson, Howard, 2006. "Artapanus Judaeus." *JJS* 57:210–21.

James, Montague R., trans., 1917. *The Biblical Antiquities of Philo*. London: S.P.C.K.

Jellicoe, Sidney, 1968. *The Septuagint and Modern Study*. Oxford: Clarendon Press.

Jellinek, Adolf, 1853–78. *Bet Ha-Midrash*, 6 vols. Leipzig: Nies.

Jeremias, Joachim, 1967. "Μωυσῆς," *TDNT* 4:848–73.

Jones, Peter Rhea, 1979. "The Figure of Moses as a Heuristic Device for Understanding the Pastoral Intent of Hebrews." *REx* 76:95–107.

de Jonge, Marianus, 1966. "The Use of the Word 'Anointed' in the Time of Jesus." *NT* 8:132–48.

Juster, Jean, 1914. *Les Juifs dans l'Empire romain: Leur condition juridique, économique et sociale*, 2 vols. Paris: Geuthner.

Kahn, Jean-Georges, 1996. "Philo Hebraeus?" In *Jewish Studies* 36, ed. Ron Margolin, 41*–58*. Jerusalem: Forum of the World Union of Jewish Studies.

Kaunfer, Alvan, 1988. "Aaron and the Golden Calf: Biblical Tradition and Midrashic Interpretation." *Conservative Judaism* 41.1:87–94.

Kenyon, Frederick G., 1951. *Books and Readers in Ancient Greece*, 2nd ed. Oxford: Clarendon.

Klausner, Joseph, 1925. *Jesus of Nazareth*. New York: Macmillan.

Klausner, Joseph, 1955. *The Messianic Idea in Israel.* New York: Macmillan.

Kraft, Robert F., 1978. "Philo (Josephus, Sirach and Wisdom of Solomon) on Enoch." *SBLSP,* ed. Lane C. McGaughy, 1:253–57. Missoula: Society of Biblical Literature.

Krämer, Hans J., 1976. "Προφήτης." *TDNT* 6:781-96.

Krauss, Samuel, 1902. *Das Leben Jesu nach jüdischen Quellen.* Hildesheim: Olms.

Kugel, James L., 1997. *The Bible as It Was.* Cambridge, Mass.: Belknap Press.

Kugel, James L., 1998. *Traditions of the Bible.* Cambridge, Mass.: Harvard University Press.

Kügler, Joachim, 2000. "Spüren Ägyptisch-Hellenistischer Königstheologie bei Philo von Alexandria." In *Ägypten und der östliche Mittelmeerraum im 1. Jahrtausend v. Chr.: Akten des Interdisziplinärn Symposions am Institut für Ägyptologie der Universität München 25.–27.10.1996,* ed. Manfred Görg and Günther Hölbl, 231–49. Wiesbaden: Harrassowitz.

Kushelevsky, Rella, 1995. *Moses and the Angel of Death.* New York: Lang.

Ladouceur, David J., 1983. "The Language of Josephus." *JSJ* 14:18–38.

Le Déaut, Roger, 1964. "Φιλανθρωπία dans la littérature grecque jusqu'au Nouveau Testament (Tite III, 4)." In *Mélanges Eugène Tisserant,* vol. 1, 255–94. Vatican City: Bibliotheca apostolica vaticana.

Levison, John R., 1994. "Two Types of Ecstatic Prophecy according to Philo." *SPA* 6:83–89.

Levison, John R., 1995a. "Inspiration and the Divine Spirit in the Writings of Philo Judaeus." *JSJ* 26:271–323.

Levison, John R., 1995b. "The Prophetic Spirit as an Angel according to Philo." *HTR* 88:189–207.

Levison, John R., 1997. *The Spirit in First Century Judaism.* Leiden: Brill.

Lévy, Isidore, 1927. *La légende de Pythagore de Grèce en Palestine.* Paris: Champion.

Lieberman, Saul, 1950. *Hellenism in Jewish Palestine.* New York: Jewish Theological Seminary.

Lierman, John, 2002. "The New Testament Moses in the Setting of Ancient Judaism." Ph.D. diss., University of Cambridge.

Loewenstamm, Samuel E., 1967. "The Making and Destruction of the Golden Calf." *Biblica* 48:481–90.

Loewenstamm, Samuel E., 1972. "The Death of Moses." In *Studies on the Testament of Abraham,* ed. George W. E. Nickelsburg, 185–217. Septuagint and Cognate Studies, no. 6. Missoula: Scholars Press.

Loewenstamm, Samuel E., 1975. "The Making and Destruction of the Golden Calf: A Rejoinder." *Biblica* 56:330–43.

Lorenz, Siegfried, 1914. "De Progressu Notionis Philanthrōpia." Ph.D. diss., Leipzig.

Luck, Ulrich, 1974. "φιλανθρωπία." *TDNT* 9:107–12.

MacDonald, John, 1960. "The Samaritan Doctrine of Moses." *SJT* 13:149–62.

MacDonald, John, 1964. *The Theology of the Samaritans.* London: SCM Press.

Mack, Burton, 1982. "Under the Shadow of Moses: Authorship and Authority in Hellenistic Judaism." *SBLSP*, ed. Kent H. Richards, 299–318. Chico: Scholars Press.

Mack, Burton, 1984. "Philo Judaeus and Exegetical Traditions in Alexandria." *ANRW* 2.21.1:227–71.

MacRae, George W., 1965. "Miracle in *The Antiquities* of Josephus. In *Miracles: Cambridge Studies in Their Philosophy and History*, ed. Charles F. D. Moule, 127–47. London: Mowbray.

Maher, Michael, 1996. "Targum Pseudo-Jonathan on Exodus 2.21." In *Targumic and Cognate Studies: Essays in Honour of Martin McNamara*, ed. Kevin J. Cathcart and Michael Maher, 81–99. *JSOT Supplement Series* 230. Sheffield: Sheffield Academic Press.

Mandelbaum, Irving J., 1990. "Tannaitic Exegesis of the Golden Calf Episode." In *Essays on Jewish and Christian Literature and History: A Tribute to Geza Vermes*, ed. Philip R. Davies and Richard T. White, 207–23. Sheffield: Sheffield Academic Press.

Mansfeld, Jaap, 1988. "Philosophy in the Service of Scripture: Philo's Exegetical Strategies." In *The Question of "Eclecticism": Studies in Later Greek Philosophy*, ed. John M. Dillon and Anthony A. Long, 70–102. Berkeley: University of California Press.

Marcus, Ralph, 1935. "Recent Literature on Philo (1924–1934)." In *Jewish Studies in Memory of George A. Kohut*, ed. Salo W. Baron and Alexander Marx, 463–91. New York: Alexander Kohut Memorial Foundation.

Marcus, Ralph, trans., 1953. Philo, Supplement 1: *Questions and Answers on Genesis;* Supplement 2: *Questions and Answers on Exodus,* 2 vols. (Loeb Classical Library). Translated from the ancient Armenian version of the original Greek. London: Heinemann.

Marrou, Henri I., 1956. *A History of Education in Antiquity*, trans. from the French by George Lamb. New York: Sheed and Ward.

Mealand, David, 1978. "Philo of Alexandria's Attitude to Riches." *ZNW* 69:258–64.

Meeks, Wayne A., 1967. *The Prophet-King: Moses Traditions and the Johannine Christology*. Leiden: Brill.

Meeks, Wayne A., 1968. "Moses as G-d and King." In *Religions in Antiquity: Essays in Memory of Erwin Ramsdell Goodenough*, ed. Jacob Neusner, 354–71. *Studies in the History of Religions*, 14. Leiden: Brill.

Meeks, Wayne A., 1976. "The Divine Agent and His Counterfeit in Philo and the Fourth Gospel." In *Aspects of Religious Propaganda in Judaism and Early Christianity*, ed. Elisabeth Schüssler Fiorenza, 43–67. Notre Dame: University of Notre Dame Press.

Mendelson, Alan, 1982. *Secular Education in Philo of Alexandria.* Cincinnati: Hebrew Union College Press.

Mendelson, Alan, 1988. *Philo's Jewish Identity*. Atlanta: Scholars Press.

Meyer, Rudolf, 1938. "Levitische Emanzipationsbestrebungen in nachexilischer Zeit." *OLZ* 41:721–28.

Miller, Selig J., trans. and ed., 1949. *The Samaritan Molad Mosheh.* New York: Philosophical Library.

Moehring, Horst R., 1973. "Rationalization of Miracles in the Writings of Flavius Josephus." *TU* 112:376–83.

Momigliano, Arnaldo, 1971a. *The Development of Greek Biography.* Cambridge, Mass.: Harvard University Press.

Momigliano, Arnaldo, 1971b. *Second Thoughts on Greek Biography.* Amsterdam: North-Holland Publishing Co.

Mommsen, Theodor, 1885. *Römische Geschichte*, vol. 5. Berlin: Weidmann.

Muffs, Yochanan, 1975. "Joy and Love as Metaphorical Expressions of Willingness and Spontaneity in Cuneiform, Ancient Hebrew, and Related Literatures: Divine Investitures in the Midrash in the Light of Neo-Babylonian Royal Grants." In *Christianity, Judaism and Other Greco-Roman Cults: Studies for Morton Smith at Sixty*, Part 3: *Judaism before 70*, ed. Jacob Neusner, 1–36. Leiden: Brill.

Murphy, Frederick J., 1988. "Retelling the Bible: Idolatry in Pseudo-Philo." *JBL* 107:275–87.

Murphy, Frederick J., 1993. *Pseudo-Philo: Rewriting the Bible.* New York: Oxford University Press.

Mussies, Gerard, 1982. "The Interpretatio Iudaica of Thot-Hermes." In *Studies in Egyptian Religion Dedicated to Professor Jan Zandee*, ed. Matthieu S. H. G. Heerma van Vos et al., 89–120. Leiden: Brill.

Mutschmann, Hermann, 1917. "Das Genesiscitat in der Schrift *Peri Hupsous*." *Hermes* 52:161–200.

Najman, Hindy, 2003. *Seconding Sinai: The Development of Mosaic Discourse in Second Temple Judaism.* Leiden: Brill.

Neusner, Jacob, 1987. "Mishnah and Messiah." In *Judaisms and Their Messiahs at the Turn of the Christian Era*, ed. Jacob Neusner et al., 265–82. Cambridge: Cambridge University Press.

Newsom, Carol A., 1992. "4Q374: A Discourse on the Exodus/Conquest Tradition." In *The Dead Sea Scrolls: Forty Years of Research*, ed. Devorah Dimant and Uriel Rappaport, 40–52. Leiden: Brill.

Neyrey, Jerome H., 1994. "Josephus' *Vita* and the Encomium: A Native Model of Personality." *JSJ* 25:177–206.

Nickelsburg, George W. E., ed., 1973. *Studies on the Testament of Moses.* Septuagint and Cognate Studies, 4. Cambridge, Mass.: Society of Biblical Literature.

Nickelsburg, George W. E., 1980. "Good and Bad Leaders in Pseudo-Philo's *Liber Antiquitatum Biblicarum*." In *Ideal Figures in Ancient Judaism: Profiles and Paradigms*, ed. George W. E. Nickelsburg and John J. Collins, 49–65. Chico: Scholars Press.

Niehoff, Maren R., 2001. *Philo on Jewish Identity and Culture.* Tübingen: Mohr-Siebeck.

Niese, Benedictus, ed., 1885–95. *Flavii Josephi Opera*, 7 vols. Berlin: Weidmann.

Nikiprowetzky, Valentin, 1973. "L'exégèse de Philon d'Alexandrie." *RHPR* 53:309–29.

Nikiprowetzky, Valentin, 1977. *Le Commentaire de l'Écriture chez Philon d'Alexandrie: Son Caractère et sa Portée: Observations philologiques.* Leiden: Brill.

Nikiprowetzky, Valentin, 1989. "Le thème du désert chez Philon d'Alexandrie." In *Le désert: image et réalité; actes du colloque de Cartigny 1983*, ed. Yves Christie, M. Sartre, B. Urio, I. Urio, 99–113. Les cahiers de Centre d'étude du Proche-Orient Ancien 3. Leuven: Peeters.

Nikiprowetzky, Valentin, 1996. *Études Philoniennes.* Paris: Cerf.

Nock, Arthur D., 1933. *Conversion: The Old and the New in Religion from Alexander the Great to Augustine of Hippo.* Oxford: Oxford University Press.

Nodet, Étienne, 1990. *Flavius Josèphe, Les Antiquités Juives*, vol. 1: *Livres I à III.* Paris: Cerf.

Nodet, Étienne, 1995. *Flavius Josèphe, Les Antiquités Juives*, vol. 2: *Livres IV et V.* Paris: Cerf.

Norden, Eduard, 1921. "Jahve und Moses in hellenistischer Theologie." *Festgabe von Fachgenossen und Freunden A. von Harnack, zum siebzigsten Geburtstag dargebracht*, 292–301. Tübingen: Mohr; reprinted in his *Kleine Schriften zum klassischen Altertum*, ed. Bernhard Kytzler. Berlin: de Gruyter, 1966, 286–313.

Norden, Eduard, 1955. "Das Genesiscitat in der Schrift vom Erhabenen." *Abhandlungen der deutschen Akademie der Wissenschaften zu Berlin, Klasse für Sprache, Literatur und Kunst*, 1954, no. 1. Berlin: Akademie Verlag.

Oded, Bustanay, 1971. "Exodus." *EJ* 6:1042–48.

Patai, Raphael, 1994. *The Jewish Alchemists: A History and Source Book.* Princeton: Princeton University Press.

Paul, André, 1985. "Flavius Josephus' 'Antiquities of the Jews': An Anti-Christian Manifesto." *NTS* 31:473–80.

Perrot, Charles, 1967. "Les recits d'enfance dans la Haggada antérieure au IIe siècle de nôtre ère." *RecSR* 55:481–518.

Perrot, Charles, and Bogaert, Pierre-Maurice, 1976. *Pseudo-Philon, Les Antiquités Bibliques*, vol. 2. Paris: Editions du Cerf.

Perry, Ben E., 1967. *The Ancient Romances.* Berkeley: University of California Press.

Petit, Madeleine, 1976. "A Propos d'une Traversée Exemplaire du Désert du Sinai selon Philon (*Hypothetica* VI, 203, 8): Texte Biblique et Apologétique concernant Moise chez Quelques Écrivains Juifs." *Semitica* 26:137–42.

Pfister, Friedrich, 1909–12. *Der Requienkult im Altertum*, 2 vols. Giessen: Töpelmann.

Pietersma, Albert, 1992. "Jannes and Jambres." In *ABD* 3:638–40.

Pietersma, Albert, 1994. *The Apocryphon of Jannes and Jambres the Magicians.* Leiden: Brill.

Pietersma, Albert, 2000. "Yohanah and His Brother." In *Encyclopedia of the Dead Sea Scrolls*, vol. 2, ed. Lawrence H. Schiffman and James C. VanderKam, 1000–1. New York: Oxford University Press.

Porter, Joshua R., 1963. *Moses and Monarchy: A Study of the Biblical Tradition of Moses.* Oxford: Blackwell.

Porton, Gary G., 1979. "Midrash: Palestinian Jews and the Hebrew Bible in the Greco-Roman Period." *ANRW* 2.19.2:104–38.

Priessnig, Anton, 1929. "Die literarische Form der Patriarchenbiographen des Philo von Alexandrien." *MGWJ* 73:143–55.

Priest, John F., 1983. "Testament of Moses." In *The Old Testament Pseudepigrapha*, vol. 1: *Apocalyptic Literature and Testaments*, ed. James H. Charlesworth, 919–34. Garden City: Doubleday.

Purvis, James D., 1973. "Samaritan Traditions on the Death of Moses." In *Studies on the Testament of Moses: Seminar Papers*, ed. George W. E. Nickelsburg, 93–117. Septuagint and Cognate Studies, 4. Cambridge, Mass.: Society of Biblical Literature.

Rabe, Hugo, ed., 1913. *Hermogenis Opera*. Leipzig: Teubner.

Radice, Roberto; Runia, David T.; et al., 1992. *Philo of Alexandria: An Annotated Bibliography 1937–1986*. Leiden: Brill.

Radin, Max, 1915. *The Jews among the Greeks and Romans*. Philadelphia: Jewish Publication Society.

Rahlfs, Alfred, 1935. *Septuaginta*. Stuttgart: Privilegierte Würtembergische Bibelanstalt.

Rappaport, Salomo, 1930. *Agada und Exegese bei Flavius Josephus*. Wien: Alexander Kohut Memorial Foundation.

Reinach, Théodore, et al., 1900–1932. *Oeuvres complètes de Flavius Josèphe*, 7 vols. Paris: Presses Universitaires de France.

Reinhartz, Adele. 1992. "Philo on Infanticide." *SPA* 4:42–58.

Remus, Harold, 1996. "Moses and the *Thaumaturges*: Philo's *De Vita Mosis* as a Rescue Operation." *LTP* 52:665–80.

Rendtorff, Rolf, 1976. "Προφήτης: *Navi* in the Old Testament." *TDNT* 6:796–812.

Richardson, W., 1957. "The Philonic Patriarchs as Νόμος Ἔμψυχος." In *SP* 1, ed. Kurt Aland and Frank L. Cross, 515–25.

Robbins, William J., 1947. "A Study in Jewish and Hellenistic Legend with Special Reference to Philo's Life of Moses." Ph.D. diss., Brown University.

Rofé, Alexander, 1988. "Qumranic Paraphrases, the Greek Deuteronomy and the Late History of the Biblical נשיא." *Textus* 14:163–74.

Rohde, Erwin, 1925. *Psyche*. New York: Routledge and Kegan Paul.

Rokeah, David, 1968. "A New Onomasticon Fragment from Oxyrhynchus and Philo's Etymologies." *JTS* 19:70–82.

Rose, Herbert J., 1914. "Divination (Greek)." In *Encyclopedia of Religion and Ethics*, ed. James Hastings, vol. 4, 796–99. Edinburgh: Clark.

Runia, David T., 1988. "G-d and Man in Philo of Alexandria." *JTS* 39:48–75.

Runia, David T., 1990. *Exegesis and Philosophy; Studies on Philo of Alexandria*. Aldershot: Variorum.

Runia, David T., 2000. *Philo of Alexandria: An Annotated Bibliography 1987–1996*. Leiden: Brill.

Runia, David T., ed., 2001. *Philo of Alexandria: On the Creation of the Cosmos according to Moses*. Leiden: Brill.

Russell, Donald A., ed., 1964. *"Longinus," On the Sublime*. Oxford: Clarendon.

Sandmel, Samuel, 1956. *Philo's Place in Judaism: A Study of Conceptions of Abraham in Jewish Literature*. Cincinnati: Hebrew Union College Press.

Sandmel, Samuel, 1979. *Philo of Alexandria: An Introduction*. New York: Oxford University Press.

Schäfer, Peter, 1997. *Judeophobia: Attitudes toward the Jews in the Ancient World.* Cambridge, Mass.: Harvard University Press.

Schalit, Abraham, trans., 1944–63. *Josephus, Antiquitates Judaicae* [Hebrew], 3 vols. Jerusalem: Bialik.

Schart, Aaron, 1990. *Mose und Israel im Konflikt: Eine redaktionsgeschichtliche Studie zu de Wüstenerzählungen.* Fribourg: Universitätsverlag.

Scherb, Hans, 1930. *Das Motif vom starken Knaben in der Märchen der Weltliteratur: Seine religionsgeschichtliche Bedeutung und Entwicklung.* Stuttgart: Kohlhammer.

Schian, Ruth, 1973. *Untersuchungen über das argumentum e consensu omnium.* Hildesheim: Olds.

Schiffman, Lawrence H., and VanderKam, James C., 2000. *Encyclopedia of the Dead Sea Scrolls.* New York: Oxford University Press.

Schmeling, Gareth L., 1980. *Xenophon of Ephesus.* Boston: Twayne, 1980.

Schmidt, T. Ewald, 1983. "Hostility to Wealth in Philo of Alexandria." *JSNT* 19:85–97.

Schnackenburg, Rudolf, 1959. "Die Erwartung des 'Propheten' nach dem Neuen Testament und den Qumran-Texten." *SE* (Texte und Untersuchungen zur Geschichte der altchristlichen Literature), series 5, 18:622–39. Berlin: Akademie-Verlag.

Schorr, Hava, 1991. "Etymologies of Hebrew Names in Philo's Allegorical Exegeses" [Hebrew]. Ph.D. diss., Tel-Aviv University.

Schreckenberg, Heinz, 1968. *Bibliographie zu Flavius Josephus.* Leiden: Brill.

Schreckenberg, Heinz, 1979. *Bibliographie zu Flavius Josephus: Supplementband mit Gesamtregister.* Leiden: Brill.

Schur, Chava, 1991. "Etymologies of Hebrew Names in Philo's Allegorical Exegesis" [in Hebrew]. Diss., Tel Aviv University.

Schürer, Emil, 1909. *Geschichte des jüdischen Volkes im Zeitalter Jesu Christi*, vol. 3. Leipzig: Hinrichs.

Schwartz, Daniel R., 1984. "Philo's Priestly Descent." In *Nourished with Peace: Studies in Hellenistic Judaism in Memory of Samuel Sandmel*, ed. Frederick E. Greenspahn, Earle Hilgert, and Burton L. Mack, 155–71. Chico: Scholars Press.

Schwartz, Eduard, 1895. "Artapanos." *RE* 2.1:1306–7.

Schwartz, J., 1953. "Note sur la famille de Philon." *AIPhHOS* 13 = *Mélanges Isidore Lévy* (1955): 591–602.

Sedgwick, Walter B., 1948. "Sappho in 'Longinus' (X, 2, Line 13)." *AJP* 69:198–99.

Seland, Torrey, 1995. *Establishment Violence in Philo and Luke: A Study of Non-Conformity to the Torah and Jewish Vigilante Reactions.* Leiden: Brill.

Shuler, Philip L., 1990. "Philo's Moses and Matthew's Jesus: A Comparative Study in Ancient Literature." *SPA* 2:86–103.

Sigal, Phillip, 1984. "Manifestations of Hellenistic Historiography in Select Judaic Literature." *SBLSP*, ed. Kent H. Richards, 161–85. Chico: Scholars Press.

Sills, Deborah, 1992. "Vicious Rumors: Mosaic Narratives in First Century Alexandria." *SBLSP*, ed. Eugene H. Lovering, Jr., 684–94. Atlanta: Scholars Press.

Silver, Daniel J., 1982. *Images of Moses.* New York: Basic Books.

Smith, Morton, 1971. "Prolegomena to a Discussion of Aretalogies, Divine Men, the Gospels and Jesus." *JBL* 90:174–99.

Smolar, Leivy, and Aberbach, Moshe, 1968. "The Golden Calf Episode in Postbiblical Literature." *HUCA* 39:91–116.

Snowden, Frank M., 1970. *Blacks in Antiquity: Ethiopians in the Greco-Roman Experience.* Cambridge, Mass.: Belknap.

Snowden, Frank M., 1983. *Before Color Prejudice: The Ancient View of Blacks.* Cambridge, Mass.: Harvard University Press.

Spencer, John, 1685. *De Legibus Hebraeorum Ritualibus et Earum Rationibus Libri Tres.* Cambridge: Hayes.

Spengel, Leonardus, 1854. *Rhetores Graeci*, vol. 2, 60–130. Leipzig: Teubner.

Spicq, Ceslaus, 1958. "La philanthropie hellénistique, virtu divine et royale." *ST* 12:169–91.

Spicq, Ceslaus, 1978. *Notes de lexicographie néo-testamentaire*, vol. 2. Göttingen: Vandenhoeck & Ruprecht.

Spilsbury, Paul, 1998. *The Image of the Jew in Flavius Josephus' Paraphrase of the Bible.* Tübingen: Mohr Siebeck.

Starobinski-Safran, Esther, 1978. "La Prophétie de Moise et sa Portée d'après Philon." In *La Figure de Moise,* ed. Robert Martin-Archard et al., 67–80. (Publications de la Faculté de Théologie de l'Université de Genève, vol. 1. Geneva: Editions Labor et fides.

Stein, Edmund, 1931. *Philo und der Midrasch: Philos Schilderung der Gestalten des Pentateuch verglichen mit der des Midrasch.* Giessen: Töpelmann.

Stenhouse, Paul L., 1993. "Molad Moshe." In *A Companion to Samaritan Studies*, ed. Alan D. Crown, Reinhard Pummer, and Abraham Tal, 159–60. Tübingen: Mohr-Siebeck.

Sterling, Gregory E., 1992. *Historiography and Self-definition: Josephos, Luke-Acts and Apologetic Historiography.* Leiden: Brill.

Sterling, Gregory E., 1993. "Platonizing Moses: Philo and Middle Platonism." *SPA* 5:96–111.

Stern, Menahem, ed., 1974–84. *Greek and Latin Authors on Jews and Judaism*, 3 vols. Jerusalem: Israel Academy of Sciences and Humanities.

Strack, Hermann L., and Billerbeck, Paul, 1922. *Kommentar zum Neuen Testament aus Talmud und Midrasch*, vol. 1. München: Beck.

Strugnell, John, 1995. "4Q Apocryphon of Moses." In *Qumran Cave 4: Parabiblical Texts*, Part 2, ed. Magen Broshi et al., 111–36. *DJD*, 19. Oxford: Clarendon Press.

Stuart, Duane R., 1928. *Epochs of Greek and Roman Biography.* Berkeley: University of California Press.

Tabor, James D., 1989. "'Returning to the Divinity': Josephus's Portrayal of the Disappearances of Enoch, Elijah, and Moses." *JBL* 108:225–38.

Talbert, Charles H., 1975. "The Concept of Immortals in Mediterranean Antiquity." *JBL* 94:419–36.

Talbert, Charles H., 1980. "Prophecies of Future Greatness: The Contribution of Greco-Roman Biographies to an Understanding of Luke 1:5–4:15." In *The Divine Helmsman: Studies on G-d's Control of Human Events, Presented to Lou H. Silberman*, ed. James L. Crenshaw and Samuel Sandmel, 129–41. New York: Ktav.

Tcherikover, Victor, 1956. "Jewish Apologetic Literature Reconsidered." *Eos* 48:169–93

Tcherikover, Victor A.; Fuks, Alexander; and Stern, Menahem, eds., 1957–64. *Corpus Papyrorum Judaicarum*, 3 vols. Cambridge, Mass.: Harvard University Press.

Teeple, Howard M., 1957. *The Mosaic Eschatological Prophet.* Philadelphia: Society of Biblical Literature.

Thackeray, Henry St. J., 1929. *Josephus, the Man and the Historian.* New York: Jewish Institute of Religion.

Thackeray, Henry St. J., 1930. *Josephus*, vol. 4 (Loeb Classical Library). London: Heinemann.

Thompson, Stith, 1957. *Motif-Index of Folk Literature*, 6 vols. Bloomington: Indiana University Press.

Tiede, David L., 1972. *The Charismatic Figure as Miracle Worker.* Missoula: Scholars Press.

Tiede, David L., 1973. "The Figure of Moses in the Testament of Moses." In *Studies on the Testament of Moses: Seminar Papers*, ed. George W. E. Nickelsburg, 86–92. Septuagint and Cognate Studies, 4. Cambridge, Mass.: Society of Biblical Literature.

Tov, Emanuel, 1984. "The Rabbinic Tradition concerning the 'Alterations' Inserted into the Greek Pentateuch and Their Relation to the Original Text of the LXX." *JSJ* 15:65–89.

Treitel, Leopold, 1915. "Agada bei Philo." In his *Philonische Studien*, ed. Marcus Brann, 85–113. Breslau: Marcus.

Tromp, Johannes, ed., 1993. *The Assumption of Moses: A Critical Edition with Commentary.* Leiden: Brill.

Trüdinger, Karl, 1918. *Studien zur Geschichte der griechisch-römischen Ethnographie.* Basel: Birkhäuser.

Usener, Hermann K., 1912–13. *Kleine Schriften*, 4 vols. Leipzig: Teubner.

VanderKam, James C., 1984. *Enoch and the Growth of an Apocalyptic Tradition.* Washington: Catholic Biblical Association of America.

Van de Water, Rick, 2000. "Moses' Exaltation: Pre-Christian?" *JSP* 21:59–69.

van Veldhuizen, Milo, 1985. "Moses: A Model of Hellenistic Philanthropia." *RR* 38:215–24.

Vassiliev, Afanasii, 1893. *Anecdota Greco-Byzantina.* Moscow: Universitas Caesarea.

Vermes, Geza, 1969. "'He Is the Bread': Targum Neofiti Exodus 16:15." In *Neotestamentica et Semitica: Studies in Honour of Matthew Black*, ed. Edward E. Ellis and Max Wilcox, 256–63. Edinburgh: Clark.

Vermes, Geza, 1973. *Scripture and Tradition in Judaism: Haggadic Studies*, 2nd ed. Leiden: Brill.

Vogelstein, Heinemann, 1889. *Der Kampf zwischen Priestern und Leviten seit den Tagen Ezechiels: Eine historisch-kritische Untersuchung.* Stettin: Nagel.

Völker, Walther, 1938. *Fortschritt und Vollendung bei Philo von Alexandrien: Eine Studie zur Geschichte der Frömmigkeit.* Leipzig: Hinrichs.

Walzer, Richard R., 1949. *Galen on Jews and Christians.* London: Oxford University Press.

Wardman, Alan E., 1974. *Plutarch's Lives.* London: Elek.

Welles, Charles Bradford, 1955. "The Hellenistic Orient." In *The Idea of History in the Ancient Near East,* ed. Robert C. Dentan, 133–67. New Haven: Yale University Press.

Werblowsky, R. J. Zwi, 1959. "Philo and the Zohar: A Note on the Methods of the Scienza Nuova in Jewish Studies." *JJS* 10:25–44, 113–35.

Westlake, Henry D., 1968. *Individuals in Thucydides.* Cambridge: Cambridge University Press.

Wevers, John W. 1993. "The Earliest Witness to Jewish Exegesis." In *The Frank Talmage Memorial Volume* 1, ed. Barry Walfish, 115–27. Haifa: Haifa University Press.

Whitaker, George H.,: *See* Colson, Francis H., and Whitaker, George H.

Willrich, Hugo, 1900. *Judaica: Forschungen zur hellenistisch-jüdischen Geschichte und Literatur.* Göttingen: Vandenhoeck & Ruprecht.

Wieder, Naphtali, 1962. *The Judean Scrolls and Karaism.* London: Horovitz.

Winston, David, 1979. *The Wisdom of Solomon: A New Translation with Introduction and Commentary.* The Anchor Bible. Garden City: Doubleday.

Winston, David, 1983. *Two Treatises of Philo of Alexandria: A Commentary on "De Gigantibus" and "Quod Deus Sit Immutabilis."* Chico: Scholars Press.

Winston, David, 1984. "Philo's Ethical Theory." *ANRW* 2.21.1:372–416. Berlin: de Gruyter.

Winston, David, 1995. "Sage and Supersage in Philo of Alexandria." In *Pomegranates and Golden Bells: Studies in Biblical, Jewish and Near Eastern Ritual, Law and Literature in Honor of Jacob Milgrom,* ed. D. P. Wright, D. N. Freedman, and A. Hurvitz, 815–24. Winona Lake: J. E. Eisenbrauns.

Winter, Paul, 1962. "Philo, Biblical Antiquities of." In *The Interpreter's Dictionary of the Bible,* vol. 3, 795–96. New York and Nashville: Abingdon.

Wolfson, Harry A., 1947. *Philo: Foundations of Religious Philosophy in Judaism, Christianity, and Islam,* 2 vols. Cambridge, Mass.: Harvard University Press.

Wong, Chan-Kok, 1992. "Philo's Use of *Chaldaioi.*" *SPA* 4:1–14.

Ziegler, Konrat, 1915. "Das Genesiscitat in der Schrift *Peri Hupsous.*" *Hermes* 50:572–603.

Index of Ancient Texts

JEWISH SCRIPTURES

APOCRYPHA

PSEUDEPIGRAPHA

DEAD SEA SCROLLS

NEW TESTAMENT

CHURCH FATHERS

SAMARITAN WRITINGS

PHILO

PSEUDO-PHILO

OTHER (ALLEGED) GRAECO-JEWISH WRITERS

RABBINIC AND ALLIED LITERATURE

MINOR TRACTATES

TARGUMIM

MIDRASHIM

MEDIEVAL AND RENAISSANCE SOURCES

CLASSICAL GREEK AUTHORS

CLASSICAL LATIN AUTHORS

PAPYRI

Index of Names and Subjects

Index of Greek, Latin, and Hebrew Words

GREEK WORDS

LATIN WORDS

HEBREW WORDS

Index of Modern Scholars

www.ingramcontent.com/pod-product-compliance
Lightning Source LLC
Chambersburg PA
CBHW071728110726
47908CB00006B/1536

9780268159511